Cover picture: Atlantean figures, Tula

224 color photographs
90 maps and plans
1 large road map

Text:
Karl Anton von Bleyleben and Anita von Bleyleben,
San Miguel de Allende, Gto. (Introduction to
Mexico, Regions, Plant and Animal Life, Popula-
tion, Pre-Columbian Cultures, History, Literature,
The Arts, Music, Economy, Mexico from A to Z,
Practical Information)
Prof. Wolfgang Hassenpflug, Kiel (Climate)
Frank J. Klug, Neuhausen (Life in the Aztec Empire)

Editorial work:
Baedeker Stuttgart
English Language: Alec Court

Cartography:
Ingenieurbüro für Kartographie
Huber & Oberländer, Munich (maps and plans in text)
Georg Schiffner, Lahr (road map at end of book)

Design and layout:
Creativ Verlagsgessellschaft mbH, Stuttgart
Ulrich Kolb, Henk Veerkamp

Conception and general direction:
Dr Peter Baumgarten,
Baedeker Stuttgart

English translation:
James Hogarth and Alec Court
2nd edition

© Baedeker Stuttgart
Original German edition

© Jarrold and Sons Ltd
English language edition worldwide

Published in the U.S. and Canada by Prentice-Hall,
Inc., Englewood Cliffs, N.J. 07632

Licensed user:
Mairs Geographischer Verlag GmbH & Co.,
Ostfildern-Kemnat bei Stuttgart

Reproductions:
Gölz Repro-Service GmbH,
Ludwigsburg

The name *Baedeker* is a registered trademark

Mexico uses the metric system. Throughout the
country you will encounter only metric measurements.
Conversion is easy. Multiply kilometers by 0.62 to
obtain miles, meters by 3.3 to obtain feet, liters by 0.26
to obtain gallons.

In a time of rapid change it is difficult to ensure that all
the information given is entirely accurate and up to
date, and the possibility of error can never be entirely
eliminated. Although the publishers can accept no
responsibility for inaccuracies and omissions they are
always grateful for corrections and suggestions for
improvement.

Printed in Great Britain by Jarrold and Sons Ltd,
Norwich. ★

0-13-056069-3 Paperback

Source of illustrations:

Ferdinand Anton, Munich (pp. 11 foot, 29, 35, 53 left,
112 foot, 146 top, 149 top, 151, 172, 180 right, 184,
208 left, 219, 236 foot, 264, 294, 307).
Christian Baedeker, Tübingen (pp. 209, 217, 236 top,
238 two).
Bavaria-Verlag Gauting (pp. 12 two, 42, 61, 104, 146,
foot, 147, 156 foot, 157, 211, 223, 247, 262, 286,
311).
Karl Anton von Bleyleben, San Miguel de Allende,
Gto. (pp. 25, 28, 32, 37, 39 two, 47, 53 left, 60, 70
top, 80, 82, 86, 93, 94, 103, 112 top, 121, 123, 124,
127, 128, 131 two, 135 two, 139, 144, 149 lower,
167, 179, 185, 192, 193, 205, 226, 249, 254, 269
right, 270, 275, 278, 281, 290, 292 left, 304).
Gerald Charm (p. 134).
Consejo Nacional de Turismo, Ciudad de México,
D.F. (pp. 17, 55 right, 66 foot, 78, 88, 100 foot, 114,
130, 133, 143, 156 top, 165, 169, 178, 214, 228,
244, 259 two, 326 left).
Dieter Grathwohl, Stuttgart (pp. 7, 10, 26 right, 51
right, 58, 74 top, 106, 142, 162–163, 173, 188, 222,
271 top, 274, 326 right, 327, 328, 329 foot).
Stefan Kober (pp. 197, 271 foot, 280, 281).
Lufthansa-Bildarchiv (pp. 11 top, 177, 180 top, 195,
196, 271 left, 283, 329 top).
Bildagentur Mauritius, Mittenwald (pp. 52, 68, 218,
221 left, 227, 241).
México Desconocido (pp. 74 foot, 81, 90, 110, 136
foot, 154, 155 foot, 212, 240, 251, 257, 289, 297).
Vera Rettenmaier, Mössingen (pp. 33 foot, 99 foot,
194, 277).
Guillermo Rode (pp. 26 left, 33 top, 52 right, 54, 55
three, 56 three, 62, 65, 70 foot, 72, 83, 91, 98, 99
foot, 100 upper, 101, 118 two, 126, 136 top, 159,
189, 190, 200, 206, 208 right, 210, 213, 216, 232,
234, 263 two, 265, 269 left, 276, 279, 284, 292
right, 295 two, 302).
Bildarchiv Karlheinz Schuster, Oberursel (p. 266).
Mexican National Tourist Council, Frankfurt am Main
(pp. 220, 325).
Zentrale Farbild Agentur GmbH (ZEFA), Düsseldorf
(pp. 14, 59, 66 foot, 155 top, 176, 221 right, 242,
253).

How to Use this Guide

The Mexican states, principal towns and areas of
tourist interest are described in alphabetical order. The
names of other places referred to under these general
headings can be found in the very full index.

Following the tradition estblished by Karl Baedeker in
1844, sights of particular interest and hotels and
restaurants of particular quality are distinguished by
either one or two asterisks.

Hotels are classified in the categories shown on
p. 319. SP=swimming pool. Only a selection of hotels
and restaurants can be given: no reflection is implied,
therefore, on establishments not included.

In Mexican addresses the word Calle (street) is
commonly omitted before the name of the street. Two
street names linked by a *y* (and) mean that the
building is situated on the corner of the two streets.

The symbol ⓘ at the beginning of an entry or on a
town plan indicates the local tourist office or other
organization from which further information can be
obtained. The post-horn symbol on a town plan
indicates a post office.

This guidebook forms part of a completely new series of the world-famous Baedeker Guides.

Each volume is the result of long and careful preparation and, true to the traditions of Baedeker, is designed in every respect to meet the needs and expectations of the modern traveler.

The name of Baedeker has long been identified in the field of guidebooks with reliable, comprehensive and up-to-date information, prepared by expert writers who work from detailed, first-hand knowledge of the country concerned. Following a tradition that goes back over 150 years to the date when Karl Baedeker published the first of his handbooks for travelers, these guides have been planned to give the tourist all the essential information about the country and its inhabitants: where to go, how to get there and what to see. Baedeker's account of a country was always based on his personal observation and experience during his travels in that country. This tradition of writing a guidebook in the field rather than at an office desk has been maintained by Baedeker ever since.

Lavishly illustrated with superb color photographs and numerous specially drawn maps and street plans of the major towns, the new Baedeker Guides concentrate on making available to the modern traveler all the information he needs in a format that is both attractive and easy to follow. For every place that appears in the gazetteer, the principal features of architectural, artistic and historic interest are described, as are its main areas of scenic beauty. Selected hotels and restaurants are also included. Features of exceptional merit are indicated by either one or two asterisks.

A special section at the end of each book contains practical information, details of leisure activities and useful addresses. The separate road map will prove an invaluable aid to planning your route and your travel within the country.

I am honored to be able to express my gratitude to the firm of Baedeker for their excellent contribution over the past 150 years to a better understanding of the ins and outs of traveling in Mexico.

Writing an accurate guide to Mexico is no small undertaking in such a fast changing country where new destinations, hotels and services spring up and develop quickly. It is also difficult to document and describe a country of such vastness and variety in terms of natural beauty, in terms of the various Pre-Columbian cultures, the Spanish heritage, the cosmopolitan vibrancy of our cities in contrast to the peaceful beauty of the many beaches.

It is hard to do justice to the way history in Mexico comes alive, not only in our pyramids, national monuments, ancient churches, our folk art and great murals, but in all forms of artistic expression.

We are grateful for the careful field work and personal experience that has gone into this book in order to make it a useful tool for the traveler to plan successfully and enjoy a friendly, rewarding visit to a great country, a great people.

Antonio Enriquez Savignac
Mexican Government Minister for Tourism

4   Contents

Introduction to Mexico

Involved as it is in the transition from a developing country to an industrialized nation, Mexico is in process of rapid change in many different respects. Its economy is being steadily expanded, so that it is difficult to be sure that the details of practical information – statistical data, road conditions, the availability of accommodation, etc. – are always up to date; and even the information provided by official sources is not always complete. On the other hand the archaeological and historical investigation of Mexico's splendid past is making steady progress, and a single archaeological find can throw fresh light on a whole phase of the country's development and lead to radical changes in the historical account. On both these grounds, therefore, the publishers are always grateful for information and suggestions about new developments which will enable them to bring this Guide more fully up to date.

Under the shadow of Iztaccíhuatl

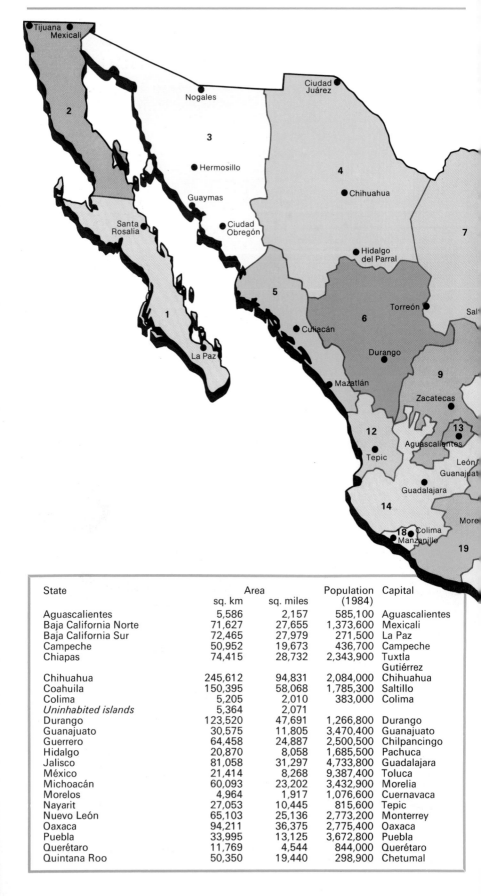

State	Area		Population (1984)	Capital
	sq. km	sq. miles		
Aguascalientes	5,586	2,157	585,100	Aguascalientes
Baja California Norte	71,627	27,655	1,373,600	Mexicali
Baja California Sur	72,465	27,979	271,500	La Paz
Campeche	50,952	19,673	436,700	Campeche
Chiapas	74,415	28,732	2,343,900	Tuxtla Gutiérrez
Chihuahua	245,612	94,831	2,084,000	Chihuahua
Coahuila	150,395	58,068	1,785,300	Saltillo
Colima	5,205	2,010	383,000	Colima
Uninhabited islands	5,364	2,071		
Durango	123,520	47,691	1,266,800	Durango
Guanajuato	30,575	11,805	3,470,400	Guanajuato
Guerrero	64,458	24,887	2,500,500	Chilpancingo
Hidalgo	20,870	8,058	1,685,500	Pachuca
Jalisco	81,058	31,297	4,733,800	Guadalajara
México	21,414	8,268	9,387,400	Toluca
Michoacán	60,093	23,202	3,432,900	Morelia
Morelos	4,964	1,917	1,076,600	Cuernavaca
Nayarit	27,053	10,445	815,600	Tepic
Nuevo León	65,103	25,136	2,773,200	Monterrey
Oaxaca	94,211	36,375	2,775,400	Oaxaca
Puebla	33,995	13,125	3,672,800	Puebla
Querétaro	11,769	4,544	844,000	Querétaro
Quintana Roo	50,350	19,440	298,900	Chetumal

Mexico
México

United Mexican States
Estados Unidos Mexicanos

States
Estados

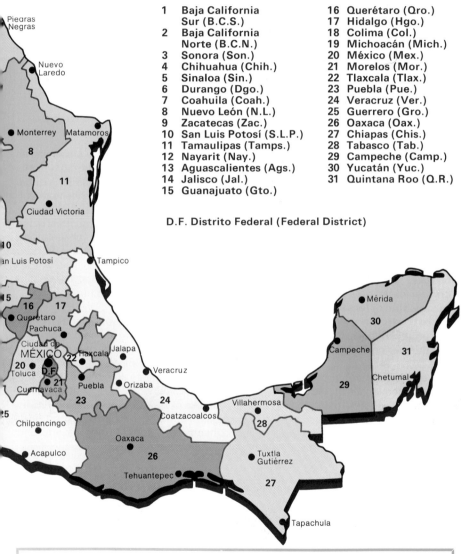

1 Baja California Sur (B.C.S.)	16 Querétaro (Qro.)
2 Baja California Norte (B.C.N.)	17 Hidalgo (Hgo.)
3 Sonora (Son.)	18 Colima (Col.)
4 Chihuahua (Chih.)	19 Michoacán (Mich.)
5 Sinaloa (Sin.)	20 México (Mex.)
6 Durango (Dgo.)	21 Morelos (Mor.)
7 Coahuila (Coah.)	22 Tlaxcala (Tlax.)
8 Nuevo León (N.L.)	23 Puebla (Pue.)
9 Zacatecas (Zac.)	24 Veracruz (Ver.)
10 San Luis Potosí (S.L.P.)	25 Guerrero (Gro.)
11 Tamaulipas (Tamps.)	26 Oaxaca (Oax.)
12 Nayarit (Nay.)	27 Chiapas (Chis.)
13 Aguascalientes (Ags.)	28 Tabasco (Tab.)
14 Jalisco (Jal.)	29 Campeche (Camp.)
15 Guanajuato (Gto.)	30 Yucatán (Yuc.)
	31 Quintana Roo (Q.R.)

D.F. Distrito Federal (Federal District)

State	Area sq. km	sq. miles	Population (1984)	Capital
San Luis Potosí	63,231	24,414	1,869,300	San Luis Potosí
Sinaloa	58,488	22,582	2,192,200	Culiacán
Sonora	182,553	70,484	1,694,500	Hermosillo
Tabasco	25,337	9,783	1,354,200	Villahermosa
Tamaulipas	79,602	30,734	2,144,300	Ciudad Victoria
Tlaxcala	4,027	1,555	613,100	Tlaxcala
Veracruz	71,896	27,759	6,022,200	Jalapa
Yucatán	38,508	14,868	1,161,700	Mérida
Zacatecas	73,454	28,361	1,244,500	Zacatecas
Distrito Federal	1,483	573	10,499,800	Ciudad de México
Estados Unidos de Mexico	1,969,344	760,365	76,791,800	Ciudad de México

Under the Constitution of February 5, 1917 the **United Mexican States** (*Estados Unidos Mexicanos*) are a presidential republic made up of 31 **states** (*estados*) and a **Federal District** (*Distrito Federal*, abbreviated *D.F.*) comprising the capital, Mexico City (Ciudad de México) and its surrounding area.

The head of state is the **President** (*Presidente*: at present Miguel de la Madrid Hurtado), elected for a single term of six years, who is also head of the government. He appoints the ministers who make up his Cabinet and the governor of the Federal District, who is also mayor of Mexico City.

The legislative body is the **Congress of the Union** (*Congreso de la Unión*), consisting of the *Chamber of Deputies* (Cámara de Diputados), the members of which are elected every three years, and the *Senate* (Cámara de Senadores) of 64 members elected for a three-year term. – By far the strongest political party is the Partido Revolucionario-Institucional (PRI), to which the present head of state belongs. The opposition parties are the Catholic and conservative Party of National Action (PAN), the pro-Communist Socialist Union Party (PSUM), the Revolutionary Workers' Party (PRT), the right-wing Mexican Democratic Party (PDM) and the Socialist Workers' Party (PST).

The **states** enjoy regional self-government and have their own constitutions. Each state is headed by a *governor* (gobernador).

Mexico is a member of the United Nations, the Organizations of American States (OAS), the General Agreement on Tariffs and Trade (GATT), the Alliance for Progress and many other international organizations and institutions. It has a trade agreement with the European Community and a cooperation agreement with Comecon.

Although in the past most of Mexico's foreign visitors came from the United States and Canada, in recent years it has attracted increasing numbers of tourists from Europe, who find the long journey well worth while for the sake of making aquaintance with a country which in addition to scenery of great beauty, extensive sandy beaches, crystal-clear seas and an abundance of sunshine offers a cultural heritage of extraordinary variety and, not infrequently, impressive scale and magnificence.

Three different cultural periods have left their distinctive mark on Mexico – the pre-Columbian cultures, the colonial period and the modern age. The **archeological sites** of Teotihuacán and Tula, within easy reach of Mexico City, of Monte Albán and Mitla near the town of Oaxaca, of El Tajín and Zempoala in the state of Veracruz, and the Maya sites in the states of Chiapas and Yucatán (Chichén Itzá, Palenque, Uxmal, etc.) are among the most fascinating of Mexico's tourist attractions; and a visit to the archeological sites in the Yucatán peninsula can be combined with a stay at one of the seaside resorts on the Caribbean coast, many of them developed only in quite recent years (Cancún, Cozumel, Isla Mujeres, etc.).

An excellent general view of the pre-Columbian cultures can be obtained by visiting the magnificent National Museum of Anthropology in **Mexico City**; and every visitor's program must of course include a stay in the capital, preserving as it does striking remains and monuments from all three cultural periods. Visitors with a taste for art and architecture will find a wealth of interest in the remains of the colonial period – whole quarters of the city, numerous churches, chapels and religious houses as well as fine palaces and other secular buildings – no less than in the remarkable achievements of modern architecture and mural painting.

No less notable for the attractions it offers to visitors is the **Pacific coast** of Mexico. *Acapulco* has long been famed as a vacation resort of international reputation; but in addition to this fashionable and often overcrowded resort there are a number of quieter places on the Pacific coast such as Puerto Escondido, Zihuatanejo-Ixtapa, Puerto Vallarta and Mazatlán, as well as numerous smaller

Square of the Three Cultures, Mexico City

The Pacific coast at Acapulco

places, some of them admittedly lacking adequate facilities for tourists. There are still hundreds of miles of magnificent beaches which offer little or no facilities for visitors. – The beaches on the Gulf of Mexico, attractive as they are, are less popular because of their changeable weather.

Among Mexico's great scenic attractions are the girdle of **volcanoes** fringing the huge central plateau, whose peaks (Popocatépetl, 5452 m (17,888 ft); Iztaccíhuatl, 5286 m – 17,343 ft) rear up to the SE of Mexico City, and the mighty *Barranca del Cobre* ("Copper Canyon") in the northern foothills of the Western Sierra Madre. – North-western Mexico, largely barren, offers relatively little in the way of scenic attractions, but even the steppe-land and the desert have a charm of their own. Interesting features in this region are the old mining settlements, some of them real "ghost towns", and the abandoned silver-mines.

Visitors to Mexico will be struck by the great variety of scenery and vegetation they encounter on their journey. They may pass within a relatively short distance – particularly where there are variations in altitude – from areas of markedly tropical vegetation to zones of subtropical type.

Mexico is a paradise for those interested in folk traditions and customs. In recent years there has been much commercialization in this field; but the old ways are still preserved in the many colorful markets to which the Indians from outlying areas flock to sell their wares. The authentic Indian way of life is best seen in the states of Jalisco, Nayarit, in the Barranca del Cobre, in the states of Hidalgo, Puebla, Oaxaca and Chiapas and in some parts of the Yucatán peninsula.

The Mexicans are a friendly and hospitable people, and a trip to Mexico will leave a lasting impression of a country with a pattern of life very different from that of Europe or North America, where there is no place for haste or hustle: a country with its own rich cultural traditions, its own ideas and attitudes.

Indians in San Cristóbal market

Mountain scenery in the Sierra Volcánica near Tuxpan (Michoacán state)

The Regions of Mexico

Mexico lies between latitude 32°43' and 14°14' N and between longitude 86°46' and 117°7' W, with an area of 1,970,000 sq. km (760,000 sq. miles), occupying the southern part of the North American continent and, SE of the Isthmus of Tehuantepec, part of the Central American land bridge, together with most of the adjoining peninsula of Yucatán. The country is bounded on the W by the Pacific Ocean and on the E by the Gulf of Mexico and the Caribbean Sea, offshoots of the Atlantic Ocean. Mexico's Pacific coast is 7338 km (4560 miles) in length, its Atlantic coast 2805 km (1743 miles). Its greatest extent from N to S is 3170 km (1970 miles), from W to E 1200 km (745 miles). At its narrowest point, the Isthmus of Tehuantepec, it is only 225 km (140 miles) across. To the N Mexico is bounded by the United States, to the S by Guatemala and Belize (formerly British Honduras).

The heartland of this extensive territory, with its richly contrasting geological and geographical pattern, is the huge region known as the **MEXICAN HIGHLANDS** or **Altiplano** which occupies the northern and central parts of the country. This high plateau, rising from 900 m (2950 ft) in the N to 2400–3000 m (8000–10,000 ft) in the S, is enclosed between the Western Sierra Madre (Sierra Madre Occidental) and the Eastern Sierra Madre (Sierra Madre Oriental), and only a small amount of rainfall passes over these mighty mountain barriers to reach the interior of the country. The plateau is by no means uniform in structure, but consists of seven large valley basins traversed by chains of hills and rift valleys. The rainfall, mostly occurring during the marked rainy season, pours down through these gorges and drains away.

The lower **Northern Highlands** are made up mainly of broad featureless depressions (*bolsones*) without outlet to the sea, the largest of which are the bolsones of Mapimí and San Luis Potosí.

In the Mexican highlands

The right-bank tributaries of the Río Bravo del Norte (Río Grande) drain into the Gulf of Mexico. In the northern section of this area the wide alluvial valley floor, lying at altitudes of between 900 and 1200 m (3000 and 4000 ft), is variegated by lakes, sand-dunes, salt steppe-land and, on the lower slopes of the hills, expanses of alluvial soil. In general the hills rise some 600–900 m (2000–3000 ft) above the desert basin. The ranges of hills run N–S and NW–SE. In this region there are numerous deposits of gold, silver, lead, zinc, mercury, oil-shale, coal and iron ore. Railways and roads cut through the hills, linking the "oases" and mining centers with one another and with towns in the United States and central Mexico. The "oases" are watered by the rivers Casas Grandes, Conchos, Nazas and Aguanaval, all rising in the Western Sierra Madre. When these rivers flow into the depressions they lose much of their water by evaporation, seepage and diverson. The Laguna district around Torreón is an important area watered by the rivers Nazas and Aguanaval. In addition to such irrigated areas there are a number of "oases" created by the flooding of low-lying land, like those of Ciudad Juarez and Ojinaga.

The **Southern Central Highlands** are centered on a number of broad alluvial valley basins, the most important being those of Bajío, Toluca, México and Puebla, with soil formed by deposits of lava and volcanic ash. The valleys are separated from one another and from southern Mexico by an upland region formed of gently rounded hills as well as rugged volcanic peaks. The blocking of the drainage by lava flows has led to the formation of lakes and swamps and the emergence of hot springs in the basins lying between 1500 and 2600 m (5000 and 8500 ft). The best known of these lakes are Lakes Chapala, Cuitzeo and Pátzcuaro. Three of Mexico's principal river systems flow out of this region towards the sea – the Mezcala-Balsas system from Puebla, the Río Lerma and Río Grande de Santiago from the area W of the México basin and the Río Moctezuma–Río Pánuco system from the México basin. This large region was already densely populated in the pre-Hispanic period. One of the most fertile corn-growing areas in the country is the Bajío, the region extending along the Río Lerma which falls mainly within the states of Michoacán and Guanajuato. Agriculture has also supported a considerable population for many centuries in the Puebla, México and Morelos regions.

The Southern Central Highlands are traversed by a volcanic range, the **SISTEMA VOLCÁNICA TRANSVERSAL**, which extends from San Blas on the Pacific Ocean to Veracruz on the coast of the Gulf of Mexico. In this belt of hills, which cuts off northern and central Mexico from the southern part of the country, are Mexico's highest mountains – *Citlaltépetl* (Pico de Orizaba (5700 m – 18,700 ft), *Popocatépetl* (5452 m – 17,888 ft), *Iztaccíhuatl* (5286 m – 17,343 ft), Nevado de Toluca (4575 m – 15,011 ft) and La Malinche (4461 m – 14,637 ft)). The southern slopes of the volcanic range are much fissured, and the volcanic rock has been eroded away by the tributaries of the Río Mezcala. – A similar picture is shown by the Sierra Mixteca, which links the highland region with the Southern Sierra Madre.

The **WESTERN SIERRA MADRE (Sierra Madre Occidental)** extends NW to SE for a distance of some 1100 km (700 miles), with a breadth of some 160 km (100 miles). Most of the peaks rise to over 1800 m (6000 ft), and the highest reach the 3000 m (10,000 ft) mark. The configuration of the main mountain chains and gorges is largely determined by the folding movements of the Mesozoic era and the more ancient stratifications of the basement rocks. In the western part of the range there are gorges (*barrancas*) over 1500 m (5000 ft) deep, scarcely less magnificent than the Grand Canyon on the Colorado River. Only two main roads, together with a very recently constructed railway line, run through the mountains, linking the highland region with the plains of Sinaloa and Sonora. The "oases" of the highland region and the depressions bordering the Gulf of California are watered by rivers flowing down from the Sierra Madre Occidental – the rivers Carmen, Conchos, Nazas and Aguanaval in the highlands, the Yaqui, Mayo, Fuerte, Sinaloa and Culiacán to the W of the mountains.

From the great bend in the Río Bravo del Norte (Río Grande) a series of relatively low hills formed by the folding of sedimentary strata run SE. S of Monterrey

The Regions of Mexico

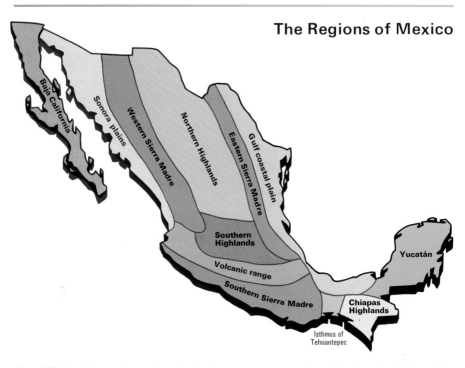

Baja California

Sonora plains

Western Sierra Madre

Northern Highlands

Eastern Sierra Madre

Gulf coastal plain

Southern Highlands

Volcanic range

Southern Sierra Madre

Chiapas Highlands

Yucatán

Isthmus of Tehuantepec

these hills rise into an imposing chain, the **EASTERN SIERRA MADRE (Sierra Madre Oriental)**, formed during the late Mesozoic. Most of the peaks are around 2100 m (7000 ft), with some rising to 3000 m (10,000 ft). The valleys are narrow and steep-sided, often running N–S. Of the rivers which have carved a way through the eastern flanks of the highland region to reach the Gulf of Mexico the most important is the Pánuco.

The **NORTHERN PACIFIC REGION** consists of parallel ranges of hills and broad valleys in the state of Sonora, the narrow strip of coastal plain, the peninsula of Baja California and the long Gulf of California (Mar de Cortés). Its origins go back to the middle and late Tertiary. The Sonora basins are flanked by chains of hills which rise toward the NE. The coast is predominantly straight, flat and sandy, with a number of lagoons and deep-water bays surrounded by rocky hills. Between the Río Sonora and the Río Colorado there are only a few rivers which reach the sea. In the southern part of the region, however, there are fertile "oases" in which cotton, wheat, rice, sugar-cane, fruit and vegetables are cultivated. In the extreme NE are a number of mining centers (mainly copper-mining).

Baja California (Lower California) is a long narrow peninsula which extends for a distance of some 1250 (775 miles) with

an average breadth of only 90 km (55 miles). The rocks date from the Cretaceous and Tertiary periods; in the southern part of the peninsula they are mainly marine deposits and volcanic formations of the Pleistocene and Holocene. The backbone of Baja California is a range of crystalline hills, mostly over 1500 m (5000 ft), with some reaching 3000 m

Desert scene near El Arco (Baja California)

(10,000 ft). This is a region of plateaus, with broad strips of desert country on either side of the Sierra de Santa Clara. On both sides of the peninsula there are bays which form excellent natural harbors. At the head of the Gulf of California is the delta of the Río Colorado.

The **COASTAL PLAIN ON THE GULF OF MEXICO** merges gradually into the fringes of the Eastern Sierra Madre in the SW. In the northern and central parts of the plain the basic formations date from the Cretaceous period. In this region, too, there are low hills, rarely more than 200 m (650 ft) high, formed of sedimentary deposits. This pattern is seen particularly in the large area known as the Huasteca S of Tampico. The coastal plain shows a succession of long beaches, sandbanks, areas of swamp and lagoons. The northern part of the coast has no good natural harbors. In the central part of Veracruz state the coastal plain is reduced by the foothills of the Eastern Sierra Madre to a width of less than 15 km (10 miles). The level pattern of the plain is broken by a stretch of rocky coast and an upland region around San Andrés Tuxtla. The northern part of the coastal plain is traversed by two great rivers, the Río Bravo del Norte, which forms the frontier with the United States (where it is known as the Río Grande), and the Tamesí-Pánuco. To the S and E of the port of Veracruz the rivers Papaloapán, Coatza-coalcos, Grijalva and Usumacinta fan out into extensive areas of swamp before reaching the sea. This coastal region, mainly consisting of sandbanks and la-goons, offers little shelter for ships to anchor, so that most of the harbors are on the rivers. Even the port of Veracruz owes its development more to its proximity to the Mexican heartland than to the quality of its harbor.

The lowland region reaches its greatest breadth (some 450 m – 280 miles) in the limestone plateau of the **Yucatán penin-sula**. Geologically this is the youngest part of Mexico, dated to the Miocene and Pliocene (i.e., the middle and late Ter-tiary). Part of the limestone formations lie under water (the Campeche Bank). The highest points in Yucatán are in the center of the peninsula (some of them being in Guatemala), but even these rarely rise above 150 m (500 ft). There is practically no drainage by rivers in this region, since the rainfall seeps away through the porous and soluble rock. This has given rise to underground caverns and water-holes (*cenotes*) formed by the colapse of the rock overlying a cavern. The northern and western coasts have numerous sand-banks and lagoons, while the eastern coasts are fringed by coral reefs; and there are many mangrove swamps.

SOUTHERN MEXICO is a mountainous region extending for over 1500 km (900 miles) from NW to SE, with a maximum breadth of some 350 km (200 miles). It runs from Cabo Corrientes to the Guate-malan frontier, passing to the S of the Sierra Volcánica Transversal, the Gulf coastal plain and the Yucatán peninsula. It is in three parts – the Southern Sierra Madre, the Isthmus of Tehuantepec and the Chiapas Highlands.

The **Southern Sierra Madre** (*Sierra Madre del Sur*) is a labyrinth of narrow ridges of hills and deep valleys. The base rock of this much fissured mountain range is made up of Cretaceous sediments; the volcanic deposits with which it was overlaid in the Mesozoic have largely been eroded away. Most of the peaks rise above 2000 m (6500 ft), a few to more than 3000 m (9500 ft). There is practically no flat land. On the E the region comes to an abrupt end at the steep escarpment falling down to the Isthmus of Tehuan-tepec. The central mountain range is enclosed between a narrow and discon-tinuous coastal plain to the SW and the depression watered by the Balsas-Mezcala river system to the N. Along the E side of this depression runs the *Sierra Mixteca*, which forms a bridge between the Sierra Volcánica Transversal and the Southern Sierra Madre. This section of the Pacific coast follows the line of the Sierra Madre. In places the coast is steep and rocky, forming first-class natural harbors like those of Acapulco and Manzanillo. There are only a few roads running through the mountains to the sea, and there is not yet any railway line. There are deposits of iron ore, lead, silver and gold in the mountains. The relative inaccessibility of this region has enabled the local Indians to retain much of their distinctive character and way of life.

The rounded hills of the **Isthmus of Tehuantepec** (*Istmo de Tehuantepec*) are similar in form to those found in the plains along the Gulf of Mexico. Geologi-cally, however, this area shows affinities

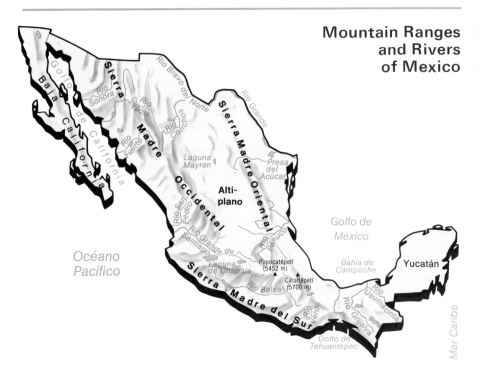

**Mountain Ranges
and Rivers
of Mexico**

with the neighboring regions to the W (Southern Sierra Madre) and E (Chiapas Highlands). The hills came into being in the late Pliocene and the Pleistocene. This low-lying, gently rolling region closes the gap between two great mountain regions and has since time immemorial been a natural area of transit, now utilized by roads, railway lines and oil pipelines. The plan to construct a canal between the Pacific and the Atlantic at Mexico's narrowest point (225 km – 140 miles) is centuries old, but has never been put into execution.

Only 40 km (25 miles) inland from the coast the **Chiapas Highlands** reach a height of over 1500 m (5000 ft); some peaks, including the volcano Tacaná, exceed 3000 m (10,000 ft). The central plateau (Meseta Central), consisting mainly of limestones and sandstones. came into being in the Pliocene. The

formation of the Sierra Madre de Chiapas dates back to the Pre-Cambrian; the foldings took place in the Pliocene. The mountain chain is made up of Pre-Cambrian and Palaeozoic crystalline rocks, Mesozoic sedimentary deposits and volcanic eruptions of later date. A number of rivers rise in the hills and reach the lagoon-fringed coastal plain after relatively short courses.

Between the two main mountain ranges lies a wide depression, mainly formed by the valley of the Río Grijalva, lying between 300 and 600 m (1000 and 2000 ft). The land in the Chiapas region is mainly arable, forest and pasture; coffee is grown in the areas betwen the hills. The isolation of this part of Mexico has been brought to an end only within the last twenty years by the construction of roads and a railway line in the Pacific coastal plain.

Climate

Mexico lies on the northern edge of the tropical zone, with the Tropic of Cancer cutting across the middle of the country. The principal topographical feature is an upland plateau sloping down from 2500 m (8000 ft) in the S to 1300 m (400 ft) in the N. The differences between different **climatic regions** result from the interplay of a variety of factors:

The southern regions have a tropically hot and moist climate (in the lowland areas). Towards the N the climate becomes steadily drier, as the land reaches into the steppe and desert zone around latitude 30°N. The eastern regions along the Atlantic coast and on the seaward slopes of the Sierra Madre Oriental have a moist and muggy climate with luxuriant tropical forests, the results of the onshore trade winds which blow throughout the year. The Pacific coastal region is much drier.

Farther away from the sea and on the leeward side of mountain ranges the rainfall becomes lower.

The climate becomes cooler with increasing altitude, giving rise to changes in the natural vegetation and the scope for agriculture. The names applied to the various zones by the Spaniards when they conquered Mexico are still used:

The lowest zone, the **Tierra Caliente** or Hot Zone, extends up to 800 m (2500 ft), the highest point at which cacao can be grown. In this zone the natural vegetation in southern Mexico, where there is sufficient humidity, is tropical rain forest. From 800 m (2500 ft) to 1700 m (5500 ft) extends the **Tierra Templada** or Temperate Zone, reaching up to the boundary for the cultivation of coffee, cotton and sugar-cane. Above 1700 m (5500 ft) is the **Tierra Fría** or Cool Zone. Finally there are the highest volcanic peaks, which are snow-covered throughout the year.

The following climatic regions can be distinguished:
The *Southern Central Highlands*, with a humid summer climate and moderate temperatures (Ciudad de México weather bureau).
The *Northern Central Highlands*, with a humid summer climate of steppe type and a subtropical semi-desert and desert climate (Ciudad Juárez weather bureau).
The *Southern Gulf Coast* region, including the Yucatán peninsula, with a climatic range extending from the continually humid rain forest of the S to the humid but changeable climates farther N (Mérida weather bureau).
The *Northern Gulf Coast* region, with a subtropical humid summer climate of steppe type (Matamoros weather bureau).
The *Southern Pacific Coast*, with tropical humid but changeable savanna climates (Mazatlán weather bureau).
The coastal region around the *Gulf of California*, with a subtropical semi-desert and desert climate (Guaymas weather bureau).
The extreme *North-West*, with rain in winter (Tijuana weather bureau).

Regional climatic patterns are illustrated in the diagrams on pp. 18–19, which show variations in temperature and rainfall over the year. The blue bars show the rainfall per month in inches, in accordance with the blue scale to the right of the chart. The orange band shows the temperature in °F, in accordance with the red scale; the upper red line gives the average maximum day temperature (reached in the early afternoon), the lower line the average minimum night temperature.

The figures for the seven selected weather bureaus apply also to the areas around these stations. For areas between two stations the figures will normally be intermediate between those shown in the diagrams, having regard to the incidence of the four factors mentioned at the beginning of this section. It should also be borne in mind, however, that variations in altitude can produce considerable variations in temperature and rainfall over a relatively short distance.

Southern Central Highlands
(Ciudad de México weather bureau)

Almost half of Mexico lies above 1500 m (5000 ft). The capital, Mexico City (Ciudad de México), lies at an altitude of 2240 m (7350 ft). Like most of the Mexican highlands, Mexico City is in the *tierra fría* or cool zone; and accordingly in spite of its tropical setting local temperatures are not tropically high. The heavy rain and muggy atmosphere characteristic of the tropics are rare, thanks to the shelter afforded by the mountains.

The climatic diagram shows the characteristics of the various months, so that the prospective visitor can see what kind of climate to expect in a particular month and can plan his trip accordingly.

The breadth of the orange band reflects the high daily temperature variations of 16–20 degrees Centigrade (29–36 degrees Fahrenheit). As is generally the case in the tropics, the differences in temperature between different seasons are relatively low.

The bars in the upper part of the diagram show the monthly rainfall figures. As in the rest of Mexico, most of the rain falls during the summer (June to September), primarily in the form of cloudbursts. During the rest of the year it is much drier than in Europe, and this period of drought sees frequent dust storms, which blow up over the dried-up basin on which Mexico City is built. These storms further intensify the haze of smog (mainly due to exhaust gases) which frequently blankets the city, so that the snow-covered volcano of Popocatépetl (5452 m – 17,888 ft), 60 km (40 miles) away, is frequently concealed from sight.

Other features of the climate are a consequence of altitude. Thus the air pressure is markedly lower (under 600 mm – 24 in.). The thin air can lead in some cases to respiratory and circulatory difficulties, and a period of acclimatization (if possible of some three weeks) is advisable for all visitors. At this altitude, too, solar radiation is much stronger than in the lowland areas: even with temperatures of 10–15 °C (50–60 °F)

A sombrero – good protection against the sun

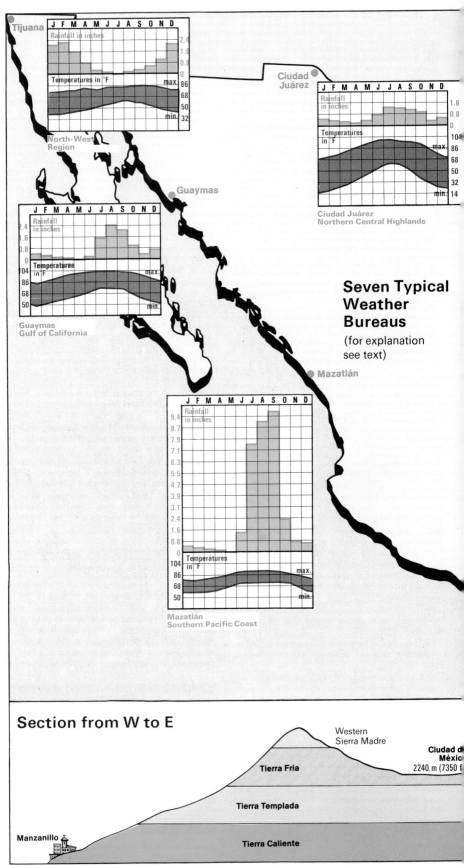

Tijuana
North-West Region

Ciudad Juárez
Northern Central Highlands

Guaymas
Gulf of California

Guaymas

Mazatlán

Seven Typical Weather Bureaus
(for explanation see text)

Mazatlán
Southern Pacific Coast

Section from W to E

Western Sierra Madre

Tierra Fria

Ciudad de México
2240. m (7350 f

Tierra Templada

Manzanillo

Tierra Caliente

Presentation by Prof. Dr. Wolfgang Hassenpflug

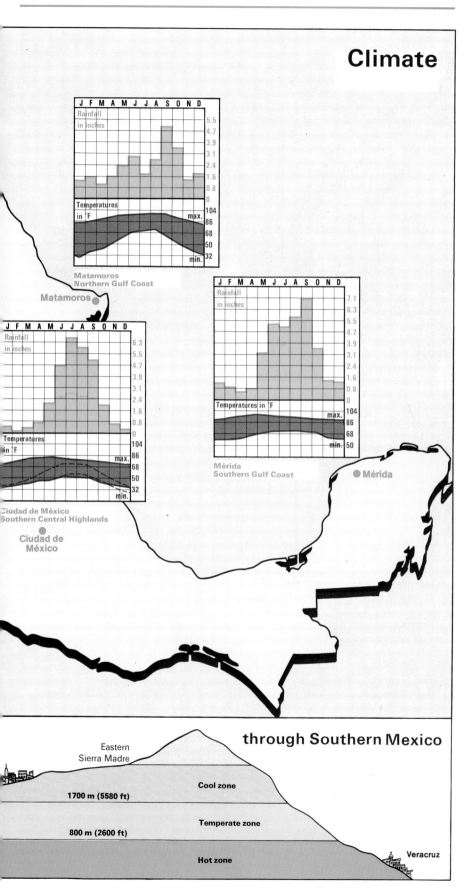

Climate

Matamoros
Northern Gulf Coast

Matamoros

Ciudad de México
Southern Central Highlands

Ciudad de
México

Mérida
Southern Gulf Coast

Mérida

through Southern Mexico

Eastern
Sierra Madre

Cool zone

1700 m (5580 ft)

Temperate zone

800 m (2600 ft)

Hot zone

Veracruz

Climatic Zones in Mexico

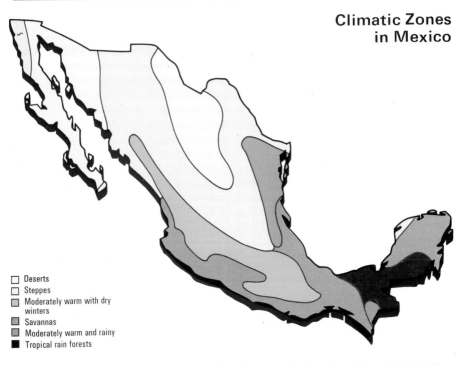

- ☐ Deserts
- ☐ Steppes
- ▦ Moderately warm with dry winters
- ▨ Savannas
- ▨ Moderately warm and rainy
- ■ Tropical rain forests

the sun will appear warm. Moreover, since the sun is very high in the sky and in the southern parts of the country is almost vertically overhead at midday the use of sun-glasses is essential and proper protection against sunburn is required. The typical Mexican sombrero is thus very valuable for protection. Conversely the loss of heat at night is rapid at high altitude, so that there is a sharp fall in temperature after dark. The low humidity of the air at this altitude may also affect some visitors with hoarseness.

Northern Central Highlands
(*Ciudad Juárez weather bureau*)

The central highlands of Mexico slope down towards the N and come increasingly into a zone of subtropical high pressure, so that the climate becomes dry and steppe-like and in the central area desert-like. The Ciudad Juárez weather bureau, on the United States frontier opposite El Paso, shows the climatic variations in this region as compared with Mexico City. The orange band is more sharply curved: i.e., the temperature differences between summer and winter are much greater here. The minimum night temperature in January has fallen to −8 °C (17.6 °F), while the maximum day temperature in summer is just under 40 °C (104 °F). The band is markedly broader than at Mexico City, the daily temperature variation having risen to almost 30 degrees Centigrade (54 degrees Fahrenheit). Thus, while even in winter it is almost as warm at midday as in Mexico City, during the night it is bitterly cold.

Here, too, most of the rain falls in summer; but the rainfall is much lower than farther S (33 m (1.3 in.) in July).

For highland areas between Mexico City in the S and Ciudad Juárez in the N the temperature and rainfall figures lie between those shown in these two diagrams.

Southern Gulf Coast and Yucatán Peninsula
(*Mérida weather bureau*)

This region has a tropical climate, hot and humid, with a period of winter drought which increases in intensity toward the N. On the whole it is an unhealthy climate. Between October and March there are frequent incursions of cold air from the N, leading to sharp falls in temperature. On the slopes of the mountains W of Veracruz the trade winds coming in from the sea bring rain, and the level of rainfall rises from 1500 mm (60 in.) in the lowlands to more than 4000 mm (160 in.) at an altitude of 2000 m (6500 ft). In this region all altitudes are represented, from the tropical rain forest to the eternal snow and ice on the summits of the great volcanoes.

Mérida weather bureau lies in the drier NW part of the Yucatán peninsula. Here most of the rain falls between May and October, and while the maximum day temperatures, at 34 °C (93 °F), are 3 degrees Centigrade (5 degrees Fahrenheit) lower than in May they are very trying because of the high humidity of the air. Only 10–30 metres (yards) above the ground (or above the scrub forest) a refreshing wind blows throughout the year, so that it is pleasantly cool on the summits of the Maya pyramids; the wind also provides the motive power for windmills.

Between July and October hurricanes from the Gulf of Mexico or the Caribbean occasionally pass over southern Mexico.

The island of Cozumel off the E coast of Yucatán shows similar temperature patterns to Mérida, but, like the eastern part of Yucatán which is exposed to the trade winds, has higher rainfall (an annual total of 1553 mm (61 in.) as against 928 mm (37 in.); July 200 mm (8 in.) against 130 mm (5 in.); September and October 243 mm (10 in.) and 234 mm (9 in.) against 180 mm (7 in.) and 91 mm – 4 in.). Tourists, particularly visitors from the United States, like Cozumel for the sunny and summer-like climate which they find there in winter.

NW of Mérida toward the Río Grande, the frontier with the United States, the climate of the Gulf Coast changes in a number of respects. The maximum day temperatures are still high (28 °C (82 °F) in January, 36 °C (97 °F) in July–August), but the minimum night temperatures fall to −1 °C (30 °F) in January. Summer rainfall decreases toward the N, while winter rains increase, being brought particularly by the *nortes* (inflows of cold air from the N), so that the climate – mild in winter and hot in summer – is humid throughout the year.

The whole of the southern Pacific coast of Mexico has high temperatures throughout the year and its highest rainfall in summer. The rest of the year is sunny and practically rainless. Frequent winds off the sea bring coolness.

Compared with Mexico City, lying some 2500 m (8200 ft) higher, the minimum night temperatures are consistently 10 degrees Centigrade (18 degrees Fahrenheit) higher and the maximum day temperatures in the second half of the year up to 7 degrees Centigrade (13 degrees Fahrenheit) higher. The daily temperature variations on the coast are much less than in the interior.

Tolerable day temperatures, warm water and an abundance of sun are the attractions which bring visitors to resorts like Acapulco and Mazatlán, particularly in winter. The temperatures at Acapulco are higher than at Mazatlán, showing little variation (2.3 degrees Centigrade – 4 degrees Fahrenheit) over the year, with day maxima of 35 °C (95 °F) and night minima of 17 °C (63 °F); the rainfall (1377 mm (54 in.)) is higher than at Mazatlán, occuring almost exclusively between June and October.

The tropical climate of southern Mexico, with its high temperatures and summer rainfall, may show local variations reflecting differences in altitude or in situation (to windward or leeward of the sea winds).

This region has a subtropical semi-desert and desert climate. In summer the Colorado delta, with the town of Mexicali and the Sonora desert, is one of the hottest places on earth. Here the sun shines for an average of $10\frac{1}{2}$ hours daily. The diagram shows the figures for Guaymas, which lies on the southern fringe of the region and is by no means one of its hottest spots, with 8 hours of sunshine daily and a certain amount of rain in summer. While at Veracruz on the Gulf of Mexico, for example, air-conditioning plants have to reduce the water content of the air, on the Gulf of California it is necessary to add humidity.

The climate of the peninsula of Baja California is influenced, particularly on the W side, by the cold California Current. This "water-cooling" system and the cool sea breezes, combined with the abundance of sunshine, have led to the very considerable development of seaside resorts, particularly at the S end of this long straggling peninsula.

The extreme NW of Mexico has a winter rainfall similar to that of the adjoining state of California with its Mediterranean climate. The Spaniards, coming from a region of winter rain to Mexico, a country of summer rain, gave the name of *invierno* ("winter") to the rainy period from June to October and *verano* ("summer") to the dry and sunny period from November to April, even though at the season the sun was lower in the sky.

Plant and Animal Life

The distribution of plant and animal life in Mexico reflects the country's different climatic zones, which in turn are affected by differences in altitude.

The Mexican **plant life** comprises a wide range of species, and many plants useful to man originated here (maize, tomatoes, tobacco, etc.).

The desert and semi-desert regions, predominantly in the NE of the country but also in Baja California, are inhabited by species equipped to cope with drought conditions, for example the succulents, which can store considerable quantities of water in their fibers. Prickly pears (*Opuntia*) are common in these regions.

The grassland and scrub steppe regions have a more abundant growth of vegetation, and after a reasonably heavy fall of rain can produce a luxuriant but short-lived growth of grass. Here, too, there are numerous species of cactus, as well as the mesquite (a straggling leguminous plant), the chaparral (a thorny shrub), yuccas, agaves and the hallucinogenic cactus known to the Indians as peyotl. There are tracts of steppe in the Southern Highlands of central Mexico.

The Western, Eastern and Southern Sierra Madre and the Sierra Volcánica Transversal, which enclose the Central Highlands, have rich growths of deciduous and

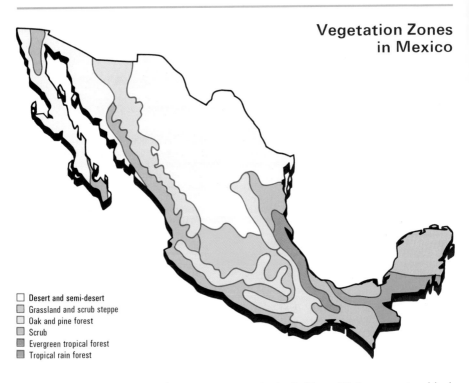

Vegetation Zones in Mexico

- ☐ Desert and semi-desert
- ☐ Grassland and scrub steppe
- ☐ Oak and pine forest
- ☐ Scrub
- ■ Evergreen tropical forest
- ■ Tropical rain forest

coniferous forest, with both evergreen and deciduous species of oak, arbor vitae and junipers as well as pines and other conifers. The ground cover consists of coarse grasses and close-growing plants.

Evergreen tropical forest is found mainly on and near the southwestern coastal strip along the Gulf of Mexico. In the amphibious coastal regions – part land, part water – are found swamp plants, bamboos and mangroves. The trees are covered with creeping plants and air-growing ferns; and there are also orchids and swamp cypresses, such as the ahuehuetl (Náhuatl, "old man of the water").

Extensive areas of scrub are characteristic of the Pacific coasts of central and southern Mexico and the northern part of Yucatán. The grassland is interspersed with low shrubby vegetation.

Tropical rain forest is found in the S of the Yucatán peninsula and in Chiapas, Tabasco and Veracruz. The species include mahogany, the kapok tree, campeche (logwood) and the chicle tree which yields the raw material for chewing-gum; and trees are frequently covered with climbing and air-growing plants.

The **animals** of Mexico also show great variety. Since the Pliocene era the animal life of North and South America has met and mingled here. Wolves, coyotes, black bears and beavers found their way into Mexico from the N and established themselves in the highland regions, while the lowlands attracted jaguars, pumas, monkeys and other South American species. Other animals found in Mexico include ocelots, lynxes, badgers, otters, armadillos, bighorn sheep, sloths, raccoons, squirrels, tapirs and ant-bears, as well as several species of wild pig, deer and small rodents. Bats and vampires (a type of South American bat), are feared as carriers of livestock diseases and are subject to pest control.

Among reptiles and amphibians there are iguanas, various smaller species of lizards, alligators and turtles as well as various frogs and toads. The Gila monster or heloderm, a poisonous lizard, is found in the NW of the country. A zoological curiosity is the axolotl, a species of salamander which lives in subterranean waters and propagates itself in the larval stage. – Poisonous snakes found in Mexico include several species of rattlesnake, the coral snake, the bushmaster and the fer-de-lance. There is also the boa constrictor, a non-poisonous snake which crushes its prey in its coils; it can attain a length of several yards.

Birds played a great part in the mythology of the ancient Indians, who were impressed by their magical ability to fly. The quetzal, whose feathers were used to make ceremonial garments for the rulers of the Indians, has now become extremely rare, as has the eagle, Mexico's heraldic animal. The humming-bird and parrot also feature in Mexican mythology. Other birds found in Mexico include the turkey, the vulture, the buzzard, the cormorant, the pelican, the toucan, the heron and the flamingo. In addition there are migrants from the N, including the woodpecker, wild geese and wild ducks, pigeons, snipe, seagulls, swallows and partridges.

Mexico's insects and spiders can sometimes be troublesome, among them various species of gnats and mosquitoes, flies, ticks and mites. In almost all the dry parts of the country there are scorpions, whose sting can be unpleasant and dangerous. There are also a number of poisonous spiders, including the bird spider and the black widow. The red ant (*Hormiga roja*) gives a painful bite. – Mexico has an abundance of butterflies and moths, among them the admiral, monarch, copperhead, malachite, emperor, morpho and calico.

The oceans bordering Mexico contain a wide variety of life. Near the coast of the N Pacific sea-lions and sometimes gray whales can be observed, and in the shallow water zone there are prawns (an important export), crayfish and flatfish. Sea-fish include the sea bass, mackerel, mullet, sardine, tuna, bonito, barracuda, swordfish, moray and various species of shark and ray. Dolphins sometimes come close inshore, particularly on remote stretches of the Pacific coast. – Fresh-water fish include trout, perch, carp, eels and catfish.

Population

Mexico is often cited, with some justification, as the most successful example of the mingling of races in modern history. Out of the approximate 6 million indigenous Indians who occupied the country at the time of the Spanish conquest, some 200,000 Spanish incomers and about the same number of negro slaves brought in during the colonial period, has developed the present Mexican nation of over 80 million people.

In the absence of exact figures it can be estimated that 75–80% of the present-day population of Mexico consists of **mestizos** (people of mixed blood, predominantly a mingling of Indian and Spanish, sometimes with a slight addition of African or East Asian blood), 10 to 12% of **Indians** and some 10% of **whites**, mostly of old Spanish descent (Criollos, Creoles). Even as late as 1870 pure-blooded Indians made up a majority of the population, and in 1921 they still represented 30–35% of the total population. Now the percentage is not much more than 10% of the total population.

Most of the native population (*indígenas*) is concentrated in the Central Highlands (México, Hidalgo, Puebla), in the S (Guerrero, Oaxaca, Chiapas), on the Gulf coast (Veracruz) and in the E (Yucatán peninsula). It is estimated that of the 8–9 million Mexican Indians about a quarter have no Spanish and speak only an Indian language. Of the old native languages, originally at least 130 in number, 82 Indian groups with about 270 different dialects have remained, including more than 20 different Maya and 6 Náhuatl languages. Among the largest and best known Indian tribes, still maintaining some degree of independent life are the *Nahua, Otomí, Tarascans* (Purépecha), *Huicholes, Cora, Tarahumara, Mayo, Yaqui, Totonacs, Huaxtecs* or *Huastecs, Matlatzinca, Mazatecs, Mazahua, Amuzgo, Trique, Mixtecs, Zapotecs, Chinantecs, Tzeltal, Tzotzil, Tajolabal, Chol* and *Yucatán Maya*. Over two dozen Indian tribes enjoy a considerable measure of self-government within their home areas. In recent years attempts to integrate the Indians have suffered some setbacks, and in certain tribes a new consciousness of their specific "Indian-ness" has been growing.

The overwhelming majority of the population (97%) profess the *Roman Catholic faith* – a statistic which covers a wide range of religious feeling, from purely formal membership of the Church to the most profound piety. This latter characteristic is found particularly among the Indians, although their Catholicism still leaves room for considerable elements and rituals belonging to the ancient Indian faith. On historical grounds the attitude of the government to the Church tends to range between neutral and hostile, though in recent years there has been an increasing easing of Church-state relationships.

In spite of government efforts to reduce the birth rate the annual rate of *population increase* is still running at an estimated 3%, although the government claims to have reduced it to 2.4%. The rapid growth in population and the present economic crisis have already led to considerable

The Indian Peoples of Mexico

Grupos indígenas de México

Source: Instituto Nacional Indigenista

1 Kumiai
2 Cucapá
3 Paipai (akwa'ala)
4 Cochimí
5 Kiliwa
6 Seri
7 Tequistlateco/ Chontal de Oaxaca
8 Tlapaneco
9 Pame
10 Chichimeco Jonaz
11 Otomí
12 Mazahua
13 Matlatzinca
14 Ocuilteco
15 Mazateco
16 Popoloca
17 Ixcateco
18 Chocho-Pooloca
19 Mixteco
20 Cuicateco
21 Trique
22 Amuzgo
23 Chatino
24 Zapoteco
25 Chinanteco
26 Huave
27 Pápago
28 Pima Alto
29 Pima Bajo
30 Tepehuano
31 Yaqui
32 Mayo
33 Tarahumara
34 Guarijio
35 Cora
36 Huichol
37 Nahua
38 Huasteco
39 Maya Peninsular
40 Lacandón
41 Chontal (de Tabasco)
42 Chol
43 Tzeltal
44 Tzotzil
45 Tojolabal
46 Chuj
47 Jacalteco
48 Mame
49 Motozintleco
50 Mixe
51 Popoluca
52 Zoque
53 Totonaco
54 Tepehua
55 Purépecha/ Tarasco
56 Kikapú

unemployment: it is estimated, that more than half of the working population of about 28 million people is either wholly unemployed (18%) or only occasionally employed (35%). The problém is aggravated by the fact that 43% of the population is under 15 years old, and there are not enough new jobs available for the approximate 900,000 young people coming on to the labor market. In consequence many of the younger members of the population try to find work in the United States, where between 5 and 7 million Mexican immigrants – "wetbacks" or "braceros", many of whom have entered the country illegally – are employed.

The main centers of economic progress are the towns and industrial regions, and this has led to an alarming *drift from the land*. Although not so long ago the

A Maya Indian woman from Yucatán

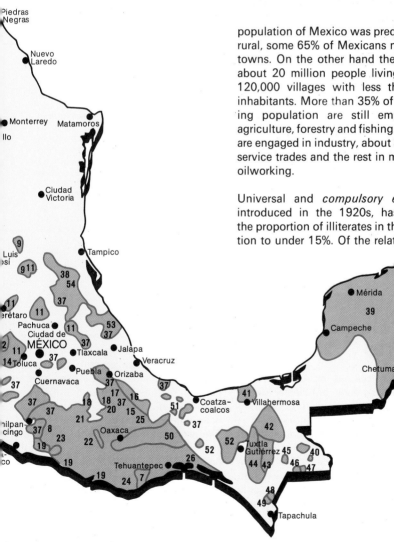

population of Mexico was predominantly rural, some 65% of Mexicans now live in towns. On the other hand there are still about 20 million people living in some 120,000 villages with less than 2,500 inhabitants. More than 35% of the working population are still employed in agriculture, forestry and fishing. Over 25% are engaged in industry, about 30% in the service trades and the rest in mining and oilworking.

Universal and *compulsory education*, introduced in the 1920s, has reduced the proportion of illiterates in the population to under 15%. Of the relatively high

Indian girl

A small Indian of Huixtán

and the urban proletariat of immigrants to the towns, who have remained under-privileged in both economic and social terms. In addition to unemployment and inflation Mexico's great social problem is the failure to involve the small peasants and land workers in a productive economic process.

number of university students those on technical courses are very much in a minority.

Unlike many other Latin American countries, Mexico has a relatively large middle class which, of course, has greatly suffered through the crisis existing since 1982; but there is still a great gulf between the small and enormously rich upper stratum of the population on the one hand and on the other, the rural population, some of them living in acute poverty,

Population Trends
in the *Aztec empire*, *New Spain* and *Mexico*

1519	5–6 million
1600	2 million
1810	6–6.5 million
1910	15 million
1920	14 million
1960	35 million
1980	70 million
1982	73 million
1984	77 million
1985	78.5 million
1986	80.3 million[1]
2000	121 million[2]

[1] Estimate
[2] Based on 3% annual increase

Pre-Columbian Cultures

The origins of the old Indian cultures of Meso-America are still not clearly identified, since reliable sources for this period are lacking. In Indian traditions there is usually a mingling of historical fact with mythology and legend, and in consequence the evidential value of the material is subject to considerable doubt. A further difficulty is that the only developed script of the pre-Hispanic period, that of the Mayas, has until recently been deciphered only to a limited extent. Accordingly – in spite of the considerable progress that had been made in American studies – our historical picture of Meso-America is still incomplete. Some 13,000 archeological sites have so far been recorded in Mexico, but only an insignificant proportion of these have been excavated and scientifically studied. The excavations of recent years have yielded steadily earlier datings, so that the history of the New World may well have to be considerably rewritten. It is already clear that there were active contacts and significant mutual influences between the various advanced cultures. Some of these cultures overlapped considerably in time.

The Pre-Columbian Cultures of Mexico

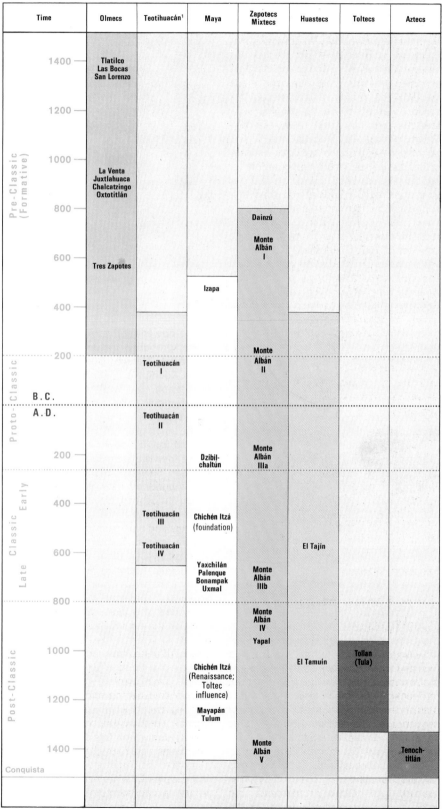

Time	Olmecs	Teotihuacán[1]	Maya	Zapotecs Mixtecs	Huastecs	Toltecs	Aztecs
1400	Tlatilco Las Bocas San Lorenzo						
1200							
1000	La Venta Juxtlahuaca Chalcatzingo Oxtotitlán						
800				Dainzú Monte Albán I			
600	Tres Zapotes						
400			Izapa				
200		Teotihuacán I		Monte Albán II			
B.C.							
A.D.		Teotihuacán II					
200			Dzibil-chaltún	Monte Albán IIIa			
400		Teotihuacán III	Chichén Itzá (foundation)				
600		Teotihuacán IV	Yaxchilán Palenque Bonampak Uxmal	Monte Albán IIIb	El Tajín		
800				Monte Albán IV Yapal			
1000			Chichén Itzá (Renaissance; Toltec influence)		El Tamuín	Tollan (Tula)	
1200			Mayapán Tulum				
1400				Monte Albán V			Tenoch-titlán

(Left-margin period labels: Pre-Classic (Formative); Proto-Classic; Classic — Early, Late; Post-Classic; Conquista)

[1] Radiocarbon dating (not universally accepted)

The chronology of the pre-Columbian cultures still presents problems. Although the temporal sequence within the Meso-American cultural area can be established – much information having been yielded by the study of pottery fragments – it is much more difficult to fit the various sequences into our chronological scheme. Great progress has been made through the refinement of the radio-carbon method of dating organic sub-stances and by the new thermo-luminescence test process, and it has become clear that the previous datings, often based on mere speculation or hypothesis, assigned the Indian cultures to a considerably later period than that suggested by new determinations.

It is important to bear in mind that the concept of "pre-Columbian" does not in any sense apply to a period which ended abruptly with Columbus's discovery of America in 1492. Each of the pre-Columbian cultures came to an end only when the Spanish conquistadors made their entry into the territory where it flourished; and the last of the pre-Columbian advanced cultures, that of the Aztecs, ended in 1521, a full generation after Columbus.

The advanced cultures of Meso-America developed mainly in four principal regions – along the coast of the Gulf of Mexico (Tabasco, Veracruz), in the Central High-lands (Distrito Federal, México, Puebla, Hidalgo), in the S (Oaxaca, Chiapas; also in Guatemala, El Salvador and Honduras) and in the E (Campeche, Yucatán, Quin-tana Roo; also in Belize, the former British Honduras). In the present state of know-ledge their origins can be dated to the transition between the Archaic and the so-called Formative period (c. 1500 B.C.).

The Olmecs and the La Venta culture

(1200–400 B.C.) – Little is known about the Olmecs (Náhuatl, "the people from the land of rubber"). The city states founded by the Olmecs on the Gulf coast (for example San Lorenzo Tenochtitlán, La Venta, Tres Zapotes) were the first cult and residential centers of any con-sequence in the region, with a glyphic script and a numerical system.

Olmec influence is found in many places far apart from one another – in many cases probably not Olmec settlements but religious and mercantile outposts of the

Colossal Olmec head (Jalapa Museum)

Olmec power centers on the Gulf coast. These probably included Las Bocas, Tlapacoya, Tlatilco, Chalcatzingo, Gua-lupita, Xochipala, Juxtlahuaca, Oxtotitlán and Izapa, as well as Monte Alto (Guatemala) and Las Victorias (El Salvador). It is believed that in their quest for the much sought after jade the Olmecs pressed forward to the Pacific coast and found their way via Chiapas, Guatemala and San Salvador into Costa Rica. The sites mentioned have yielded Olmec or Olmec-influenced clay, stone and jade figures (mostly found in burials) and relief carvings and wall paintings on rock faces and in caves. Some authorities have detected stylistic affinities (human figures with jaguar features) with the roughly contemporaneous Chavín culture in Peru. However that may be, these two cultures developed the first distinctive artistic styles on the American continent.

Olmec influence on later Meso-American cultures like those of the Mayas, Monte Albán I, Dainzú and El Tajín is seen most notably in relief carving, the system of numbers and the glyphic script. Part of the Olmec pantheon (Xipe Tótec, Quetzal-cóatl, Huehuetéotl, etc.) was also taken over by later cultures.

The people of the Gulf coast were highly skilled in the working of hard stone, demonstrating their mastery in the famous colossal basalt heads (probably representing priestly rulers), massive altars weighing up to 50 tons, stelae, stone vessels and delicately carved jade figures. Ubiquitous among these works is the strange and distinctive representation of a jaguar with more or less markedly human features, probably an effigy of the rain god. The characteristic facial type found in the Olmec figures, with thick lips and a broad fleshy nose, has given rise to speculation about a possible negroid element.

The oldest exact date glyph found so far in the Olmec culture is on Stela C from Tres Zapotes (September 2, 31 B.C.).

Material of the Olmec period can be seen in the museums of Villahermosa and Santiago Tuxtla, the Jalapa and Tres Zapotes open-air museums and the National Museum of Anthropology in Mexico City. Only those with a serious interest in archeology will want to visit the original sites, which are difficult to reach.

Temple of the Sun, Palenque

Teotihuacán (*c.* 200 B.C.–A.D. 750). – During the Classic period the great religious and urban center of Teotihuacán was the most important religious, political and economic metropolis in Meso-America. Hardly anything is known about the founders of this great center, but it is supposed that they came from the N and later mingled with incomers from Cuicuilco, Copilco and the Huasteca region. Astonishingly, this highly developed culture has left no evidence of a written script.

The development of Teotihuacán went through a number of phases. The first lasted until the end of the pre-Christian era, the second until about A.D. 350. During the third phase (until about A.D. 650) the town reached its peak. In this period it had cultural exchanges with Monte Albán, Pánuco, El Tajín and the Maya region – evidently based not merely on trading contracts but on the establishment of colonies of artists and craftsmen. It is now known that Teotihuacán directly controlled, at least for a time, such distant places as Kaminaljuyú in Guatemala (1100 km (680 miles) away as the crow flies) and some of the lowland Maya settlements. It is not known whether this control was merely political and commercial or was also maintained by military force. Teotihuacán also exerted influence on the cult sites of Xochicalco and Cholula and on many places in the state of Guerrero. – About A.D. 750, evidently as a result of enemy attack, the great city fell and was abandoned.

Teotihuacán is notable particularly for its magnificent architecture, comprising not only pyramids, temples and palaces but also houses for workers and peasants. Characteristic of this architecture was the *talud-tablero* principle (the use of inclined bearing walls, with horizontal cornices to ensure structural stability and optical effect), which was also adopted by other peoples, usually in modified form.

In comparison with the monumental architecture of Teotihuacán, sculpture played a relatively minor role. Apart from carved snakes' heads and stone reliefs, artistic activity was concentrated on splendid masks, often in inlaid work, and on stone figures. The craftsmen of Teotihuacán also produced pottery – incense-burners with brightly colored figural decoration, painted cylindrical vessels with lids and figurines, of which as a rule only the heads have survived. The fine pottery known as "thin orange ware" which is also found at Teotihuacán (figured vessels, representations of animals, etc.) probably came from Puebla or the Maya region in the way of trade. – The numerous wall paintings show an astonishing variety of themes, depicting gods, animals, cult scenes and much else. The dominating figures of Teotihuacán mythology are the gods of maize, rain and fire, frequently in animal form.

The Mayas (500 B.C.–A.D. 1450). – The origin of the Mayas is also obscure. Until recently it was believed that this tribe first appeared about 500 B.C. in the temperate highlands of Chiapas and Guatemala and the Petén lowlands. The results of recent research, however, have shown that a considerable Maya center had already existed in Cuello (Belize) as early as 2000 B.C. and that this existed until A.D. 200. A tribe which later developed into the Huastecs seems to have split off in the Early Formative period and settled on the northern coast of the Gulf of Mexico. The classical territory of the Mayas was already densely settled by about 1500 B.C., but it is not clear whether, and if so to what extent, the sites of Chiapa de Corzo, Izapa, Ocós and El Baúl were associated with the development of Maya culture. In this region independent cultures of which we know nothing mingled with those of the Olmecs and the Mayas, now emerging here into the light of history. The first settlements of any size were established at Dzibilchaltún (northern Yucatán) and Petén (Guatemala), where stone temples began to be built in the 3rd c. B.C. During the Formative period cult sites came into being at Xacuná, Uaxactún and Tikal (Guatemala) and at Kaminaljuyú. Early Maya influence also reached Oaxaca (Monte Albán II) and later, in the Classic period, Teotihuacán, Cacaxtla and Xochicalco. Between A.D. 400 and 600 there was a current in the opposite direction, and Teotihuacán influence was felt in some of the Maya sites.

The greatest achievements of the Mayas, who were without metal tools or implements, had no draft or pack animals and used the wheel only as a child's toy, date from the Classic period (A.D. 300–900) and are found mainly in the central part

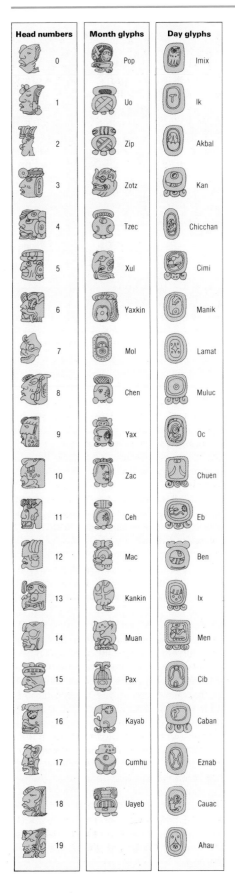

Head numbers	Month glyphs	Day glyphs
0	Pop	Imix
1	Uo	Ik
2	Zip	Akbal
3	Zotz	Kan
4	Tzec	Chicchan
5	Xul	Cimi
6	Yaxkin	Manik
7	Mol	Lamat
8	Chen	Muluc
9	Yax	Oc
10	Zac	Chuen
11	Ceh	Eb
12	Mac	Ben
13	Kankin	Ix
14	Muan	Men
15	Pax	Cib
16	Kayab	Caban
17	Cumhu	Eznab
18	Uayeb	Cauac
19		Ahau

of their area of settlement on sites such as Palenque, Bonampak, Yaxchilán and Chinkultic in Chiapas state and in Guatemala, Belize (formerly British Honduras) and Honduras. At Tikal in Guatemala the highest pyramid in the New World was built (65 m – 213 ft). The Mayas erected palaces, ball courts, altars and stelae, exactly dated according to their calendar. The stelae, works of consummate craftsmanship, are carved in low relief with glyphs, dates, figures of priestly rulers and historical scenes, and may also be in full relief. The Maya calendar was the most perfectly devised of its period, and Maya astronomy was highly developed. Maya mathematics used zero and figures varying in value according to their position; the numbering system was based on the figure 20. Among the finest achievements of Maya art are the fine wall paintings (Bonampak, Cacaxtla; Tikal and Uaxactún in Guatemala), the delicate polychrome pottery and the jade objects.

The Maya Calendar

The Mayas possessed two different calendar systems – also found, modified in varying degree, in other Meso-American cultures.

The **ritual calendar** was based on a year of 260 days, divided up by the interplay of the numbers 1 to 13 with 20 "day glyphs". Each day both the number count and the series of glyphs moved one place forward, the number count starting again at the 14th glyph, so that each of the 260 days had its own combination of number and glyph.

The **solar calendar** was divided up into 18 months of 20 days each, with the addition of five "empty" days, which were regarded as unlucky, to bring the total into line with the earth's orbit around the sun of approximately 365 days. – The next highest unit above the year (*tun*) was a span of 20 years (*katun*). – The "calendar round", a cycle of 52 solar years or 18,980 days, ended when the last day of the year in both the ritual and solar calendars fell on the same date.

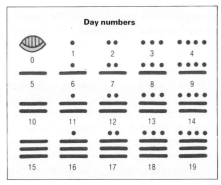

Day numbers

Dates in the solar calendar were recorded with the aid of 19 numerical signs or *head figures*, 21 *day glyphs* and 19 *month glyphs* (including one for the "empty" days), which made possible a unique combination for each day of the year. The name of the year in the solar calendar was determined by the date in the ritual calendar on which the first day in the 365-day cycle fell.

The calendar was of great importance in the religion and mythology of the Mayas, which were closely dependent on astronomy and astrology. The days, months and years were each dedicated to particular divinities, and every date was regarded as lucky or unlucky according to the divine forces which held sway. Before embarking on any major undertaking it was necessary to consult the calendar; for even the gods were subject to the influence of the constellations.

This complex system of chronology could accommodate very long periods of time, and the Mayas were able to calculate dates going back several million years. It seems likely, indeed, that they had some conception of the infinite duration of time.

Sculptural decoration in the Puuc style (Kabah)

The settlements in the central Maya territory were suddenly abandoned about A.D. 900, and in a very short space of time were swallowed up by vegetation. We can only speculate about the reasons: it is supposed, however, that the great cult system lost its hold, thus destroying the power of the priestly caste, and that internal strife brought about the collapse of the culture. Recent research has also revealed that external pressure by incoming foreign tribes accelerated the collapse.

The Classic period was also the heyday of Maya settlements in the N of their territory, including Kohunlich and areas in southern Campeche (El Hormiguero, Xpuhil, Becán, Chicaná) which are classified as belonging to the Río Bec style. In the Late Classic phase of this region, when the carved stelae almost disappeared, a number of styles flourished in northern Yucatán, for example the Chenes style (Hochob, Dzibilnocac) and the Puuc style (Uxmal, Kabah, Sayil, Labná, Jaina, Cobá). They are notable for the rich decoration applied to buildings in the form of hundreds of small sculptured elements fitted together in complex patterns. The principal motif is the rain god Chac. These settlements too came to an end in the 10th c.

With the advance of the Toltecs into Northern Yucatán there was a further burst of creative activity. The mingling of Toltec and Maya stylistic features is found most notably at Chichén Itzá, for example in large stone sculptures of Chac-mool and Atlantean figures. The motif of the feathered serpent predominates. The practice of human sacrifice and an increase in military activity are also to be attributed to Toltec influence.

The great days of Chichén Itzá came to an end about 1200, when it was overshadowed by Mayapán; but this last great Maya metropolis in turn fell about 1450, and with it disappeared the 2000-year-old Maya culture.

Zapotecs and Mixtecs (800 B.C. to A.D. 1521). – The history of the great cult center in the Oaxaca valley in southern Mexico is divided into five phases (Monte Albán I, II, III, IV and V). The stone reliefs, tombs and pottery dating from before the Christian era show the influence of Olmec and later of Maya culture. Around the time of Christ the Zapotecs, who left their mark on the cult center in the Classic period, made their appearance. Between A.D. 300 and 600 there were active cultural exchanges with Teotihuacán. Between 900 and 1200 there was a period of stagnation and then of decline, and it seems likely that Monte Albán was abandoned by the Zapotecs and taken over by the Mixtecs, who used it only as a place of burial – Mitla, SE of Oaxaca, was alternately under the influence of the Zapotecs, the Mixtecs and another culture of which we know nothing.

From the pre-Christian period date large and impressive terracottas of standing human figures and jaguars and the low-relief figures known as "Los Danzantes". – It has not been possible to decipher the script used by these cultures.

During the Classic period, in addition to monumental architecture influenced by Teotihuacán, there are anthropomorphic vessels, mostly representing priest gods, which were found in tombs. The cult of the dead was of great importance: the tomb chambers, cruciform in plan, were decorated with paintings and reliefs and contained rich grave goods. The Mixtecs produced very fine jewelry and poly-chrome pottery, and their pictographic manuscripts have yielded valuable historical information.

Gold mask from Tomb 7, Monte Albán

The principal gods of the pantheon worshipped in the Oaxaca valley were the rain god Cocijo, the maize god Pitao Cozobi, the wind god Quetzalcóatl and Xipe Tótec, the god of renewal and of jewelers.

Towards the end of the 15th c. the Oaxaca region was conquered by the Aztecs.

El Tajín (300–1100). – The cult center of El Tajín, situated between Tampico and Veracruz near the Gulf of Mexico, was formerly attributed to the Totonacs; but this people came into the area only about the beginning of the 13th c., when the site had already been abandoned. It is still not known with certainty who founded the settlement, but late Olmec features and Teotihuacán influence have been identified here. Some authorities ascribe El Tajín to the Huastecs, who belong to the Maya linguistic group and may therefore have come into this area from the S in the Archaic or Early Formative period.

Grupo de las Iglesias, Mitla

The heyday of El Tajín appears to have lain between A.D. 500 and 800. It developed a distinctive style of architecture, with a very limited area of diffusion, the most striking example of this being the six-story pyramid with niches. Other typical items are the carved stone objects, often elaborately ornamented, known as the *yugo* (yoke), *hacha* (axe) and *palma* (palm) – probably reproductions of wooden protective shields used in the ritual ball game. The ball game was of great importance in the religious life of the inhabitants: in El Tajín alone eleven ball courts have been found. It is believed that the losers of the game were sacrificed to the gods.

The Toltecs (950–1300). – The post-Classic period of the pre-Columbian cultures begins with the establishments of the Toltec city of Tollan (Tula). The people called Toltecs probably consisted of two groups, the Náhuatl-speaking primitive Chichimecs who came in from the NW, and the civilized Nonoalca from Tabasco.

The town of Tollan was founded in A.D. 968 by the Toltecs under their ruler Ce Acatl Topiltzín, who later took the name of the god king Quetzalcóatl, the Feathered Serpent. Some twenty years later he is believed to have left Tollan after some internal conflict and made his way with a group of followers via Cholula to the Gulf coast of Yucatán; and it is significant that about A.D. 1000 there began, notably at Chichén Itzá, the impressive mingling of Toltec and Maya culture under the god king Kukulcán (Maya, "Feathered Serpent"). The Toltecs, who preserved many elements of the Classic culture, also exerted influence – no doubt with the help of commercial and military force – on the Mixtec region, on Xochicalco, Malinalco, La Quemada and Chalchihuites, and possibly even on Casas Grandes.

Stylistically this period was distinguished from the preceding Classic phase by the relative coarseness of the architecture and sculpture. – The priests must now have lost their directing role to the warrior caste.

The relatively short flowering of Toltec culture ended in 1175 with the rapid decline of Tula, attributable to internal conflicts and pressure from a new wave of Chichimec incomers. Some of the Toltecs who were now driven out settled in the

Mexico valley (Culhuacán, and also in Cholula), while others moved S along the coast into what is now Nicaragua.

Among the most notable monuments of Toltec culture are the large pillared halls, the colossal Atlantean figures up to 4.60 m (15 ft) high, the curious recumbent figures of Chac-mool, the Serpent Wall (Coatepantli) and the Wall of Skulls (Tzompantli). The warlike bent of this culture, represented by the military orders of the Eagle Knights and Jaguar Knights, is evident in the reliefs of skulls and scenes of war and sacrifice. The finest examples of Toltec art in Yucatán are to be seen at Chichén Itzá, where the basic conception is clearly of Toltec origin but the decoration has been carried out by Maya artists. Also dated to the Tollan period are the first examples of metalworking, a craft brought in from Guerrero, and the introduction of the spinning whorl.

In the Toltec pantheon a predominant role was played by Quetzalcóatl in his various forms and symbols. His brother and counterpart was Tezcatlipoca ("Smoking Mirror"), god of the night sky, of magicians and of retributive justice. More generally, astral and military divinities now began to displace the earth and vegetation gods of the Classic period.

The Magic of Jade

The Mexican Indians of the pre-Hispanic period ascribed magical qualities to certain minerals. Thus the semi-precious stone **jadeite**, known to the Indians as *chalchihuitl* or *quetzalitzli*, was more highly prized than gold – no doubt partly because of its resemblance to the metallic green sheen of the plumage of their sacred bird, the quetzal.

The Aztecs (1300–1521). – The Aztec culture, the least artistically oriented of the advanced pre-Columbian cultures, owed its success mainly to its highly developed technical, economic and religious organization. For the most part the Aztecs took over the foundations of their culture from their predecessors or their neighbors and carried them to a higher pitch of development.

Around the middle of the 14th c. the Aztecs ("people from the land of Aztlán"), who had come into the Mexico valley from the NW, established their capital, Tenochtitlán, on an island in Lake Tex-

Aztec sculpture – a snake carved from stone

The most important surviving remains of Aztec art are pieces of monumental stone sculpture (the Sun Stone or "Stone of the Fifth Sun" or Calendar Stone; the Stone of Tizoc; statue of the earth goddess Coatlicue).

Life in the Aztec Empire before the Spanish Conquest

When the Spanish conquerors first saw Tenochtitlán, the huge capital city of the Aztec empire, they were amazed by its size, magnificence and well-ordered layout. They were particularly impressed by the markets. Even Cortés, who was not given to overstatement, later wrote to the Emperor Charles V about the market of Tlatelolco: "There were soldiers among us who had seen much of the world, who had been in Constantinople and all over Italy, even at Rome, and they said that they had never seen such a well-ordered market, one so large and so overflowing with goods and with people." Bernal Díaz del Castillo recorded that 25,000 people came to this market every day, but that every five days a market was held which drew between 40,000 and 50,000 people.

coco. After its foundation the term "Mexica" came into use, applied by the Aztecs to themselves. During the following 150 years they extended their rule to the N and E as far as the coastal regions on the Gulf of Mexico inhabited by the Huastecs and to the SW and S from Colima by way of Oaxaca to the borders of what is now Guatemala. Their dominions, however, did not form a unified state but, outside the central heartland, were made up of forty provinces whose inhabitants paid tribute to the Aztecs. The invasion of Aztec territory by the Spaniards and their Indian allies between 1519 and 1521 brought their culture – the last of the advanced cultures of Meso-America – to a sudden end.

The Aztecs regarded themselves as successors to the Toltecs, and this relationship is reflected in their architecture and sculpture. They took over artistic techniques from their subject peoples, either importing their works or bringing in their craftsmen. Many objects found in the Aztec heartland have come from the regions of Mexteca-Puebla, Huastec or Purépecha (Tarascan) culture. – Most of the great Aztec cult centers were demolished by the Spanish conquerors, who used the material in their own buildings, so that very little Aztec work has survived. In recent years parts of the temples of Tenochtitlán and Tlatelolco have been brought to light within Mexico City.

At the time of the Spanish conquest **Tenochtitlán** ("place of the cactus fruit") and the neighboring *Tlatelolco*, which it had conquered in 1473, were divided into four large districts, and this division was maintained long after the conquest. The traditional administrative units, however, were the smaller *calpulli*, neighborhoods which owned their land in common and elected their own head man.

The island city was traversed by a network of canals and linked with the shores of the lake by three great causeways. The northern highroad, leaving from Tlatelolco, reached the mainland at Tepeyacac, near the pilgrimage church of Guadalupe; the western causeway linked Tenochtitlán with Tlacopan; and the southern causeway had two branches, one running SW to Coyoacán, the other E to Iztapalapan. There were also two aqueducts, one running from Chapultepec to the city center, the other bringing drinking water from Coyoacán along the Iztapalapan road.

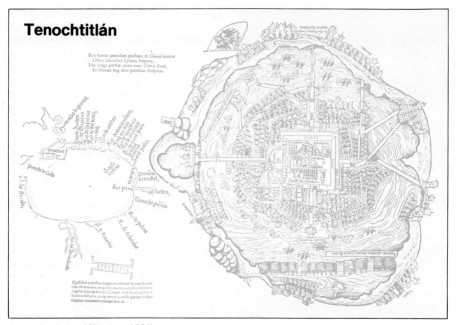

Tenochtitlán

Town plan (printed Nürnberg 1564)

The *social structure* of the Aztecs was hierarchical, but offered ample scope for rising up the social scale. The members of the highest stratum of the army, the administration and the judicature were addressed as *tecuhtli* ("lord", "dignitary") – a title which was also borne by the emperor. In an earlier period these dignitaries had been appointed on the basis of merit, but in the final phase before the coming of the Spaniards they were for the most part selected by the emperor, usually from among the heirs of the last holder of the post. The emperor also bore the titles of *Tlatoani* ("Speaker": i.e., leader of the Tlatocan or Supreme Council) and *Tlacatecuhtli* ("Lord of the Warriors" or commander-in-chief), and was elected in Tenochtitlán by an electoral college of dignitaries. From the time of Moctezuma I the emperor was assisted by a senior official known as the *Cihua-cóatl* ("Serpent Lady", from the name of a goddess). Immediately below the emperor and the Cihuacóatl were four other high dignitaries and counsellors, and below these again came the *Tlatocan* or Supreme Council.

All offices and dignities in the Aztec empire were held for life. There was no hereditary nobility: the son of a *tecuhtli*, known as *pilli* ("child", "son"), had no right to a title but had to earn rank and dignity by his own merits, particularly in the military field. The only advantage he enjoyed was easier access to the *Cal-mecac*, an institution of higher education. Normally the upper ranks of society were recruited from the *macehuatlin* (singular *macehualli*) or "plebeians". A plebeian, but not a merchant (see below), could attain the rank of *lyac* by the capture of an enemy in combat; but if he served in two or three campaigns without achieving any further distinction he was required to leave the service and remained a *mace-hualli*. If, however, he killed or captured four enemy warriors he was promoted to the rank of *tequia*, which meant that he received a share of the enemy tribute (*tequitl*). The higher ranks took their titles from the rough warlike tribes of the north – Quauhchichimecatl ("Chichimec eagle") and Otomitl ("Otomí warrior").

Among the merchants, who were known as *pochteca* after the commercial district of Pochtlan in Tlatelolco, trades were hereditary. The military career was closed to them, but on their adventurous trading trips into remote regions they performed the function of spies or scouts. They frequently acquired considerable wealth through their monopoly of external trade, but took care to avoid ostentatious display lest they should incur the jealousy of the privileged priestly and military castes.

Recruits for the priestly class, which enjoyed equal rights with the military and civil dignitaries of the empire, were trained in the higher educational establishments known as *calmecac*. At the age of 22 the novice, who was required to remain celibate, could attain the statue of *tlamacazqui* (priest). The highest ecclesiastical dignitaries were two high priests, *Quetzalcóatl Tótec Tlamacazqui* ("Feathered Serpent Priest of our Lord"), for the cult of the sun and war god Huitzilopochtli, and *Quetzalcóatl Tláloc Tlamacazqui* ("Feathered Serpent Priest of Tláloc"), for the cult of the rain god. For the female divinities there were priestesses.

Another important category was the craftsman, who were known to the Aztecs as *tolteca*, since the development of the craftsmen's skills (*toltecayotl*, "Toltec trades") was ascribed to the Toltecs. The most important craftsmen's guilds were the feather-weavers (*amanteca*) and the goldsmiths (*teocuitlahuaque*); the "writers" of *tlacuilo* (actually book painters) were held in particularly high regard.

There were also slaves (*tlatlacotin*, singular *tlacotli*), who were much more humanely treated than their counterparts in Europe. They were permitted to possess property, save money and purchase their freedom, and marriages between free citizens and slaves were allowed. The slaves were recruited from prisoners of war who were not sacrificed or from persons convicted of an offence; but most of them seem to have embraced slavery willingly, the purchase price being paid to the prospective slave, who then remained in freedom until the money was spent, perhaps a year later.

In the *cosmology* of the Aztecs, as in that of other Meso-American peoples, it was held that this present world had been preceded by other worlds which had been destroyed by cosmic catastrophes. The Aztecs believed that the present world was the fifth: hence the name "Stone of the Fifth Sun" given to the famous Calendar Stone. After the destruction of the fourth world by a flood, it was believed

"La Gran Tenochtitlán", mural by Diego Rivera (National Palace, Mexico City)

the gods had assembled in Teotihuacán. Then one of the gods cremated himself and gave rise to the new sun, but at first this remained without movement. Thereupon the other gods sacrificed themelves and their vital force was thus transferred to the sun, which was now set in motion. But since the universe had been started on its course by sacrifices of this kind its continuance could be ensured only by the sacrifice of human blood, known in Náhuatl as *chalchiuatl* ("precious water"). This was the reasoning that lay behind the practice of *human sacrifice*, which the Spaniards, ignorant of the religious background, saw merely as senseless cruelty.

The Aztec Calendar Stone

These human sacrifices were of particular importance at the end of a Mexican "century" of 52 years (see the account of the Mexican calendar on p. 31). The beginning of the year could fall only on four of the 20 "day glyphs", and these, multiplied by the 13 basic numbers, gave 52 "new year's days", after which the first day of the year had the same glyph and the same number. The Aztecs believed that at that moment the danger of a cosmic catastrophe was particularly great: accordingly fires were extinguished throughout the country and the painted stucco facings of pyramids and temples were broken up. During the night the high priests made their way to the summit of Uixachetecatl, a hill near the capital, in order to observe the constellations. If these were found to be continuing in their courses a flame was lit with a fire-stick in the breast of a sacrificial victim and the "new fire" was carried by messengers over the territory of the empire. Thereafter the sanctuaries were given a new stucco facing.

At the time of the Spanish conquest the Aztec empire had reached its greatest extent, and further military campaigns were rarely undertaken, so that there was a shortage of prisoners of war for the sacrifices. Accordingly the dominant city states of Tenochtitlán, Texcoco and Tlacopan agreed with the tributary provinces of Tlaxcala, Huejotzingo and Cholula to fight ritual battles at regular intervals with the sole purpose of obtaining prisoners of war for sacrifice. These battles were known as the "flower war" (*xochiyáoyotl*). The republic of Tlaxcala had to pay a particularly heavy toll of blood in this way, and the accumulated resentment of the Tlaxcalans led them to ally themselves with the invading Spaniards against the Aztecs – and without this assistance the Spaniards might well have been unable to achieve the conquest of Tenochtitlán.

Accounts of the earlier campaigns of conquest by the Aztecs show that they had a quite different conception of the *art of war* from that accepted in Europe. In their wars there were no surprise attacks: a declaration of war was always preceded by the sending of embassies to the enemy and by long-drawn-out negotiations during which they were repeatedly offered the choice between voluntary submission and war. When war came the object was not to kill the enemy but to take them prisoner, and once the principal temple of the enemy city was captured this was accepted as a divine judgment: Huitzilopochtli, the war god of the Aztecs, had shown himself to be stronger than his counterpart. Thereupon the fighting stopped and the bargaining over the amount of tribute to be paid began. This was fixed at a level which left the economic structure of the defeated people intact; and they were also allowed to retain their own customs and way of life. These practices explain why the Aztecs were at such a loss when confronted with the Spaniards' method of waging war: their tactics were quite unsuited to coping with the ruthlessness of the conquistadors, who felt justified in using any methods to bring about the annihilation or total subjugation of the "pagans".

Our information about the life of the Aztecs is derived not only from the accounts of the conquistadors themselves and of the first monks sent to the New World but also on original sources, the

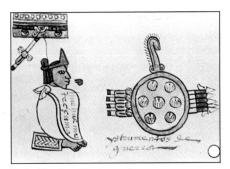

Codex Mendoza: Moctezuma I

codices. The most important of these are the *Codex Mendoza*, the *Codex Magliabecchiano*, the *Codex Rios* and its parallel volume the *Codex Telleriano* – all provided, by priests familiar with the Náhuatl language, with Latin transcriptions of the ideographs and commentaries in Spanish. Other codices, without such commentaries, are the *Codex Florentino* and the *Codex Nuttall*.

These explanations were very necessary, since the texts are written in an *ideographic script*: thus to express the fact that the Aztec emperor Moctezuma made preparations for war the book depicted the seated emperor, with his name glyph, accompanied by weapons. A script of this kind was, of course, unable to express the finer points of Náhuatl literature, which had considerable achievements to its credit in the fields of rhetoric, lyric and epic writing. It was necessary, therefore, for the students at a priestly school (*calmecac*) to learn long texts by heart, using the ideographic script merely as an aide-mémoire. Fortunately the monks who went to Mexico after the conquest to instruct the Indians in the Christian faith found a sufficient number of young men of the upper ranks of Aztec society, from whose dictation they were able to write down the Náhuatl texts in Latin transcription or to whom they could teach the method of phonetic transcription.

It is significant, however, that the Aztecs also used glyphs with a particular significance to express the same syllables with another meaning. They had thus taken the first step toward evolving a phonetic or syllabic script; and it may be supposed that they would soon have developed such a script if their culture had not been brought to a sudden end by the Spanish conquest. One is tempted to indulge in similar speculations in other fields. But even as it is the cultural achievements of the Meso-American peoples are astonishing when it is considered that their technological and economic level was still basically that of the Stone Age.

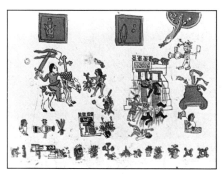

Codex Telleriano: the Conquista

History

Prehistory (40000–5000 B.C.). – During the *Ice Ages* of the Pleistocene the level of the sea falls and allows human beings and animals, *c.* 50000 B.C., to cross the broad Bering land bridge from Asia to the American continent. These "Palaeo-Indian" hunters and food-gatherers move S and are believed to have reached Tierra del Fuego, at the southern tip of America, *c.* 10000 B.C.

About 29000 B.C.   First traces of human beings in Latin America. Worked-on bones and stones found at El Cedral, S.L.P., Mexico.

About 10000 B.C.   *Tepexpan Man*, the oldest human remains in Mexico.

About 7000 B.C.   First traces of agricultural crops (gourds, avocados, chili peppers, cotton) in the Tehuacán valley.

Archaic period (5000–1500 B.C.). – Permanent settlements of some size are established, providing the basis for the *pre-Columbian cultures*.

About 3000 B.C.   The first communal settlements appear. Farming methods and craft processes are refined and lead to the production of the first Obsidian blades and the earliest ceramic figures (about 2500 B.C.). About 2000 B.C. the first Maya center of Cuello (Belize) develops.

1200–400 B.C.   Flowering of OLMEC culture.

800 B.C.   **Monte Albán I**.

500 B.C.   First established appearance of the MAYAS.

350 B.C.   Foundation of **Teotihuacán**. – Establishment of El Tajín.

31 B.C.   Stela C, *Tres Zapotes* (the earliest dated evidence of the Olmec culture).

Classic period (A.D. 200–900). – The advanced cultures of Mexico reach the zenith of their development. Although draft and pack animals and metal tools are unknown, and the wheel is not used as a practical device, these cultures produce magnificent achievements in architecture, sculpture, pottery, painting and jewelry. Astronomy and mathematics are highly developed.

About A.D. 400   Beginning of the rise of **El Tajín**.

Post-Classical period (900–1521). – "Barbarian" tribes begin to advance into central Mexico from the N. The priestly rulers, who had hitherto possessed almost unlimited power, are now increasingly displaced by the warrior caste. Human sacrifice plays a large part in cult rituals. The tremendous cultural advance of the Classic period comes to a halt, and the arts show a coarsening of style. The craft of metalworking spreads. – The Spanish **Conquest** puts an end to Indian cultures.

About 900   Decline of the cities in the Maya heartland.

968   Foundation of the Toltec city of **Tollan** (Tula).

1000–1200   Heyday of **Chichén Itzá**.

1168   Fall of Tollan (Tula).

About 1300   Coming of the AZTECS, who *c.* 1350 establish their capital, **Tenochtitlán**, on the site now occupied by Mexico City.

About 1450   End of the Maya culture.

1492   Discovery of the New World by **Christopher Columbus** (*Cristóbal Colón*).

1512   First contacts between Spanish navigators and Maya Indians on the coast of Yucatán. *Gonzalo Guerrero* and a priest, *Jerónimo de Aguilar*, are taken prisoner by the Indians.

1517–18   The conquistadors *Hernández de Córdoba* and *Juan de Grijalva* reconnoitre the coast of Yucatán and the Gulf of Mexico.

1519   *Hernán* **Cortés**, then aged 34, sails SW from Cuba, without the governor's authority, with 11 ships, 100 sailors and 508 soldiers. After calling in at the Caribbean island of Cozumel he frees Jerónimo de Aguilar, who thereafter performs a useful service as an interpreter. Cortés sails around the Yucatán peninsula and lands on the Tabasco coast, but leaves again after a fight with the Mayas. He takes with him an Indian girl named *Malinche* (Malintzín), who is baptized under the name of Marina and becomes a valuable adviser and interpreter.

Near the present town of Veracruz Cortés receives envoys from the Aztec ruler **Moctezuma II** (the "wrathful prince": usually known as *Montezuma*), who have been sent to establish whether Cortés and his men are the god-king Quetzalcóatl and his retinue returning to their country. – Many of the rulers of territories subject to the Aztecs offer their support to Cortés. After founding the town of Villa Rica de la Vera Cruz the Spaniards advance towards Tenochtitlán and capture Cholula, where they massacre the population and destroy the temple of Quetzalcóatl. They are received by Moctezuma in his capital as guests, but soon afterwards take him prisoner.

1520   *Pánfilo de Narváez* arrives at Veracruz, having been sent by the governor of Cuba to call Cortés to account for his insubordination. Cortés leaves *Pedro de Alvarado* in Tenochtitlán with 80 men, hurries down to the coast and on May 20 defeats Narváez at Zempoala. He then returns to Tenochtitlán, where during his absence Pedro de Alvarado and his men have killed 200 members of the Aztec ruling class. This leads to a rising against the Spaniards, whereupon Moctezuma is deposed and *Cuitláhuac* declared his successor. Three months later Cuitláhuac dies of smallpox and is succeeded by the uncompromising **Cuauhtémoc** ("Swooping Eagle"), the last Aztec ruler. On June 27 Moctezuma is killed by his subjects, and on June 30, the "Noche triste" ("sad night"), the Spaniards leave the town, suffering heavy losses. Soon afterwards Cortés defeats a large force at Otumba. The Spaniards have a period of rest with their allies the Tlaxcalans and prepare for the siege of Tenochtitlán.

1521   On August 13 the Spaniards and their Indian allies capture and destroy Tenochtitlán. Cuauhtémoc is taken prisoner. Three years later Cortés takes Cuauhtémoc with him on an expedition to Honduras and has him executed in 1525 on the pretext of his treachery.

Spanish colonial rule (1522–1821). – At first Cortés rules New Spain under the Spanish crown, as governor and commander-in-chief (Capitán General). From 1527 to 1535 the country is governed by a strong Audiencia (court exercising military and civil jurisdiction). Thereafter until the end of the colonial period, it is ruled by Viceroys appointed by the crown. – The native population is almost completely converted to Christianity, and the first phase of the mingling of Indian, Iberian and African races begins. – European cereals are cultivated and stock-farming is introduced. The Mexican silver-mines become one of Spain's major source of revenue.

1522 Cortés has the old capital of Tenochtitlán, which had been completely destroyed, rebuilt as the future colonial capital, under the name of México. The Emperor *Charles V* appoints Cortés governor of NEW SPAIN.

1522–4 Cortés and his lieutenants conquer almost all the territories ruled by the Aztecs, extending as far as Honduras and El Salvador. In 1523 the first 3 and in 1524 another 12 *Franciscan friars* arrive in Mexico and set about evangelizing the population and founding religious houses. – Members of the Spanish forces are granted *encomiendas*, estates covering large areas of land and Indian villages, with the obligation (not always observed) not to exploit the population but to protect them and convert them to the Christian faith. Although the *encomiendas* are formally abolished in 1542, in practice they continue to exist, in greater or lesser degree, until the beginning of the 18th c.

1526 *Dominican monks* come to New Spain, establishing themselves mainly in the S, in the territory of the Mixtecs and Zapotecs. Later *Augustinians* and *Jesuits* join in this missionary activity, and within a decade millions of Indians are converted. Although they destroy the pre-Columbian temples and other buildings and prohibit the old rites, they study the Indian languages and record the way of life and customs of their flock. They build hospitals and construct irrigation systems, teach the Indians European crafts and farming techniques and protect them against harsh treatment by Spanish soldiers and settlers. Notable among them are *Juan de Zumárraga*, *Vasco de Quiroga*, *Bartolomé de las Casas*, *Diego de Landa* and *Bernardino de Sahagún*, whose writings contain much valuable historical information. – After 1555, when the Spanish crown establishes its authority more strongly, the rights and freedom of action of the missionaries are increasingly restricted and their work brought under the control of the bishops.

1527 Cortés returns to Spain to defend himself against accusations of malgovernment in Mexico. He is deprived of his post as governor but is granted the title of Marqués del Valle de Oaxaca. The government of New Spain is entrusted to the **Audiencia**, a five-man commission responsible for both administration and justice.

1530 Cortés goes back to Mexico and undertakes a number of unsuccessful naval expeditions along the Pacific coast. *Nuño Beltrán de Guzmán* conquers territories on the Pacific coast, including what is now the state of Jalisco. *Francisco de Montejo* fails in an attempt to subjugate the Mayas of Yucatán, who put up a fierce resistance; ten years later his son, with the same name, succeeds where his father had failed.

1531 An Indian, *Juan Diego*, claims to have seen an apparition of the Virgin at Guadalupe on December 12. As Nuestra Señora de Guadalupe, the Virgin becomes the patroness of the Mexican Indians.

1535 The Emperor Charles V appoints the very able *Antonio de Mendoza* as the first **Viceroy** of New Spain, with authority also over the Antilles and Philippines. Within Mexico the Viceroy is the highest administrative and judicial authority, patron of the Church and commander-in-chief of the forces. Until independence (1821) Mexico is ruled by 62 Viceroys. New Spain is divided into provinces ruled by governors-general. Supreme authority over the new colonies still rests with the king, who is advised by a council on colonial affairs. The main tasks of the new administration in Mexico are to maintain the absolute authority of the crown, to exploit the

country's economic resources and to protect and convert the natives. For this purpose special Indian laws are promulgated in 1542, but these are only very imperfectly enforced.

1535–65 Campaigns of conquest by *Ponce de León*, *Pánfilo de Narváez* (Florida), *Alvaro Núñez Cabeza de Vaca* (Texas and New Mexico), *Hernán de Soto* (from the Atlantic to the Mississippi) and *Francisco Vázquez de Coronado* (from the Gulf of Mexico to Kansas) extend the area of Spanish rule still farther. – The first negro slaves are brought to New Spain.

1547 Cortés dies in Spain, solitary and embittered.

1551 The first university on American soil is established in Mexico City. – Mining, particularly of silver, develops on a considerable scale.

1571 The Santa Inquisición, the supreme court in matters of faith, is established in Mexico City.

About 1600 The Spaniards have now established their authority over the whole mainland of present-day Mexico. – The Indian population has been reduced to about a third of its former size, mainly as a result of diseases brought in from Europe. Some 30% of the country's area is in the hands of the Church. The large, economically self-supporting estates known as *haciendas* are established. Alongside them there survive the *ejidos*, Indian settlements with communally owned land which date from pre-Columbian times.

About 1650 Economic decline of New Spain, due to a fall in the output of silver.

1697 Conquest by Tayasal (Peten) of the last independent Indian state (Itza-Maya).

1700 King *Charles II*, last of the Spanish Hapsburgs, dies, and the crown passes to the **Bourbons**, who seek, with varying success, to reform colonial policy.

1767 The Jesuits are expelled from Mexico (as well as from Spain).

About 1800 New Spain reaches its greatest extent: with an area of some 4,000,000 sq. km (1,500,000 sq. miles), it is the largest country in America after Brazil. The population is estimated at 6 million (15% Spaniards, 25% mestizos, 60% Indians). The Spaniards are known as *Gachupines* if they were born in Spain and as *Criollos* (Creoles) if they were born in the colonies. The Gachupines enjoy preferential treatment, particularly in government service. – The ideas of the French and American revolutions penetrate into New Spain and give rise to demands for increased independence.

1803–4 *Alexander von Humboldt* visits Mexico. – The Spanish crown takes over Church property. The Criollos and many churchmen lose faith in Spain.

1808 *Napoleon* invades Spain and his brother *Joseph Bonaparte* becomes king. New Spain refuses to recognize him. There are differences of view about the political consequences of this action: a small group favour declaring Mexican independence of Spain, but the majority advocate carrying on the government in the name of the deposed king *Ferdinand VII*. The Viceroy, *José de Iturrigaray*, counting on the support of the Criollos, seeks to have himself proclaimed king, but is carried off to Veracruz and then to Spain by a group of Spaniards and imprisoned.

1810–21 *War of Independence*. A group of Criollos led by *Miguel Hidalgo y Costilla*, a priest of advanced ideas from Dolores, and *Ignacio Allende* of San Miguel, a captain in the army, launch the first

Hidalgo Monument, Dolores Hidalgo

national rising with the "Call of Dolores" ("Gritto de Dolores") on September 16 at 5 a.m. Their watchword is "Vivan las Américas, muera el mal gobierno, mueran los Gachupines!"

1811　After gaining some initial military successes the rebels are defeated. Hidalgo and Allende are taken prisoner and executed. A second rising breaks out under the leadership of an energetic priest, *José María Morelos*.

1813　The rebels issue a **declaration of independence** at Chilpancingo, promising a new constitution to establish the unlimited sovereignty of the people and universal suffrage, the abolition of slavery, the class system, torture and the government monopoly, and the recognition of Catholicism as the state religion. – The rebels are defeated by loyalist troops led by Agustín de Iturbide in the battle of Morelia. Morelos is captured in 1815 and is shot in Mexico City.

1820　A revolution by the "Liberales" in Spain compels Ferdinand VII to bring into force the constitution adopted at Cádiz in 1812. This strengthens the movement for independence in New Spain.

From Independence to the War of Intervention (1821–67). – The independence of Mexico, won in battle and confirmed by treaties between the rebels and loyalists, is not recognized by Spain until 1836. This first phase of Mexican independence, usually regarded as lasting until 1857, is marked by internal conflicts, wars with the United States and attempts at foreign intervention. This leads to the Guerra de la Reforma, a civil war which is followed by the intervention of European powers, concerned about their claims on the Mexican state.

1821　The energetic General *Agustín de Iturbide* mediates between rebels and royalists and, having secured the support of the most powerful forces in the country, puts forward the "Iguala Plan" declaring **Mexican independence**. On August 24 Iturbide and the Viceroy, *Juan O'Donojú*, sign the treaty of Córdoba giving Mexico national sovereignty.

1822　The Spanish parliament rejects the treaty of Córdoba. Iturbide is elected **emperor** by the new Mexican Congress and takes the title of *Agustín I*.

1823　Risings against the government, led by Vicente Guerrero, Guadalupe Victoria, Nicolás Bravo and Antonio López de Santa Ana. Iturbide abdicates and leaves the country. The monarchy is abolished and the Central American provinces declare their independence (United States of Central America, 1823–39).

1824　Promulgation of a **constitution** similar to that of the United States of America. The revolutionary leader *Guadalupe Victoria* becomes first President of the **Republic**, with *Nicolás Bravo* as Vice-President. Iturbide, having returned to the country, is court-martialed and shot.

1925–8　The last Spanish stronghold, the fort of San Juan de Ulúa (Veracruz), is taken by the Mexicans. – The Mexican government encourages settlers from North America in Texas, still largely unpopulated. Political conflicts between the conservative Centralists and the liberal Federalists, together with intervention by Britain and the United States in Mexico's internal affairs, hamper the effectiveness of the government. Vicente Guerrero, a federalist, is defeated in an election but is nevertheless appointed the new President.

1829　Guerrero is overthrown and flees to Acapulco, but is betrayed and executed in 1831 for high treason. He is succeeded by the Vice-President, *Anastasio Bustamante*.

1832　General *Antonio López de Santa Ana*, in alliance with the Liberals, overthrows Bustamante and becomes President and finally **Dictator**. – Increased tension in Texas between immigrants from North America and the Mexicans, now increasingly in the minority.

1836　Bitter conflicts between immigrants and Mexicans. Texas secedes from Mexico. Santa Ana moves N with his troops and takes San Antonia. In the battle for the old Franciscan mission station of the Alamo all the American rebels holding it are killed and Santa Ana's victorious force suffers heavy losses. A few weeks later they are defeated in the battle of the San Jacinto river by American troops under General *Sam Houston*, and Santa Ana is taken prisoner. Texan independence is thus, de facto, achieved (the "Lone Star Republic").

1845　The United States annex Texas, which becomes the 28th state in the Union.

1847　Outbreak of the "War of the Castes", the uprising of the Yucatan Maya tribes, which lasts until the beginning of the 20th century.

1846–8　The Texas conflict leads to *war between the United States and Mexico*. Santa Ana's forces are defeated in bitter fighting. Mexico City falls at the end of September 1847 after a heroic resistance by young cadets (the "Niños Héroes") in Chapultepec Castle. Santa Ana resigns as President and his successor *Herrera* signs the peace treaty of Guadalupe Hidalgo, under which Mexico gives up Texas and cedes northern California, Arizona and New Mexico to the United States in return for a payment of $18,250,000. The territory of Mexico is thus reduced by more than half.

1849–55 Defeat exacerbates the political tensions between the clerical Conservatives and the anti-clerical Liberals in Mexico. In 1853 Santa Ana comes back as Dictator, but after two years returns into exile for good.

1856–7 The Liberals, led by General *Ignacio Comonfort* and his associates *Benito Juárez, Miguel Lerdo de Tejada* and *Melchor Ocampo*, take over the government and draft radical **reform laws**. These provide among other things for the abolition of the privileges of the Church and the army, the replacement of the *hacienda* and *ejido* systems by the private ownership of land and programs for the development of industry and the transfer of responsibility for education to the state. The compulsory sales of former Church property and the redistribution of the Indian *ejidos* meet with determined opposition from the Church and lead to the further impoverishment of the Indians, who cannot cope with the private ownership of land. – The long-standing conflicts between Conservatives and Liberals end in civil war.

1858–61 *Guerra de la Reforma* (the "Reform War"). During the Presidency of *Benito Juárez*, a proud and uncompromising Xapotec from Oaxaca, fighting breaks out. In the first year the forces of the Conservatives, under the leadership of Generals *Miguel Miramón, Tomás Mejía* and *Leonardo Márquez*, are victorious. Juárez moves his Liberal government first to Guadalajara and then to Vera-cruz. In terms of the reform laws he promulgates measures for the expropriation of Church property without compensation, the abolition of the religious orders, the introduction of civil marriage and the take-over of cemeteries by the state. The separation of Church and state is now complete.

1860 The fortunes of war favor the Liberals.

1861 Liberal forces led by General *González Ortega* enter Mexico City, and ten days later Juárez and his cabinet return to the capital. In view of the desperate state of the country's finances the President freezes repayments of external debts for two years. Britain, Spain and France protest and decide to enforce payment by joint military intervention. In December the first allied units land at Veracruz.

1862–7 *European intervention*. The Mexican government successfully negotiates the withdrawal of British and Spanish forces, but *Napoleon III* of France seizes the opportunity to continue his aggressive foreign policy. His plan is to establish a monarchic alliance, a Latin league to counter the expansion of the United States, and to restore France's former influence in the New World.

1862 The French troops in Mexico are reinforced and advance against Mexico City. On May 5 they are defeated by General *Ignacio Zaragoza* at Puebla, but in further fighting Mexican forces are almost wiped out.

1863 The French enter Mexico City, and the Juárez government flees to the N of the country. On July 10 a **monarchy** is proclaimed in the capital. Napoleon III and Mexican conservative politicians in exile offer the imperial throne to the Habsburg Archduke *Ferdinand Maximilian*, who accepts the regency only after a plebiscite in his favor.

1864 The **Emperor Maximilian** arrives in Mexico on May 28 with his wife, the Belgian Princess Charlotte. To the disappointment of the Conservatives he leaves the reform laws in force, proposes measures to improve the legal status of the peasants (*peones*) and seeks to alleviate the situation of the Indians; but the desperate financial position, mainly due to the heavy costs of the French army of intervention, makes any effective government action almost impossible. Further difficulty is caused by conflicts with the Conservatives who had invited him to come to Mexico and with the French commander-in-chief, Marshal *Bazaine*.

1865 By the spring the French have driven almost all Juárez's forces out of Mexico. – In the United States, where the Civil War has been won by the northern states, the French intervention is seen as infringing the Monroe Doctrine, and the US government calls for the immediate withdrawal of French forces.

1866 Prussia's victory over Austria at Königgrätz and the resultant threat to France leads Napoleon III to begin withdrawing the French forces. In July the Empress Charlotte travels to Europe in an attempt to make Napoleon change his mind and to seek help from Pope Pius IX. She is unsuccessful in this mission and becomes mentally deranged.

1867 The last French troops leave Mexico in March. Maximilian refuses to abandon "his" people and takes command of the loyalist Mexican forces; but these are no match for the Liberal forces led by Generals *Mariano Escobedo* and *Ramón Corona* and *Porfirio Díaz*. On May 15 his small army is encircled at Querétaro, and he himself is taken prisoner and, in spite of numerous international appeals, court-martialed and shot together with his two generals *Miguel Miramón* and *Tomás Mejía*.

Restoration of the Republic (1867–76). – The Liberals, restored to power, take up their policies at the point where they were interrupted by the French intervention. The government is faced with grave difficulties arising from the devastation caused by the war, unemployment among the discharged soldiers and an increasing split within the Liberal camp itself. Two leading aims of the Juárez government are the revival of the economy and the reorganization of the educational system.

1867 *Benito Juárez* is confirmed as President. He seeks to preserve at least some of the *ejidos*, the Indian communes, although this is contrary to the reform laws. – British engineers resume work on the railway between Veracruz and Mexico City, which had been suspended; it is completed in 1873.

1871–6 Juárez is re-elected in 1871 but dies in the following year. He is succeeded by the intelligent but indecisive *Sebastián Lerdo de Tejada*, who in the main continues Juárez's policies but aims at greater centralization. On his initiative the parliamentary system is changed to provide for two chambers (House of Representatives and Senate).

The age of Porfirio Díaz (1876–1911). – These years of autocratic rule by Porfirio Díaz are the longest period of peace enjoyed by Mexico in the first hundred years of independence. This period sees the first great wave of modernization of the country, and a considerable economic advance begins. Mexico acquires – partly with the help of foreign capital – new industrial plants, railways, telephone and telegraph services, and new mines are opened up.

1876 *Porfirio* **Díaz**, a mestizo of very modest origins but of great ability, takes over the government. Lerdo resigns and flees the country.

1877   Repeated frontier violations by Mexican bandits and groups of Indians lead the United States to ask Díaz's permission to pursue them into Mexican territory. Díaz refuses to allow this on the ground that it would offend against Mexican sovereignty, but strengthens his own frontier forces in order to prevent further intrusions. Thereupon the United States officially recognizes the Díaz government.

1880–4   Since the Mexican constitution prevents a President from being re-elected for an immediate second term, a protégé of Díaz's, *Manuel González*, takes over the government after an election victory. During his period of office investment in modernization exceeds the budgetary resources available, and in order to meet his foreign obligations he cuts the pay of government officials. The consequence is a considerable increase in corruption, and public opinion turns against the President.

1884–1911   *Porfirio Díaz* is re-elected and thereafter remains continuously in power. Although originally a Liberal, he is able to win over the Conservatives to his support and to keep opposing groups (including the Indians) in check. While the upper stratum of society is involved in the redevelopment of the country, there is little change in the situation of the poorer members of the population. The ownership of land is concentrated in the hands of the few, and industry and mining are largely financed by foreign capital. In 1910 Díaz stands for election for the last time, promising greater political freedom; but when he fails to keep his promise he is forced into resignation (1911). He dies in exile in Paris.

The Mexican revolution (1910–20). – Mexican historians describe the history of the country from 1910 to the present time as a period of "permanent revolution". The first decade of this period, the decade of "revolution and destruction" during which a million Mexicans lose their lives, is the bloodiest period in the history of independent Mexico.

1910–15   The first revolutionary movement is led by the liberally minded son of a large landowner, *Francisco Madero*, who allies himself with the cruel *Francisco (Pancho) Villa* (Doroteo Arango), a former bandit leader. After Díaz's resignation Madero, an idealistic but weak man, becomes President in 1911. He is overthrown by a rising led by General *Victoriano Huerta* and shot in 1913. Huerta, ruling as a dictator, becomes involved in a civil war with the constitutionalists, who are led by *Venustiano Carranza* (Coahuila), *Alvaro Obregón* (Sonora) and Pancho Villa (Chihuahua). In the S the altruistic *Emiliano Zapata* stirs up an Indian peasant revolt, which calls for radical land reform with the battlecry "Tierra y Libertad" ("Land and Liberty"). The United States, under Woodrow Wilson, support the constitutionalists and in 1914 occupy Veracruz. In July Huerta seeks refuge abroad. Carranza allies himself with Obregón, who in 1914 is the first to reach the Capital, now without a government. Villa, in temporary alliance with Zapata, is defeated in 1915 by Obregón at Celaya in the bloodiest battle in Mexican history and flees to the N.

1916–20   Carranza, who is recognized as President by the United States, succeeds in pacifying most of the country under his authority. Only Zapata continues the fight until he is murdered in 1919. In 1916 Pancho Villa invades New Mexico, and thereafter General John Pershing leads an unsuccessful United States punitive expedition into Mexico. Villa is shot in 1923.

1917   A new constitution is drafted in Querétaro. Largely based on the 1857 constitution, it abolishes the hacienda system, declares the country's minerals to be the property of the Mexican people, contains far-reaching provisions for the protection of workers and limits the President to a single four-year term. The constitution is brought into force on February 5.

The political turmoil continues. The United States withdraw support from Carranza, since he refuses to enter the First World War on the side of the Allies. Within Mexico opposition to Carranza intensifies, and in April 1920 he is murdered. He is succeeded by Alvaro Obregón.

Consolidation of the revolution (1921–33). – During this period the leaders of the revolutionary wars, the "Caudillos", continue to play a major part. The objectives of the old constitution and of the revolution – redistribution of land, development of the educational system, limitation of the power of the Church – are still pursued.

1921–4   During the Presidency of *Alvaro Obregón* the trade union movement develops, schools are built and revolutionary painting flourishes (Dr Atl, Diego Rivera, José Clement Orozco, etc.). Large estates are confiscated and the *ejidos* taken over. The leading personality in the Cabinet is the energetic minister of education, *José Vasconcelos*, a philosopher and writer, who promotes cultural nationalism and creates the new school system. – A rising led by *Adolfo de la Huerta* is suppressed with United States help.

1924–8   The self-confident *Plutarco Elías Calles* becomes President and pursues in autocratic fashion the reforms initiated by Obregón. The continuing conflict with the Church leads to the bloody *Cristero War*, after which religious life is driven underground for years to come. – The constitution is amended to extend the President's term to six years and to permit a second Presidential term provided it does not immediately follow the first. This enables Obregón to be re-elected, but he is murdered soon after taking office.

1929–33   Three Presidents – *Emilio Portes Gil*, *Pascual Ortíz Rubio* and *Abelardo Rodríguez* – who are much under the influence of the powerful ex-President Calles. – Foundation of the National Revolutionary Party (PNR), bringing together the country's most important political forces. All subsequent Presidents of Mexico have been members of this party (several times renamed and reformed).

The period of nationalism (1934–40). – During this period an end is put to the continuing dominance of foreign capital in important branches of the economy. Although nationalization brings economic setbacks it strengthens the national self-confidence.

1934   During the Presidency of *Lázaro Cárdenas*, the first head of state not to be drawn from among the leaders of the revolution, there is a distinct move to the left, as the President appeals increasingly to the masses of workers and peasants. Calles, who at first supports Cárdenas in the hope of influencing him, sees his expectations disappointed. Cárdenas begins to reform the army, on which Calles had relied for support.

1935   Cárdenas eliminates supporters of the ex-President from his government and administration. Calles publicly criticizes the government in violent terms, and in 1936 is expelled from the country.

1938   United States and British oil companies in Mexico are expropriated and their property nationalized. This action is enthusiastically welcomed by the population as a major step toward economic independence.

Contemporary Mexico (since 1940). – The first great economic upswing since the revolution is made possible by Mexico's favorable position in the Second World War, by the un-doctrinaire, economically oriented policies of Presidents Camacho and Alemán and by the absence of coups d'état and internal unrest. Officially the main part of the revolution is complete, though there is some doubt about its practical realization. This gives the government scope for departing from the form and content of radical laws, to the advantage of the country's economic development. The infrastructure is improved, but the distribution and working of the land still present problems, as does the creation of additional jobs for the rapidly increasing population.

1940   *Manuel Avila Camacho* is elected President. He slows down the land reform and promotes the bringing in of foreign capital and the formation of private property. The US armament industry's demand for raw materials opens up a large export trade and brings in high revenues. In the following six years the Mexican gross domestic product doubles.

1942   Mexico declares war on the Axis powers.

1946–52   *Miguel Alemán Valdés* becomes President – the first civilian President since the revolution. The country's economic development continues to forge ahead. Huge irrigation systems and a steadily increasing road network promote the development of agriculture and communications. Between 1946 and 1952 both the gross domestic product and investment in industry increase by over 80%, and by 1952 Mexico is self-sufficient in agricultural produce.

1952–64   The economic upsurge continues under the presidencies of *Adolfo Ruíz Cortines* and *Adolfo López Mateos*. Problems are, however, created by increasing inflation, the illegal entry into the United States of Mexican agricultural workers ("wetbacks" or "braceros") and corruption in the government service. The inequalities between the different social classes as regards participation in the country's economic growth still remain. – The annual rate of population increase rises from 2.7% to 3.4%.

1964–70   Presidency of *Gustavo Díaz Ordaz*. The country's self-confidence is given a boost by the Summer Olympics of 1968 and the (football) World Cup of 1970, which are staged in Mexico. The ruthless repression of student demonstrations in Tlatelolco shortly before the Olympics, however, has remained an unhappy political legacy.

1970–6   Under the ambitious President *Luis Alvarez Echeverría* the move towards the left is accentuated. The redistribution of land and decentralization of industry are continued, new tourist centers established and government expenditure considerably increased. Mexico aspires to play a leading role in the Third World; under the Treaty of Tlatelolco the atomic neutrality of Latin America is recognized.

The continuing inflation and reduced competitiveness of Mexican products in world markets lead to great economic difficulties, and Mexico becomes too expensive for foreign tourists. When a massive flight of capital begins, the exchange rate of the Mexican peso against the US dollar is increased (August 31, 1976), and later the peso is allowed to find its own level. This change of monetary policy, the first for 22 years, leads to a devaluation of almost 50%. During this period there is a wave of *terrorism* (assassinations and assassination attempts, kidnappings, bank raids).

1976–82   The new President, *José López Portillo* introduces at once anti-inflationary measures, which reduce the rate of inflation from 35% to 20%. The discovery of large new oil reserves and the quick increase of oil- and gas-production makes Mexico already in 1980 the fourth biggest oil-producer in the world. Oil export income jumps between 1976 and 1981 from $500 million to 13.3 billion. A new general boom and enormous, often wasteful public investments take place. Based on the new national wealth López Portillo endeavours to increase Mexico's political and economic role in the world, particularly its independence from the USA. Political support for Cuba and Nicaragua and attempts to become autark in food supplies are the main points of his policy. In October 1981 the President is host to a North–South Summit Conference in Cancún which he had initiated. – In order to answer dissatisfaction with "guided democracy", López Portillo allows more political groups in addition to "official" opposition parties. He also reforms election laws to the extent, that of 400 parliamentary seats, 100 are reserved for the opposition.

The huge income from oil and lavish foreign credits, heavily pushed by foreign banks, heat up inflation again. Uneconomic investments in agriculture and state-owned companies, mismanagement and corruption drive the country into a dangerous situation as the budget deficit and foreign indebtness become uncontrollable. The overvalued peso and the loss of confidence in the government lead to massive capital flight. It is estimated that between 1976 and 1982 not much less than $40 billion left the country. Under all these pressures the government is forced on February 18, 1982 to devalue the currency from 27 peso to 44 peso for the dollar. In August 1982 there are no currency reserves left and newly established strict regulations create a black market for the dollar, and also partly paralyze industry, trade and foreign tourism. At the same time, legally existing dollar accounts in Mexican banks, estimated at about $13 billion, are forcibly turned into pesos at a low rate of exchange. On September 1, 1982 the President spontaneously announces, for interior political reasons, the expropriation of the strong private bank sector. By this, at the time unconstitutional act, the long existing sensitive balance between the state and the private sector is shaken. López Portillo's presidency ends with the country's worst political and economic crisis in fifty years.

1982–86   On December 1, 1982 *Miguel de la Madrid Hurtado* becomes President. – As the first Mexican, the diplomat *Alfonso García Robles* receives the Nobel Prize for Peace. – The President faces a difficult heritage: $86 billion in foreign debts, no currency reserves, a steep 150 peso rate for the dollar, a budget deficit of 18% of the gross national product, an inflation rate of 100% as well as a demoralized population. The government immediately negotiates an agreement with the International Monetary Fund (IMF) and with the creditor banks on rescheduling the debts; the USA assists with a substantial cash infusion. Mexico commits itself to hard austerity measures like cutting public spending, lowering subsidies as well as restricting imports and pushing exports. A good part of these measures is carried out, and until the middle of 1984 a currency reserve of almost $7 billion is accumulated. The deficit is curtailed by 60% and the inflation rate drops to 65% p.a. On the other hand unemployment increases and the average Mexican, particularly the new middle class suffers a painful loss of purchasing power. During 1982 and 1983 the GNP falls by almost 6%. – In 1984 and 1985 debts are rescheduled again, though on a smaller scale. However, government spending and hence the budget deficit go up again, leading to a new inflation thrust. In 1986, reaching about 105% at the end of the year. As oil prices collapse, Mexico looses more than half of its oil income from exports and 40% of its tax revenue. In order to keep the country financially afloat, a substantial rescue action for 1987 is agreed upon by international institutions and creditor banks.

At the beginning of his presidency Miguel de la Madrid puts "moral renovation" on his political banner. Some higher officials of the previous administration are charged with corruption and put into jail. Later on this "cleaning" campaign slows down noticeably. The people's dissatisfaction with the dominant party PRI, which has been ruling the country for two generations, leads in 1983 and 1984 to election victories for the conservative opposition party PAN in some state capitals and in other cities. In 1985 and 1986, however, the PRI succeeds in winning back these municipalities and in keeping hard fought over governorships. The opposition parties claim election fraud and cause some unrest, particularly in the northern states and in Oaxaca. – In the parliamentary elections on July 7, 1985, the ruling PRI gains almost 65%, the conservative PAN 15.5% and the communist-leftist PSUM 3.2% of the popular vote. In the new legislature of the 300 relative mayority deputies, 289 are from the PRI, 9 from the PAN and 2 from the PARM. Of the 100 proportional representation deputies, 32 are from the PAN, 12 from the PDM, 12 from the PSUM, 12 from the PST, 11 from the PPS, 9 from the PARM, 6 each from the PRT and PMT.

As his predecessors, Miguel de la Madrid tries to follow a foreign policy independent from the USA. Being a member of the "Contadora Group", Mexico cooperates with Venezuela, Columbia and Panama for a peaceful solution of the conflicts in Central America. – The guerilla war in Guatemala drives between 1978 and 1982 some 45,000 refugees, mainly Maya Indians over the Mexican border into Chiapas. Since 1984 almost half of them have been resettled in Campeche and in Quintana Roo. It is estimated that about 4,000 refugees have returned recently to Guatemala. – On September 19, 1985 a massive 8.1 scale earthquake hits Mexico City and some limited areas in Jalisco, Michoacán, Colima and Guerrero. According to the official statistics 8,000 people die, more than 100,000 are left homeless and an estimated $4 billion in material damage is sustained. Although tourists were hardly affected, tourism in general suffers from this natural disaster. Great efforts by the Mexican people and foreign assistance relieve the situation in a relatively short time. – In May 1986 Mexico hosts for the second time the Football World Cup in Mexico City and in eight other cities. – In July 1986 the country becomes a full member of the General Agreement on Tariffs and Trade (GATT).

Although Mexico is trying hard to control the problem of drugs, illegally produced here or shipped through, it is often criticized by the United States for not cooperating sufficiently with its authorities. The US-Mexican relations are also bedevilled by the problem of illegal Mexican workers in the USA. On the one hand many plantations in the southern and western US and also small enterprises are dependent on the supply of cheap labour, while on the other the US trade unions object to this unorganised competition. In Mexico the "wetbacks" or "braceros" are seen as relieving the pressure on jobs but there is resentment that these immigrant workers have no rights in the neighbor country. After several years of political bickering, a new US Immigration Law (Simpson-Rodino Act) comes into effect in November 1986. It includes an amnesty program for illegal aliens who have been US residents since 1982 and penalties for employers who hire undocumented workers in the future.

Literature

Although countless Indian documents and records were destroyed by the Spaniards during the Conquest – for example in the middle of the 16th c. the Bishop of Mérida, Diego de Landa, caused almost the entire corpus of Maya writings in hieroglyphic script to be burned in a gigantic auto-da-fé – much important material, particularly from the region of Aztec culture, was nevertheless preserved for posterity. The credit for this must go mainly to a number of enlightened Spanish ecclesiastics who, while disapproving of the content of these writings, were able to recognize their great importance in the industry of human culture.

Bernardino de Sahagún

Of the greatest importance for the study of Náhuatl literature (i.e., the literature of the Aztecs and related peoples) are the writings of the Spanish monk Fray **Bernardino de Sahagún** (1500–90). His four most important collections of sources are the "Veinte poemas rituales" ("Twenty Ritual Poems"), the "Manuscrito de los romances de los señores de la Nueva España" ("Manuscript of the Romances of the Lords of New Spain"), the "Cantares mexicanos" ("Mexican Epics") and the "Manuscrito de Cantares ("Manuscript of Epic Poems"). These are mainly works of heroic and religious poetry, but there are also some subjective poems expressing the writer's feelings which come close to lyric poetry. Much use is made of refrains, and the language is often rich in metaphor and symbolism. A popular genre was a form of play accompanied by music and dancing, often with a religious theme and not infrequently associated with contests and human sacrifice.

Particular mention should be made of the works, translated into Spanish after the Conquest, of the legendary poet-king **Netzahualcóyotl** of Texcoco (1402–72), who was renowned as a wise ruler, a philosopher and a poet. No less respected was his son Netzahualpilli (1464–1515), some of whose poems were recorded by Sahagún in his 'Cantares mexicanos". Other important Náhuatl poets of the period of the Conquest were Tecayehuatzin, king of Huejotzingo, and Temilotzin, an Aztec warrier prince who lived in the reign of Cuauhtémoc, last ruler of Tenochtitlán.

Numerous Náhuatl texts were translated into German by Eduard Georg Seler, director of the International Archeological Institute in Mexico in 1910–11. His collected articles on American linguistics and archeology ("Gesammelte Abhandlungen zur amerikanischen Sprach- und Altertumskunde", 1902–23) give an excellent general view of pre-Columbian literature.

Hardly any Maya literature has come down to us. Only a single dramatic work, the "Rabinal-Achi", survived the Conquest: it is an interesting piece of evidence on Maya-Quiché culture and yields much information about the life and customs of the Mayas. Another important document is the "Popul-Vuh" ("Book of Counsel"), which was preserved by oral transmission and was written down by a Quiché Indian soon after the Conquest, in the original language but in the Latin alphabet. It was translated in the early 18th c. by Fray Francisco Ximénez, a friar from Guatemala who knew the Maya language and several of its dialects, and gives valuable information on the mythology, traditions and development of the various Maya tribes. Similar in form and content are the Yucatán Maya chronicles known as "Chilam Balam" ("Book of the Jaguar Prophet"), a mixture of history, oracular pronouncements and mythology. Bishop Diego de Landa, mentioned at the beginning of this section as the destroyer of Maya writings of incalculable value, later – evidently stricken with remorse – made a major contribution to our knowledge of the Maya world with his "Relación de las cosas de Yucatán" ("Account of the Affairs of Yucatán").

The period of the **Conquest** produced a whole host of chroniclers; but it can also be seen as the time when Mexican literature written in Spanish came into being. One of Cortés's companions, *Bernal Díaz del Castillo* (1492–1580), gives a vivid account in his "Historia verdadera de la conquista de la Nueva España" ("True History of the Conquest of New Spain") of the historic clash between Spanish and Indian civilization during the Conquista. Other major historians of this period, apart from *Hernán Cortés* (1485–1547) himself, whose "Cartas de relación", addressed to the Emperor Charles V, is an informative and well-arranged but not entirely objective and dispassionate eyewitness account, were *Bartolomé de las Casas* (1474–1566), *Jerónimo de Mendieta* (1525–1604) and *Antonio de Solís* (1610–86). In addition to these Spanish chroniclers there were also a number of Indian historians writing in Spanish, which they had learned in convent schools – *Fernando de Alvarado Tezozómoc*, a nephew of Moctezuma Xocoyotzin, and *Fernando de Alva Ixtlixóchitl*, a descendant of Netzahualcóyotl, author of the important "Historia chichimeca" (1648).

During the **colonial period**, apart from the not wholly objective historical writings, conditions were not favorable to the development of an independent and original Mexican literature. Spanish influence was ubiquitous, and the process of integration was carried on vigorously and not infrequently by force. Western culture and the Roman Catholic faith were the great imperatives to which all else must give place.

Nevertheless, a number of outstanding writers came to the fore in the late 16th and the 17th c. The Mexican-born dramatist *Juan Ruiz de Alarcón y Mendoza* (1581–1639), whose principal works were written in Spain, made notable contributions to a genre, the comedy of character, which he helped to create, though in character and attitudes he was at odds with the intellectual mood of the day in Spain. One of the leading poetesses writing in Spanish in the 17th c. was the nun *Sor Juana* **Inés de la Cruz** (1648–95), whose religious plays ("El Cetro de José", "Joseph's Sceptre") and comedies ("Amor es mas laberinto", "The Labyrinth of Love") enjoyed considerable success. Inés de la Cruz also wrote numerous love poems, still regarded as among the finest and tenderest ever

written by a woman. A leading exponent of the Baroque literature of New Spain was the poet, essayist and philosopher *Carlos de Sigüenza y Góngora* (1645–1700), who in order to combat superstition wrote a "Philosophical Manifesto against Comets" (1680).

The *18th c.* was a time of social commitment, marked also by the rise of science and the quest for a national identity – trends which overlaid the literary ambitions of the writers of the period. Some authors took over the French neoclassical manner, but this bore little fruit in Mexico. The only name deserving mention in this connection is that of *José Manuel Martínez de Navarrete* (1768–1809).

The early part of the *19th c.* was dominated by the national rising of 1810, and most of the works of the period were concerned in one way or another with this theme, no matter whether the authors were for or against independence. *José Joaquín Fernández de* **Lizardi** (1776–1827), the outstanding figure of the first quarter of the century, who inveighed in numerous newspaper articles against the wrongs and abuses of the colonial period, was a committed supporter of Mexican independence and fought for the underprivileged classes of the population. In his novel of social criticism "El Periquillo Sarniento" ("The Itching Parrot") he gives expression to his views within the framework of the picaresque novel and under the cloak of frivolity.

Important representatives of the realist novel in Mexico were *Emilio Rabasa* (1856–1930: "La Bola", "Turmoil"; "El cuarto poder", "The Fourth Power"), *López Portillo y Rojas* (1850–1923): "La Parcela", "The Plot of Land"; "Los Precursores", "The Forerunners") and *Rafael Delgado* (1853–1914: "La Calandria", "The Lark"; "Angelina"). *Heriberto Frías* (1870–1925) tackled a historical theme, the rising of the Tomochitec Indians, in his novel "Tomochic" (1894).

Towards the end of the 19th c. a number of major writers, like *Manuel Acuña* (1849–73), *Guillermo Prieto* (1818–97) and *Justo Sierra* (1848–1912), aligned themselves with the Romantic schools in France and Spain. – The desire for renewal and reaction against Romanticism soon led to the emergence of the trend known as **Modernism**, Latin America's first important contribution to world literature. The Modernist school was cosmopolitan in attitude, seeking its subjects in the remotest regions, and was constantly concerned to seek refinement and originality of language, *Manuel Gutiérrez* **Nájera** (1859–95), an admirer of French art and literature, ranks as the father of all modern Mexican literature, and his poems influenced generations of later writers. Other important representatives of the Modernist school are *Amado Nervo* (1870–1919), *Luis G. Urbina* (1864–1934) and *Enrique González Martínez* (1871–1952), the last exponent of this trend.

Contemporary literature has finally established the international status of Mexican writing. The 1910 revolution inspired a series of works on tropical themes, often with an autobiographical element and giving expression to strong national feeling. *Mariano Azuela* (1873–1952) falls into this group. In his novel of social criticism, "Los de abajo" ("The Underdogs"), he describes the revolution in its most violent phase. *Martin Luis Guzmán* (b. 1887) takes as his subject some of the great figures of the revolution, as in his "Memorias de Pancho Villa" ("Memoirs of Pancho Villa") and "La Sombra del Caudillo" ("The Shadow of the Caudillo"). *José Vasconcelos* (1882–1959) paints an exact picture of these years of turmoil in his novels "La Tormenta" ("The Storm"), "Ulises criollo" ("The Creole Ulysses") and "El Proconsulado" ("The Proconsulate").

The 1920s saw a revival of interest in the colonial period. *Artemio de Valle Arizpe* (1888–1961) took a leading place among writers who concerned themelves with Mexico's colonial past. *Gregorio López y Fuentes* (b. 1897) depicted for the first time, in a highly pessimistic tone, the

tragedy of an Indian village in his novel, "El Indio" ("The Indian", 1935). Many other writers followed a similar line, like *Ramón Rubín* in "El callado dolor de los Tzotziles" ("The Mute Suffering of the Tzotziles"), *Francisco Rojas Gonzáles* in "El Diosero" ("The God-Maker") and *Rosario Castellanos* (b. 1925) in "Balun Canan" ("The New Watchmen").

Carlos Fuentes (b. 1928), author of "Where the Air is Clear", "The Death of Artemio Cruz", "The Old Gringo", and *José Revueltas* (b. 1914) wrote novels of social criticism. *Agustín Yáñez* (b. 1904: "Al Filo del Agua") and *Juan Rulfo* (1918–86) "Pedro Páramo", "The Plain on Fire" analysed the atmosphere in rural Mexico against the background of the revolutionary turmoil.

Juan José Arreola (b. 1918) established himself with a volume of stories, "Varia invención y confabulario". *Alfonso Reyes* (1889–1959) and *Octavio* **Paz** (b. 1914), whose "The Labyrinth of Solitude" and "The Other Mexico" have been translated into the languages of the world, are the great masters of the Mexican essay. – Leading dramatists of the period are *Rodolfo Usigli* (b. 1905), *Xavier Villaurrutia* (1903–50), *Salvador Novo* (b. 1904) and *Jorge Ibargüengoitia*.

Notable among contemporary lyric poets are *Bernardo Ortiz de Montellano* (1899–1949), *Ali Chumacero* (b. 1918), *Rosario Castellanos* (b. 1925) and *Jaime Sabines* (b. 1925).

The "**Espiga Amotinada**" group, founded in 1960, includes a number of young and talented authors like *Augusto Shelley, Jaime Labastidas, Juan Buñuelos, Oscar Olivas* and *Eraclio Zepedas,* who are concerned to renew contemporary lyric poetry.

The Arts

Painting

The period before the Spanish conquest, until about 1520, is notable particularly for the **pre-Columbian wall painting**. Magnificent examples of this painting can be seen in the Maya temple at Bonampak and at Teotihuacán, Tepantitla, Atetelco, Cacaxtla and Cholula. Unfortunately only a few of these old Indian paintings have survived. The red and orange tones, the gold and the famous Maya blue in the Bonampak frescoes give some impression of the high standards of painting technique in the period of the classical Maya culture. In addition to the frescoes elaborately painted pottery has been found. – To this period, too, belong the **codices**, the illuminated manuscripts with their figural representations and pictographs (reproductions, p. 39).

Soon after the Conquest European artists began to teach at the school in Mexico City founded by Franciscan friars. Like most of the painters of the period, these artists were under the influence of the Dutch school. The only significant painter of this period was a Fleming living in Mexico, *Simón Pereyns* (1566–1603).

An independent **colonial art** did not come into being until the beginning of the 17th c.; it is exemplified in the work of *Baltazar de Echave Orío* (1548–1620), *Baltazar de Echave Ibía* (1585–1645) and *Luis Juárez* (1600–35). The works of these artists are now principally to be found in churches, convents and museums in Mexico City, Querétaro, Tepotzotlán, Morelia and Guadalajara. They were followed by *José Juárez* (1615–67), *Baltazar de Echave Rioja* (1632–82) and *Pedro Ramírez* (1650–78), who combined elements from such diverse European painters as Murillo and Rubens with their own distinctive style. Their works can be seen in Mexico City, Texcoco, Puebla, San Miguel de Allende and Guadalajara.

Notable painters of the first phase of the Mexican *Baroque* (late 17th and early 18th c.) are *Cristóbal de Villalpando* (1652–1714), *Juan Correa* (1674–1739) and *Juan Rodríguez Juárez* (1675–1728). Their works are to be seen mainly in Mexico City, Puebla, San Miguel de Allende, Atotonilco, Tepotzotlán, Aguascalientes and Querétaro. Two of Correa's pupils, *José Maria de Ibarra* (1688–1756) and *Miguel Cabrera* (1695–1768), dominated Mexican painting in the 18th c.; their numerous works are to be found mainly in museums in Mexico City, Puebla, Morelia, Tepotzotlán, San Miguel de Allende and Taxco. – In contrast to Mexican architecture and the mestizo schools of Cuzco and Potosí in South America, the Mexican painting of this period is almost wholly free of Indian influence.

Leading figures of the middle and second half of the *19th c.* were two primitive painters, the portraitist *José María Estrada* (1830–62) and the landscapist *José María Velasco* (1840–1912), one of whose pupils was Diego Rivera. – In the provinces there developed in this period a vigorous and appealing style at its best in numerous village chapels.

In the late 19th and early 20th c. the influence of Impressionism began to make itself more strongly felt, as in the landscapes of *Joaquín Claussel* (1866–1935) and *Mateos Saldaña*.

The next period of Mexican painting began in the *20th c.* during the revolutionary period (1910–20). A new and independent art form was evolved in the form of **Muralismo**. The starting point of this school was a "secessionist" exhibition in 1910, in which *Gérardo Murillo* (1875–1964), who took the name of *Dr Atl* (Náhuatl, "water"), played a leading part; in fact, however, he is better known for his landscapes than for his frescoes. Also of importance was *Francisco Guitía* (1884–1960) who portrayed in Expressionism the fate of human beings in the War of Revolution. A forerunner of the new trend was the engraver and political caricaturist *José Guadalupe Posada* (1852–1913).

Painters now turned to the old folk art which was vigorously practiced. Taking over colors, forms and themes from pre-Columbian art, they painted murals which were ideologically directed toward the instruction of the illiterate masses of the population but for the most part managed to avoid falling into an empty "socialist realism". The scenes they depicted glorified the old Indian heritage and the events of the revolution and derided the conservative Spanish element in the Mexican

"Man in Flames" by Orozco, Guadalajara

past. Although the artists took up extreme anti-clerical attitudes they were unable to break entirely free of their Catholic roots. Scope for the diffusion of the new art was provided in the early 1920s by the minister of education, José Vasconcelos, who allowed the artists to paint the walls of schools and other public buildings. In 1923 Mexican painters published a manifesto declaring their belief in monumental art in preference to the easel painting.

The three most famous Mexican painters of this period, best known as "muralists", are José Clemente Orozco, Diego Rivera and David Alfaro Siqueiros. Outstanding among these three is *José Clemente* **Orozco** (1883–1949), whose numerous works (including drawings, engravings and paintings as well as murals) display a hard and ruthless realism in the depiction of vigorous and dramatic scenes. Orozco's painting shows the influence of the Baroque, but his technique and subject-matter also show affinities with European Expressionism. In contrast, however, to Rivera and Siqueiros, who are more open to a variety of stylistic influences, he is a painter of a very individual and personal style. His finest work is the ceiling frescoes in the Hospicio Cabañas, Guadalajara (1938–9), in particular the painting of "Man in Flames" in the dome. He also painted the staircase of the Government Place in Guadalajara. In Mexico City he created impressive murals for the Escuela Preparatoria Nacional and the Palacio Nacional de Bellas Artes.

As a young painter *Diego* **Rivera** (1886–1957) went through a variety of phases, from Neo-Impressionism by way of Fauvism to Cubism. Later he painted huge murals depicting scenes from Mexican political and social life. Taking the fresco painting of the Italian Renaissance as his starting point and much influenced in his choice of themes by the art of the Mayas

and Aztecs, he developed his own very clear and subtle style. Outstanding among his numerous murals are those in the Palacio Nacional and Solidarity Park in Mexico City and in the Escuela Nacional de la Agricultura in Chapingo. Others are to be seen in the Ministry of Education, the Palacio Nacional de Bellas Artes and the Ministry of Health in Mexico City and the Palacio de Cortes in Cuernavaca.

David Alfaro **Siqueiros** (1896–1974) incorporated Baroque elements in his work – reflected, for example, in the sense of movement in his paintings. Under the influence of Futurism he painted machinery and depicted the achievements of technology, and he was commissioned by various government departments to decorate public buildings with murals of monumental effect. His work is to be seen mainly in Mexico City – e.g., in the Hospital de la Raza, the Palacio Nacional, the Palacio Nacional de Bellas Artes and the Rector's Office of the University. He also designed and decorated the Polyforum.

The grand old man of the **contemporary school** is the Zapotec *Rufino* **Tamayo** (b. 1899), Mexico's best known living painter, who combines elements of Mexican folk art with features influenced by modern painting, particularly Cubism. Like Rivera, he supports the cause of an "Indian Renaissance". Tamayo belongs to a group of artists which also includes *Carlos Mérida* (1891–1984), *Ricardo Martínez* (b. 1918), *Juan Soriano* (b. 1920) and *Pedro Coronel* (b. 1922).

"Juego de niños" by Rufino Tamayo

Tamayo and Mérida, together with *Miguel Covarrubias* (1904–57), *Roberto Montenegro* (1886–1968), *Juan O'Gorman* (1905–82), *Jorge González Camarena* (b. 1908), *José Chávez Morado* (b. 1909), *Pablo O'Higgins* (1904–83) and *Federico Cantú* (b. 1909), are "muralists"; among Tamayo's work in this genre are the frescoes on the staircase of the Conservatoire in Mexico City.

Other painters who have come to the fore in recent decades are *Frida Kahlo* (1907–54, wife of Diego Rivera), *Manuel Rodríguez Lozano* (1896–1972), *Gunter Gerzo* (b. 1915), *Leonora Carrington* (b. 1917), *Francisco Zúñiga* (b. 1913), *Romeo Tabuena* (b. 1921), *Rafael Coronel* (b. 1923), *Guillermo Rode* (b. 1933), *Pedro Friedeberg* (b. 1937), *José Luis Cuevas* (b. 1933) and *Francisco Toledo* (b. 1940). They represent a variety of stylistic trends.

Sculpture

Among the Mayas, the Aztecs and the other peoples of ancient America, sculpture, like painting, was mainly used in the decoration of temples and sanctuaries; and the art of the *pre-Columbian cultures* was principally concerned with religious rituals and the worship of the gods. Sculpture might be in stone, in stucco or in terracotta. The sculpture found in the temples includes figural representations, such as the famous "Danzantes" of Monte Albán, and geometric relief decoration of walls, often in patterns which show affinities with those of textiles, as, for example, at Mitla.

During the classical period of **Maya** culture stone and stucco sculpture of the highest quality was produced, particularly notable being the stucco reliefs at Palenque. The Mayas added natural rubber to the mixture of plaster and water in order to give the stucco a particularly hard surface which could be polished.

The magnificent art of the **Olmecs** (the *La Venta culture*) produced monumental stone sculpture. Particularly impressive are the colossal heads, up to 3 m (10 ft) high, with broad flat noses and thick lips.

In the field of small sculpture there were both simple everyday objects and elaborate items found mainly as grave goods. Small female figures, generally interpreted as fertility goddesses, are particularly common. The ideal of beauty changes in the course of time: in the early period the figurines are opulently proportioned but thereafter become steadily more graceful. The clay figures, often no more than 20 cm (8 in) high, usually take the form of anthropomorphic or zoomorphic vessels. The painted terracotta figures include some clad only in a loincloth or belt round the hips and others in rich garments. Differences can also be observed in attitude and facial expression. – The Olmecs also produced notable small sculpture, including jade objects in which the surface treatment is reduced to the minimum number of lines.

The Mayas also produced small sculptures of high quality, as the numerous finds in tombs on the island of Jaina have shown. The small painted terracottas show what priests and warriors looked like and how members of the higher classes of society dressed. – The sculpture included not only work in stone and terracotta but also goldsmith's work, including masks and jewelry and feather mosaics. For this purpose the feathers were dyed and inserted into a fabric base in accordance with a sketched pattern. One particularly fine example of this work depicts a prairie wolf on a shield. There are also headdresses, cloaks and totem signs in feather-work.

In sculpture as in painting and architecture the Spanish conquest marked a sharp break. Apart from the decorative sculpture on public buildings and churches the

Stone relief, Palenque

Colossal Olmec head

sculpture of the *colonial period* in Mexico is lacking in individual expression. A sculptor who achieved fame after coming to Mexico at the beginning of the 18th c. was *Jerónimo Balbás*, who carved the splendid Altar of the Kings in the Cathedral in Mexico City. His work had considerable influence on other Mexican sculptors. In the late 18th and early 19th c. sculpture, particularly figures in churches, showed a steady decline in refinement and plastic quality. One work of non-religious sculpture which deserves mention is *Manuel Tolsá*'s "Caballito", a bronze equestrian statue modelled on one by Girardon. About the middle of the 19th c. *José Antonio Villegas de Cora* (1713–85), his nephew *Zacarías de Cora* and his adopted son *José Villegas*, working in Puebla, and *Mariano Perusquía, Mariano Arce* and *Mariano Montenegro*, working in Querétaro, sought to give fresh impulses to sculpture. Their work can be seen in Puebla and Querétaro. – A simple but original and distinctively Mexican form of sculpture which developed during this period is represented by the peasant altars and sacred effigies to be found in large numbers in churches.

In the *20th c.* after the revolution (1910–20), the emphasis was on monumental sculpture, frequently reflecting some political concern. – During the last thirty years or so a new generation of sculptors has come forward, producing imaginative and original work which can be seen in Mexico City and other towns – *Juan F. Olaguíbel* (1889–1971; "Diana the Huntress" fountain in Mexico City, with a bronze statue of the goddess; Monumento al Rey de Coliman, Colima), *Germán Cueto* (1893–1975; "La Tehuana", Palacio Nacional de Bellas Artes, Mexico City), *Ignacio Asúnsulo* (1890–1965; Obregón memorial in San Angel, Mexico City), *Rodrigo Arena Betancourt*

(b. 1919; figure of Prometheus in the University City, Mexico City), *Jorge Gonzáles Camarena* (b. 1908; I.M.S.S. building, Paseo de la Reforma, Mexico City), *Ernesto Tamariz* (b. 1904; Monumento a los Niños Héroes, Cuauhtémoc Park, Mexico City), *Federico Canessi* (b. 1906; Monumento de la Bandera, Iguala) and *Francisco Zúñiga* (b. 1913; "Yucatecas en el Parque", Galería Tasende, Acapulco).

Architecture

The very numerous examples of **colonial architecture** in Mexico, built within a relatively short space of time, reflect the ready availability of building materials and the large reservoir of cheap labor which the Spanish conquerors had at their disposal. A particularly versatile material was the porous volcanic stone known as *tezontle* (Náhuatl, "petrified hair"), found particularly in the Central Highlands. This stone, ranging in color from pink to dark brown, was already being worked in Aztec times, and can still be seen in most of the palaces in Mexico City. There are also various colored limestones, attractively toned and easily worked. These building stones are known by the general name of *cantera*. – After the Spanish conquest of Mexico, which began in 1519, many fine works of Indian architecture and sculpture were destroyed or lost to sight. During the next 400 years a variety of architectural styles were introduced into the New World from Europe, mainly from Spain, often developing local variants.

In the first generation after the Conquest a form of architecture developed which can be defined as a **medieval convent-fortress**. The churches and convents

Fortified convent, Acatzingo

Open chapel, Teposcolula

Some features of the Spanish **Mudéjar style** (a mingling of Moorish and Gothic elements, named after the Mudéjares – Moors who stayed in Spain after the Spanish reconquest) are found also in Mexican buildings. One of the trademarks of this style is the *alfiz*, a rectangular framing of a Moorish arched doorway in the form of a narrow frieze. In many 16th c. buildings the *alfiz* incorporates an imitation of the Franciscan rope girdle (e.g., the *posas* at Huejotzingo). Other features of the Mexican Mudéjar style which appear only at a later stage are the use of *azulejos* (glazed tiles), the distinctive forms of door arches and ceilings and the timber panelling (*alfarje* and *artesonado*).

In the 16th c. the early form of the **Plateresque style** (from Spanish *platero*, silversmith) came to Mexico. The intricately carved stonework, found principally on doorways, incorporates heraldic elements, flowers and arabesques in its decorative patterns, originally based on those of Spanish silversmiths. The Plateresque style also assimilates Mudéjar features and late Gothic and Renaissance decorative forms. In New Spain it developed a number of variants based on pure Renaissance with Italian features, found for example at Actopán and Teposcolula and in the church of San Francisco at Morelia; *Spanish Plateresque*, with Spanish Renaissance elements, as in the *posas* of Heujotzingo, the Palacio Montejo in Mérida and at Acolman; *Colonial Plateresque*, a local interpretation of Spanish techniques, as at Tepoztlán, in the side doorway of Cuernavaca Cathedral and the N entrance to the church at Huejotzingo; and *Indian Plateresque*, combining pre-Columbian skills with a local interpretation of the style, as in the main and side doorways of the church at Yuriria, the façade and N doorway of the parish church of Xochimilco and the open chapel at Tlalmanalco.

erected by the Spanish missionaries, in the first place by the Franciscans, frequently occupied the sites of Indian pyramids or temples, often using as material parts of the earlier buildings which had been demolished. With their strong walls and massive buttresses, these early religious buldings, sometimes still showing Romanesque and Gothic features, served also as fortresses. The few windows were set high and far apart, and the roof was a simple ribbed or barrel-vaulted structure. Other features of the 16th c. convents are the walled *atrium* and the *capillas posas* which are found only in Mexico – small processional chapels at the four corners of the courtyard. Another special architectural form was the *capilla abierta* (open chapel) opening up to the atrium, which, like the atrium itself and the *posas*, took account of the Indians' dislike for enclosed places of worship. This came about because entry to a church was often denied them before baptism. Of course there were individual priests who stood out against the majority.

Fine examples of atriums and *posas* can be seen at Huejotzingo, Calpan, Izamal and Tlaxcala (San Francisco). The most interesting open chapels are at Tlalmanalco, Teposcolula, Coixtlahuaca, Tlaxcala (San Francisco), Cuitzeo, Cuernavaca (Cathedral) and Acropán.

The 17th c. brought the gradual emergence of the **Baroque**, at first in a relatively restrained form (e.g., La Soledad, Oaxaca). Into this phase, too, fell the main constructional work on the great *cathedrals* of Mexico City, Puebla, Morelia, Guadalajara, San Luis Potosí and Oaxaca. During the same period *nunneries* and numerous *parish churches* were built. These buildings reflect the growing power of the Church, under the

Alfíz on the Huejotzingo *posa*

direct patronage of the Spanish crown, while the influence of the independent religious orders was declining. The development of Mexican Baroque in ever greater luxuriance and in varying styles also reflects the increasing strength of the Mexican-border Spaniards (Criollos) as compred with the incomers from Spain (Gachupines).

In the 18th c. the Mexican High Baroque reached its finest form in the **Churrigueresque style**, named after the Spanish architect *José Benito Churriguera* (1665–1723) and his brothers (whose work was considerably more restrained). Characteristic of the Churrigueresque style, mainly found on towers, doorways and altars, is its unrestrained exuberance of ornamentation. The column, still clearly recognizable as such in the Baroque style, is broken up

into such a variety of forms and so much altered in character that the original form is sometimes completely lost. The main distinguishing characteristic of the style is the pilaster (*estípite*) in the form of a truncated pyramid standing on its smaller end – a feature frequently found on church façades and, within the church, on altar screens. Among the many examples of Churrigueresque to be found in New Spain the following may be cited: the façades of the Sagrario Metropolitano, the church of La Santísima, the Casa de los Mascarones and the Altar of the Kings in

Santa Prisco, Taxco

the Cathedral, all in Mexico City; the church of San Francisco Xavier in Tepotzotlán; the Basilica of Ocotlán, Tlaxcala; the church of San Sebastián and Santa Prisco, Taxco; the parish church of Dolores Hidalgo; the church of La Valenciana, Guanajuato; the Aránzazu chapel, San Luis Potosí; and Zacatecas Cathedral.

A particularly original variant of the Mexican Baroque is the **Poblano style** (named after the town of Puebla), the characteristic regional style of Puebla and Tlaxcala. In this style exuberant stucco ornament, often of Indian type, is combined with colored tiles and red brick. In addition to the shrine at Ocotlán, which has already been mentioned, outstanding examples of this style can be seen in the churches of San Francisco de Acatepec, Santa María de Tonantzintla and San Bernardino de Tlaxcalancingo; the church of La Merced and the Rosary Chapel in Atlixco; the Casa del Alfeñique and the

Posa, Huejotzingo

Churrigueresque decoration, Tlaxcala

devastating consequences – to strip the churches of their rich ornamental forms in order to assimilate them to the neo-classical style. He was also, however, responsible for the magnificent equestrian statue of the Emperor Charles IV, El Caballito (the "Little Horse"), in Mexico City and designed the School of Engineering (Palacio de Minería) in the capital. Also very fine is his work on the dome of Mexico City Cathedral, with paintings by Rafael Jimeno y Planes.

The leading personality of the new school was the versatile *Francisco Eduardo Tresguerras* (1759–1833), famous as a poet, musician, painter, sculptor, engraver and architect. Among his finest works are the church of El Carmen in Celaya, the rebuilding of the church of Santa Clara in

chapel of San Antonio, Puebla; and the Casa de los Azulejos in Mexico City.

In the latter part of the 18th c, the **neoclassical style** came to Mexico from Europe. It was seen as a welcome means – with political overtones – of breaking away from the over-powerful Spanish cultural heritage. Thus the Spanish-born architect and sculptor *Manuel Tolsá* (1759–1816) sought – sometimes with

Façade of Sagrario Metropolitano, Mexico City

Façade in Poblano style, Acatepec

Querétaro and the Casa Rul in Guanajuato. – An important work of neo-classical art, with evident Baroque antecedents, is the high altar of the Sagrario Metropolitano in Mexico City, by *Pedro Patino Ixilinque* (1774–1835), an Indian pupil of Manuel Tolsá. Another notable architect of the period was *José Damián Ortiz de Castro* (1750–93), who was responsible for the bell-towers and the last alterations to the façade of the Cathedral in Mexico City.

During the hundred years between the achievement of independence and the revolution (1910–20) there was no significant development in Mexican architecture. Exceptions to this general statement are provided by various embellishments to older buildings carried out in the reign of the Emperor Maximilian, the very original (mainly neo-Gothic) work of *Ceferino Gutiérrez* (d. 1896) and a few examples of Art Nouveau.

After the revolutionary wars Mexican architects began, under the influence of the Bauhaus, to take an interest in the modern **functional style**. The monumental structures built during this phase are not universally admired, and it was not until the 1950s amd 1960s that Mexican architects, under the influence of Le Corbusier and Oscar Niemeyer, began to produce buildings of impressive quality: *Enrique de la Mora y Palomar* (b. 1907; church of La Purísima, Monterrey); in Mexico City *José García Villagrán* (b. 1901), *Mario Pani* (b. 1911) and *Enrique del Moral* (b. 1906; University City, Ministry of Water Supply, Mercado La Merced); *Luis Barragán* (b. 1902; apartment buildings; El Pedregal, Las Arboledas); *Felix Candela* (b. 1910; churches of La Milagrosa and Santa Mónica); *Mathias Goeritz* (b. 1915; towers in Ciudad Satélite, Seven Stations of the Cross in the church of Santiago Tlaltelolco, lattice-work hotel Camino Real); *Pedro Ramírez Vázquez* (b. 1919) and *Rafael Mijares* (b. 1924; Museum of Modern Art, National Museum of Anthropology, rebuilding of Basilica of Guadalupe, Instituto Nacional de la Vivienda).

Music

Present-day Mexican music incorporates features going back to **pre-Columbian music**, mainly in relation to the percussion instruments which are used to accompany dances. Little is known about the old music of the Indians, but it evidently played a major role in dances and singing of cult significance. The Aztecs, for example, had a "House of Song" (Cuicacalli), in which children received a compulsory musical education from the age of 12. Poems were always sung or declaimed with a musical accompaniment. The principal instruments used were percussion instruments – drums (of terracotta, wood or tortoiseshell), rasps of notched bone or wood, various kinds of rattles and also simple flutes or conch shells – which were also used for transmitting orders during military operations. Some of these old instruments are still used, mainly on the occasion of ceremonial dances, by a few Indian tribes including the Seri, Yaqui, Huicholes and Tzotziles. The flutes now used, made of bone, clay or reeds, differ very little from those of the pre-Hispanic period.

The *jarabe tapatío* dance, with mariachis

Present-day Mexican **folk music** also uses more modern instruments such as brass trumpets, guitars, violins, harps and, in the S of the country, marimbas. The marimba, based on West African models, consists of a series of strips of wood of different lengths with gourds as resonators. Although almost untouched by European influence, the folk music of the isolated Tarascans of Michoacán and the Yaqui and Seri Indians of Sonora is strikingly melodious.

The traditional songs and melodies of the various regions consists for the most part of a mingling of Spanish and Indian elements; in some cases also Moorish, African and European (non-Spanish) influences can be detected. As any visitor will soon discover, the Mexicans are very fond of singing; and they have a wide range of songs. Notable among these are the popular ballads known as *corridos*, which before the coming of the mass media were used for the diffusion of news. The wandering bard retails a variety of local gossip, but he also sings on historical themes and about love and death. Many of the old *corridos* have remained popular to the present day. From this type of ballad there developed the *canción ranchera*, a melancholy song which takes as its themes sorrow, violence and unrequited love. The tunes are usually taken from 19th c. Spanish songs, "Mexicanized" for the purpose. The songs of many regions (e.g. Jalisco, Veracruz, Oaxaca and Tehuantepec) have a ring of quite unmistakable individuality.

The best known type of Mexican folk music is that of the **mariachi** bands, which is of Spanish origin, enriched by French and mid-European elements. The name is probably a corruption of the French word "mariage", since the French troops in Mexico erroneously believed that these bands played mainly at weddings. The band, which may be large or small, usually consists of violinists, guitar-players, trumpeters and a singer. Originally these wandering musicians were found mainly in Jalisco state, and particularly in its capital, Guadalajara, but they can now be encountered in most parts of the central highlands, wearing the traditional ranchero costume. Their music, usually with a fairly brisk tempo, has a very characteristic and immediately recognizable rhythm. The meeting-place of the mariachis in Mexico City is the Plaza de Garibaldi; in Guadalajara it is the Plazuela de los Mariachis, near the Mercado Libertad.

From the beginning of the colonial period until quite recently Mexican musical life, apart from folk music, looked toward Europe for its inspiration. Composers and performers came from Europe to Mexico, where they had a great influence on the work of local musicians. It was only in the early years of the 20th c. that Mexican music began to develop any national individuality. *Manuel Ponce* (1886–1948) was the first to write orchestral works, chamber music and songs incorporating elements taken from folk music ("Chapultepec", "Ferial", "Estrellita"). Peraps the most gifted Mexican composer was *Silvestre Revueltas* (1899–1940), who wrote orchestral works, string quartets and ballets ("Cuauhnáhuac", "Sensemaya", "Janítzio", "Magueyes", "Homenaje e Federico García Lorca"). The outstanding figure in Mexican music, however, was *Carlos* **Chávez** (1899–1978), who had a great reputation not only as a composer but as a conductor and a musical scholar. In his works ("Concerto for Piano and Orchestra", "H.P.", "Sinfonia India", "Four Suns", "The New Fire", "El Amor Propiciado", "Pánfilo y Lauretta" – the last two works being operas) he frequently used old Indian tunes and legends. *Julián Carillo* (1875–1965) was noted as a composer of 13-tone music ("Preludio a Cristóbal Colón", "Tetepán"). Other important Mexican composers are *José Pablo Moncayo* ("Huapango"), *Miguel Bernal Jiménez*, *Luis Sandi* and *Blas Galindo*.

Among leading composers of light music are *Tata Nacho, Agustín Lara, Guti Cárdenas* and *Manuel M. Ponce*.

Economy

Mexico is one of the few developing countries which seemed to be on its way to achieve a sufficiently rapid economic development to take it out of this category. However, in 1982, the country got into a very serious crisis (see also History 1976–82 and 1982–86), which since then stopped economic growth and reduced the gross national product and purchasing power. While Mexico's GNP rose between 1971 and 1981 at an average of 6.5% a year, this index showed a combined minus of 2% during the period of 1982–86. According to official statistics the inflation rate (rounded up) amounted in 1982 to 100%, in 1983 to 81%, in 1984 to 59%, in 1985 to 64% and is likely to surpass 105% by the end of 1986. The purchasing power during this period showed a loss of over 50%. At the close of 1986 the minimum wage ranged between $2.25 and $2.65 per day. – Since the introduction of a value-added tax at the beginning of 1980, some changes occur in 1984. The general rate is 15% and there is a top rate of 20% for several luxury items; a few basic foods and services are free of taxation, whereas some enjoy a preferable rate of 6%.

At the end of 1986, Mexico's foreign debts amounted to $103 billion, thus drawing level with Brazil as the world's largest debtor country. Income losses from fallen oil prices will cut export revenues in 1986 by about $7.5 billion. Though foreign sales of manufactured goods and of agricultural produce have increased considerably, total value of the 1986 exports will not exceed $15.5 billion compared to $21.8 billion in 1985. Petroleum's share of foreign sales will be down from 68% in 1984 to quite less than 40% in 1986. Mexico's trade surplus in 1986 will probably dip to $3 billion or less compared to $7.8 billion in 1985 and $13.1 billion in 1984. Contrary to a surplus in 1985, the balance of payment for 1986 will show a deficit of some $2 billion. Therefore Mexico is forced to negotiate a financial rescue package of $12 billion in new loans for 1987. The IMF, the World Bank and other institutions as well as some 600 creditor banks finally agree to this request and on rescheduling $52.88 billion government debts.

Mexico's leading trade partner is the USA with roughly two-thirds of its total exports

Guanajuato, a mining town

and imports. But Mexico is also the fourth largest customer and supplier of the States. Japan is Mexico's second and Germany its third most important trading partner. In 1985 Germany's exports to Mexico totalled $817 million, whereas Mexico's sales to Germany amounted to $334 million. It is expected that figures for 1986 will be somewhat higher.

Due to Mexico's debt and currency problems the government recently softened its laws on foreign investments. The 51% to 49% clause in favor of Mexican capital is not as strictly handled anymore. As of early 1986, total foreign investments in the country were $14.8 billion of which the USA held 68%, the Federal Republic of Germany 8.1%, Japan 6.0%, Switzerland 4.6%, the United Kingdom and Spain 2.6% each.

Mining, an important branch of the economy already before World War I, still plays a major role, although there has been hardly any progress in output in recent years. The mining industry employs 223,000 persons, a number which has been stable for the past four years. Mexico is the world's largest producer of silver, and fluorite, graphite and celestite; in the production of arsenic it takes second place, of antimony and bismuth third place and fourth place in sulphur, barite, mercury molybdenum and zinc. Other minerals in Mexico include gold, tin, lead, manganese, iron and coal. The country's uranium-ore reserves are considered to be substantial.

Already at the beginning of this century, Mexico belonged to the leading producers of crude oil in the world. After the nationalization of the foreign oil companies in 1938, production fell to an extent that the country could hardly satisfy its own demand. Very successful oil drilling operations at the end of the seventies led to an enormous expansion of production. Presently the country's oil reserves are given at more than 52 billion barrels, the 6th or 7th largest in the world. The state corporation PEMEX (Petróleos Mexicanos) earned from its exports: $3.8 billion in 1979, 9.4 in 1980, 13.3 in 1981, 15.6 in 1982, 14.8 in 1983, 15.0 in 1984 and 13.3 billion in 1985. It is expected that in 1986 PEMEX will produce 2.7 million barrels of crude a day, of which 1.3 million barrels will have been exported at an average price of $12 per barrel. This would

amount to a foreign sales income of approximately $5.7 billion. – Mexico's main oil customer is the USA which at present buys close to 55% of the exported crude. Until the end of 1984 Mexico was the USA's main oil supplier but it fell back to 3rd place last year. Spain purchases about 11% of the Mexican crude exports, followed by Japan with 10%, France with 5.5%, Israel with 3.3% and Canada with 2.5%. – Although Mexico is not a member of the Organisation of Petroleum Exporting Countries (OPEC), it usually sold its oil at OPEC price levels. In 1986, however, it had to adjust its prices to market conditions. – Most of Mexico's crude is found in the states of Veracruz, Tabasco and Chiapas as well as in the off-shore fields, most of it in the Gulf of Mexico near Campeche and less off the coasts of Nayarit and Baja California.

Mexico's minerals have long been the country's economic backbone. There are deposits of a wide range of minerals in every Mexican state except Tabasco, Campeche and Yucatán: over 20,000 have been officially registered. But since there has been no systematic prospecting, no detailed survey of the country's resources is available, and a large proportion of the sites have not been developed. The concentration on commercially productive mineral deposits and oilfields has led to the neglect of less important sites, particularly those yielding *precious stones* and semi-precious stones. Stones which have been found in substantial quantities include opal, amethyst, rock crystal, apatite, agate, garnet, topaz, jadeite, nephrite, onyx and obsidian; only small workable deposits of sapphires, emeralds, rubies and diamonds have been found.

Industry, has been considerably developed until 1982, in which year it supplied about 30% of the GNP. In 1982–83 industrial production suffered a drop of up to 50%. Ever since it has been an up and down rather differing from branch to branch. Losses were particularly heavy in Mexico's primary industry which in its majority is nationalized and in other state-owned enterprises. Some of these were shut down and a limited number was sold to private entrepreneurs. Most of the country's manufacturing is located in the area of Mexico City (about 55% of the plants), in Guadalajara, Jal., in Monterrey,

N.L., in the region Coatzacoalcos-Minatitlán, Ver. (petrochemical works), in Monclovia, Coah. and Lázaro Cárdenas, Mich. (steel production. – Despite the general crisis, a new and highly successful in-bond assembly industry ("Maquiladora") has sprung up in the larger cities bordering the USA, particularly in Ciudad Juárez, Chih., Matamoros, Tamps., Nogales, Son., Tijuana, B.C. and Chihuahua, Chih. In 1986 exports from these 1,100 off-shore plants (1985: 760 plants) with some 300,000 employees will have reached $1.5 billion, thus surpassing the net income from tourism as the second largest foreign currency earner. – The, until 1982, flourishing automotive industry has been in a crisis ever since. Some plants had to be shut down, others are concentrating now more on exports than on the dwindling domestic market. As to the number of cars produced, Volkswagen de México still maintains the number one spot in the country, followed by Nissan Mexicana, Chrysler de México, Ford Motor Company and General Motors de México. Whereas the American companies were able to increase their exports in 1986 compared to the two previous years, Volkswagen's foreign sales dropped considerably, particularly as it stopped producing and exporting the legendary "beetle" in 1985.

Energy supply is mainly in the hands of a state corporation, the Comisión Federal de Electricidad (CFE). Almost 90% of the total energy production is supplied by hydrocarbons of which crude oil provides 70%, natural gas 3% and other gases 2%. Energy sources like carbon and hydro-energy made up the rest of the output. – The large and controversial nuclear power plant at Laguna Verde, Ver., is supposed to become partly operative some time in 1987.

The situation in **agriculture and forestry** is consistently problematic. Only about 16% of the country's total area is suitable for agriculture, and almost 10 million of the rural population still live in remote villages with less than 500 inhabitants. More than half the agricultural land is worked in the form of ejidos, by peasants or communities which were allotted land from the expropriated haciendas. Most of the approximately 27,000 ejidos with 3 million families lack the capital resources to pay for the machinery, fertilizers and irrigation systems required to increase productivity. A more productive form of agriculture, on larger holdings, is found, among other places, in the Sonora and Sinaloa valleys, where winter vegetables (tomatoes, aubergines, peppers, cucumbers, onions, gourds, chick-peas, etc.) and fruit are grown, principally for export. Other exports include agricultural products (primarily coffee, cocoa, tobacco, honey, cotton and sisal) as well as animals for slaughter. Over the last 20 years or so the agricultural development has stagnated except for the export crops. Up to 10 million tons of corn and other cereals, beans sugar and seeds etc. had to be imported regularly. In 1986, however, domestic drops increased to some extent making imports of a few staples unnecessary.

The Mexican **fishing industry** has been severely hampered in recent years by a shortage of boats and equipment, 1986 seems to become a better year compared to the recent past. According to official sources the total catch could reach 1.47 million tons. Foreign sales mainly consist of shrimps, lobsters, tuna, sardines and mussels.

An important branch of the Mexican economy – important particularly as a source of foreign currency is **tourism**. Since the end of the Second World War Mexico's great range of scenic and cultural attractions has drawn many visitors, especially from the United States and Canada and in past years from Europe. Tourism dropped in 1981 and particularly in 1982, increased again in 1983 and 1984. In 1985 the number of visitors sank from 4.7 million to 4.29 million. Projections for 1986 are quite better and it is

Oil derrick, Villahermosa

Pilgrims outside the shrine of Guadalupe, Mexico City

expected that, border traffic excluded, up to 4.6 million foreigners will visit Mexico and will spend in excess of $2 billion. Of these tourists about 84% are from the USA, 7% from Latin America, 4.5% from Canada and Europe each. During the last years between 100,000 and 130,000 tourists a year originated in the Federal Republic of Germany, Austria and Switzerland.

It is accepted that in the next two years Mexico will succeed in putting behind it the severe economic crisis. The pre-requirements for this are a speedy reduction in inflation and the attainment of a healthy rate of economic growth accompanied by an acceptable level of borrowing from abroad. There remains the problem of the ever increasing population, in consequence of which 800,000–900,000 job seekers annually come on to the market.

Mexico A to Z

The Basilica of Ocotlán, Tlaxcala

Acapulco

State: Guerrero (Gro.).
Altitude: 2 m (6 ft). – Population: 1,000,000.
Telephone dialing code: 9 17 48.
ⓘ **Coordinación Federal de Turismo,**
Costera Miguel Alemán 187;
tel. 5 11 78, 5 13 03, 5 14 28, 5 10 22.

HOTELS. – *Villa Vera Hotel and Raquet Club*, Lomas del Mar, L, SP, tennis; *Acapulco Princess*, Playa Revolcadero, L, SP, tennis, riding; *Las Brisas*, Carretera Escénica, 5255, L, SP, tennis; *Pierre Marquéz Princess*, Playa Revolcadero, L, SP, golf; *Exelaris Hyatt Regency Acapulco*, Costera Alemán 1, L, SP, tennis; *Acapulco Plaza Holiday Inn*, Costera Alemán, L, SP; *El Mirador*, Quebrada 74, I, SP, (Quebrada divers); *ElCano*, Costera M. Alemán, I, SP; *De Gante*, Costera M. Alemán 268, I, SP; *El Cid*, Costera M. Alemán 248, I, SP; *Embassy*, Costera M. Alemán, I, SP; *Linda Vista*, Playa Caleta, II, SP; *Los Flamingos*, Av. López Mateos, II, SP; *Caribe*, Av. López Mateos 10, II; *Astoria*, Costera M. Alemán y La Suiza, II; *De La Costera*, Costera M. Alemán y G. Sandoval, II; *Bungalows Marbrisa*, Lirios 153, III; *Asturias*, Quebrada 45, III.

RESTAURANTS in most hotels; also *Armando's Taj Mahal*, Costera M. Alemán 2330; *Las Madeiras*, Carretera Escénica 39; *Embarcadero*, Costera M. Alemán 25; *Villa Demos*, Av. Del Prado 6; *Coyuca 22*, Coyuca 22; *Barbas Negras*, Costera M. Alemán/Playa Condesa; *Carlos 'n' Charlie's*, Costera M. Alemán 999; *Los Rancheros*, Carretera Escénica; *Antojitos Mayab*, Costera M. Alemán/corner Aviles, Playa Los Hornos; *Suntory*, Costera M. Alemán 36; *Famous Steve's Hideaway*, Sunset Beach, Coyuca Lagune.

RECREATION and SPORTS. – Swimming, snorkeling, diving, water skiing, para-sailing, sailing, surfing, fishing, deep-sea fishing, boat and canoe trips, shooting, riding, golf, tennis, jai alai, squash.

EVENTS. – Fiestas: March 19, Día del Señor San José; May 15, Día de San Isidro Labrador; July 25, Fiesta del Santo de Coyuca de Benítez; September 28, Día de Santiago Apóstol; December 12, Día de Nuestra Señora de Guadalupe.

Para-sailing, Condesa Beach

ACCESS. – By air from Mexico City and other Mexican and foreign airports; by road from Mexico City 415 km (258 miles), from Zihuatanejo-Ixtapa 240 km (150 miles).

The world-famous sun-drenched bathing resort of **Acapulco extends along the wide crescent-shaped Acapulco Bay – not only a scenic paradise, with its blue sea, white beaches, green hills and rugged cliffs, but a magnificent natural harbor. Although overrun by tourists in recent years, it still provides a memorable vacation, and its immediate surroundings offer plenty

Acapulco

of opportunities for getting away from the crowds.

HISTORY. – Although the Acapulco area (Náhuatl, "place where the grasses are destroyed") was probably settled in very early times, the name first appears in the records only after the *Aztec conquest* at the end of the 15th c. According to some theories Peruvian vessels may have reached this region at an even earlier date. The first European to discover the bay was apparently the Spanish conquistador *Gil Gonzales Avila* in 1521. In subsequent years Acapulco became a supply base for expeditions along the Pacific coast to the N and to South America. At the end of the 16th c. it became the home port of the ships which carried on trade with the Philippines, China and India as well as with South America. From the East Asian countries came silk, porcelain and spices, from South America silver and gold. The main exports from New Spain were silver, textiles and cacao. The goods brought in to Acapulco were transported to Mexico City on a road built by the Spaniards and from there to the port of Veracruz on the Gulf of Mexico, from which they were shipped to Europe. In the 17th and 18th c. the shipping routes from Acapulco, like other seaways in those days, were much exposed to the attentions of pirates. The decline of the port began when a new trade route from the Philippines across the Indian Ocean and around the Cape of Good Hope to Spain was opened up at the end of the 18th c. After Mexico achieved independence Acapulco lost all importance, and it was only after the construction of a motor road linking it with Mexico City in 1927 that the town began to revive. Its boom years began after the Second World War when it was discovered by American tourists.

SIGHTS. – Apart from its magnificent setting and its chain of great hotels Acapulco has few features of particular note. Of interest is *Fort San Diego (Fuerte de San Diego)*, originally built between 1615 and 1617 and rebuilt after an earthquake in 1776. The present museum was once used principally as a refuge against attacks by pirates. In the *Zócalo* (main square) stands the *Cathedral*, a building in Moorish-Byzantine style erected in the 1930s; and the **Cultural and Convention Center** *(Centro Acapulco)* at the E end of the town, with conference halls, a theater, an exhibition of folk art (articles for sale) and a small archeological museum.

The life of the resort is concentrated along the **Avenida Costera Miguel Alemán**, on which most of the large hotels, restaurants, night spots and shops are to be found. There are more than 20 *beaches* in Acapulco and its immediate surroundings, the finest of which are *Caleta* and *Caletilla* (popular in the mornings: calm

water, underwater life, glass-bottomed boats); the island of *La Roqueta*, with the beach of the same name is reached by boat from Playa Caleta; this island has been converted into a magnificent nature reserve; offshore, underwater, is a bronze statue of the Virgin of Guadalupe; *Hornos* and *Hornitos* (busy in the afternoon: surfing); *Condesa* (popular in the afternoon and evening; at present particularly fashionable); *Puerto Marqués*, at the fishing village of that name, 13 km (8 miles) E of Acapulco (beautiful bay, busy in the mornings, calm water); *Revolcadero*, 1 km (¾ mile) farther on (beautiful and quiet, but surf and undertow; surfing); *Pie de la Cuesta*, 12 km (7½ miles) NW of Acapulco (heavy surf and undertow, magnificent sunsets); and *Laguna de Coyuca* (dense tropical vegetation, freshwater fishes and exotic birds). There are other good beaches at *La Angosta*, *Honda*, *Manzanillo*, *Redonda* and *Icacos*. A new attraction, very popular with local people, is the *Parque Papagayo*, in which there are shows, animals and exhibits of art.

Every visitor should see the performance put on several times a day by the *Quebrada divers, who leap down from a 40 m (130 ft) high cliff into the waves which surge in and out between the rocks. – Another local spectacle is provided by the *voladores*, Totonac Indians from Papantla who on most evenings perform their ritual leap from a high pole to which they are attached by a rope. – A popular outing in the evening is a drive along the coast road in one of the little horse-drawn carriages known as *calandrias*.

Acapulco to Puerto Escondido along the coast. – Road 200 runs E from Acapulco along the **Costa**

Quebrada diver, Acapulco

Chica, as this stretch of coast is called. Soon after leaving the city there is a superb *view of Acapulco Bay from the *Carretera Escénica*. The road then runs past the *Puerto Marqués* bay and comes to the picturesque lagoon of *Tres Palos*. Then follows an interesting but still little known stretch of country between the Sierra Madre del Sur and the Pacific, with the towns of *Crus Grande* (about 120 km – 75 miles), *San Luis Acatlán* (turn off about 27 km – 16 miles), *Ometepec* (turn off 16 km – 10 miles), *Cuajinicuilapa* (about 234 km – 145 miles), *Montecillos* (turn off 16 km – 10 miles) and *Punto Maldonado* (turn off 14 km – 8 miles). The interest of this region lies in its tropical vegetation and its numerous rivers, lagoons and rock formations. Parts of the area are inhabited by the descendants of runaway negro slaves, most of whom intermarried with the local Indians. At the end of the 19th c. a German-American named Johann Schmidt established himself in this region as a kind of petty king, maintaining his position until the 1910 revolution. – Just over the border of Oaxaca state is the town of *Pinotepa Nacional* (about 284 km – 177 miles; population 40,000; hotels: Carmón and Marisol). 6 km (4 miles) short of the town Road 125 leads to the Convent Road of the *Mixteca Alta* (see Oaxaca Town). From Pinotepa Nacional it is another 145 km (90 miles) on Road 200 to the resort of **Puerto Escondido** (p. 227).

Acatepec

State: Puebla (Pue.).
Altitude: 2200 m (7220 ft). – Population: 2000.
ⓘ **Coordinación Federal de Turismo de Puebla,**
   Blvd. Hermanos Serdan y Blvd. Norte;
   Puebla, Pue.;
   tel. (91 22) 48 29 77, 48 31 77, 48 30 44.

ACCESS. – The village is 16 km (10 miles) from Puebla on the road to Atlixco Oaxaca (No. 190).

The *church of San Francisco de Acatepec is one of the finest examples of the regional High Baroque style in Mexico. The façade of the church, which is of no great size, is completely covered with glazed bricks and tiles (azulejos) in the Poblano style.

HISTORY. – Little is known about the origins of the church, but it is believed that the present building was erected about 1730 and that the azulejos were specially designed and produced in Puebla for the decoration of the church. Part of the interior was destroyed by fire at the end of the 1930s, and the restoration, carried out with great zeal by local craftsmen, has not entirely reproduced the original 18th c. splendour. – The magnificence of the churches to be found in quite small places in this region reflects the fact that the Spaniards were able to enlist the skills of the local Indian artists and craftsmen.

THE CHURCH. – An imposing *arch* in neo-Mudéjar style gives access to the church. The whole *façade* is covered with bricks and azulejos and is divided

The church of San Francisco de Acatepec (Poblano style)

into three parts. The *doorway*, framed in an irregular arch, is flanked by three Corinthian columns on either side. In niches between the groups of columns are sculptured figures. In the central section the columns are replaced by pilasters in the form of inverted and truncated pyramids (*estípites*, one of the main features of the Churrigueresque style). The large window in the middle bears the symbol of St Francis. In the upper part of the façade the pilasters at the sides of the middle section are continued upward by volutes to form a kind of gable. In the star-shaped niche is a figure of St Francis, and above this, on the highest point of the façade, a representation of the Trinity. – At the corners of the right-hand tower are Solomonic (twisted) columns, decorated with bands of blue and yellow azulejos. The left-hand tower, set at an angle, has an almost jaunty effect.

*INTERIOR. – The church contains a profusion of *stucco* and *wood sculpture*, painted and gilded,

typical of the 18th c. Poblano style. There is an interesting 17th c. *retablo* in which the gilded and painted figures (the *estofado* technique) almost disappear in the riot of gold Solomonic columns and other ornamentation. The extraordinary complex and luxuriant decoration of the doorway into the *baptistry* is another notable feature. The rest of the interior is more restrained and shows less Indian influence than the neighboring church of Santa María de Tonantzintla.

SURROUNDINGS. – Less than 1 km (¾ mile) W lies the village of *Tonantzintla* (alt. 2200 m (7220 ft); pop. 2000; fiesta August 15, Assumption). – If the façade of San Francisco de Acatepec is one of the great achievements of the Poblano style, the church of **Santa Maria de Tonantzintla** is an equally remarkable example of the style applied to a church interior. The relatively simple red façade of Santa María is in two parts and is decorated with blue and white tiles and sculpture.

The exuberantly Baroque **INTERIOR, a riot of color in a blending of Indian and European styles, was the work of unknown local artists and craftsmen. It reflects the pre-Columbian practice of covering the whole surface of a structure with ornamentation and the native liking for the decorative use of fruits, flowers and birds, here mingled with Christian elements. In the *choir*, for example, is a representation of an orchestra of Indian musicians and also stucco

Stucco ornament, Santa María de Tonantzintla

Acolman de Netzahualcóyotl

State: México (Mex.).
Altitude: 2215 m (7267 ft). – Population: 3000
(i) **Coordinación Federal de Turismo,**
Av. Vincente Villada 123,
Col. Centro,
Toluca;
tel. (9 17 21) 4 42 49, 4 89 61, 4 03 04.
Secretaría de Turismo,
Av. Presidente Masaryk 172,
Ciudad de México;
tel. (9 15) 2 50 85 55.

ACCESS. – The village is 40 km (25 miles) from Mexico City on Road 85D or 85 (10 km (6 miles) before Teotihuacán) and 25 km (15 miles) from Texcoco, Mex., on Road 136.

frames containing figures in relief of Christ, the Virgin and St Christopher. In the *nave* are figures of St Francis, St James and St Antony. In the *dome* a host of angels' heads peer down from amid a profusion of gilded foliage. Note also the remarkable stucco decoration on the *chancel arch*, with richly ornamented Atlas figures and crowned figures of devils spewing out fruit.

Near the church is a national *observatory* (1942) with a Schmidt telescope. The building contains frescoes by Miguel Prieto.

Returning to Acatepec and continuing on Road 190 toward Puebla, we come in 4 km (2½ miles) to the little town of **Tlaxcalancingo** (alt. 2200 m (7220 ft), pop. 4000). On the right is the 18th c. church of San Bernardino, another fine example of the Poblano style. The magnificent *façade with its curved gable is completely covered with red bricks and azulejos; on the left is an elegant tower with a tiled dome and roof cap.

From here it is only 12 km (8 miles) to **Puebla** (p. 224).

The magnificent Augustinian house at *Acolman, situated on a plateau, is a typical example of the fortified convents built in New Spain in the 16th c. The general design of the building is Ibero-Gothic, but the façade of the church is a fine example of the Plateresque style, influenced by the Renaissance. In contrast to the façade many features of the interior show surprisingly primitive characteristics.

HISTORY. – The foundation stone of the convent of Acolman (Náhuatl, "surrounded by water") was laid in 1539, but the church was not begun until the middle of the century. The façade dates from 1560; the building of the convent was completed in 1571, but the church was then still unfinished. In 1580 there were 24 monks in the convent, 19 of them engaged in study and 5 in missionary activity among the Indians. During the 19th c. and again in the 1930s the convent suffered damage from flooding.

The fortified convent of Acolman

THE BUILDINGS. – In the architecture of the 16th c. particular importance was attached to the façade containing the main doorway, and this is well exemplified by Acolman, designed in pure Plateresque style. The delicately carved arch of the **doorway** is flanked on either side by two classical columns in the manner of the Italian Renaissance, and in between each pair of columns is the statue of a saint under a richly decorated canopy – an arrangement unknown elsewhere in Mexico. Above the cornice are three niches containing statues, and above these again is a *window* in the same style as the doorway, surmounted by an ornate carving of the Augustinian heraldic device. To the left of the window is the coat of arms of the kingdom of Castile and León, to the right that of Acolman. The façade is topped by battlements, above which rises the simple *bell-turret*.

The INTERIOR of the church has the fortress-like character typical of the period. The nave measures 57 by 12.5 m (187 by 41 ft). Only one of the altars dates from the period of foundation; the others were added in the 17th and 18th c. At the end of the nave and in the cloisters are frescoes in grey, black and ochre dating from about 1600.

The *cloisters* show evidence of having been the work of several different architects. – On the right of the church façade, under a plain arch, is an *open pulpit*, the interior of which is decorated with frescoes. – The *posas* (processional chapels) were destroyed by flooding, but one has been reconstructed. Outside the present *atrium* stands a fine carved stone cross, with a figure of Christ as the Man of Sorrows, the symbols of the Passion and flower ornament. Many details, such as the skull at the foot of the cross, show a remarkably primitive style.

A small *museum* in the convent contains religious pictures.

SURROUNDINGS. – A short distance SW is the village of **Tepexpan**, where a fossilized human skeleton about 11,000 years old was found in 1949. There is a small museum containing the remains of a mammoth dating from the same period which was found nearby in 1952, together with stone tools and implements.

10 km (6 miles) from Acolman are the magnificent remains of the city of ****Teotihuacán** (p. 257).

Actopán

State: Hidalgo (Hgo.).
Altitude: 2050 m (6725 ft). – Population: 45,000.
(i) **Coordinación Federal de Turismo,**
Plaza de la Independencia 110, 3rd floor,
Pachuca, Hgo.;
tel. (9 17 71) 2 59 60, 2 48 60, 2 32 89

ACCESS. – From Mexico City on Road 85 via Pachuca 92 km – 57 miles); distance 130 km (81 miles).

MARKET DAY. – Wednesday.

HOTELS. – *Jardin*, Independencia 10, II; *Reforma*, Escobedo 7, II.

RESTAURANTS. – *Centro Camionero*, on the Mexico City–Laredo road; *Glorieta*, Zaragoza.

EVENTS. – Fiestas: September 10, Día de San Nicolás Tolentino; December 12, Día de Nuestra Señora de Guadalupe.

The large convent of *Actopán is situated in the town of the same name, largely inhabited by Otomí Indians. It is a fine example of the fortified convents built in New Spain in the 16th c.

HISTORY. – The convent was founded by Augustinians in 1548 in the village of Actopán (Náhuatl, "place of fertile land"). It was built by a self-taught architect, Father *Andrés de Mata*, with the help of the two Indian headmen of the village, *Juan Mica Actopán* and *Pedro Izcuitloapilco*. The church was dedicated to St Nicholas of Tolentino.

THE CONVENT. – An unusual feature of the beautiful *Renaissance façade*, with Plateresque elements, is that the inner framing of the doorway is repeated on a larger scale in the outer framing. On either side is a pair of Corinthian columns. Above the smaller columns rises a fan-like arch, with coffering. The outer columns support a cornice with a beautiful frieze, above which is the window of the choir. The fortress-like character of the **church** is emphasized by the battlements on the roof and the stylized lookout posts. The massive square tower shows Moorish influence. – The nave of the church, with Gothic vaulting, is over 24 m (75 ft) high and ends in an angular apse. The interior has been much altered and is now predominantly neo-classical. – In the *sacristy* are a fine font and a statue of St John the Baptist.

To the left of the church, surrounded by a defensive wall, is the former cemetery, at the end of which is an ***open chapel**, the *Bóveda de Actopán* ("vault of Actopán").

Fresco in the convent of Actopán

This consists of a large, boldly vaulted arch, decorated with wall mosaics and Biblical and historical scenes on the sides.

To the right of the church doorway is the entrance to the **convent**, in front of which is a porch (*portería*) with a very unusual façade. This has three coffered arches borne on massive fluted columns, with pilasters, balustrades, medallions (decorated panels), two Augustinian heraldic devices and an ornate cross completing the effect. Immediately to the right is a small room, the *Sala de Profundis*, with beautiful frescoes depicting, in medieval style, the history of the convent. – The interior is predominantly Gothic, with pointed arches and ribbed vaulting.

In contrast to these Gothic features are the *Renaissance frescoes, in a variable state of preservation, to be seen on most of the walls in the convent; only the figures show occasional traces of Gothic influence. The frescoes, which are the finest of the period in Mexico, depict primarily fathers of the Church and saints of the Augustinian order, together with friezes of heraldic animals, garlands and other decorative elements. Under the staircase is a figure of *Martín de Acevedo* with two Indian nobles. He played an important part in the building of Actopán and is believed to have painted some of the frescoes. Notable both for its form and decoration is the *refectory*, with frescoed barrel-vaulting and a polygonal pulpit. – In one of the convent buildings is a *museum* of Otomí folk art. – Temporary exhibitons of religious art are put on in the former presbytery office.

The huge *atrium*, now almost completely built over, originally measured 290 by 180 m (950 by 590 ft), and is said to have been capable of accommodating between 40,000 and 50,000 worshippers.

SURROUNDINGS. – 45 km (28 miles) NW of Actopán is **Ixmiquilpan** (alt. 1750 m (5740 ft); pop. 28,000; hotels: Club Alcanara, SP, Hostería del Cortijo; market day Monday). The town, capital of the Otomí Indians in pre-Columbian times, has an interesting Augustinian convent, built between 1550 and 1554 by Father Andrés de Mata, the architect of Actopán. The church, dedicated to the Archangel Michael, has a beautiful Renaissance (Plateresque) façade with Corinthian columns and a coffered arch. In 1960 unusual frescoes were discovered in the church and conventual buildings, the themes of which showed them to be evidently the work of an Indian artist, they include scenes of battle between Indian warriors and mythological figures from earlier times. Other features of interest in the town are the church of El Carmen (Churrigueresque façade, Baroque retablos), two bridges of the colonial period and the local folk art (miniature musical instruments, decorated mirrors and combs, embroidered blouses and purses). – In the surrounding area are several health resorts, including *Tzindijeh* (hotel), 2 km (1 mile) outside Tasquillo.

40 km (25 miles) NW of Ixmiquilpan on Road 85 is the old mining town of **Zimapán** (alt. 1950 m (6400 ft); pop. 5500; hotels: La Fundición, SP, Posada de Rey, SP; fiesta June 24, St John the Baptist; market days Saturday and Sunday); the town has a fine parish church with a 17th c.: Baroque façade and neoclassical retablos.

Road 85 continues N through magnificent mountain scenery with stretches of luxuriant vegetation to *Tamazunchale*, 152 km (94 miles) distant (p. 252).

Aguascalientes (State)

State of Aguascalientes (Ags.). – Capital: Aguascalientes.
Area: 5486 sq. km (2118 sq. miles).
Population: 585,100.

(i) **Coordinación Federal de Turismo**,
Av. Circunvalación Sur y Mahatma G.,
1st floor,
Aguascalientes, Ags.;
tel. (9 14 91) 6 01 23, 5 11 55.

Aguascalientes, bounded on the N, W and E by Zacatecas and on the S by Jalisco, is one of the smallest states in Mexico. It lies within the central Mexican highlands at an average altitude of 1800 m (5900 ft) and is bordered on the W by the foothills of the Sierra Madre. One large river and numerous smaller ones make it one of the most fertile parts of Mexico. The population is almost wholly of Spanish descent.

HISTORY. – In pre-Columbian times this region was occupied by the semi-nomadic *Chichimecs* ("descended from a dog"). This rather disparaging name was given to them by the Indian peoples of more advanced culture, and was not so much a tribal or ethnic designation as a general term for primitive tribes

Mexico
United Mexican States
Estados Unidos Mexicanos

Aguascalientes

States
Estados

1a Baja California Sur	12 Aguascalientes
1b Baja California Norte	13 Jalisco
2 Sonora	14 Guanajuato
3 Chihuahua	15 Querétaro
4 Sinaloa	16 Hidalgo
5 Durango	17 Colima
6 Coahuila	18 Michoacán
7 Nuevo León	19 México
8 Zacatecas	20 Morelos
9 San Luis Potosí	21 Tlaxcala
10 Tamaulipas	22 Puebla
11 Nayarit	23 Veracruz

24 Guerrero	26 Chiapas
25 Oaxaca	27 Tabasco
	28 Campeche
	29 Yucatán
	30 Quintana Roo

D.F. Distrito Federal (Federal District)

which were still at the hunting and food-gathering stage of development. These barbarian peoples, belonging to the *Náhuatl* linguistic group, made repeated incursions into the central highlands from the 8th c. onwards, and were for the most part absorbed into the more advanced peoples who had established themselves there. The destruction of the Toltec capital of Tollan (Tula: see p. 272) in 1168 was probably the work of Chichimec raiders. The *Aztecs* who began to come into prominence in the 13th c. were also of Chichimec origin. This region was apparently never influenced by the cultural centers of the central highlands or La Quemada.

The first Spaniard to come into this area was Cortés's companion *Pedro de Alvarado*, but on his first expedition he was compelled to withdraw. It took some decades for the Spaniards to destroy the local Indians or drive them into the mountains; and thereafter they were obliged to resettle the land and build new towns themselves. From the colonial period onwards the inhabitants of this region, particularly of the capital, were well known for their activity in both politics and culture, and accordingly they played a prominent part in the *War of Independence* (1810–21). Until 1789 Aguascalientes wa part of the province of Nueva Galicia and subsequently it was joined with Zacatecas; not until 1857 did it become a separate state of the Mexican Republic. Lying as it did in the middle of the country, Aguascalientes was the scene of bitter fighting between the contending parties during the *revolutionary wars* (1910–20).

ECONOMY. – In the fertile valleys, cereals (including maize), fruit, vegetables and vines are cultivated; on the plateau there is large-scale livestock-farming (horses, fighting bulls). The mines produce gold, silver, copper, lead and antimony. Textiles, leather goods, pottery, tobacco processing and the distillation of brandy are also of some importance in the economy. Tourists are primarily attracted to the popular health resorts and to the spring festival, Feria de San Marcos, in the capital.

Aguascalientes (Town)

State: Aguascalientes (Ags.).
Altitude: 1889 m (6198 ft).
Population: 370,000
Telephone dialing code: 9 14 91.
ⓘ **Coordinación Federal de Turismo,**
Av. Circunvalación Sur y Mahatma G., 1st floor, tel. 6 01 23, 5 11 55.

HOTELS. – *Medrano Continental* (motel), José María Chávez 904, I, SP; *Francia*, Plaza Principal 113, I; *París*, Plaza Principal Norte, I; *Internacional* (motel), José María Chávez 1111, II; *La Jolla* (motel), José María Chávez 21, II; *La Joya* (motel), Carretera 45, Salida Sur de la Ciudad, II.

RESTAURANTS in most hotels; also *Birriería El Cabrito*, Circunvalación Nte. 704; *El Caballo Loco*, V. Carranza 310; *Ostería del Jardín*, M. Ponce 130.

RECREATION and SPORTS. – Swimming, tennis, riding, golf.

EVENTS. – April 25 to May 5, Feria (Festival) de San Marcos; August 15, Feast of the Assumption of the Blessed Virgin Mary.

The pleasant colonial town of Aguascalients has an agreeable climate and is surrounded by orchards, vineyards and haciendas on which fighting bulls are bred. This very Spanish-looking town in the heart of Mexico is noted for its attractive pottery, embroidery and textiles and has been famous for a long time for its lively and colorful

Bullfight

spring fair, the Feria de San Marcos, celebrated in many old folk songs.

Aguascalientes is also known as the *Ciudad Perforada*, the "city riddled with holes", on account of the labyrinth of passages under the town – catacombs hewn by pre-Hispanic Indians of unknown origin. The passages are at present closed to visitors.

HISTORY. – In 1575, after bitter fighting with the semi-nomadic natives, the Spaniards were finally able to establish a town here with the imposing name of *Nuestra Señora de las Asunción de las Aguas Calientes*, the last part of the name ("hot waters") referring to the numerous hot springs in the area. The new settlement was for a long time no more than an outpost providing defense against hostile Indian tribes. In 1857 Aguascalientes became the capital of the newly established state of the same name. As an important railroad junction it was hotly disputed

Aguascalientes Cathedral

during the revolutionary years (1910–20), passing repeatedly from the control of one faction to the other.

SIGHTS. – Aguascalientes is best known for the healing *thermal springs in the town and surrounding area, which attract large numbers of visitors from Mexico and abroad. It has several beautiful parks and 18th c. churches in typical Churrigueresque style.

In the main square, the **Zócalo** or **Plaza Principal**, stand the *Town Hall* (17th c.) (Palacio Municipal) and the **Government Palace** (*Palacio de Gobernación*; 18th c.). The latter, formerly the palace of the Marqués de Guadalupe, is a magnificent Baroque building, with murals by Osvaldo Barra, a pupil of Rivera, in the inner courtyard. – Interesting religious buildings include the 18th c. **Cathedral**, the churches of **San Marcos** (picture, "Adoration of the Kings"; by José Alzibar), **El Encino** (Black Christ, pictures by Andrés López) and **San Antonio** (neo-Byzantine, 20th c.), and the convent of **San Diego** (fine pictures).

Most visitors are attracted to Aguascalientes by the annual **Feria de San Marcos**, held since 1604 in honor of the town's patron saint (bullfights, cockfights, charreadas, serenades, fireworks, etc.). – Some visitors may be interested in seeing one of the haciendas in the surrounding area where fighting bulls are bred.

Akumal

State: Quintana Roo (Q.R.).
Altitude: sea level.

HOTELS. – *Aventuras Akumal*, L; *Akumal Caribe*, L; *Las Casitas de Akumal*, I; *Hotel Club Akumal Caribe*, L; *Villas Maya*, II.

RECREATION and SPORTS. – Swimming, snorkeling, diving, fishing, boat trips and jungle expeditions; Akumal Caribe diving station.

ACCESS. – 100 km (60 miles) from Cancún on Road 307; 36 km (22 miles) S of Playa del Carmen (passenger ferry from Cozumel); 25 km (15 miles) N of Tulum (air taxi).

*Akumal, consisting of a small settlement, a hotel complex and a club, is the only seaside resort of any size S of Cancún on the coast of Quintana Roo state. It lies in a crescent-shaped bay with a palm-fringed beach of snow-white sand 15 km (10 miles) long. It is one of the most beautiful and one of the best equipped bathing places on the E coast of the Yucatán peninsula.

HISTORY. – Akumal (from the Maya word for turtle) was originally a small Maya settlement, which became known only when the Mexican association known as CEDAM began to operate here some 25 years ago and later made the bay its headquarters. The association, which is mainly concerned with underwater archaeology, has, in the course of numerous expeditions, discovered many Maya sites both along the coast and under water and raised old Spanish wrecks from the sea bottom. In association with the National Geographic Society and the Instituto Nacional de Arqueología e Historia (INAH) it has also carried out diving operations in the sacred cenote at Chichén Itzá. A cenote is a natural underground reservoir; these were used by the Mayas as sacrificial wells.

SIGHTS. – In addition to the wide range of facilities for water sports, fishing and excursions, visitors can see the remains of *wrecks* (cannon, anchors, chests, etc.), some of them dating from the 16th and 17th c., lying in shallow water near the shore. To the left of the entrance to the hotel is a small *museum* containing objects recovered from the sea.

SURROUNDINGS. – Along the coast S and N of Akumal are numerous Maya sites with the remains of buildings, cenotes and quiet little bays. Thanks to the geological structure of the Yucatán peninsula most of the cenotes and lagoons on the limestone plateau, which has practically no rivers, are connected with the sea by underground channels. In the small coastal bays and the lagoons near the sea fresh water mingles with salt water, producing a submarine fauna of mixed type and offering snorkelers and divers a unique experience. On the sea-floor can be seen crevices in the rock through which freshwater emerges from the channels in the limestone.

2 km (1¼ miles) N of Akumal is the beautiful lagoon of **Yal-ku** ("son of the god" in Maya), which offers excellent swimming and snorkeling. – 12 km (7½ miles) farther N on Road 307 a side road goes off on the right to the beautifully situted lagoon of **Chakalal**, with an interesting Maya temple. – Another 5 km (3 miles) along Road 307 a road leads to the beach of *Pamuul* (Cabañas), with unexcavated Maya remains.

11 km (7 miles) along the coast road an unsurfaced side road branches off to ***Xcaret**, where visitors can bathe in two Maya cenotes and in the picturesque bay and can watch the turtles in a small lagoon.There are also a number of Maya sites concealed in the jungle around Xcaret. – 6 km (4 miles) beyond this is the port of **Playa del Carmen** (p. 89).

Álamos

See under Guaymas

Amecameca de Juárez

State: México (Mex.).
Altitude: 2468 m (8098 ft). – Population 28,000.
(i) **Coordinación Federal de Turismo,**
Av. Vicente Villada 123,
Co. Centro,
Toluca, Mex.;
tel. (9 17 21) 4 42 49, 4 89 61, 4 03 04.
Secretaría de Turismo,
Av. Presidente Masaryk 172,
Ciudad de México;
tel. (9 15) 2 50 01 23
Coordinación Federal de Turismo,
Blvd. Hermanos Serdan y Blvd. Norte,
Puebla, Pue.
tel. (91 22) 48 29 77. 48 31 77, 48 30 44.
Coordinación Federal de Turismo,
I. Comonfort 12,
Cuernavaca, Mor.
tel. (9 17 31) 2 18 15, 2 52 39, 2 54 14

HOTELS. – *San Carlos*, ii.

RESTAURANTS in hotel; also *La Flecha Roja*; *La Montaña*.

RECREATION and SPORTS. – Walking, climbing.

EVENTS. – Pilgrimage to the Señor de Sacromonte (Ash Wednesday); Sunday market.

ACCESS. – Road 190 from Mexico City to exit for Chalco, then Road 115; distance to Amecameca 60 km (37 miles). – 44 km (27 miles) from Cuautla on Road 115.

The little town of Amecameca lies at the foot of the two snow-covered volcanoes, **Popocatépetl and **Iztaccíhuatl. Its situation in austere mountain scenery and its proximity to notable examples of colonial art make it a good center for

climbs and excursions of various kinds.

HISTORY. – In the Late Classic period Amecameca (Náhuatl, "old water-holes") was a member, second only to Chalco in importance, of a powerful league of city states. In 1464 the *Aztecs* captured the town, and a year later achieved final victory over their great enemies the Chalca. – The *Spaniards* of Cortés's force passed through the town in 1519 on their march to Tenochtitlán. The region was envangelized at a very early stage by Franciscan missionaries.

SIGHTS. – In the main square is the *parish church*, which has beautiful Baroque altars. The *Dominican convent* (16th c.) associated with the church has a well-preserved cloister.

On Ash Wednesday the **Sacromonte** ("sacred hill") which rises 150 m (500 ft) above the town is crowded with pilgrims and visitors, and there is a lively and colorful market in the town below. A *Way of the Cross*, with Stations of the Cross in brightly colored tiles, runs up to a small *church* on top of the hill where a figure of Christ which is believed to work miracles is kept. The church was built in honor of a hermit named Martín de Valencia, one of the first Franciscan friars to come to New Spain, who lived in a cave here. Higher up is a *chapel*, dedicated to the Virgin of Guadalupe; it is built on the old Indian cult site of Teteoinán. – From the top of the hill there is a magnificent *view of the Mexico valley and the surrounding mountains.

SURROUNDINGS. – 10 km (6 miles) NW is **Tlalmanalco** (Náhuatl, "on the plain": pop. 8800), with a Franciscan friary founded in 1525. The porch leads into a cloister which contains remains of frescoes. The late 16th c. church. with a Renaissance façade, has a fine Baroque altar and a number of pictures. There is also an incompletely preserved *open chapel built between 1558 and 1564, with richly decorated pillars and arches, which is one of the finest examples of Indian Plateresque art in Mexico.

From Tlalmanalco it is 12 km (7½ miles) to **Chalco** (Náhuatl, "many months": alt. 2270 m (7448 ft); pop. 21,000), once chief town of an important Nahua tribe which for over a century fought with the towns of Atzcapotzalco and Tenochtitlán for predominance in the Valley of Mexico. This long-standing feud led the Chalca tribe to ally themselves with the Spaniards against the Mexica people of Tenochtitlán. – The town is connected by a network of canals with the "floating gardens" of Xochimilco (see under Mexico City). The only feature of interest is a 16th c. Franciscan friary with a church, the façade of which was rebuilt in Baroque style in the 18th c.

10 km (6 miles) NW of Chalco, near the village of *Ayotla*, is the archeological site of **Tlapacoya**, the excavation of which has thrown fresh light on early pre-Columbian history. A six-story pyramid, probably dating from the 6th–4th c. B.C., and numerous tombs with figurines dating back to 1200 B.C. suggest that this was an early Olmec site. The earliest evidence so far discovered of human activity in Mexico, dating from about 23000 B.C. was also found here.

2 km (1¼ miles) S of Amecameca a road goes off to the Paso de Cortés and to Tlamacas and La Joya, at the foot of the **Popocatépetl-Iztaccíhuatl massif** (see p. 221). – 10 km (6 miles) farther S on Road 115 (the Cuautla road) is **Ozumba de Alzate** (pop. 8000), which has a 16th c. Franciscan friary with interesting frescoes depicting the reception of the first twelve Franciscan friars in New Spain by Cortés in 1523. The church, which has a Baroque altar, was rebuilt in the 18th c. Nearby are the waterfall of *Salto de Chimal* and the little town of *Chimalhuacán*, set amid beautiful gardens.

Atotonilco
See under San Miguel Allende

Atotonilco el Grande
See under Pachuca

Baja California
Baja California Norte

State of Baja California Norte (B.C.N.).
Capital: Mexicali.
Area: 71,627 sq. km (27,655 sq. miles).
Population: 1,373,600.
ⓘ **Coordinación Federal de Turismo,**
Linea Internacional,
Puerta México, Planta Alta, Col. Federal,
Tijuana, B.C.N.;
tel. (91 66) 82 33 47–9, 86 54 01–05.

Baja California Sur

State of Baja California Sur (B.C.S.). – Capital: La Paz.
Area: 72,465 sq. km (27,979 sq. miles).
Population: 271,500.
ⓘ **Coordinación Federal de Turismo,**
Paseo Alvaro Abregon 2130,
La Paz, B.C.S.;
tel. (9 16 82) 2 11 90, 2 11 99 and 2 79 75.

The peninsula of Baja California (Lower California), 1250 km (775 miles) long with an average breadth of 90 km (55 miles), is bounded on the N by the United States (state of California), on the W by the Pacific and on the E by the Gulf of California. It is divided between two states, Baja California Norte and Baja California Sur, the boundary between

Mexico
United Mexican States
Estados Unidos Mexicanos

Baja California Norte
Baja California Sur

States
Estados

1a	Baja California Sur	12	Aguascalientes
1b	Baja California Norte	13	Jalisco
		14	Guanajuato
2	Sonora	15	Querétaro
3	Chihuahua	16	Hidalgo
4	Sinaloa	17	Colima
5	Durango	18	Michoacán
6	Coahuila	19	México
7	Nuevo León	20	Morelos
8	Zacatecas	21	Tlaxcala
9	San Luis Potosí	22	Puebla
10	Tamaulipas	23	Veracruz
11	Nayarit	24	Guerrero
		25	Oaxaca

26	Chiapas
27	Tabasco
28	Campeche
29	Yucatán
30	Quintana Roo

D.F. Distrito Federal (Federal District)

the two running along the 28th parallel. It is a hot and arid region, with ranges of mountains and a much indented coastline.

The principal chain of mountains is the Sierra de San Pedro Mártir which runs almost due N–S, the highest point being the Cerro de la Encantada (3080 m – 10,105 ft). The boundary with the state of Sonora is formed by the Río Colorado, which flows into the northern tip of the Gulf of California. The peninsula is primarily inhabited by whites and mestizos; the Indian tribes (Cucapá, Kiliwa, Pai-Pai, Cochimí, Ki-nai, etc.) have been almost completely exterminated, being now represented by barely 1000 Indians.

Except for a number of mission stations the peninsula, now served by a through road from N to S (the Carretera Transpeninsular, completed in 1974), has little that is typically Mexican to offer the visitor. The proximity of the United States and the great influx of tourists from the north have given its towns a largely North American character. The tourist attractions of Baja California are its desert cactuses, the majestic outlines of its rugged mountains and its endless expanses of coast with their alternation of sandy beaches, cliffs and lagoons. Apart from a few crowded tourist resorts Baja California is a region of bare and solitary landscapes. It has rich and varied animal life, including pumas, coyotes, foxes, deer, hares, wild geese, wild ducks and seabirds of all kinds, as well as grey whales (to be seen in the Laguna San Ignacio), sealions, seals, swordfish, dolphins, barracudas and tuna.

Apart from a number of rock paintings, as at San Borjita, San Ignacio and Calimalí, Baja California has little of archeological interest. Caves occupied in prehistoric times have been found at Caguama and Metate Comondú and on the Isla de Cedros.

In addition to **Tijuana** (p. 266) the main places of tourist interest not on the Carretera Transpeninsular are Tecate, Mexicali and San Felipe (see under Tijuana).

HISTORY. – Traces of human settlement dating back to about 7500 B.C. have been found in Baja California. Practically nothing is known about the fairly primitive cultures of the early Indian inhabitants of the peninsula. – In 1535 Hernán Cortés landed in the La Paz area during his quest for a legendary paradise of Amazons ruled by a black queen named Calafia. The Spaniards who later followed in his footsteps met fierce resistance from the local Indians and were unable to establish themselves in this region, which they named California after the elusive queen. Settlement began only after 1697, when three Jesuit missionaries, Francisco Eusebio Kino, Juan María de Salvatierra and Juan de Ugarte, came to Baja California. After the expulsion of the Jesuits in 1767 their missionary task was taken over by Franciscans, who were in turn succeeded by Dominicans in 1772. In 1804 Baja California was separated from California, and during the war with the United States the

A natural rock arch on the coast of Baja California

peninsula was occupied by American troops (1847–8). In 1931 Baja California was divided into a northern and a southern territory. Baja California Norte became an independent state in 1952, Baja California Sur in 1974.

ECONOMY. – A considerable contribution is made to the economy of Baja California by *tourism*. In addition cotton, maize, wheat, alfalfa, vegetables and fruit are grown in areas where there is artificial irrigation. The main forms of *industry* are the processing of agricultural and fish products and the mining of gold, copper, iron, silver and salt. Fishing is potentially a promising source of revenue, but is hampered by shortage of boats and processing facilities.

To Cabo San Lucas on the Carretera Transpeninsular. – The starting-point of Road 1, which runs down the whole length of the peninsula for a distance of 1700 km (1050 miles), is Baja California's largest town, **Tijuana** (p. 266).

108 km (67 miles) from Tijuana is **Ensenada** (pop. 220,000; hotels: San Nicolás Resort Hotel, I, SP; La Pinta, I, SP; Ensenada Travel Lodge, II, SP; Estero Beach, II, tennis; restaurants: El Rey del Sol, Bronco Steakhouse, Mariscos Bahía Ensenada). This fishing port, now a popular tourist resort, lies on the beautiful bay of Todos los Santos, which was discovered in 1542 by the Portuguese navigator Rodríguez Cabrillo. After the separation of the northern and southern parts of the peninsula Ensenada was capital of the northern part from 1888 to 1910, when it was superseded by Mexicali.

Some 35 km (22 miles) SW of Ensenada, at Punta la Banda, a natural phenomenon which is common on the Pacific coast can be observed. The force of the waves drives water through a narrow opening in the rocks with enormous force and tosses it up to a height of 20 m (65 ft), creating a thunderous noise. The place is known as *La Bufadora* (from *bufar*, to snort).

Returning to the main road, we continue to San Quintín, a distance of some 185 km (115 miles),

passing on the way a number of old mission stations including *Santo Tomás* (El Palomar Motel), *San Vicente* and Vicente Guerrero (Meling Ranch) and the Colchimí Indian settlements of *La Huerta* and *San Miguel*.

The farming and fishing town of **San Quintín** (hotel: La Pinta, I, SP, tennis), situated in a fertile valley on the flat bay of the same name, has beautiful beaches of white sand. – Continuing S, the road leaves the coast at *El Rosario* (Espinosas Motel) and runs through the interior of the peninsula. In addition to El Rosario there are several other mission stations along this part of the road, including *San Fernando, San Agustín, Cataviña* (hotel: La Pinta, I, SP, tennis) and *Santa María*. – The road continues past the *Laguna Chapala* and comes in another 50 km (30 miles) to a side road on the left which leads to the beautiful *Bahía de los Angeles* (Hotel Cabañas Díaz; fishing), 70 km (45 miles) away.

Returning to Road 1, we continue via *Rosarito* and come in another 80 km (50 miles) to **Guerrero Negro** (landing strip for light aircraft; Hotel La Pinta, I), in Baja California Sur. Near the town are large deposits of salt. Of interest to visitors are the lagoons on the *Bahía Sebastián Vizcaíno* (Scammon, Ojo de Liebre) and the easily accessible lagoon of *San Ignacio*, to the S of the Sierra Vizcaíno, in the calm waters of which the grey whales mate and produce their young between the end of December and March every year; (limited opportunities for tourists to visit the breeding grounds by boat).

The **grey whales**, which weigh up to 25 tons, begin their long journey in the Arctic seas in autumn. Since grey whales have a gestation period of 13 months, the young are born to some pairs at the same time as others are mating. The mating process brings together two males and one female; the dominant male mates with the female, while the other male helps her to find a suitable place.

From Guerrero Negro the road runs inland and in 100 km (60 miles) reaches the attractive little town of **San Ignacio** (hotel: La Pinta, I, SP.), which has a Jesuit *church built in 1728, the best preserved church in Baja California. From here an excursion (guide required) can be made to some interesting *cave paintings* (human figures, animals, etc.), the age and origin of which have not been established. – From here the road continues E to the coast passing on the left a still active volcano, *Las Tres Virgenes* (2180 m – 7153 ft).

74 km (46 miles) from San Ignacio is the little port of **Santa Rosalía** (pop. 10,000; hotels: Frances, El Centro, El Morro), founded in the mid 19th c. The church of Santa Rosalía was built by the French settlers who formerly owned the local copper-mines, using iron parts imported for the purpose; it is said to have been designed by Gustave Eiffel, who also designed the Eiffel Tower in Paris, France. The town has several beautiful beaches. An antique ore-transport train can be seen. This unusual place has several beaches and a ferry service to Guaymas in Sonora state.

In about another 40 km (25 miles) the road forks (turning on R to Hacienda Baltasar), and in about 22 km (14 miles) reaches the great *caves of San Borjitas* (by cross-country vehicle; the last stretch on foot). Here can be seen *interesting colored rock paintings of hunting and warlike scenes, partly life size. – In the surrounding area there are other caves (La Trinidad, San José de los Arce, El Coyote, La Esperanza) with similar though less impressive paintings.

The next place of any size is the charmingly situated little town of *Mulegé* on the Gulf of California (pop. 5000; hotels: Terrazas, Old Hacienda Mulegé, outside the town: Serenidad), with the Jesuit mission of Santa Rosalía de Mulegé (1705) and a reproduction of the old prison of Cananea, Son. (without bars or locked doors) which is frequently celebrated in folksongs and street ballads. The town has several beaches and good fishing.

The next 40 km (25 miles) S of Mulegé along the *Bahia Concepion* offers particularly charming scenery and attractive beaches, for example *Santispac, El Coyote, El Requeson, Los Muertos*; (accommodations: Recreo Playa Cocos, Posada Concepión).

135 km (84 miles) farther on is the picturesque little town of **Loreto** (pop. 5400; hotels: La Pinta, I, SP; Misión de Loreto, I, SP; Playa Loreto, I, SP; 11 km (7 miles) S, El Presidente, I, SP; fiesta of Our Lady of Loreto on September 8), where the Jesuits settled in 1697. The beautifully restored mission church is the oldest Jesuit foundation on the peninsula. There is an interesting little mission museum. Loreto was for a time the capital of Baja California. It is now a popular base for trips to the offshore islands and for deep-sea fishing, diving and shooting. – An excursion can be made from Loreto to *San Javier*, which has a well-preserved mission church dedicated to St Francis Xavier (first half of 18th c.); the church has a beautiful Baroque façade and a gilded high altar.

In another 40 km (25 miles) the road turns inland again and in 120 km (75 miles) comes to the settlement of *Villa Insurgentes*. From here a side road leads to *Puerto A. López Mateos* on the broad *Bahía de Magdalena* on the Pacific coast. Like the Bahía Sebastian Vizcaíno this is a **breeding place of a school of grey whales which come here every winter

to mate and produce their young. Another convenient place for boat trips to observe the whales is the fishing village of *Puerta San Carlos* to the S (accommodation: Las Brisas). This place is most conveniently reached from Ciudad Constitución, about 55 km (34 miles) to the W. The *Isla de Santa Margarita*, in the bay, is the haunt of large numbers of sealions. Returning on the Carretera Transpeninsular, it is about another 210 km (130 miles) to **La Paz** (p. 152).

From La Paz Road 1 continues via *San Pedro* (woodcarving), the old mining town of *El Triunfo* and the fishing village and resort of **Los Barriles** (landing strip; hotels: Palmas do Cortés, fishing, water skiing; Playa Hermosa, fishing, water skiing; 15 km – 9 miles N Punta Pescadora, landing strip, SP, fishing, scuba diving, sailing) to **Buenavista** 110 km (62 miles) distant (landing strip; hotels: Club Spa Buenavista, SP, fishing, tennis, water skiing, thermal bath; Rancho Buenavista, SP, fishing, tennis, hunting, water skiing).

30 km (18 miles) farther on is *Miraflores*, an old Pericúe Indian settlement noted for its beautiful leatherwork. From here it is about 44 km (28 miles) to **San José del Cabo** (pop. 16,000; hotels: Calinda Costa Aquamarina, I, SP, tennis, fishing; El Presidente Los Cabos, I, SP, tennis; Las Cruces Palmilla, I, landing strip, SP, tennis, fishing, riding; Castel Cabo San José, I, SP; Nuevo Sol, II, SP; some hotels closed in summer; fiesta on March 19, Día de San José), an old mission station and fishing village which is now an important market town for this agricultural region. It has several beaches (some of them exposed to heavy seas) and offers good fishing. The House of Culture contains a small museum and library.

About 35 km (21 miles) beyond this is **Cabo San Lucas** (p. 84), at the end of the Carretera Transpeninsular.

Barranca del Cobre

State: Chihuahua (Chih.).

(i) **Coordinación Federal de Turismo,**
Edif. de la Unidad Admva. Municipal
"Lic. Benito Juárez" Av. Malecón y F. Villa,
Ciudad Juárez, Chih.
tel. (9 11 61) 4 66 92, 4 01 23, 4 08 37, 4 06 07.

ACCESS. – *By road* from Chihuahua via Cuauhtemoc (102 km – 63 miles) to La Junta (152 km – 94 miles); the road from there to Creel (262 km – 163 miles) is in places not good; the stretch Cuauhtemoc–Carichic–Creel is in course of improvement. – *By rail* (cars carried; advance reservation advisable) from Chihuahua via Creel (297 km – 185 miles), Divisadero (354 km – 185 miles), Cuiteco and Bahuichivo to Los Mochis (653 km – 406 miles). The same journey can be made in the opposite direction (Los Mochis–Chihuahua. – *Light aircraft*).

The name of **Barranca del Cobre ("Copper Canyon") is given to a series of twelve or more large gorges in the Sierra Madre Occidental. This wild and rugged range of mountains, also known as the

Barranca del Cobre
at Divisadero Barrancas

Sierra Tarahumara after the name of the local Indians, can be traversed in a breathtaking rail journey of 12 or 13 hours (86 tunnels, 39 bridges).

HISTORY. – In pre-Columbian times this region was inhabited by semi-nomadic Indians, the ancestors of the present-day Tarahumara. The remains of cave dwellings and huge vessels for the storage of provisions which have been found here have been dated to A.D. 1000. – At the beginning of the 17th c. Jesuit missionaries in quest of copper discovered the area and gave it its present name. The region, difficult of access, was occupied by the *Tarahumara* Indians when they were driven off the plateau by the large landowners. The Spaniards found silver, gold, opals and other minerals in the gorges. – The idea of building a railroad linking the United States (Texas) and northern Mexico with the Pacific was first considered in 1903, but the plan was not carried out until 1953–61, when the present boldly engineered line was built.

Tarahumara Indians

SIGHTS. – The railroad from Chihuahua to the Pacific passes through an extraordinary variety of scenery – from plateaus covered with cactuses, through hills and mountains clad with coniferous forest, past bizarre rock formations and gorges, mountainsides with a luxuriant growth of vegetation and subtropical plantations to groves of palms and bamboos. The most scenically interesting part of the journey is the stretch from Los Mochis to Creel. The mighty canyons are up to 1200 m (4000 ft) deep and 1500 m (4920 ft) across and vie in grandeur with the famous Grand Canyon in Arizona. While the summits are frequently bare, or in places covered with coniferous forest, and in winter with snow, the floors of the canyons are luxuriant with tropical vegetation (citrus fruits, bananas). The finest gorges are those of Urique, Cobre, La Bufa, Batopilas, Oteros, Sinforosa and Río San Miguel.

Places of interest in this region, or bases for excursions (by car, on muleback or on foot) in the Tarahumara gorges, are the following:

Creel (alt. 2300 m (7546 ft); pop. 5000; hotels: Nuevo, Korachi, Cabaña Cañon del Cobre; outside the town; mission church; Lake Arareco, 8 km (5 miles) S). – *Cuzasare* (18th c. mission church; small Indian Museum; waterfall and cave drawings in vicinity). – *Basihuare, Urique, La Bufa* and *Batopilas*. – Other Tarahumara villages in this area are *Aboreáchic, Rocheáchic, Norogáchic* and *Guachóchic*.

Divisadero (alt. 2300 m (7546 ft); 15-minute photo stop on railway; Hotel Cabañas Divisadera Barrancas). From here there is a particularly fine *view of the grandiose panorama of the Barranca del Cobre.

Other railway stations where accommodation is available are Cuiteco (H.C.C. Cuiteco Hotel) and Bahuichivo (Hotel Misión).

The area of settlement of the **Tarahumara Indians**, some 50,000 in number, covers 60,000 sq. km (23,000 sq. miles), mostly in the state of Chihuahua. The Tarahumara, who call themselves the Rarámuri ("runners"), belong to the large Uto-Aztec language family and are most nearly related to the Pima (see under Hermosillo). Little is known about their past history, but it is established that before the Conquest they occupied large territories in Chihuahua. After bitter fighting with the whites and mestizos which continued into the 20th c. they were driven back into these inaccessible regions in the Sierra Madre Occidental, where they were able to preserve a measure of independence. The first European in modern times to study the Barrancas and their inhabitants was a Norwegian, Carl Lumholtz, about 1900.

In addition to the places already mentioned the Tarahumara live in the villages of *Bocoyna, Carichic, Guazápares* and *Guanacevi*. During the winter many of them occupy cave dwellings on the floor of the gorges. The Tarahumara, now to some extent farmers and stock-herders as well as hunters, are – formally, at any rate – largely converted to Christianity, though the old Indian religion is still predominant.

Their principal divinities are the Sun and the Moon. As with the Huicholes (see under Nayarit) the peyotl cactus is a sacred plant, the intoxicating properties of which are supposed to be reserved to the elders and medicine-men of the tribe. They believe that the souls of the dead return and have the power to turn men into beasts; accordingly when a member of the tribe dies a secret ceremony has to be performed to appease the soul of the dead man. Among the Christian festivals celebrated by the Tarahumara are Holy Week, Corpus Christi, All Souls and Christmas. Their best known dances are the "Moors and Christians" dance, the Matachines and the peyotl dance. Special events in the Tarahumara year are races, usually lasting several days and covering extraordinary distances and often involving the driving of a wooden ball.

Each village is governed by an elected council of three. The men wear their hair long, with a white or red head-band, and their clothing consists of a simple cloak or cape and a kind of loincloth. The women wear a sack-like tunic and a full woolen skirt with a belt. The handicrafts of the Tarahumara include incense burners, basketwork, wooden masks representing human beings or animals, hand-woven belts and woolen blankets.

The Barranca del Cobre (Chihuahua)

Bonampak

State: Chiapas (Chis.).
Altitude: 350 m (1150 ft).

ACCESS. – From Villahermosa, Tenosique, Palenque, San Cristóbal de las Casas by *air-taxi*. – There is a *road* (130 km – 81 miles) from Palenque to Bonampak, but this is frequently quite impassable and even at its best is suitable only for cross-country vehicles (jeeps, etc.).

The relatively small Maya site of Bonampak lies on a hill near the Río Lacan-há in the dense rain forest of eastern Chiapas. Although architecturally the site is of minor importance, it caused a world sensation when it was discovered some 35 years ago, because of the magnificent **wall paintings in one of the buildings which have yielded a wealth of information about the life and mythology of the Mayas.

Relief on Stela 1

HISTORY. – Bonampak ("painted walls" in Maya), so named by the Maya scholar Sylvanus G. Morley, dates from the *Classic period* (A.D. 300–900), which reached its peak here between 650 and 850. Although only part of the site has so far been excavated, it seems clear that this temple town was of lesser religious and political importance than the great centers in this region such as Palenque and Yaxchilán in Chiapas and Piedras Negras in Guatemala. Since the emblem glyph (sculptured symbol) of Yaxchilán was found associated with one of the most prominently represented female figures in the Bonampak frescoes, it is believed that these temples were dependent on the great cult center of Yaxchilán. No doubt we shall never know why these magnificent frescoes – artistically the finest as well as the largest in area in Meso-America – were painted in a quite simple building in a relatively unimportant settlement like Bonampak. – The site was discovered in February 1946 by two Americans, Charles H. Frey and John Bourne; the temple with the wall paintings was found and photographed three months later by Giles C. Healey. The frescoes, which were excellently preserved – the humidity of the climate having laid a protective coating of lime over the colors – were copied by Antonio Tejeda with the sponsorship of the Carnegie Institution. During the years after the discovery Bonampak and the surround-

ing area were the target of several scientific expeditions, as well as of adventurers attracted by the sensational find.

THE SITE. – The principal buildings stand on a hill which has been artificially terraced. In front is a rectangular plaza measuring 90 by 110 m (295 by 360 ft), in the middle of which is **Stela 1** (found broken but now re-erected), which stands 6 m (20 ft) high and bears the figure of a richly attired priest-ruler; the date on the stela was deciphered as A.D. 785. The other two important stelae are on the flight of steps leading to the plaza. **Stela 2** (to the left) has a very delicately carved relief of a ruler attended by two figures of lesser importance. Particularly notable features are the rich garments and the tall headdress. On the upper part of the stela are glyphs. The steps lead to the next level, on which, to the left, is *Building III*. The stucco head lying on the floor of the building was formerly on the façade of one of the temples.

On the right is *Building I* (Edificio I), the **Temple of the Frescoes** (*Templo de las Pinturas*), now protected by a corrugated iron roof. It has three doors, all with lintels similar to those in Building 44 at Yaxchilán. Above the central doorway are three niches which once held seated stucco figures. The upper part of the building was originally decorated with stucco reliefs, of which little now survives. The three rooms are all of the same size,

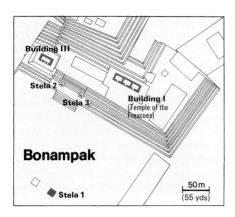

Bonampak

and their walls are covered with the world-famous **wall paintings. They are in classical fresco technique: i.e., the colors, mixed with water, were painted on to a thick coat of fresh plaster. When first found they were in brilliant colors; they depict with consummate draftsmanship scenes from Maya life in the Classic period.

THE PAINTINGS. – *Room 1*. To the left are **dignitaries engaged in some ceremony, wearing white robes and decked with shells (symbols of the earth and the underworld). On a rather higher platform sits the *Halachuinic* ("real man" – the ruler of the city state), flanked by two women, while to one side stands a servant holding the ruler's child in his arms. Three chieftains of lower rank are surrounded by servants. In the middle of the lower part the three chieftains appear again, now wearing great headdresses of quetzal plumes. – To the left is a troupe of musicians playing drums, trumpets, whistles, rattles and turtle-shells together with two figures bearing parasols. Also among the musicians are six grotesquely masked figures representing the crocodile, crab, earth, fertility and maize gods and one other god who has not been identified. To the right are spectators, also with parasols.

Room 2 contains **scenes of fighting** between richly arrayed warriors armed with lances and naked unarmed men – probably a surprise attack by the warriors of Bonampak with the object of capturing prisoners for sacrifice, as was the normal military practice of the period. Another scene shows a parade of prisoners. The Halachuinic stands on a platform clad in a jaguar-skin jacket and leggings and decked with jade and quetzal plumes, surrounded by subordinate chieftains and dignitaries. In front of him and below him are the almost naked prisoners; some of them have blood dripping from their fingers, and close by can be seen a severed head resting on green leaves.

Room 3 depicts **preparations for a festival**. Here again we see the chief, who is now offering a blood sacrifice, attended by three women. He is piercing his tongue with a sharp thorn, while a servant holds other thorns ready. Between the two figures is a vessel for catching the blood. Also apparently associated with this scene are ten dignitaries engaged in lively conversation, some of them wearing white cloaks, and nine other figures sitting below them. – In another scene, higher up, twelve men are carrying on a bier a small figure with grotesque features, probably the earth god. – Most of the wall space in this room is occupied by the final scene depicting a **human sacrifice** accompanied by dancers. On the two topmost tiers of a pyramid are the three principal dancers, with seven others on a lower level. They are richly attired, with huge headdresses of quetzal plumes. The hands and feet of a naked man who has evidently just been sacrificed are being united by two attendants. To the left of this central scene are four figures wearing headdresses, who have probably been taking part in the blood-taking ceremony, and to the right are eight other figures, some with musical instruments and others with parasols.

The original frescoes, painted about A.D. 800, are still in situ but in very poor condition, and it remains to be seen whether they can be successfully restored. The best plan, therefore, is to see one of the excellent reproductions in the National Museum of Anthropology in Mexico City or the Museo del Estado de Tabasco in Villahermosa.

SURROÙNDINGS. – From Bonampak an excursion can be made to the nearby hamlet of **Lacan-há** (airstrip) on the Río Lacan-há, home of the last few families of *Lacandón Mayas* ("Ah Acantun"=in Yucateca-Maya "those who set up the stones") who were believed until recently to be the last descendants of the Mayas who had remained untouched by civilization. They lived a nomadic life in the area of rain forest named after them (Selva Lacandona) or carried on a primitive form of agriculture at their temporary settlements. The Lacandones call themselves Caribs, and their settlements are given the general name of "Caribal". They now number barely more than 300, living chiefly in Lacan-há (in Maya="at the river of snakes"), Na-há ("mighty water"), which can be reached by air taxi or by cross-country vehicle from Palenque in about 100 km (62 miles) and Mensabak ("powder maker"). They grow their hair long and wear long white garments. Until very recently they still hunted with bow and arrow and performed their ancient rites in the ruins of the temples built by their ancestors; but, having become the quarry of missionaries, ethnologists and tourists, they have largely lost their former sturdy independence. The tribe, now dying out, was once numbered in thousands, and never came into contact with the Spaniards. About their origins there can only be speculation. It is supposed that they are descended from a Maya tribe which moved into the region from southern Yucatán early in the 18th c.

Wall painting

Cabo San Lucas

State: Baja California Sur (B.C.S.).
Altitude: sea level. – Population: 7,500.
Telephone dialing code: 9 16 84.

(i) **Coordinación Federal de Turismo,**
Paseo Álvaro Abregon 2130,
La Paz, B.C.S.
tel. (9 16 82) 2 11 90, 2 11 99, 2 79 75.

ACCESS. – *By road:* Carretera Transpeninsular from Tijuana via Ensenada, Mulegé, Loreto, La Paz and San José del Cabo. – *Ferry* from Puerto Vallarta in Jalisco state (sometimes suspended). – *By air:* domestic and international services to San José del Cabo.

HOTELS. – *Calinda Cabo Baja*, Cabo Bello y Cabo San Lucas, L, SP, tennis, fishing, sailing; *Cabo San Lucas*, Bahía Chileno, L, SP, tennis, fishing, hunting; *Twin Dolphin*, Bahía de Santa Marta, L, SP, tennis, fishing, riding; *Finisterra*, Bahía Cabo San Lucas, I, SP, fishing; *Hacienda*, Bahía Cabo San Lucas, I, SP, tennis, riding, water skiing, scuba diving, fishing; *Solmar*, southern point of Bahía San Lucas, I, SP, fishing; *Mar de Cortés*, L, Cárdenas y U. Guerrero, II, SP. (some hotels closed in summer).

RESTAURANTS in most hotels; also *Balandra*, Morelos y 16 de Septiembre; *El Corral*, Hidalgo y Malecón de Marino; *Playa Brujita*, El Medano; *Taquería San Lucas*, Hidalgo.

RECREATION and SPORTS. – Swimming, snorkeling, diving, water skiing, deep-sea fishing, boat trips, tennis, golf, shooting, riding.

EVENTS. – Fiesta March 19, Día de San José.

The modern *vacation center of Cabo San Lucas lies at the southern tip of the Baja California peninsula, an area without vegetation. With its spectacular rock formations, varied range of beaches, excellent deep-sea fishing and first-rate hotels and other vacation facilities, this is one of the finest beach resorts in Mexico.

Cabo San Lucas, situated in magnificent seclusion at the end of the 1700 km (1050 mile) long *Carretera Transpeninsular (see under Baja California), consists of a small harbor, a few houses, hotels, restaurants and shops, and offers facilities for all kinds of water sports. – A boat trip can be made to *El Arco, a natural arch hewn from the cliffs by the sea at the point where the Gulf of California meets the Pacific. The beaches and bays on either side of the cape (El Médano, Amor, Sol, Santa María, Colorado, etc.) vary in character, some being sandy and others rocky, some with calm water and others with heavy surf; but everywhere there is an abundance of fish. There is endless scope for divers and snorkelers, among

particular features of interest being a curious underwater *cascade of sand and an area on the sea-bottom which is covered with lumps of manganese.

SURROUNDINGS. – Road No. 9 to Todos Santos (45 km) passes attractive beaches and interesting coastal scenery. From *Todos Santos* (Jesuit mission church of 1734; small museum), it continues via *San Pedro* to **La Paz** (82 km – 51 miles); see p. 152.

35 km (21 miles) NE of Cabo San Lucas is the little port of *San José del Cabo* (see under Baja California).

Cacahuamilpa Caves
See under Taxco

Campeche (State)

State of Campeche (Camp.). – Capital: Campeche.
Area: 50,952 sq. km (19,673 sq. miles).
Population: 436,700.

(i) **Coordinación Federal de Turismo,**
Av. Republica 159,
Frente a la Alemeda,
Campeche, Camp.;
tel. (9 19 81) 6 31 97 and 6 55 93.

The state of Campeche occupies the south-western part of the Yucatán peninsula, and is bounded on the N and E by Yucatán state, on the NW by the Gulf of Mexico, on the SW to Tabasco state, on the S by Guatemala and on the SE by the state of Quintana Roo. It lies on the low Yucatán plateau, with hills rising out of the plateau to the N. The northern half is relatively arid, depending for its water supply on underground lakes and rivers. The southern and eastern parts of the state have heavy rainfall and are covered with luxuriant rain forest. The rivers in the S flow into the Laguna de Términos. Along the coast of the Gulf of Mexico there are many beautiful beaches, with some areas of swamp. The state is primarily inhabited by Maya Indians and mestizos.

Among the principal Maya sites in Campeche are *Edzná* (p. 124), *Hochob*, *Dzibilnocac, Nocuchich, Xcalunkin, Calakmul, Hormiguero, Becán, Chicaná, Xpuhil* (see under Chetumal) and *Río*

Mexico
United Mexican States
Estados Unidos Mexicanos

Campeche

States
Estados

1a Baja California Sur	12 Aguascalientes
1b Baja California Norte	13 Jalisco
	14 Guanajuato
2 Sonora	15 Querétaro
3 Chihuahua	16 Hidalgo
4 Sinaloa	17 Colima
5 Durango	18 Michoacán
6 Coahuila	19 México
7 Nuevo León	20 Morelos
8 Zacatecas	21 Tlaxcala
9 San Luis Potosí	22 Puebla
10 Tamaulipas	23 Veracruz
11 Nayarit	24 Guerrero
	25 Oaxaca

26	Chiapas
27	Tabasco
28	Campeche
29	Yucatán
30	Quintana Roo

D.F. Distrito Federal (Federal District)

Bec. – One site of particular interest is **Jaina**, a small limestone island off the N coast of Campeche which in Maya times was used as a place of burial. It can be visited with special permission. Since only a few buildings, poor and meagre in comparison with the great numbers of rich tombs, were found on the island it is supposed that Jaina was used solely as the burial-place of the Maya nobles of the Puuc area. The delicately modelled painted clay figurines found here – all are hollow and fitted with whistles on their backs – rank among the finest pottery produced in pre-Columbian times.

The scrub and the rain forests of Campeche are still inhabited by varied *animal life*. Among the species found here are jaguars, ocelots, tapirs, wild pigs, armadillos and roe-deer; the birds include pheasants, wild ducks, wild turkeys, many species of parrot, heron and flamingoe; the reptiles include alligators, turtles, iguanas and boa constrictors. The coastal waters are among the most abundantly stocked with fish in the whole of Mexico (tuna, barracuda, shark, mackerel, swordfish, dolphin, snapper; crustaceans, including prawns and shrimps; many species of shellfish).

HISTORY. – Like other parts of the Yucatán peninsula, Campeche had many Maya centers of the *Classic period* (A.D. 300–900), and the archeological evidence indicates that some of these sites were already occupied in the Pre-Classical period (300 B.C.

to A.D. 300). Little is known about Indian history between A.D. 1000 and 1500, but many settlements on the Gulf coast were undoubtedly centers of trade between central and southern Mexico and the N and E of the Yucatán peninsula. – The first European, Francisco Hernández de Córdoba, landed on the coast near present-day Champotón in 1517. After a brief but hard-fought encounter the Spaniards were driven off by the local Indians, and Córdoba himself later died of his wounds. Although Juan de Grijalva established a temporary foothold in 1518, followed by Cortés himself in 1519, it was another twenty years before Francisco de Montejo was able to conquer at least part of the territory of Campeche. During the colonial period and the first thirty years of the Republic, Campeche was part of the state of Yucatán. It became an independent state in 1863.

ECONOMY. – Until about thirty years ago, as a result of its poor communications with the rest of the country, Campeche played only a small part in the economy of Mexico. Its only resources of any significance were its *precious woods*, as well as the logwood or campeche wood, which was formerly used in the manufacture of a dye, and the sapodilla tree (*Achras sapota*), which yields chicle, the raw material used in making chewing gum. In recent years the considerable development of the *fisheries* and the discovery of *oil* off the coasts of Campeche have given a tremendous boost to its economy. The government has begun to promote the development of farming and livestock-rearing. In addition to this, Campeche's interesting archeological sites, beautiful beaches and ample scope for fishing and hunting are likely to lead to a considerable growth of *tourism* in the near future.

Campeche (Town)

State: Campeche (Camp.).
Altitude: 16 m (52 ft). – Population: 147,000.
Telephone dialing code: 9 19 81.

(i) **Coordinación Federal de Turismo,**
Av. Republica 159,
Frente a la Alameda;
tel. 6 31 97 and 6 55 93.

HOTELS. – ON THE COAST ROAD: *El Presidente*, Av.
Ruiz Cortines 51, I, SP; *Baluartes*, Av. Ruiz Cortines,
I, SP; *López*, Calle 12 No. 189, II; *Señorial*, Calle 10
No. 132, II; *México*, Calle 10 No. 329, III. – 40 km
(25 miles) SW on the road to Champotón (No. 180):
Misión Si-ho-Playa, I, SP.

RESTAURANTS in most hotels; also *Miramar*, corner
of 16 Septiembre and Calle 59; *La Perla*, Calle 57,
between Calles 10 and 12; *Kalua*, Calle 12 No. 150.

RECREATION and SPORTS. – Swimming, water
skiing, sailing, fishing, shooting.

EVENTS. – August 7, Campeche National Holiday;
September 14–30, Fiesta de San Román; October
4–13, Fiesta de San Francisco.

Fort in the town of Campeche

**Campeche, capital of the state of the
same name, lies in the Gulf of
Mexico, on the W coast of the
Yucatán peninsula. The town is an
attractive mixture of older buildings
from its romantic past and modern
districts. The oil boom of recent
years, however, has had a somewhat
unfortunate effect on the townscape.**

HISTORY. – The first European to land here was the
Spanish conquistador Hernández de Córdoba in
1517. The town was founded on October 4, 1540 by
Francisco de Montejo the Younger ("El Mozo") and
named Campeche after the Maya settlement of *Ah-
kin-pech* ("place of the snake and the tick"). During
the 16th c. it developed into the principal port on the
Yucatán peninsula. In the 16th and 17th c. it was
repeatedly raided by pirates, the worst attacks being
those of William Park in 1597, Diego el Mulato in
1631, Laurent van Graff ("Lorencillo") in 1672 and
1685 and L'Olonois ("El Olonés"); and during this
period the town was partly destroyed and the
population decimated on many occasions. Visitors
can still see many of the underground passages in
which women and children sought refuge during
these raids. Finally, between 1686 and 1704, the town
was surrounded by a wall 2.5 km (1¾ miles) long,
2.5 m (8 ft) thick and up to 8 m (25 ft) high, defended
by eight forts, and thereafter it was secure against
pirates. In 1777 Campeche was granted a municipal
charter by King Charles III of Spain. A hurricane
destroyed many buildings in the town in 1807. In
1867 Campeche became capital of the state of the
same name.

SIGHTS. – In the *Plaza Principal* (Plaza
de Independencia) are some fine old
colonial houses and the **Cathedral of
La Concepción**, begun in 1540 but

not completed until 1705, with a plain
Baroque façade.

Near the square is one of the bastions on
the town walls (still largely preserved),
the **Baluarte de la Soledad**, which now
houses the *Museo de Historia*, containing
pictures and drawings illustrating the
history of the town and a collection of
arms and armor. – Turning right into
Calle 8, we pass one of the town gates,
the *Puerta de Mar*, and the modern
Palacio de Gobierno or Edificio de
Poderes and come to the *Cámara de
Diputados*, the state parliament. Between
the two government buildings and the
coast road is a man-made *lake* surrounded
by modern buildings, including the
Theater. – Calle 8 now comes to the
Fuerte San Carlos, one of the oldest and
best preserved of the town's forts, which
contains a *Museum of Applied Art*. Near
the Puerta de Tierra, in the Casa del
Teniente del Rey, one finds the new
Regional Museum (Museo Regional)
showing history and archeology of Campeche including interesting tomb contents from Calakmul, e.g. a precious
mosaic mask.

On Calles 59 and 16 is the interesting
church of San Francisco, with five
carved wooden altars. To the N, on the
Malecón (Quay) Miguel Alemán, is the
Convent of San Francisco, on the spot
where the first Christian mass on Mexican
soil is said to have been celebrated

in 1517. Hernán Cortés's grandson Jerónimo (b. 1562) was baptized here; the font is still in use. – The **market** (*mercado*) is well worth a visit, particularly during the fiesta. Souvenirs which may tempt visitors include *jipis* (a kind of panama hat) and articles made from turtle-shell, seashells and hardwoods.

On the southern outskirts of the town a road branches off the coast road and runs up to the *Fuerte de San Miguel*, finely situated above the town. The fort, which is entered over a drawbridge, still retains its cannon. It houses a small but very interesting *Archeological Museum (Museo de Arqueología)* containing much Maya material. Particularly notable are the terracotta figurines from Jaina and the excellently arranged tables showing all the pre-Columbian cultures.

Campeche to Villahermosa by the coast road. – Road 180 runs S via the little ports and fishing towns of *Lerma* (8 km – 5 miles) and *Seybaplaya* (33 km – 20 miles) and comes to **Champotón** (pop. 40,000); Snook Inn, SP; D'Venetia.

In pre-Hispanic times this port town was the center of a large area of Indian settlement which played an important part in the cultural exchanges between Guatemala, Yucatán and central Mexico. Probably the culture of the Toltecs mingled here with the cultures of their subject Maya tribes, who from the 10th c. onward moved E and joined the Maya peoples settled there. According to the old chronicles – not always to be uncritically believed – the *Itzá* and *Xiú* tribes established temporary settlements in this region at various times. – Champotón is now primarily a fishing port and a good base for deep-sea fishing and hunting expeditions in the interior.

105 km (65 miles) from Champotón is *Isla Aguada* (Hotel Tarpón Tropical; La Cabaña Motel and Trailer Park), from which there is a ferry to the **Isla del Carmen.** The N coast of this island looks out on *Campeche Bay* (Bahía de Campeche), while its S coast bounds the *Laguna de Términos*, a large fresh-water lagoon fed by several rivers. The island, resembling a huge sandbank, was formerly known as the *Isla de Tris* and from 1558 to 1717 was a favourite pirates' haunt, providing them with a convenient base for raids on the Spanish ports in the Gulf of Mexico. At the SW end of the island, which is 40 km (25 miles) long, is **Ciudad del Carmen** (pop. 95,000; hotels: Lossandes, Lli-re, Isla del Carmen, Lino's; restaurants: Flamingos, Carmelo, Pepe's; fiesta July 15–31).

The town was given its name (after the Virgin of Mount Carmel, its patroness) by Alfonso Felipe de Andrade, who expelled the pirates in 1717. It is now an important center for the prawn fisheries, and in recent years has become the principal port handling the oil produced in the Gulf of Mexico. The Cathedral of the Virgin del Carmen is notable for its fine stained glass. In the Liceo Carmelita is a small archeological museum chiefly containing Maya pottery.

From here there is another ferry to the little fishing port of *El Zacatal* on the mainland. A short distance beyond this the road passes the lighthouse of *Xicalango*, a township which in pre-Columbian times was an important center of trade between central Mexico and Yucatán. Cortés landed here on the way to Veracruz and carried off the Indian girl known as La Malinche, whose services as interpreter and adviser were of great assistance during the conquest of Mexico. – 30 km (19 miles) farther on there is a ferry over the *Río San Pedro y Pablo*, and 24 km (15 miles) beyond this another ferry over the *Río Grijalva* at *Frontera*. The road then turns inland and in 75 km (47 miles) reaches Villahermosa (p. 289).

Campeche to Mérida by the western route. – Leave on Road 180, which runs E past the airport, and in 30 km (19 miles) turn N into Road 261. This passes through *Tenabo* and *Pomuch* and comes in another 47 km (29 miles) to **Hecelchakán,** which has a Franciscan church of 1620 and the *Museo del Camino Real*. The museum contains a notable collection of clay figures from the island of Jaina and, in the patio, stelae and door lintels from excavations in the surrounding area. – Around Hecelchakán are a whole series of Maya sites, the most notable being *Kocha* and *Xcalumkín* (Holactún).

The road continues to two places of some size, *Calkiní* (23 km – 14 miles) and *Becal* (32 km – 20 miles). Becal is a center of production of *jipis*, the light tropical hats, which are kept in damp rooms under the patios to "mature" before being put on the market.

From Becal it is 30 km (19 miles) to *Maxcanú* (p. 285) and 95 km (59 miles) to *Merida* (p. 157).

Campeche to Mérida by the eastern route (via Hopelchén). – Leave on Road 180, which runs E to *Cayal* (45 km – 28 miles), from which a road runs S to the Maya site of **Edzná** (p. 124).

40 km (25 miles) E of Cayal is **Hopelchén** ("five fountains" in Maya), with a 16th c. fortified church.

From here visitors with an interest in archeology will want to take a trip S into the area of the *Chenes culture* (so called after the commonest ending of place-names, -*chen*, "fountain"). In this area are the sites of *Dzehkabtún*, *El Tabasqueño* and *Dzibalchén* (San Pedro). 13 km (8 miles) SW of Dzibalchén, a dirt road, usable only in the dry season, leads via Chenkoh to **Hochob,** an interesting Maya site in Chenes style. Among the buildings surrounding the central plaza is a well-preserved temple on the N side. This has three chambers, the central chamber still having the remains of its roof-comb. The doors are framed in large masks; the rest of the façade is covered with stylized snakes. There is a scale model of this temple in the National Museum of Anthropology in Mexico City.

From Dzibalchén there is a road (20 km – 12½ miles) to *Iturbide*, near which is the site of **Dzibilnocac,** one of the largest in Chenes territory. The principal temple has a façade similar to that of the Hochob temple.

From Hopelchén Road 180 continues N, coming in 33 km (20 miles) to *Bolonchén* ("nine fountains") *de Rejón*. From here there is a road to the nearby *Grutas Xtacumbil-xunan* (the "hidden woman" in Maya), a huge system of stalactitic caves and cenotes, the full extent of which cannot yet be estimated. There is a legend of a beautiful mestizo girl who, after an unhappy love affair, ended her life as a hermit in these gloomy caverns. The caves were first explored and recorded by John L. Stephens and Frederick Catherwood. They should be visited only with a knowledgeable guide.

Near Bolonchén are the ruined temples of *Kichmool* and *Itzimté*, the architecture of which shows a mingling of the Chenes and Puuc styles.

Some 150 km (95 miles) from Campeche (24 km (15 miles) N of Bolonchén) the road enters the state of Yucatán. From here there are two alternative routes to Mérida. One goes via *Kebah (8 km (5 miles): see p. 148), **Uxmal (31 km (19 miles): see p. 282) and *Muna* (46 km – 29 miles). The other route turns right off the main road in 3 km (2 miles) and continues via *Sayil (6 km (4 miles): p. 244), *Xlapak* (10 km (6 miles); p. 245), *Labná (14 km (9 miles): p. 150), *Loltún (32 km (20 miles): p. 151), *Oxkutzcab (41 km – 25 miles), *Tikul (58 km – 36 miles) and *Muna* (79 km – 49 miles) to *Mérida (138 km (86 miles): p. 157).

Cancún

State: Quintana Roo (Q.R.).
Altitude: sea level. – Population: 90,000.
Telephone dialing code: 9 19 88.
ⓘ **Coordinación Federal de Turismo,**
  Av. Tulum 81,
  Edificio Fira;
  tel. 4 32 38.

HOTELS. – IN THE RESORT AREA: *Camino Real*, L, SP, tennis; *El Presidente*, L, SP, tennis, golf; *Exelaris Hyatt Cancún*, L, SP, tennis, golf; *Aristos*, L, SP, tennis; *Cancún Sheraton*, L, SP, tennis; *Calinda Cancún*, L, SP; *Cancún Viva*, L, SP, tennis; *Krystal Cancún*, L, SP, tennis; *Club Mediterranée* (Punta Nizuc), L. – YOUTH HOSTEL: *CREA Albergue Cancún* (Bahia de Mujeres Beach). – IN THE TOWN: *Plaza Caribe*, Av. Uxmal/Tulum, I, SP; *María de Lourdes*, Av. Xachilán 1357, I, SP; *Suites Flamboyanes*, Av. Carlos Nader, I, SP, tennis; *Ántillano*, Av. Tulum y Claveles 37, II, SP; *Soberanis*, Av. Cobá 5 & 7, II; *Rivemar*, Tulum, Manz 22 Lte. 49, III; *Tulum*, Tulum 41, III.
RESTAURANTS in most hotels; also IN THE RESORT

AREA: *Mauna Loa*, opposite the Convention Center; *ChacMool*, Chac-Mool Beach; Cancún 1900, near the Convention Center; *Maxime*, Pez Volador 8; *Augustus Pizza*, Convention Center. – IN THE TOWN: *El Potrero*, Av. Yazchilán 50; *La Habichuela*, Margaritas 27; *Los Pericos*, Av. Yaxchilán 71; *Brujos*, Claveles 9; *Hugo's*, Av. Cobá 89; *Chocko's y Tere*, Claveles 7; *Las Almendras*, Av. Bonampak Sur/Sayil.

RECREATION and SPORTS. – All kinds of water sports; fishing, golf, tennis, squash, hunting.

EVENTS. – Golf and tennis tournaments, windsurfing and fishing competitions.

The L-shaped island of Cancún, 21 km (12 miles) long by 400 m ($\frac{1}{4}$ mile) across, lying off the N coast of Yucatán, is now a well-planned modern beach resort with excellent hotels and other facilities for tourists. The large *resort area, which has grown up in recent years, lies amid superb beaches of white sand, palm-groves and banks of coral. It has an equable climate with relatively little rainfall. The resort area is linked by a causeway to the mainland, on which the modern town of Cancún has been built.

HISTORY. – Originally a *Maya settlement*, the site was first described by Stephens and Catherwood in 1843 and named *Can-cune* ("vessel at the end of the rainbow" in Maya). In 1970, when the new development was being planned, the only inhabitants were about 100 Mayas, who gained their subsistence by fishing and gathering chicle. The Mexican government, in association with private interests, selected the area as a suitable site for an international holiday

Part of the resort area on the island of Cancún

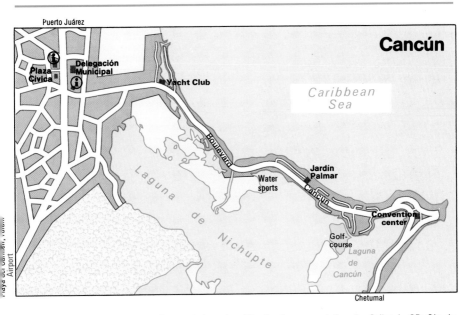

center, which was carefully planned as a whole and has been completed within the last few years. The resort which provides 5800 hotel rooms was visited in 1983 by 750,000 tourists and provided no less than 10% of the total foreign tourist income of Mexico.

SIGHTS. – The modern TOWN of Cancún (Ciudad de Cancún) has little of tourist interest to offer, but it is a successful experiment in the planning of an entirely new town, complete with all necessary services, shops, hotels, restaurants, etc. – The RESORT AREA, on the island of Cancún, has, in addition to its large modern hotels, vacation houses and privately owned dwellings, a *Convention Center* (Centro de Convenciones) with an auditorium seating 2000 which is also used for cultural events. In the town center can be found the museum (Museo de Antropología). Nearby are two shopping complexes.

Between Punta Cancún and Punta Nizuc are a number of interesting Maya remains, mostly in the Puuc style. They are usually known as **El Rey** (=Kinich Ahau-Boniz), but are occasionally referred to under other names – *Pinturas, San Miguel, Yamilum, Pok-ta-poc* or *El Conchero*. The remains include truncated pyramids topped by temples, some of which have rounded corners, and over fifty tombs which illustrate Maya forms of burial.

A regular service by hovercraft to the island of Cozumel (see p. 114) has recently been established from Cancún (near the Convention Center).

Cancún to Playa del Carmen by the coast road.
– Road 307 runs S past Cancún *airport* (17 km – 11 miles) and comes in 35 km (22 miles) to *Puerto*

Morelos (accommodation: La Ceiba, L, SP; Ojo de Agua, I SP; Posada Amor, III). From this little port there are passenger and car ferries to Cozumel.

25 km (16 miles) farther on is *Punta Beté*, from which two field tracks, running almost parallel, lead to three beautifully situated beaches (accommodations: Cabañas Capitán Lafitte, *KaiLuum, Cabañas El Marlin Azul).

From here it is another 8 km (5 miles) to the little port of **Playa del Carmen** (hotels: Balam-ha, Posada Lily, Molcas), from which there is a ferry to Cozumel. The town has a beautiful beach and a number of small fish restaurants.

From Playa del Carmen it is 36 km (22 miles) to *Akumal (p. 75), 46 km (29 miles) to *Xel-há (p. 291) and 65 km (40 miles) to *Tulum (p. 275).

Casas Grandes
See under Chihuahua (state)

Laguna de Catemaco

State: Veracruz (Ver.).
ⓘ **Coordinación Federal de Turismo,** Av. Ignacio Zaragoza 20 Altos Centro, **Veracruz,** Ver.;
Tel. (91 29) 32 70 26, 32 16 13.

HOTELS. – BY THE LAKE: *Motel Playa Azul,* I, SP; *La Finca,* I; *Motel Posada Koniapán,* I, ; *Del Lago,* I. – IN CATEMACO: *Catemaco,* I, SP; *Berthangel,* I; *Acuario,* II; *Ymalca,* II.

RECREATION and SPORTS. – Swimming, sailing, rowing, water skiing, fishing, boat trips and hunting.

Laguna de Catemaco

10 km (6 miles) SE of San Andrés Tuxtla on the Veracruz–Coatzacoalcos road (No. 180) and some 35 km (22 miles) from the Gulf of Mexico lies the **Laguna de Catemaco, surrounded by hills of volcanic origin. One of the most beautiful lakes in Mexico, it is 16 km (10 miles) long and has an area of 130 sq. km (50 sq. miles). In the lake are the islands of Ténapi and Agaltepec.

The Catemaco region is separated by the *Sierra de los Tuxtlas* from the hot and humid lowlands on the Gulf coast and accordingly has an agreeably equable climate. For this reason, and because of its European-type scenery, Alexander von Humboldt, visiting it at the beginning of the 19th c., called it the *Suiza Veracruzana*, the Switzerland of Veracruz. The highest peak in the surrounding area is the extinct volcano of *San Martín* (1850 m – 6070 ft). The abundance of water in the region, unusual for Mexico, is apparent in the vigorous flow of the *Río Cuetzalapa* and the waterfalls of *Tepetapan, Chilapa* and *Eyipantla* (8 km (5 miles) S of San Andrés Tuxtla: 41 m (135 ft) high). On the slopes of Mt San Martín, E of Acayucan, there are still a few villages of the Popolaca Indians, who belong to the Nahua language group (*Mecayapan, Soteapan*).

The principal place on the lake is the little town of **Catemaco** (alt. 370 m (1212 ft); pop. 40,000) on its NW shore. The church

of the Virgen del Carmen in the main plaza is a popular place of pilgrimage (fiesta July 16), as can be seen from the votive offerings hung in the doorway. – The town's main sources of income are fishing and tourism. The area is also popular with Mexican guests because of its healers (curanderos) and witches (brujas).

Catemaco to Veracruz. – 15 km (9 miles) W on Road 180 is **San Andrés Tuxtla** (alt. 370 m (1214 ft); pop. 50,000; hotels: San Andrés, Del Parque, Zamfer). This old colonial town, lying in a basin-shaped valley surrounded by volcanic hills, was known in pre-Hispanic times as *Zacoalcos* (Náhuatl, "enclosed place"). It has two interesting churches, San José and Santa Rosa. In 1902 a jade figure of a priest 20 cm (8 in.) high was found near the town; it is an Olmec work bearing the date A.D. 162, which is now in Washington, D.C. – San Andrés is a center of cigar manufacture, and there are large banana plantations around the town.

Near San Andrés, but so far not accessible to car traffic is the round crater lake known as the **Laguna Encantada** or Enchanted Lake. Paradoxically, the level of the lake, which has a circumference of 2.5 km (1¼ miles), falls during the rainy season and rises during the dry period. From time to time the water becomes so hot as a result of volcanic influences that the fish in the lake die; but as soon as the temperature falls the fish stock is renewed.

Continuing NW from San Andrés, Road 180 comes in another 10 km (6 miles) to **Santiago Tuxtla** (alt. 350 m (1180 ft), pop. 35,000; Hotel Castellanos; fiestas: June 24, San Juan; July 23–25, Santiago Apóstol), which lies astride the *Río Tuxtla* on the edge of the tropical forest. In the plaza is a colossal Olmec head. The small but very interesting Tuxteco-Museum contains other Olmec material, particularly stone sculpture, from the Olmec center of *Tres Zapotes*. This place, 24 km (15 miles) away, can be reached via Villa Isla. Here you will find a new small museum worthwhile visiting for the archeological fan. There is an Olmec colossal head, stone figures and stelae, including the recently discovered upper part of Stela C. At Tres Zapotes were found two huge basalt heads and Stela C, which bears the oldest date so far known in Olmec history (31 B.C.). Most of the material discovered is now in museums but recently a very interesting museum was opened in Tres Zapotes itself. It is reached by taking the road to Isla from Santiago Tuxtla in a SW direction for 9 km (5 miles) and then taking the road to the right at a crossing to Tres Zapotes, about 14 km (8 miles) distant.

70 km (43 miles) NW of Santiago Tuxtla, Road 180 reaches the Gulf coast at *Alvarado* (pop. 32,000; hotels: Lefty, María Isela), situated on a spit of land between the Gulf and the *Laguna de Alvarado*.

Augustinian convent, Yuriria

Visitors with an interest in archaeology will want to branch off the main road 40 km (25 miles) NW of Alvarado into Road 150 to visit the site of **Cerro de las Mesas** ("Hill of the Altars"), situated on the flood plain of the *Río Blanco* between the townships of *Piedras Negras* and *Ignacio de la Llave*. The extensive archaeological area is covered with hundreds of artificial mounds, only some of which have been excavated. Excavations were carried out here in the 1940s by the US Bureau of American Ethnology and the National Geographic Society under the direction of Matthew W. Sterling and brought to light small pyramids, temple platforms, altars, stone sculpture, stelae (the oldest dated to A.D. 206), pottery and 782 intricately carved jade objects. The finds are now in museums in Mexico and the United States, so that the site has little to attract the ordinary visitor.

From Alvarado it is 70 km (44 miles) to **Veracruz** (p. 286).

Catemaco to Villahermosa. – 80 km (50 miles) SE of Catemaco on Road 180 is the important road junction of *Acayucan* (alt. 160 m (525 ft); pop. 27,000; hotels: Plaza, Joalicia), where Road 185 branches off and runs S across the Isthmus of Tehuantepec to *Juchitán* (195 km – 121 miles), **Tehuantepec** (220 km (137 miles): see p. 255) and *Salina Cruz* (235 km – 146 miles).

40 km (25 miles) NE of Acayucan, off Road 180, is **Minatitlán** (alt. 65 m (213 ft); pop. 136,000; hotels: Trópico, Oasis, Suites Hotel Mina), which in recent years, thanks to the oil boom and the working of sulphur in the area, has developed into an industrial center. It has little to offer the tourist.

About 45 km (28 miles) SW of Minatitlán, on the *Río Chiquito*, is the site of **San Lorenzo Tenochtitlán** (access difficult), where a number of statues and nine Olmec heads were discovered. Some of the statues had been mutilated and buried. The site was dated by carbon-14 to between 1200 and 900 B.C. Finds from San Lorenzo can now be seen in museums in Mexico (particularly in Jalapa) and abroad.

25 km (16 miles) NE of Minatitlán lies the important port and industrial town of **Coatzacoalcos** (pop. 160,000; hotels: Club Terranova, Margón, Valgrande, Gireya), which is handling an increasing trade in agricultural produce and oil products.

About 40 km (25 miles) SE of Coatzacoalcos the road crosses the *Río Tonalá* to enter the state of Tabasco. 4.5 km (3 miles) farther on the highway there is a branchroad to the left leading to the village of La Venta, 6 km (4 miles) away. This is a swampy region, now in an oilfield, and on the outskirts of the town there is the historically important Olmec site of **La Venta**. The first excavations here were carried out in the 1920s by Frans Blom and Oliver La Farge of Tulane University, and their work was continued by M. W. Stirling fifteen years later. La Venta seems to have been the principal political and religious center of the Olmecs, and the Olmec period is often referred to as that of the *La Venta culture*. The influence of this, the earliest advanced culture of Meso-America, extended from the Gulf coast through central Mexico (Tlatilco and Tlapacoya) to the W coast (Guerrero) and reached S as far as El Salvador, influencing the early phases of the cultures of Monte Albán and the Mayas. Nothing is known of the Olmecs themselves: all that we have is the magnificent works of art which they left behind, above all in San Lorenzo Tenochtitlán (1200–900 B.C.) and here in La Venta which reached its zenith between 900 and 400 B.C., but was still in existence at the beginning of the Christian era. More than any other Olmec site it has yielded material of outstanding importance and interest. Near the remains of a once mighty temple pyramid built up of clay to a height of 30 m (100 ft) were found four of the familiar colossal heads, stone altars and stelae, and terracotta and jade figures. Practically all the material from La Venta is now to be seen in museums, particularly the **La Venta Open-Air Museum** at Villahermosa (p. 289).

From Coatzacoalcos to **Villahermosa** it is 175 km (110 miles).

Celaya

State: Guanajuato (Gto.).
Altitude: 1800 m (5905 ft). – Population: 120,000.
Telephone dialing code: 9 14 61.

ⓘ **Coordinación Federal de Turismo,**
    Galarza 90,
    Guanajuato, Gto.;
    tel. (9 14 73) 2 01 23, 2 02 14, 2 02 44, 2 01 19.

HOTELS. – *Calinda Celaya Plaza,* Blvd. López Mateos y Carr. Panamericana, L, SP; *Posada Real,* 2.5 km (1 mile) on Salvatierra Road, I; *Mary,* Blvd. A. López Mateos y Zaragoza, I; *Motel El Cid,* Blvd. A. López Mateos 1548 Pte., II; *Isabel,* Hidalgo 207, II; *Allenda,* Allende 208, III.

RESTAURANTS. – In most hotels; also *Michelson,* Río Juárez 106; *Mariscos,* Río Juárez 313 A; *La Cueva del Perico,* Tabachines y Puerta de Oro; *La Perla,* Cuauhtémoc 201 C.

RECREATION and SPORTS. – Swimming, tennis, golf, riding.

EVENT. – Fiesta on July 16, Dia de la Virgen del Carmen.

The busy town of **Celaya** lies in the fertile valley basin known as the Bajío. Although not particularly favoured by nature in its situation, the town has beautiful parks and squares and a number of notable examples of Baroque and neo-Classical architecture. Its economic importance is growing steadily.

HISTORY. – Celaya ("flat land" in Basque) was founded in 1570 by sixteen Basque families from Spain, and was granted a municipal charter in the mid 17th c. Celaya's most famous son was the poet, musician, architect and artist Francisco Eduardo Tresguerras (1759–1833). Like most towns in Guanajuato state, Celaya played an important part in the war of Mexican independence (1810–21). In 1915, during the revolutionary wars, it was the scene of the bloodiest battle in Mexican history, in which Alvaro Obregón, later to become President of Mexico, decisively defeated Francisco (Pancho) Villa.

SIGHTS. – In the arcaded **Plaza Principal** or *Jardín* is the new *Palacio Municipal* (Town Hall). – Nearby is the old *Plaza de Armas*, with a fine *Independence Monument* (Monumento a la Independencia) by Francisco Eduardo Tresguerras. Here, too, are the *Church of the Third Order* (Iglesia de la Tercer Orden) and the *Church of the Cross* (Iglesia de la Cruz).

At the corner of Calle Miguel Doblado and Calle Guadalupe Victoria stands the 17th c. *church of San Francisco*, the façade, towers and high altar of which were altered by Tresguerras. The masterpiece of this versatile artist, however, is the neo-Classical *church of Nuestra Señora del Carmen* (1803–7), which in spite of its size has an appealing elegance and harmony. Particularly fine is the principal dome; the church contains notable sculpture, retablos and frescoes by Tresguerras. The finest of his wall paintings are in the Chapel of the Last Judgment (Capilla del Juicio), in which the raising of Lazarus and the burial of Tobias are depicted in addition to the principal scene. – Tresguerras also designed the unusual *bridge over the Río Laja*, outside the town.

SURROUNDINGS. – 70 km (45 miles) SW of Celaya on Road 43 (Salamanca–Morelia), (situated on the Laguna de Yuriria, a crater lake) lies **Yuriria** (alt. 1733 m (5686 ft); pop. 55,000; Hotel El Rinconcito; fiesta on January 3, Día de la Preciosa Sangre de Cristo). It was the old Tarascan town of *Yuririapúndaro*. It has an imposing *Augustinian convent, built between 1556 and 1567 by Fathers Diego Chávez y Alvarado (a relative of the conquistador Pedro de Alvarado) and Pedro del Toro, which for many years provided a place of refuge for monks and Christian Indians against the frequent attacks by hostile Indians. Built in the medieval and Gothic tradition, the church has a transept – an unusual feature for the 16th c. The exterior is dominated by the massive tower with its open bell-turret, its battlemented roof and its powerful buttresses. The main façade, displaying all the luxuriant fancy of Indian artists, is a magnificent example of the Plateresque style, although the typical lines are blurred by a complicated pattern of flowers and foliage; on either side of the doorway are statues of SS. Peter and Paul. The side entrance is a smaller version of the principal doorway, with a statue above the cornice of St Nicholas of Tolentino, an Augustinian saint and patron of the province. Part of the interior was destroyed by a fire in the early 19th c. and later restored. – The convent's magnificent two-story cloister has Gothic arcading and a monumental open staircase.

Cempoala (Zempoala)
See under Veracruz (town)

Laguna de Chapala

State: Jalisco (Jal.).

ⓘ **Coordinación Federal de Turismo,** Lázaro Cárdenas 3289, 1st floor, Colonia Chapalita, **Guadalajara,** Jal.; tel. (91 36) 22 41 30, 22 41 52, 22 41 67, 22 41 90.

HOTELS (along the N side of the lake from E to W). – *Nuevo Hotel*, Chapala, Madero 200, II; *El Nido*, Madero 202, II, SP; *Chapala Haciendas*, Carr. Chapala-Ajijic, I, SP; *Motel Chula Vista*, Carr. Chapala-Ajijic, I; *Real de Chapala*, Ajijic, Paseo del Prado 20, L, SP, tennis; *Posada Ajijic*, Ajijic, 16 de Septiembre 4, II; *Posada Las Calandrias*, Ajijic, II, SP; *Motel Las Casitas*, Carr. Ajijic-Jocotepec, II, SP; *Posada del Pescador*, Jocotepec, II, SP.

RESTAURANTS in most hotels; also IN CHAPALA *La Viuda, Café Paris, Don Juan, Cazadores*; IN AJIJIC: *Italo Pizza*.

RECREATION and SPORTS. – Swimming, rowing, sailing, water skiing, tennis, golf, riding.

Mexico's largest natural lake (82 km (51 miles) long and an average of 28 km (17 miles) across), the Laguna de Chapala, lies some 50 km (30 miles) SE of Guadalajara. Most of the lake is in Jalisco state, only the south-eastern part being in Michoacán. It contains three islands – **Chapala** (Alacranes), **Mezcala** (Presidio) and **Maltaraña.**

Sunset over the Laguna de Chapala

The lake is surrounded by low hills, most of them bare of vegetation. Although subject at times to considerable pollution which makes swimming unattractive it offers a wide range of facilities for water sports. Among the fish which can be caught in the lake are carp, mojarra, catfish (bagre) and whitefish (pescado blanco).

The lake's beautiful setting and pleasant climate has attracted large numbers of foreigners, particularly North Americans, to settle on the NW shore of the lake.

The principal places on the lake are:
Chapala (Náhuatl, "splashing waves"; alt. 1500 m (4922 ft); pop. 29,000), which together with the adjoining commune of *Chula Vista* has the largest colony of foreigners.
Ajijic (alt. 1500 m (4922 ft); pop. 9000), a picturesque fishing village with an artists' colony. There is a small archeological museum, and hand-woven fabrics and embroidery are on sale. There are also thermal baths.
Jocotepec (alt. 1444 m (4738 ft); pop. 30,000; Fiesta de los Dulces Nombres, January 14–15), an attractive little fishing town founded in 1528 with an artists' colony; noted for its white *sarapes*.

Chetumal

State: Quintana Roo (Q.R.).
Altitude: sea level.
Population: 90,000.
Telephone dialing code: 9 19 83.
(i) **Coordinación Federal de Turismo,**
   Av. Tulum 81,
   Edificio Fira,
   Cancún;
   tel. (9 19 88) 4 32 38.

HOTELS. – *El Presidente*, Av. de los Héroes/Av. Chapultepec, I, SP; *Continental Caribe*, Av. de los Héroes 171, I, SP; *Real Azteca*, Calle Bélice 186, II; *Jacaranda*, Av. de los Héroes/Av. Obregón, III. YOUTH HOSTEL: *CREA*, Albergue Chetumal, Av. A. Obregón y General Anaya.

RESTAURANTS in most hotels; also *Los Portales*, Av. de los Héroes 46; *Campeche*, Av. A. Obregón y Héroes; *Señorial*, Av. Obregón; *El Caribe*, on the harbor.

RECREATION and SPORTS. – Swimming, diving, fishing, tennis, golf.

Chetumal, capital of the state of Quintana Roo, lies at the most southerly point on the E coast of Yucatán at the mouth of the Río Hondo, which forms the border with Belize (formerly British Honduras). With the improvement of communications by road and the establishment of a free port the town has developed by leaps and bounds.

HISTORY. – Chetumal has had a long and eventful history. Originally named *Chactemal* ("place where the redwood grows" in Maya), it was for many centuries a Maya boatbuilding center and port. The first Spaniards to arrive here were Gerónimo de Aguilar and Gonzalo Guerrero, who were shipwrecked on the coast and became slaves of the Mayas. Aguilar was later freed by Cortés and performed valuable service as an interpreter, while Guerrero married a Maya princess and for some years fought on the Maya side against the Spanish invaders. The Spanish history of Chetumal began in 1898, when the town was founded by Captain Othón P. Blanco under the name of *Payo Obispo*. The main purpose of the new foundation was to suppress the smuggling of weapons and ammunition to rebel Indians during the "Caste War". The inhabitants of the town, originally a straggling settlement of wooden houses, gained a modest subsistence from farming and fishing. In 1954 the town was almost completely destroyed by a hurricane, and the central government then built a new and more pleasant town which is now of some importance as the market center for the E side of the Yucatán peninsula.

The "false towers" of the Maya palace at Xpuhil (Campeche state)

SIGHTS. – Apart from a few old wooden houses the modern town of Chetumal has few features of particular note. It attracts many Mexican visitors, who come to shop in the free port for goods imported via Panama. In recent years it has also developed some importance as a base for tourists visiting the numerous archeological sites in the area or enjoying the beauties of the surrounding lagoons and reefs.

SURROUNDINGS. – 153 km (95 miles) N of Chetumal on coast road 307 lies the road junction of Felipe Carillo Puerto (pop. 30,000; Hotel Chan Santa Cruz). This place is historically interesting, since in its time it was called Chan Santa Cruz ("little holy cross") and was the center of the cult of the "Speaking Cross". This Indian movement was the motive force behind the "War of the Castes" (1847–1901). Chan Santa Cruz was also from time to time the political capital of the independent Maya state of Yucatán. Remains of the original Temple of the Speaking Cross can be found at the western edge of the town; on the main square stands the great church of the cult, built in 1858, from which the "voice of the cross" spoke to the Indians and directed their destiny. The voice was either that of a ventriloquist or of a hidden trickster.

About 50 km (31 miles) S of Felipe Carillo Puerto, near Cafetal, a new road leads SE towards the coast to Majahual. Those who appreciate unspoiled coastal scenery or who enjoy diving should continue to the little fishing village of Xcalak (no accommodation at present) at the southern tip of the peninsula and facing the reefs of the Banco Chinchorro.

35 km (22 miles) NW of Chetumal on Road 307 is the *Laguna Bacalar, a fresh-water lake 56 km (35 miles) long whose calm waters offer scope for fishing and all kinds of water sports. Around the shores of the lake are Maya ruins and the remains of Spanish settlements. At the SW end of the lake is Bacalar (hotels: Bac-Halal, Laguna), with a 17th c. Spanish fort. An interesting fiesta (San Joaquín) takes place on August 13–16. 3 km (2 miles) from the town is the *Cenote Azul (bathing; fish and game restaurant).

There is good fishing in Chetumal Bay.

Chetumal to Villahermosa via Escárcega. – Road 186 runs through the almost uninhabited territory of southern Yucatán, most of it covered by dense scrub and great expanses of savanna. 58 km (36 miles) W of Chetumal, at Francisco Villa, a road goes off on the left to the excellently restored Maya site of *Kohunlich (p. 149) 9 km (6 miles) away.

About 60 km (37 miles) W of Francisco Villa, just off the road to the right, is the archeological site of *Xpuhil, in Campeche state. The excavated remains date from the Late Classic period (A.D. 600–900), although Xpuhil and other neighboring sites were also inhabited at an earlier stge. The principal building is a palace with three towers, one at either side and the middle one set back from the others. These towers have no function: they are purely decorative features, imitating the fronts of the temple pyramids found in Petén (Guatemala). Here, however, the towers are solid structures and the steps are so narrow and steep that they cannot be climbed. The façade above the doors was once decorated with huge stylized masks. This combination of "false towers" with the decoration of the façade, showing affinities with the Chenes culture, is known as the Río Bec style. On the two side towers of the place at Xpuhil the remains of large masks can still be seen.

4 km (2½ miles) farther on, also a little way off the road to the right, is *Becán, which also has buildings in the Río Bec style. The remains include palaces with the two typical "false towers", a pyramid crowned by a temple, altars and a ball court. Most of the buildings are wholly or partly overgrown by tropical vegetation. An interesting feature is that the site was surrounded by an artificial ditch, constructed at the beginning of the Classic period but never finished.

1¼ miles farther along the main road a side road on the left (5 minutes' drive) leads to the interesting site of *Chicanná, with many widely scattered buildings.

Mexico
United Mexican States
Estados Unidos Mexicanos

Chiapas

States
Estados

1a	Baja California Sur	12	Aguascalientes
1b	Baja California Norte	13	Jalisco
		14	Guanajuato
2	Sonora	15	Querétaro
3	Chihuahua	16	Hidalgo
4	Sinaloa	17	Colima
5	Durango	18	Michoacán
6	Coahuila	19	México
7	Nuevo León	20	Morelos
8	Zacatecas	21	Tlaxcala
9	San Luis Potosí	22	Puebla
10	Tamaulipas	23	Veracruz
11	Nayarit	24	Guerrero
		25	Oaxaca

26	Chiapas
27	Tabasco
28	Campeche
29	Yucatán
30	Quintana Roo

D.F. Distrito Federal (Federal District)

Some of the richly decorated façades are well preserved or have been restored, so that the site affords an opportunity of studying some outstanding examples of the Río Bec style. In the first plaza is a building with one of the characteristic huge masks on the upper part of the façade, the open jaws forming the doorway. Also typical of the style is the decoration of stylized motifs on the whole of the central part of the façade, reaching right down to the terrace. The corners of the temples are also notable, being formed of superimposed masks of the rain god Chac with the characteristic trunk-like nose. Little is left of the once richly decorated roof-combs.

Between these three sites and the Guatemalan frontier to the S are about twenty other Maya sites, accessible only on poor tracks and during the dry season (December to April). Among the most important are *Hormiguero*, one of the largest Maya sites in Mexico; *Calakmul*, where 103 stelae were found; *Río Bec*, the type site which gave its name to the style; *Chan-há*; and *La Muñeca*.

From Chetumal to the road junction of *Francisco Escárcega* (accommodation: Ah Kim-Pech, at the Pemex gas station; María Isabel, Calle 32) it is a total of 273 km −170 miles (157 km (98 miles) from the turning for Chicaná). Here Road 261, coming from Campeche and Champotón, joins Road 186, which continues SW and after crossing the *Río Usumacinta* (150 km – 93 miles) comes to *Catazaja* (161 km – 100 miles), where a road goes off on the left to **Palenque** (p. 213), 35 km (22 miles) away.

From Catazaja it is another 119 km (74 miles) to **Villahermosa** (p. 289). Just before reaching the town the road crosses the *Río Grijalva*.

Chiapas

State of Chiapas (Chis.).
Capital: Tuxtla Gutiérrez.
Area: 74,415 sq. km (28,732 sq. miles).
Population: 2,343,900.

ⓘ **Coordinación Federal de Turismo,**
Av. Central Pte. 1454,
Col. Moctezuma;
Tuxtla Gutiérrez;
tel. (9 19 61) 2 45 35, 2 55 09.

Chiapas, Mexico's most south-easterly state, extends in the W, where it is bounded by the states of Oaxaca and Veracruz, almost to the Isthmus of Tehuantepec. The boundary with Tabasco and Campeche to the N runs through hot and humid lowlands (valley of the Río Grijalva). The border with Guatemala to the E is formed in the central section by the Río Usumacinta, flowing through impenetrable rain forest, while farther S an upland region extends on both sides of the border, occupying most of the state of Chiapas. The hills in this region are the rugged outliers of the Sierra Madre del Sur, which average some 1500 m (4900 ft) in height, with some peaks such as Tacaná rising above 3000 m (9800 ft). On the S the sierra falls steeply down to the Pacific.

Chiapas, lying on the periphery of the country, has until recent years been little involved in the process of modernization which has been taking place in the central regions. Hence the old peasant culture of tribes belonging to the Maya language group, including the Zoque, Tzotzil, Tzeltal, Chol and Lacandón Indians (see under Bonampak), with their rich heritage of customs and traditions, has been better preserved than in most other parts of the country.

Important pre-Columbian Maya sites in Chiapas are *Chiapa de Corzo*, *Toniná, *Chinkultic (see under Lagunas de Montebello), *Bonampak (p. 82), *Yaxchilán (p. 296), **Palenque (p. 213) and *Izapa*.

HISTORY. – The first inhabitants of this region in the early period were probably the *Olmecs*, who were succeeded in the Pre-Classic period by the *Mayas*. The heyday of Maya culture here was between A.D. 300 and 900. After the Mayas abandoned their great cities they dispersed into numerous smaller settlements, most of which had to pay tribute to the *Aztecs* toward the end of the 15th c. The *Spaniards* first appeared in Chiapas in 1524 and succeeded after bitter fighting in subjugating the southeastern part of what is now Mexico.

In 1544 *Bartolomé de Las Casas* became bishop of Chiapas. He abolished the enslavement of the Indians by the Spaniards and used his influence at the Spanish court to secure legal protection for the Indians in the newly conquered regions of America. Although his efforts had only limited success, he is still regarded as the great patron of the Indians. From 1543 until Mexico achieved independence in 1822 Chiapas was governed by the Spanish administration in Guatemala. During the colonial period and also under the Republic there were repeated Indian risings against the government, the last of these being the rising of the Tzotzil and Tzeltal Indians in 1911.

ECONOMY. – In addition to the traditional agriculture – the working of tropical timbers – chicle, salt and the growing of coffee and cacao make a major contribution to the state's economy. In recent years the mining of gold, silver and copper and above all the extraction of oil have increased greatly in importance. There has also been a considerable development of tourism.

From the Isthmus to Guatemala via Tonalá and Tapachula. – This route follows the coast road (No. 200), which can be joined in Oaxaca state by turning right off the Tuxtla Gutiérrez road (No. 190) beyond San Pedro Tepanatepec in the direction of Arriage (44 km – 27 miles). It is also possible to turn off Road 190 farther N, at *Las Cruces*, into a road which runs via *Tiltepec* (23 km – 14 miles) to **Arriaga** (pop. 17,000; Motel El Parador, SP). From there it is 23 km (14 miles) to **Tonalá** (pop. 19,000; Hotel Grajanda), a little town surrounded by luxuriant tropical vegetation, with a small archaeological museum. From Tonalá a road runs S to the little fishing port of *Puerto Arista* (17 km – 11 miles), near which is an excavation site with remains showing early Aztec influence.

180 km (112 miles) beyond Tonalá is *Huixtla*, from which it is another 41 km (25 miles) to **Tapachula**

(alt. 190 m (624 ft); pop. 160,000; hotels: Loma Real, SP; San Francisco; Kamico, SP; Fénix), beautifully situated at the foot of an extinct volcano some 4093 m (13,433 ft) high, *Tacaná*. The town is the economic center of the surrounding area, in which there are considerable coffee plantations at the higher altitudes. It has a zoo and an archeological museum.

Near Tapachula is the interesting archeological zone of **Izapa** ("ditch in the plain"), with almost 100 temple platforms. This was a very ancient cult center which flourished from about 1000 B.C. to A.D. 300, during the Pre-Classic and Classic periods. The stelae found here, with carving in bas-relief, including the representation of a curious "long-lipped" god, point to Olmec influence, and form a transition to the later Maya style. In a later phase works of art in the Maya style were produced here.

27 km (17 miles) S of Tapachula is **Puerto Madero**, a port and a popular beach resort. There are border crossings into Guatemala at *Puente Talismán* (18 km – 11 miles) and *Ciudad Hidalgo* (38 km – 24 miles). – The railroad from Salina Cruz via Tehuantepec (p. 255) into Guatemala runs roughly parallel to the coast road.

Chichén Itzá

State Yucatán (Yuc.).
Altitude: 10 m (33 ft).

HOTELS. – *Mayaland, I, SP; Villas Arqueológicas, I, SP, tennis; IN PISTÉ: Misión Inn Chichén Itzá, I, SP; Pirámide Inn, I, SP; Motel Posanda Novelo, II; Cunanchén, II; Motel Dolores Alba, II, 3 km (2 miles) towards the ruins on Road 180.

**Chichén Itza, 120 km (75 miles) E of Mérida, is one of the largest and best restored archeological sites in Mexico. For more than 700 years, with only brief interruptions, it was a sacred center of the Mayas, and later, in the 11th and 12th c. A.D., the political and religious center of a revived Maya empire under Toltec dominance.

HISTORY. – Chichén Itzá ("near the fountain of the Itzá people" in Maya) was probably founded about A.D. 450 by Maya tribes which had come into the region from the S. It is now believed that the site was not abandoned at the end of the Classic period (c. A.D. 900), as were other much more important places in the central and southern parts of Maya territory (Campeche, Chiapas, Guatemala, Honduras). The most recent research suggests that some centuries earlier tribes from the central Mexican highlands had moved into this region and mingled with the Mayas. Previously the view had been that the Toltecs had come here from Tollan (now Tula: see p. 272), 1200 km (750 miles) away, about A.D. 1000 and had settled at this site, then probably still known as *Uucil-abnal* ("seven bushes" in Maya). According to the ancient Nahua chronicles the incomers were led by the legendary prince Ce Acatl Topiltzín – known, like a number of Toltec rulers, as Quetzalcóatl or

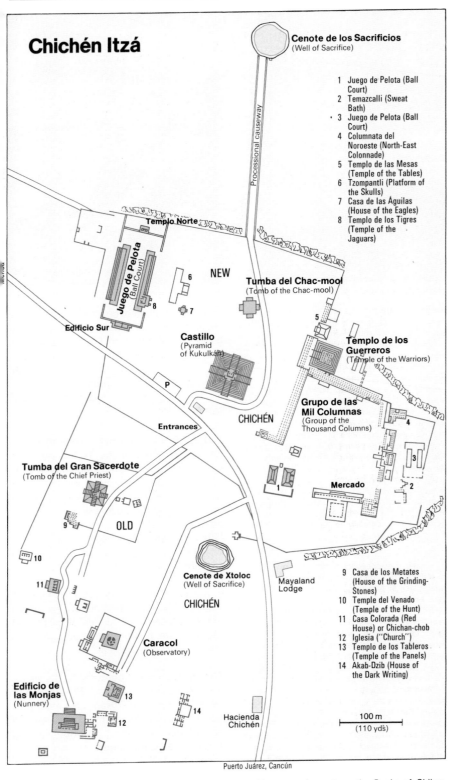

Chichén Itzá

Cenote de los Sacrificios
(Well of Sacrifice)

1 Juego de Pelota (Ball Court)
2 Temazcalli (Sweat Bath)
3 Juego de Pelota (Ball Court)
4 Columnata del Noroeste (North-East Colonnade)
5 Templo de las Mesas (Temple of the Tables)
6 Tzompantli (Platform of the Skulls)
7 Casa de las Águilas (House of the Eagles)
8 Templo de los Tigres (Temple of the Jaguars)

Processional causeway

Templo Norte

Juego de Pelota
(Ball Court)

NEW

Tumba del Chac-mool
(Tomb of the Chac-mool)

Edificio Sur

Castillo
(Pyramid of Kukulkán)

P

Templo de los Guerreros
(Temple of the Warriors)

Grupo de las Mil Columnas
(Group of the Thousand Columns)

CHICHÉN

Entrances

Tumba del Gran Sacerdote
(Tomb of the Chief Priest)

OLD

Mercado

Cenote de Xtoloc
(Well of Sacrifice)

Mayaland Lodge

CHICHÉN

Caracol
(Observatory)

9 Casa de los Metates (House of the Grinding-Stones)
10 Temple del Venado (Temple of the Hunt)
11 Casa Colorada (Red House) or Chichan-chob
12 Iglesia ("Church")
13 Templo de los Tableros (Temple of the Panels)
14 Akab-Dzib (House of the Dark Writing)

Edificio de las Monjas
(Nunnery)

Hacienda Chichén

100 m
(110 yds)

Puerto Juárez, Cancún

Kukulkán ("feathered serpent" in Náhuatl and Maya) – who had been driven out of Tula because of his unwarlike disposition.

During the following two centuries the mingling of the advanced cultures of the Toltecs and the Mayas led to the Post-Classic renaissance of Maya architec-

ture. Maya records, such as the Books of Chilam Balam (the "Jaguar Soothsayer") – which are often at variance with the Nahua chronicles – tell us that between A.D. 1007 and 1194 Chichén Itzá was allied with Uxmal and Mayapán in the "League of Mayapán"; but modern research has thrown doubt on this statement, since Uxmal had already been

El Castillo (Pyramid of Kukulkán), Chichén Itzá

abandoned by the 11th c. and Mayapán was probably not founded until the early 13th c. In Chichén Itzá's heyday Toltec stylistic influences predominated, so that the buildings of this period, in spite of many Maya features, show remarkable similarities to those in the old Toltec capital of Tollan. There are also contradictory accounts of the end of Chichén Itzá: most probably it was abandoned about A.D. 1200. The cause of its decline is stated to have been a second wave of Maya incomers under the influence of the highland cultures, who gave Chichén Itzá its present name. Once again the leader of the conquerors is said to have borne the name of Kukulkán or Quetzalcóatl, thus linking him also with the Toltec tradition. Soon afterwards the Itzá people split up, and one group led by the Cocom tribe founded the town of Mayapán, from which they ruled the northern part of the peninsula until about 1450. During this period Chichén Itzá was evidently of no great importance, since there was practically no new building and much of the site was abandoned.

At the time of its conquest by the Spaniards in 1533 the town had few inhabitants but was still a much visited place of pilgrimage. Bishop Diego de Landa came here and described some of the buildings (1566). The site was investigated by John L. Stephens in 1841–2, and in 1875 a French archeologist, Le Plongeon, worked on it. They were followed by an Englishman, A. P. Maudslay, and an Austrian, Teobert Maler. In 1855 Edward Thompson, United States consul in Mérida, acquired the whole area, and in 1904–7 he carried out diving operations in the Sacred Cenote on behalf of the Peabody Museum in search of votive offerings. In the 1920s another American, Sylvanus Morley, carried out extensive excavation and restoration work. Finally in the 1960s further exploration was carried out by the US National Geographic Society and the Mexican Institute of Anthropology and History (INAH).

The archeological zone, which is traversed by the Mérida–Puerto Juárez road (No. 180), extends over an area of some 8 sq. km (3 sq. miles). As on almost all pre-Columbian sites, only part of the remains has been excavated, and most of the area is still concealed under a luxuriant growth of vegetation. The names of the various buildings are often misleading, stemming as they do from early Spanish sources or from the reports of archeologists: the original Maya names are almost all lost.

THE SITE. – In the **northern section** of the site features of the Toltec style are particularly prominent. Characteristic of this style is the *Chac-mool*, a stone figure lying on its back in a semi-reclining position and holding a bowl for sacrificial offerings – probably a temple guardian. Other typically Toltec features are the so-called *Atlantean figures* – standing figures of warriors which supported temple roofs or altars. The constantly recurring symbol of the *feathered serpent* (Maya *Kukulkán*) displaced representations of the Maya rain god Chac; and scenes of battle and sacrifice are much more common here than in classical Maya art.

The first feature encountered by the visitor is the building known as ****El Castillo** or the *Pyramid of Kulkulkán*. Like most pre-Columbian buildings, this was erected in accordance with strict astronomical and astrological requirements.

Excellently restored and exceedingly impressive in its classical simplicity, this square ****pyramid** altogether 30 m (98 ft) high, has *nine terraces* and *four staircases*, symbolizing the nine heavens and the four cardinal points. Each of the staircases has 91 steps, making a total of 364; including the summit platform as the final step, the total becomes 365, the number of days in the year. On each of the staircases is a large snake's head. After climbing up one of the staircases, which rise at an angle of 45°, we arrive at the platform on which stands the **Temple of Kukulkán**. From here there is a magnificent *view of the whole site. The main entrance is flanked by two typically Toltec *serpent columns*. During the restoration of the Castillo a temple in pure Maya style was discovered in the interior; it stands on an earlier pyramid which had been buried within the later one. At the entrance to this temple was a stone *Chac-mool* and a throne in the form of a jaguar, painted red and inlaid with pieces of jade. The temple is reached through a passage leading to the inner pyramid (open only at certain times).

At the equinoxes (March 21 and September 22) the pyramid is the scene of a spectacular **phenomenon. The reflection of light and shade on these two afternoons penetrates the angles of the nine terraces of the staircase on the NW side and produce a wave effect which glides up to the snake heads. Through the refined architecture of the Castillo the appearance of the great snake becomes a symbol of the descending Kukulcán, the sun-god, as he brings the time of sowing and ends the season of rain.

E of the Castillo is the *Temple of the Warriors (Templo de los Guerreros)*, a magnificent building on a terraced platform surrounded by large colonnaded halls. It is evidently a copy, on a larger scale, of Pyramid B at Tula. After passing through several rows of pillars the visitor climbs the staircase, at the top of which is a *Chac-mool*. The entrance to the *principal temple* is flanked by two large serpent columns, with the snakes' heads on the ground and their tails, which originally supported the lintel, rising vertically into the air. Beyond this are four Atlantean figures supporting a large stone altar. Remains of a smaller earlier temple were found within the pyramid.

In the Temple of the Warriors, Chichén Itzá

Below the Temple of the Warriors is the **Group of the Thousand Columns** (*Grupo de las Mil Columnas*), the original function of which is not known: it may have been a market hall or a place of assembly. Beside it are a small *Ball Court* (Juego de Pelota), the so-called Market (Mercado) and a *Sweat Bath* (Temazcalli).

N of the Castillo is the *Tomb of the Chacmool* (Tumba del Chac-mool)), also known as the Platform of Venus. It is named after a stone figure, found by Le Plongeon over 100 years ago, to which he gave the name of Chac-mool. On the platform are interesting reliefs combining the symbol of Kukulkán with that of the planet Venus.

300 m (330 yds) farther N, approached by a causeway 6 m (20 ft) wide, is the large *Sacred Cenote or Well of Sacrifice

Temple of the Warriors and Group of the Thousand Columns

Sacred Cenote

(*Cenote Sagrado, Cenote de los Sacri-ficios*), the existence of which probably led the Mayas to establish themselves on this site. This circular natural water-hole has a diameter of 60 m (200 ft), and its walls rise over 20 m (65 ft) above the surface of the water; up till now its greatest depth has been measured as 82 m (269 ft).

The *Cenote was probably used from the 7th c. until after the Spanish conquest as a place of sacrifice and of pilgrimage. A *sweat bath* on the edge of the pool probably served for ritual purifications. In time of drought living human victims and precious objects were thrown into the water as sacrifices to the gods, particularly to the rain god Chac. As long ago as 1904–7 Bowditch and Thompson dived into the pool and found 50 human skeletons as well as numerous objects of terracotta, stone, gold, copper, jade and obsidian. Further exploration in the 1960s, going down into the deeper reaches of the pool, recovered 4000 more objects of the same kind, together with pieces of copal resin, rubber and wooden dolls, and human and animal bones. The legend that most of the sacrificial victims were beautiful maidens was dis-proved by the examination of the skeletons recovered, which were mainly of men and children.

Returning from the Cenote, we pass on the right a large rectangular platform known as the **Tzompantli** (Náhuatl, "wall of skulls"). This originally had a palisade on which the skulls of victims sacrificed to the gods were displayed.

Ball Court

There are relief carvings of skulls on the masonry.

Adjoining this is a smaller platform known as the **House of the Eagles** (*Casa de las Aguilas*). The staircase has carvings of snakes, and the walls bear reliefs of eagles and jaguars holding human hearts in their claws – symbols of the two military orders of the Nahua Indians, the Eagle and Jaguar Knights.

Like almost all Maya cities, Chichén Itzá has several courts for the ritual ball game. The ****Great Ball Court** (*Juego de Pelota*) at the NW end of the plaza is the most imposing so far discovered in Meso-America.

The PLAYING FIELD is almost 85 m (280 ft) long and some 35 m (115 ft) across, with vertical walls 8 m (25 ft) high along the sides. Half-way along each side, at a height of over 7 m (22 ft), is a heavy *stone ring* decorated with serpents. The object of the game was to drive a hard rubber ball through the rings, using only the elbows, knees and hips. The ball, as a symbol of the sun, had to be kept in the air all the time, since otherwise the symbolic course of the sun would have been interrupted. It is supposed that the losing side were sacrificed. Along the foot of the walls are relief panels depicting the players being conducted to the sacrifice.

Two small temples at the ends of the court, the *Edificio Sur* and the *Templo Norte*, are believed by some authorities to have been dedicated to the gods of the sun and the moon.

Built up against the SE wall of the ball court is the **Temple of the Jaguars** (*Templo de los Jaguars*). On the side open to the large plaza is a carved stone *jaguar* serving as an altar. The upper story of the structure, reached by a steep stair-case, opens on the W side onto the ball court. The entrance is flanked, like that of the Temple of the Warriors, by serpent columns, and the façade is decorated with several friezes, mostly depicting jaguars. The interior contains wall paint-ings evidently showing a fight between Mayas and Toltecs.

The **southern section** of the site, which includes the area known as OLD CHICHEN (*Chichén Viejo*), is reached by crossing the Mérida–Puerto Juárez road. On the right of the track is the **Tomb of the Chief Priest** (*Tumba del Gran Sacerdote*), a much damaged pyramid 10 m (33 ft) high, which was found to contain seven burials, with skeletons and valuable grave goods.

The Caracol ("Snail")

To the left is the *Caracol ("Snail"), one of the most interesting buildings on the site, evidently an observatory. It is built on a two-tier platform and has a spiral ramp winding its way up inside on an easy gradient. Its narrow slit windows allow the rays of the sun to penetrate into the center of the building for a few seconds on only two occasions in the year, thus giving the priests of Chichén Itzá a simple but reliable means of marking the passage of time. Architecturally the building shows stylistic forms derived from the central highlands as well as classical Maya features.

Farther S is the **Nunnery** (*Edificio de las Monjas*), erroneously so named by the Spaniards. The richly decorated building and its associated structures are in classical Chenes style. The carved ornamentation which covers almost the whole of the façade symbolizes the Maya god Chac. The adjoining building known as the "Church" (*Iglesia*) shows the characteristics of the Puuc style, an early style in which the façades are decorated not only with the classic Chac masks but also with a profusion of geometric and animal ornamentation. Between the Chac masks can be seen a prawn and an armadillo, a snail and a turtle, representing the four creatures which support the sky in Maya mythology.

Other notable buildings in this part of the site are the *Temple of the Panels* (Templo de los Tableros), the *House of the Dark Writing* (Akab Dzib), the *Temple of the Lintels* (Templo de los Dinteles), the *Red House* (Casa Colorada or Chichan-chob), the *House of the Grinding-Stones* (Casa de los Metates), the *Temple of the Hunt* (Templo del Venado), another *ball court* and the *Cenote de Xtoloc*.

SURROUNDINGS. – 5 km (3 miles) E on road 180 (to Valladolid and Puerto Juárez) is the stalactitic cave of *Balankanché ("throne of the jaguar priest"), discovered by chance in 1959 after remaining undisturbed for many centuries. The entrance to this cult and burial site had been blocked with large boulders. It is probably part of a much larger complex of underground caverns and watercourses which still awaits investigation. In the caves, now open to the public and provided with lighting, visitors see the cult utensils as they were left by the priests – numerous pottery dishes and plates, *metates* (maize grinding stones), copal incense-burners, etc. Many of the objects are decorated with the face of the Toltec-Aztec rain god Tláloc, suggesting that the cave was a purely Toltec burial site. The central feature is a chamber containing an altar, with a stalactitic formation resembling a ceiba, the sacred tree of the Mayas. A narrow passage leads into a chamber on a lower level, at the end of which is a pool of crystal-clear water with an altar dedicated to Tláloc. The pool contains small prawns and sightless fish.

42 km (26 miles) E of Chichén Itzá is **Valladolid** (hotels: San Clemente, SP; Zaci, SP; El Mesón del Marqués; María de la Luz, SP; Don Luis, SP.), the second largest town in Yucatán. The church of San Bernardino, founded by Franciscans in 1552, is one of the few colonial buildings which survived the civil war in the second half of the 19th c. Other notable features are the cenotes of Sis-ha and Zac-hi; a path leads down to the water 45 m (150 ft) below, offering the chance of a swim.

From Valladolid a road runs N to *Tizimin* (52 km – 32 miles), where from December 30 to January 6 there are great celebrations in honour of the Three Kings.

55 km (34 miles) farther N, on the coast, is the little town of **Río Lagartos**. The beautiful surrounding area offers good hunting and fishing. At *Las Coloradas*, at the mouth of Río Lagartos and Río Celestún is a bird sanctuary with a large colony of flamingoes. To the E of the town is the sulphur spring of Chiquila – a rare feature in Yucatán. To the W is the fishing village of *San Felipe*, from which an interesting boat trip can be made to the *Isla de los Pájaros* ("Island of Birds").

From Valladolid a new road runs via *Chemax* to *Cobá (p. 109).

Chihuahua (State)

State of Chihuahua (Chih.). – Capital: Chihuahua.
Area: 245,612 sq. km (94,831 sq. miles).
Population: 2,084,000.

(i) **Coordinación Federal de Turismo,**
Edif. de la Unidad Admva. Municipal "Lic. Benito Juárez" Av. Malecon y F. Villa, **Ciudad Juárez**, Chih.;
tel. (9 11 61) 4 66 92, 4 01 23, 4 08 37, 4 06 07.

Chihuahua, one of the largest and richest states in Mexico, is bounded on the N and NE by the United States (New Mexico and Texas), on the E by

Mexico
United Mexican States
Estados Unidos Mexicanos

Chihuahua

States
Estados

1a Baja California Sur	12 Aguascalientes	
1b Baja California Norte	13 Jalisco	
2 Sonora	14 Guanajuato	
3 Chihuahua	15 Querétaro	
4 Sinaloa	16 Hidalgo	
5 Durango	17 Colima	
6 Coahuila	18 Michoacán	
7 Nuevo León	19 México	
8 Zacatecas	20 Morelos	
9 San Luis Potosí	21 Tlaxcala	26 Chiapas
10 Tamaulipas	22 Puebla	27 Tabasco
11 Nayarit	23 Veracruz	28 Campeche
	24 Guerrero	29 Yucatán
	25 Oaxaca	30 Quintana Roo

D.F. Distrito Federal (Federal District)

Coahuila, on the S by Durango and on the W by Sinaloa and Sonora. The boundary with Texas is formed by the Río Bravo del Norte (Río Grande del Norte), of which Chihuahua's largest river, the Río Conchos, is a tributary. The main part of the state consists of a high plateau lying between 1200 m (3900 ft) and 2400 m (7800 ft), while in the W are the mountains of the Sierra Madre Occidental, slashed by deep gorges. The population consists mainly of mestizos and whites; the local Indian tribes, including the Guarijio in the W, the Tarahumara in the mountainous SW and the Tepehuano in the S, were driven back into these peripheral areas after the Spanish conquest.

In addition to the archeological zone of *Casas Grandes* there are pre-Columbian sites around *Pacheco* (El Willy, Cueva de la Olla), around *Ciudad Madera* (Huaynopa, Vallecito, Cuarenta Casas) and in the *Sierra Tarahumara* (Arroyo de Guaynopa). For the most part these consist of cliff dwellings or cave dwellings, often difficult of access.

HISTORY. – This region must undoubtedly have had a long pre-Columbian past, the chronology of which has not been established with any certainty. The main influences most probably came from the southwestern United States, and only later to a limited extent from central Mexico. *Casas Grandes* was an important cult center for some 700 years. – In the final period before the Spanish conquest the Nahua peoples living in Chihuahua were driven back by tribes coming from the N, such as the *Apaches*. At this stage, however, the *Tarahumara* were probably already the strongest group. – The first *Spaniard* to come here was Alvaro Núñez Cabeza de Vaca in 1528. Although the Spaniards found the minerals for which they were looking, most of their settlements in the 16th c. were unable to hold out against the constant Indian attacks. Prominent among the hostile Indian tribes were the *Comanches* of Texas, whose regular raids continued into the 19th c., taking them through Chihuahua and as far S as Zacatecas. During the colonial period Chihuahua, together with Durango, formed the province of *Nueva Vizcaya*. After Mexico became independent, the history of the state was closely bound up with that of its capital. In 1823 Chihuahua was separated from Durango, and in the following year it became an independent state.

ECONOMY. – The most important branch of the economy is *livestock-farming* (mainly cattle). In areas with artificial irrigation it is possible to grow corn, cotton, beans, alfalfa, fruit and vegetables. *Mining* (iron, antimony, gold, silver, copper, lead, coal) also makes a considerable contribution, and there is also a certain amount of *forestry*.

Apart from the capital, **Chihuahua** (see below), the towns of *Cuauhtémoc, Ciudad Camargo* and *Hidalgo del Parral* (p. 105) and the magnificent ****Barranca del Cobre** (p. 79), the state of Chihuahua has few places to attract the particular interest of tourists.

Near the modern farming settlement of *Nuevo Casas Grandes* (small archeological museum) is the most important pre-Columbian site in northern Mexico, **Casas Grandes** (*Paquimé*), which shows affinities with the cultures of the southwestern United States rather than with those of Meso-America.

Casas Grandes is one of the "oasis cultures", the most important of which are those of Casa Grande (Arizona), Mesa Verde (Colorado) and Pueblo Bonito (New Mexico). Little is known about the people who created these cultures of about their dates. Casas Grandes itself was probably established between the 7th and 8th c. and achieved a first flowering of culture around A.D. 1000. Recent finds indicate that it fell under the influence of the culture of the central highlands in the 13th c. Thereafter there are further traces of influences from the N, ascribed to the *Anasazi culture*. It is uncertain what part was played in the history of this culture by the Tarahumara, the Pima and the Apaches, but it is believed by some authorities that the Apaches were responsible for its collapse, probably in the 15th c.

The *archeological zone* has yielded remains dating from the different phases of development at Casas Grandes. The early period is represented by semi-subterranean dwellings, the first pottery and under-ground cult chambers (*kivas*); the middle period by the remains of houses of several stories, staircases and irrigation channels; the late period by Anasazi pottery and a variety of buldings in Toltec-Aztec style, including ball courts, platforms, remains of pyramids and representations of Quetzalcóatl.

NW of Nuevo Casas Grandes, on the United States border, is **Ciudad Juárez** (alt. 1144 m (3753 ft); pop. 700,000; hotels: *El Presidente, L, SP; Plaza Juárez, L, SP; *Motel Colonial Las Fuentes, L, SP; Sylvia's, I, SP; Mónaco, I, SP; Imperial, II; Motel Flamingo, II; restaurants: Cortijo Los Colorines; Florida; La Parilla Suiza; Las Vacas; fiestas: December 4, Día de Santa Bárbara; December 5–12, foun-

dation of the town; August 10–20, Cotton Fair), the fifth largest city in Mexico, situated on the S bank of the Río Grande opposite El Paso in Texas. The town, formerly called *Paso del Norte*, was renamed in 1888 in honour of Benito Juárez who had his headquarters here during the War of Intervention in 1865–6. During the revolutionary wars (1910–21) it was the base of the revolutionary hero and bandit chieftain Francisco (Pancho) Villa. Ciudad Juárez is now of importance as a commercial and frontier town. Features of interest are the mid-17th c. mission church of Guadalupe and the new Cultural Center, with an archeological and historical museum (pottery from Casas Grandes, mementoes of the revolutionary wars) and exhibitions of folk art.

Chihuahua (Town)

State: Chihuahua (Chih.).
Altitude: 1430 m (4693 ft). – Population: 700,000.
Telephone dialing code: 9 11 41.
ⓘ **Coordinacion Federal de Turismo,**
Edif. de la Unidad Admva. Municipal "Lic. Benito Juárez" Av. Malecon y F. Villa, **Ciudad Juarez**, Chih.;
tel. (9 11 61) 4 66 92, 4 01 23, 4 08 37, 4 06 07.

HOTELS. – *Exelaris Hyatt Chihuahua*, Av. Independencia 500, L, SP; *El Presidente, Calle Libertad 9, L, SP; El Mirador, Av. Universidad 1309, I, SP; Posada Tierra Blanca, Av. de Independencia y Niños Héroes, I, SP; Motel Nieves, Av. Technológico y Ahuehuete, II, SP; Apolo, Av. Juárez 907, II; Roma, Libertad 1015, III.

RESTAURANTS in most hotels; also *Robin Hood de Mexico*, E. Talavera 208; *La Olla de Chihuahua*, Av. Juárez 3331; *Caballo Loco*, Av. Niños Héroes y 3a; *La Hacienda*, Av. Reforma y 20 s.

RECREATION and SPORTS. – Swimming, tennis, golf.

EVENTS. – May 22, Fiesta de Santa Rita; September 15–16, Cotton Fair.

Chihuahua, capital of the large state of the same name, is attractively situated in a valley open to the N and enclosed on the other sides by the hills of the Sierra Madre Occidental. In earlier days primarily a mining town, it is now a busy industrial and commercial center.

HISTORY. – In pre-Columbian times and in later periods the area of Chihuahua was frequently traversed by raiding Indians from the N, the *Apaches* of Arizona and the *Comanches* of Texas. The first

Church of Guadalupe, Ciudad Juárez

View of the town of Chihuahua

attempts by the *Spaniards* to settle here and evangelize the population were unsuccessful, and it was not until 1709 that a settlement was founded on the site of Chihuahua by Antonio de Deza y Ulloa and named *San Francisco de Cuéllar*. In 1718 it was given the name of *San Felipe el Real de Chihuahua* ("dry place" in Tarahumara). Rich finds of silver brought prosperity to the town, but its development was hampered by constant Indian attacks. In 1811 the "father of Mexican independence", Miguel Hidalgo y Costilla and his companions, were court-martialed and shot here, after being captured by Spanish troops. During the war with the United States (1846–8) and the War of Intervention (1862–6) the town was temporarily occupied by US troops. Benito Juárez lived for some time in Chihuahua. The rising which started here at the end of 1910 led to the abdication of President Porfirio Díaz and to the revolutionary war (1910–21). The revolutionary leaders in northern Mexico were Abraham Gonzáles and Pancho Villa; the latter took the town in 1913 with his "División del Norte" and made it his headquarters.

After suffering an annihilating defeat at the hands of Alvaro Obregón at Celaya in 1915 Villa fled to the mountains, from where he mounted many raids, even thrusting into the United States. In 1920 he made peace with the Mexican government and was granted a large hacienda in Durango, but was shot in an ambush at Hidalgo del Parral in 1923.

SIGHTS. – In the *Plaza de la Constitución* stands the **Cathedral*, dedicated to St Francis of Assisi, which was built between 1717 and 1826. With its Baroque façade, bearing statues of the twelve Apostles, it is the most impressive religious building in northern Mexico. – A short distance away, in the *Plaza Hidalgo*, is the **Government Palace** (*Palacio de Gobierno*), an old Jesuit college which was rebuilt in the 19th c. Here Hidalgo and his principal lieutenants were captured and executed in 1811, their severed heads being later displayed in Guanajuato. Also in the Plaza Hidalgo is the *Palacio Federal*, in which Hidalgo was confined during his trial. In *Calle Libertad* is the **church of San Francisco** (1721–41), in which Hidalgo's remains lay buried until their transfer to Mexico City in 1823.

At the corner of Bolívar and Calle 2 in the former Palace of Justice is the **State Regional Museum** (*Museo Regional del Estado*). This building, known as the **Quinta Gameros**, was erected at the turn of the century and represents one of the best examples of Art Nouveau in Mexico. Among its exhibits are completely furnished rooms in the style of this period, archeological material from the surrounding area (Casas Grandes, Hohokam, Mogollón, Anasazi, etc.) as well as exhibits illustrating the advanced cultures of other parts of Mexico. The museum also has an ethnological collection and examples of folk art. – At No. 3014 in Calle 10 Norte is the **Quinta Luz*, the palace once occupied by Pancho Villa, formerly a museum run by his family but now part of the **Historical Museum of the Revolution* (*Museo Histórico de la Revolución*) of the Mexican army. The Pancho Villa Museum contains, in addition to his death mask, many souvenirs of the famous or notorious bandit and revolutionary hero (weapons, photographs, uniforms, flags, etc., as well as the car in which he was shot).

Other notable features in Chihuahua are the churches of *Santa Rita* (1731) and *Guadalupe* (1826) and a disused *aqueduct*, 5583 m ($3\frac{1}{2}$ miles) long, constructed between 1754 and 1864.

The tiny hairless dogs named after the town (*perritos chihuahuenses*), weighing

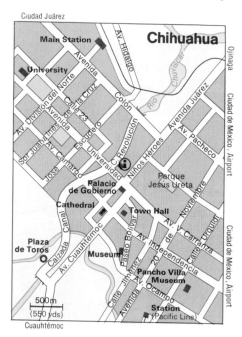

only 600–1200 g (20–40 ounces) and with an average body temperature of 40 °C (104 °F), are offered for sale in the Sunday markets. The breed probably originated in Europe or Africa and not in Chihuahua.

SURROUNDINGS. – Around the town are a number of artificial lakes (Presa Francisco Madero, Las Virgenes, Chuviscar) which offer facilities for bathing and fishing. Some of the old silver-mines (Santa Eulalia, Aquiles Serdán) are also worth a visit.

102 km (63 miles) W of Chihuahua is **Cuauhtémoc** (alt. 2100 m (6890 ft); pop. 30,000; hotels: Posada del Sol; Motel Tarahumara Inn; Romo; fiesta June 13, Día de San Antonio). The population of the surrounding area consists mainly of German-speaking Mennonites about 80,000 engaged in farming and livestock-rearing.

Members of this Protestant sect, founded by a Frisian named *Menno Simons* in the 16th c. and originally established chiefly in Switzerland, Germany and the Netherlands, emigrated in the 17th c. to the United States and in the 18th c. to Russia. About the middle of the 19th c. the **Mennonites** of Russia emigrated to the United States and Canada in order to avoid the compulsory military service which they rejected along with other state-imposed obligations. About 1921, groups of Mennonites left their new homes, where they were not allowed to have German-language schools, and settled in Chihuahua, establishing farming settlements of exemplary quality. Many of the stricter Mennonites were compelled to move once again in 1976, this time to Texas, as a result of new measures introduced by the Mexican government.

From Cuauhtémoc it is some 50 km (30 miles) to *La Junta*, from which Creel in the **Barranca del Cobre** (p. 79) can be reached by rail or on the road which has been recently brought up to modern standards. – There is also a new road W to *Yepáchic* (170 km – 105 miles). To the S of this town, at *Ocampo*, are the *Basaseáchic* falls, one of the most impressive waterfalls in Mexico. The falls, in a beautiful setting of forest-covered mountains, drop down 310 m (1020 ft) into a gorge on the Basaseáchic river.

150 km (95 miles) SE of Chihuahua on Raod 45 is **Ciudad Camargo** (alt. 1200 m (3940 ft); pop. 30,000; fiesta September 4, Día de Santa Rosalía; markets Tuesday and Saturday). The town founded in 1740, was destroyed by the Apaches in 1797. Until 1897 it was known as Santa Rodalía. The town's economy is centered on the livestock-farming of the ranchos in the surrounding area and the processing of cotton. Within the surrounding area there are also a number of thermal springs (*Ojo de Jabalí, Ojo Caliente, Ojo Salado*) and the man-made lake of *Boquilla*.

From Ciudad Camargo it is another 150 km (95 miles) on Road 45 to the mining town of **Hidalgo del Parral** (alt. 1660 m (5446 ft); pop. 73,000; hotels: Chihuahua, San José), which has three interesting churches – the parish church (1710, with a Churrigueresque altar), El Rayo (18th c., with Churrigueresque retablos), a place of pilgrimage much frequented by the Indians, and La Fátima (20th c.). Pancho Villa was shot in Hidalgo del Parral in 1923, an event commemorated by a small museum and a memorial tablet.

Chilpancingo de los Bravos

State: Guerrero (Gro.).
Altitude: 1360 m (4462 ft). – Population: 80,000.
Telephone dialing code: 9 17 47.
ⓘ **Coordinación Federal de Turismo,**
Costera Miguel Alemán 187,
Acapulco, Gro.;
tel. (9 17 48) 5 11 78, 5 13 03, 5 41 28, 5 10 22.

HOTELS. – *Posada Meléndez*, Juárez 50, I, SP; *Bravo*, Trujano 6, II; Outside the town on the Acapulco road: *Parador del Marquez*, II; *Motel Las Cabaños*, II, SP.

RESTAURANTS in most hotels; also *Colonial*, Mexico City–Acapulco road, 272; *La Fuente*, Zapata 2 Altos.

RECREATION and SPORTS. – Swimming, tennis, riding.

EVENT. – December 25 to January 2, Feria de San Mateo.

Chilpancingo de los Bravos, capital of the state of Guerrero, lies in a valley on the slopes of the Sierra Madre del Sur. The town has little of tourist interest, but its situation on the Cuernavaca–Acapulco road makes it an excellent base for excursions into the unspoiled mountain regions in the surrounding area.

HISTORY. – The area around Chilpancingo (Náhuatl, "place of wasps") was occupied from the Archaic period by various Indian peoples, the earliest to have left their mark being the *Olmecs*. During the *colonial period* the town was primarily of importance as a staging point on the road from the Pacific into the central highlands. In 1813 it was the meeting-place of the first Mexican National Congress under the presidency of José María Morelos. The style "de los Bravos" was added to the town's name in 1825 in honour of the Bravo brothers, who had distinguished themselves in the fight for independence. Chilpancingo is now the center of the surrounding agricultural and forest region.

Apart from the *Government Palace* (Palacio de Gobierno), which contains frescoes of scenes from Mexican history, the *parish church* and a *zoo* there are few features of interest in the town.

SURROUNDINGS. – 60 km (37 miles) E of Chilpancingo is **Chilapa**, formerly state capital of Guerrero (pop. 15,000; Hotel Las Brisas; fiesta June 3–4, with folk dancing; Sunday market; Cathedral built of concrete; 16th c. Augustinian convent).

7 km (4 miles) N of Chilapa lies the village of *Acatlán* near which (45-minute climb) are the **Oxtotitlán Caves**, discovered in 1968. In two stalactitic caves, about 30 m (98 ft) deep can be seen interesting wall paintings (900–700 B.C.); the subjects (a man sitting on a jaguar throne, jaguars' heads, children's faces, etc.) point to an Olmec origin.

60 km (37 miles) E of Chilapa is the Tlanpanec village of *Atliztac* (Indian dances). – 66 km (41 miles) farther on is **Tlapa** (16th c. Augustinian convent), another settlement of the Tlapanecs, who probably came into the area from the southwestern United States in the 9th c.

34 km (21 miles) from Atliztac on the road to Talapa a turning on the left leads in 35 km (22 miles) to *Olinalá*, a village which until recently could not be reached by car. Olinalá is noted for its *lacquerware on wood and gourds, the technique of which goes back to pre-Spanish times. Olinalá work can also be obtained from many shops and markets in the larger towns. The huge area between the Chilapa–Tlapa road and the Pacific coast, which has no roads giving access to it, is one of the least known parts of Mexico.

11 km (7 miles) S of Chilpancingo is *Petaquillas*, where a road goes off on the left to *Colotlipa* (40 km – 25 miles). 8 km (5 miles) from this village are the *Juxtlahuaca Caves*, discovered in the 1930s but not explored until 1966. These stalactitic caves (to be visited only with a guide) were found to contain wall paintings 3000 years old, together with pottery and the remains of skeletons. The paintings, which are found at 1050 and 1150 m (1150 and 1260 yards) from the entrance, depict Olmec motifs (figures of rulers, feathered serpents, etc.) in black, red, yellow and green. Apart from the finds of Indian material these caves contain magnificent stalactitic specimens and promise, on further exploration, to be among the most interesting of their kind in North America.

Chinkultic

See under Lagunas de Montebello

Cholula

State: Puebla (Pue.).
Altitude: 2150 m (7054 ft). – Population: 26,000
(i) **Coordinación Federal de Turismo,**
    Blvd. Hermanos Serdan y Blvd. Norte,
    Puebla, Pue.
    tel. (91 22) 48 29 77, 48 31 77, 48 30 44.

HOTELS. – *Villas Arqueológicas*, L, SP; *Campestre Los Sauces*, I.

RESTAURANTS in the hotels; also *Tío Nico, La Fuente, La Pirámide*.

EVENTS. – Fiestas: February 2, Fiesta de la Candelaria; August 15, Día de la Asunción de la Virgen María; September 8, Día de la Virgen de los Remedios.

Cholula, situated on the same plateau as Puebla, 12 km (7½ miles) away, was once one of the most important religious, economic and political centers of ancient Mexico. Little now remains of its former splendor except a gigantic earth mound under which is concealed the largest pyramid in the world. From

Excavations of the pyramid at Cholula

the top of the pyramid, now crowned by a church, there is a striking view of the numerous spires and domes of the churches built by the Spaniards after the Conquest on the sites of pyramids and temples: there are said to be at least 365 of them in Cholula.

HISTORY. – It is not known who were the original builders and inhabitants of Cholula (from the Náhuatl name Atcholollan, "place from which the water flows"), but there was certainly a settlement of some size here by 400–300 B.C. At the beginning of the Christian era the influence of the great Classic culture of Teotihuacán began to make itself felt – an influence which was to last for five centuries. It finds expression in the pyramidal platforms with vertical rectangular panels (*tableros*) and long horizontals, and is confirmed by comparisons of the early pottery.

As a result of Cholula's situation at a meeting-place of several pre-Columbian cultures some of the stylistic features of the later Monte Albán IIIb and El Tajín cultures are also found here. In the 7th c. A.D. the town fell under the control of the *Olmec-Xicalanca* people (who were not the same as the Pre-Classic Olmecs). Between the fall of Teotihuacán (c. A.D. 750) and the rise of Toltec Tula (c. 950) Cholula was the leading city in central Mexico. Shortly before A.D. 1000 the legendary god-king Quetzalcóatl (Ce Acatl Topiltzin) is said to have stayed for some time in Cholula after his expulsion from Tula before moving on to Yucatán. After the fall of Tula (A.D. 1168) *Toltecs* and *Chichimecs* thrust into the Cholula area, eventually compelling the rulers of Cholula to flee to the coast of the Gulf of Mexico.

Mixtec influence in art, which had been evident in the earlier period, now became more powerful, and there came into being the *Mixteca-Puebla culture*, notable particularly for its magnificent glazed polychrome pottery. Although temporarily occupied by neighboring peoples – for example by *Huexotzinco* in 1359 and by the *Aztecs* (Mexica) a hundred years later – Cholula remained relatively undisturbed in its role as a religious center during the long period of its history before the Spanish conquest. – In 1519 Cortés and his forces, with their Tlaxcalan auxiliaries, came to Cholula, whose population they estimated at 100,000. Fearing a trap, they carried out a massacre of the inhabitants in which between 3000 and 6000 people are believed to have lost their lives. They also destroyed the principal pyramid dedicated to Quetzalcóatl. When this catastrophe was followed in 1544–6 by a great epidemic of plague which wiped out a large part of the population, the greatness of Cholula was finally at an end.

The excavation of the gigantic pyramid was begun in 1931 under the direction of José Reygadad Vértiz and continued by Ignacio Marquina on behalf of the Instituto Nacional de Antropología e Historia (INAH). INAH has also carried out interesting excavations in recent years, and further work may be expected to yield much valuable information.

SIGHTS. – The *Pyramid, still almost entirely covered by earth and vegetation, is the largest structure of the kind in the world.

The *temple pyramid was dedicated to the god Quetzalcóatl, the "Feathered Serpent", the light-skinned and bearded god of the wind, the morning and evening stars and the techniques of civilization, who had brought to Meso-America the knowledge of art, learning and agriculture. The pyramid, seven times built over in the course of some 1500 years, was 425 m (1395 ft) square at the base, originally stood over 62 m (200 ft) high and covered an area of 17 hectares (42 acres).

The excavations carried out so far, in the course of which some 9 km (5¾ miles) of tunnels have been cut through the structure, have revealed the remains of a number of platforms, residential apartments, temple walls and patios. Also discovered were an unusual peripheral staircase, interesting *Frescoes (about A.D. 200) including representations of butterflies and grasshoppers in the style of Teotihuacán and a magnificent colored painting 50 m (165 ft) long depicting life-size figures engaged in drinking (sometimes closed to the public). – Visitors can see the excavated areas and some of the tunnels which are still negotiable. There is also a small museum.

Even after the Conquest the Indian population remained faithful to the cult of Quetzalcóatl and their other divinities, and so the Spaniards built their churches either on, or on the site of, the old shrines. Thus on the summit of the principal pyramid they erected the chruch of Nuestra Señora de los Remedios (Our Lady of Perpetual Succor), which was begun in 1666, continued in the 18th c. and later almost completely destroyed by an earthquake. Rebuilt in 1873 in Neo-classic style, the church contains in a glass case above the altar the statue of a Madonna which is believed to have been a gift from Cortés to the Franciscan monks. From the church there is a fine *view of the town.

The site of another ancient temple is occupied by the massive Convent of San Gabriel, built by Franciscans in 1549. Notable features are the large atrium, the Plateresque doorway, the substantial doors and the Gothic arches. The Capilla Real (Chapel Royal), in a style influenced by the Great Mosque in Córdoba, dates from the mid-16th c. (restored in the 17th c.). It is an imposing structure with 7 aisles and 49 small domes and opens into a spacious atrium with 3 finely decorated posas (processional chapels).

Of Cholula's numerous other churches the most notable are San Andrés, San Miguel Tianguistengo, Guadalupe, Santiago Mixquitla and San Miguelito. – Cholula is also the seat of the University of the Americas, which was moved here from Mexico City in 1970.

SURROUNDINGS. – It is only a few miles S to *Tonantzintla (p. 69), *Acatepec (p. 68) and Tlaxcalancingo (p. 70). – 16 km (10 miles) NW is *Huejotzingo (p. 141) and beyond this *Calpan (p. 142).

Citlaltépetl (Pico de Orizaba)
See under Puebla (town)

Ciudad del Carmen
See under Campeche (town)

Ciudad de México
See Mexico City

Ciudad Juárez
See under Chihuahua (town)

Ciudad Obregón
See under Guaymas

Ciudad Victoria
See under Tamaulipas

Coahuila de Zaragoza

State of Coahuila (Coah.). – Capital: Saltillo.
Area: 150,395 sq. km (58,068 sq. miles).
Population: 1,785,300

ⓘ **Coordinación Federal de Turismo,**
Blvd. V. Carranza 2454, 3rd floor,
Saltillo, Coah.
tel. (9 18 41) 3 83 22.

Coahuila, Mexico's third largest state (after Chihuahua and Sonora), is bounded on the N by the United States (Texas), on the W by Chihuahua and Durango, on the S by Zacatecas and on the E by Nuevo León. It consists primarily of a vast rolling plateau traversed by several ranges of hills. The climate is predominantly hot and arid, and the only fertile land is in the valleys and depressions, which are artificially irrigated. The inhabitants of the state are mainly mestizos and Spaniards, but there are also some Indians in the remoter areas.

HISTORY. – The first European to come to this region, then chiefly inhabited by nomads, was Alvaro Núñez Cabeza de Vaca, in the course of his eight years of exploration on foot. The first significant settlement in Coahuila (Náhuatl, "naked snake") was established by Francisco de Urdiñola in 1575 on the site now occupied by Saltillo. In order to provide protection from attacks by hostile Indians he settled the *Tlaxcalans* here – allies of the Spaniards who enjoyed privileges denied to other Indians. From here the Spaniards pushed steadily northward into what is now the United States. When Mexico achieved independence Coahuila and Texas formed a single state with its capital at Monclova or Saltillo until the Texan territories were separated in 1836. During this and the following period there were disturbances amounting almost to civil war and then, during the war with the United States, military engagements between Mexican forces under General Antonio López de Santa Ana and US forces under General Zachary Taylor. In 1857 Coahuila was joined with Nuevo León, but in 1868 it was made an independent state. In 1863 Benito Juárez set up temporary headquarters in Saltillo when retreating before the advance of French troops.

ECONOMY. – The state has good communications and a well-balanced economy, with a considerable output of *steel*, substantial supplies of *minerals* (silver, lead, coal, copper, iron) and a varied pattern of *agriculture* (maize, wheat, beans, cotton, sugar-cane, wine) and *livestock-farming*.

The capital of Coahuila is **Saltillo** (alt. 1550 m (5086 ft); pop. 238,000; hotels: *Camino Real, Carr. 57 at km 865, L, SP; Arizpe Sainz, Victoria 418, I, SP; Motel San Jorge, M. Acuña 240 Nte., I, SP; Poza Rica, Allende Nte. 436, II, SP; Motel El Paso, Blvd. V. Carranza Nte. 3101, 11, SP; restaurants: La Canasta, Blvd. V. Carranza 2485; Principal, Allende Nte. 702; El Tapanco, Allende Sur 225; fiesta; Santo Cristo de la Capilla, August 6; mass, August 13). In the main square is the Cathedral of Santiago, a handsome Churrigueresque building (1746–1801). Other features of interest are the church of San Esteban (1592) and a picturesque square, the Alameda. Saltillo is noted for its

Mexico
United Mexican States
Estados Unidos Mexicanos

Coahuila

**States
Estados**

1a Baja California Sur	12 Aguascalientes
1b Baja California Norte	13 Jalisco
	14 Guanajuato
2 Sonora	15 Querétaro
3 Chihuahua	16 Hidalgo
4 Sinaloa	17 Colima
5 Durango	18 Michoacán
6 Coahuila	19 México
7 Nuevo León	20 Morelos
8 Zacatecas	21 Tlaxcala
9 San Luis Potosí	22 Puebla
10 Tamaulipas	23 Veracruz
11 Nayarit	24 Guerrero
	25 Oaxaca
26 Chiapas	
27 Tabasco	
28 Campeche	
29 Yucatán	
30 Quintana Roo	

D.F. Distrito Federal (Federal District)

hand-woven woolen fabrics (*sarapes*) and for its University (summer courses for foreigners).

In the SW corner of the state is the largest town, **Torreón** (alt. 1137 m (3730 ft); pop. 317,000; hotels: Palacio Real, Av. Morelos 1280 Pte, I, SP; Calvete, Juárez y Ramón Corona, I, SP; Río Nazas, Morelos y Trevino, II, Salvador, Hidalgo 1353 Pte., III; restaurants: Casa Doña Julia, Matamoros 1094; La Calesa, Morelos 1119 Pte.; El Chalet, Matamoros y Colón). This industrial town, which has grown up around a traffic junction, is barely a hundred years old and has little to offer the tourist.

The surrounding country is exceedingly arid but has been made fertile by irrigation, producing mainly wheat and cotton. Its industries are concerned with processing the local products (minerals, wheat, grapes).

Another important industrial town is **Monclova** (alt. 600 m (1969 ft); pop. 130,000; hotels: Chulavista, Av. Frontera 100, I, SP; Gil Cantú, V. Carranmza 410, I, SP; Doris, Av. V. Carranza 207, II, SP; restaurants: El Cid, Dela Fuente Ote. 306; Jardín, Morelos y V. Blanco), which has one of the largest iron and steel works in Mexico.

Other towns in Coahuila are **Piedras Negras** (border crossing into the United States), on the Eagle Pass; **Parras**, the oldest town in northern Mexico, a wine-producing center; and *Sabinas*, from which there is a road to the man-made lake of Don Martín.

Visitors interested in ethnology will find it worthwhile to make an excursion from *Melchor Múzquiz*, 50 km (30 miles) W of Sabinas, to the village of *Nacimiento de los Negros*, around which there are settlements of Kikapú Indians. Now numbering only a few hundreds, they belong to a tribe of Algonquin Indians, formerly living in the eastern United States, who moved into this area about 200 years ago.

Coatzacoalcos
See under Laguna de Catemaco

Cobá

State: Quintana Roo (Q.R.).
Altitude: 8 m (26 ft).

HOTEL and RESTAURANT. – *Villas Arqueológicas*, on Lago Cobá, L, SP, tennis.

ACCESS. – From the E, branch off Road 307 at Tulum, then 42 km (26 miles) on a good road to Cobá. From the NW, branch off Road 180 (Mérida–Chichén Itzá–Valladolid) at Nuevo X-can; the road from there is usable now.

Amid a group of small lakes in the dense scrub of Quintana Roo is *Cobá, one of the largest Maya sites. This ceremonial center and settlement, almost completely overgrown, remained in occupation for a very long time, from the Early to the Late Classic period, thanks to an abundance of water unusual in Yucatán peninsula.

HISTORY. – On present evidence Cobá ("wind-ruffled water" in Maya) seems to have enjoyed its most prosperous age in the Maya *Classic period* (A.D. 600–900), though some of the buildings date from the Post-Classic (900–1450). Although the site was evidently still occupied when the Spaniards arrived in Mexico, they never discovered it. – The first white man to come to Cobá was an Austrian, Teobert Maler, the great loner among Maya archeologists, who visited the site in 1891. Between 1926 and 1929 it was excavated by the leading Americanists of the day, both British and American – Thomas Gann, Sylvanus G. Morley, J. Eric Thompson and H. D. Pollock, working on behalf of the Carnegie Institution. Since 1973 Mexican archeologists have been working at Cobá.

In the huge area, of a minimum of 70 sq. km (27 sq. miles), covered by the site, about 50 roads and over 6000 buildings have so far been identified and 32 stelae of the Classic period, most of them carved with reliefs, have been found. The oldest date found is A.D. 623 (on Stela 6), though the architecture of many buildings, resembling that of Petén (Guatemala) suggests that they may date from the Early Classic period (A.D. 300–600). The importance of Cobá as a metropolis is confirmed by the large number of "white roads" (*sacbeob*, singular *sacbe*) found here. These roads, surfaced with a concrete-like mass of limestone, formed a dense network linking the center of the city with the outlying districts. Unusual features are that some of the roads are as much as 10 m (33 ft) wide and that one of them ran for almost 100 km (65 miles) to *Yaxuná*, a cult center SW of Chichén Itzá. The road system around Cobá was the densest in Meso-America.

THE SITE.– Many of the pyramids, temples and stelae that have been excavated still have no names, while others are known only by the numbers or letters given them by the excavators. It should also be noted that the tracks leading to the various buildings are subject to frequent changes.

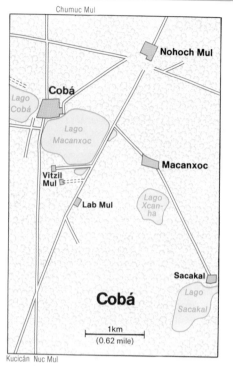

Cobá

1km
(0.62 mile)

steps. Finally two narrower steps only 1 m (3 ft) wide lead up to the *temple* (Structure I) which crowns the pyramid. The pyramid itself is in the style of the Classic period, while the temple resembles those of Tulum and thus belongs to a considerably later period, probably the 14th or 15th c. In front of the temple is a small altar. In the upper frieze of the temple are three rectangular recesses, each originally containing a figure of the "Diving God"; two of the figures are still in place. The only entrance leads into a chamber with corbelled vaulting. From this temple there is a superb *view.

At the foot of the pyramid are the remains of *Temple 10*, in front of which is the magnificent **Stela 20**, bearing the date A.D. 684. The relief shows the richly attired figure of a ruler with his feet resting on two crouching slaves. He carries a ceremonial staff, which is held at an angle – a feature typical of the Cobá style. The sides and upper part of the stela are covered with glyphs.

Going back a little way and taking a turning to the left, we come to the **Group of the Paintings** (*Grupo de las Pinturas*). The principal structure is a pyramid, which is crowned by a small **temple**. The temple has doors at the E and W ends and a main entrance on the N side, divided into two by a column. The lintel of the doorway and the three horizontal ledges above it still show distinct traces of the original painting. The codex-like *frescoes* have representations of numbers and divinities. Through the E doorway there is a good view of the Castillo in the Nohoch Mul Group.

Going a little way farther back and taking another road to the left, we come to the **Macanxoc Group** also called Group A, between Lakes Macanxoc and Xcantha. Here, at a short distance from one another, are five well-preserved **stelae** 3 m (10 ft) high and 1.50 m (5 ft) wide, almost all with figures of rulers or chief priests and glyphic Maya inscriptions.

On entering the archeological zone visitors see on the right a series of buildings known as the **Cobá Group** (*Grupo de Cobá*) or *Group B*. The large pyramid (partly restored) is known as the **Church** (*Iglesia*). It stands 24 m (80 ft) high, on a base measuring 40 m (130 ft) from E to W and 50 m (165 ft) from N to S. It has nine terraces with rounded corners, and above the seventh terrace is a wall supporting the highest platform on which stands a small temple. From here there is a magnificent *view over the Cobá area with its numerous pyramids, temples and lakes. – At the foot of the staircase of the "Church" is *Stela 11*, 1.40 m (4½ ft) high and 90 cm (3 ft) wide with many glyphs, no longer legible, on one side. To the left of the pyramid is a small group of buildings, including one with a corbelled vault. – Nearby, best seen from the road, are the remains of a *ball court* (juego de pelota).

Following the road in a northeasterly direction, we come to the **Nohoch Mul Group** or *Group C* (on the left). The commanding pyramid known as *El Castillo is 42 m (138 ft) high – the highest accessible Indian structure in the Yucatán peninsula.

The base of the *pyramid measures 55 by 60 m (180 by 200 ft). The staircase, 11 m (36 ft) wide, has 120 steps leading up the six terraces to the summit platform. Note the shell motifs carved on many of the

Pyramid in the Cobá Group

There are other interesting remains at Cobá, but the decision whether to visit them must be taken on the spot, having regard to the accessibility and state of restoration of the buildings.

Colima (State)

State of Colima (Col.). – Capital: Colima.
Area: 5205 sq. km (2010 sq. miles).
Population: 383,000.

ⓘ Coordinación Federal de Turismo,
Juárez 244, 4th floor,
Manzanillo, Col.;
tel. (9 13 33) 2 01 81, 2 20 90.

The little state of Colima, on the Pacific coast, is bounded on the N and NW by Jalisco and on the E by Michoacán. Most of its area consists of a flat coastal plain, rising in the NE into the foothills of the Sierra Madre, built up of tectonic rocks. The Islas Revilla Gigedo (Socorro, San Benedicto, Roca Partida and Clarión), lying some 800 km (500 miles) W, are also included in Colima state. The population consists of the descendants of Spaniards, mestizos and Nahua Indians.

The most important of the archeological sites in the state – for the most part merely cemeteries – are *El Chanal*, *Los Ortices* and *Periquillos*.

HISTORY. – Practically nothing is known about the early Indian peoples who created the art of which remains have been found in Colima and the surrounding regions. Many authorities simply call them the *Teca*. In the Late Classic and Post-Classic periods there were probably settlements of *Nahua* peoples at various times.

On the basis of the grave goods recovered from numerous burials, which included well-preserved pieces of the attractive and unusually naturalistic pottery of the region, it has been possible to identify a number of different cultural phases. The Classic period, to which the name of the *Los Ortices-Las Animas* phase is given, was artistically the most fertile; dated between A.D. 200 and 850, it developed in parallel with the corresponding phase at Teotihuacán. The next phase, the *Armería-Colima* phase, lasted from about 850 to 1250 – i.e., during the early Post-Classic period – and shows Toltec influences. The last or *Periquillo* phase (1250–1521) developed under the influence of the *Chimalhuacán League*, an alliance of four states, including Colima ("conquered by our grandfathers" in Náhuatl). In the second half of the 15th c. the allied city-states came under attack from the *Purépecha* (Tarascans). The settlement of *Cajitlán* ("place where pottery is made" in Náhuatl), which is said to have been founded in the 11th c. and later became a town of some consequence in the region, probably occupied the site of present-day Tecomán.

A year after the fall of Tenochtitlán (1521) the Spaniards arrived in the Colima area under the leadership of Gonzalo de Sandoval and Juan Alvarez Chico. The first successful conquests in this region, however, were achieved by Francisco Cortés de San Buenaventura, a nephew of Hernán Cortés. During the colonial period Colima was part of the province of *Nueva Galicia*, which was governed from Guadalajara. – Miguel Hidalgo, the pioneer of Mexican independence, was parish priest in Colima in 1792. After forming part of the state of Michoacán for a time Colima became a separate territory and in 1857 an independent state.

Mexico
United Mexican States
Estados Unidos Mexicanos

Colima

States
Estados

1a Baja California Sur
1b Baja California Norte
2 Sonora
3 Chihuahua
4 Sinaloa
5 Durango
6 Coahuila
7 Nuevo León
8 Zacatecas
9 San Luis Potosí
10 Tamaulipas
11 Nayarit

12 Aguascalientes
13 Jalisco
14 Guanajuato
15 Querétaro
16 Hidalgo
17 Colima
18 Michoacán
19 México
20 Morelos
21 Tlaxcala
22 Puebla
23 Veracruz
24 Guerrero
25 Oaxaca

26 Chiapas
27 Tabasco
28 Campeche
29 Yucatán
30 Quintana Roo

D.F. Distrito Federal (Federal District)

ECONOMY. – *Livestock-farming* is practiced in the higher parts of the state. The most important *agricultural products* are cane sugar, rice, maize, copra and coffee. The principal *minerals* worked are copper, lead, iron and salt. Other sources of revenue are *forestry, fishing* and *tourism*. The Islas Revilla Gigedos produce sulfur, guano, timber, fruit, sheep and fish.

In addition to the capital, **Colima** (see below), and the port and beach resort of **Manzanillo** (p. 155), the only towns of any considerable size are *Armería* and *Tecomán* (alt. 80 m (262 ft); pop. 40,000; Real Motel; fiestas: February 2, Día de la Candelaria; December 12, Día de Nuestra Señora de Guadalupe).

Colima (Town)

State: Colima (Col.).
Altitude: 508 m (1667 ft). – Population: 115,000.
Telephone dialling code: 9 13 31.
(i) **Coordinación Federal de Turismo,**
Juarez 244, 4th floor,
Manzanillo, Col.;
tel. (13 33) 2 01 81, 2 20 90.

HOTELS. – *Villa del Rey,* on the Guadalajara road, I, SP; *Motel Costeño,* on the Manzanillo road, I, SP; *Los Candiles,* Bul. Camino Real, I, SP; *Ceballos,* Constitución 5, II; *Casiono,* Portal Morales, II.

RESTAURANTS in most hotels; also *La Cabaña,* Blvd. Las Palmas 699; *Los Naranjos,* Gabino Barreda 34; *Carrusel,* at km 1 on Tonilá Road.

RECREATION and SPORTS. – Swimming, hunting.

EVENTS. – Fiestas: February 2, Día de la Virgen de la Salud; February 5, Fiesta Brava.

Colima, capital of the state of the same name, lies on the slopes of a fertile valley watered by two rivers. Within sight of two magnificent mountain peaks, Colima is an attractive town of simple colonial buildings and luxuriant gardens where life is lived at a quiet and leisurely pace.

40 km (25 miles) N of Colima, in the state of Jalisco, are the **Nevado de Colima** (4380 m – 14,371 ft) and the ***Volcán de Colima** (3900 m – 12,796 ft). The Nevado, also known as *Zapotépetl* ("mountain of the sapodilla trees"), is Mexico's sixth highest mountain. The frequently smoking Volcán de Colima (diameter of crater 1800 m/5908 ft; depth 250 m/820 ft), also known as the "fiery volcano" (Volcán de Fuego), last erupted in 1941, causing considerable devastation. The Nevado is reached from Ciudad Guzmán by way of El Fresnito and the

Terracotta dogs from Colima

Albergue de la joya, a mountain hut (3560 m – 11,680 ft); the Volcán via Atenquique and El Playón (3130 m – 10,270 ft). At the foot of the mountains is the beautiful *Lake Carrizalillos* (boat trips and pony-treks).

HISTORY. – The Colima area no doubt had a long pre-Columbian history, but little is known of the peoples who lived here. – The Spaniards who came to this area in 1522 under Gonzalo de Sandoval found an Indian settlement on the site, near which they established the town of *San Sebastián de Caballeros*. In course of time, particularly in the 18th c. and during the last few

Terracotta model of a temple from Colima

decades, the town developed into a center for the marketing and processing of livestock, timber and agricultural produce from the ranchos and haciendas of the surrounding area.

SIGHTS. – The principal feature of interest is the **Museum of the Cultures of the West** (*Museo de las Culturas de Occidente*), notable for its collection of material belonging to the Colima culture.

There is also an interesting **Museum of Old Cars** (*Museo de Automóviles Antiguos*), with over 100 vehicles dating between 1912 and 1950.

Other notable buildings in the town are the *Government Palace* (Palacio de Gobierno), the *Cathedral* and the *churches* of *San José, Fátima* and *El Sagrado Corazón*.

SURROUNDINGS. – 15 km (9 miles) SE is *Agua Caliente*, one of the many health resorts in this area. – 10 km (6 miles) N is the attractively situated little town of *Comalá*, noted for its craft products (furniture painted articles, wrought-iron work).

Córdoba

State: Veracruz (Ver.).
Altitude: 920 m (3019 ft). – Population: 155,000.
Telephone dialing code: 9 12 71.
(i) **Coordinación Federal de Turismo,**
Av. I. Zaragoza 20 Altos Centro,
Veracruz, Ver.;
tel. (91 29) 32 70 26, 32 16 13.

HOTELS. – *Real Villa Florida*, Av. 1, 3002, L, SP; *Palacia*, Av. 3 y Calle 2, I, SP; *Las Palmas*, Carr. a Fortín, I, SP; *Virreinal*, Av. 1 y Calle 5, II; *Marina*, Av. 2 y Calle 11, II.

RESTAURANTS in most hotels; also *El Cordobés*, Av. 1 y Calle 3; *El Portal*, Av. 3 Nr. 304; *Oasis*, Av. 3 Nr. 1510.

RECREATION and SPORTS. – Golf, tennis.

EVENTS. – August 24, Freedom Day; May 11–22, Trade Fair.

The picturesque town of Córdoba lies amid luxuriant vegetation in the valley of the Río Seco, at the end of the still unfinished highway from Mexico City to Puebla and from Orizaba to Córdoba which is to be extended to Verucruz. Tropical fruits grow in the lowlands extending toward the hot coastal plain, coffee and tobacco in the intermediate zone; the mountainsides are still largely covered with mighty cedars and walnut trees.

HISTORY. – Córdoba was founded by the Spaniards in 1618 and named after the old Moorish city in Andalusia. Here on August 24 1821 General Agustín de Iturbide, later emperor of Mexico, and the last Spanish viceroy, Juan O'Donojú, signed the *Treaty of Córdoba* recognizing the independence of Mexico – a treaty which was at first rejected by King Ferdinand of Spain.

SIGHTS. – Many houses in the town still show strong Andalusian and Moorish influence – for example, in their massive old wooden doors, window grilles and wooden balconies. In the arcaded main square, the **Zócalo**, is the neo-classical *Town Hall* (Palacio Municipal), and on one side of the square stands the historic *Palacio Zevallos*, now a hotel, in which the treaty of Córdoba was signed. Another building with historical associations is the Casa Quemada ("Burnt House"), at the corner of Calle 7 and Avenida 5, in which a small force of Mexican freedom fighters was wiped out by Spanish troops at the beginning of the war of independence. – The small *Municipal Museum* (Museo de la Ciudad de Córdoba) at 303 Calle 3 is notable mainly for its Totonac material. – There is an interesting **market** (*Mercado Juárez*), between Calles 7 and 9 and Avenidas 8 and 10, which draws crowds of people from the surrounding area, particularly on Saturdays and Sundays.

SURROUNDINGS. – 6 km (4 miles) W on Road 150 is *Fortín de las Flores ("Fort of Flowers": alt. 1010 m (3314 ft); pop. 16,000; hotels: *Ruiz Galindo, L, SP, golf, tennis, Las Animas garden; Posada Trini, I, SP; Posada Loma Motel, outside the town, I, SP, tropical garden). During the colonial period there was a Spanish fort here; it is now a very pleasant little town with an equable climate and a profusion of flowers, both subtropical and temperate. The beautiful main square consists of two areas of public garden separated by a narrow street. In the square are the Town Hall and the Public Library. The town is surrounded by coffee plantations on the higher slopes of the hills, while tropical fruits (mangoes, oranges, bananas, pineapples and papaws) flourish on the lower ground. On a clear day, particularly in the early morning, there is a magnificent *view of the snow-capped *Pico de Orizaba (Citlaltépetl, "Mountain of the Star": see p. 227)., Mexico's highest mountain (5700 m – 18,700 ft). It is well worth while visiting some of the haciendas and the Sunday market. – Between January and May there is a period of relief from the area's frequent showers of rain – which are unusual in Mexico; from May to September there is heavy rain; and from October to the end of December the rain is lighter but persistent.

Cozumel

State: Quintana Roo (Q.R.).
Area of island: 490 sq. km (189 sq. miles). –
Population: 32,000.
Telephone dialing code: 9 19 87.

(i) **Coordinación Federal de Turismo,**
Fideicaribe,
tel. 2 09 64.

Coordinación Federal de Turismo,
Av. Tulum 81,
Edificio Fira,
Cancún, Q.R.;
tel. (9 19 88) 4 32 38.

HOTELS. – ON THE SEASHORE: *Sol Caribe,* Playa Paraíso, L, SP, tennis; *Cozumel Caribe,* Playa San Juan, L, SP, tennis; *El Presidente,* 6 km (4 miles) S of San Miguel de Cozumel, Playa San Francisco, L, SP, tennis, golf; *El Cozumeleño,* Playa Santa Pilar, L, SP, tennis; Cabañas del Caribe, Playa Santa Pilar, L, SP; La Ceiba, Playa Paraíso, L, SP, tennis; Mara, Playa San Juan, I, SP; Cantarel, 1·5 km (1 mile) N of San Miguel de Cozumel, I, SP; Galápagos Inn, 1·5 km (1 mile) S from San Miguel, II; Barracuda, 1 km (¾ mile) from the Pier, II. – IN THE TOWN: Mesón San Miguel, I, SP; Maya Cozumel, I, SP; El Marquez, II, SP; Mary Carmen, II; Bahía, II; El Pirata, III.

RESTAURANTS in most hotels; also *Morgan's; Pepe's Grill; El Acuario; *Casa Denis; El Portal; Soberanis; Pepe's; El Ranchito; Carlos 'n' Charlie's; Las Palmeras.

RECREATION and SPORTS. – Snorkeling, diving, sailing, water skiing, wind-surfing, fishing, riding, tennis, golf.

EVENT. – Fiesta September 20, Día de San Miguel.

ACCESS. – Passenger and car ferry from Puerto Morelos, passenger ferry from Playa del Carmen; hovercraft connection from Cancún; (bus services from Mérida, Puerto Juárez and Cancún; and from Chetumal and Felipe Carillo Puerto). – Air services from Mérida, Isla Mujeres and Cancún and from some other Mexican and foreign airports.

Cozumel is one of Mexico's largest islands, 45 km (28 miles) long and up to 18 km (11 miles) across. Located 20 km (12 miles) off the NE coast of the Yucatán peninsula, it is flat and almost entirely covered by dense green scrub forest. It has magnificent *beaches of white sand, many of them fringed by palms, which stand out brilliantly against the blue-green of the sea. The *water, over a sea-floor of fine white coral sand, is crystal clear.

HISTORY. – Cozumel, originally Ah-cuzamil ("land of the swallows" in Maya), appears to have been of considerable importance in the Maya Post-Classic period, particularly between A.D. 1000 and 1200. As the most easterly of the Maya sites it may have been a sanctuary dedicated to the rising sun. According to the ancient chronicles it was also the base from which Maya peoples such as the Itzá made their way to the mainland. Cozumel, like Izamal, seems to have been an important shrine of the fertility goddess Ixchel, the patroness of birth, medicine and weaving. As the moon goddess and the consort of Itzamná, the sun god and supreme ruler of the universe, she played an important part in the Maya mythology of Yucatán. The shrines of Ixchel were particularly revered by women.

The first Spaniard to discover the island (in 1518) was Juan de Grijalva, followed in 1519 by Cortés and in 1527 by Francisco de Montejo, who made it a base for his attempt to conquer Yucatán. When Cortés landed here the island was said to have a population of 40,000. – In the 17th, 18th and 19th c. Cozumel was a pirates' and smugglers' lair, frequented by Henry Morgan, Laurent de Graff and Jean Lafitte among many others. In the second half of the 19th c., during the "Caste War", many refugees from the mainland came to Cozumel. – During the Second World War the old town of San Miguel was demolished to make room for a United States air base. – In the late 1950s the island began to be developed as a tourist center offering magnificent scope for divers and snorkelers.

A beach on the island of Cozumel (Quintana Roo)

San Miguel de Cozumel

SIGHTS. – the town of **San Miguel de Cozumel**, in the NW of the island, offers little of particular interest apart from an attractive little aquarium and a museum with material illustrating Cozumel's past. – Among the most beautiful and popular *beaches on Cozumel are the *Playa San Juan* in the NW and the *Playa San Francisco* in the SW. Other good beaches are to be found at *Encantada, Hanan, Bonita, Punta Morena* and *Chen Río* on the E (Caribbean) side of the island. Bathers should be wary of the heavy seas and strong currents which sometimes occur.

A popular trip from San Miguel is to the *Chancanab* lagoon (in Maya "little sea") a small fresh-water lake 7 km (4 miles) S which is connected with the sea by underground channels. With its crystal-clear water and variety of aquatic animal life it is a paradise for swimmers and snorkelers. In recent years a nature reserve with a botanical garden (restaurant) has been established here. – On the *Isla de la Pasión* (N coast) a wild-life reserve is being set up.

Although the marine life in the seas around Cozumel has been decimated in recent years, particularly by underwater hunters armed with harpoons, there is still much to attract snorkelers and scuba divers. One of the best diving areas is the ***Palancar Reef** at the SW tip of the island, which rises from a depth of 80 m (260 ft) to just under the surface. Other similar areas near the island are the *González, Punta Norte* and *Maracaibo* reefs.

More than thirty small Maya sites have been found on the island but only a few have been excavated. Although they are of no great significance architecturally and are mostly difficult to reach, it is well worthwhile looking out for at least one of them. The following is a brief selection: *Miramar* (N of San Miguel de Cozumel), *Aguada Grande* (in the N of the island), *El Real, Hanán* and *Las Grecas* (in the NE), *San Severo* and *San Gervasio* (in the northern central area) and *Punta Islote* (in the S).

Cuauhtémoc

See under Chihuahua (town)

Cuautla

State: Morelos (Mor.).
Altitude: 1280 m (4200 ft). – Population: 84,000.
Telephone dialing code: 9 17 35.
(i) **Coordinación Federal de Turismo,**
　I. Comonfort 12,
　Cuernavaca, Mor.;
　tel. (9 17 31) 2 18 15, 2 52 39, 2 54 14.

HOTELS. – *Hacienda Cocoyoc,* 6 km (4 miles) outside the town, L, SP, riding, tennis, golf; *De Cautla,* Batalla 19 de Febrero 114, I, SP; *Vasco,* Esteban Pérez 40, I, SP; *Internacional,* Gral. Gabriel Tepepa 124, I, SP; *Jardines de Cautla,* 2 de Mayo 94, II; *Servilla,* Conspiradores 9, II, *Posada El Asturiano,* at 124 km on Mexiko–Oaxaca Road, II; *Colonial,* José Perdiz 18, III; *Quinta Los Arcos,* Carr. Mexiko-Oaxaca 150, III.

RESTAURANTS in most hotels; also *Valgrande,* Reforma 522; *El Oasis,* Galeana 32; *Flamart,* Av. Reforma 135; *Fonda Cholita,* Tavera 289; *La Aurora,* Av. Insurgentes 206.

RECREATION and SPORTS. – Swimming, tennis, golf, riding.

EVENTS. – May 1, "Batalla de Cuautla"; September 30, birthday of José María Morelos. – Sunday market.

Cuautla, long renowned as a health resort, lies in a region of subtropical climate and luxuriant vegetation. Located as it is at the intersection of major traffic routes, the town is a good base for excursions to the places of interest in the surrounding area, in particular the numerous convents (see under Morelos).

HISTORY. – Cuautla (Náhuatl *Cuauhtlán,* "place of eagles") was noted for its thermal springs even in pre-Columbian times, and at the beginning of the 17th c. it developed into a fashionable spa for well-to-do Spaniards. During the war of independence, in 1812, it was the scene of a battle between José María Morelos's freedom fighters and royalist troops. – Emiliano Zapata, leader of the great peasant revolt during the revolutionary wars (1910–20), came from the Cuautla area.

SIGHTS. – The town has little in the way of colonial art and architecture. The best known churches are *San Diego* and *Santiago,* both 17th c. The *Casa de Morelos* contains relics and mementos of the war of independence. – The best known spa establishments in and around Cuautla, mostly with hot sulphur springs, are **Agua Hedionda,** *Agua Linda, Casa-sano* and *El Almeal.*

SURROUNDINGS. – Leave on Road 140 (signposted to Puebla) and in 20 km (12½ miles) take a side road which runs 8 km (5 miles) N to **Zacualpan de Amilpas,** a picturesque village which has an Augustinian convent with a 16th c. fortified church. At the four corners of the atrium are *posas* (processional chapels), and the cloister contains frescoes which were restored in the 19th c. The architecture and details of the adjoining chapel are also interesting.

Branching off to the right from Road 140 not far from Amayuca towards the S, one comes in 2 km (1 mile) to a road on the left leading in barely 4 km (2½ miles) to the village of **Chalcatzingo.** Here stands the beautiful colonial church of San Mateo with sculpture and ornament on the façade showing Indian influence. From here it is another 2 km (1 mile) to a pre-Columbian site on the *Cerro de la Cantera.*

The ***reliefs** carved from the rock on this site are among the finest of their kind. Since the subjects are of Olmec type it is supposed that the site was either occupied by Olmecs or at least under Olmec influence. Following recent dating it is believed that the heyday of this cult site was between 1100 and 500 B.C. The most important reliefs would have been carved between 900 and 700 B.C., perhaps even earlier. The most interesting is *Petroglyph 1* ("El Rey"), almost 3 m (10 ft) high, which depicts a richly adorned seated figure in a cave (perhaps representing the jaws of a gigantic jaguar). On one side are sprouting maize shoots, and in the upper part of the scene are clouds from which rain is falling. *Petroglyph 2* shows a bearded prisoner threatened by two Olmec warriors with jaguar masks, *Petroglyph 4* jaguars attacking prostrate human figures, *Petroglyph 5* a strange kind of snake swallowing a recumbent human figure (perhaps an early allusion to the cult of Quetzalcóatl). At the base of the rock lies the so-called Complex III which consists of a number of platforms and altars. 3 km (2 miles) from Chalcatzingo lies the archeological site Las Pilas.

About 3 km (2 miles) SW is *Jonacatepec,* with a 16th c. Augustinian convent. – Another 5 km (3 miles) S a short side road on the right leads to the attractive health resort of **Atotonilco.** – About 15 km (9 miles) farther SW is the little town of **Tepalcingo** (pop. 14,000; Sunday market).

The finest of the town's six churches is the **shrine of Jesús Nazareno** (1759–89), a magnificent example of Mexican-Indian Baroque. The richly carved *façade differs from other Baroque and Churrigueresque façades in Mexico in lacking the characteristic pilasters (*estípites*) and Solomonic (twisted) columns. It is decorated with sculpture in the manner of a retablo, with New Testament scenes depicted in Indian style. The church contains pictures imitating retablos (*c.* 1800) which are ascribed to Juan de Sáenz. – On the third Friday in Lent there is a great pilgrimage to Tepalcingo, combined with a lively fair. In the market craft articles from remote and inaccessible villages (e.g. lacquerware from Olinalá) are offered for sale.

Cuernavaca

State: Morelos (Mor.).
Altitude: 1540 m (5053 ft). – Population: 325,000.
Telephone dialing code: 9 17 31.
(i) **Coordinación Federal de Turismo,**
　I. Comonfort 12,
　tel. 2 18 15, 2 52 39, 2 54 14.

HOTELS. – *Cuernavaca Racquet Club,* Francisco Villa 100, L, SP, tennis; *Las Mañanitas,* R. Linares 107, L, SP; *Casino de la Selva,* L. Valle 26, L, SP; *Posada Jacarandas,* Av. Cuauhtémoc 105, L, SP, tennis, golf; *Hostería Las Quintas*, Av. Las Quintas 107, I, SP; *Posada San Angelo*, Privada La Selva 100, I, SP; *María Cristina*, A. Obregon 329, III, SP; *Iberia*, Calle Rayón 9, II; *Palacio*, Calle Morrow 204, II; *Royal*, Matamoros 19, III.

RESTAURANTS in most hotels; also *Lancer*'s, Morrow 13; *La India Bonita*, Morrow 6B; *Harry's Bar*, Gutenberg 1; *Moby Dick*, Plan de Ayala 383; *El Fogón Gaucho*, Humboldt 618; *Los Armandos*, Plan de Ayala 1104-B; *Vienes*, Lerdo de Tejada 4; *Viena*, Guerrero 104.

RECREATION and SPORTS. – Swimming, riding, tennis, golf.

EVENTS. – May 2, Festival of Flowers; May 15, Día de San Isidro Labrador; September 8, Día del Nacimiento de la Virgen María (Nativity of the Virgin).

Scarcely an hour's drive from Mexico City is Cuernavaca, capital of Morelos state. Its mild subtropical climate, its profusion of flowers and the colonial charm of its *old town have made it a popular vacation resort and a retreat much favored by the retired. With the growth of industry and the increasing numbers of visitors, however, it has begun to lose something of its old intimate atmosphere.

HISTORY. – Cuernavaca (Náhuatl *Cuauhnáhuac*, "near the trees") has a long pre-Conquest history, probably going back to the Olmecs. From about A.D. 1200 it was the chief town of the *Tlahuica* ("people of the earth" in Náhuatl), who at the beginning of the 15th c. were conquered by the *Aztecs* under Itzcóatl. There is a story – probably legendary – that there had been an earlier liaison between the Aztec chief Huitzilíhuitl and Miahuaxihuitl, daughter of the ruler of Cuernavaca, who was famed as a magician, and that the great Aztec ruler Moctezuma I was their son. Until the Spanish conquest the Aztec rulers had splendid summer residences in Cuernavaca. The town was captured and destroyed by the *Spaniards* under Cortés in 1521. After his fall from power Cortés, as Count of Cuernavaca, spent some time here before finally returning to Spain in 1540. During the colonial period Cuernavaca was a favorite residence of the Spanish ruling classes; and the Emperor Maximilian and his wife Carlota (Charlotte) stayed several times in Cuernavaca during their short reign (1864–7). During the revolutionary war (1910–20) the rebellious peasants were led by Emiliano Zapata. He called for the splitting up of the huge estates of the large landowners with the battle-cry "Tierra y Libertad" ("Land and Liberty") and destroyed many haciendas in the surrounding area.

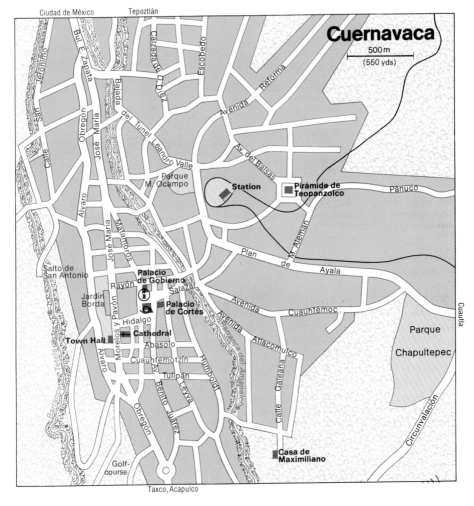

SIGHTS. – Near the main square, the **Zócalo** or *Plaza Morelos*, is the massive bulk of the ***Palacio Cortés**, which was begun about 1530 and much altered in later periods. Originally built as Cortés's residence, it was later used as municipal offices and now houses the *Cuauhnáhuac Historical Museum*. From the loggias on the first floor there are magnificent *views of the town and surrounding area. The frescoes by Diego Rivera (1929–30), which were commissioned by the US ambassador Dwight Morrow (father-in-law of Charles Lindbergh), depict scenes from the story of the Spanish conquest, the history of Cuernavaca, the war of independence and the revolutionary wars.

Palacio Cortés, Cuernavaca

The ***Cathedral**, at the corner of Calle Hidalgo and Avenida Morelos, originally belonged to a Franciscan friary founded in 1529. This fortress-like structure, begun in 1533, dates back to the time of Cortés. The side doorway is in colonial-Platersque style, and above the pediment are a crown, a cross and a skull and cross bones, all enclosed within an *alfix* (Moorish frame).

The INTERIOR of the Cathedral was restored in the 1950s, when early *wall paintings* were discovered. They depict the embarkation of Franciscan friars on a missionary voyage to Japan and the martyrdom (1597) of the only Mexican saint, San Felipe de Jesús – A popular mariachi mass is celebrated in the Cathedral on Sundays at 11.

In the rear range of conventual buildings is a *Chapel of the Third Order* with a typically Mexican Baroque façade. The beautiful carved wooden altar (1735) shows strong Indian influence. – Abutting on the Cathedral is a spacious *open chapel*, its vaulting borne on three arches; the middle columns are reinforced by two buttresses. – In the *cloister* are remains of wall paintings depicting the genealogical trees of the Franciscan order.

Opposite the Cathedral is the **Borda Garden** (*Jardín Borda*), laid out in the second half of the 18th c. by the "silver king" of the mining town of Taxco, José de la Borda. It contains terraced gardens, ponds and fountains. The Emperor Maximilian and his wife Carlota gave splendid fêtes here. Their summer residence was the *Casa de Maximiliano* in Calle Galeana (restored 1960). – About 1.5 km (1 mile) S of the town center lies the former village, now part of the town, of Acapatzingo. Here stands the *"*Casa Olinda*" and its park in peaceful, rustic surroundings. The

building, now a museum of herbs (Museo de la Herbolería), was built by the Emperor Maximilian and was used by him as a private retreat which he shared with his Indian mistress, India Bonita.

On the W side of the town is the **Salto de San Antón**, a 30 m (100 ft) high waterfall in a picturesque setting.

On the E side of the town, near the station, is the pre-Columbian site of **Teopanzolco** ("abandoned temple"), dating from the late Post-Classic period (1250–1521), which was not discovered until 1910. This last relic of the capital of the Tlahuica people is in typical Aztec style. It consists of two temple pyramids of different periods, one built over the other. A double staircase leads up to the summit of the pyramid, on which there are the

Chapel of the Third Order, Cuernavaca

remains of walls belonging to two temples. Built into the walls can be seen primitive stone animals' heads, originally covered with stucco.

SURROUNDINGS. – 40 km (25 miles) S, amid subtropical vegetation, is the crater lake of **Tequesquitengo**, on the E side of which lies the town of the same name (alt. 914 m (2999 ft); pop. 3800; hotels: Ski Club Paraíso, SP; Playa Brujo' *Hacienda Vista Hermosa; San José Vista Hermosa, SP. tennis, riding). At the edge of the township there is one of the most important private *Museum of Mussels in the world (Museo Malacologico; 30,000 examples; visiting hours restricted). The lake offers facilities for a variety of water sports.

12 km (7½ miles) NE of Tequesquitengo is **Tlaquiltenango**, with a convent founded in 1530 by Franciscans and taken over by Dominicans forty years later. Features of particular interest are the atrium, the *posas* (processional chapels) and the colonial Plateresque side doorway, which resembles that of Cuenavaca Cathedral. – 20 km (12 miles) N of Tlaquiltenango by way of Tlatizapán is the source of the Río Yautepec, with *Las Estacas*, a group of holiday bungalows (snorkeling).

35 km (22 miles) SW of Cuernavaca is the site of *Xochicalco (p. 292).

In the eastern part of Morelos state there are many places of interest, in particular a series of 16th c. convents (see p. 199).

Culiacán
See under Sinaloa

Distrito Federal (Federal District)

Abbreviation: D.F.
Area: 1483 sq. km (572 sq. miles).
Population: 10,449,800.
ⓘ **Secretaría de Turismo,**
Av. Presidente Masaryk 172,
Cuidad de México;
tel. (9 15) 2 50 85 55.

Like the District of Columbia in the United States, the Distrito Federal (Federal District) around the capital was created in order to ensure that the central government would not be subject to the influence of any of the federal states, and its administration is directly answerable to the President. The Federal District occupies the SE corner of the Valley of Mexico, being enclosed on three sides by the state of México and bounded on the S by Morelos state. Its natural boundaries are the

Sierra Guadalope in the N; the foothills of the Sierra Volcánica Transversal (here also called the Sierra Nevada on account of the two snow-capped giants Popocatépetl and Iztacíhuatl) in the E; the Las Cruces massif in the W; and in the S, where Mounts Ajusco and Cuautzin rear up, the Pass of the Three Maries (Tres Marías), near the hill of the same name. The population consists of mestizos, Creoles (descendants of Spaniards), the local Indians, who belong to the Nahua group, and members of other Indian tribes who have moved into the area.

The most interesting archeological sites, *Cuicuilco* and *Copilco*, are near the University City on the edge of the *Pedregal* lava field, which covers the southern part of the territory of Mexico City (which in turn occupies almost the whole of the northern half of the Federal District). These sites date from the Pre-Classic or Archaic period. The peak period of Aztec civilization is represented only by a few relatively insignificant remains, owing to the systematic work of destruction carried out by the Spanish conquerors: the best impression of the buildings of this period can be gained from the excavations at the corner of Calle Argentina and Av. Guatemala, near the Zócalo, and the reconstructions in the Plaza de las Tres Culturas in Tlatelolco (see under Mexico City).

HISTORY. – As the sites of El Arbolillo, Ticomán, Zacatenco, Cuicuilco and Copilco show, the Valley of Mexico (or Valley of Anáhuac) was already occupied in the Pre-Classic period (Early Formative and Middle Formative), between 1500 and 800 B.C., by tribes practicing the most primitive form of agriculture. *Tlatilco*, near the present-day Federal District, was from 1300–800 B.C. an important settlement within the Olmec cultural horizon. – During the Classic period (A.D. 300–900) the area was for a time under the influence of Teotihuacán. After the fall of Toltec Tollan (Tula) in the second half of the 13th c. a number of different tribes began to move into the Valley of Anáhuac, establishing a series of petty states, the most important of which were those of the *Tepanecs* of Atzcapotzalco ("place of the ant-hill"), the *Acolhua* of Coatlichán, the *Chichimecs* ("descended from the dog" – i.e. barbarian tribes) of Tenayuca and later of Texcoco, and the *Toltecs* of Culhuacán (Náhuatl, "place of the grandfathers").

But the people which were to rule this central valley and large territories elsewhere in Mexico during the last 150 years before the coming of the Spaniards were the Náhuatl-speaking **Aztecs** (*Tenocha* or *Mexica*). About A.D. 1111, according to the traditional account, they left their mysterious island home of Aztlán or Aztatlán (Náhuatl, "place of herons") – probably an

Mexico
United Mexican States
Estados Unidos Mexicanos

Distrito Federal

States
Estados

1a Baja California Sur	12 Aguascalientes	
1b Baja California Norte	13 Jalisco	
	14 Guanajuato	
2 Sonora	15 Querétaro	
3 Chihuahua	16 Hidalgo	
4 Sinaloa	17 Colima	
5 Durango	18 Michoacán	
6 Coahuila	19 México	
7 Nuevo León	20 Morelos	
8 Zacatecas	21 Tlaxcala	26 Chiapas
9 San Luis Potosí	22 Puebla	27 Tabasco
10 Tamaulipas	23 Veracruz	28 Campeche
11 Nayarit	24 Guerrero	29 Yucatán
	25 Oaxaca	30 Quintana Roo

D.F. Distrito Federal (Federal District)

island in a lagoon on the NW coast of Mexico – and, under the leadership of their chieftain and god Huitzilopochtli ("Humming-Bird of the South"), moved by way of Chicomoztoc ("seven caves"), the legendary starting-point of all migratory movements by Nahua peoples in the mid-12th c., into the Valley of Mexico. In 1299 this barbarian tribe, now calling themselves the *Mexica*, reached *Chapultepec* ("hill of grasshoppers"). After being subjugated by the Tepanecs they fled to Culhuacán, were driven out again and finally, in 1325 (or 1345), founded *Tenochtitlán* ("place of the cactus fruit") on an island in Lake Texcoco. According to legend Huitzilopochtli had told them to settle at the spot where they found an eagle sitting on a cactus and eating a snake. The eagle symbolizes the sun, and thus Huitzilopochtli, while the red cactus fruit represents the human heart which is consumed by the sun. These symbols still feature in the Mexican coat of arms. – Within a short time the Mexica, boldly claiming to be successors to the great Toltecs, whose cultural achievements they had taken over and made their own, were able, under the leadership of their chief priest Tenoch, to transform a swampy and inhospitable island into an economically self-sufficient community, creating *chinampas* (artificial islands: see p. 184) to provide areas of cultivable soil. In 1358 the town of *Tlatelolco* ("earthen mound") was established on a subsidiary island, and remained a rival to Tenochtitlán until it was finally brought under the authority of that city and thereafter played an important part in the Aztec empire as a trading center.

In 1372 *Acamapichtli* (Náhuatl, "a handful of reeds"), a Toltec prince from Culhuacán, ascended the throne, founding the Aztec dynasty which lasted, under eleven rulers, until the conquest of Tenochtitlán by the Spaniards in 1521. On the initiative of the Mexica a Tepanec prince was installed as ruler of Tlatelolco. In the course of the next 150 years, through marriages, changing alliances and numerous wars, the Mexica contrived not only to make themselves the dominant power in the Valley of Anáhuac (see under Texcoco) but to establish their authority over large parts of what

is now Mexico, extending almost to Guatemala. Mainly during the reigns of three warlike rulers, *Moctezuma I* ("Wrathful Lord": 1440–68), *Axayácatl* ("Water-Face": 1468–81) and *Ahuizotl* ("Ghostly Water-Face": 1486–1502), their armies conquered extensive territories in the states of México, Hidalgo, Morelos, Guerrero, Veracruz, Puebla, Oaxaca and Chiapas and exacted tribute from them. Only the lands of the *Purépecha* (Tarascans) in Michoacán and the states of *Tlaxcala* and *Meztitlán* remained unconquered and were able to preserve their independence. The last Aztec ruler was *Moctezuma II*, Cortés's adversary, who came to the throne in 1502. The peoples subjugated by the Aztecs, either by war or by threats, were required to pay large tributes to Tenochtitlán, mainly in the form of goods, slaves and military service. Permanent Aztec garrisons at strategic points, special tax-collectors and travelling Aztec merchants ensured that treaty obligations were fulfilled and promoted the spread of *Náhuatl*, which now became the lingua franca of Meso-America. – In 1517 the first Spaniard, *Francesco Hernández de Córdoba*, landed on the coast of the Yucatán peninsula, and in 1519 *Hernán Cortés* set foot on Mexican soil. This marked the beginning of the end of the Aztec empire – in which risings by the oppressed Indian peoples also played a part.

The extraordinary success of a small band of primitive nomads in creating within a few generations an empire which in the western hemisphere could be compared only with that of the Incas of Peru was mainly due to their aggressive attitude of mind, economic resources of their area of settlement and their socio-political organization. The central figure in their religion was *Huitzilopochtli*, god of war and symbol of the sun who, like the sun, died every evening and was reborn every morning. In order to ensure that the sun should pursue its daily course, and thus that human existence should continue, Huitzilopochtli had to be nourished on the most precious available substance, the blood of human beings; and accordingly one of the main objectives of war was to take prisoners who could be sacrificed to the gods.

The "Flower Wars" which were fought principally with the republican state of Tlaxcala had this as their sole purpose. In return the sun god, who was also god of war, promised the Nahua authority over the world, and his priesthood gave impetus to the expansionist urges of the Aztecs. In the course of time the scale of the sacrifices grew beyond all reason: thus it is said that during the ceremonies of Ahuítzotl's coronation no fewer than 80,000 prisoners were sacrificed by having their hearts cut out with a stone knife. Among other gods in the Aztec pantheon, many of them taken over from the subject peoples, were *Tláloc* (from *tlalli*, "earth"), god of rain and of growth; *Tezcatlipoca* ("Smoking Mirror"), god of the night sky, of destruction, of magic and of retributive justice; *Xipe Tótec* ("Our Lord the Flayed One"), god of natural renewal and of jewelers; *Quetzalcóatl* ("Feathered Serpent"), the versatile god of the morning star, the winds and the techniques of civilization; *Coatlicue* or Tonantzín ("She of the Serpent Apron"), earth goddess and mother of Huitzilopochtli; and Coatlicue's daughter *Coyolxauhqui*, goddess of the moon and of night.

The sacred calendar cycle of the Mexica covered a period of 52 years without repeating the same combination of date glyphs. At the end of this period the ceremony of the "New Fire" was performed, involving the relighting of the fire, the renewal of utensils and equipment and the re-facing of the temple pyramids. – The *chinampa* system of cultivation and the tribute paid by the subject peoples enabled the Aztecs to maintain food supplies for a large city like Tenochititlán, which had an estimated population of between 150,000 and 300,000 at the time of the Spanish conquest.

At the head of the empire was the elected king, who in practice usually came from one of the ruling families. The nobility, who gained this status from relationship to the royal house or as a reward for special military exploits, provided the empire's military and political leaders. The middle class was made up of craftsmen (*tolteca*), who were highly regarded, and the powerful guild of merchants (*pochteca*), who in addition to their commercial role also played an important part in the establishment and maintenance of the Aztec colonial empire as ambassadors and spies. Below this class were free workers and peasants, as well as non-hereditary serfs – who, however, were able to achieve promotion to a higher class by military valor. The distribution of the population between different quarters of the city (*calpulii*, "large houses"), which formed relatively independent communities within Tenochtitlán and other towns, established the basic units of military and political organization. A bureaucracy of priests and clerks administered the whole of the huge empire, collecting the tribute from the subject peoples and managing the country's trade.

The history of the Federal District, which was created by a decree of President Guadalupe Victoria, both during and after the colonial period, is identical with that of Mexico and its capital.

ECONOMY. – More than 50% of Mexico's total *industrial capacity* is concentrated in the Federal District, and the attempts made in recent years to promote decentralization are unlikely to make such difference in this respect. The most important branches of industry are iron and steel, building, automobile construction, textiles, papermaking, chemicals, glass and ceramics, machinery, electrical apparatus and foodstuffs. In addition to the central government and the headquarters of *government*

departments, the principal *banks* and *insurance corporations* have their head offices in Mexico City. The capital is also the country's main traffic junction – for *rail services*, *air services* and a considerable network of *bus services*. As the largest market and largest producer of consumption goods, it is Mexico's leading *commercial center*. Finally the numerous features of interest is Mexico City and the surrounding area and the capital's well-developed facilities of all kinds make *tourism* an important element in the economy of the Federal District.

Dolores Hidalgo
See under San Miguel de Allende

Durango (State)

State of Durango (Dgo.). – Capital: Durango.
Area: 123,520 sq. km (47,691 sq. miles).
Population: 1,266,800.

(i) **Coordinación Federal de Turismo,**
Bruno Martínez 403 Sur 305,
Durango, Dgo.
tel. (9 11 81) 2 76 44, 1 56 81.

The large and thinly populated state of Durango is bounded on the N by Chihuahua, on the W by Sinaloa, on the S by Nayarit and on the E by Zacatecas and Coahuila. Lying on the slopes of the Western Sierra Madre, it consists mainly of arid plateaus covered with lava rocks and slashed by deep gorges. The

Durango Cathedral

Mexico
United Mexican States
Estados Unidos Mexicanos

Durango

States
Estados

1a Baja California Sur	12 Aguascalientes
1b Baja California Norte	13 Jalisco
	14 Guanajuato
2 Sonora	15 Querétaro
3 Chihuahua	16 Hidalgo
4 Sinaloa	17 Colima
5 Durango	18 Michoacán
6 Coahuila	19 México
7 Nuevo León	20 Morelos
8 Zacatecas	21 Tlaxcala
9 San Luis Potosí	22 Puebla
10 Tamaulipas	23 Veracruz
11 Nayarit	24 Guerrero
	25 Oaxaca

26 Chiapas
27 Tabasco
28 Campeche
29 Yucatán
30 Quintana Roo

D.F. Distrito Federal (Federal District)

population is made up of Mestizos and Creoles (descendants of Spaniards), with some Tepehuano Indians in remote parts of the state.

There are no pre-Columbian remains in Durango. Visits can be paid to some of the settlements of te *Tepehuano Indians* (belonging to the Nahua group), which are found in only two areas (Tepehuanes and Mesquital).

HISTORY. – In pre-Hispanic times this region was inhabited by semi-nomadic tribes of *Tepehuano* and *Acaxe* Indians. The first Spaniard to come here is believed to have been the conquistador Ginés Vázquez del Mercado, who passed through the region in 1551 in a quest for precious metals. He was followed by Francisco de Ibarra, a Basque, who founded the first settlements, including Nombre de Dios (1555) and Durango (1563). Fighting with the Indians continued until 1616, when the Tepehuanos suffered a decisive defeat, but until the late 19th c. there were repeated native risings. Until 1823 Durango and Chihuahua formed the province of *Nueva Vizcaya*; thereafter they became independent states.

ECONOMY. – Durango is rich in *minerals*, including gold, silver, copper, iron, tin, sulphur and antimony. Areas watered by rivers or by artificial irrigation grow *agricultural crops* such as cotton, wheat, maize, tobacco, sugar-cane and vegetables. Contributions are also made to the economy by *livestock-farming* and *industries* processing agricultural produce. In recent years film-producers have frequently shot westerns on location in the state. *Tourism* is now also a factor of some importance, sportsmen being particularly attacted by the game available here (wild cats, bears, wolves, wild duck).

Durango (Town)

State: Durango (Dgo.).
Altitude: 1890 m (6201 ft). – Population: 320,000.
Telephone dialling code: 9 11 81.

ⓘ **Coordinación Federal de Turismo,**
Bruno Martinez 403 Sur 305,
tel. 2 76 44, 1 56 81.

HOTELS. *El Presidente*, Av. 20 Noviembre 257 Ote., L, SP, tennis; *Motel Los Arcos*, Av. 20 Noviembre 2204 Ote., I; *Posada Durán*, Av. 20 Noviembre 506 Pte., I; *Roma*, Av. 20 Noviembre Pte. 705, II; *Reyes*, Av. 20 Noviembre 220 Ote, III.

RESTAURANTS in most hotels; also *Mansión*, Juárez 315 Sur; *Mario's*, L. Cárdenas 416 Nte.; *Palapas*, F. Sarabia 112.

RECREATION and SPORTS. – Swimming, tennis, fishing, hunting.

EVENT. – July 4–12, commemoration of town's foundation.

Situated on an eastern outlier of the Sierra Madre Occidental, the town of Durango (de Victoria) commands the picturesque and fertile Guadiana valley. It has a dry and agreeable climate, and still preserves something of the atmosphere of old Spain. It is an important regional and industrial center, mainly engaged in processing the products of the surrounding area.

95. HISTORY. – In 1556 Father Diego de la Cadena founded a settlement here under the name of *San Juan de Analco*. In 1563 it was formally renamed *Durango* by Francisco de Ibarra and Alonso Pacheco; but in practice it was known only as *Villa de Guadiana* until the 18th c. As an outpost for Spaniards seeking precious metals the town was for long exposed to raids by hostile Indians, particularly the Tepehuanos. In the 17th c. peace came to the region and the establishment of an episcopal see in Durango led to a considerable cultural upsurge. In the 19th c. the town stagnated economically, and it is only in recent decades that any substantial progress has been made in this respect.

SIGHTS. – Durango is a quiet country town. In the main square (*Zócalo*) is the fine **Cathedral**, built between 1695 and 1777, which reflects the development of the Mexican Baroque during that period. Also worth seeing are the Baroque Jesuit *church of the Sagrario* and the *Casa del Conde de Suchil.*

To the N of the town is the *Cerro del Mercado*, a hill just over 200 m (650 ft) high which consists almost entirely of iron ore (haematite). Although the existence of this ore was known to the conquistadors of the 16th c. it began to be worked only in 1828. In recent years the daily output has been running at over 300 tons, and it is estimated that there is enough ore to last another hundred years.

SURROUNDINGS. – Within easy reach of Durango are a number of health resorts (chalybeate and sulfureous water), such as *Navacoyan* and *El Saltito*. – Near the town there are a series of man-made lakes (reservoirs) which offer facilities for water sports and fishing (Garabitos, La Tinaja, Guadalupe Victoria, Peña del Águila, etc. – Film enthusiasts will want to visit the area where numerous westerns have been shot. It lies N of the 12 km mark (8 miles) on Road 45 and includes part of the village of *Chupadores*.

The *road from Durango via *El Salto* (100 km/62 miles) to **Mazatlán** (320 km (200 miles): see p. 156) traverses magnificent scenery; the first part of the trip can also be done by rail. The road through this wild mountain region has many stretches with numerous bends. – On the road to Hidalgo del Parral (No. 45) an excursion can be made from *La Zarca* (about 250 km – 150 miles) on Road 30 to **Mapimí** (about 100 km – 60 miles). This old mining town is a good place to buy rare minerals. Here, in the *Sierra del Rosario*, are the so-called *Red Caves* (colored by iron oxide).

Dzibilchaltún

State: Yucatán (Yuc.).
Altitude: 12 m (39 ft.).
(i) **Coordinación Federal de Turismo,**
Itzaes 590, corner of Calle 59,
Mérida, Yuc.;
tel. (9 19 92) 1 59 89 and 3 00 95.

The site of Dzibilchaltún, only 17 km (11 miles) N of Mérida near the road to Progreso, was for a long time neglected by archeologists on account of its unspectacular architecture. Only within the last twenty years has it been established by excavation that Dzibilchaltún was the largest pre-Columbian town on the Yucatán peninsula and the one which remained in occupation for the longest period.

HISTORY. – Sporadic excavations in the 1940s showed that his was a very extensive and long-established settlement. Some time later, in 1956, Tulane University and the National Georgraphic Society began a major excavation campaign under the direction of E. Wyllys Andrews IV. Since then it has been established that Dzibilchatún ("where the flat stones bear writing" in Maya) was occupied from at least 600 B.C. and covered an area of over 50 sq. km (20 sq. miles). These facts, together with the more than 8000 buildings identified on the site, make Dzibilchaltún not only the largest and oldest Indian site in Yucatán, and probably in the whole of Mexico, but also the one with the longest continuous period of occupation. It is quite possible that the foundation of the town dates back to the Archaic period (i.e., before 1500 B.C.); and it is known that the site was still occupied when the Spaniards arrived in Mexico. It seems likely that Dzibilchatún was both a place of pilgrimage and an important political center.

Many of the excavated buildings date from the *Pre-Classic* period (3rd–1st c. B.C.), but some of them were rebuilt in the *Late Classic* period (A.D. 600–900). Here, too, were discovered for the first time a considerable number of dated stelae of the type found in southern central Mexico. The evidence produced by the excavations points to the existence of a very early independent Maya culture in Yucatán – contradicting the previously accepted view that the flourishing Classic culture (A.D. 300–900) of the southern central regions (Chiapas, Tabasco; Guatemala, Honduras) was carried northward. Extensive further excavation

Temple of the Seven Dolls, Dzibilchaltún

on this and other sites in Yucatán will be required before the revised account of early Maya history which is now evidently necessary can be written.

THE SITE. – The archeological zone contains a number of different ceremonial sites, once linked with one another by *sacbeob* ("white roads"). Only a few buildings within this extensive area have been sufficiently restored to be worth visiting. – One structure of unique type is the **Temple of the Seven Dolls** (*Templo de las Siete Muñecas*), also known as *Building 1 sub.*

The Five-Story Building, Edzná

Radiocarbon tests on remains of wood have shown that the TEMPLE dates from the 7th c. A.D. It differs from the normal type of Maya architecture not only in its simple style but also in having a square ground-plan and two *windows* on either side of the entrance – the first windows to be found in any Maya building. The *roof-comb* also departs from the traditional type, taking the form of a truncated pyramid: probably an early form designed to accommodate the internal vaulting to the square ground-plan. The temple takes its name from seven primitive *terracotta figurines* found within the building. Together with a number of smaller buildings, it stands on a platform measuring 250 by 90 m (820 by 295 ft), with staircases on all four sides.

In the *Central Group* near the present entrance to the archaeological zone is a temple, known simply as *Building 38*, with sculptured ornament and scanty remains of wall paintings. Other features of interest are the *Palacio*, the *Templo del Pedestal*, the ruins of a *church* built in 1590 and the *Museum*.

A major feature of the site was the **Cenote of Xlacah** ("Old Town") which is 30 m (100 ft) in diameter and has an estimated depth of 45 m (150 ft). From the depths of this pool divers recovered no fewer than 30,000 items of archeological interest, including pottery vessels and figurines, jewelry and a few human bones. This suggests that human sacrifice was not practiced here to any great extent. The cenote is now used for bathing.

In the center of the main square are the remains of a large Spanish open chapel, dating from the end of the 16th c. and the priest's house nearby. The position and size of the chapel show that Dzibilchaltún must have had a considerable population at the beginning of the colonial era. – At the entrance to the site is a small museum (stelae, sculptures, bones, pottery, etc. including items recovered from the cenote).

Edzná

State: Campeche (Camp.).
Altitude: sea level.

(i) **Coordinación Federal de Turismo,**
   Av. Republica 159,
   Frente a la Alameda,
   6 31 97
   Campeche, Camp.;
   tel. (9 19 81) 6 31 97 and 6 55 93.

ACCESS. – From Campeche Road 180 E to Chencoyí; then N on Road 261 to Cayal (45 km – 28 miles); from there a good road (to right) leads in 19 km (12 miles) to Edzná.

The interesting archeological site of *Edzná lies on the fringes of the Chenes cultural area (named after the place-name ending *chen*, "fountain", which is common in this region). This Maya site lies in a wide valley covered with scrub forest and areas of cultivated land and bounded on the N and E by a low range of hills.

HISTORY. – Since only a small part of the site of Edzná ("house of grimaces" in Maya) has been excavated little is known of its early history. It was clearly a settlement of the *Classic* period. The pottery found here included the familiar wares of the Early and Late Classic phases but also suggested that there was a settlement on the site before the beginning of the Christian era. The stelae excavated at Edzná are dated between A.D. 672 and 810. No evidence has so far been found of the Post-Classic period (A.D. 1000 onwards).

In the 1920s the site was studied by an American and a Mexican archeologist, Sylvanus G. Morley and Enrique Juan Palacios, who were particularly concerned with deciphering the glyphs. In the 1940s two Mexican archeologists, Alberto Ruz l'Huillier and Raúl Pavón Abreu, worked on the site, and the latter continued during the fifties and sixties, primarily with restoration work. The most recent excavations have been carried out by the New World Archeological Foundation and the Instituto Nacional de Antropologia e Historia.

THE SITE. – The archeological zone covers an area of some 6 sq. km (2½ sq. miles). Most of the buildings have not yet been excavated or have been overgrown after earlier excavations. As on many Maya sites, some of the structures were rebuilt several times, leading to difficulties in dating them. The most interesting buildings are those around the *Plaza Central*, in the center of which is a square *altar* with a small superstructure on the W side known as "La Picota".

On the E side of the plaza is the most interesting of the accessible monuments of Edzná, the ***Five-Story Building** (*Edificio de los Cinco Pisos*). This is a pyramid on an almost square base measuring 60 by 58 m (200 by 190 ft), with a staircase to the first four stories, each 4.60 m (15 ft) high. The fifth story is formed by the *temple*, which stands 5 m (16 ft) high and is topped by a roof-comb 6 m (20 ft) high. The total height of the structure is 31 m (102 ft).

It is supposed that the first four stories contained the dwellings of the priests and that the actual shrine was the temple on the top with its altar. The lowest story has masonry columns reminiscent of the Río Bec style, while the fourth story has monolithic columns with capitals, of a type common in the Puuc style. On the first floor, under the staircase, is a corbel-vaulted passage containing the entrance to the central inner chamber. – This imposing building is an example of the restrained architectural style, with plain cornices and undecorated façades, which was favored at Edzná, in sharp contrast to the architecture of the cult sites in the Chenes and Puuc cultural areas. Only the roof-comb was richly decorated with stucco figures.

On the W side of the plaza is the restored **House of the Moon** (*Casa de la Luna*, in Maya *Paal u'ná*), built on a platform and topped by the remains of a temple. The broad staircase is flanked by six tiers on either side. – At one corner of the plaza is the **Southwestern Temple** (*Templo del Suroeste*). This consists of a rectangular platform from which battered walls reminiscent of the architecture of Petén lead up to the summit terrace, on which are remains of the actual temple. – The other corner of the plaza on the same side is occupied by the *Northwestern Temple* (Temple del Noroeste) and its associated structures. Adjoining this temple is a *sweat bath* (temazcalli).

Around another plaza is a series of structures known as the *Grupo del Centro Ceremonial*, some of them not yet excavated and others excavated but overgrown with vegetation. On the E side of the plaza is the "*Great Acropolis*" (Gran Acrópolis), on the W side the *Great House* (Casa Grande or Nohol'ná), on the N side

the *Platform of the Knives* (Plataforma de los Cuchillos) and on the S side the *Southern Temple* (Templo del Sur).

Since part of the site lay under sea level, provision had to be made for drainage, and the Mayas achieved this by an ingenious system of underground channels and collecting basins.

El Sumidero
See under Tuxtla Gutiérrez

El Tajín

State: Veracruz (Ver.).
Altitude: 298 m (978 ft).
ⓘ **Coordinación Federal de Turismo,**
Av. I. Zaragoza 20 Altos Centro,
Veracruz, Ver.
tel. (91 29) 32 70 26, 32 16 13.

ACCESS. – The site is reached from Mexico City on Road 85 via Pachuca (90 km – 56 miles); then NE of Road 130 (the "Vanilla Road") to Huauchinango (170 km – 106 miles) and Poza Rica (290 km – 180 miles); from there it is 20 km (12 miles) to El Tajín. From Veracruz either via Jalapa or by the coast road (No. 180) via Nautla and Papantla. From the N (Tampico) Road 180 via Naranjos, Tuxpan and Poza Rica. – It is possible also to fly to Poza Rica and rent a car or take a taxi from there.

* El Tajín lies amid vanilla plantations in a green and hilly region with a warm and humid climate. It is one of the most important pre-Columbian sites in Mexico covering a total area of some 10 sq. km (4 sq. miles), only a small part of which has been excavated.

HISTORY. – Since the area round El Tajín ("lightning" in Totonac) was inhabited by *Totonacs* at the time of the Spanish conquest, it has been ascribed to them, but probably the site had been previously occupied and then abandoned at least 400 years before the Conquest. It may have been a late Olmec or Proro-Maya foundation in association with the Huastecs.

The beginning of major building works at El Tajín is dated to the 4th and 5th c. A.D. – i.e., to the Early Classic period. The most important structures, which show substantial influences from the *Teotihuacán culture*, were evidently built in the 6th and 7th c. In the 11th c., the final building phase, Toltec stylistic features can be detected. At the beginning of the 12th c. El Tajín ceased to exist as a city and cult center; traces of destruction and fire suggest that it was conquered by some enemy state. Thereafter this part of Veracruz state was occupied by the Totonacs, who came under the influence of the *Aztecs* in the 15th c. and were compelled to pay tribute to Tenochtitlán.

Edificio de las Columnas (Building of the Columns)

Pirámide de los Nichos (Pyramid of the Niches)

El Tajín

100 m
(110 yds)

☐ Excavated structures   Entrance

1 Juego de Pelota (Ball Court)
2 Juego de Pelota Sur (South Ball Court)
3 Monumento V
4 Monumento II
5 Plaza de la Piramide de los Nichos
6 Monumento III
7 Monumento IV
8 Juego de Pelota (Ball Court)
9 Plaza del Tajin Chico
10 Plataforma
11 Edificio C
12 Edificio B
13 Edificio A
14 Edificio E
15 Edificio D
16 Juego de Pelota Norte

After the Spanish conquest (1519–21) no attention was paid to El Tajin. The first *Spaniard* to visit it and give some account of the site was Diego Ruiz in 1785. Later it was also visited by Alexander von Humboldt (1811) and the Austrian traveller W. Dupaix (1836). Systematic excavation began only in 1934 under the direction of a Mexican archeologist, José Garcia Payón, and was continued by S. Jeffrey K. Wilkerson. Of the archeological site extending over some 12 hectares (30 acres) it is estimated that only about one tenth has been uncovered.

THE SITE. – Just inside the entrance to the site is the *Plaza del Arroyo*, surrounded by four mounds of earth concealing pyramids which have not yet been excavated. Here, too, likewise concealed under the earth, is the first of the eleven ball courts so far identified at El Tajín. – Just beyond this is the impressive *South Ball Court (Juego de Pelota Sur)*. At the ends of the side walls are panels of *bas-reliefs*, lying between horizontal friezes of stylized serpent motifs. There are four principal scenes – the dedication of a young warrior, who is shown standing in front of gods or priests; a ball-player being held on a sacrificial altar by one priest while

another plunges an obsidian knife in his breast; two ball-players conversing with one another, holding a *yugo* and *palma*, watched by divinities, one of whom is masked; and the dedication of a ball-player, shown lying on a bench, probably to the god of the ball game (*tlachtli*), who is symbolized by the sun bird hovering above.

The remains found at El Tajín indicate that this was a **center of the ball game** which originated on the Gulf coast and was played over an immense area in Meso-America. Characteristic of the Indian cultures of the Gulf coast and particularly of El Tajín are the objects known as *yugos* (yokes), *hachas* (axes) and *palmas* (palms). The *yugos* are richly decorated horseshoe-shaped objects carved from stone which may weigh up to 30 kg (65 lbs); the *hachas* are thin axe-like stone blades, usually decorated with human faces and openwork ornament; the *palmas* are finely carved triangular wedges which were added to *yugos* as ornamental features. All three are now believed to have been reproductions in stone of wooden items of equipment used in the ball game. They are among the most artistic and elaborate achievements of the pre-Columbian sculptors.

In the *Plaza of the Pyramid of the Niches* there are a number of structures in addition to the main pyramid – Monuments II, III, IV and V, the most notable being *II* and *V*. On the W side of the plaza is the unique ****Pyramid of the Niches** (*Pirámide de los Nichos*), 25 m (82 ft) high, on a base 35 m (115 ft) square, which was dedicated to the rain and wind gods.

The pyramid, built between the 6th and 7th c., has seven stories, including the temple. Around the sides, tier upon tier, are 365 shallow square niches symbolizing the 365 days of the year, each niche being surrounded by a frame of projecting stone slabs. Until recently it was thought that these niches originally held figures, but the present view is that they served a purely decorative purpose. The exterior of the stucture was originally faced with colored stucco and the niches were painted in brilliant colors, probably to create a mystical effect of light and shade.

Pyramid of the Niches, El Tajín

The "flying men" of Papantla

On either side of the 10 m (33 ft) wide staircase is a *balustrade* decorated with carved meander (irregular mosaic) patterns. The staircase was a later addition and has more of the character of a ladder than of a staircase. Set at regular intervals up the staircase are five groups of three smaller niches. – As so frequently happened in this pre-Columbian architecture, the pyramid was built over an earlier structure of the same type.

The mast which formerly stood on the plaza has been moved outside the archeological area; at certain times it is used for the *Dance of the Flying Men* (Danza de los Voladores).

A road runs N to the later part of the site and the *Plaza El Tajín Chico*. The structures first encountered here are Buildings K, C, B, A and Q, the most notable of which are *Buildings C, A* and *Q*. The finest structure in this area is the **Building of the Columns** (*Edificio de las Columnas*), which covers an area of 35,000 sq. m (42,000 sq. yds). It stands on a small mound, which is partly man-made and thus reaches a total height of 45 m (150 ft) above the plaza.

The *niches* on this building are decorated with meander patterns. The *cornices* seem to defy the laws of gravity. An extraordinary feature is that the massive *staircases* could not be used to climb to the top but served purely as decoration. It is now known that ladders had to be used to enter the rooms on the higher levels. The roofs are covered with a kind of concrete found nowhere else in Meso-America. – At the base of the building are a number of huge **column drums** 1.20 m (4 ft) in diameter, originally belonging to a gallery which ran along the front of the building. They are decorated with bas-reliefs depicting scenes involving warriors and priests, human sacrifices and hieroglyphs. Toltec stylistic features are frequently evident. On the E side of the topmost story are panels with *cruciform reliefs*. From the summit of the structure there is a magnificent view of the whole archeological zone.

In the same group is the *Tunnel Building* (Edificio de los Túneles), from which two underground passages lead to a large courtyard to the W of the structure.

SURROUNDINGS. – 16 km (10 miles) from the site is **Papantla** (alt. 290 m (950 ft); pop. 50,000; hotels: Totonacapán; Tajín; Papantla; San Antonio; fiestas: New Year, Corpus Christi, early June Fiesta de la Vainilla, All Saints), an attractive town in a hilly region of dense tropical forests, surrounded by the largest vanilla plantations in America. Papantla is famous for its *voladores*, the "fliers" who perform their astonishing act on special festivals, particularly during the week-long fiesta of Corpus Christi.

The ceremony was originally part of an ancient religious drama based on the myth of the young maize which is depicted in pictographic writings of the pre-Hispanic period. Four dancers and a musician climb up a tall mast; the musician then plays and dances on a small platform on the top, while the four "flying men" (*Tocotines*) – who have ropes wound around their bodies and tied to their feet, the other end being attached to a rotating device on top of the pole – launch themselves off the platform and swing down, head first, circling around as the ropes unwind until they reach the ground. This ritual ceremony is mainly performed by the Totonacs, but also by the Huastecs and Otomí. Similar performances are found among the Chorti in Honduras and the Quiché in Guatemala.

It is 40 km (25 miles) on Road 180 to **Tecolutla** (hotels: Marsol, SP; Posada del Virrey, SP; Playa), on the Gulf coast. This pleasant little town, surrounded by luxuriant vegetation, is a favorite family resort, with a flat sandy beach.

19 km (12 miles) NW of El Tajín is **Poza Rica** (alt. 60 m (197 ft); pop. 150,000; hotels: Poza Rica, Robert Prince, Aurora, Tapatico), which has grown in size in recent years with the development of the oil industry.

18 km (11 miles) N of Poza Rica lies Tihuatlán, from which a road lead to Teayo (20 km – 12 miles).

In the main square of the village stands a well-restored pyramid, the **Castillo de Teayo**, a three-story structure with the remains of a rectangular temple on top. Pieces of sculpture, mostly of Aztec origin and mostly found in the neighborhood, are displayed along the sides of the pyramid, and there are other similar pieces to be seen in the districts of Zapotitlán and La Cruz. It had earlier been believed that the pyramid was built by the Aztecs in the 15th c. at this base in Totonac territory, but the view is now held by a number of archeologists that it was erected centuries earlier by Toltecs from Tula. The present village was established only just over a century ago, and the inhabitants used material from the old Indian structure to build their houses.

58 km (36 miles) N of Poza Rica, 10 km (6 miles) inland, is the river port of **Tuxpan** (pop. 85,000; hotels: Plaza, Playa Azul, Posada El Campanario; outside the town Tajín), noted for the first-rate fresh-water and deep-sea fishing it offers. Popular fishing competitions are held here at the end of June and beginning of July.

Ensenada
See under Baja California

Federal District
See Distrito Federal

Guadalajara

State: Jalisco (Jal.).
Altitude: 1552 m (5092 ft). – Population: 3,800,000.
Telephone dialing code: 91 36.

(i) **Coordinación Federal de Turismo,**
Lázaro Cárdenas 3289, 1st floor,
Col. Chapalita;
tel. 22 41 30, 22 41 52, 22 41 67, 22 41 90.

HOTELS. – *Fiesta Americana*, Aurelio Aleves 225, L,
SP, tennis; *Camino Real*, Av. Vallarta 5005, L, SP,
tennis; *El Tapatio*, Bulevar Aeropuerto 4275, L, SP,
tennis, golf; *Guadalajara Sheraton*, Av. Niños Héroes,
L, SP; *Holiday Inn*, López Mateos 2500, L, SP, golf;
Fénix, Av. Corona 160, I, SP; *Castel Plaza del Sol*, Av.
M. Otero y López Mateos, I, SP; *Calinda Roma*, Av.
Juárez 170, I, SP; *Colón*, Av. Revolución Pte, 12, II;
Motel Colonial, López Mateos Sur 1617, II; *Morales*,
Av. Corona 243, II; *Ana-Isabel*, Calle Javier Mina 164,
III; *Posada España*, López Cotilla 594, III.

RESTAURANTS in most hotels; also *Cazadores*,
Niños Héroes 62 and Golfo de Mexico 606; *Hacienda
de la Flor*, Aurelio Ortega 764; *Le Bistrot*, Av. Vallarta
1275; *Tecare*, Av. 16 Septiembre 157; *Recco*, Av.
Libertad 1973; *Fulano's* Av. de la Paz 2155; *La Copa
de Leche*, Av. Juárez 414.

RECREATION and SPORTS. – Swimming, tennis,
golf, riding, shooting.

EVENT. – October 4–12, Fiesta de la Virgen de
Zapopan.

**Guadalajara, Mexico's second lar-
gest city, lies on a low hill in the
fertile high valley of Atemajac and
enjoys an equable subtropical climate. As a result of its long period of
isolation from the Mexican capital
it has been able, as chief town
of Jalisco state, to preserve the
independent character of a town
conscious of its own traditions with
something of a European atmosphere. The Tapatíos, as the people
of Guadalajara call themselves, have
contrived, thanks to their prosperity
and their artistic sense, to create an
attractive city of broad avenues,
carefully tended parks and trim
light-colored buildings. Even the
drive for modernization of recent
years has done little to spoil the**
friendly, comfortable *atmosphere
of Guadalajara.

Guadalajara is not only a center of
mariachi music but a stronghold of the
charreadas (the Mexican version of the
rodeo) and the popular folk dance,
the *Jarabe Tapatío* – three things which to
the foreigner express the very essence of
Mexican folk traditions.

HISTORY. – The history of Guadalajara in pre-
Columbian times paralleled that of Jalisco (see
p. 146) and neighboring regions. – The first temporary
settlements established by the Spanish conquistadors
in this western region were abandoned between 1530
and 1542, but in the latter year Pérez de la Torre
founded Guadalajara (named after the Spanish town
of that name) on its present site. In 1560 it became
capital of the province of *Nueva Galicia*. Its distance
from Mexico City and its isolated situation preserved
Guadalajara from any major setbacks during the wars
of the 19th and 20th c. Notable events in the history of
the town were Miguel Hidalgo's declaration on the
abolition of slavery in 1810, the defeat of Hidalgo and
Allende by Spanish forces in 1811 and the occupation
by French troops between 1863 and 1866. Guadalajara was not connected with Mexico City by rail until
the end of the 19th c.

SIGHTS. – The central feature of Guadalajara is a magnificent group of four squares
arranged in the form of a cross, with the
city's principal public buildings set
around them. In the finest of the four
squares, the *Plaza de Armas*, is the
Government Palace (*Palacio de Gobierno*, 1643–1774), a splendid Baroque
building (columns with zigzag ornamentation, large volutes, Churrigueresque
estípites). On the staircase and in one of
the council chambers are *murals (Hidalgo in the war of independence, 1936–9;
heroes of the three great Mexican wars,
1948–9) by the famous fresco-painter
José Clemente Orozco, a native of
Jalisco.

Government Palace, Guadalajara

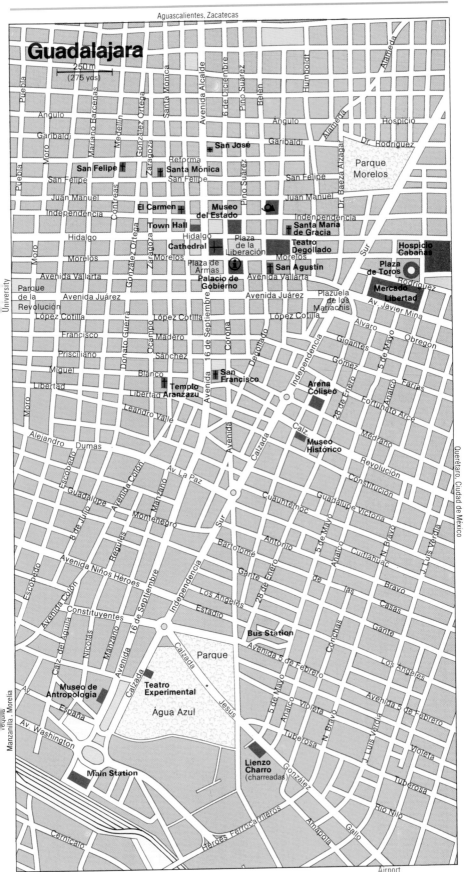

Plaza de la Liberación and Cathedral, Guadalajara

On the N side of the Plaza de Armas, with its façade fronting the square to the W (large fountain), is the **Cathedral**, with the *Sagrario*. Built between 1558 and 1616 and much altered in later periods, the Cathedral is basically Baroque but shows a remarkable mingling of different styles (naive Gothic, neo-classical, etc.). In the chapels and the Sagrario are pictures attributed to Cristóbal de Villalpando, Miguel Cabrera and Murillo. A painting ascribed to Murillo hangs over the doorway of the sacristy.

To the NW is the modern colonial-style *Town Hall*. Three blocks farther NW stands the ***church of Santa Mónica** (first half of 17th c.). The Baroque façade, with Solomonic (twisted) columns, is covered with rich and intricately carved ornamentation (grapes, cobs of maize, angels, double eagles, symbols of religious orders). At the corner is an early and impressive *statue of St Christopher*. – Other Baroque churches in Guadalajara are *San Francisco* (17th c.), *San Felipe Neri* (17th c.), *Aránzazu* (17th–18th c.: Churrigueresque retablos), *San Juan de Dios* (18th c.) and *San Agustín* (16th–17th c.).

In a former seminary in the *Plaza de la Rotunda*, to the N of the Cathedral, is the *Regional Museum* (Museo del Estado de Jalisco), which covers a wide range including archeology (western states and W coast), ethnography (Huicholes, Cora Indians), pictures (colonial art of the 17th–19th c., European painters of the 16th–19th c., modern Mexican pictures and frescoes), religious objects, historical collections and paleontology, – SE of the Museum, in the Plaza de la Liberación, is the mid-19th c. **Teatro Degollado** (formerly *Teatro Alarcón*) a large neo-classical building with frescoes by Gerardo Suárez (scenes from Dante's "Divine Comedy") in the dome.

Four blocks E of the Theater is the **Hospicio Cabañas** (now part of the recently created Plaza Tapatío), a neo-classical orphanage built by Manuel Tolsá at the beginning of the 19th c., with no fewer than twenty-three patios. In a former chapel can be seen what are probably Orozco's finest **frescoes, painted in 1938–9 (the Elements; Art and Sciences; the Conquest; the Four Riders of the Apocalypse). There are other interesting murals (Dante's "Inferno") in the auditorium of the *University* in Avenida Vallarta. – A little way SW of the Hospicio is the huge **Market Hall** (*Mercado Libertad*), where in addition to the usual wares regional costumes and pottery, paper flowers, musical instruments and live birds are offered for sale. – Between Avenida Javier Mina and Calle Obregón is the *Plazuela de los Mariachis*, in which mariachi orchestras demonstrate their skill and are available for hire.

From here the Calzada Independencia runs SW to the beautiful **Parque Agua Azul**, around which are the *Casa de las*

Artesanías (exhibition and sale of folk arts and crafts), a small *Anthropological Museum*, an *open-air theater*, a *bird park*, a *flower market* and the *House of Culture*. – In Avenida Vallarta, to the W, stands the former home and studio of the painter José Clemente Orozco (1883–1949), now an **Orozco Museum**, with many pictures and drawings by Orozco.

On the outskirts of Guadalajara, near the new residential district of LAS FUENTES, is the *Pyramid of Ixtépete*, which measures 44 by 36 m (144 by 118 ft) at the base.

SURROUNDINGS. – Some 6 km (4 miles) SE of the city center is the suburb of *San Pedro Tlaquepaque (small Ceramic Museum, shops selling ceramics, glass and antiques). This was a great pottery center even before the Conquest, and still is today. – 7 km (4½ miles) beyond this is **Tonalá**, noted for its fine pottery, in characteristic patterns and a variety of forms. In pre-Columbian times Tonalá was capital of the state of Tonalán.

Tlaquepaque pottery

8 km (5 miles) NW of the city center is **Zapopan**, an old Indian settlement, now also a suburb of Guadalajara. It is widely famed for its 17th c. Baroque Franciscan church dedicated to the city's patroness, the Virgin of Zapopan. During the summer the statue of the Virgin is set up in various churches in the city in rotation, and on October 4 it is brought back to Zapopan in an impressive procession (dancers, charros, mariachi orchestras, etc.). There is also a Huichol Indian museum in this district.

50 km (30 miles) SE of Guadalajara lies the **Laguna de Chapala** (p. 92), with a number of picturesque little places around its shores which are popular with summer vacationers.

Guanajuato (State)

State of Guanajuato (Gto.). – Capital: Guanajuato.
Area: 30,575 sq. km (11,805 sq. miles).
Population: 3,470,400.
(i) **Coordinación Federal de Turismo,**
Galarza 90,
Guanajuato, Gto.;
tel. (9 14 73) 2 01 23, 2 01 19, 2 02 14,
2 02 44.

Guanajuato, the heartland of Mexico during the colonial period, is bounded on the N by the state of San Luis Potosí, on the W by Jalisco, on the S by Michoacán and on the E by Querétaro. Predominantly mountainous, with fertile valleys and plains, it is part of the Bajío, the granary of the central Mexican plateau. In addition to its capital, Guanajuato, the state has several handsome colonial towns which together with its beautiful scenery and numerous health resorts make it a popular tourist region. The population includes Creoles, mestizos and Indians of the Otomí and Chichimeco-Jonaz tribes as well as Tarascans. There are small archeological sites in Ibarilla near León, Aquaespinoza near Dolores Hidalgo, Cañada de la Virgen near San Miguel de Allende and Oduña near Comonfort.

HISTORY. – At an early stage the Otomí mingled with the Chichimecs in this region; then in the 15th c. *Tarascans* (Purépecha) and *Aztecs* (Mexica) moved in and eventually became dominant. After the fall of the Aztec empire the first *Spaniards*, led by Nuño Beltrán de Guzmán, arrived (*c.* 1526) in what is now the state of Guanajuato (Tarascan *Cuanax-huato*, "hilly place of the frogs"). Simultaneously with the first discoveries of minerals, areas of fertile land were granted to Spanish settlers as encomiendas. The subsequent history of the region during the colonial period and after Independence is substantially that of the larger towns in the state. Until 1824 Guanajuato

Characteristic Guanajuato pottery

Mexico
United Mexican States
Estados Unidos Mexicanos

Guanajuato

States
Estados

1a Baja California Sur	12 Aguascalientes
1b Baja California Norte	13 Jalisco
2 Sonora	14 Guanajuato
3 Chihuahua	15 Querétaro
4 Sinaloa	16 Hidalgo
5 Durango	17 Colima
6 Coahuila	18 Michoacán
7 Nuevo León	19 México
8 Zacatecas	20 Morelos
9 San Luis Potosí	21 Tlaxcala
10 Tamaulipas	22 Puebla
11 Nayarit	23 Veracruz
	24 Guerrero
	25 Oaxaca

26 Chiapas
27 Tabasco
28 Campeche
29 Yucatán
30 Quintana Roo

D.F. Distrito Federal (Federal District)

was joined with Querétaro as an administrative unit under Spanish control.

ECONOMY. – The state has a well-developed system of *communications* by road and rail. Guanajuato once had the most productive *silver mines* in the world, now largely worked out. Other *minerals* worked include gold, tin, lead, copper, mercury and opals. *Industry* is mainly concerned with the processing of wheat, cotton, sheep's wool and alcohol; there are also some smelting works and pottery production. In the fertile southern part of the state there is a productive *agriculture* (maize, wheat, tobacco), and *livestock farming* also makes a contribution to the economy. *Tourism* now also plays an important part.

In addition to the capital, ****Guanajuato** (see below), the state has numerous other places of interest to the tourist, including ****San Miguel de Allende** (p. 241), ***Atotonilco** (p. 244), **Dolores Hidalgo** (p. 244), **Celaya** (p. 91), ***Yuriria** (p. 92), **Salamanca** (p. 234), **Irapuato** (p. 235) **León** (p. 153) and **Acámbaro** (alt. 1947 m (6388 ft); pop. 66,000; hotels: Posada Virrey de Mendoza, Paris; small archeological museum, Tarasces, Otomi, Mazahua).

Guanajuato (Town)

State: Guanajuato (Gto.).
Altitude: 2050 m (6726 ft). – Population: 82,000.
Telephone dialing code: 9 14 73.
ⓘ **Coordinación Federal de Turismo,**
Galarza 90;
tel. 2 01 23, 2 01 19, 2 02 14, 2 02 44.

HOTELS. – **El Presidente*, Carr. Vieja a Marfil 2 km, L, SP, tennis; **Castillo de Santa Cecilia*, 1 km (¾ mile) on Dolores Hidalgo road, L, SP; **Parador San Javier*, Plaza Aldama, L, SP; **Real de Minas*, Nejayote 17, L, SP; *Villa de la Plata*, 1.5 km (1 mile) on Dolores Hidalgo road, I, SP; *San Diego*, Jardin de la Unión 1, I; *Motel Valenciana*, 2.5 km (1½ miles) on Dolores Hidalgo road, I, SP; *Hosteria del Frayle*, Sopena 3, II; *Hacienda de Cobos*, Padre Hidalgo 3, II.

RESTAURANTS in most hotels; also *L'Antorcha*, Carr. Panoramica near the El Pípila statue; *La Tasca de los Santos*, Plaza de la Paz 28; *Valadéz*, Jardín de la Unión; *La Manzana*, Plazuela San Fernando 27.

RECREATION and SPORTS. – Swimming, tennis, golf, boat trips.

EVENTS. – January 20, Día de San Sebastián; second half October–early November, International Cervantes Festival (opening times vary); June 23, Fiesta de la Olla; July 31, Fiesta de la Bufa.

**Guanajuato, capital of the state of the same name, extends along a narrow valley and up the lower slopes of the bare hills on either side. The trim houses, often painted in bright colours, the narrow streets and lanes, the snug little squares and the old colonial buildings give the town a charm which is all its own; and its rich cultural life combines with the visual attractions of the townscape to make Guanajuato one of the most popular tourist centers in Mexico.

HISTORY. – In pre-Columbian times the region was occupied by Tarascans, who called the settlement here *Cuanax-huato* ("hilly place of the frogs"). – Between 1526 and 1529 the region was conquered and settled by the Spaniards, led by Nuño Beltrán de Guzmán. By the middle of the 16th c. the first silver mines were opened up, establishing the prosperity of the town. In 1557 the settlement was given the name of *Santa Fé y Real de Minas de Quanaxhuato*, and in 1741 was granted a municipal charter.

Shortly after the declaration of Mexican independence in 1810 Ignacio de Allende succeeded in occupying the town after Juan José de los Reyes Martínez, known as El Pípila (the "Turkeycock"), had blown up the entrance to the Spanish fort of Alhóndiga de Granaditas and compelled the garrison to surrender, but the town was soon afterwards retaken by royalist forces under General Félix M. Calleja. In 1811 the severed heads of the leaders of the fight for independence – Hidalgo, Allende, Jiménez and Aldama – were hung at the corners of the Alhóndiga de Granaditas, remaining there until Mexico achieved independence in 1821. – During the Guerra de la Reforma (1857–60) Guanajuato was capital of the Republic for a month at the beginning of 1858. – During the dictatorship of Porfirio Díaz (1876–1911) foreign capital flowed into the mines, and the town enjoyed a great surge of prosperity, during which many public buildings such as the Teatro Juárez, the Mercado Hidalgo and the Palacio Legislativo were erected. – Guanjuato, with its Festival and its University, is now a center of intellectual life.

SIGHTS. – In the beautiful main square, the *Jardín de la Unión* or *Zócalo*, stands the **Teatro Juárez**, an opera house in neo-classical style with Doric columns, which was opened in 1903, having taken thirty years to complete. Beside it is the elegant *church of San Diego, altered and rebuilt during the 17th and 18th c., with a Churrigueresque façade.

From here the Avenida Benito Juárez leads to the *Plaza de la Paz* (Peace Square), in which, to the right, is the Baroque **Basilica of Nuestra Señora de Guanajuato**, formerly the parish church. In the church, originally 17th c. but much altered thereafter, is a much revered statue of the *Virgin of Guanajuato, a carved wooden figure on a silver base which is believed to date from the 7th c. and was presented to Guanajuato by King Philip II of Spain in 1557.

Also in the Plaza de la Paz is the **Casa Rul y Valenciana**, a neo-classical mansion built by Francisco Eduardo Tresguerras at the end of the 18th c. for the Conde de Rul, a wealthy mine owner. Alexander von Humboldt stayed in this house for a short time in 1803. – On either side of the Avenida Juárez are a number of picturesque little squares or *plazuelas*. Off the Plazuela de los Angeles (to left) opens the *Callejón del Beso* ("Kissing Lane"), so called because the narrowness of the lane, which is only 68 cm (2 ft 3 in.) wide, allowed a loving couple to kiss from windows on opposite sides. Farther along, on the left, is the *Mercado Hidalgo*, a market hall opened in 1910. – Opposite the market is a street leading to the *Templo de Belén* (Bethlehem), a conventual church begun in 1773, with a Churrigueresque façade.

View of the center of Guanajuato

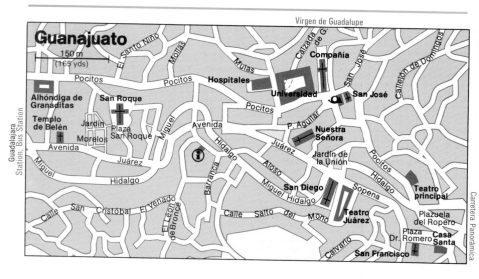

A picturesque lane in old Guanajuato

A little way N is the **Alhóndiga de Granaditas** (1799), a plain and unadorned building which was originally a granary. Thereafter it was used as a prison and a fort, the gate of which was blown up by "El Pípila", Guanajuato's folk hero. It now houses the museum of the same name containing archeological and ethnological material from the region (e.g. Chupícuaro), as well as relics and souvenirs of the political, sociological and economic history of the district. On the staircase are murals by José Chávez Morado (1955–66) depicting scenes from the fight for independence, the revolutionary wars and folk tradition. At the corners of the Alhóndiga can be seen the hooks on which the heads of the executed freedom fighters were displayed in iron cages for ten years.

In Calle de los Pocitos, at the corner of Calle Mollas, is the *birthplace* of the famous mural painter *Diego Rivera* (1886–1957), now a museum devoted to the artist and his work. – To the SW in the *Plaza San Roque* stands the Baroque church of San Roque. This square makes a picturesque setting for performances – given annually by the University on special occasions – as, for example, during the Cervantes Festival – of the "Entremeses Cervantinos" ("Cervantine Interludes"), one-act plays by Miguel de Cervantes Saavedra (1547–1616), better known as the author of "Don Quixote", who gave this genre its definitive form. – Near the end of Calle de los Pocitos stands the former residence of the Marqués San Juan de Royas, built in 1776 and now the *Municipal Museum* (Museo del Pueblo de Guanajuato). In this museum the exhibits on display are changed from time to time (works by the painter José Chávez Morado; collections of folk art, etc.).

To the N of the Museum the main building of the **University** (rebuilt 1955) is approached by an impressive flight of steps; it is built of white stone in a colonial style showing Moorish influence which fits very naturally into the townscape of Guanajuato. – On the E side of the University is the massive bulk of the

church of La Compañía de Jesús, a Jesuit foundation of 1747. The façade is in Churrigueresque style, the mighty dome neo-classical. The church contains two pictures by the great Mexican painter Miguel Cabrera.

On the way back to the main square we pass the *Plazuela del Barratillo*, with an attractive fountain presented to the town by the Emperor Maximilian.

It is worth driving along the *Avenida Miguel Hidalgo* (which follows the line of an old river bed, running underground for part of the way) into the *Carretera Panorámica*, from which there are magnificent *views of the town and surroundings. Along this road to the SW is a **Monument to El Pípila**. – Also worth seeing are the *churches* of *San Francisco, Guadalupe, Cata and Pardo* (which has the façade of the old church of San Juan Rayas).

The Baroque church of La Valenciana

In the Mummy Museum

SURROUNDINGS. – The Calzada de Tepetapa runs past the station, in the direction of Guadalajara, to the *Municipal Cemetery* (Panteón Municipal), which has a macabre *Mummy Museum* (*Museo de las Monias*). Here, in a crypt, mummified bodies are displayed in glass cases, their excellent state of preservation being apparently due to mineral salts contained in the soil of the cemetery. – 4 km (2½ miles) farther on is **Marfil** (hotels: El Laurel, Villa Cervantinas), an old mining town in which some of the old houses have been restored and reoccupied by new owners, including foreigners. The gardens and the old chapel (now part of the hotel El Presidente) of the *Hacienda San Gabriel* are worth a visit.

16 km (10 miles) beyond this on the road to Silao a side road branches off on the right to the *Cerro del Cubilete* (2700 m – 8860 ft), on which is a conspicuous statue of Christ the King (El Cristo Rey) almost 23 m (75 ft) high. The statue (by Fidias Elzondo and Carlos Olvera, 1922–9) is much visited by pilgrims and day-trippers and affords a superb

panoramic *view of the Bajío and the forest-covered hills of Tarascan territory. The Cerro del Cubilete is regarded as the geographical center of Mexico.

5 km (3 miles) from Guanajuato on the Dolores Hidalgo road is the **church of La Valenciana* or *San Cayetano*, built by the Conde de Valenciana, Antonio Obregón y Alcocer, owner of the famous silver mine of La Valenciana (below).

The church, built in pink *cantera* stone and consecrated in 1788, represents the great final period of the Mexican "Ultra-Baroque". It has only one of the intended two towers, the other not having been built. The façade is in late Churrigueresque style, while the windows along the sides have neo-Mudéjar arches. Particularly attractive is the side doorway into the church from the garden, with an elaborately shaped and decorated scallop shell and a statue of St Joseph. – The church contains three splendid Churrigueresque retablos, partly gilded and partly polychrome. Note also the fine intarsia work of ivory and precious woods on the pulpit. Another striking feature is the doorway into the sacristy, with a carved stone lambrequin above the Mudéjar arch. The arches are particularly elegant, with their bands of intricate ornamentation in *tezontle* stone.

Near the church is the interesting *La Valenciana silver mine*, which has recently been reopened. It was discovered in 1766 by Antonio Obregón y Alcocer, a miner who became a mine owner and Conde de Valencia rapidly became the most productive mine in the world, employing up to 3300 miners in shafts penetrating to a depth of 500 m (1650 ft). Some of the old buildings have fallen into ruin or disappeared altogether, but visitors can still see the pyramid-shaped walls over which Indian workers hauled the ropes bringing up the baskets of ore.

Guaymas

State: Sonora (Son.).
Altitude: 8 m (26 ft). – Population: 135,000.
Telephone dialling code: 9 16 22.

(i) **Coordinación Federal de Turismo,**
Blvd. Eusebio Kino/Esq. Roman,
Yocupicio Edif. Pitic– 6,
Hermosillo, Son.;
tel. (9 16 21) 4 63 04, 2 78 84, 2 79 90.

Guaymas, on the Gulf of California

HOTELS. – *IN THE TOWN: Motel del Puerto, Yañéz 92,
II; Impala, Calle 21 Nr. 40, II; Motels on Carretera
Internacional: Flamingos, II, SP; Malibu, II, SP;
Guadalajara, II; on Carretera al Varadero Nacional: Las
Playitas, II (trailer park); Bahía Bacochibampo (Playa
Miramar): *Playa de Cortés, I, SP, tennis; Bahía San
Carlos: Fiesta San Carlos, I, SP; Nueva Posada de San
Carlos, I, SP; Solimar, I, SP; El Crestón, I, SP.

RESTAURANTS in most hotels; also IN THE TOWN: El
Paraiso, Av. Rodríguez 20. – IN SAN CARLOS: Country
Club, El Yate, El Patio Mexicano de Shangri-La, Jax
Snax.

RECREATION and SPORTS. – Swimming, water
skiing, diving, fishing, deep-sea fishing, tennis, golf,
riding, hunting.

EVENTS. – Fiestas: May 18, Día de San José; June 24,
Día de San Juan Bautista. – Sailing regattas, fishing
competitions.

**The port of Guaymas lies in a quiet
bay in the Mar de Cortés, as the Gulf
of California is called here, surrounded by an impressive landscape of
bare hills. A ridge of high ground
separates the port area from the
popular bathing beaches in the bays
of Bacochibampo and San Carlos.**

HISTORY. – The first Spaniards explored the bay in
1535 and named it Guaima after a tribe of Seri Indians.
About 1700 Father Francisco Eusebio Kino founded
the mission station of San José de Guaymas near the
present harbor, but the little township of Guaymas de
Zaragoza was not established until 1769. As a port
shipping large quantities of precious metals from the
hinterland, Guaymas frequently attracted the attentions of pirates and adventurers and the intervention of
foreign countries. In 1847-8, during the war with the
United States, it was occupied by US troops; and six
years later a French expedition under Comte Gaston
Raousset de Boulbon tried to seize Guaymas in order
to found a private colony in Sonora – an attempt which
was unsuccessful and ended in the capture and
shooting of the count. In 1865, during the War of
Intervention, the town was occupied by French
troops. Its later history is that of the state of Sonora.

SIGHTS. – The town has few features of
great tourist interest apart from the church
of San Fernando, the offices of the Banco
de Sonora and the Town Hall (Palacio
Municipal). It is, however, a very popular
holiday resort on account of the facilities
it offers for water sports of all kinds,
particularly *deep-sea fishing (sailfish,
fanfish, swordfish, etc.). Among the most
popular beaches are Miramar, San

Plaza de Armas, Alamos (Sonora state)

Francisco, San Carlos, Lalo and *Catch 22.*
Worthwhile excursions can be made to
the islands of San Nicolás, Santa Catalina
and San Pedro where there are now good
facilities for diving and for observing the
birds and sealions.

In recent years an attractive tourist center,
especially for fishing and diving enthusiasts, has developed around the village of
San Carlos (pop. 3000), 20 km (12 miles)
from Guaymas.

SURROUNDINGS. – Around the town are a number
of interesting old haciendas. – Some 10 km (6 miles)
N of Guaymas is the village of *San José de Guaymas*,
with an 18th c. Jesuit pilgrimage church. – 36 km
(22 miles) N of Guaymas is the *Selva Encantada
("Enchanted Forest"), a huge cactus grove which is
the nesting-place of many parrots. Some 80 km (50
miles) N of Guaymas on Road 15 a minor road bears
left and in a further 6 km (4 miles) comes to *La
Pintada*. From here it is a 20-minute climb along the
walls of a gorge where there are *interesting rock
paintings attributed to the Seri Indians. Predominantly
in black, yellow ochre and red are scenes of hunting,
dancing, riding and boating as well as representations
of animals and heraldic devices. There is a ferry service
from Guaymas to *Santa Rosalía* in Baja California.

SE of Guaymas, along the lower course of the Rio
Yaqui between Ciudad Obregón and the Gulf of
California, are eight villages – *Cócorit, Bácum, Tórim,
Belém, Vicam, Pótam, Ráhum and Huírivis* – occupied
by **Yaqui Indians**, a tribe numbering over 15,000
which belongs to the large Uto-Aztec language
family. The origins of this once warlike people, never
completely subjugated by the Spaniards, are buried in
obscurity, but until the middle of the 19th c. they were
widely distributed over the state of Sonora. At the turn
of the century numbers of rebellious Yaquis were
deported to Yucatán by the Mexican government, but
later almost all of them returned. In 1927 there was
another Yaqui rising against the government, which
ended with the death of their last war leader, Luis
Matuz. The Yaquis are now mainly occupied in
farming, hunting and fishing.

The religious practices of the Yaquis are a mixture of
Indian and Catholic elements. An important part is
played in their social structure by various "frater-
nities", particularly that of the magicians and
soothsayers, who on the one hand are medicine-men
able to drive out evil spirits and on the other hand take
part in church festivals. Most social and religious rites
involve *dances*, the best known of which is the Stag
Dance (*danza del venado*). To the Yaquis and the
related Mayo tribe the stag is sacred as the incarnation
of the Forces of Good. Features of Yaqui music,
particularly its rhythms, have been used by modern
Mexican composers, including Carlos Chávez, in
symphonic works. Among the principal festivals
celebrated by the Yaquis are Holy Week, June 24 (St
John the Baptist), October 4 (St Francis) and
Christmas week.

The self-government of the village communities and
the region of which they form part is based on both
Indian and Jesuit models. – The dress of the men
differs very little from that of other countryfolk in
Sonora, but they frequently carry knives, pistols or
ammunition pouches on their leather belts. The

women wear brightly coloured cotton blouses, skirts
and *rebozos* (shawls), the ends of which hang down
over their backs; their long hair is decked with colored
ribbons. – The most notable products of Yaqui folk art
are the beautifully made wood and paper masks,
usually representing animals, which are worn in the
old folk dances.

About 130 km (80 miles) SE of Guaymas is the
modern town of **Ciudad Obregón** (alt. 35 m
(115 ft); pop. 250,000; hotels: Valle Grande Obregón,
I, SP; Costa de Oro, SP; Motel San Jorge, SP; El Cid),
which was known until 1924 as *Cajeme* (after a Yaqui
chieftain). It is an important center for the processing
of the agricultural produce of the surrounding area.
The creation of *Lake Alvaro Obregón*, a large reservoir,
has made possible the cultivation of corn, cotton,
alfalfa, rice and other crops.

68 km (42 miles) SE is *Navojoa* (alt. 36 m (118 ft);
pop. 56,000; hotels: Nuevo Hotel del Río; Motel
Colonial; Motel El Rancho), a rapidly growing modern
town which is the center of an agricultural region
made productive by irrigation (cotton, fruit, vegetables).

Around *Alamos, Navojoa* and *Huatabampo* and in the
villages of *Tesila, Guasave* and *San Miguel Zapotitlán*
in Sonora state and the surrounding towns of *El
Fuerte, San Blas* and *Los Mochis* in Sinaloa extends
the large area of settlement of the **Mayo Indians**, a
tribe belonging to the Uto-Aztec language family and
related to the Yaquis which still numbers some
28,000. As with most of the Indian peoples of this
region, very little is known about their origin. Probably
they arrived in the area between A.D. 1100 and 1300
during the great migration of the Nahua peoples. Their
first encounters with the Spanish conquistadors took
place between 1530 and 1540, but this warlike tribe
was not pacified until about 1700, when they were
evangelized by a Jesuit mission under the celebrated
explorer Father Eusebio Francisco Kino. There were
serious risings by Mayo and Yaqui Indans at the end of
the 18th c. against the Spaniards and during the
19th c. against the Mexican government, but about
1900 the Mayo gave up the struggle and turned to
farming.

As with other Indian tribes in this region, Mayo
religious beliefs are a mingling of ancient Indian and
Catholic practices, with the latter predominating. Like
the Yaquis, they have a Stag Dance (*danza del
venado*) as well as another dance known as the
Pascola. The principal religious festivals in which
dancing plays a part are May 3 (Día de la Santa Cruz),
June 24 (St John the Baptist) and October 4 (St
Francis). – The traditional self-government system of
the Mayo Indians based on the village community,
with village headmen and tribal chiefs, is now
gradually breaking up. – Mayo dress is very much the
same as that of their non-Indian neighbors.

Inland, 53 km (33 miles) E of Navojoa, is the old
mining town of *Álamos* (alt. 410 m (1345 ft); pop.
8000; hotels: Casa de los Tesoros, I, SP; Los Portales,
II, SB; Somar, II; Dolisa, II, trailer park), now protected
as a national monument. After the discovery of gold
and silver here in 1680 the town grew rapidly and 100
years later had a population of over 30,000. Its decline
began with the fall in silver prices, and thereafter
frequent raids by the warlike Mayo Indians and the
turmoil of the revolutionary wars reduced it to a mere
ghost town. Then after the Second World War a group
of artists from the United States settled in Álamos and
began to restore some of the old buildings. The Casa

de los Tesoros and the Palacio Almada are now hotels. Other features of interest·are the parish church, the House of Mexican Folk Art and the pottery center of La Uvulama. In the last few years many retired people from the United States have come to Álamos, building houses in an "Americanized" version of the colonial style.

Guerrero

State of Guerrero (Gro.). – Capital: Chilpancingo.
Area: 64,458 sq. km (24,887 sq. miles).
Population: 2,360,000.
(i) **Coordinación Federal de Turismo,**
Costera M. Aleman 187,
Acapulco, Gro.;
tel. (9 17 48) 5 11 78, 5 13 03, 5 41 28,
5 22 84, 5 10 93, 5 15 95.

The state of Guerrero is bounded on the N by the states of México and Morelos, on the NW by Michoacán, on the NE and E by Puebla and Oaxaca and on the S and W by the Pacific. It lies on both sides of the Sierra Madre del Sur and is thus one of the most mountainous and most unspoiled regions in Mexico, although a series of major tourist resorts have developed along its coast. Apart from the great river system of the Río Balsas and the Río Papagayo it has a number of smaller rivers flowing into the Pacific.

Guerrero is mainly inhabited by mestizos and various Indian tribes including the Nahua, Tlapanecs, Mixtecs and Chatino; in the SE there are still some descendants of negro slaves, who have mingled with the Indians only to a limited extent.

A large number of archeological sites have been discovered in the state, but they have either not been excavated or are of relatively little interest. Among them are Los Monos, Momoxtli, Ixcateopan and Xochipala. – The caves of Juxtlahuaca and Oxtotitlán (pre-Columbian rock paintings; see p. 105–6) are well worth a visit.

HISTORY. – The region was probably already settled in the Archaic period. The first archeological remains were left by the mysterious Olmecs, who came to this area about 1000 B.C. from the Gulf coast by way of the central highlands, probably questing for jade, and left traces of their presence in the form of rock paintings and terracotta and jade figures. Practically nothing is known of the people which created the Mezcala style (stylized geometric figures carved in various kinds of stone). In this area Olmec and Teotihuacán influences evidently fused to produce a new artistic whole. Figurines and masks in pure Teotihuacán style have

also, however, been found in Guerrero. The later development of metalworking in central Mexico is attributed to possible influences from Peru, Colombia and Costa Rica, passing by way of Guerrero. In the Post-Classic period (950–1521) the predominant cultural influences were those of the Mixtecs and later the Aztecs, who conquered part of Guerrero in the mid 15th c.

Between 1522 and 1532 the Spanish conquistadors, under Cristóbal de Olid, Gonzalo de Sandoval and Hurtado de Mendoza, conquered parts of Guerrero and advanced to the coast. During the colonial period the important route from the Pacific port of Acapulco to Mexico City and on to the Gulf of Mexico ran through Guerrero. – The state of Guerrero was established in 1849 and named after Vicente Guerrero, one of the leading fighters for Mexican independence and the second President of the Republic.

ECONOMY. – In addition to mining (silver, gold, mercury, lead, tin, zinc and sulfur) the main elements in the economy of Guerrero are agriculture (sugar-cane, cotton, coffee, tobacco, vanilla and corn) and forestry (hardwood, rubber). Tourism also makes a major contribution, the great tourist centers being Taxco, Acapulco and Zihuatanejo-Ixtapa.

In addition to the capital, **Chilpancingo** (p. 105), and the major tourist centers of ****Taxco** (p. 252), ***Acapulco** (p. 66) and ***Zihuatanejo-Ixtapa** (p. 303) there is also the town of **Iguala** (alt. 731 m (2398 ft); pop. 58,000; hotels: La Cabaña, María Luisa, San Luis; fiestas: February 24, Día de la Bandera; May 3, Día de la Santa Cruz; market Saturday and Sunday), where Agustín Iturbide promulgated the "Iguala Plan" which laid the foundations for the practical achievement of Mexican independence.

Hermosillo

State: Sonora (Son.).
Altitude: 237 m (778 ft). – Population: 335,000.
Telephone dialing code: 9 16 21.
(i) **Coordinación Federal de Turismo,**
Blvd. Eusebio Kino/Pitic-6,
tel. 4 63 04, 2 78 84, 2 79 90.

HOTELS. – *Holiday Inn, Blvd. E. Kino 369, L, SP; Internacional, Av. Rosales y Morelia, I, SP; Posada del Mar, Blvd. Rodríguez y Veracruz, I, SP; Janitzio, Zacatecas 20, II; Regis, M. González 94, II.

RESTAURANTS in most hotels; also Blocky's, Blvd. E. Kino y Juán José Ríos; El Palomito, Blvd. Transversal y Bahía; Henry's. Blvd. E. Kino 904; Cazadores del Noroeste, Blvd. E. Kino y Cabral.

RECREATION and SPORTS. – Swimming, tennis, golf, fishing, shooting.

EVENT. – June 21–26, Fiesta de la Vendimia (Vintage Festival).

Mexico,
United Mexican States
Estados Unidos Mexicanos

Guerrero

States
Estados

1a	Baja California Sur	12 Aguascalientes
1b	Baja California Norte	13 Jalisco
		14 Guanajuato
2	Sonora	15 Querétaro
3	Chihuahua	16 Hidalgo
4	Sinaloa	17 Colima
5	Durango	18 Michoacán
6	Coahuila	19 México
7	Nuevo León	20 Morelos
8	Zacatecas	21 Tlaxcala
9	San Luis Potosí	22 Puebla
10	Tamaulipas	23 Veracruz
11	Nayarit	24 Guerrero
		25 Oaxaca

26	Chiapas
27	Tabasco
28	Campeche
29	Yucatán
30	Quintana Roo

D.F. Distrito Federal (Federal District)

Hermosillo, capital of the state of Sonora, is located on the shores of a lake at the confluence of the Río Sonora and Río Zanjón, surrounded by fertile fruit-orchards, market gardens and arable land. Few old colonial buildings survive, since the town has developed rapidly in recent years and has largely been modernized. The stretch of coast opposite the Isla Tiburón attracts many visitors with its agreeable winter climate.

HISTORY. – The first Spaniards arrived in this region in 1531 and encountered stiff resistance from the warlike nomadic Indian tribes. It was more than 200 years before the first fortified settlement was established here by Agustín de Vildósola in 1742 under the name of *El Real Presidio de la Santísima Trinidad de Pític*. In 1828 the town was given its present name in honor of the General José María Gonzáles Hermosillo

a hero of the war of independence. In 1879 Hermosillo finally became capital of Sonora state, having previously been its provisional capital.

SIGHTS. – The town has few buildings of tourist interest. Notable features are the 19th c. neo-classical *Cathedral*, the *Government Palace* (Palacio de Gobierno, also 19th c.), the *Madero Park* and the *Mirador* (outlook tower) on the *Cerro de la Campana*.

On the campus of the modern University is the *Museo Regional de Historia de Sonora*, which contains archeological material from Sonora and ethnological collections illustrating the local Indian cultures (Seri, Pima, Opata, Yaqui). Particularly notable is a mummified body some 12,000 years old, found in a cave near the village of Yécora.

SURROUNDINGS. – Some 110 km (68 miles) W of Hermosillo is a beautiful bay, the *Bahía Kino* (Hotel Kino Bay, SP; Condominios Jaquelynn; Posada del Mar, SP), with the fishing villages of *Viejo Kino* and *Nuevo Kino*. The names commemorate the famous Jesuit missionary and explorer Eusebio Francisco Kino (1644–1711), who established more than twenty-five missions in Sonora at the end of the 17th and beginning of the 18th c. and thus helped to open up the region. It was he who proved that Baja California was not an island but a peninsula. The area offers excellent facilities for water sports (fishing, diving) and the opportunity of visiting the last Seri Indians in the coastal region.

The **Isla Tiburón** ("island of sharks"), Mexico's largest island (60 km (40 miles) long and up to 30 km (20 miles) across), lies just off the coast of Sonora in

Government Palace, Hermosillo

the Mar de Cortés (Gulf of California). Discovered by Fernando de Alarcón in 1540, it was for a long time inhabited by Seri Indians, but since 1976 it has been an uninhabited *nature reserve*, with rich animal and plant life, which can be visited only with special permission.

The **Seri Indians**, now dying out and numbering fewer than 300, are still semi-nomadic hunters, fishermen and food-gatherers. They are now mainly to be found at *Punta Chueca* and *El Desemboque*. Practically nothing is known about the origin of these tall Indians, whose language belongs to the Sioux group. Although they were converted to Christianity by the Jesuits they still worship the sun, the moon and various animal demons. Their ceremonies, which usually involve dancing, are intended to ensure success in hunting and fishing, and they also attach importance to girls' puberty rituals. Lacking any well-defined social hierarchy, they recognize women as having great authority, but in times of crisis they elect the boldest hunter as their leader. Nowadays only the women paint their faces in bright colors on special occasions; their jewelry is mostly made from shells, bones and seeds. Their traditional crafts are confined to elaborately woven baskets and carved ironwood figures of animals.

E of Hermosillo, around the settlements of *Ures, El Novilla, Sahuaripa, Yécora* and *Maycoba* on the slopes of the Sierra Madre Occidental, live the **Pima Indians**, some 1500 in number. The Pima, whose language belongs to the Uto-Aztec family and is thus similar to Náhuatl, originally lived a nomadic life in Sonora and Arizona. Toward the end of the 17th c. they were pacified with the help of the Jesuits, and thereafter they fought with the Spaniards against the Seri, and their hereditary enemies the Comanches. They now live mainly by farming and livestock-herding. Their principal fiesta is October 4 (Día de San Francisco).

NE of Hermosillo, near the villages of *Ures, Nacori Grande, Terapa* and *Ponida* between the Río Sonora and the Río Bavispe, live the **Ópata Indians**, now very few in number. They also belong to the Uto-Aztec language family, being related to the Pima and Tarahumara, and are believed to be descended from the Aztecs. Although they, too, were converted by the Jesuits at the end of the 17th c., they still preserve many ancient Indian rituals, and they believe in a kind of transmigration of souls. Their dances represent battles with the Apaches and their first encounters with the Spaniards. Like the Tarahumara, they go in for long-distance races and contests of skill. They now live mainly by farming and silkworm breeding.

Some 140 km (90 miles) S of Hermosillo is the port of **Guaymas** (p. 136).

Hidalgo

State of Hidalgo (Hgo.). – Capital: Pachuca.
Area; 20,870 sq. km (8058 sq. miles).
Population: 1,685,500

ⓘ **Coordinación Federal de Turismo,**
Plaza de la Independencia 110, 3rd floor,
Pachuca, Hgo.;
tel. (9 17 71) 2 59 60, 2 48 60, 2 32 89.

The state of Hidalgo, most of which lies in the central Mexican highlands, is bounded on the N by the states of San Luis Potosí and Veracruz, on the W by Querétaro, on the S by México state and Tlaxcala, and on the E by Puebla. The northern and eastern parts of the state are mountainous, while to the S and W is a relatively flat plateau. The population consists of whites, mestizos and a considerable proportion of Indians – Otomí, Nahua and Huastecs.

Mexico
United Mexican States
Estados Unidos Mexicanos

Hidalgo

States
Estados

1a Baja California Sur	12 Aguascalientes
1b Baja California Norte	13 Jalisco
	14 Guanajuato
2 Sonora	15 Querétaro
3 Chihuahua	16 Hidalgo
4 Sinaloa	17 Colima
5 Durango	18 Michoacán
6 Coahuila	19 México
7 Nuevo León	20 Morelos
8 Zacatecas	21 Tlaxcala
9 San Luis Potosí	22 Puebla
10 Tamaulipas	23 Veracruz
11 Nayarit	24 Guerrero
	25 Oaxaca
26 Chiapas	
27 Tabasco	
28 Campeche	
29 Yucatán	
30 Quintana Roo	

D.F. Distrito Federal (Federal District)

In addition to the great Toltec site of *Tula (p. 272) Hidalgo has a number of archeological sites of lesser importance (*Tepeapulco, Tepeyahualco, Huapacalco*).

HISTORY. – In pre-Columbian times the Hidalgo area was mainly under the influence of *Teotihuacán* and to a lesser degree *El Tajín* during the Classic period. Later the city of *Tula* (Tollan) became the center of the splendid Toltec culture (A. D. 968–1168). The Otomí and Huastecs, who settled here after the departure of the Toltecs, fell under the dominance of the *Aztecs* in the second half of the 15th c. – The history of Hidalgo during the *colonial period* was for the most part that of its capital, Pachuca. Under the Republic it was part of México state until 1869, when it became an independent state under the name of the hero of Mexican independence, Miguel Hidalgo y Costilla (1753–1811).

ECONOMY. – In terms of mineral resources Hidalgo is one of the richest states in Mexico, with *mines* yielding silver, gold, mercury, copper, iron, lead, zinc and antimony. Its *agriculture* and *forestry* produce rice, wheat, coffee, agaves, tobacco, mahogany and ebony. In the S of the state is a considerable concentration of *industry* (textiles, cement, goods wagons, motor vehicles, machinery). Hidalgo also has a large oil refinery. *Tourism* is making an increasing contribution to the economy.

Places of interest in Hidalgo include the archeological sites already mentioned, the state capital of **Pachuca** (p. 211), *Actopán (p. 71), *Ixmiquilpan* and *Zimapán* (p. 72), *Tepeji del Río* (p. 275) and the following towns:

Tulacingo (alt. 2200 m (7200 ft); pop. 70,000; hotels: Colonial, SP; Señorial; fiesta August 2, Día de Nuestra Señora de los Angeles), an industrial and agricultural center noted for the production of *sarapes* and apple juice. Near the town is the archeological site of *Huapacalco.*

Huichapan (alt. 2100 m (6900 ft); pop. 20,000; Hotel Jardín; fiestas: March 19, Día del Señor San José; September 21, Día de San Mateo; market Sunday), with a 16th c. parish church (Indian-Plateresque doorway, stone *cross, Baroque tower).

Two interesting towns a short distance apart are **Epazoyucan**, with a 16th c. Augustinian *convent (atrium with a stone cross, Spanish-Plateresque *posas* and open chapels, church with Renaissance façade; interesting frescoes, some of them in many colors, in cloister, baptistery and sacristy), and **Singuilucan**, with an Augustinian *convent of 1540 (Plateresque doorway and

interesting cloister, Baroque church with 18th c. retablos) and a Franciscan friary of 1527 (frescoes in cloister; church altered and restored in 17th c., with Spanish-Plateresque façade; Indian carved stone cross, 16th c.).

Hidalgo del Parral
See under Chihuahua (town)

Huejotzingo (Huexotzingo)

State: Puebla (Pue.).
Altitude: 2304 m (7559 ft.). – Population: 28,000
ⓘ **Coordinación Federal de Turismo,**
Blvd. Hermanos Serdán y Blvd. Norte
Puebla, Pue.;
tel. (91 22) 48 29 77, 48 31 77, 48 30 44.

EVENTS. – Rose Monday; Carnival Tuesday; July 16, Fiesta de la Virgen del Carmen; September 23 to October 1, Apple Juice Festival. – Market on Tuesday and Saturday.

ACCESS. – 26 km (16 miles) NW of Puebla on Road 190, 14 km (9 miles) from Cholula.

Huejotzingo lies amid fruit plantations on a fertile plateau at the foot of the snow-capped volcano of Iztaccíhuatl (5286 m – 17,343 ft). The old pre-Columbian town of Huexotzingo played a leading role in this area during the Post-Classic period.

Huejotzingo is noted as a center of manufacture of apple juice and *sarapes.*

HISTORY. – Huexotzingo made its first appearance in Indian history in the 14th c. A.D., when Náhuatl-speaking nomads from the N (Chichimecs) settled in this area. Thereafter they built up an independent state which for a time dominated the rival states of Cholula and Tlaxcala. In the second half of the 15th c. they came into conflict with the *Aztecs* (Mexica) and the neighboring town of Tlaxcala and took part in the "Flower Wars", the purpose of which was not to win territory but to capture prisoners for sacrifice to the gods. After suffering defeats at the hands of the Tlaxcalans, Huejotzingo finally, in 1518, entered into an alliance with them against the Aztecs of Tenochtitlán. – When the *Spaniards* came to Huejotzingo in 1519 on their way to Tenochtitlán the people of the town (which then had a population of 40,000) gave them assistance, as did the Tlaxcalans. Recognizing the importance of Huejotzingo as an Indian center, the Spaniards built one of their earliest and most imposing convents just outside the old town.

Danza de los Viejitos, Huejotzingo

SIGHTS. – The *Convent of San Francisco de Huejotzingo, built by Father Juan de Alameda and Toribio de Alcazar between 1529 and 1570, is one of the oldest and finest in New Spain. On the way to the convent we pass through the *atrium*, which is entered by way of a broad flight of steps and a doorway with three Plateresque arches. In the middle is a carved stone cross, and at the four corners are *posas* (processional chapels) which are among the finest of the kind in Mexico; with their pyramidal roofs and their pattern of ornamentation they are in the Spanish Plateresque tradition. Note the arms of the Franciscan order and the *alfiz* ("hood-mould" framing a doorway), here usually in the form of the Franciscan rope girdle – a characteristic of the Mudéjar style.

The *façade* of the typical **fortified church** is decorated in Spanish-Plateresque style with columns and symbols of the order. The framing of the *N doorway* (now walled up) is a fine example of colonial-Plateresque: here again the doorway arch is enclosed by an *alfiz* and the exuberantly but harmoniously ornamented façade bears the arms of the Franciscans. The triangular merlons, with openings, of the battlements are found only at Huejotzingo. – In the spacious nave of the *church*, with its magnificent Gothic ribbed vaulting, is a large four-part *retablo* with fourteen statues (1586), another fine example of the Plateresque tradition. Its seven oil paintings are by the Flemish artist Simón Pereyns, who went to New Spain in 1566. Some remains of the frescoes which once covered the walls can still be seen. The wall of the entrance to the sacristy has Mudéjar ornament.

The *Convent* is entered through a door on the right-hand side of the church. In the porch is the Trinity Chapel, adjoining which is the cloister. The friezes in the

corridors and cells are in Renaissance style. The interesting *frescoes* include representations of the Immaculate Conception, the arrival of the first twelve Franciscans in New Spain in 1524 (Sala De Profundis) and scenes from the life of St Francis.

Another notable building in Huejotzingo is the 16th c. *church of San Diego*, with a richly carved early 17th c. sacristy roof, a font with Franciscan symbols and ornamentation on the façade similar to that at Calpan (below).

SURROUNDINGS. – 10 km (6 miles) from Huejotzingo on an unsurfaced road is **Calpan** (Náhuatl, "in the houses"), now also known as San Andrés Calpan, which has another interesting *Franciscan friary founded in 1548. The Plateresque façade of the church has sculptured decoration, including representations of agave plants. In the interior is a triumphal arch decorated with the Franciscan rope girdle. At the corners of the atrium are four fine *posas* richly decorated with sculpture (flowers, geometric patterns, the Annunciation, the Last Judgment, Franciscan symbols, etc.). – The parish church of Calpan is also well worth a visit.

Isla Mujeres

State: Quintana Roo (Q.R.).
Population: 8000.
Telephone dialing code: 9 19 88.
(i) **Coordinación Federal de Turismo,**
   Av. Tulum 81,
   Edificio Fira,
   Cancun, Q.R.;
   tel. (9 19 88) 4 32 38.

HOTELS. – *El Presidente Caribe, L, SP; Zazil-há, L, SP; Posada del Mar, I; Berny, I, SB; Rocas del Caribe, I; Rocamar, I, SP; Martinez, II; Cabañas (Playa Cocos), II. – YOUTH HOSTEL: Poc-ná.

RESTAURANTS in most hotels; also Ciro's, Gomar, Villa del Mar, Kim-há, French María's.

RECREATION and SPORTS. – Snorkeling, diving, water skiing, fishing.

EVENT. – Fiesta December 1–12.

ACCESS. – Passenger ferry from Puerto Juárez, car and passenger ferry from Punta Sam (bus services from Mérida and Chetumal); air services from Mérida, Cancún and Cozumel.

The Isla Mujeres (Island of Women), 8 km (5 miles) long and up to 2 km (1¼ miles) across, lies in the Caribbean off the coast of the Yucatán peninsula. It offers the visitor beautiful *beaches of white sand fringed by coconut palms, lagoons of crystal-clear water and *coral reefs with an abundance of fish.

HISTORY. – Little is known of the island's history in pre-Conquest days. the *Mayas* have left traces of their presence in remains of buildings, some of which date from the 8th and 9th c. A.D. (the Late Classic period). Most of the temples that have been found are thought to have been dedicated to Ixchel, goddess of the moon and of fertility. – The island was discovered in 1517 – two years before Cortés landed in Mexico – by a Spanish expedition under Francisco Hernández de Córdoba, who named it the Island of Women after the large numbers of terracotta female figurines which he and his men found in the Maya ruins. In later periods the Isla Mujeres, like most of the Caribbean islands, was a pirates' and smugglers' lair. It is only within the last twenty years or so that tourism has come to the island and turned a sleepy fishing settlement into a popular vacation resort. Unlike the neighboring island of Cozumel and the modern bathing resort of Cancún, the Isla Mujeres has remained relatively unspoiled and not too crowded. In order to promote its trade the island has been made a free port.

SIGHTS. – The island's main attractions lie on and in the sea. The best bathing place is the **Playa Cocos** on the N side of the island; and at the northern tip begin the coral reefs which provide such splendid opportunities for snorkelers. The E coast, on the Caribbean, also has beautiful beaches and reefs, for example *Playa Pancholo*, but strong currents make bathing hazardous.

At the S end of the island is a charming bay, *El Garrafón (the "Carafe"), which can be reached either by road or by boat. In this statutorily protected underwater area countless tropical fish, denizens of the coral reef, can be observed. At one spot in the bay can be seen, just under the water, a huge shoal of fish which, extraordinarily, has remained almost in

Coral-diver, Isla Mujeres

the same place for many years. There are restaurants serving simple fish meals.

Farther out is a reef known as **Los Manchones** which attracts many diving enthusiasts. For experienced scuba divers a boat trip can be arranged to the *Caves of the Sleeping Sharks*, 20–30 m (65–100 ft) under water, which were discovered at the end of the 60s by a local fisherman, "Valvula" and became widely known through television films. – On the way to El Garrafón it is well worthwhile paying a visit to the *turtle farm*.

An experience of a different kind is provided by a visit to the *Hacienda Mundaca*, with the remains of the house and garden of the 19th c. Basque pirate and slave-dealer Antonio de Mundaca.

The most interesting *Maya remains* on the Isla Mujeres lie beyond the lighthouse at the southern tip of the island. They are believed to represent an observatory dedicated to the goddess Ixchel. From here there is a magnificent *view of the Caribbean Sea and Cancún.

SURROUNDINGS. – An interesting day trip by boat is to the **Isla Contoy** to the N of the Isla Mujeres, a bird sanctuary under statutory protection. Here visitors can observe flamingoes, frigate birds, pelicans, ducks and other species. Fishermen, too, will be well rewarded if they pursue their hobby in the waters to the NW between *Cabo Catoche* and the *Isla Holbox* (marlin, shark, sailfish, barracuda, sea bass, mackerel, etc.). Holbox can also be reached by car and boat from the mainland (side road to Chiquila off the Valladolid–Puerto Juárez road, then boat).

Isla Mujeres

Caribbean Sea

Matamoros
Av. Juárez
Av. R. Medina
Town Hall
Quay for ferry boats
Juárez

Caribbean Sea

Turtle Farm

Lighthouse

El Garrafón

Ixtaccíhuatl

See Popocatépetl and Iztaccíhuatl

Ixtapa

See Zihuatanejo and Ixtapa

Izamal

State: Yucatán (Yuc.).
Altitude: 13 m (43 ft). – Population: 20,000.

ACCOMMODATIONS of adequate standard not yet available.

EVENTS. – Fiestas: April 3, San Ildefonso; May 3–5, Santa Cruz (Holy Cross); August 15, Virgin of Izamal.

Izamal, one of the most interesting places in Yucatán but still hardly discovered by tourists, lies only 26 km (16 miles) N of Road 180 from Mérida to Chichén Itzá. With its remains of Maya pyramids and temples and its 16th c. Franciscan churches and convents it is a dramatic illustration of the encounter between pre-Columbian and Spanish culture.

HISTORY. – Although Izamal ("city of hills" in Maya) has been the subject of little archeological investiga-

tion, it is believed to have reached its peak in the Maya *Classic period* (A.D. 300–900). According to legend it was founded by Itzamná ("Dew from Heaven"), later revered as a sky god. After his death his body is said to have been divided into three parts, which were then buried under the three hills of Izamal. On these hills were built three huge temples, the principal temple being known as Kinich-kakmó ("Sun-Bird with the Fiery Face"). Izamal then became a place of pilgrimage frequented by worshippers of the sun god Kinich-kakmó and the sky god Itzamná, from all over the country. Along with other sacred sites such as Cozumel and above all Chichén Itzá, Izamal later developed, perhaps under the rule of the legendary Itzá ("Mayanised" Toltecs or "Toltecised" Mayas), into an important political center.

The chronicles tell of the abduction by Chac-xib-chac, ruler of Chichén Itzá, of the betrothed wife of Ah-ulil, ruler of Izamal, and of the subsequent war which ended in the expulsion of the population of Chichén Itzá about A.D. 1200. This war seems also, however, to have initiated the political decline of Izamal. At the same time began the rise of Mayapán, the last stage in the development of Maya civilization.

Izamal's importance as a place of pilgrimage led the Spaniards to take strong measures when they captured it around 1540. They at once pulled down most of the pyramids and used the stone to construct their own religious buildings.

SIGHTS. – From the main square of the town a broad flight of steps leads up to the Franciscan *Convent of San Antonio de Padua, built by Juan de Mérida between 1553 and 1561. The huge *atrium*, with an area of some 8000 sq. m (9500 sq. yds), is surrounded by an arcade of 75 arches. It is said to be exceeded in size only by St Peter's Square in Rome.

The **church** with a very plain façade is a typical example of the fortress-like churches built by the

Convent of San Antonio de Padua, Izamal, seen from the atrium

Franciscans in the 16th c. The horseshoe-shaped arch above the arcade dates from the 19th c. On the walls of the nave are oil paintings of archbishops of Mérida. The original *altar* of the Virgin of Izamal, patroness of Yucatán, which came from Guatemala, was destroyed by fire in 1829; the present altar, a skilful copy, has ten niches, most of which contain effigies of saints. In the convent courtyard is an old Maya sun stone.

The atrium, church and convent are built on the foundations of the large Maya temple of *Popol-chac*, which the Spaniards called the "Castle of the Kings" (Castillo de los Reyes).

Most of the twelve pyramids which originally stood here were destroyed by the Spaniards or by natural causes. The three principal pyramids were known by the names of *Itza-matul, Kab-ul* and **Kinich-kakmó**, only the last of which still conveys some impression of its original imposing bulk. One of the largest pyramids in Mexico, it is notable for the steepness of the staircase leading up to the summit. From the top there are superb panoramic *views of the town and surrounding area.

SURROUNDINGS. – Returning to Road 180 at Katonil and going E in the direction of Chichén Itzá and Valladolid, we come in 26 km (16 miles) to *Libre Unión*, from which a road runs S to Yaxcabá. 3 km (2 miles) down this road a side road branches off to the beautiful *Cenote Xtojil*, 1 km (¾ mile) away. 15 km (9 miles) beyond the turning is **Yaxcabá**, which has an interesting parish church with an unusual façade and three towers. Also in the village is a *cenote*, into which the local people threw their weapons, jewelry and money to save them from looting during the 19th c. "Caste War"; most of the objects were later recovered.

Iztaccíhuatl
See Popocatépetl and Iztaccíhuatl

Jalapa (Xalapa)

State: Veracruz (Ver.).
Altitude: 1420 m (4659 ft). – Population: 335,000.
Telephone dialing code: 9 12 81.
ⓘ **Coordinación Federal de Turismo,**
Av. I. Zaragoza 20 Altos Centro,
Veracruz, Ver.;
tel. (91 29) 32 70 26, 32 16 13.

HOTELS. – *Xalapa*, Victoria Esq. Bustamante, I, SP; *María Victoria*, Zaragoza 6, I, Sp; *San Bernardo*, Altamirano 2, II; *Limón*, Revolución 8, II; *Estancia*, J. Carillo 11, II.

RESTAURANTS in most hotels; also *La Nueva Pérgola*, Pérgola y Vista Hermosa; *La Madriguera del*
Conejo, Ignacio de la Llave 19; *Luigis Queso, Pan y Vino*, A. Camacho 95.

RECREATION and SPORTS. – Swimming, tennis, golf.

EVENT. – May 1–6, Trade Fair.

Jalapa, capital of Veracruz state, is built on a number of hills in a garden-like region at the foot of the Cerro de Macuiltepec. It is surrounded by high mountains, with the Cofre de Perote (Nauhcampatépetl) overtopping the others, and to the S can be seen the Pico de Orizaba (Citlaltépetl), Mexico's highest mountain. This situation gives the region an abundant rainfall and at times a heavy cloud cover, promoting a luxuriant growth of vegetation. Jalapa has modern districts as well as old colonial parts of the town. It has a university, and has developed in recent years into a considerable cultural and intellectual center.

HISTORY. – When *Cortés* passed through Jalapa (Náhuatl *Xalla-apan*, "river in the sand") in 1519 on his way to Tenochtitlán, it was a flourishing Indian settlement under *Aztec* influence. After the Conquest Spaniards settled here in large numbers. During the colonial period Jalapa was famed for its important annual fair, at which goods brought from Spain by the returning "silver ships" were sold. Lying 120 km (75 miles) from Veracruz and 300 km (185 miles) from Mexico City, it later became a staging point on the mailcoach route. The town also played a part in the movement for Mexican independence.

SIGHTS. – The Spanish period has left a legacy of narrow streets and lanes, colorful houses and luxuriant gardens which are in striking contrast to the broad avenues and modern buildings in the newer parts of the town. There are few major buildings of the colonial period.

One notable building of that period is the massive late 18th c. **Cathedral** (*Catedral Metropolitana de Jalapa:* restored) which stands near the *Parque Juárez*. On the other side is the **Government Palace** (*Palacio de Gobierno*), in light-colored stone, which contains interesting frescoes. – Another attractive park is the *Parque Hidalgo* (Paseo de los Berros). Some blocks E are the new *Stadium* (Estadio Jalapeño) and the *University*, which runs summer courses for foreigners.

In the NW of the town, on the left of the Mexico City road, is the important *Museum of Anthropology* (*Museo de*

Terracotta figure, Jalapa Museum

Antropología de Jalapa). It has been newly landscaped and restored and re-opened in October 1986. This museum is already considered perhaps to be the most beautiful in the country. In the park are colossal Olmec heads from San Lorenzo. The large pieces of Olmec sculpture found at La Venta are to be seen in the Open-Air Museum at Villahermosa (p. 290). Also displayed in the park are other impressive pieces of Olmec sculpture and examples of Aztec and Huastec work. The museum itself contains a large collection of stelae, sculpture and cult objects of stone, pottery vessels and figures and articles made from semi-precious stones. There are also two rooms of ethnological material on the Indian peoples of the region.

SURROUNDINGS. – 7 km (4½ miles) NW on the Puebla road (No. 140) is the garden city of

Maize Stone, Jalapa Museum

Banderilla (Motel Banderilla), with the beautiful *Jardín Lecuona, a botanic garden with more than 200 species of orchids alone.

46 km (29 miles) farther on is *Perote* (alt. 2400 m (7875 ft); pop 30,000), at the foot of the volcano known from its shape as the Cofre ("coffer, chest") **de Perote** (*Nauhcampetépetl*, "square mountain": 4282 m – 14,049 ft). On the outskirts of the town is the forbidding Fort San Carlos de Perote, built in the 18th c. to control bandits and rebels and later used as a prison.

16 km (10 miles) S of Jalapa is *Coatepec*, and old Indian village surrounded by tropical forests with abundant plant life which will interest the botanically minded.

Jalisco

State of Jalisco (Jal.). – Capital: Guadalajara.
Area: 81,058 sq. km (31,297 sq. miles).
Population: 4,581,000.
ⓘ **Coordinación Federal de Turismo,**
Lazaro Cardenas 3289, 1st floor, Col. Chapalita, tel. (91 36) 22 41 30, 22 41 52, 22 41 67, 22 41 90.

The state of Jalisco is bounded on the N by Zacatecas and Aguascalientes, on the W by Nayarit and the Pacific, on the S by Colima and Michoacán and on the E by Guanajuato. It is a region of varied scenery, with an extensive high plateau, ranges of hills in the sierra Madre Occidental, deep gorges, numerous lakes and a coastal region of luxuriant tropical vegetation. The mountains, many of them volcanic, rise to their highest points in the S, with the Nevado de Colima (4380 m – 14,371 ft) and the Volcán de Colima (3900 m – 12,796 ft). The population is made up of whites, mestizos and a considerable proportion of Indians, mainly Nahua, Huicholes and Purépecha (Tarascans).

A number of pre-Columbian sites have been identified, many of them merely cemeteries. Among them are *Ixtepete, Teuchtitlán, Etzatlán, Tuxacuesco* and *Ameca*.

HISTORY. – The pre-Columbian history of Jalisco (Náhuatl, "place in front of the sand") began in the Pre-Classic period and continued in the Classic. Since very little is known of the peoples who created these cultures they are referred to simply as the *cultures of the West* (Occidente). Their most notable products are the lifelike terracotta figures of Jalisco, Colima and Nayarit. During the Post-Classic period there grew up in this region a number of Indian states, including *Coliman, Zapotlán, Xalisco and Tollan*, which were

Upland scenery, Unión de Tula

conquered in the second half of the 15th c. by the *Purépecha* (Tarascans) under their king, Tzitzic Pandácuaro.

The first of the Spanish conquistadors to arrive in this area, in 1524, was Francisco Cortés de San Buenaventura, who encountered the *Chimalhuacanes*, then dominant over the other local tribes. It was left to the notorious Nuño Beltrán de Guzmán, however, to conquer the greater part of the region between 1530 and 1535. After the dismissal and arrest of Guzmán, Pérez de la Torre was made governor of the province of *Nueva Galicia*, to which Aguascalientes and Zacatecas also belonged until 1789. In subsequent years there was bitter fighting between the Spaniards and rebellious Indians, who entrenched themselves in the old strongholds (*peñoles*) originally built by the Tarascans. After the pacification of the area and the discovery of minerals, the state, with its capital at Guadalajara, became independent and prosperous. In 1889 Jalisco gave up part of its coastal territory,

including the town of Tepic, and this developed into the state of Nayarit. The worst of the fighting in the bloody Cristero War (1926–29) took place around Los Altos, the NE part of Jalisco. It was an uprising of country Catholics against the suppression of the church under Presidents Plutarco Elías Calles and Emilio Portes Gil.

ECONOMY. – The state has a richly productive *agriculture* (maize, beans, wheat, sugar-cane, cotton, agaves, rice, indigo, tobacco). The coastal regions have rubber and copra, and there is also much *livestock-farming*. *Minerals* worked include gold, silver, cinnabar, copper and semi-precious stones. *Industry*, mainly in Guadalajara, produces textiles, leather goods, chemicals, tobacco, glass, pottery, cement and drinks. The state's growing *tourist trade* is centered on Guadalajara, the area around the Laguna de Chapala and the beach resorts on the Pacific.

In addition to ***Guadalajara** (p. 128), the **Laguna de Chapala** area (p. 92) and the bathing resort of ***Puerto Vallarta** (p. 228), the following towns in Jalisco are of interest:

Tequila (the Náhuatl name for a drink made from mezcal: alt. 1218 m (3996 ft); pop. 35,000; fiestas: May 2, Día de la Santa Cruz; December 12, Día de la Virgen de Guadalupe), with the beautiful church of San Francisco. The town is a center of tequila and mezcal production. These potent liquors are made from the fermented juice of the mezcal agave or maguey. The distilleries in the town, which can be visited, obtain their supplies from the large agave plantations in the surrounding area.

Mexico
United Mexican States
Estados Unidos Mexicanos

Jalisco

States
Estados

1a Baja California Sur	12 Aguascalientes	
1b Baja California Norte	13 Jalisco	
2 Sonora	14 Guanajuato	
3 Chihuahua	15 Querétaro	
4 Sinaloa	16 Hidalgo	
5 Durango	17 Colima	
6 Coahuila	18 Michoacán	
7 Nuevo León	19 México	
8 Zacatecas	20 Morelos	
9 San Luis Potosí	21 Tlaxcala	26 Chiapas
10 Tamaulipas	22 Puebla	27 Tabasco
11 Nayarit	23 Veracruz	28 Campeche
	24 Guerrero	29 Yucatán
	25 Oaxaca	30 Quintana Roo

D.F. Distrito Federal (Federal District)

Ciudad Guzmán (formerly *Zapotlán*: alt. 1507 m (4944 ft); pop. 110,000; fiesta October 22–25, Día del Señor San José). The town has a small archeological museum which also contains pictures by José Clemente Orozco. It is a good base for climbing the Nevado de Colima and the Volcán de Colima (see under Colima).

San Juan de los Lagos (alt. 1864 m (6116 ft); pop. 55,000; Motel Las Palmas, Casa Blanca; fiestas: February 2, Candlemas; December 8, Immaculate Conception). The wonder-working statue of the Virgen de la Candelaria in the parish church draws thousands of pilgrims from all over Mexico, particularly at the beginning of February, and the pilgrimages are the occasion of great *fiestas (mariachis, dancing, bullfights, cockfights, etc.). The town is also noted for its embroidery and its horse market (November 20 to December 13).

Barra de Navidad (pop. 4500; hotels: Cabo Blanco, I, SP; Barrade Navidad, I, SP; Tropical, II, SP; Sand's, II, Delfin, II.), a fishing village which is famous as the starting point in 1564 of Miguel López de Legazpi's voyage of exploration across the Pacific, in the course of which he reached the Philippines and founded the first Spanish settlement there. In recent years the town, together with the neighboring *San Patricio Melaque* (hotels: Melaque, I, SP; Posada López de Legazpi, II, SB; Las Brisas, SP; Bungalows Vista Hermosa, II, SP; Posada Las Gaviotas, II, SP.), has developed, thanks to its beautiful beaches, into a very popular vacation resort, particularly for Mexicans.

Playa de Tenacatita (hotels: Tenacatita, I, SP, tennis, trailer park; Tecuán, II), lies about 35 km (22 miles) N of Barra de Navidad. About 25 km (16 miles) further on in the direction of Puerto Vallarta is the Costa Careyes with the *Playa Rose* (hotel Plaza Careyes, L, SP, tennis) and the *Playa Blanca* (Club Mediterranée, L, SP), both bays with beautiful extensive *beaches, still largely unspoiled.

Kabah

State: Yucatán (Yuc.).
Altitude: 25 m (82 ft).

The very interesting Maya site of Kabah, rather neglected by archeo-logists in recent years, lies 20 km (12 miles) SE of Uxmal on the Mérida–Campeche road. Although the buildings so far excavated at Kabah are in the traditional Puuc style, they have revealed unusual features which are attributed to Chenes influence.

HISTORY. – Little is known about the history of Kabah. It seems to have been a dependency of the great city of Uxmal, with which it is linked by a *sacbe*, one of the Maya "white roads" mostly used for ceremonial purposes. The site was explored in the mid 19th c. by the indefatigable J. L. Stephens and Frederick Catherwood, but the first systematic excavations were carried out by Teobert Maler toward the end of the century. These and later investigations have shown that the principal buildings on the site date from the 9th c. (i.e., the Late Classic period).

THE SITE. – In the southern part of the site, E of the road, is the *Palace of the Masks* or *Codz-pop* ("rolled-up mat"), the most interesting of the structures so far excavated. The Maya name comes from the trunk-like nose, resembling a rolled-up mat, of the rain god Chac, here used as a staircase.

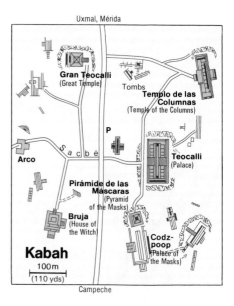

Kabah
100m
(110 yds)

The TEMPLE, 45 m (150 ft) long and 6 m (20 ft) high, stands on a low platform, the front of which is decorated with a horizontal row of stylized *masks. The palace is unique in Puuc architecture in having the façade of the substructure as well as the main structure covered with decoration – a feature attributed to the influence of the Chenes style from the S. Above a richly ornamented sill is a continuous row of masks with huge trunk-like noses, now mostly broken off; above this a cornice decorated with geometric patterns, and above this again three further continuous rows of masks. Practically nothing is left of the roof-comb, once 3 m (10 ft) high, with its rectangular apertures. Bizarre and overloaded with decoration as the façade appears, with more than 250 masks, the

Palace of the Masks, Kabah

technical mastery which it displays is no less astonishing.

A little way N of the Palace of the Masks is the **Teocalli** or *Palace* (Palacio). This two-story building, the lower story of which is destroyed, shows a plain and unadorned style of architecture which is in striking contrast to the over-decorated façade of the Codz-pop. The decoration here mainly consists of panels of close-set columns between two projecting moldings. – Beyond the Teocalli is the much ruined *Temple of the Columns* (Templo de las Columnas), which shows some affinity to the Governor's Palace at Uxmal.

W of the road is the fine ***Arch of Kabah** (*Arco de Kabah*), a notable example of the corbelled or "false" arch so typical of Maya architecture, formed by allowing

The Arch of Kabah

each successive course of stone on either side of the opening to project over the one below until they met at the top. This undecorated arch was presumably the entrance to the main cult center, and there was probably a *sacbe* ("white road") running through the arch to Uxmal. These Maya ceremonial highways, constructed of limestone with a cement surface, stood between 0.50 m (1½ ft) and 2.50 m (8 ft) above the ground and were an average 4.50 m (15 ft) wide.

In the western part of the site is a largely unexcavated area containing the *Great Temple* (Gran Teocalli), the *Western Quadrangle* (Cuadrángulo del Oeste) and the *Temple of the Lintels* (Templo de los Dinteles).

SURROUNDINGS. – Near Santa Elena, some 5 km (3 miles) N of Kabah, is the small site of *Mul-chic*, where excavation brought to light a building containing remains of wall paintings (now barely visible). – A short distance along the Campeche road (No. 261) a side road diverges on the left to the archeological sites of *Sayil (p. 244), *Xlapak* (p. 245) and ***Labná** (p. 150) and the *Loltún Caves (p. 151).

Kohunlich

State: Quintana Roo (Q.R.).
Altitude: 85 m (279 ft).

ACCESS. – From Chetumal 58 km (36 miles) W on Road 186 to Francisco Villa; then road on left (9 km – 6 miles) to site.

The excavated area in the center of the Maya site of *Kohunlich lies amid primeval tropical forest, but in spite of its isolated situation it is one of the best maintained excavation sites in Mexico. This little known site of the early Classic period is easily accessible, and is well worth visiting for its beautiful setting as well as its archeological interest.

HISTORY. – The name Kohunlich is a garbled version of the English name *Cohoon Ridge*; the Spanish name is *Aserradero* ("sawmill"). – Little is known of the early history of the site, or of the neighboring Río Bec area. Kohunlich was undoubtedly occupied for several centuries before the beginning of the Christian era and continued in occupation until the 13th c. (i.e., from the Formative to the Post-Classic period). Its heyday as a religious and political center lay between A.D. 400 and 700: basically, therefore, it is a site of the *Classic period*.

The site was first recorded by the US archeologist R. E. Merwin in the course of an archeological survey of the neighboring area of southern Campeche in

1912. The real discovery of the site, however, came in 1968, when plunderers were caught in the act of stealing the large masks on the Temple of the Masks. Since then exemplary excavation and restoration work has been carried out under the direction of Victor Segovia.

THE SITE. – The area so far explored at Kohunlich covers more than 2 sq. km (¾ sq. mile). The earlier occupants of the site leveled and consolidated almost half the total area, using and extending natural ditches and depressions to channel rainwater into collecting basins for use during the dry period.

The large *Plaza of the Stelae* (Plaza de las Estelas) is named after the four monolithic *stelae* which were found in the **East Building** (*Edificio Oriente*) and are now set on either side of the staircase. The East Building, like the three others around the square, dates from the 8th c. A.D. It is 60 m (200 ft) long, with nine tiers leading up to the temple on the summit. Of the original three doors only the middle one, the main entrance, survives.

The **South Building** (*Edificio Sur*) is 87 m (285 ft) long and has a very long staircase formed of nine unusually broad steps. – The *West Building* (Edificio Poniente), almost 50 m (165 ft) long, has a short side staircase of five steps which leads through a small passage to the front platform, evidently intended to serve as a stage for ceremonies. – The *North Building* (Edificio Norte), 70 m (230 ft) long, has a staircase leading to another plaza on the W side of the building, which gives access to a patio 10 m (33 ft) above ground level with an area of 2500 sq. m (3000 sq. yds).

The **Ball Court** (*Juego de Pelota*) has a wall 33 m (110 ft) long, with no stone rings. It is similar in structure to the ball courts of Copán (Honduras) and Becán (Campeche).

The most interesting structure at Kohunlich, unique of its kind in Maya territory, is the *Pyramid of the Masks* (*Pirámide de los Mascarones*). Flanking the staircase are eight large stucco masks, originally found by tomb robbers, which are still *in situ* but are now protected from the weather by roofs.

The PYRAMID and the masks date from the 5th c. A.D. Within the upper part of the pyramid, on different levels, were found four tomb chambers which had been looted by tomb robbers. The four *masks, all different, are 1·50 m (5 ft) high and appear to represent the sun god. In their tall headdresses is a mythological creature with eyes of spiral form. Some of the eyes bear the glyph *chuen*, representing the *tzolkin*, the Maya ritual year of 260 days. As was usual with Maya nobles, the noses are ornamented with rings. The teeth originally had an L-shaped inlay, now barely visible, representing the glyph *ik* ("wind"). Interestingly, the feline-like mouths, with the twirling moustaches of the rain god, show Olmec characteristics. All the masks have ear-rings and ear-plugs, the sides of which are formed by snakes, perhaps representing rain. Traces of red paint can be detected on the masks.

In 1968 one of the masks was stolen and after being hardened with artificial resin was cut into small pieces and flown to the United States in a private aircraft. There it was put together again and offered to a New York museum for a considerable sum. The museum informed the Mexican government, which was then able to recover the mask. It can now be seen in the National Museum of Anthropology in Mexico City.

A little way below the excavated area is a picturesque little *lagoon.*

SURROUNDINGS. – Archeological enthusiasts will want to visit the sites of *Xpuhil, *Becán and *Chicaná, some 60 km (40 miles) W on Road 186 (see under Chetumal).

Labná

State: Yucatán (Yuc.).
Altitude: 28 m (92 ft).

ACCESS. – About 5 km (3 miles) S of Kabah on Road 261 a new road branches off L via Sayil to Labná, some 13 km (8 miles) distant

*Labná – buried, like the neighboring places of Sayil and Xlapak, among dense tropical vegetation – was an important Maya center, the full extent of which has not yet

Labná

Palacio (Palace)

Sacbé (Ceremonial Way)

East Temple

Sacbé

Arco (Arch)

Mirador (Temple Pyramid)

The Arch of Labná

free-standing façade. We know from Stephens's account that it was originally decorated with a large seated figure in brightly painted stucco. The projecting stones on the front of the roof-comb provided a base for the stucco. The only surviving remnant of decoration on the temple is the lower half of a figure at the SW corner of the building.

The best-known feature of the site is the magnificent *Arch of Labná (*Arco de Labná*), SW of the Mirador.

been explored. Labná is a classical example of the Puuc style of architecture.

HISTORY. – As with Sayil and Xlapak, little is known of the history of this interesting site. The few datings that have been established indicate that the principal structures at Labná ("broken houses" in Maya) were built in the 9th c. A.D., during the *Late Classic period*. Here as at most Maya sites we owe the first account of the remains to John L. Stephens and Frederick Catherwood, who visited Labná in the mid 19th c. The large numbers of *chultunes* (cisterns), over sixty of which were found, suggest that the town had a considerable population. – In recent years the Carnegie Institute and various Mexican institutions have done excellent restoration work at Labná as well as the neighboring sites of Sayil and Xlapak.

THE SITE. – The group of structures in the northern part of the site known as the **Palace** (*Palacio*) is one of the largest temple precincts in Puuc territory. The group, haphazard and asymmetrical in layout, has a total length of almost 135 m (445 ft) and stands on a *terrace* 167 m (550 ft) long. In front of it is a huge plaza, crossed by the remains of a *sacbe* (ceremonial way).

The FAÇADE of the eastern range is decorated with groups of three clustered columns, bands of geometric ornamentation and nose masks. At the SE corner, above a cluster of three columns, is an unusual **Chac mask** with a snake's jaws, wide open, disgorging a human head. The trunk-like nose is curled up over the forehead. Here one of the two year glyphs so far recorded at Labná was found. – The façades of the other parts of the palace are, with one or two exceptions, in similar style but simpler in form. On the upper level is a *rainwater collecting basin*, linked with a cistern in front of the group.

The southern group of structures is dominated by a pyramid (not yet properly restored) topped by a temple known as the **Mirador** ("Lookout"). Above the two restored platforms and the temple rears the imposing roof-comb, like a

Since the Mayas were ignorant of the true arch they used the corbelled or false arch formed by the overlapping of successive courses of stone and topped by a cover-slab. The richly decorated *Arch of Labná, which is 3 m (10 ft) deep and has an interior height of 5 m (16 ft), is flanked by two small chambers with entrances on the NW side. The frieze along the front of the arch, with mosaic patterns reminiscent of those at Uxmal, is framed by projecting sills. Above the entrances to the two lateral chambers are representations in high relief of two typical Maya huts, with thatched roofs in feather patterns; originally there were probably figures at the doors of the huts. On the stepped roof of the higher middle section the remains of the open roof-comb can still be seen. – The rear of the arch is much plainer. Above a sill with similar decoration to that on the front of the arch is a striking frieze with a meander pattern against a background of clustered columns.

By following the road via Cooperativa to Oxcutzcab one reaches in 20 km (12 miles) the *Caves (*Grutas*) of Loltún (Maya: "flower of stone"). On the outer rock face, near the Nahkab – (Colmena) entrance to the caves, can be seen a larger than life bas relief figure of a richly adorned Maya warrior. The lettering, which has not yet been deciphered, could be of very early, perhaps Pre-Classic origin. In these stalactitic caves, which are among the largest and most interesting in Mexico, can be seen, among other things, the remains of wall-painting and rock drawings as well as a stone 'head of Loltún' with Olmec-like features. Recent tests have shown that the caves were probably used as early as 2500 B.C. Pottery dating from 1200–600 B.C. has been discovered as well as artifacts from the Classical Maya period and later. It is presumed that the caves served as a refuge for the Indians from the Spanish invaders. Tours of the caves take place only at specified times (at present until 1.30 p.m.).

From *Oxkutzcab*, a short distance beyond Loltún, it is worth making a detour to the little town of **Maní**, 10 km (6 miles) N.

Historically this was a place of some importance. About A.D. 1450, after the destruction of Mayapán, the Xiú tribe, coming from the Uxmal area, founded the town, prophetically calling it Maní ("it is all over" in Maya). The subsequent period, until the arrival of the Spaniards, saw the decline of the great Maya civilization, and the disintegration of the Maya empire into some twenty warring city states, the most important of which was the Xiú city of Maní. The fall of the Maya empire facilitated the Spanish conquest of the country. The last ruler of Maní, Titul-Xiú, surrendered to the conqueror of Yucatán, Francisco de Montejo, in 1542 and became a convert to Christianity.

In 1562 the main square of Maní was the scene of the great *auto-da-fé* in which Bishop Diego de Landa burned all known Maya manuscripts, with the exception of three codices, as works of the devil. – The imposing church of San Miguel was founded by the Franciscans. Maní also has a cenote which is the subject of many legends.

Another 14 km (9 miles) NE is **Teabo**, with the interesting church of San Pedro y San Pablo. From here a poor road continues another 13 km (8 miles) NE to *Mayapán* (p. 159).

La Paz

State: Baja California Sur (B.C.S.).
Altitude: 30 m (98 ft). – Population: 145,000.
Telephone dialing code: 9 16 82.
(i) **Coordinación Federal de Turismo,**
Paseo Alvaro Obregon 2130,
tel. 2 11 90, 2 11 99 and 2 79 75

HOTELS. – *Gran Hotel Baja*, Calle Rangel, I, SP, tennis; *Castel Palmira*, 2.5 km (1½ miles) on the road to Pichilingue, I, SP, tennis; *Los Arcos*, A. Obregón 498, I, SP; *El Presidente*, 5 km (3 miles) on the road to Pichilingue, I, SP, beach; *Gardenias*, Av. Achiles Serdán 520 Nte., II, SP; *La Posada*, Reforma y Playa Sur, II, SP; *Perla*, Av. A. Obregón 1570, II, SP; *La Purísima*, 16 de Septiembre 408, III; *Del Principe*, 16 de Septiembre y M. Rubio, III.

RESTAURANTS in most hotels; also *Las Brisas*, A. Obregón y Frontera; *Cielo Azul*, Bravo 601 Pte.; *Miramar*, Serdán y 5 de Mayo; *Bismark*, 16 de Septiembre y A. Serdán; *la Arboleda*, Ocampo.

RECREATION and SPORTS. – Swimming, diving, water skiing, fishing, tennis, golf, hunting.

EVENTS. – May 3, celebrations of the foundation of the town; September, fishing competitions

La Paz, capital of the state of Baja California Sur, lies in the bay of the same name on the Mar de Cortés (Gulf of California). Some ten years ago a quiet old-world fishing port, known only to fishermen, it has now developed into a considerable town, mainly owing to the construction of the new N–S route, the Carretera Transpeninsular. In spite of this hectic growth La Paz has managed to preserve something of the restful atmosphere of earlier days.

HISTORY. – Before the Conquest the southern part of Baja California was inhabited by Indian tribes, including the *Pericúe*, Cochimi and *Guaicura*, who at first gave the Spaniards a friendly reception but later tried to prevent the first attempts at settlement. Hernán Cortés is said to have been the first Spaniard to set foot on the peninsula, near the site of present-day La Paz, in 1535. The Jesuit mission station established here in 1720 had to be abandoned in 1745 because of water shortage and illness, and a permanent settlement was not established until 1800. In 1830 La Paz became

capital of the southern territory of Baja California. In 1847–8, during the war with the United States, it was occupied by US troops.

In 1853 an American adventurer named William Walker seized the harbor in an unsuccessful bid to set up an independent state. La Paz was for a long time a center of the pearl fisheries (black and pink pearls), but pearl-fishing is now of little importance. The town's principal sources of revenue are tourism, fishing, commerce and a developing processing industry.

SIGHTS. – This new town has few features of tourist interest apart from the *parish church* (19th c.), the *Government Palace* (20th c.), the *House of Folk Art*, the *Anthropological and Historical Museum*, the *shell market* and the harbor promenade (*Malecón*); but La Paz is an excellent base for deep-sea fishing and diving expeditions and trips to the many beautiful beaches in the surrounding area. It has also acquired importance as a free port.

Among the many *beaches* near La Paz, some close to the town and others rather farther away, are *Playa Sur* to the S, *Centenario* to the W and *Costa Baja*, *Eréndira*, *Pichilingue*, *El Tecolote* and *Puerto Balandra* to the N and NE; near **Las Cruzes** are *El Saltito*, *El Palo*, *Los Muertos* and *El Rosarito*. Excursions by boat to the offshore islands are recommended, especially to *Espíritu Santo*, *La Partida* and *Islotes*, which have good facilities for diving and on which sea lions and many species of birds can be observed.

Another interesting excursion from La Paz is via Los Planes to *Punta Arena Las Ventanas* (about 65 km/40 miles; hotel: Las Arenas, landing strip, SP, fishing) and *Ensenada de los Muertos* with beautiful quiet beaches.

There are regular ferry services between La Paz and Topolobampo and between La Paz and Mazatlán.

From La Paz it is 220 km (140 miles) on Road 1, the Carretera Transpeninsular (see under Baja California), to *****Cabo San Lucas** (p. 84).

La Venta
See under Laguna de Catemaco

León de los Aldamas

State: Guanajuato (Gto.).
Altitude: 1884 m (6181 ft).
Population: 920,000.
Telephone dialing code: 9 14 71.

ⓘ **Coordinación Federal de Turismo,**
Garalza 90,
Cuanajuato, Gto.;
tel. (9 14 73) 2 01 23, 2 01 19, 2 02 14,
2 02 44.

HOTELS. – *Real de Minas*, López Mateos, I, SP;
Condesa, Portal Bravo 14, I; *León*, Madero 113, I, golf;
La Estancia (motel), López Mateos y Estrella. *Motel
Calzada*, Calz. de los Héroes 107, II; *El Dorado*, B.
Domínguez 320, II.

RESTAURANTS in most hotels; also *Los Venados*,
Blvd. López Mateos 511 Ote.; *La Historia*, Blvd. López
Mateos 208 Ote.; *Los Delfines*, M. Alemán 1308.

RECREATION and SPORTS. – Swimming, tennis,
golf.

EVENT. – January 20–30, Feria de San Sebastián.

**León lies on the banks of the Río
Turbio in a fertile valley with an
equable climate. It is the largest
town and principal industrial center
of the state of Guanajuato, producing mainly leather goods (shoes,
saddles, etc.), textiles, soap and
steel products. It is surrounded by a
rich wheat-growing region.**

HISTORY. – In pre-Columbian times the population of
this area was a mixture of *Otomí Indians* and the
nomadic tribes from the N known as *Chichimecs*. In
the second half of the 15th c. these were displaced by
Tarascans and *Aztecs*. The *Spaniards* established their
first settlement here in 1552, and this was followed in
1576 by the official foundation of a town, which
received its municipal charter in 1836. The words "de
los Aldamas" were then added to its name in honor of
Juan Aldama, one of the prominent figures, together
with Hidalgo and Allende, in the struggle for Mexican
independence. – Thereafter the town developed
rapidly, but suffered several times from severe
flooding, as in 1888, when much of the town was
destroyed. It is now protected by a dyke.

SIGHTS. – Although León is now predominantly a modern industrial city it has a
number of handsome colonial buildings.
The main square (*Zócalo*), with the
Baroque *Cathedral* (18th c.), is surrounded by arcades.

The **Town Hall** (*Palacio Municipal*) has
a richly carved façade. – A notable 20th c.
church is the neo-Gothic **Templo Ex-
piatorio**, which has more than twenty
altars and numerous chapels, etc., in the
undercroft.

Also of interest are the *Market*, the *Ciudad
Deportiva* (City of Sport) and, 40 km (25
miles) away, the spa of *Comanjilla* (sulfur
springs).

Malinalco

State: México (Mex.).
Altitude: 1750 m (5742 ft). – Population: 18,000.

ⓘ **Coordinación Federal de Turismo,**
Av. Vincente Villada 123,
Col Centro,
Toluca, Mex.
tel. (9 17 21) 4 42 49, 4 89 61.

ACCESS. – From Mexico City on Road 95D to Tres
Marias 44 km (27 miles) then turn right via the
Lagunas de Zempoala (14 km – 9 miles) and Chalma
(40 km – 25 miles) to Malinalco. From Toluca, 65 km
(40 miles) W of Mexico City, 13 km (8 miles) S on
Road 55 to Tenango; then road on left to Malinalco
(27 km – 17 miles). From the parking lot it is a
30 minute climb to the site of the ruins.

**The pre-Columbian site of *Malin-
alco lies on the Cerro de los Ídolos
("Hill of Idolos"), 220 m (720 ft)
above the village of the same name,
in a region of green forests and
rugged rock formations. This Aztec
cult site is unique in having one
of the very few rock-cut pre-
Columbian structures in Meso-
America.**

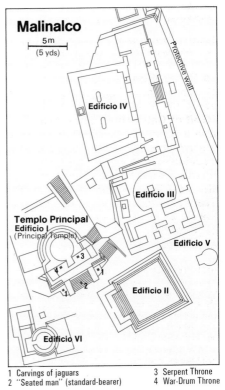

Malinalco

1 Carvings of jaguars   3 Serpent Throne
2 "Seated man" (standard-bearer)   4 War-Drum Throne

HISTORY. – Finds of pottery in Teotihuacán style indicate that the site was occupied in the early Classic period. Later it appears to have been under the influence of the *Toltecs*. In the 12th c. A.D. one of the Nahua tribes moving from Aztlán to the Anáhuac valley settled in Malinalco (Náhuatl, "place of the *malinalli* herb"). The town was taken by the *Aztecs* (Mexica) under Axayácatl in 1476, and the building of the main cult structures probably began twenty-five years later. – When the *Spaniards*, led by Andrés de Tapia, captured Malinalco in 1521 the ceremonial center was not yet complete. Augustinian missionaries established themselves here in 1537. – The excavation and restoration of the site was begun by José García Payón on behalf of INAH in the 1930s and continued thirty years later by César A. Sáenz.

THE SITE. – At the SW corner of a group of buildings on a narrow platform cut into the hillside is *Building VI* (Edificio VI), the construction of which was interrupted by the Spanish conquest. Immediately N of this is ***Building I** (*Edificio I*), the **Templo Principal**.

The temple, which is entirely hewn from the rock, thus being the only one of this type in Meso-America, was originally faced with a thin coating of colored stucco. As the **House of the Eagle** (*Cuauhcalli*), it was used for the initiation of members of the religious military orders, the Eagle Knights and Jaguar Knights. The *staircase* is flanked by the remains of carved *jaguars*; in the middle is the damaged figure of a standard-bearer.

The TEMPLE which stands on the platform is now protected by a palm-leaf roof. The entrance to the circular *shrine* is carved in low relief to resemble the open jaws of a snake, on either side of which are a serpent throne and war-drum throne. The temple chamber, 6 m (20 ft) in diameter, contains three figures of sacred animals hewn from the native rock: to left and right eagles and in the middle, to the rear, a jaguar. In the center of the semicircle is a carved representation of an eagle's skin, and behind this is a cavity in which the hearts of the sacrificial victims were probably deposited.

NE of the House of the Eagle and to the N of *Building II* is *Building III*, which consists of an antechamber and a round chamber containing an altar hollowed out of the rock. This was probably a *tzincalli*,

House of the Eagle, Malinalco

a temple in which the "messenger of the Sun" – the warrior killed in battle or sacrificed by the enemies of the Aztecs – was cremated and "deified". The Aztecs believed that the souls of warriors killed in this way became stars.

In the ante-chamber are the remains of interesting frescoes, probably depicting warriors who had been transformed into stars.

The large *Building IV*, partly hewn from the rock, which lies immediately N of Building III, is believed to have been a temple of the Sun. – A remarkable wooden drum (*tlapanhuéhuetl*) with finely carved figures and glyphs of the eagle and the jaguar associated with the "messenger of the Sun" was found here; it is now in the museum in Tenango.

The village of Malinalco has an interesting *church* belonging to an Augustinian convent, with a plain Renaissance doorway and early frescoes (past the entrance on the right on the rear wall).

SURROUNDINGS. – 11 km (7 miles) E is the village of **Chalma**, one of Mexico's principal places of pilgrimage. In pre-Columbian times a statue of Oztoteótl, the god of caves, was worshipped here, and when this was destroyed by Augustinian monks in 1533 and replaced by a large crucifix, popular devotion was transferred to this new object. The church, built in 1683, in which the Christ of Chalma (El Santo Señor de Chalma) is now worshipped, attracts many thousands of pilgrims on the great festivals, particularly on the first Friday in Lent, at Ascension and on August 28 (St Augustine). On these occasions there is a fascinating mixture of Catholic and ancient Indian rituals (ceremonies, processions, dances, purifying baths, etc.). – 40 km (25 miles) NE of Chalma are the seven *Lagunas de Zempoala*, in a magnificent setting reminiscent of the Alps.

15 km (9 miles) W of Malinalco is **Tenancingo** ("place of the little walls"; alt. 2040 m (6693 ft); pop. 26,000; Hotel San Carlos; fiestas: May 15, Día de San Isidro Labrador; October 4, Día de San Francisco; December 8, Immaculate Conception), which has an 18th c. Carmelite convent, the Convento del Santo Desierto de Tenancingo. The town is noted for its wooden furniture and its *rebozos* (shawls).

33 km (21 miles) S of Tenancingo on Road 55 is the spa of **Ixtapan de la Sal** (alt. 1900 m (6234 ft); pop. 10,000; hotels: Ixtapan, SP, golf, tennis, riding; Kiss, SP; Casa Raúl; Vista Hermosa, SP; Belisama, SP; Casa Blanca, SP; Lolita, SP; fiesta on second Friday in Lent, Día del Señor de la Misericordia). This attractively situated resort draws many visitors with its radioactive mineral springs and the facilities it offers for a variety of sports.

Manzanillo

State: Colima (Col.).
Altitude: sea level.
Population: 80,000.
Telephone dialing code: 9 13 33.

ⓘ **Coordinación Federal de Turismo,**
Juárez 244, 4th floor,
tel. 2 01 81, 2 2 90, 2 20 91.

HOTELS. – *Las Hadas*, Peninsula Santiago, L, SP, tennis, golf; *Club Maeva*, at 12 km on road to Barra Navidad, L, SP, tennis; *La Posada*, at 2 km on old road to Santiago, I, SP; *Playa de Santiago*, Playa de Santiago, I, SP, tennis; *Colonial*, Av. Mexico 100, II; *Las Brisas*, Lote 4, Manzana 15, II; *Anita*, Playa Santiago, III.

RESTAURANTS in most hotels; also *Los Girasoles*, Av. Mexico 79; *Belén*, Independencia 18; *Las Hamacas*, Playa de Mirador; *El Plato*, at 10.5 km on Salagua Road; *El Dorado*, at 9 km on Santiago Road; *L'Recif*, Fracc. Vida del Mar.

RECREATION and SPORTS. – Swimming, diving, surfing, water skiing, fishing, deep-sea fishing, tennis, golf, riding, hunting.

EVENTS. – Fishing competitions; sailing regattas. – Fiesta December 12, Día de la Virgen de Guadalupe.

Manzanillo lies on a peninsula at the S end of two curving bays, the Bahía de Santiago and the Bahía de Manzanillo, surrounded by luxuriant jungle and by banana and coconut plantations. It is an important Pacific port, but has also developed into a popular vacation resort in recent years, thanks to its extensive beaches and above all to the excellent deep-sea fishing.

HISTORY. – Near the site of Manzanillo there stood in pre-Columbian times the settlement of *Tzalahua* (Náhuatl, "where cloth is laid out to dry"), at one time capital of the Indian state of Coliman. It has been

Las Hadas beach, Manzanillo

suggested that during this period the port was already engaged in trade with Peru, Ecuador and Colombia. – In 1526 Cortés and his Spaniards reached Tzalahua, and soon afterwards founded a settlement there, *Santiago de Buena Esperanza*. From here they sailed along the coast as far as the Gulf of California. After 1560 the Spanish vessels which sailed to East Asia (e.g., for the conquest of the Philippines) were built and fitted out here. It is only within recent decades, however, that the building of roads and railways and the establishment of air services have enabled Manzanillo to develop to its present size.

The town has a charming main square (Zócalo) and a number of churches, but its main attractions lie in its setting and its surroundings, with their luxuriant vegetation and beautiful beaches and lagoons.

Fishermen are magnificently catered for (sea raven, catfish, mojarra, sea bass, snapper, etc.), with excellent deep-sea fishing (sailfish, fanfish, bonito, devil ray, shark, etc.).

Las Hadas vacation center, Manzanillo

Manzanillo has a whole range of fine *beaches* on the open sea. To the S are the *Playa de Campos de Coco* and *Playa de Ventana* (waves and current); to the N the *Playa de Oro*; in the Bahía de Manzanillo the beaches of *Rompeolas, San Pedrito* (near the town: popular), the very large *Playa Azul, Las Hadas* (with a well-designed modern vacation center); and in the Bahía de Santiago *La Audiencia, Santiago Olas Altas* and *Miramar*.

SURROUNDINGS. – SE of the town is the *Laguna de Cuyutlán*, with interesting animal and plant life. *Cuyutlán*, 45 km (28 miles) from Manzanillo, and *Los Pascuales*, 15 km (9 miles) farther away, are noted for the high waves which come in from the Pacific; these are known as the "green waves" from the coloring sometimes given to them by phosphorescent marine organisms.

Matamoros
See under Tamaulipas

Matehuala
See under San Luis Potosí (state)

Mazatlán

State: Sinaloa (Sin.).
Altitude: sea level. – Population: 255,000.
Telephone dialing code: 9 16 78.
ⓘ **Coordinación Federal de Turismo,** Av. del Mar 1000;
tel. 1 42 12, 1 42 11, 1 42 10.

Mazatlán, on the Pacific Ocean

In the town of Mazatlán

HOTELS. – *Camino Real,* Punta del Sábalo, L, SP, tennis; *El Cid Resort,* Calz. Camarón – Sábalo, L, SP, tennis, golf; *Holiday Inn,* Calz. Camarón – Sábalo, L, SP; *Hacienda Mazatlán,* Av. del Mar y Flamingos, I, SP, tennis; *El Pescador,* Calz. Camarón – Sábalo y Atún, I, SP; *Aquamarina,* Av. del Mar 10, I, SP; *Sand's,* Av. del Mar, II; *Casa Blanca,* Albatros 206, II; *Fiesta,* Tamazula y Rio Presidio, II; *Olas Altas,* Centenario 14, II; *Santa Barbara,* Juárez y 16 Septiembre, II; *San Jorge,* A. Serdán 2710, III.

RESTAURANTS in most hotels; also *Mamucas,* S. Bolívar 73; *Casa Loma,* Av. Gaviotas 104; *Ney's,* Av. del Mar 548; *El Patio,* Av. Del Mar 301; *La Copa de Leche,* Olas Altas Sur 33; *La Cueva,* Av. Del Mar 2002; *Rolf's,* Av. del Mar 225.

RECREATION and SPORTS. – Swimming, snorkeling, diving, water skiing, para-sailing, sailing, fishing (including deep-sea fishing), surfing, boat and canoe trips, shooting, riding, golf, tennis.

EVENTS. – Fishing competitions; Carnival. – Fiesta December 8, Immaculate Conception.

Mazatlán lies in a natural bay on a projecting tongue of land just to the S of the Tropic of Cancer. It is the largest Mexican commercial and fishing port on the Pacific, as well as a considerable industrial town and a popular beach resort.

HISTORY. – Mazatlán (Náhuatl, "place of the deer") was an area of Indian settlement long before the Conquest. The Spaniards were already here in 1576 under Hernando de Bazán, but the town in its present form was not founded until 1806. Mazatlán and the surrounding area had previously been exposed to frequent pirate raids, and at times served as a buccaneers' lair. The foundations of the town's subsequent development were laid in the mid 19th c. by German settlers, who improved the harbor in order to facilitate the export of their agricultural produce and the import of farming equipment.

SIGHTS. – Local features of interest are the *lighthouse* (El Faro), one of the highest in the world (almost 160 m – 525 ft), the *Aquarium* (Av. de los Deportes III) and the "death divers" who launch themselves into the sea from the *Mirador*. A drive in an *araña*, a two-wheeled horse carriage, along the coast roads makes an attractive outing. – The main attractions for visitors are the facilities for all kinds of water sports, chief among them deep-sea fishing (sailfish, fanfish, shark, swordfish, tarpon, etc.).

Among the most popular *beaches*, to the N of the town, are *Olas Altas, Norte, Avenida El Mar, Las Gaviotas, Sábalo Camarones, Sábalo Cerritos* and *Escondida*. Some of the beaches offer good surfing, while others are more suitable for swimming and water skiing.

Also very popular are trips to the offshore islands, some of them used as nesting places by large numbers of birds. Among them are the *Piedras, Dos Hermanas, Pájaros, Lobos* and *Venados* islands.

There is a daily service between Mazatlán and La Paz, capital of Baja California Sur. From Mazatlán it is some 225 km (140 miles) NW to *Culiacán*, capital of Sinaloa state (p. 245).

Mérida

State: Yucatán (Yuc.).
Altitude: 8 m (26 ft). – Population: 430,000.
Telephone dialing code: 9 19 92.
ⓘ **Coordinación Federal de Turismo,**
Av. Itzaes 501;
tel. 3 60 75, 3 69 75, 4 65 96, 4 53 67

HOTELS. – *El Castellano*, Calle 57 Nr. 513, I, SP; *María del Carmen*, Calle 63 Nr. 550, I, SP; *Holiday Inn*, Av. Colón y Calle 60, I, SP; *Casa del Balam*, Calle 60 Nr. 488, I, SP; *Hacienda Inn*, Av. Aviación 709, I, SP; *Autel 59*, Calle 59 Nr. 546, I, SP; *Montejo Palace*, Calle 56 Nr. 483, I. SP; *Colón*, Calle 62 Nr. 483, II, SP; *Colonial*, Calle 62 Nr. 476, II, SP; *Caribe*, Calle 59 Nr. 500, II; *Del Gobernadoc*, Calle 57 Nr. 535, II; *Nacional*, Calle 61 Nr. 474, II, SP; *Posada Central*, Calle 55 Nr. 446, III; *Margarita*, Calle 66 Nr. 506, III; *Mucuy*, Calle 57 Nr. 481, III.

RESTAURANTS in most hotels; also *Alberto's Patio Continental*, Calle 64 Nr. 482; *El Faisán y el Venado*, Calle 59 Nr. 617; *Los Portales*, Calle 60 Nr. 466; *Siqueff*, Calle 59 Nr. 553; *Los Almendros*, Calle 59 Nr. 434; *Soberanis*, Calle 60 Nr. 483; *Taquería El Cangrejito*, Calle 62 Nr. 487A.

RECREATION and SPORTS. – Swimming, tennis, golf, hunting, fishing.

EVENTS. – Carnival. – Fiesta December 12, Día de Nuestra Señora de Guadalupe. – Daily market.

*Mérida, capital of the state of Yucatán, lies at the N end of a plateau of porous limestone which is well suited to the cultivation of a type of agave yielding henequen (sisal) fibers. Before the development of man-made fibers the hennequen industry brought prosperity to the town, whose trade connections linked it wit̀ Europe and particularly with France. During this period it became known as the "ciudad blanca", the "white city", since the people of Mérida liked to dress in white and took pride in keeping their town trim and clean. Thanks to its warm and humid climate this attractive town is gay with flowers, and life goes at a leisurely pace.

In the center of Mérida

HISTORY. – The town was founded on January 6, 1542 by the conquistador Francisco Montejo, known as "El Mozo" (the "Boy") to distinguish him from his father, "El Adelantado" (the "Governor"). After bitter fighting with the Maya tribes the younger Montejo conquered most of Yucatán within the following four years. Mérida was built on the site of the Maya town of *Tihó*, using material from the demolished temples. In the year in which it was founded the last Maya ruler of the area, Titul-Xiú, cacique or chief of Maní, surrendered to the Spaniards. A prominent role in the history of Mexico was played by the second bishop of Mérida, Diego de Landa, who tried by all the means in his power to eradicate the old Indian culture – burning, for example, a great number of irreplaceable Maya manuscripts. He did, however, write a valuable "Relación de las Cosas de Yucatán", an account of the conquest of Yucatán and the civilization of the Mayas as seen by Spanish eyes. He died in Mérida in 1579.

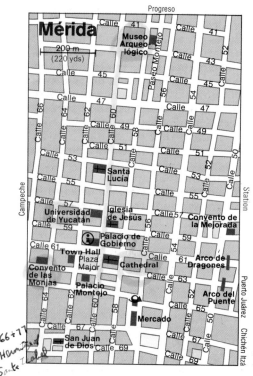

In 1648 Mérida and Yucatán were ravaged by an epidemic of yellow fever brought by Negro slaves from Africa. – During the struggle for independence from 1810 onwards Mérida and Yucatán, owing to their remoteness, played little part. There were, however, some movements aimed at securing the independence of Yucatán from Mexico. In the second half of the 19th c. there was a ruthless civil war when the Maya tribes rebelled against Mexico rule. The peninsula was not finally pacified until the early years of the 20th c.

SIGHTS. – Unlike most other Mexican towns, Mérida has a regular layout with the streets running at right angles to one another. The streets have numbers instead of names, those running from N to S having even numbers and those running from E to W odd numbers.

The **Plaza Mayor (Plaza de la Independencia)** is the commercial and cultural center of Mérida. On the E side of the square, occupying the site of an earlier Maya temple, stands the **Cathedral**, built by Pedro de Aulestia and Miguel de Aguero between 1561 and 1598.

The largest church in the Yucatán peninsula, it has few architectural features of particular note. – Above a doorway in the INTERIOR hangs a picture of the Maya ruler of Maní, Titul-Xiú, visiting the conquistador Francisco Montejo in Tihó. To the left of the high altar is the *Chapel of the Christ of the Blisters* (Capilla del Cristo de las Ampollas), with a 16th c. Indian woodcarving. According to the legend this was made from the wood of a tree which the Indians once saw burning all night long without showing any trace of the fire. The statue originally stood in a church at

Ichmul which was burned down, and after the fire was found black and covered with blisters. It has been in the Cathedral since 1645, and is the subject of special veneration at the beginning of October every year.

Adjoining the Cathedral but now separated from it by an intervening street is the *Archbishop's Palace*, which is occupied by various government offices.

In the middle of the S side of the Plaza Mayor is the ***Palacio Montejo**, one of the finest examples of Spanish colonial architecture, built in 1549 as the residence of the Montejo family. Originally the palace, with its magnificent Plateresque façade, extended along the whole of the S side of the square. The large and handsome rooms are laid out around two patios and furnished with antique furniture imported from Europe. Note the coat of arms of the Montejo family and the stone sculptures of conquistadors standing with one foot on the head of a conquered Maya. Until quite recently the house was still owned by descendants of the Montejo family.

Opposite the Cathedral is the **Town Hall** (*Palacio Municipal*), a 16th c. building with colonnades and a clock tower. – At the NE corner of the square is the **Government Palace** (*Palacio de Gobierno*), built in 1892, which has interesting murals by Fernando Castro Pacheco (1971–4).

One block W of the Town Hall is a handsome conventual building, a relic of the *Convento de las Monjas*, founded at the end of the 16th c.

In the *Parque Cepeda Peraza*, one block N of the Plaza Mayor on Calle 60, is the **Jesus Church** (*Iglesia de Jesús*) or *Church of the Third Order*, a favorite church for weddings. On the left of the high altar is an altarpiece of carved and gilded wood in Plateresque style. Near the church, with it entrance on Calle 59, is the *Pinacoteca Gamboa Guzmán* which houses primarily pictures of the 19th and 20th c., including portraits and religious subjects as well as works by Gamboa Guzmán. The park also serves as a "cabrank" for Mérida's *calesas* (horse-drawn carriages).

The *Ermita de Santa Isabel church*, at the corner of Calles 66 and 77, is notable mainly for the gardens in which it stands, with their Maya statues. The hermitage was once much frequented by travelers to and from Campeche, who prayed here for a safe journey or gave thanks for a safe return. – Another church of historical interest is *Santa Lucía*, at the corner of Calles 60 and 55; it was originally built by the Spaniards for the exclusive use of their Negro and mulatto slaves.

During Mérida's heyday at the beginning of the 20th c. the *Paseo Montejo* was laid out on the model of the Paris boulevards. It runs through a select residential district and is flanked by monuments; the most striking and interesting of them is the **Monument to the Fatherland** (*Monumento a la Patria*) which took the Columbian sculptor Rómulo Rozo eleven years (1946–57) to complete. This curious and gigantic work, sympathetic to the Maya style, portrays substantial periods of Mexican history and its characters.

At the corner of the Paseo Montejo and Calle 43, in a former government building known as the Palacio del General Cantón, is the ***Museum of Archeology and History** (*Museo de Arqueología e Historia*). This imposing 19th c. building contains a fine collection of material mostly from the great days of Maya civilization, but the other advanced cultures of pre-Columbian Mexico are also well represented. – At the corner of Calles 57 and 60 is the *University of Yucatán*, originally a Jesuit foundation (1618), which runs summer courses for visitors in a variety of subjects, including Spanish and archeology.

The **Mercado Municipal* (Municipal Market), a little way S of the Plaza Mayor, is well worth a visit. The main products on sale here are articles made from sisal (hammocks, panama hats, bags, carpets, sandals), together with *huipiles* (Maya-style dresses with brightly colored embroidery around the neck) for women and *guayabera* shirts for men.

SURROUNDINGS. – Mérida is a good base for excursions to most of the archeological sites in Yucatán, such as **Dzibilchaltún** (p. 123), ****Uxmal** (p. 282), ***Kabah** (p. 148), **Izamal** (p. 144) and ****Chichén Itzá** (p. 96).

35 km (22 miles) from Mérida is **Progreso** (hotels: Yuxcatún, Costa Maya, Malecón; restaurants: Soberanis, La Terraza, Carabela.), Yucatán's principal port, with a pier 2 km (1¼ miles) long.

To the E of Progreso, near *Chicxulub*, are the summer beach resorts traditionally favored by the people of Mérida. Also very popular are the beaches W of Progreso, with the little ports of *Yucalpetén* and *Chelem*. In addition to bungalow hotels there are also furnished houses available for hiring at very reasonable rents between September and June. It must be admitted, however, that this coast does not compare with the coasts on the Caribbean side of Yucatán.

SE of Mérida are a number of small places, some of which have interesting churches and convents of the colonial period which are worth a visit (see Yucatán p.– 299). While in this area the visitor should not fail to see the former Maya town of Mayapán, 48 km (30 miles) from Mérida. In the same direction, 22 km (14 miles) from Mérida, is the little town of **Acanceh**, which has remains of a pre-Hispanic pyramid and a palace. From here it is another 20 km (12 miles) S to **Mayapán**.

The Maya chronicles tell contradictory stories about the origin and development of Mayapán. It seems probable that the *Itzá* (who are now believed to have been a "Toltecized" Chontal-Maya people from Tabasco) came to Yucatán about 1200, resettled the abandoned site of Chichén Itzá and finally founded **Mayapán** ("banner of the Maya"). Thereafter for almost 250 years Mayapán, under the *Cocom* dynasty, was the predominant power in Yucatán. Its end came around 1450, when the town was destroyed during a rising by the *Xiú* tribe, who had previously been settled at Uxmal. This led to the final collapse of Maya civilization, when the empire broke up into some 20 unimportant petty states. – In its heyday Mayapán covered an area of about 6.5 sq. km (2½ sq. miles), with some 3500 buildings, and was surrounded by a strong town wall. Architecturally Mayapán is a smaller copy of Chichén Itzá and has only been excavated and restored to a limited extent. The first thing one sees is the Old Man's House (Casa del Viejo) and then the Tzompantli (Náhuatl, "wall of the skull"); half left is the Palace of Pillars (Palacio de las Mil Columnas) with a large stone mask and two figures. Dominating the site is the *Castillo* (Pyramid of the Kukulcán) with an interesting view of the overgrown site. A path on the E side of the Castillo leads to the left to a low structure which is decorated in the most intriguing

Convento de las Monjas, Mérida

manner with masks of the rain-goddess Chac in the purest Puuc style, that is in a style which had its heyday at least 400 years earlier.

An interesting visit can be paid to one of the haciendas near Mérida which still grow henequen – perhaps combined with an excursion to Chichén Itzá or another place of interest.

Mexicali
See under Baja California

México (State)

State of México (Mex.). – Capital: Toluca.
Area: 21,414 sq. km (8268 sq. miles).
Population: 9,387,400.

ⓘ **Coordinación Federal de Turismo,**
Av. Vicente Villada 123,
Col. Centro.
Toluca, Mex.;
tel. (9 17 21) 4 42 49, 4 89 61.

The state of México (Estado de México) – not to be confused with the name of the country or with the Federal District which contains Mexico City – is bounded on the N by the states of Hidalgo and Querétaro, on the W by Michoacán, on the S by Guerrero and Morelos and on the E by Puebla and Tlaxcala, and encloses the Federal District on three sides. The eastern half of the state is hilly, the western part flat. **Although in process of industrial development, México state has much beautiful scenery – snow-capped mountains, lakes and forests – and there are a number of national parks within its boundaries. It also has many works of colonial art and architecture and many archeological sites. In addition to whites and mestizos its population includes several Indian tribes, including the Otomí, Matlatzinca, Ocuilteca and Nahua.**

The state has an unusually large number of pre-Columbian sites, the most important of which are ****Teotihuacán** (p. 257), *Tepexpan* (p. 71), *Texcotzingo*, *Huexotla* and *San Miguel Coatlinchán* (p. 265), *Tlapacoya* (p. 74), **Tenayuca* (p. 256), *Santa Cecilia Acatitlán* (p. 257), *Calixtlahuaca* and *Teotenango* (p. 272) and **Malinalco** (p. 153).

In addition to these archeological sites – at some of which examples of colonial art and architecture can also be seen – the main places of interest in México state are *Toluca* (the capital), **Tepotzotlán*, **Acolman*, **Texcoco** and **Amecameca** (see the entries for these places).

HISTORY. – The history of human settlement and culture in the state of México goes back a long way, as the finds at Tepexpan and Tlapacoya have shown. On the whole its historical development has been the

Mexico
United Mexican States
Estados Unidos Mexicanos

México

States
Estados

1a Baja California Sur	12 Aguascalientes
1b Baja California Norte	13 Jalisco
	14 Guanajuato
2 Sonora	15 Querétaro
3 Chihuahua	16 Hidalgo
4 Sinaloa	17 Colima
5 Durango	18 Michoacán
6 Coahuila	19 México
7 Nuevo León	20 Morelos
8 Zacatecas	21 Tlaxcala
9 San Luis Potosí	22 Puebla
10 Tamaulipas	23 Veracruz
11 Nayarit	24 Guerrero
	25 Oaxaca

26 Chiapas	
27 Tabasco	
28 Campeche	
29 Yucatán	
30 Quintana Roo	

D.F. Distrito Federal (Federal District)

same as that of Mexico City and the principal towns within the state. – As part of the Viceroyalty of New Spain and later as the *Intendencia de México*, with Mexico City as its capital, that state had a considerably larger area than it now has. It was given its present boundaries only after Mexico became independent.

ECONOMY. – The state's main forms of *industry* are cement manufacture, iron and steel, aluminium processing and motor vehicle assembly. the principal *agricultural crops* are wheat, maize, agaves, sugarcane, coffee, fruit and vegetables; *dairy farming* also flourishes. Substantial contributions are made to the economy by *forestry* and *tourism*.

Mexico City/ Ciudad de México

Distrito Federal (D.F.).
Altitude: 2240 m (7349 ft).
Population (with suburbs): 18,100,000 (estimate for 1984).
Telephone dialing code: 9 15.

(i) **Secretaría de Turismo,**
Av. Presidente Masaryk 172;
tel. 2 50 01 23.
Information Office,
Av. Juárez 92; tel. 5 85 58 45.

EMBASSIES. – *United Kingdom,* Lerma 71 (tel. 5 11 48 80, 5 14 33 27, 5 14 38 86, 5 14 36 86). – *United States of America:* Paseo de la Reforma 305 (tel. 5 53 33 33). – *Canada* Schiller 529 (tel. 2 54 32 88).

HOTELS. – IN THE CENTER (on both sides of Av. Juárez, from intersection with Paseo de la Reforma to Zócalo and around Zócalo): *Alfer,* Revillagigedo 18, *Bamer,* Av. Juárez 52, I; *Gran Hotel Ciudad de México,* 16 de Septiembre 82, I; *De Cortés,* Hidalgo 85, II; *Ambassador,* Humboldt 38, II; *Majestic,* Av. Madero 73, II; *Ritz,* Madero 30, II; *Metropol,* Luis Moya 39, II; *Marlowe,* Independencia 17, II; *Guadalupe,* Revillagigedo 36, II.

ON PASEO DE LA REFORMA (from intersection with Av. Juárez to Angel): *María Isabel Sheraton,* Paseo de la Reforma 325, L, SP; *El Presidente,* Hamburgo 135, L SP; *Fiesta Palace,* Paseo de la Reforma, 80, L, SP; *Krystal,* Liverpool 155, L, SP; *Galería Plaza,* Hamburgo 195, L; *Emporio,* Paseo de la Reforma 124, I; *Aristos,* Paseo de la Reforma 276, I; *Calinda* Geneve, Londres 130, I; *Century Zona Rosa,* Liverpool 152, I, SP; *Reforma,* Reforma y Paris, I; *María Cristina,* Río Lerma 31, II; *Reqente,* Paris 9, II; *Sevilla,* Serapio Rendón 126, II; *Del Angel,* Rio Lerma 154, II; *El Ejecutivo,* Viena 8, II; *Internacional Havre,* Havre 21, II; *Jardín Amazonas,* Río Amazonas 73, II; *Viena,* Marsella 28, II; *Corinto,* Vallarta 24, II; *Vasco de Quiroga,* Londres 15, II; *Versailles,* General Prim 59, II.

ADJOINING AREAS IN CITY CENTRE: *Camino Real,* Mariano Escobedo 700, L, SP, tennis; *El Presidente Chapultepec,* Campos Eliseos 218, L, SP; *Park Villa,* Gómez Pedraza 68, II; *Polanco,* Edgar Allan Poe 8, II.

OUTER DISTRICTS: *Holiday Inn,* Blvd. Aeropuerto 502, I; *El Diplomático,* Insurgentes Sur 1105, I; *Virreyes,* J. M. Izazaga 8, 11; *Brasilia,* Av. Cien Metros 482, II;

Cien Metros, Av. Cien Metros 1119, II; *Finisterre,* Calzada Tlalpan 2043, II; *Montreal,* Calzada Tlalpan 2073, II. *Fiesta Americana Aeropuerto,* Calle Fundidora de Monterrey 85.

RESTAURANTS in most hotels; also *Hacienda de los Morales,* Vázquez de Mella 525; *San Angel Inn,* Palmas 50; *Rivoli,* Hamburgo 123; *Del Lago,* Chapultepec Park; *Ambassadeurs,* Paseo de la Reforma 12; *Champs Elysées,* Reforma y Amberes; *Bellinghausen,* Londres 95; *Delmónico's,* Londres 78; *Fonda del Refugio,* Liverpool 166; *Château de la Palma,* Providencia 726; *Focolare,* Hamburgo 87; *Richelieu,* Paseo de la Reforma 336; *Tokio,* Hamburgo 134; *La Trucha Vagabunda,* Londres 104; *Loredo,* Hamburgo 29; *Nuevo Acapulco,* Lopez 9; *Danubio,* Uruguay 3; *Piccolo Suizo,* Mariano Escobedo 539; *Viena,* Amberes 4; *Café de Paris,* Plaza Melchor Ocampo 11; *La Marinera,* Liverpool 183; *Fuji,* Río Pánuco 128.

RECREATION and SPORTS. – Swimming, tennis, squash, jai alai, badminton, golf, riding, skating, polo.

EVENTS. – July 16, Día de la Virgen del Carmen; August 13, commemoration of defence of Mexico City; September 15–16, Independence Day (Noche del Grito); November 20, anniversary of 1910 revolution; December 12, Día de Nuestra Señora de Guadalupe.

**Mexico City (Ciudad de México), the Mexican capital and seat of the central government, lies at an altitude of over 2200 m (7300 ft) in the Valley of Mexico or Valley of Anáhuac, a high valley surrounded by mighty mountain ranges. Owing to the city's high altitude it has an equable climate which suits visitors from more northerly regions, and its situation is breathtaking, lying as it does at the foot of two magnificent snow-covered volcanoes rising to over 5000 m (16,000 ft), Popocatépetl and Iztaccíhuatl. The city preserves countless reminders of its past of more than 650 years, though pre-Columbian art and architecture exist almost solely in isolated fragments and museum reproductions, since the conquistadors built the nucleus of their new town on the ruins of the old Aztec metropolis of Tenochtitlán which they had destroyed. Against this, however, there are many churches and palaces of the colonial period, mainly in the Baroque style; and modern Mexican architecture is represented by numbers of fine buildings, particularly those of quite recent years.

The city area extends for almost 40 km (25 miles) from N to S, with an average extent of 25 km (15 miles) from E to W. The

Distrito Federal (*Federal District:* see p. 119), which is headed by a Regente directly responsible to the President, was created to establish the capital as a separate administrative unit but is no longer adequate to contain the city's northward growth, so that its new industrial suburbs extend into the neighboring state of Mexico.

The city's rate of growth, primarily due to the influx of population from the agricultural regions of the N with their harsh climate, is enormous. The present population of Mexico City is estimated at 17 million, making it the most populous city in the world. This over-population, combined with the increasing growth of industry – which, however, still fails to produce enough jobs for those who need them – creates serious economic and social difficulties. Traffic problems have been eased by the construction of the

Metro and intersection-free roads (the Anillo Periférico, a highway round the city), but conditions are still chaotic at peak periods. The once crystal-clear mountain air of this high valley has given place to an industrial haze, a smog laden with exhaust gases, which usually blankets the view of the city's tremendous mountain backdrop.

The Growth of Mexico City	
(Rounded figures, including suburbs)	
1910	0.8 million
1920	1.0 million
1950	3.0 million
1960	5.0 million
1970	7.5 million
1980	15.0 million
1986	18.1 million[1]
2000	31.2 million[2]

[1] It is estimated that 11.3 million are living in the Federal District and 6.8 million in the state of Mexico.
[2] Projection on the 2.5% natural increase rate plus 350,000 new immigrants per year.

Panoramic view of Mexico City,

Although the new housing areas are built in a style of nondescript uniformity and there are expanses of slums in the outer districts, Mexico City nevertheless holds an abundance of fascination for the visitor – the style and dignity of the Paseo de la Reforma, the treasures of art in its many museums, the numerous parks with their magnificent old trees, the secluded little nooks and corners with their old Spanish atmosphere which can be found only a few hundred yards from the noisy swirl of city traffic.

HISTORY. – Apart from the culture center in the Formative period which has been found at Cuicuilco the pre-Columbian history of the area around Mexico City centers mainly on the Náhuatl-speaking *Aztecs* or *Mexica*, who in 1325 (or 1345) founded their capital of *Tenochtitlán* (Náhuatl, "place of the cactus fruit") on a swampy island in Lake Texcoco, which until the Spanish conquest covered the eastern part of the present city area. Clustered around the capital were a number of other, originally independent, towns occupied by other Chichimec peoples including *Tenayuca* (see p. 248), *Texcoco* (Acolhua tribe),

Chalco (Chalca tribe), *Tlatelolco, Coyoacán, Tlacopán* (now Tacuba), *Atzcapotzalco* (Tepaneca tribe), *Xochimilco* and *Culhuacán* (Colhua tribe). Three great causeways and an aqueduct linked the island city, which was crisscrossed by numerous canals, with the mainland. In the center of the city stood the massive principal pyramid, with two temples dedicated to the war and sun god Huitzilopochtli and the rain god Tláloc. The ceremonial precinct (Teocalli), surrounded by the "Serpent Wall" (Coatepantli), also contained the temples of other important gods (Tezcatlipoca, Xochiquetzal, Quetzalcóatl, Cihuacóatl). The remains of all these magnificent buildings lie under the present Zócalo (Plaza de la Constitución) and the immediately surrounding area. Outside the cult center were the royal palaces, the residential areas with their market squares and smaller groups of temples. – The older town of Tlatelolco, the rival and later the ally of Tenochtitlán, also had a pyramid similar to that of Tenayuca on which the remains of temples dedicated to the gods Tláloc and Quetzalcóatl were found. Tlatelolco's main importance, however, was as the principal trading center of the Aztec empire. The site of pre-Cortesian Tlatelolco is now covered by the La Lagunilla market, the church of Santiago, the Foreign Ministry and modern apartment buildings; some remains were brought to light in the Square of the Three Cultures. On the lake around the two towns were the artificial islands

with Iztaccíhuatl and Popocatépetl in the background

(*chinampas*) which provided areas of cultivable land. Relics of this method of cultivation can still be seen in the "floating gardens" of Xochimilco. No doubt similar methods were employed on the lakes of Chalco to the S and Xaltocán and Tzompanco (now Zumpango) to the N.

On November 8, 1519, Hernán Cortés with his small force of Spaniards and more numerous Tlaxcalan allies set foot for the first time in the Aztec capital. After the imprisonment of the Aztec ruler, Moctezuma II, in his own palace and his violent death, Cortés was driven out by Tenochtitlán by the Mexica; during their flight, on what came to be known as the "Noche Triste" ("Sad Night", June 30, 1520), the Spaniards lost more than half their strength as well as their booty. After reorganizing their forces, securing reinforcements in the form of native auxiliaries and building thirteen brigantines to control the shores of the lake the Spaniards laid siege to Tenochtitlán in May 1521; and on August 13, 1521, after the capture of the last Aztec ruler Cuauhtémoc, the city was compelled to surrender. Thereafter its buildings were razed to the ground and its canals filled in with rubble.

In 1522 the Spaniards began to build a new town, to which they gave the name of *Méjico*, on the ruins of the Aztec temples, using material from the demolished buildings. In the following year the town was granted its municipal coat of arms. In 1535 Franciscan friars established in Santiago Tlatelolco the Colegio de Santa Cruz, later to achieve wide reputation, in which the children of the Aztec nobility were educated. In the same year the Viceroyalty of New Spain, in which Mexico played a leading part, was created. By 1537 the population of the town had risen again to some 100,000 Indians and 2000 Spaniards. Now capital of New Spain, it became in 1546 the see of an archbishop, with Juan de Zumárraga as the first incumbent. In 1551 the first university on the American continent was founded here.

During the Indian risings of 1692 several public buildings were devastated by fire, including the viceregal palace, which had originally been Cortés's residence. During the war of independence (1810–21) the supporters of independence were for a long time unable to dislodge the royalist forces who held the capital, and it was only after Agustin de Iturbide joined the movement that the garrison was finally obliged to surrender (1821). After Iturbide's episodic "empire" there was a long struggle for power between Liberals and Conservatives and between supporters of the "centralist" and federal systems. During the war between Mexico and the United States (1846–8) the town was occupied for a time by US troops.

In 1863 French troops captured the capital, and from 1864 to 1867 the Archduke Maximilian reigned as emperor from Chapultepec Castle. During this period the city's finest boulevard, the Paseo de la Reforma, was laid out. After the defeat of the French invaders and the shooting of Maximilian at Querétaro, the dispossessed President Benito Jaúrez returned to the city. During the dictatorship of Profirio Díaz (1876–1911) Mexico City was modernized in a style which owed much to foreign and particularly to French influence, and there was a period of intense building activity. During the following decade Mexico was racked by bloody conflicts between the various revolutionary leaders – Francisco Madero, Victoriano Huerta, Álvaro Obregón, Pancho Villa, Emiliano Zapata – and it was only in the post-revolutionary period that the city could again begin to forge ahead.

During and after the Second World War the modernization and industralization of Mexico City made great strides. In 1968 the Summer Olympics were held in the city and in 1970 the World Cup. The finest achievements of modern architecture, painting and sculpture in the Mexican capital are also of recent date.

Sightseeing in Mexico City

Mexico City is divided into sixteen main administrative units called DELAGACIONES or wards, with names such as Álvaro Obregón, Benito Juárez, Cuauhtémoc, Coyoacán, Atzcapoltzalco and Xochimilco. The wards are in turn subdivided into 240 COLONIAS or neighborhoods, often with street names of a particular type (e.g., named after well-known rivers, philosophers, European cities, etc.). Although Mexico City, like all Spanish colonial towns, was originally laid out on a regular plan, the city's frenetic pace of development has wrought such havoc with the system that visitors may sometimes have difficulty in getting their bearings. In general the *avenidas* (avenues) run from E to W and the *calles* (streets) from N to S, but there are also other designations like *bulevar* (boulevard), *calzada* (originally a causeway), *callejón* (lane), *prolongación* (extension), *eje vial* (expressway) and urban motorway. Only the largest and most important thoroughfares retain the same name throughout their length, including the great N–S axis the Avenida de los Insurgentes and the Paseo de la Reforma, running from NE to W. Another important N–S connection is formed by the Calzada Vallejo, Avenida San Juan de Letrán (now Lázaro Cárdenas), Calzada Niño Perdido and Avenida Universidad, and a second E–W axis is provided by the Avenidas Chapultepec, Dr Río de la Loza and Fray Servando Teresa de Mier. There is also a ring road (partly of highway standard) formed by the Calzada Melchor Ocampo, Avenida Río Consulado, Bulevar Puerto Aéreo and Viaductor Miguel Alemán. On the S side this ring is supplemented by the Avenida Río Churubusco, which, like the Viaducto, runs into the outer ring road, the Anillo Periférico (the SE part of which is not yet complete).

Forms of transport in Mexico City include three kinds of *taxis* – the normal type, others which can be hired only from a taxi rank (*sitio*) and communal or collective taxis (*peseros, colectivos*; Setta mini-buses to airport); various types of municipal *buses*; the modern *underground* (Metro: small hand baggage only). A few figures will illustrate the enormous transportation requirements of this huge city: 2.8 million private automobiles, 90,000 taxis, 4800 buses, a subway system with 6 routes, 104 km (65 miles) long, carry 4 million passengers every day.

Between the Alameda and the Zócalo

Before setting out on a sightseeing expedition it is a good idea to get a general impression of the city from the viewing terrace (bar, restaurant) of the 177 m (580 ft) high 43-storey **Torre Latinoamericana** at the corner of Avenida

Madero and San Juan de Letrán (now Lázaro Cárdenas), which affords a magnificent *view of the city.

Going E along *Avenida Francisco I. Madero*, we come to the **church of San Francisco**, with a handsome Churrigueresque doorway of the early 18th c. This is a remnant of a large convent founded by Cortés in 1524 which was destroyed by the Reform government in 1856. The remains of Cortés are said to have lain in this church from 1629 to 1794. – Opposite the church is the *Casa de los Azulejos* (House of Tiles), originally built in 1596 and decorated by the Conde del Valle de Orizaba 150 years later with blue and white tiles from Puebla. It is now a shop and restaurant, with frescoes by José Clemente Orozco (1925) on the staircase.

Beyond this, on the right, is the *Palacio de Iturbide**, an excellently restored 18th c. Baroque palace now occupied by a bank. Originally the residence of the Conde de San Mateo de Valparaiso, it was occupied in 1821–2 by Agustín de Iturbide, who was proclaimed emperor while living here. – On the left, at the corner of Madero and Isabel la Católica, is the fine Baroque **church of La Profesa** (1720). – Father S, at the corner of Isabel la Católica and Uruguay, is a former Augustinian church which housed the National Library until its recent move to the University City. In front of the library stands a statue of Alexander von Humboldt, the gift of the German Emperor.

Going E along the next cross street, *Avenida República del Salvador*, we cross Avenida Pino Suárez and come to the *Museum of Mexico City** (*Museo de la Ciudad de México*), in the imposing Palacio de los Condes de Santiago de Calimaya. This has an interesting collection of material on the history of the city from prehistoric times to the present day. Notable items are a model of the Teocalli, the cult center of ancient Tenochtitlán, and another of the present-day city. – Opposite the Museum is the 17th c. Baroque **church of Jesús Nazareno**, which has *frescoes* by Orozco (1944) in the dome.

Torre Latinoamericana, Mexico City

It was either here or at the church of Santa Cruz Acatlán that Cortés is said to have met the Aztec ruler Moctezuma II for the first time on November 8, 1519. The body of Cortés, who died at Seville in 1547, now rests in the Jesús Nazareno church. Adjoining the church is the **Hospital de Jesús** (originally called the Hospital of the Purísima Concepción), the first of its kind in America, which was founded by Cortés in 1524 and was until recently under the management of his descendants. – In the Pino Suárez underground station, to the S, is a circular Aztec pyramid which was excavated here.

Some blocks (*cuadras*) farther E along Avenida del Salvador is the ***Mercado de la Merced**, a modern market hall designed by Enrique del Moral y Palomar. Until recently it was the largest market of its kind in the city (principally foodstuffs). The market was officially closed in 1982 and moved in stages to the SE district of Iztapalapa, where it occupies an area of 327 hectares (808 acres; *Central de Abastos de Iztapalapa*). Iztapalapa is also renowned for its great *Passion Play* at Eastertide. – In the area of the former market it is worth looking in at the ***Convent of La Merced** (rebuilt 1634), at the corner of Uruguay and Jesús María. The fine cloister shows a mingling of styles, including in particular Mudéjar. – Farther along Avenida Uruguay is the *Capilla Manzanares*, primarily frequented by the market folk, which has a beautiful 18th c. Churrigueresque façade. – SW of La Merced in Calle San Jerónimo is the former *Convent of San Jerónimo* (recently restored). The great poetess and painter Juana Inés de la Cruz (1651–95) lived in this convent, and her remains were recently discovered in the church. The building, dedicated to her is now a museum (library, film shows, excavated relics, etc.).

One block S on Isabel la Católica is the *Avenida José Maria de Izazaga*, in which, near the Isabel la Católica underground station, is the little *church of Nuestra Señora de Monserrat*. The former convent now houses the *Charro Museum* (Museo de la Charrería). – Returning to Calle San Jerónimo and going W along this street, we come, just before the Avenida San Juan de Letrán (recently renamed Lázaro Cárdenas), to the *Colegio de las Vizcainas* or *Colegio de San Ignacio*, a Baroque structure built by Miguel José de Quiera between 1734 and 1786 as a girls' school. It has a very beautiful Churrigueresque chapel which, like the N front, is attributed to Lorenzo Rodríguez. There is a small religious *museum* open at certain times to the public.

At the W end of Calle Izazaga, on the Avenida Lázaro Cárdenas, is the mid-18th c. *church of La Purísima*, with a richly decorated doorway. In the square in front of the church is the *Salto de Agua* fountain, the original of which, dating from colonial times, was removed some sixty years ago to Tepotzotlán. – NW of the square is the *Mercado San Juan, one of the city's oldest and largest markets (foodstuffs, flowers, household requisites, folk art).

Around the Zócalo

The central feature of Mexico City is the **Zócalo (Plaza de la Constitución)**. Measuring some 240 m (260 yds) each way, it is one of the largest squares in the world. The Spaniards began to lay out the square immediately after the conquest of Tenochtitlán, with its northern half overlying the southern part of the demolished Aztec temple precinct, the Teocalli. In the early colonial period the square served a variety of purposes – as a bullfighting arena, a market and a place of public execution among other things. In 1980 the administration designated an area of 9 sq. km (3½ sq. miles) with 1436 representative buildings of the city from the 16th to the 19th century to be the *Historic Center* of the city (El Centro Histórico de la Ciudad) which has been placed under protection as an ancient monument. It is bounded on the W by the streets Abraham Gonzales and Paseo de la Reforma, on the E by Calle Amfora, by Bartolome de Las Casas in the N and by J. Ma. Izazaga in the S. The buildings are soon to undergo extensive restoration. – If we begin our tour on the S side of the square, at the end of the Avenida 20 de Noviembre, we have on the left the *Old Town Hall* (Palacio del Ayuntamiento), a building of the colonial period which was altered around 1700, and on the right the *New Town Hall*. Both of these house Federal District offices. On the SE corner of the Zócalo is the *Supreme Court* (Suprema Corte de Justicia), a modern building in colonial style, with frescoes by José Clemente Orozco on the staircase.

The whole of the E side of the square is occupied by the *National Palace (Palacio Nacional), with a façade over 200 m (650 ft) long. Built of reddish tezontle stone, it is the official residence of the President and houses various government offices. Originally built by Cortés in 1523 on the site of Moctezuma II's "New Palace", it was the seat of the Spanish Viceroys during the colonial period. Much altered and enlarged over the years and partly destroyed during the 1692 rising, it is one of the oldest and finest buildings in the city.

Above the large central doorway, surmounted by the Mexican coat of arms, hangs the *Freedom Bell*, rung by Miguel Hidalgo at Dolores on September 15, 1810 at the start of the war of independence. Every year on September 15 the bell is rung at 11 p.m. and the "Grito de Dolores" is repeated from the balcony.

INTERIOR. – The National Palace has a large number of handsome rooms laid out around seventeen court-yards (only some of which are open to visitors). The most notable feature of the arcaded **Grand Court-yard* is the **frescoes** by Diego Rivera (1929–45) on the staircase and first floor. Covering a total area of 450 sq. m (4850 sq. ft), they depict themes from the history of Mexico from Indian times to the period after the revolution. In picturing this wide span of historical events and their principal actors Rivera gives expression to his very "Indian" social and political attitudes.

Also in the National Palace are the main State Archives, with interesting historical documents; the Biblioteca Miguel Lerdo de Tejada, one of the largest and most important libraries in the country; the Benito Juárez Museum, in the room in which Juárez died in 1872; and the Recinto Constitucional, with the Constitutions of 1857 and 1917.

The N side of the Zócalo is occupied by the Cathedral and the **Sagrario Metro-politano** which adjoins it on the E. The Sagrario, built to the design of Lorenzo Rodriguez, was consecrated in 1768. It is a parish church, quite independent of the Cathedral, and one of the finest examples of Mexican Churrigueresque. On the *façade geometric ornamentation predominates, in the form of the pilasters known as estípites. The harmonious transition from the high central part of the

National Palace, Mexico City

The Cathedral and Sagrario Metropolitano, floodlit

façade to the lower side elements is contrived with consummate skill. A particularly notable feature of the interior is the *high altar* (1829) by Pedro Patiño Ixtolinque, an Indian pupil of Manuel Tolsá's who is also credited with the altar in the chapel of the Virgen Dolorosa. – Part of the interior was destroyed by fire and earthquake in the 18th c. Here, as in many other buildings in Mexico City, the foundations are sinking on one side as a result of the settlement of the subsoil of the drained lake. – On the E side of the Sagrario various craftsmen tender their services, with their tools laid out in front of them. On this side, too, there stood until quite recently a beautiful *fountain* commemorating the great patron of the Indians, Bartolomé de las Casas.

The *Cathedral*, which dominates the square on the N side as the National Palace does on the E, is one of the oldest and largest churches in the western hemisphere. It stands on the southwestern part of the old Aztec temple precinct, once occupied by the Wall of Skulls (Tzompantli) and the temple of Xipe Tótec. The original building, begun in 1525, was later partly demolished and partly rebuilt; the present structure dates from 1563, though the definitive plans were prepared at the end of the 16th c. and the beginning of the 17th by Claudio de Arciniega, Juan Gómez de Mora and Alonso Pérez de Castañeda. Although the

construction of this massive building of basalt and grey sandstone extended over more than 250 years and thus shows a mingling of various styles it creates an effect of notable harmony. In spite of the two openwork towers in neo-classical style and certain other features, the *façade* creates a predominantly Baroque impression with its massive volutes and pairs of twisted columns. The *bell-towers*, by José Damián Ortiz de Castro, were completed in 1793; the statues (attributed to Manuel Tolsá) of Faith, Hope and Charity on the clock-tower and the dome in 1813. The bells are unusual in their method of hanging and vary greatly in size; one of them, known as "Guadalupe", weighs no less than 5600 kg (5½ tons).

*INTERIOR. – The Cathedral, which has two lateral aisles on either side, is 118 m (387 ft) long, 54 m (177 ft) wide and 55 m (180 ft) high. There are fourteen subsidiary altars as well as the high altar. Like the exterior, the interior shows a mingling of all the different styles and fashions prevailing during the colonial period. Its great glory is the **Altar of the Kings** (*Altar de los Reyes*, 1718–39) behind the high altar, with a *retablo* by Jerónimo de Balbás, a sculptor of the Churrigueresque school from Seville. The retablo, which follows the form of the apse, has paintings by Juan Rodríguez y Juárez, including an Adoration of the Kings and an Assumption (to which the Cathedral is dedicated). The chapel W of the high altar contains the remains of Agustín de Iturbide, briefly emperor of Mexico. Opposite the main entrance, closing the S end of the choir, is the *Altar del Perdón*, the Churrigueresque retablo of which (by Jerónimo de Balbás), with a painting of the Virgin by Simón Pereyns (1568), was damaged by a fire in 1967; it has since been restored. The other chapels

Calle de Guatemala

Calle del Seminario

Plaza de la Constitución

**Cathedral,
Mexico City**

**Catedral
Metropolitana**

30 m
(33 yds)

Sagrario
Metropolitano

1 Capilla de Nuestra Señora de las Angustias de Granada
2 Capilla de San Isidro
3 Capilla de Santa Ana y la Purísima Concepción
4 Capilla de Nuestra Señora de Guadalupe
5 Capilla de Nuestra Señora de la Antigua
6 Capilla de San Pedro
7 Capilla del Santo Cristo o de las Reliquias
8 Sacristía
9 Altar Mayor
10 Altar de los Reyes
11 Sala Capitular
12 Capilla de San Felipe de Jesús
13 Capilla de los Dolores
14 Capilla de San Eligio o del Señor del Buen Despacho
15 Capilla de la Soledad
16 Capilla de San José
17 Capilla de los Santos Cosme y Damián
18 Capilla de San Miguel o de los Ángeles
19 Organ galleries

and side altars contain some notable pictures, mainly of the Baroque period.

The very fine carved cedarwood **choir-stalls** (by Juan de Rojas, 1696) were also destroyed in the fire and have been restored. In the *sacristy, which has 16th c. Gothic groined vaulting, are pictures painted about 1665 by Cristóbal de Villalpando ("Immaculate Conception", "Triumph of the Church") and Juan Correa ("Coronation of the Virgin", "St Michael and the Dragon", "Entry into Jerusalem"). – In the *crypt* are the tombs of most of the archbishops of Mexico City, among them Juan de Zumárraga, the great teacher of the Indians, who was the first incumbent of the see. –Adjoining the Cathedral is a *Museum of Religious Art** containing many precious objects.

W of the Cathedral is a much altered building of the colonial period, now occupied by the **Monte de Piedad**, the state pawnshop, founded in 1775 by Pedro Tomero de Terreros. Here articles of all kinds can be purchased, either at periodic auctions or in the sales department.

Behind the Cathedral, at the corner of Calles Argentina and Guatemala, are remains of the TEMPLE PRECINCT of Tenochtitlán which were discovered some years ago and left *in situ*. Near here a carved stone was found in the spring of 1978, a round disc more than 3 m (10 ft) in diameter and weighing 8500 kg ($8\frac{1}{2}$ tons), finely carved with a relief of the beheaded and dismembered goddess Coyolxauhqui. In Nahua mythology she was the sister of the god-king Huitzilopochtli and was defeated and killed by her brother during a struggle for predominance after the Nahua people left the legendary city of Aztlán.

This find stimulated the *excavation of the **Gran Teocalli**, the principal pyramid of Tenochtitlán. The excavations, which are still in progress and have involved the demolition of a whole block of houses, began on the main front of the pyramid with its double staircase, roughly on the line of the E side of Calle Argentina. It was discovered that this side of the pyramid had been built over no fewer than eleven times, while on the other sides there were only five rebuildings. Nothing has survived of the two temples, dedicated respectively to Tláloc and Huitzilopochtli, which originally stood on top of the pyramid.

In the fifth top layer, however, was found the summit platform of an earlier pyramid with the well-preserved walls of two temples. In front of the left-hand temple, dedicated to Tláloc, was a figure of *Chac-mool*, still preserving most of its vividly colored painting. To the right, in front of the temple of Huitzilopochtli, was a *sacrificial altar*. From the height of the walls and the material used it is deduced that these temples were probably erected before the Aztecs gained control of the Anáhuac valley in 1428. There may well be even older temples at lower levels, but it seems improbable that they will be brought to light.

Buried between different building levels were found the *skulls* of sacrificial victims and over fifty vessels containing *votive offerings*. An interesting feature is that only a fraction of the objects found, which numbered several thousand, were of Aztec origin, most of them coming from the territory of other Indian peoples. Probably these represent tribute from the Aztecs' subject peoples, offered to the gods before the completion of a new pyramid.

From the NE corner of the Zócalo, *Calle Moneda* runs E. Going along this street, we see on the left, at the corner of Calle Licenciado Verdad, the Baroque *Archbishop's Palace* (Palacio del Arzobispado). On the other side of this cross street is a building in which Viceroy Antonio de Mendoza set up the first printing office in New Spain in 1536. – On the right, at Calle Moneda 13, is the *Antigua Casa de la Moneda*, a building with an attractive patio which housed the government Mint from 1734 onwards. It now contains the *Museum of the Cultures* (Museo de las Culturas), with works of art and applied art from many countries.

One block farther on, beyond Calle Academia, is the *Academia de San Carlos*, once the most important art school in the country. The building, which was altered in the 19th c., now houses reproductions of European sculpture of the classical period. – In the continuation of Calle Moneda, *Calle Emiliano Zapata*, is the **church of La Santísima** (on left), with a Churrigueresque *façade* (1755–89) which is one of the finest in the city; the first stage in its construction is attributed to Lorenzo Rodríguez, the architect of the Sagrario Metropolitano. A notable feature is the bell-tower in the form of a papal tiara.

To the NW, reached by way of Calle Loreto, is the Plaza Loreto, in which stands the **church of Nuestra Señora de Loreto**, one of the most interesting

neo-classical churches in Mexico, built by Ignacio de Castera and José Agustín Paz between 1809 and 1816. Notable features are the elegant dome, the large windows between the buttresses and, in the sacristy, a reproduction of the Santa Casa of Loreto, with fine pictures of the colonial period by Miguel Cabrera and other artists. It says a great deal for the solidity of the church's structure that it shows no significant damage, although on account of the unstable subsoil the E end, built of heavy stone, has sunk quite considerably while the W end, in the lighter volcanic *tezontle*, has subsided very little.

Two blocks W, at Calle Ildelfonso 43, is a Baroque building, erected in 1749 as a

Jesuit college, which now houses the Gabino Barreda **Escuela Nacional Preparatoria**, the most famous of Mexico's state secondary schools. It is notable particularly for the *frescoes on the walls of the patio and the staircase by Fermín Revueltas, Ramón Alva de la Canal, Fernando Leal, Jean Charlot, David Alfaro Siqueiros and José Clemente Orozco, who were invited in 1921 by the then Minister of Education, José Vasconcelos, to decorate the school. This marked the birth of the world-famous school of Mexican wall painting (Muralismo). The finest of the murals here are those painted by Orozco between 1922 and 1927, which combine spiritual and religious themes with the revolutionary history of Mexico. In the great hall of the school, known as "El Generalito", are the *choir-stalls, recovered after a fire, of the Augustinian church which formerly housed the National Library. The carving of these stalls, which are of walnut wood, is among the finest of the kind depicting scenes from the Old and New Testaments; it was the work of Salvador de Ocampo, son of the great Indian sculptor Tomás Xuárez, and dates from 1701–2.

To the NW, in Calle República Argentina between Calles Venezuela and L. G. Obregón, is the **Ministry of Education** (*Secretaría de Educación Pública*), on the site of the mid-17th c. Convent of the Incarnation. The Baroque church which

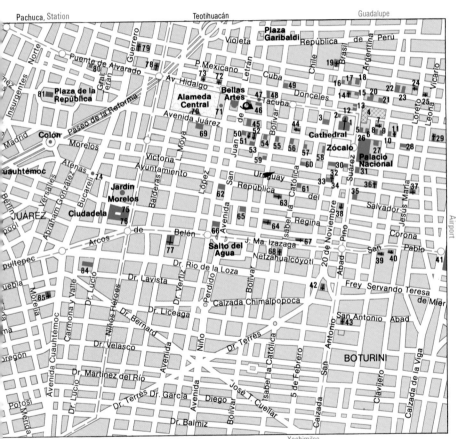

formerly belonged to the convent now houses the *Ibero-American Library* (Biblioteca Iberoamericana). The Ministry is decorated with magnificent *murals, mainly by Diego Rivera but also by Amado de la Cueva, Juan O'Gorman, Carlos Mérida and others. Rivera's frescoes, mostly concerned with the life and work of the Indians, were done between 1923 and 1928 and reflect the spirit of social criticism prevalent at that time. In the publications section of the Ministry visitors can obtain publications and informative material about the land and people of Mexico.

In Calle Justo Sierra, one block S in the direction of the Cathedral, stands the **church of La Enseñanza Antigua**, a Baroque conventual church built by Francisco Guerrero y Torres in the second half of the 18th c. The *interior is notable for its magnificent Churrigueresque retablos and pictures of the Mexican colonial school.

One block N, to the W of the Avenida República de Brasil, lies the *Plaza de Santo Domingo*, a square of the colonial period which has preserved much of its Spanish atmosphere. Under the arches on one side of the square sit the public letter-writers (*evangelistas*), offering their services to illiterate customers. On the edge of the square, at Calle Cuba 95, is a tablet recording that the Indian woman known as Malinche or Doña María, who was Cortés's interpreter, adviser and mistress, lived in the house in 1527 with her husband, Juan de Jaramillo. In the square are two monuments – a seated figure of Josefa Ortiz de Domínguez, known as "La Corregidora", one of the heroines of the fight for independence, after whom the square was formerly named the Jardín de la Corregidora; and, in front of the church, a statue of Manuel Carmon y Valle, a well-known doctor and dean of the medical faculty.

On the N side of the square is the handsome Baroque **church of Santo Domingo**, the only remnant of a once powerful Dominican convent. The present building, in red *tezontle*, dates from the first half of the 18th c., and is notable for its elegant azulejo-decorated tower, harmonious façade, two Churrigueresque retablos and neo-classical high altar by Manuel Tolsá. – On the E side of the square, at the corner of Calles Brasil and Venezuela, stands an 18th c. palace housing the *Antigua Escuela Nacional de Medicina*. During the colonial period the building was used as a prison by the Inquisition, the highest court of judgment in matters of faith (although it had no authority over the Indians). The Inquisition was introduced into New Spain in 1571 and remained active until 1815.

The Palacio de Bellas Artes and Alameda

From the Salto del Agua fountain the Avenida Lázaro Cárdenas runs past the *Mercado de Curiosidades* (on the left, at the corner of Calle Ayuntamiento) to the ***Palacio de Bellas Artes** (*Palace of Fine Art*). Commissioned during the presidency of Porfirio Díaz, this massive marble building designed by Adamo Boari is in a very eclectic style which shows Art Nouveau influence. Although begun in 1900 it was not completed until 1934. The weight of the heavy Carrara marble has caused it to sink more than 4 m (13 ft) into the ground, in spite of an attempt to lighten it by removing part of the facing of the dome. The headquarters since 1946 of the *Instituto Nacional de Bellas Artes*, the palace now serves primarily as an opera-house and concert hall.

The great hall, known as the **Teatro de Bellas Artes**, can seat an audience of 3500. The stage has a *glass mosaic curtain* weighing 22 tons designed by Dr Atl (Gerardo Murillo) and made by Tiffany's of New York. It depicts, with carefully contrived lighting effects, the landscape of the Valley of Mexico with the two mighty volcanoes, Popocatépetl and Iztaccíhuatl, rearing

Palacio de Bellas Artes, Mexico City

Torre Latinoamericana

above it. – The famous Ballet Folclórico performs in the theater twice weekly.

In the same building is the **Museum of Art** (*Museo de Artes Plásticas*), which is notable for its collection of works by Mexican artists of the 19th and 20th c. It also has rooms for periodic special exhibitions and a number of lecture and concert halls. On the second and third floors are *murals by the leading Mexican exponents of this genre. In the corridors on the second floor are two large works by Rufino Tamayo, "The Birth of Our Nationality" and "Mexico Today". On the third floor is a painting by Diego Rivera, "Man at the Turning-Point" (1934), a copy of the painting done for the Rockefeller Center in New York which was painted over because of its Marxist trend. There is also an interesting series of frescoes by David Alfaro Siqueiros depicting Democracy and the last Aztec ruler Cuauhtémoc, done in the then new technique using a spray-gun. Here, too, is a rather cynically conceived work by José Clemente Orozco entitled "Catharsis" (1934).

The *Avenida Benito Juárez* links the Paseo de la Reforma with the Avenida San Juan de Letrán (Lázaro Cárdenas); to the E of the Palacio de Bellas Artes where there are many elegant shops (silver, leather goods, folk art), offices, hotels and restaurants, the avenue takes the name of Francisco I Madero. At No. 44, in the former Corpus Christi church, is the **Museum of Folk Arts and Crafts** (*Museo de Artes e Industrias Populares*), where the products of the different parts of Mexico are displayed and can be bought (frescoes by Miguel Covarrubias). – The famous mural "Dream on a Sunday Afternoon in the Alameda Park" (1947–48) by Diego Rivera has been moved to a

new home on the Solidarity Park, adjacent to the Alameda Park and created after the 1985 earthquake. The moral caricatures figures in the history of Mexico whom the artist regarded as enemies of the people. When first shown the picture gave rise to a great furore, since it bore the inscription "Dios no existe" ("God does not exist"). For years the painting was covered over, until in 1958, amid a blaze of publicity, Rivera painted out the offending words. In other parts of the hotel are frescoes by Roberto Montenegro and illustrated maps of Mexico by Miguel Covarrubias. Near the Hotel Del Prado and on Avenida B. Juárez 89 and 92 are stalls exhibiting and selling articles under the auspices of FONART, the national development fund for handcrafted art.

On the N side of the Avenida Juárez extends the **Parque Alameda Central,** a shady and beautifully kept park with fine old trees, benches, numerous fountains and pieces of sculpture, and a bandstand; it was originally laid out in 1592 and in pre-Columbian times was a market square (*tianguis*). In the early colonial period it was also used as a drill-ground and as a place of execution for heretics condemned by the Inquisition. Always crowded with visitors and hawkers, the park is at its busiest and gayest at Christmas, when it is illuminated and decorated and becomes a popular amusement park. In the park is a semicircular memorial to the reforming President Benito Juárez (1806–72), the *Hemiciclo Juárez,* erected in 1910.

North of the Alameda

On the far side of the *Avenida Hidalgo,* which bounds the Alameda on the N, is the little Plaza Morelos (Plaza 2 de Abril or Plazuela de San Juan de Dios), in which are two churches. The **Santa Veracruz church,** on the E side of the square, occupies the site of an earlier church of the mid 16th c.; the present building was consecrated in 1764. The once richly decorated interior has suffered from the attentions of robbers, but still has a fine crucifix on the high altar which was presented to the church by Charles V. The famous architect and sculptor Manuel Tolsá is buried in the atrium. – On the other side of the square stands the **church of San Juan de Dios** (1727). It has an interesting façade in the form of a huge niche with a conch-like top and several statues in smaller niches, creating a remarkably harmonious total effect. Adjoining the church is a former hospital in which craft goods are now offered for sale. – Behind the Palacio de Bellas Artes and the two aforementioned churches one finds the new *Franz Mayer Museum, opened in August 1986, and which is the only one in Mexico dedicated to applied art.

At the W end of the Alameda is the Pinacoteca Virreinal (Viceregal Picture Gallery), housed in the old conventual church of San Diego (1595–1621). The *pictures displayed in the church, the chapels and the cloister are by leading artists of the colonial period (16th–19th c.), including Simón Pereyns, Baltazar de Echave Orio, Cristóbal de Villalpando, Juna Rodríguez Juárez, José María de Ibarra, Miguel Cabrera and José María Tresguerras.

The Avenida Hidalgo runs W into the Paseo de la Reforma. Just beyond the intersection, on the right, is the church of San Hipólito – a massive early 17th c. building with a Baroque façade – dedicated to Mexico City's patron saint. – Two blocks farther W, to the right, lies the Plaza San Fernando, on the N side of which is the church of San Fernando, a mid-18th c. building with a relatively plain Baroque façade. In the churchyard are the graves of famous Mexicans, including Benito Juárez.

Two blocks W of the Plaza San Fernando, at the corner of Calle Puente Alvarado (No. 50, on left), stands the neo-classical Palacio de Buenavista, an early 19th c. building by Manuel Tolsá. In 1865 the Emperor Maximilian presented the palace to the French Marshal Bazaine, commander of the French troops in Mexico. It now houses the *Museum San Carlos (Museo de San Carlos), containing pictures mostly by Mexican and foreign artists which were formerly displayed in the Academia San Carlos.

E of the Palacio de Bellas Artes, at the intersection of Avenida Ruiz de Alarcón (the continuation of Avenida San Juan de Letrán to the N) with Calle Tacuba, is the Head Post Office (Correo Mayor, Dirección General de Correos), a building in neo-Renaissance style with Gothic features (1902–8), designed by Adamo Boari, architect of the Palacio de Bellas Artes. On the upper floors is a Postal Museum (Museo Postal). There is a special counter for the sale of commemorative stamps.

W of the Post Office, fronting on to Calle Tacuba, is the Palacio de Minería, built about 1800 by Manuel Tolsá in the French-influenced neo-classical style of the period, which until 1954 housed the College of Mining. – In front of the palace stands the famous bronze equestrian statue of Charles IV of Spain, popularly known as "El Caballito" (the "Little Horse"); also by Manuel Tolsá, it was modeled on a statue by the French sculptor Girardon. The statue formerly stood at the intersection of the Paseo de la Reforma and the Avenida Juárez, so that the whole square was – and sometimes still is – known as the "Caballito". The imposing building opposite (Calle Tacuba 8), dating from the beginning of the 20th c. to the design of the Italian architect, Silvio Contri, was for a long time the offices of the Ministry of Transportation and Public Works. Since 1982 it has housed the new *National Museum of Art (Museo Nacional de Arte). In 22 rooms on two floors a broad cross-section of Mexican art, from Maya sculptures on religious themes of the colonial era, rural paintings of the 19th c. right up to present-day works are displayed.

NW of the Palacio de Minería are the buildings occupied by the two houses of the Mexican Parliament – at the corner of Calles Donceles and Xicoténcatl, the Cámara de Senadores (Senate), with murals by Jorge González Camarena on the staircase; and at the corner of Donceles (N side) and Calle Allende, the Cámara de Diputados.

Two blocks NE, on the N side of Calle Belisario Domínguez, is the Plaza de la Concepción, with a small octagonal chapel in the center. In this square is the Convent of the Concepción, the first nunnery to be built in the town; it was founded by Bishop Juan de Zumárraga in 1540. The convent was altered and added to down the centuries, and now shows a whole range of styles from early Baroque to the neo-classicism of the 19th c.

Two blocks farther N, between Calles Montero, Ecuador, Allende and Santa María la Redonda, is the picturesque

*Plaza Garibaldi (reached direct from the Palacio de Bellas Artes by way of the northward continuation of Lázaro Cárdenas; six blocks up Aquiles Serdán, then turn right), surrounded by cafés and restaurants much favored by tourists. In these and in the square itself groups of musicians play folk music. Most of these groups are mariachis from Jalisco (charro costume; trumpets, violins, guitars and the *guitarrón* or bass guitar), but there are usually also groups from Veracruz (white costumes with straw hats; harps and small guitars) and other regions. Payment is expected for each song, but it is also possible to arrange for a longer performance (bargaining required!) or to hire a group for a private party.

A short distance E, on the N side of the Calle República de Honduras, is the **Mercado de la Lagunilla**. Now that most of the stalls are in a modern market hall this has lost much of its old "flea market" atmosphere. On Sundays, however, "antiques" (rarely genuine) are on sale. – To the NE, round Calle de Toltecas, is the **Mercado de Tepito**, where, around the modern market hall, secondhand articles are offered at very reasonable prices by reputable dealers but also by smugglers.

Tlatelolco

To the E of the Tepito market, reached direct by way of the Paseo de la Reforma, is the TLATELOLCO district, extending N of the Buenavista railway station. In this area is the large modern housing scheme known as the *Conjunto Urbano Nonoalco-Tlatelolco*, covering an area of almost 1,000,000 sq. m – 250 acres (reached by going along the Paseo de la Reforma to the third roundabout after the intersection with the Avenida Juárez and turning left into the Calzada Nonoalco). The central feature and principal sight of this redeveloped quarter is the *Square of the Three Cultures (Plaza de las Tres Culturas or Plaza Santiago de Tlatelolco: photograph, p. 10).

The *Plaza de las Tres Culturas occupies roughly the same place as the main square of the pre-Columbian town of Tlatelolco, Tenochtitlán's great rival until 1473, when the Aztecs captured the town and killed its ruler, Moquihuix, by throwing him down from the principal pyramid. However, Tlatelolco still remained the most important trading town in the region, with a market which, according to the accounts of the conquistadors, was frequented by Raza60,000 people every day. During the siege of Tenochtitlán by the Spaniards in 1521 Tlatelolco was the scene of the last desperate stand by the Aztecs.

The square takes its name from the fascinating juxtaposition of buildings of three different periods – Aztec pyramids and temples, a Spanish conventual church and modern tower blocks. It was designed by Mario Pani and completed in 1964. The Aztec remains include, in addition to the principal pyramid which shows fourteen superimposed structures, other pyramids, platforms, staircases, walls and altars, and a *tzompantli* ("wall of skulls"). On one of the subsidiary pyramids are fine reliefs of Aztec calendar signs.

In the middle of the spacious square is the **church of Santiago de Tlatelolco**, in unadorned Baroque style. The present church (rather unhappily restored) was built at the beginning of the 17th c. on the site of a small chapel of 1535 belonging to the Franciscan convent of Santiago. Adjoining the church is one of the old conventual buildings, formerly the famous *Colegio Imperial de Santa Cruz*, in which the Franciscans taught the gifted sons of the Aztec nobility. One of the most notable teachers in the college was Bernardino de Sahagún, the great chronicler of the history of New Spain before and after the Conquest. – On the SW side of the square is the modern office block of the *Foreign Ministry* (Secretaría de Relaciones Exteriores), the building of which entailed the destruction of the pyramid of Quetzalcóatl and part of another cult building.

The Basilica of Guadalupe

From Tlatelolco the pilgrimage churches of Guadalupe can be reached by either of two routes. The more easterly route is by the **Calzada de Guadalupe**, which begins at the Glorieta de la Reforma. At this intersection stands a statue of the last Inca of Peru, Atahualpa, brought here from the Peruvian town of Cuzco in exchange for a figure of the last-but-one Aztec ruler Cuitláhuac which now stands in the Plaza de Armas in Cuzco.

The westerly route leads from Buenavista station along the *Avenida Insurgentes Norte* to the junction with the Calzada Vallejo, a busy traffic intersection, with the massive pyramidal **Monumento a la Raza**, a monument to the mingling of the European and Indian races (1964) by a team of sculptors under the direction of Luis Lelo de Larrea. Every year on October 12, the date on which Columbus discovered the New World, the Día de la Raza

Basilica of Guadalupe

is celebrated here. – Nearby is the *Hospital de la Raza*, with frescoes by David Alfaro Siqueiros and Diego Rivera chiefly on the theme of the history of medicine.

8 km (5 miles) away via the Calzada Vallego is the pre-Columbian site of *Tenayuca* (p. 256). – At the end of Insurgentes Norte, on the left, is the *Rancho Grande* (Lienzo Grande), where *charreadas* (the Mexican equivalent of the rodeo) are held regularly. – A short distance beyond this, at the beginning of the road to **Teotihuacán** (p. 257), are two bronze statues, one on either side, known as the *Indios Verdes* ("Green Indians") – the Aztec rulers Itzcóatl (1426–40) and Ahuítzotl (1486–1502). – To reach the churches of Guadalupe, turn off Insurgentes Norte at the Glorieta Lindavista into Calle Montevideo, going E.

The **Old Basilica of Nuestra Señora de Guadalupe** was built in 1709 on the site of an earlier 16th c. church and several times altered in later periods. The exterior is unremarkable, but the interior (now closed) is impressive, with its wide nave and the contrast between the white marble and the gilded ornamentation; it made an even deeper impression on the observer when it was thronged with pilgrims, imbued with the profound native piety of the ordinary Mexicans. When this church sank ever deeper into the swampy subsoil and became dangerous it was replaced by the *New Basilica, a modern structure of concrete and marble which was designed by Pedro Ramírez Vázquez, architect of the National Museum of Anthropology, and consecrated in 1976.

The spacious interior, which apart from the figure of the Virgin of Guadalupe contains no statues or pictures, can accommodate a congregation of 20,000. A passage on a lower level by the side of the high altar allows visitors to see the Virgin without disturbing worshippers in the church.

The basilica is visited by many thousands of pilgrims throughout the year, but on December 12, the anniversary of the Virgin's second apparition, the square in front of the church, as well as the church itself, is filled to overflowing with a great mass of the faithful. The colorfully garbed dancers and mimes who are everywhere to be seen help to create the atmosphere of a great popular fiesta. The Virgin of Guadalupe is venerated by all classes of the Mexican population, and in addition draws pilgrims from many other countries in Latin America. These manifestations of popular faith have been called the *culto guadalupano*, and it is a notable fact that many of its aspects lie outside the bounds of Catholic dogma and frequently show affinities with pre-Christian myths.

According to the legend the Virgin appeared on December 9, 1531 to Juan Diego, a baptized Aztec, in the form of a dark-skinned Indian woman and charged him to ask the bishop to have a chapel built for her on a particular spot. Bishop Juan de Zumárraga did not believe the story and asked for proof. Thereupon the Virgin appeared to Juan Diego a second time on December 12 and caused roses to bloom on a bare hilltop, although it was then the season of drought. Juan Diego plucked the roses and took them to the bishop, but when he opened the folds of the cloak in which he had been carrying it was seen to bear an image of the Virgin surrounded by a radiant halo. This, it is believed, is the wonderworking *image of the Virgin of Guadalupe* which now hangs above the high altar in the new Basilica. Bishop of Zumárraga caused a shrine to be built on the hill of *Tepeyac*, on the site of an earlier Aztec temple of the earth-mother Tonantzin. Soon the church and the image of the Virgin began to attract large numbers of pilgrims; and even the Indians, who had been disillusioned with Christianity by the cruelties of the colonial regime, became more willing to accept the Christian faith. After being venerated for centuries as the patroness of the Indians and Mestizos, the Virgin of Guadalupe was invoked in support of the struggle for Mexican independence, and in 1810 Miguel Hidalgo inscribed her image on the banner of the insurgents.

Beside the old basilica is the late 18th c. *Capilla del Pocito* (Chapel of the Spring), designed by Francisco de Guerrero y Torres; the dome is faced with azulejos. Bubbling out of the rock inside the chapel is a spring credited with healing powers, and the faithful come here to fill their bottles with its water. – An old *Capuchin* *church* now contains a *Museum of Religious Art* which displays treasures from the old basilica and large numbers of votive offerings, mainly of silver. – On the hill of Tepeyac, from which there are fine *views of the surrounding area, is the *Capilla del Tepeyac*, with frescoes by Fernando Leal depicting the miracle. It was built in the 18th c. on the spot where the Virgin appeared to Juan Diego.

The Paseo de la Reforma

The *Paseo de la Reforma, the principal E–W traffic artery of Mexico City, extends for a total distance of 15 km (9 miles) from Tlatelolco to the residential district of Las Lomas ("The Hills") on the city's western boundary. The main section, however, is the stretch from the intersection with the Avenida Benito Juárez to Chapultepec Park. The boulevard is 60 m (200 ft) wide, with 6–8 traffic lanes, a green strip in the middle, busts of famous men (mostly heroes of the War of Independence and the War of Intervention) along the sides and large roundabouts (*glorietas*) at the intersections, with monuments or groups of trees. The patrician houses of the colonial period which once flanked the street have almost all disappeared, and it is now lined by tall modern blocks containing offices, hotels, restaurants, movie theaters and shops. This magnificent avenue was originally laid out during the reign of the Emperor Maximilian to provide a direct link between his residence in Chapultepec Castle and the official seat of government on the Zócalo. It takes its present name from the reforming laws promulgated by Benito Juárez in 1861; it was previously known as the Calzada del Emperador ("of the Emperor") and Paseo de los Hombres Ilustres ("of Famous Men").

Going SW down the Paseo de la Reforma from the Avenida Juárez, we come to the first intersection, the Glorieta de Cristóbal

Colón, with the *Columbus Monument* by the French sculptor Charles Cordier, erected in 1877. On the base of the statue are the figures of the learned monks, Juan Pérez de Marchena, Diego de Deza, Pedro de Gante and Bartolomé de Las Casas, who played a leading part in the settlement of Mexico and the integration of the Indians.

From the intersection Calle Ignacio Ramírez, to the right, runs N to the *Plaza de la República*, with the huge *Monumento a la Revolución*, commemorating the 1910 revolution. This was formed out of an unfinished building originally commissioned by Porfirio Díaz to house lawcourts. Two of the columns contain the remains of the revolutionary Presidents Francisco I. Madero, Venustiano Carranza, Francisco Villa, Lázaro Cárdenas and Plutarco Elías Calles. – To the SE of the Glorieta de Cristóbal Colón is the *Citadel* (Ciudadela), a neo-classical building completed in 1807 in which the independence leader José María Morelos was confined before his execution. It now houses the **National Institute of Handicrafts** (*Instituto Nacional de Artesanía*), with a school for the training of craftsmen, an exhibition of articles for sale and a library, the Biblioteca México.

In the center of the next glorieta on the Paseo de la Reforma is a *statue of Cuauhtémoc*, the last Aztec ruler. Here the Paseo is crossed by the 26 km (16 mile)

Paseo de la Reforma, with the Columbus Monument

Independence Monument ("El Angel")

as sales points for FONART, the national development fund for Artesanía, on Londres 6 and 136, Altos "A".

The next-but-one glorieta is dominated by the *Independence Monument* (Monumento a la Independencia), known as "El Angel" from the figure of a winged goddess of victory which stands on top of a tall column. At the foot of the column, among other figures, is a statue of Miguel Hidalgo, the first leader of the struggle against colonial rule. It is interesting to note that this monument rests on a very thick concrete base, to prevent general subsidence (the town sinks on average about 20 cm (8 ins) a year). Consequently the monument regularly "climbs" above its surroundings, so that in practice a new step has to be added annually. – Beyond the next glorieta, on the left, is the *Institute of Social Security* (Instituto Mexicano del Seguro Social, IMSS). The entrance is decorated with relief carving and sculpture by Jorge González Camarena, and the interior has frescoes by Camarena and Federico Cantú. Beyond this, on the edge of Chapultepec Park (on left), is the *Ministry of Health* (Secretaría de Salubridad), which has frescoes and stained glass by Diego Rivera in some of the rooms. To the right, in a small triangular garden, are the *Diana Fountain* (Fuente de Diana Cazadora) and a monument to Venustiano Carranza, and beyond this, at the entrance to the park, is a statue of Simón Bolívar, the hero of South American independence.

long *Avenida de los Insurgentes*, the city's main N–S axis. – Beyond the intersection, on the left of the Paseo, is the district known as the ZONA ROSA ("Pink Zone") or Colonia Juárez, which is bounded on the S by the Avenida Chapultepec. In this area, in which the streets are named after European cities, there is a great concentration of hotels, restaurants, cafés, night spots, art galleries and elegant shops. In addition there is in this zone and on the edge of it the *Municipal Wax Museum* (Museo de Cera de La Ciudad de México), Londres 6, and, at Liverpool 16, the *National Music Center* ("Carlos Chávez"); including an exhibition of old and contemporary musical instruments, and a market (Mexican clothing and handcrafted articles, etc.) on Londres, between Amberes and Florencia, as well

Chapultepec Park

The *Bosque de Chapultepec* (Náhuatl, "hill of the grasshoppers") is Mexico City's principal park and, with an area of 4 sq. km (2½ sq. miles), its largest. It was once a stronghold of the Toltecs, and the last Toltec ruler, Huémac, is said to have hanged himself here in 1177 after fleeing from Tula. In 1200 the Aztecs (Mexica) settled on the hill after their long wanderings but were driven away again twenty years later by the neighboring tribes. Legend has it that the park was originally laid out in the first half of the 15th c. by Netzahualcóyotl, the poet king of Texcoco. As the power of Tenochtitlán increased, the hill became a summer residence of the Aztec rulers, and water from the springs here was conveyed in an aqueduct to the temple precinct in the capital. Portraits of the Aztec rulers were carved from the rock on the slopes of the hill, and remains of these sculptures can still be seen on the E side.

The park still preserves numbers of fine old trees, the most imposing being some massive specimens of cedars and ahuehuetes (swamp cypresses: Náhuatl for "old man of the water"). Its lakes, sports facilities, botanic garden, zoo, museums and castle attract crowds of city-dwellers, particularly at weekends, to walk, ride, picnic or enjoy the wide range of entertainments available here (concerts, theater, children's programs, etc.).

Just beyond the entrance to the park, on the left, is the important *Museum of Modern Art (Museo de Arte Moderno), designed by Rafael Mijares and Pedro Ramírez Vázquez and opened in 1964. Apart from a retrospective look at Mexican art before and during the colonial period, the museum is notable primarily for its collection of pictures and sculpture by Mexican artists of the 19th and 20th c. There are periodic special exhibitions of work by Mexican and foreign artists. – Immediately S of the Museum is the Monumento a los Niños Héroes (Monument to the Young Heroes), a semicircular structure of six columns, with fountains, commemorating the last stand by the young cadets in Chapultepec Castle during the siege by US forces in 1847.

On the hill at the SE corner of the park (access on foot, by bus or by lift) is Chapultepec Castle (Castillo de Chapultepec). Before entering the castle courtyard it is worth visiting the Galería de Histoira, housed in a circular white modern building, with displays illustrating the history of Mexico from the struggle for independence (1810–21) to the post-revolutionary period. – On a lower level is "Moctezuma's Tree" (Arbol de Moctezuma), an ahuehuete 50 m (165 ft) high and 15 m (50 ft) in circumference, which is said to date from Aztec times.

Chapultepec Castle was built at the end of the 18th c. by the Spanish Viceroy, Conde de Gálvaz, as a summer residence, on a site once occupied by Aztec buildings and later by a Spanish hermitage. In 1841 it became a military academy, which six years later was to be the last Mexican stronghold during the attack by US troops. Maximilian and Carlota made the castle their residence and carried out various alterations in 1863–4. The dictator Porfirio Díaz also used it as a summer residence from 1884 onwards.

Chapultepec Castle after dark

In 1944 Chapultepec Castle finally became the *National Historical Museum (Museo Nacional de Historia). The Museum's nineteen rooms contain, in addition to a collection of pre-Columbian material and reproductions of codices, a vast range of exhibits illustrating the history of Mexico since the Spanish conquest. These include arms and armor, documents, maps and plans of the Conquest period and its immediate aftermath; furniture, ceramics, clothing, jewelry and coins of three centuries; relics and souvenirs of the struggle for independence and the revolutionary wars; portraits of leading figures in Mexican history; frescoes by Orozco, Siqueiros, O'Gorman and other artists, and a number of state carriages, including those used by Benito Juárez and the Emperor Maximilian. The apartments occupied by Maximilian and Carlota, decorated in neoclassical style, contain the furniture which they brought from Europe. – From the castle terrace there is a superb *view of the city.

N of the Castle is the Lago Antiguo, which is divided into two parts by the Gran Avenida. On the W side of the lake is the Casa del Lago ("House on the Lake"), now belonging to the University, used for certain courses and cultural events. – The road along the E side of the lake cuts across the Paseo de la Reforma to the National Museum of Anthropology. To the W of the lake are the Zoo (Parque Zoológico), Botanic Garden (Jardín Botánico) and, in the newer part of the park, the Auditorio Nacional, a huge hall with accommodation for 15,000 spectators, which is used for cultural events, sports contests, etc. – SW of the lake is the Fountain of Netzahualcóyotl (Fuente de Netzahualcóyotl), commemorating the ruler of Texcoco who also made a name for himself as a poet and philosopher.

The Calzada Molino runs S to Los Pinos ("The Pines"), residence of the President of Mexico. To the W of this road and the Anillo Periférico extends the new part of Chapultepec Park, with the artificial Lago del Nuevo Bosque. S of this is the Fuente Lerma, a fountain with a basin containing an underwater mosaic by Diego Rivera.

To the E is the Amusement Park, to the SW the modern Museum of Natural History (Museo de Historia Natural), the Museum of Technology (Museo Tecnológico) and

Monolithic figure of Tláloc (or Chalchiuhtlicue?)

The *Museum was designed by Pedro Ramírez Vázquez and built in 1963–4. A strikingly successful example of contemporary architecture, of notably harmonious effect, it is one of the world's great museums, with its treasures of Indian art magnificently displayed. A notable feature is the *Central Patio, part of which is roofed over by a kind of gigantic stone umbrella borne on a column 11 m (36 ft) high. From the top of the column a curtain of water falls into the basin below and is then pumped up again, symbolizing the eternally continuing cycle of life.

In the Entrance Hall is the museum shop (on left), where catalogs, brochures, books and reproductions of pre-Columbian objects can be bought. The best idea is to buy a good guide and then join one of the conducted tours with explanations in English. – On the right-hand wall is a mural by Rufino Tamayo depicting a feathered serpent and a jaguar, the two central symbols of the ancient Indian gods. Also to the right are rooms in which occasional special exhibitions are held.

On the LOWER GROUND FLOOR is the Sala de Resúmen (Orientation Room), in which films and slides on the Museum and its contents are shown. – The Central Patio is enclosed on three sides by two-

a cemetery, the Panteón de Dolores. – Just outside the park, at Avenida Constituyentes 500, is a lienzo charro in which charreadas (Mexican rodeos) are regularly held.

On the other side of the Paseo de la Reforma, in the northern section of Chapultepec Park, is the **National Museum of Anthropology (Museo Nacional de Antropología). At the entrance is a huge monolithic figure hitherto identified as the rain god Tláloc but in fact, according to the latest theories, more probably his sister, the water goddess Chalchiuhtlicue. This colossal figure, weighing 167 tons, which is unfinished, was found near San Miguel Coatlinchán (p. 265) and transported to its present site with the greatest difficulty.

A realistic Aztec head

story wings containing the main display rooms. After an "Introduction to Anthropology", the twelve rooms on the ground floor display the archeological finds; the rooms on the upper floor contain the corresponding ethnological material. The individual rooms are devoted to particular cultures and particular tribal groups.

If we begin the tour of the GROUND FLOOR in the rooms to the right, we pass successively through the following rooms: Introduction to Anthropology; Cultures of Meso-America; Prehistory (the origins of man in America); Pre-Classic Period in the Central Highlands; Teotihuacán; Toltecs; Mexica (Aztecs); Oaxaca; Gulf of Mexico; Mayas (with an outdoor

The goddess Coyolxauhqui

National Museum of Anthropology
Museo Nacional de Antropología

Ciudad de México

I Sala del Resumen
(Film, etc., displays)

II Special exhibitions

III Auditorium

IV Recent excavations

V Introduction to Anthropology
An outline of anthropology and its auxiliary disciplines; models, dioramas, maps, displays, etc.

VI Cultures of Meso-America
Hunting (weapons, game animals), development of agriculture, population, rituals (forms of burial, festivals, music), cultural achievements (numerical system, calendar, script, medicine, architecture, painting).

VII Sala de Preistoria
(Prehistory)
Migration over the Bering Strait, development of the hunting and collecting cultures (human and animal fossils), beginnings of agriculture in the Valley of Mexico.

VIII Sala del Período Preclásico
(Pre-Classic or Formative period)
Development of pottery and other crafts; good examples of the figures from Tlatilco, particularly the female figures known as the "mujer bonita"; the "Acrobat Vase"; model of the Cuicuilco pyramid.

IX Sala de Teotihuacán
Classification of the different phases of this important culture on the basis of artistic techniques, particularly in pottery; sculpture (Xipe Tótec from Tlamimilolpan, Chalchiuhtlicue, Huehuetéotl); reconstruction of the "Paradise of Tláloc" fresco; masks.

X Sala de Tula
(Toltec Classic period)
Stelae, Atlas figures, sculpture (Chac-mool), pottery.

XI Sala Mexica
(Aztec Post-Classic period)
From the coming of the Chichimecs to the fall of Tenochtitlán: Calendar Stone ("Stone of the Fifth Sun"), Stone of Tizoc, codices, maps, magnificent sculpture (Coatlicue, Xochipilli), diorama of the market of Tlatelolco.

XII Sala de Oaxaca
(Zapotec-Mixtec culture)
Pottery from Monte Albán, stelae, urns, masks, Mixtec jewelry.

XIII Sala de las Culturas del Golfo de México
From the early Olmec material to the El Tajín culture and the Huaxtec excavations: pottery and stone sculpture from La Venta, hachas ("axes" – ceremonial objects), palmas and yugos ("palms" and "yokes" – stone objects, probably connected with the ritual ball game), stelae, objects made from jade.
Outside: colossal sculpture.

XIV Sala Maya
Stelae, stucco heads, terracotta figures (particularly fine examples from the island of Jaina), copies of the famous Bonampak frescoes, Atlas figures and delicate stone carving from Chichén Itzá.

XV Sala de las Culturas del Norte
(Cultures of northern Mexico)
Grave goods, everyday objects, pottery, material from Casas Grandes.

XVI Sala de las Culturas del Occidente
(Cultures of western Mexico)
Fine terracotta figures from Jalisco, Nayarit and Colima, which give a picture of daily life in the period before the arrival of the Spaniards; Tarascan material.

XVII Salón de Venta
(Museum shop)
Publications, transparencies, handicrafts; reproductions of exhibits; guides to the Museum.

XVIII Monolith
The gigantic figure known as Tláloc, but probably in fact his sister Chalchiuhtlicue.

section containing a stela from Guatemala, an altar and reproductions of a Chenes-style temple at Hochob and a temple with copies of the famous wall paintings of Bonampak); Northern Mexico; and Western Mexico.

The ethnological collections on the UPPER FLOOR are arranged in the following order: Introduction to Ethnology, Cora and Huichol Indians, Tarascans (Purépecha), Otomí-Pame, Puebla, Oaxaca, Totonacs, Huaxtecs, Mayas, North-Western Mexico and Modern Indian Art.

The Museum also contains the *National Library of Anthropology*, founded by Lucas Alamán in 1831 and developed by the Emperor Maximilian; it now has more than 300,000 volumes. The National School of Anthropology moved a few years ago to the residential quarter (Colonia) of Isidro Favela (Periférico Sur y Zapote). In 1983 a new section was opened which includes gardens, workshops and exhibitions.

Not far E of the Museum of Anthropology (Paseo de la Reforma/Calzada Gandhi) stands the newest museum of the city, the *Rufino Tamayo Museum* (Museo Rufino Tamayo) named after the most famous Mexican painter still living. The building, created and internally arranged by Abraham Zabludovsky and Teodore González de León, is practically without windows; it was dedicated in 1981. As well as works

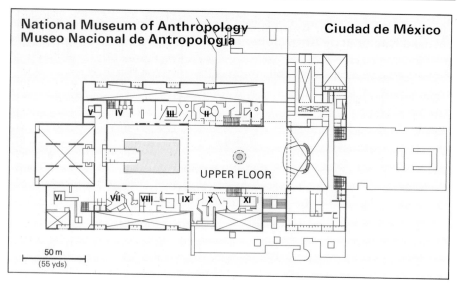

National Museum of Anthropology
Museo Nacional de Antropología
        Ciudad de México

UPPER FLOOR

50 m
(55 yds)

by Tamayo and interesting special exhibitions, the museum has its own collection of several hundred works (paintings, graphics, sculptures, tapestries etc.) by contemporary artists from all over the world. N of the National Museum of Anthropology in the residential district (Colonia) of Polanco, at Tres Picos 29, one finds the public studio of David Álfaro Siqueiros (Museo Sala de Arte Público David Alfaro Siqueiros). In this former home of the Siqueiros family can be seen pictures, drawings, photographs, decorations and documents of this famous muralist and Communist politician.

In an impressive red-bricked building next to the Hotel Presidente Chapultepec is Televisa's new museum called The Centro Cultural de Arte Contemporaneo. It is destined to show mainly collections of contemporary – and pre-Hispanic art as well as photography.

The Northern Outskirts

At the NW end of Chapultepec Park the Paseo de la Reforma passes the *Fuente de Petróleos*, a fountain erected to commemorate the nationalization of foreign oil companies in 1938. – The Paseo now crosses the Anillo Periférico and turns SW to run through the elegant residential district of LOMAS DE CHAPULTEPEC. – If we follow the *Anillo Periférico*, which becomes the Bulevar Avila Camacho, to the NW we pass on the left the *Hipódromo de las Américas*, a racetrack which can accommodate 60,000 spectators, and the *Olympic Sports Center* (Centro Olímpico Mexicano). Beyond this, on the right, is the *El Toreo* bullring, with seating for 35,000 spectators (reconstruction in progress).

To the right extends the district of TACUBA (formerly Tlacopan), and farther N the industrial district of ATZCAP-OTZALCO, which in pre-Columbian times was capital of the Tepanec kingdom for three generations until the defeat of the Tepanecs by other Nahua peoples in 1428. The victorious cities of Tenochtitlán, Texcoco and Tlacopan then formed an alliance which lasted until the Mexica established their predominant authority. In the middle of Tacuba is the *Arbol de la Noche Triste* ("Tree of the Sad Night": recently badly damaged by fire), an ahuehuete (Montezuma cypress) under which Cortés is said to have lamented his defeat of June 30, 1520. – In the Avenida Ribera de San Cosme, which ends in Tacuba, at No. 71, is the **House of the Masks** (*Casa de los Mascarones*), with the finest Churrigueresque façade on any secular building in the city.

2 km (1¼ miles) N of the Toreo the Bulevar Ávila Camacho comes to a junction with the Avenida 16 de Septiembre. Going left along this and continuing along Calle de los Remedios, we come to the **church of the Virgen de los Remedios** (consecrated in 1629), a place of pilgrimage in which a statue of the Virgin brought from

Spain by the conquistadors is venerated. During the war of independence (1810–21), the royalist troops carried flags bearing the image of this Virgin of Perpetual Succor, while the victorious Mexicans fought under the banner of the Virgin of Guadalupe. There is an annual fiesta in honour of the Virgen de los Remedios on September 8.

Returning to the main road (No. 57) and going N, away from the city, we come, at the entrance to the new suburb known as the CIUDAD SATELITE, to the *Goeritz Towers* (1957) – five colored prismatic obelisks of different heights which represent an interesting attempt by the Danzig artist and architect, Mathias Goeritz, to combine sculpture and architecture.

The Southern Districts

The southern part of the city can be reached either on the *Anillo Periférico Sur*, which cuts across Chapultepec Park, or by taking the *Avenida de los Insurgentes Sur* from the Cuauhtémoc monument on the Paseo de la Reforma. Among the features of interest in the southern districts (Tacuba, Mixcoac, Coyoacán, San Ángel, San Jerónimo, El Pedregal, Tlalpan and Xochimilco) are a number of interesting museums, large sports grounds, the University City, the archeological site of Cuicuilco and the "floating gardens" of Xochimilco.

About 3 km (2 miles) from the intersection with the Paseo de la Reforma, on the right of Avenida Insurgentes Sur, is the *Parque de la Lama*, with the still unfinished Hotel de México (fine panoramic *view of the city from the top floor). Nearby at the corner of Filadelfia is the very modern *Polyforum Cultural Siqueiros* (1965–9), a twelve-sided mushroom-like building designed by José David Alfaro Siqueiros (1886–1974), who was also responsible for the "plastic" mural (2400 sq. m – 2870 sq. yds), "The March of Mankind", in the large egg-shaped hall in the interior. There are regular *son et lumière* shows in this hall. The building also includes a dance hall and conference, exhibition and sales rooms for objets d'art and craftwork. – 3 km (2 miles) farther on is the CIUDAD DE LOS DEPORTES ("City of Sport"), with a football stadium accommodating 65,000 spectators and the *Plaza México*, the largest building in the world (60,000 seats).

At the junction of Avenidas Río Mixcoac and Río Churubusco take Río Churubusco and continue along the Avenida Universidad into the district of COYOACÁN, which has preserved much of the tranquil atmosphere of colonial times. At the corner of Avenida Universidad and Calle Francisco Sosa are the modern *church of El Altillo* ("The Hillock") and the little 18th c. Baroque *Capilla de San Antonio* (Panzacola). *Calle Francisco Sosa*, lined by handsome 17th and 18th c. houses, leads to the main square, *Plaza Hidalgo*, in which is the **church of San Juan Bautista**, built by Dominicans in 1538. Very typical of the style of the period, it has a fine richly carved doorway leading into the atrium, which has Indian-Plataresque decoration. Inside on the left is the interesting High-Baroque *Capilla de Santisima*.

Londres, we come to the **Frida Kahlo Museum**, at No. 247 on the left. This was the birthplace of the painter Frida Kahlo (1910–54), who lived here with her husband Diego Rivera from 1929 until her death. Leon Trotsky stayed in the house as a guest after his arrival in Mexico in 1937. In addition to personal mementoes and works by Frida Kahlo and Diego Rivera, the museum contains pictures and sculpture by the 18th and 19th c. Mexican artists, as well as pre-Columbian objects and examples of Mexican folk art from Frida Kahlo's private collection. – At the corner of Calles Viena and Morelos is the **Leon Trotsky Museum**. In this house, which he had converted into a real fortress, Trotsky lived in exile until his murder by an agent of Stalin on August 20, 1940. In the garden can be seen the grave of the great revolutionary and his wife. Trotsky's study is kept as it was on the day of his death. On the walls of the austere bedroom there remain the bullet holes of an earlier attack on the house by the Stalinists, an attack in which the muralist David Álfaro Siqueiros had taken part. A plaque by the front door commemorates Trotsky's bodyguard who was shot in the attack.

Going NW and crossing the Avenida Division del Norte, we come to the Museo de Las Intervenciones de Churubusco on Calle 20 de Agosto and Xicotenatl. The museum, housed in an old Franciscan friary, contains relics of the War of Intervention and special exhibitions. – Returning to the Avenida Division del

Norte and following it S, we bear right in 5 km (2 miles) into the Calle del Museo. At No. 150 is the Diego Rivera Museum or *Anahuacalli (*House of Anáhuac*), a pyramid-like structure designed by Rivera himself; it contains his very fine collection of pre-Columbian material, notably pottery of the west culture and Aztec stone sculptures. The development of Rivera's artistic career is illustrated in a reproduction of his studio. – From here the Calzada Tlalpan runs S to the modern *Aztec Statium* (Estadio Aztecá), which has seating for 100,000 spectators.

A little way S is the Glorieta de Huipulco, with an *equestrian statue of Emiliano Zapata*, from which it is 7 km (4½ miles) to *XOCHIMILCO ("place of the flower-fields" in Náhuatl).

The little town of **Xochimilco** on the outskirts of Mexico City, with a population which still includes many Nahua Indians, was probably founded at the end of the 12th c. by Toltec refugees from Tula. In the 13th c. a Náthuatl-speaking nomadic tribe related to the Aztecs settled here; they later became known as *Chinampanecs* owing to the chinampa system of cultivation which they practiced. In this system the crops were planted on small rafts covered with mud and water plants and held together by a retaining screen of interwoven reeds, which were eventually anchored to the lake bottom by the growth of roots. The abundance of water and the fertilizing effect of the mud enabled these "floating gardens" to produce up to seven crops per year. The rich yields obtained here and elsewhere on the lake where the same methods were applied insured a plentiful food supply for Tenochtitlán.

About 1430, Xochimilco was conquered by the Aztecs. The town was the scene of bitter fighting during the Conquest (1521), and was finally burned down by the Spaniards. – The area immediately surrounding Mexico City is still an important vegetable- and flower-growing region. In recent years the productivity of the region has suffered a recession through polution and a decrease in the area of water, but the Xochimilco area, which attracts large numbers of visitors, particularly on Sundays, is still crisscrossed by numerous canals. Visitors can sail along these waterways on brightly painted flower-decked boats known as *trajineras*, accompanied by boats selling food, drinks and handmade articles or bearing bands of mariachi musicians.

In the main square of Xochimilco is the fine *parish church of San Bernardino. The present church, on the site of an earlier Franciscan foundation (1535), was probably built in 1590, and is thus one of the oldest in the country. Notable features are the Indian-Plateresque façade of the main doorway, a 16th c. Renaissance retablo, 17th c. choir-stalls and a crucifix with a figure of Christ formed from maize stems in a typically Indian technique (*de caña*). There is an interesting *Saturday market*.

Continuing S on Avenida Insurgentes Sur from the intersection with Avenidas Río Mixcoac and Río Churubusco, we see on the right the modern **Teatro de los Insurgentes**, a circular building with a mosaic by Diego Rivera on the façade depicting the history of the Mexican theater. To the right extends the district of TLACOPAC.

The Avenida Insurgentes Sur continues S to the district of VILLA OBREGON, passing on the left the *Alvaro Obregón Monument* which commemorates the revolutionary hero and President, murdered here in 1928. The sculpture and relief carving on this massive granite memorial are by Ignacio Asúnsolo. – The eastern part of the district, to the right of the avenue, is known as *San Ángel. One block W of the Obregón monument, in the Avenida Revolución, is the **Museo Colonial del Carmen**. It is housed in a former Carmelite convent (1617) dedicated to the martyr, San Angelo, from whom the little town takes its name. The museum contains articles of religious art and pictures. Notable features of the building, which is richly decorated with azulejos, are the patio with its tiled fountain, the crypt, which contains a number of mummified bodies, and the sacristy, with a beautifully paneled ceiling.

To the W is the picturesque *Plaza San Jacinto*, in which the *Bazar Sábado* is held on Saturdays. In a 17th c. building in the square is a shop selling traditional handicraft articles, as well as modern art. – On

Flower-decked boats, Xochimilco

Central Library, University City

the N side of the square is the *Casa del Risco* ("House of the Cliff"), an 18th c. palace furnished with valuable antiques especially furniture and paintings of the Colonial era. It has an interesting two-tier fountain faced with tiles and ceramics. – In 1847, during the war between Mexico and the United States, sixteen Irish deserters from the US army who had fought on the Mexican side were captured and hanged in the square. – At Alta Vista and Palma one discovers a functional building of 1929 designed by Juan O'Gorman which houses the new Museo Casa Estudio Diego Rivera. Here the artist lived between 1933 and 1957; Rivera's personal documents, clothes and furniture as well as photographs, drawings, paintings and archeological artifacts are exhibited.

From San Ángel the Calzada del Desierto de los Leones leads to the **Desierto de los Leones** national park, some 25 km (15 miles) away. This magnificent expanse of coniferous forest (alt. around 3000 m – 9800 ft) surrounding a beautiful 17th c. Carmelite convent, is a popular resort of the people of Mexico City.

The Avenida Insurgentes Sur continues S from Villa Obregón to the district of COPILCO, lying on the fringes of **El Pedregal**, a vast sheet of lava 6–8 m (20–25 ft) thick covering an area of some 40 sq. km (15 sq. miles). The lava was deposited shortly before the beginning of the Christian era by an eruption of

the volcano *Xitle* (3120 m – 10,237 ft). On this great lava field are the University City and the residential district of EL PEDREGAL DE SAN ÁNGEL to the W; the local lava was used in the construction of many of the buildings. Excavation has revealed evidence of a culture which was brought to an abrupt end by the eruption of the volcanoes. – Taking the Avenida Copilco, which runs E off Avenida Insurgentes Sur, and turning left into Calle Victoria; where, at No. 110, we come to the office of INAH (Instituto Nacional de Antropología e Historia), which is associated with the archeological site at Copilco. Here, under a 3 m (10 ft) thick layer of lava, were found a number of tombs containing skeletons, stone implements, pottery and figurines, some of them dating from the Archaic period (before 1500 B.C.). The site museum contains the finds, some of them still *in situ*.

Immediately S is the large *CIUDAD UNIVERSITARIA (University City). Begun during the presidency of Miguel Alemán, it covers a 3 sq. km (1 sq. mile) area and consists of more than eighty buildings erected between 1950 and 1955. The complex was primarily planned by José Garcia Villagrán, Mario Pani and Enrique del Moral, and some 150 architects were involved in the work. Among the principal buildings, many of them decorated with old Indian symbols, are the *Rector's Office*, with its harmonious alternation of horizontal and vertical features (frescoes by Siqueiros); the **Central Library**, with its windowless ten-story book stack, the *façade* of which has a mosaic in natural stone by Juan O'Gorman; the *Auditorium of the Science Faculty*, with a glass mosaic by José Chávez Morado; and the Faculty of Medicine, with a mural by Francisco Eppens Huelguera. There are extensive sports facilities, including a large swimming pool, football and baseball fields, tennis and jai alai courts. – To the S of the main University buildings is a concert hall seating 2500, the *Sala de Netzahualcóyotl.* – On the W side of the Avenida Insurgentes is the *Olympic Stadium* (Estadio Olímpico), decorated with colored stone reliefs by Diego Rivera. It seats more than 80,000 spectators and, like some other buildings on the University campus, it incorporates features taken from pre-Columbian architecture. – Near the Olympic Stadium, to the right, is the University *Botanic Garden.*

About 2 km (1¼ miles) S, beyond the underpass under the Anilla Periférico, a road branches off on the left to the archeological site of **Cuicuilco** (Náhuatl, "place of singing and dancing"). The circular *pyramid*, now 18 m (60 ft) high, has a diameter of 112 m (365 ft), and since the eruption of the volcano Xitle shortly before the beginning of the Christian era has been covered and surrounded by lava. During the difficult process of excavation, part of the sculpture was destroyed, and the restoration is of doubtful authenticity. The pyramid seems to have originally been an artificial earth mound, which was subsequently built over on several occasions. The primitive fortress-like style of the pyramid reflects the very beginnings of pre-Columbian monumental religious architecture.

Probably first established by a farming people of the Formative period about 900 B.C., Cuicuilco enjoyed its most flourishing period between 600 and 300 B.C. when, with 20,000 inhabitants, it played a dominant role in the region. The site was abandoned before the final volcanic eruption: presumably the inhabitants moved to Teotihuacán and Tlapacoya.

The **pyramid** consists of five circular tiers of decreasing size, ending in a platform with the remains of an altar. There were probably two staircases leading up to the top of the pyramid, originally 27 m (90 ft) high. – In addition to the principal pyramid, excavations in recent years have brought to light the remains of at least a dozen buildings, some of which may be even earlier than the pyramid. Of special interest are the remains of an altar in the shape of a horseshoe, embellished with stones polished by the action of water, and to the right of the main entrance a room

constructed of stone blocks on which remains of red drawings can be seen. The central deity of Cuicuilco seems to have been the old fire god Huehuetéotl, who would naturally be associated with the active volcanoes in the surrounding area. – The recently erected **museum** contains material (mainly terracottas) of the Pre-Classic period from the Valley of Mexico, Michoacán, Guanajuato and the Gulf of Mexico.

To the S of the site is the attractive suburb of *TLALPAN (Náhuatl, "footprint of man"), a quiet residential area which is also a popular weekend resort. Between 1827 and 1830 it was capital of México state. It has a number of fine colonial buildings, including the 16th c. *church of San Agustín de las Cuevas* and the *Casa Chata* (now a restaurant).

Distrito Federal (Federal District): see p. 119, – **México state:** p. 160.

Michoacán

State of Michoacán (Mich.). – Capital: Morelia.
Area: 60,093 sq. km (23,202 sq. miles).
Population: 3432900.
ⓘ **Coordinación Federal de Turismo,**
Santos Degollado 340 Altos 1,
Morelia, Mich.;
tel. (9 14 51) 2 05 22, 2 01 23, 2 84 98.

Michoacán is bounded on the N by Guanajuato and Jalisco, on the W by Jalisco and Colima, on the S by the Pacific Ocean and Guerrero and on the E by México state and Querétaro. Its sharp contrasts – plateaus with their lakes and volcanoes, subtropical valleys with their rivers, waterfalls and gorges, unspoiled beaches of white sand – make it a region of great scenic attraction. The mountains of Michoacán, mostly forest-covered, reach their highest point in the Pico de Tancítaro (3850 m – 12,632 ft). The state is crossed by the rivers Lerma, Tepalcatepec and Balsas, draining into the Pacific. The population is primarily composed of Mestizos and Tarascan (Purépecha) Indians, with smaller numbers of Nahua Indians.

There are a number of pre-Columbian (mostly Tarascan) sites in Michoacán, such as *Tzintzuntan (p. 279), *Ihuatzio* (p. 280), *Zacapu* (p. 220), *Tingambato* and *Los Alzati* (near Zitácuaro).

HISTORY. – The area of Michoacán (Náhuatl, "place of the fishermen") was probably settled in the 11th

Mexico
United Mexican States
Estados Unidos Mexicanos

Michoacán

States
Estados

1a	Baja California Sur	12	Aguascalientes
1b	Baja California Norte	13	Jalisco
		14	Guanajuato
		15	Querétaro
2	Sonora	16	Hidalgo
3	Chihuahua	17	Colima
4	Sinaloa	18	Michoacán
5	Durango	19	México
6	Coahuila	20	Morelos
7	Nuevo León	21	Tlaxcala
8	Zacatecas	22	Puebla
9	San Luis Potosí	23	Veracruz
10	Tamaulipas	24	Guerrero
11	Nayarit	25	Oaxaca

26	Chiapas
27	Tabasco
28	Campeche
29	Yucatán
30	Quintana Roo

D.F. Distrito Federal (Federal District)

and 12th c. by Indians from the NW, who later called themselves the *Purépecha* and were known to the Spaniards as *Tarascans*. The pre-Columbian and colonial history of Michoacán is closely linked with that of its capital, Morelia (p. 196), and the towns of Pátzcuaro (p. 218) and Tzintzuntan (p. 279). – Some of the leading figures in the war of Mexican independence (1810–21), such as Ignacio López Rayón, Gertrudis Bocanegra and José María Morelos came from Michoacán. The name of Morelos is also associated with the convening of the first constitutional assembly and the publication of the Constitution at Apatzingán on October 22, 1814. – In December 1821 Michoacán became a state in the Republic of Mexico. Melchor Ocampo (1814–61), the Liberal co-author of the radical reform laws of 1859 during the presidency of Benito Juárez, was a native of the state; and Lázaro Cárdenas (1895–1970), who expropriated the foreign oil companies during his presidency (1934–40), came from Jiquilpan.

ECONOMY. – *Agriculture* (wheat, vegetables, fruit, coffee) plays a major part in the economy of Michoacán; and important contributions are also made by *forestry, livestock-farming* and – to a lesser extent – *mining* (gold, silver, lead, copper, iron). In recent years there has also been considerable development of *energy production* (hydroelectricity) and the *steel industry.* Also of importance are *craft products, folk art* and *tourism.* Recent decades have seen a vast improvement in communications, and Lázaro Cárdenas has become one of Mexico's busiest ports.

In addition to the well-known tourist areas and attractions such as *Morelia (p. 196), the *Lago de Pátzcuaro (p. 218), *Tzintzuntan (p. 279) and Uruapan (p. 281), there are the towns of *Zamora de Hidalgo* (alt. 1600 m (5250 ft); pop. 98,000; hotels: Jérico, SP; Ram-Val, SP; Fenix, SP), with a 19th c. neo-

classical Cathedral; *Apatzingán de la Constitución* (alt. 680 m (2230 ft); pop. 68,000; Motel Río Grande, SP); with the Museo de la Casa de la Constitución; *Lázaro Cárdenas* (pop. 150,000; hotels: Las Truchas, SP; Internacional, SP; Las Palmas, SP), a modern port and industrial town, with a steelworks; *La Piedad Cavadas* (pop. 51,000; Motel Cerro Grande, SP; Posada San Sebastian); *Jiquilpan de Juárez* (alt. 1645 m (5397 ft); pop. 20,000; Hotel Palmira), with the church of San Francisco (17th c. doorway) and the Gabino Ortiz Library (murals by José Clemente Orozco and the Casa Museo del General Lázaro Cárdenas); and *Playa Azul* (hotels: La Loma, Playa Azul, Delfín), a fishing village which has become a popular beach resort.

Mitla

State: Oaxaca (Oax.).
Altitude: 1480 m (4855 ft). – Population: 7000.

ACCOMMODATION. – *Posada La Sorpresa,* II.

EVENTS. – January 25–31, Fiesta of San Pablo; December 31, Cruz de Petición.

ACCESS. – 38 km (24 miles) E of Oaxaca on Road 190 is a side road leading (4 km – 2½ miles) to the site.

The site of *Mitla, just outside the village of the same name, is one of Mexico's best known archeological

Potter at work, Mitla

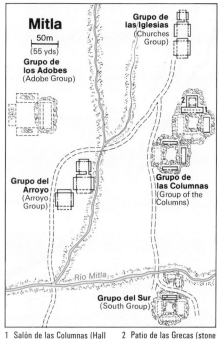

1 Salón de las Columnas (Hall   2 Patio de las Grecas (stone
  of Columns)   mosaics)

attractions. Although the site and its architecture are less imposing than other sites, the elaborate *stone mosaics here are unsurpassed in the art of Meso-America.

HISTORY. – Since the Oaxaca area lay on the route of many migrant peoples and was thus exposed to a variety of influences, it is difficult to disentangle the early history of Mitla ("place of the dead" in Náhuatl). It is believed that Mitla, like Monte Albán and Yagul, was established long before the beginning of the Chritian era. The influence of the *Zapotecs* was no doubt predominant in the Classic period, i.e. in the Monte Albán IIIA and IIIB phases (A.D. 0–900). From 900 the influence of the *Mixtecs* ("the men from the land of clouds") began to make itself felt in this area. These people, who lived mainly in northern Oaxaca and between the 10th and 12th c., were hard pressed by the *Toltecs* of Tollan (Tula). They moved gradually S into Zapotec territory and, by the time the Spaniards arrived, had gained possession, either by war or by marriage, of some 200 places of importance belonging to the Zapotecs and other peoples. It is supposed that between 900 and 1500 the Mixtecs exerted considerable influence on Mitla. During the important period of the 10th and 11th c., however, other stylistic features appear, neither Mixtec nor Zapotec, so that we still cannot establish all the influences which contributed to the delvelopment of this interesting site. The 14th c. pottery found at Mitla is almost exclusively of Mixtec origin.

In 1494 the *Aztecs* captured the town during their advance toward Oaxaca. When the *Spaniards* arrived at Mitla in 1521, it was occupied mainly by Zapotecs. – The first account of Mitla was given by Diego Garcia de Palacio in 1576, followed a hundred years later by Francisco de Burgoa, who recorded his impressions in 1679. Among later descriptions of the site were those of Alexander von Humboldt, Guillermo Dupaix, Désiré Charnay, Eduard Seler and Alfonso Caso.

THE SITE. – Within the archeological zone there are five main groups of structures, together with a large number of houses and tombs between and around these groups.

In the eastern part of the site is the most important complex, the *Group of the Columns (Grupo de las Columnas)*. This is laid out around two rectangular patios, set corner to corner, with three large halls around each patio.

In the middle of the first patio, which measures 45 by 36 m (150 by 120 ft), is an *altar*. On the N side is a flight of steps leading up to a platform on which stands the **Hall of Columns** (*Salón de las Columnas*), accessible by three doors. The hall, which was originally roofed, measures 38 by 7 m (125 by 25 ft) and has six porphyry columns 4.20 m (14 ft) high and almost 1 m (3 ft) in diameter. – From here a narrow passage with a low roof leads into a small inner patio, the *Patio de las Grecas*, which is surrounded by long narrow rooms. The walls of the patio and the rooms are decorated with the *STONE MOSAICS characteristic of Mitla, produced by covering the walls with a coat of mortar into which small pieces of stone, carefully and accurately cut, were set in particular patterns. The elaborate decorative motifs, always geometrical in form – there are no human or mythological figures at Mitla – are found in no fewer than fourteen variations, showing an alternation between cross-shaped patterns, interlace, stepped meanders, zigzags and other forms reminiscent of Greek ornament. The optical effect of the designs varies with the play of light and shade. The various forms are believed to symbolize religious concepts such as the feathered serpent, the sky and the earth. It is estimated that more than 100,000 mosaic stones were used in the decoration of this building.

Also very characteristic of the architecture of Mitla are the massive slabs of carefully dressed stone which form the lintels and uprights of the doors. The erection of these huge blocks of stone, up to 8 m (25 ft) in length and 23 tons in wieght, is an extraordinary achievement by men who were without the use of the wheel and had neither pack nor draft animals. – The building is said to have been the residence of Uija-táo ("he who sees all"), who was both chief priest and supreme judge of the region.

The adjoining *Patio of the Crosses* (Patio de las Cruces), to the S, has on the E side a building with a magnificent *pillared doorway* built of heavy ashlar blocks. In front of it is a subterranean *tomb chamber*, cruciform in shape, which is also decorated with a stone mosaic in meander pattern, constructed of larger pieces of stone. The tomb is well preserved but when excavated was found to have been robbed. The tomb chamber on the N side had a roof supported by a central column, and it is believed that visitors can measure their life expectancies by stretching their arms round this column.

The **Churches Group** (*Grupo de las Iglesias*), to the N, is so called because after the Spanish conquest a church, the *Iglasia de San Pablo*, was built in the remains of the old Indian structure. The plan of this group is similar to that of the Group of the Columns but on a smaller scale. Unfortunately, one of the patios and some of the structures around it were destroyed during the construction of the church. The northern patio is moderately well preserved; and this patio and a smaller one on the N side also have mosaic decoration on the walls and in the rooms.

Stone mosaic work, Mitla

There are remains of a frieze of wall paintings, and there were once paintings on most of the door framings. The paintings were in the style of the Mixtec pictographic manuscripts, the most famous of which are the Codex Vindobonensis (Mexicanis I) and Codex Becker I (the "Manuscript of the Cacique"), now preserved in the Austrian National Library and the Museum of Ethnography in Vienna respectively.

On the other side of the Rio Mitla is the *South Group* (Grupo del Sur), and to the W are the *Arroyo Group* (Grupo del Arroyo) and the *Adobe Group* (Grupo de los Adobes), which have not yet been fully excavated and restored.

Near the village square is the **Frissell Museum** (*Museo Frissell de Arte Zapoteca*), with an excellently displayed collection of archeological material from the state of Oaxaca, in particular Zapotec and Mixtec material.

SURROUNDINGS. – Some 5 km (3 miles) from the site, on the road to Tepuxtepec, is the *Hacienda Xaaga*, where an interesting cruciform tomb with meander ornament was found.

Monte Albán

State: Oaxaca (Oax.).
Altitude: 2000 m (6560 ft).

ACCESS. – 6 km (4 miles) W of Oaxaca.

The site of **Monte Albán at one time extended over several hills and covered an area of 40 sq. km (15 sq. miles), and over a period of almost 2500 years served a succession of different peoples as a cult and ceremonial site. The central part of the site, rising 400 m (1300 ft) above the subtropical Oaxaca valley on a man-made platform, is perhaps the most impressive pre-Columbian site in the whole of Meso-America.

HISTORY. – The origins and early history of human culture in the area around Monte Albán (the "(White Mountain") are lost in obscurity. It is known that there were human settlements here as early as 4000 B.C., but the first evidence of any kind of advanced culture dates only from about 1000 B.C. We still do not know who were the first settlers who built the cult site during the *Monte Albán I* phase (800–300 B.C.), although this phase shows features characteristic of the *Olmecs* (La Venta culture). A settlement of urban type was now

Monte Albán, a "symphony of staircases"

established, represented archeologically by simple tombs containing pottery and dressed blocks of stone with bas-reliefs of human figures and calendrical signs. There we find probably the first simple writing system in the Americas. – In the *Monte Ablán II* phase (300–0 B.C.), influences from the Pre-Classic culture of the *Mayas* to the S can be detected. Pottery of better quality, an improved calendrical system and large structures in cyclopean masonry are found during this phase. – The following phases, *Monte Albán IIIA* (until about A.D. 300) and *Monte Albán IIIB* (until about 900), which coincide with the appearance of the *Zapotecs*, were the heyday of Monte Albán. Characteristic features of this period are the use of the *talud-tablero* style (vertical panels alternating with sloping walls) in most of the major buildings and the construction of elaborate tombs with beautiful frescoes and a variety of pottery funerary urns. In the first half of the period, stylistic features derived from *Teotihuacán* on the central plateau are found, while, toward the end of the period, the *Mixtec* influence is already making itself felt. – In the *Monte Albán IV* phase (900–1200) decline set in. No new buildings were erected and the magnificent earlier structures began to decay, while other towns, including Etla, Yagul, Mitla and Zaachila were being established or developed. Monte Albán seems now to have served only as a place of burial for the Zapotecs and later for the Mixtecs. The pottery becomes plainer and the structure and furnishings of the tombs simpler. – The *Monte Albán V* phase, the last before the Spanish conquest, was primarily the work of the *Mixtecs*, who constructed numerous tombs and reused older ones. – The *Aztecs*, who established a military base on the site of Oaxaca in 1486, had no influence on the development of Monte Albán, any more than the *Spaniards* who arrived in 1521.

The first serious investigation of Monte Albán came only in the 19th c., with Désiré Charnay, Eduard Seler and W. H. Holmes among the principal archeologists. In the 20th c. major contributions have been made by the Mexican archeologists Alfonso Caso and Ignacio Bernal.

THE SITE. – The central feature of the site, which is about 10 km (6 miles) from Oaxaca, is the ****Gran Plaza**, a large level area measuring 200 by 300 m (220 by 330 yds), formed partly by the removal of soil and partly by building it up. Any blocks of stone too difficult to remove were built into the various structures, as in the North and South Platforms and Buildings G, H and I. As a result the main structures were not exactly in the middle of the plaza and the great staircases of the two platforms were not opposite one another. In order to conceal this lack of symmetry, the Zapotecs erected in phase III two small additional buildings in front of Buildings M and IV, separated by patios. – As was usual in pre-Columbian architecture, almost all the structures were several times built over, some of them as many as six times, and the walls were originally faced with coloured stucco.

The first building encountered on leaving the parking lot, to the left (i.e., on the E side of the plaza), is the **Ball Court** (*Juego de Pelota*). As at all the other ball courts in the Oaxaca region no stone rings to serve as "goals" were found here. The last rebuilding of the court was in phase IIIB.

Of the adjoining buildings, all in the style characteristic of Monte Albán III, the most notable is the **pyramid**, which has an internal staircase leading to the top. From here a tunnel ran under the plaza to the central group of buildings (G, H and I), enabling the priests to reach these buildings without being seen.

The next major building, also with a broad staircase, is the **Palace** (*Palacio*). On the summit platform nothing was left but some remains of walls, probably belonging to the priests' dwelling. Under the inner patio a cruciform tomb of phase IV was found. – Between the Palace and the central group of buildings, set in the rock, is an *altar*, in which the excavators found an unusual jade mask of the bat god, now in the National Museum of Anthropology in Mexico City.

The three main buildings of the **Central Group** (*G, H* and *I*) probably housed altars. The one in the middle (*Building H*) measures 45 by 30 m (150 by 100 ft) and has a broad staircase leading up to a two-chambered temple. On a lower level are two temple chambers with columns in front of them. The other two buildings (*G* and *I*) are almost identical: the temples stand on two platforms, the lower one having vertical and the upper one sloping walls, with their staircases leading respectively N and S.

The fourth building in the central group, standing by itself, is known as *****Mound J** (*Montículo J*). This structure is the only one which does not fit into the regular pattern of the layout as a whole, but is set at a 45° angle to the other buildings. It is also unusual in its form, with a ground-plan resembling an arrowhead, with the staircase at the end opposite the point. A vaulted tunnel runs up under the front part of the building. Tunnels of this kind in Meso-American buildings were usually designed by astronomical observations; but, curiously, the sky is not visible from this tunnel. On the wall at the end of the building are carved figures and hieroglyphs evidently recording conquests of enemy cities. The main part of this structure is thought to date from just before the beginning of the Christian era (from phase II).

The **South Platform** (*Plataforma del Sur*), which bounds the S side of the plaza, is a huge structure on which relatively little excavation has been done. A staircase 40 m (130 ft) wide leads up to a platform from which, particularly at sunset, there is a magnificent *view of

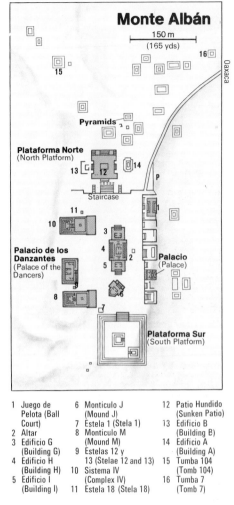

Monte Albán

150 m
(165 yds)

Oaxaca

Plataforma Norte
(North Platform)

Pyramids

Staircase

Palacio de los Danzantes
(Palace of the Dancers)

Palacio
(Palace)

Plataforma Sur
(South Platform)

1	Juego de Pelota (Ball Court)	6	Montículo J (Mound J)	12	Patio Hundido (Sunken Patio)
2	Altar	7	Estela 1 (Stela 1)	13	Edificio B (Building B)
3	Edificio G (Building G)	8	Montículo M (Mound M)	14	Edificio A (Building A)
4	Edificio H (Building H)	9	Estelas 12 y 13 (Stelae 12 and 13)	15	Tumba 104 (Tomb 104)
5	Edificio I (Building I)	10	Sistema IV (Complex IV)	16	Tumba 7 (Tomb 7)
		11	Estela 18 (Stela 18)		

the whole site, famed as a "symphony of staircases". Here were found Stelae 5 and 6, now in the National Museum of Anthropology in Mexico City. – At the NE corner of the platform is *****Stela 1**, one of the finest and best preserved of the Monte Albán stelae. To the left is a jaguar wearing the headdress of the rain god Cocijo, seated on a hill: to the right and along the top are rows of glyphs.

At the SW corner of the plaza is *Mound M* (*Montículo M*), a rectangular structure consisting of two buildings separated by a patio with a small alter. As is normal at Monte Albán, a central staircase leads up by way of two stories with four sloping walls to the summit platform, on which are the remains of four columns, once part of the temple façade. As already mentioned, the front part of the structure was added in phase III to improve the symmetry of the layout as a whole. On the N side of the main building are **Stelae 12 and 13**,

One of the "Danzantes", Monte Albán

which are covered with number glyphs and are evidently associated with the adjoining *Palace of the Dancers (*Palacio de los Danzantes*).

This, perhaps the most interesting part of the whole site, has an altar dating from the 6th–5th c. B.C. (Monté Albán I). The original structure was built over several times, and what we now see, a tall double-story building measuring 30 by 60 m (100 by 200 ft), dates from phases IIIA and IIIB. The most important features are the slabs of stone carved with reliefs of figures, the famous **Danzantes**, which originally decorated a 3 m (10 ft) high terrace wall. They are now set up in groups around the structure. The negroid features of these figures and the accompanying glyphs show considerable similarities to those of the Olmecs (La Venta culture) on the coast of the Gulf of Mexico. It is clear that even at this early stage the people of Monte Albán had a form of script and a calendrical and numerical system. It used to be thought that these figures, with their bizarre body attitudes, represented dancers: the current view is that they may be slaves undergoing torture. No doubt this would be clarified if the glyphs could be read; but so far only numbers have been deciphered. – During the past years some of these slabs have been taken to museums and were replaced by polyester reproductions. Apparently it is planned to remove all originals from the site in order to preserve them from damage.

Farther N is *Complex IV* (Sistema IV), which is very similar to Mound M. On the N side of this is the badly weathered **Stela 18**, believed to date from phase II (*c.* 300–0 B.C.). This is the only stela of phase II which has been preserved, and is probably of about the same date as the original structure of Complex IV, which is built of massive cyclopean blocks in the style characterestic of phase II. – Between

Complex IV and the North Platform is a low group of structures comprising a number of chambers and several tombs.

The massive **North Platform** (*Plataforma del Norte*), which stands 12 m (40 ft) high and covers an area 250 by 200 m (275 by 220 yds), is approached by a staircase 38 m (125 ft) wide, on either side of which was found a *cult chamber* decorated with hieroglyphs and figures and containing a tomb. Opposite the W chamber was found *Stela 9* (now in the National Museum of Anthropology, Mexico City), decorated on all four sides with reliefs; it ranks as the finest of its kind. On the platform are remains of the double row of columns 2 m (6½ ft) in diameter which once supported the roof of a huge hall. – A staircase leads down to the *Sunken Patio* (Patio Hundido), in the middle of which is a finely carved rectangular altar. On this altar stood *Stela 10*, now also in Mexico City.

To the W is *building B* (Edificio B), the superstructure of which, poorly preserved, is ascribed to the Mixtecs and is perhaps the most recent building at Monte Albán. – On the other side of the Sunken Patio is *Building A* (Edificio A), an earlier pyramid now represented only by some remains of the masonry base and staircase. – To the N of the main platform are a variety of unexcavated remains.

A path runs NW to *Tomb 104 (*Tumba 104*), the finest so far discovered at Monte Albán; it dates from about A.D. 500.

Above the elaborate entrance façade is a niche containing a **terracotta urn** in the form of a seated figure wearing the headdress of the rain god Cocijo. The *door* between the antechamber and the tomb chamber is a massive slab of stone covered with hieroglyphs. All three walls of the tomb chamber have colored **frescoes**. On the right-hand wall is the figure of Titao Cazobi, the Zapotec maize god, with a large serpent and feather headdress. On the rear wall, above a niche, is the head of an unknown red divinity with an arc-shaped headdress, the "5 turquoise" glyph and the opening of the firmament. On the left-hand wall is a figure with the features of an old man, his head, neck and waist laden with ornaments and holding a copal bag; it probably represents the god Xipe Tótec, the Zapotec, Mixtec and Aztec god of renewal, of jewelers and of the flayed. In the tomb chamber were found the remains of an adult male, a large urn representing the same figure as on the rear wall, and four smaller urns.

Under the mound containing Tomb 104 is *Tomb 172*, in which the skeleton of the dead man and the accompanying grave goods have been left exactly as they were found.

To the NE of the Gran Plaza, outside the cult center itself, is the famous **Tomb 7** (*Tumba 7*), discovered by Alfonso Caso in 1932. This tomb, probably built by the Zapotecs in phase III, contained the largest hoard of treasure ever found in Meso-America. Zapotec pottery and funerary urns were found in the antechamber, in which at a later period (probably about the middle of the 14th c.) were buried the remains of noble personages. The Mixtec **grave goods consisted of almost 500 works of excellent craftsmanship in gold, silver, jade, turquoise, rock crystal, alabaster and other materials. They are now in the Regional Museum in Oaxaca (Convent of Santo Domingo). – Another notable tomb is *Tomb 105*, on the "Plumage Hill", with a magnificent entrance doorway and interesting wall paintings.

Near the parking lot is a small *archeological exhibition* which is well worth visiting.

There is a new museum-annex to the service building, containing mainly interesting carved stelae.

Lagunas de Montebello

State: Chiapas (Chis.).
Altitude: 1500 m (4900 ft) and below.

ACCESS. – 103 km (64 miles) from San Cristóbal de las Casas and 16 km (10 miles) from Comitán de Domínguez on Road 190 (Panamericana), the road to Guatemala, a side road branches off on the left and comes in 38 km (24 miles) to the Lagunas de Montebello National Park. – A road, only the first part of which is asphalt-covered, runs through the National Park, with offshoots of varying quality leading to the various lakes.

ACCOMMODATIONS. – *Albergue* on Lago Tziscao and camp sites.

RECREATION and SPORTS. – Swimming, rowing, sailing.

The group of small and medium-sized lakes known collectively as the *Lagunas de Montebello extends E from the beginning of the National Park into Guatemala and the Selva Lacandona. There are more than a hundred lakes, with water of varying hues, scattered over a terraced, largely unspoiled, landscape – most of it covered by pine forests. In addition to the lakes, there are many

One of the Montebello lakes

swallow-holes, caves and waterfalls adding to the scenic attractions of the region.

Visitors to this large tract of wild country should hire a local guide; otherwise they may easily lose their way. – One group of lakes is known as the **Lagos de Colores** ("Colored Lakes") because of the widely varying hues of their water, from emerald-green to midnight blue: a phenomenon in which the depth of the lake, the angle of the sun, the nature of the lake bottom and the constitution of the water all play a part. The lakes and their surrounding areas are known by evocative names like *La Encantada* (the "enchanted lake"), *Ensueno* ("dream"), *Esmeralda* ("emerald"), *Bosque Azul* ("blue forest") and *Agua Tinta* ("colored water").

Near a small hamlet is the remarkable **Arco de San Rafael** (Arch of St Raphael), a natural bridge of limestone under which the Río Comitán flows into a cave and disappears. – One of the largest of the readily accessible lakes is **Lago Tziscao**, 10 km (6 miles) E, which lies on the Guatemalan frontier. This is presently the only place in the area with available accommodation for visitors.

The road E, along the Guatemalan frontier and then N to *Bonampak** (p. 79), is at present under construction.

SURROUNDINGS. – 32 km (20 miles) E of the junction with Road 190 on the road to the National Park a side road runs 2 km (1¼ miles) N to the Maya site of **Chinkultic**, at an altitude of 1600 m (5250 ft) on the rocky escarpment of a forest-covered hill and surrounded by a beautiful region of lakes and pastureland. Unexpectedly, in this area far from the karstic terrain of Yucatán, there is a cenote.

Chinkultic ("cave of the steps" in Maya) was occupied from about the beginning of the Christian era to the 13th c., with its heyday during the Maya Classic period (A.D. 300–900). The first to visit the site was the German archeologist Eduard Seler in 1895;

about 1925 it was investigated by a Dane, Frans Blom, and an American, Oliver La Farge; further excavations were carried out by Stephen F. de Borhegyi and Gareth W. Lowe. In recent years many of the excavated remains have been overgrown by vegetation.

Within the large area covered by the site, there are over 200 mounds of varying size concealing Maya remains. Of the six main groups little can now be seen. – On the W side of the site, in *Group C*, is a large *ball court*, 54 m (177 ft) long and 25 m (82 ft) across, with three sculptured stelae along the W side. (A total of nineteen stelae with relief carvings of figures and glyphs have so far been found at Chinkultic.) – To the NW is *Group A*, with the excavated *Temple 1* or *Mirador*, which tops a 40 m (131 ft) high pyramid. It stands on a terrace on which there are four platforms. The broad staircase leading up to the temple has been overgrown by scrub. – Some 50 m (55 yds) below the temple is the picturesque turquoise-blue *Cenote Agua Azul*. Assuming that this cenote, like the one at Chichén Itzá, would contain the remains of sacrificial victims and offerings to the gods, divers went down to look for material of this kind. They were unable to find anything because they were hindered by the opaque layer of silt which began just below the surface. The cenote was then drained into the neighboring Lake Chanujabab and excavations were carried out, yielding various types of pottery.

In addition to a number of interesting stelae and elaborately decorated incense-burners, the excavators found in the vicinity of the site a stone disc 55 cm (22 in.) in diameter and weighing 78 kg (172 lb), which was dated to A.D. 590. This interesting object, a marker used in the ball game, depicts a ball-player with an elaborate feather headdress and the ritual equipment used in the game, surrounded by a band of glyphs. It is now in the National Museum of Anthropology in Mexico City.

Monterrey

State: Nuevo León (N.L.).
Altitude: 538 m (1765 ft). – Population: 2,450,000.
Telephone dialling code: 91 83.
(i) **Coordinación Federal de Turismo,**
Emilio Carranza 730 Sur P.B.
tel. 44 01 72, 44 50 11, 44 11 69.

HOTELS. – *Ambassador*, Hidalgo y E. Carranza, L, SP; *Gran Hotel Ancira*, Hidalgo y Escobedo, L, SP; *Monterrey*, Morelos y Zaragoza, I, SP; *Colonial*, Hidalgo Ote. 475, II; *Nuevo León*, Amado Nervo Nte. 1007, II; *Victoria*, Av. Bernardo Reyes Nte. 1205, II; *Conde*, Reforma 419, Pte. III; *Madero*, Modero Pte. 428, III. – OUTSIDE THE TOWN: *Holiday Inn*, Universidad 101, L, SP, tennis; *Ramada Inn*, Av. Jorge del Moral, L, SP, tennis; *Motel Dorado*, Carr. a Laredo 901, I, SP; *Hotel Monterrey Plaza*, Avenida Constitución. 300 Ote, L, SP.

RESTAURANTS in most hotels; also *Luisiana*, Hidalgo 530 Ote.; *El Pastor*, Madero 1067; *Santa Rosa*, Plaza Hidalgo; *El Tío*, Hidalgo y Calle México; *La Belle Época*, extension of Madero Pte. 201; *Regio*, Gonzalitos y Vancouver; *Mérida*, Zaragoza Nte. 522.

RECREATION and SPORTS. – Swimming, tennis, golf, climbing, riding.

EVENTS. – May 20, Agricultural and Trade Fair; September 15–16, Independence celebrations.

The industrial city of Monterrey lies in the Santa Catarina valley, under the jagged peak of the Cerro de la Silla ("Hill of the Saddle", 1740 m – 5709 ft) and the Cerro de la Mitra ("Hill of the Mitre", 2380 m – 7809 ft). Capital of the state of Nuevo León, it is Mexico's third largest city (after Mexico City and Guadalajara) and its second most important industrial center. Although the town has developed into a modern industrial city, it still has a few corners which preserve an old Spanish atmosphere with narrow lanes, flat-roofed houses and picturesque patios. Monterrey is a wholly Spanish town showing no signs of Indian influence.

HISTORY. – The area around Monterrey has no pre-Columbian history. It was a land crossed only by nomads, who left little trace of their passing. The first Spaniards, led by Luis Carvajal y de la Cueva, arrived in 1584 and established the outpost of *Ojos de Santa Lucía* to provide defense against Indian attack. The first permanent settlement was eleven years later, when twelve Spanish families under the leadership of Diego de Montemayor founded a settlement which they called *Ciudad de Nuestra Señora de Monterrey* after the then Viceroy, the Conde de Monterrey. This

Monterrey

500 m
(550 yds)

isolated little township, which had still no more than 258 inhabitants in 1775, was exposed to frequent raids by nomadic Indians. During the war with the United States, in 1846, Monterrey was occupied by US troops, and in 1864, during the War of Intervention, it was occupied by the French. Economic growth began in 1882, when the railway line from Laredo to Monterrey was opened, and has continued undiminished ever since.

ECONOMY. – Thanks to its excellent communications, Monterrey has become a major area of *heavy industry*, and is also an important producer of *consumer goods*. Its principal products include glass, cement, textiles, plastics, foodstuffs and beer. Its Instituto Tecnológico is one of the largest and best colleges of technology in Latin America.

SIGHTS. – Since only a century ago Monterrey was a place of little importance, it has little in the way of colonial art and architecture, but this lively town and its surrounding area attract many tourists, particularly from the United States.

Fountains in Plaza Zaragoza, Monterrey

In the center of the city is the **Plaza Cinco de Mayo**, with a *statue of Benito Juárez*. On the N side of the square is the **Government Palace** (*Palacio de Gobierno*), built of red sandstone, the most notable features of which are its beautiful colonial patio and the state apartments, decorated with frescoes, with a small historical museum (including the guns of the firing squad which shot the Emperor Maximilian in 1867). – Almost opposite is the modern *Palacio Federal*, from the tower of which there is a good *view of the town and surrounding area.

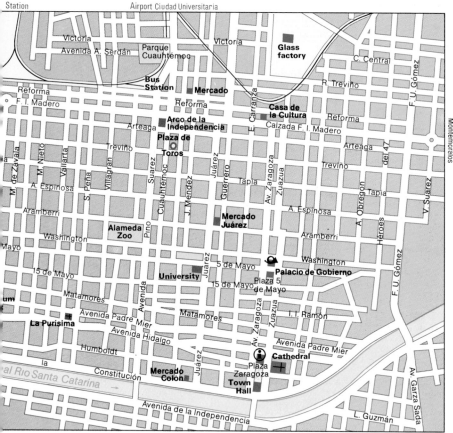

Going S along either Calle Zaragoza or Calle Sazua, we come to Monterrey's most important square, the **Plaza Zaragoza**, surrounded by hotels, restaurants and shops, which, particularly in the evening and on weekends, is the hub of the city's social life. In this square, too, are the **Town Hall** (*Palacio Municipal*), with an attractive patio and a small library, and the single-towered **Cathedral** (begun in 1603 but not completed until 1851), with a Baroque façade.

To the W, along the Avenida Hidalgo (corner of the Calle Serafín Peña), is the *church of La Purísima, one of Mexico's finest modern churches, designed by Enrique de la Mora y Polomar. – From here Calle padre Mier continues W to end at the Cerro de Obispado of Chepe Vera, on which is the **Bishop's Palace** (*Obispado*), built at the end of the 18th c. and later used as a fortress and then a hospital. In 1913 the notorious bandit and revolutionary hero, Pancho Villa, entrenched himself here. The palace now houses a *museum* illustrating the economic and cultural development of the region. Notable features are the *chapel*, with a beautiful Churrigueresque façade, and the *printing press* on which Father Servando Teresa de Mier printed pamphlets directed against Spanish rule during the war of independence (1810–21).

Other features of interest in Monterrey are the *church of Espíritu Santo*, an asym-

metric modern building designed by Armando Rauize, with a large mural mosaic; the modern *Institute of Technology* (Instituto Tecnológico: library with a large mural by Jorge González Camerena); a *Glass Museum*; an *Automobile Museum*; and the *Cuauhtémoc Brewery*.

SURROUNDINGS. – 20 km (12 miles) SW of Monterrey (leave by the Avenida Mesa Chipinque, the road to the golf-course) is the **Mesa Chipinque** (Hotel Chipinque, SP, horses for hire), a forest-covered plateau from which there is a beautiful *view of Monterrey and the surrounding area.

13 km (8 miles) from Monterrey, on the road to Saltillo (No. 40), a side road (3 km – 2 miles) goes off to the **Cañón de la Huasteca**, a sheer-sided gorge 300 m (1000 ft) deep enclosed by bizarre rock formations. – 20 km (12 miles) W of Monterrey on Road 40 a side road runs 24 km (15 miles) N to the *Grutas de García, one of the largest and finest cave systems in Mexico (cableway to entrance).

36 km (22 miles) from Monterrey on the road to Ciudad Victoria (No. 85) is *El Cercado*, where a road branches off to the **Cascadas Cola de Caballo** ("Horsetail Falls"), an impressive waterfall with a drop of 30 m – 100 ft (Hotel Cola de Caballo, SP, horses for hire). From here a detour can be made to the *Presa de la Boca*, man-made lake (reservoir) with facilities for a variety of water sports.

Morelia

State: Michoacán (Mich.).
Altitude: 1950 m (6400 ft). – Population: 570,000.
Telephone dialing code: 9 41 51.
ⓘ **Coordinación Federal de Turismo,**
Santos Degollado 340, Altos 1,
tel. 2 05 22, 2 01 23, 2 84 98.

Cathedral and Zaragoza Monument, Monterrey

HOTELS. – *Calinda Morelia*, Av. Las Camelinas, L, SP, tennis; *Virrey de Mendoza*, Portal Matamoros 16, I; *Posada de la Soledad*, Zaragoza y Ocampo, I; *Mansión de la Calle Real*, Av. Madero Ote. 766, I; *Alameda*, Av. Madero y Guillermo Prieto, I; *Condordia*, Valentín Gómez Farías, II; *Posada Morelia*, Tapía 31, II; *El Carmen*, El Ruiz 63, III. – OUTSIDE THE TOWN: *Villa Montaña*, Calle Patzinba, I, SP, tennis.

RESTAURANTS in most hotels; also *L'Escargot*, Lázaro Cárdenas 2118; *La Cabaña de Vic*, Av. Las Camelinas 1535; *Las Morelianas*, El Retajo 90; *La Huacana*, García Obeso y Aldama.

RECREATION and SPORTS. – Swimming, tennis, golf, riding.

EVENT. – September 30, birthday of José María Morelos.

Morelia Cathedral

*Morelia, the magnificent capital city of the state of Michoacán, lies on the right bank of the Río Grande de Morelia, in a wide and fertile valley basin. Located half-way between Mexico's two largest cities, Mexico City and Guadalajara, it has preserved the character of an elegant old Spanish colonial town.

HISTORY. – In pre-Columbian times the Morelia area was occupied by a tribe of *Matlatzinca* Indians who, in the mid 15th c., retreated before the Aztec advance into this region, then controlled by the *Tarascans* (Purépecha). – Soon after the Conquest the first *Spaniards* came here under Cristóbal de Olid and subjugated the Tarascans. According to the Spanish chronicles a convent was founded here in 1537 by the Franciscan friar, Juan de San Miguel; the town itself was established in 1541, under the name of *Valladolid*, by the first Viceroy of New Spain, Antonio de Mendoza, and was granted a municipal charter only six years later. There was some rivalry between the "Indian" town of Pátzcuaro, an episcopal see under Bishop Vasco de Quiroga, and the "Spanish" Valladolid; but in 1570 Valladolid also became the see of a bishop, and in 1582 it replaced Pátzcuaro as capital of Michoacán. During the 17th and 18th c. it developed into a market and commercial center for the surrounding agricultural region. – During the war of independence (1810–21) the town was for a time the operational base of the leader of the independence movement, Miguel Hidalgo y Costilla. After Mexico became independent, in 1828, it was renamed Morelia in honor of another great figure in the struggle for independence, the priest José María Morelos y Pavón (1765–1815), who was a native of the town. Inheriting the cultural traditions of Spain, Morelia eventually became one of Mexico's leading intellectual centers thanks largely to its University.

SIGHTS. – The beautiful main square of Morelia, the **Plaza de los Mártires** or *Zócalo*, is surrounded on three sides by arcades, while the E side is occupied by the *Cathedral, a magnificent building of brownish pink trachyte which was begun in 1640 and completed more than a hundred years later. In spite of the long period of construction, it shows a remarkable unity of style, predominantly severe Baroque. The dome is covered with azulejos. Notable features of the interior, which underwent some alteration at the end of the 19th c., are the neo-classical retablos, the silver font, a crucifix by Manual Tolsá, the German-made organ (1903) and a number of pictures in the choir and sacristy; these are attributed to the leading painters of the first half of the 18th c., Juan Rodríguez Juárez, José María de Ibarra and Miguel Cabrera.

Facing the Cathedral, on the other side of the Avenida Madero Oriente, is the **Government Palace** (*Palacio de Gobierno*), a Baroque building erected between 1732 and 1770 (interesting patio). It is notable for the huge mural paintings by a local artist, Alfredo Zalce, depicting the history of Mexican independence, reform and revolution.

At the corner of Calles Allende and Abasolo, in a Baroque building of the mid 18th c., is the **Regional Museum** (*Museo Regional de Michoacán*), with pre-Columbian archeological and ethnological material and pictures, weapons, implements and furniture of the colonial period. On the staircases are frescoes by Alfredo Zalce and Federico Cantú. – Turning left after leaving the Museum, we come to the *Town Hall* (Palacio Municipal), a neo-classical building of the late 18th c.

Going N along Calle Galeana and crossing the Avenida Madero Poniente, we reach the **Colegio San Nicolás**, originally founded at Pátzcuaro in 1540 and later transferred to a building on this site erected in 1580; it is the oldest college on the American continent after the Santa Cruz college in Tlatelolco (1537). The college is now part of the University. It has a large courtyard surrounded by handsome Baroque arcades. – Opposite the Colegio San Nicolás is the former *Jesuit church* (Iglesia de la Compañía, 1660–81), which now houses the *Public Library* (*Biblioteca Pública*).

On the far side of Calle Santiago Tapia, in a pretty little square, is the **church of Santa Rosa de Lima**, begun in the late 16th c. It has an interesting double doorway showing Renaissance influence, although the rest of the façade is predominantly Baroque. Baroque, too, in its Churrigueresque form, are the church's beautiful gilded and painted retablos. Attached to the church is a *Conservatoire*, the oldest in the New World. – On calle Guillermo Prieto and Santiago Tapia is the State Museum (Museo del Estado), which houses various historical objects of all centuries connected with the region. Near the Casa Cultura on Benito Juárez 240, one finds the Museum of Colonial Art (Museo de Arte Colonial) with many religious exhibits from the area.

Beyond the Plaza Valladolid is the **church of San Francisco**, built about 1540 and therefore the oldest church in the town. It has a fine Renaissance-style façade with Plateresque elements and a bell-tower with a small azulejo-clad dome. The old convent buildings now house the *Palacio de Artesanías*, in which the arts and crafts of the region are displayed. The *planetarium*, the largest and most modern in Mexico, is well worth a visit.

Other features of interest are the *churches* of *Carmen, San Agustín* and *Guadalupe, Cuauhtémoc Park* and the house once occupied by José María Morelos, now a museum. – A distinctive local landmark is an **aqueduct** built in 1785–9, 1600 m (1 mile) long, with 253 arches.

SURROUNDINGS. – 70 km (45 miles) E of Morelia, on Road 15 (the road to Toluca and Mexico City), which goes over several 3000 m (10,000 ft) passes, is **Mil Cumbres** ("A Thousand Peaks"), from which there is a breathtaking panoramic *view of the forest-covered mountains of the Sierra Madre Occidental. – Some 30 km (20 miles) beyond this is **Ciudad Hidalgo** (alt. 2360 m (7746 ft); pop. 55,000; hotels: Diplomático, Central). The parish church, which belonged to a 16th c. Franciscan convent, has a

Plateresque façade. – 30 km (20 miles) SE along the road to Zitácuaro, a side road goes off on the right to *San José Purúa, 8 km (5 miles) away, a picturesque little spa set amid tropical vegetation on the edge of a deep gorge (hotels: Spa San José Purúa, SP, tennis, golf; Spa Hotel Melia, SP, riding; Balneario Agua Blanca, SP). – From Ciudad Hidalgo it is 48 km (30 miles) on Road 15 to *Zitácuaro* (1781 m (3845 ft); pop. 50,000; hotels: Rosales del Valle, San Cayetano, Salvador) with 12 km (8 miles) away the archeological zone of *San Felipe Los Alzati* (Camají); this site which is attributed to the Malatzinca (late classic A.D. 700–900), has a gigantic pyramid 6 stories high but only partly excavated. Its estimated height of 70 m (230 ft) would make it the tallest pre-Spanish building in Mexico.

E of Zitácuaro in the direction of Toluca there is to the N of the mountain road an area to which every year huge numbers of *monarch moths come to spend the winter from December to February.

Road 43, going N from Morelia, crosses the shallow *Lake Cuitzeo* and comes in 35 km (22 miles) to the fishing village of **Cuitzeo**, which attracts many visitors to its Augustinian *convent (1551). The convent church has a beautiful and richly ornamented façade in Indian-Plateresque style. Above the doorway is a pierced heart, the emblem of the Augustinian order. The tower was built at the beginning of the 17th c. The defensive character of the church and convent, with its large enclosed atrium, is evident. In the center of the atrium wall, behind the third arch from the right, is a large niche-like recess which may have served as the open chapel. The cloister still has some remains of the original frescoes.

58 km (36 miles) SW of Morelia on the Uruapan road is *Pátzcuaro, a good base from which to visit the interesting places around the *Lago de Pátzcuaro (see p. 218).

Morelos

State of Morelos (Mor.).
Area: 4964 sq. km (1917 sq. miles).
Population: 1,076,600
(i) **Coordinación Federal de Turismo,**
  Ignacio Comonfort 12,
  Cuernavaca, Mor.;
  tel. (9 17 31) 2 18 15, 2 52 39, 2 54 14.

Morelos, Mexico's smallest state after Tlaxcala, is bounded on the N by the Federal District and México state, on the W by México state and Guerrero and on the SE by Puebla. Lying on the southern slopes of the Mexican central plateau, it is a region of forest-covered hills and valleys with a luxuriant growth of vegetation and several waterfalls. Its proximity to Mexico City and its excellent communications make Morelos one of the most popular tourist and vacation regions in Mexico. The population consists of Mestizos, together with com-

Mexico
United Mexican States
Estados Unidos Mexicanos

Morelos

States
Estados

1a Baja California Sur	12 Aguascalientes	
1b Baja California Norte	13 Jalisco	
	14 Guanajuato	
2 Sonora	15 Querétaro	
3 Chihuahua	16 Hidalgo	
4 Sinaloa	17 Colima	
5 Durango	18 Michoacán	
6 Coahuila	19 México	
7 Nuevo León	20 Morelos	
8 Zacatecas	21 Tlaxcala	26 Chiapas
9 San Luis Potosí	22 Puebla	27 Tabasco
10 Tamaulipas	23 Veracruz	28 Campeche
11 Nayarit	24 Guerrero	29 Yucatán
	25 Oaxaca	30 Quintana Roo

D.F. Distrito Federal (Federal District)

munities of **Nahua Indians** which maintain their separate identity in some parts of the state.

The most important of the pre-Columbian sites in Morelos are *Xochicalco (p. 292), *Tepoztlán (*Tepozteco*, see below), *Chalcatzingo (p. 116) and *Teopanzolco*.

HISTORY. – There is much archeological evidence (Chalcatzingo, Gualupita, La Juana, San Pablo) indicating that the area was settled or at least strongly influenced by the *Olmecs* around 1200 B.C. During the Classic period Morelos lay mainly within the sphere of influence of Teotihuacán. Thereafter it was subject to the influence of Xochicalco and later of the Toltecs. In the 11th or 12th c. the Náhuatl-speaking *Tlahuicas*, descendants of the Chichimecs, moved into the area after being driven out of the Anáhuac valley. In the first half of the 14th c. the Aztecs gained control of this territory and exacted tribute from the population. – The *Spaniards*, under Gonzalo de Sandoval, conquered parts of what is now Morelos in 1520, and in the following year Cortés took Cuernavaca after bitter fighting. In 1529 Cortés was granted large estates in this area by Charles V, and until 1540 resided mainly in Cuernavaca. The first sugar-cane plantations in New Spain were established at Tlaltenango, and Negro slaves – who in course of time were assimilated by the Indian population – were brought in to work them. During the war of independence (1810–21) some places in Morelos, such as Cuautla, played a prominent part. After the war the state was named after the great leader of the independence movement, José María Morelos. During the revolutionary wars (1910–21) Morelos was the scene of the peasant uprising led by Emiliano Zapata, who succeeded in keeping part of the state under his control until his death in an ambush near Cuautla in 1919.

ECONOMY. – Morelos depends mainly on its flourishing *agriculture*, the principal crops being sugar, rice, maize, coffee, wheat, fruit and vegetables. Its *minerals* (silver, cinnabar, iron, gold, oil and coal) have so far been little worked. *Tourism* plays an important part in the state's economy.

The Morelos Convent Route

In addition to the state capital, Cuernavaca, and the beautiful spas and health resorts of Morelos, the state's tourist attractions include a whole series of historic old convents built during the 16th c., primarily by Dominicans and Augustinians. In accordance with the policy of the conquistadors, these were usually established in important Indian areas.

Some 85 km (55 miles) from Mexico City and 25 km (15 miles) from Cuernavaca is the picturesque little town of *Tepoztlán (Náhuatl, "place of the axe"); alt. 1701 m (5581 ft); pop. 12,000; hotels: Posada del Tepozteco, SP; Tepoztlán; restaurants: Fonda La Tapatía, Los Colorine; fiestas: Carnival, Shrove Tuesday (the Tuesday before Ash Wednesday); November 1 and 2, All Saints and All Souls Days; market Sunday and Wednesday), situated under bizarre cliff-like rock formations, with a large *Dominican convent.

Convent church, Tepoztlán

This fortress-like structure, built between 1559 and 1588, was probably designed by the Spanish architect Francisco Becerra. At the corners of the atrium are interesting *posas* (processional chapels), with gables and Gothic ribbed vaulting, although the workmanship does not compare with that seen at Huejotzingo (p. 138) and Calpan. On the right, in front of the remains of an open chapel, is a 16th c. stone *cross*.

The **church** has a magnificent *doorway, a good example of colonial Plateresque showing Herrerian influence. The sculpture, carved with consummate skill, includes a representation of the Virgin between two saints and medallions with the sun, moon and planets and the Dominican cross. Above the gable, on the W front, are figures of angels which once held tablets with inscriptions. To the left of the porch are two chapels with fine Gothic groined vaulting but otherwise in Renaissance style. In these chapels and in the *posas* there are remains of frescoes. – From the church, which is aisleless, a doorway leads into the *cloister*, rather rustic in architecture.

From the upper floor of the loggia, at the NW corner of the convent, there is a fine *view of the hills around the town. – At the rear of the convent buildings is a small archeological museum which is well worth a visit.

On a steep rocky hill which rises 500 m (1650 ft) above the town, the pre-Columbian site of **Tepozteco** has a three-story temple pyramid 20 m (65 ft) erected by the Tlahuicas in honor of their harvest and pulque god Tepoztécatl. (Pulque is a fermented drink prepared from the sap of Maguey, an agave plant.) A steep path leads up to the pyramid – an hour's walk, but rewarded by the very fine *view from the top. Two staircases lead to the first level of the pyramid, a third to the second level and the entrance to a small shrine. In the interior of the pyramid are columns carved with figures and abstract patterns. The walls and the floor bear calendrical signs and symbols for pulque, water, war and blood. – Nearby are the ruins of other buildings.

Some 15 km (9 miles) S of Tepoztlán is *Yautepec* (pop. 1400; fiesta first Friday in Lent, the "Entierro del Malhumor" or "Burial of Ill Humor"), with a fortress-like Dominican convent founded in the mid 16th c. by Lorenzo de la Asunción (cross in the atrium, open chapel and remains of a posa). There is an archeological site near the town.

20 km (12 miles) W is Cocoyoc, from which a side road leads in 4 km (2½ miles) to the spa of *Oaxtepec* (alt. 1085 m (3560 ft); pop. 2000). The spa has been developed in recent years for state-run "social tourism" (vacations for workers). The Aztec ruler Moctezuma I is said to have had a summer palace here.

Here, too, there is a *Dominican convent*, founded in the first half of the 16th c., now housing a school and an occasional exhibit of archeological finds from Morelos state. Compared with other convents this one is of minor importance. In the cloister are charming primitive paintings of saints and monks and frescoes showing Mudéjar influence. The fortified church, with Gothic groined vaulting, is divided into five parts by massive columns and double arches.

Another 10 km (6 miles) N is *Tlayacapan* (Náhuatl, "in the first hills") in particularly pretty mountainous surroundings. The church San Juan Bautista and its Augustinian convent here was one of the earliest founded by the Augustinians in this region; the inhabitants put up a particularly stiff resistance to the Spanish invaders.

Convent church, Yecapixtla

Unusually, the **convent** is on the S side of the church, not on the N side as was the normal practice. At the end of the spacious atrium is the church, with a plain façade, topped by an espadaña with five niches. To the left of the church, entered through a porch, is the cloister with gothic arcades made of stones of different colours. The Sala de Profundis follows, which has 16th c. frescoes depicting scenes from the passion and figures of saints. In the refectory there is a Sala de Exposiciones containing archeological artifacts, historical documents, mummies etc.

10 km (6 miles) NW is the village of *Totolapan*, with an Augustinian convent founded by Jorge de Ávila in 1534 but not actually built until later. In the fortified church is a large atrium with a *posa*. In the convent itself, which has a plain cloister, are remains of 16th c. frescoes.

6 km (4 miles) SE of Totolapan is **Atlatlahuacan**, which has an *Augustinian convent built between 1570 and 1600. In the large atrium are two fine *posas*. The church has a plain façade and an open bell-tower. On the left is an open chapel, behind which is a tall tower of a later period. The vaulting of the cloister is frescoed.

10 km (6 miles) away is **Yecapixtla** (pop. 8000; fiestas: Easter Day; April 25, Día de San Marcos; May 3, Día de la Santa Cruz; *tianguis* (market), last Thursday in October). At the *tianguis*, just before All Saints and All Souls Days (the "Día de los Muertos"), when the Indians buy gifts to lay on graves, different colored candles are sold according to the status of the dead person (black for married persons and adults, blue for adolescents, green for children and white for young girls).

The *Augustinian convent** was founded by Father Jorge de Ávila in 1535, replacing a Franciscan hermitage established in an Indian village in 1525.

This fortress-like structure has more Gothic features than any other 16th c. convent in New Spain. The *posas* in the atrium, which are relatively plain, are topped by battlements.

The *church* has a beautiful unadorned façade topped by battlements and flanked by buttresses, the upper sections of which serve as watchtowers. The main doorway has typical colonial-Plateresque ornament (medallions, cherubs, niches, tritons, flowers). Below the gable are the emblem of the Augustinian order (a heart pierced by arrows) and the five stigmata of St Francis. The choir window has the form of a Gothic rose-window. Notable features of the interior are the Gothic groined vaulting of the choir and the 16th c. stone pulpit. – The cloister is of plain and solid construction.

Some 20 m (12 miles) farther E is the village of *Ocuituco*, with the first Augustinian convent built in New Spain (begun 1534). In the atrium is a 16th c. stone cross. The church has remains of frescoes. In the convent itself are a 16th c. hexagonal fountain with carvings of animals and remains of frescoes.

Nayarit

State of Nayarit (Nay.). – Capital: Tepic.
Area: 27,053 sq. km (10,445 sq. miles).
Population: 815,600.
ⓘ **Coordinación Federal de Turismo,**
Av. México Sur 253-A 1st floor, Local,
Tepic, Nay.;
tel. (9 13 21) 3 09 93, 2 09 45.

The state of Nayarit lies on the Pacific coast, bounded on the N by Durango and Sinaloa and on the S and E by Jalisco. Some 100 km (60 miles) off the coast are the Tres-

Penitas Marías islands (María Magdalena, María Madre and María Cleofas). From the narrow coastal strip of land the Sierra Madre Occidental rises steeply up, slashed by deep gorges and narrow valleys. The coastal region is an area of lagoons and swamp, with abundant bird life. The population is made up of Caucasians, Mestizos and considerable numbers of Indians, mainly Cora and Huicholes.

In addition to the pre-Columbian remains at *Ixtlán del Río* (p. 254) there are a number of other archeological sites, not particularly rewarding for the ordinary visitor, such as *Santa Cruz, Chacala, Amapa, Coamiles* and *Penitas*.

HISTORY. – Nayarit (named after an Indian priest-king) is usually classed in pre-Columbian archeology along with the neighboring states of Jalisco and Colima under the general term of *cultures of the West* (*cultures del Occidente*), which seem to have developed in the Pre-Classic period and reached their heyday in the Classic (*c*. A.D. 200–850). The Nayarit material, like that of Colima and Jalisco, is known primarily for its terracottas depicting scenes from everyday life. The Nayarit figures are cruder than the delicately molded figures of Colima, sometimes showing a spirit of caricature. Very little is known about this culture.

During the Post-Classic period there were sporadic movements into the region by Indian peoples like the Tepehuano, Totorano, Huicholes and Cora, but in the late Post-Classic phase (1250–1521) these incomers were driven back by Xalisco, a state belonging to the Chimalhuacán confederation. – The *Spaniards*

Mexico
United Mexican States
Estados Unidos Mexicanos

Nayarit

States
Estados

1a	Baja California Sur	
1b	Baja California Norte	
2	Sonora	
3	Chihuahua	
4	Sinaloa	
5	Durango	
6	Coahuila	
7	Nuevo León	
8	Zacatecas	
9	San Luis Potosí	
10	Tamaulipas	
11	Nayarit	
12	Aguascalientes	
13	Jalisco	
14	Guanajuato	
15	Querétaro	
16	Hidalgo	
17	Colima	
18	Michoacán	
19	México	
20	Morelos	
21	Tlaxcala	
22	Puebla	
23	Veracruz	
24	Guerrero	
25	Oaxaca	
26	Chiapas	
27	Tabasco	
28	Campeche	
29	Yucatán	
30	Quintana Roo	

D.F. Distrito Federal (Federal District)

pushed into this region in 1526 under the leadership of Francisco Cortés Buenaventura. Later, under Nuño Beltrán de Guzmán, they drove into the mountains those Indians whom they could not subdue. Throughout the colonial period, however, and after Mexico became independent, there were recurrent rebellions by the Cora and Huicholes. One of the bloodiest and longest lasting of these risings was one led by "Mariano"; it extended over the first twenty years of the 19th c. In 1854 the tribes rose against the Mexican government under the leadership of Manuel Lozada, the "Tiger of Alica", and later came out in support of the Emperor Maximilian. The rebellion was not finally quelled until 1873, when Lozada was executed. Other risings, usually led by the Huicholes, continued into the 20th c. – In 1889 Nayarit was separated from Jalisco and became the independent territory of Tepic; in 1917 it became an independent state.

ECONOMY. – Nayarit is primarily an agricultural region, the principal products of its *farming* and *forestry* being maize, tobacco, sugar-cane, cotton, beans, coffee and various types of lumber. In recent years *tourism* and the sale of *craft goods* have begun to contribute to the economy of the state.

The **Huicholes** who live in and around Nayarit have been able, owing to the remoteness of their territory, to maintain much of their traditional way of life. They belong to the large Uto-Aztec language family, but their precise origins are obscure. They probably came from the northern part of the state of San Luis Potosí, a region known to them as the sacred land of Wírikuta. Every year, between October and February, they travel 500 km (300 miles) NE into this desert region to collect the peyotl cactus (also known as peyote or hicuri), which for them represents the body of the stag god. A cult has grown up around this sacred plant, which is valued for its hallucinogenic effect. The Indians ceremonially "hunt" it (i.e., pierce it with arrows), and then consume it, believing that while under the effects of the drug they receive messages from their gods. The Huicholes are now to be found in eastern Nayarit, between La Yesca and Guadalupe de Ocotán; in northern Jalisco, at Santa Catarina, Mexquitic, San Andrés Cohamiapa, San Sebastián, Tuxpan de Bolanos, etc.; at Colotlán in Zacatecas and at Huazamote in Durango. Although largely converted to Christianity they still practice polygamy and worship various divinities of nature (the sun, fire, water, fertility, etc.). – Among the great festivals of the Huicholes are the change of local headman around January 1, Carnival, Holy Week and various harvest celebrations – all with their special rituals, involving special foods, drinks, music, dances, offerings, etc. – Although the local costume varies from village to village, the typical feature of Huichol dress is a cotton shirt embroidered in cross-stitch with brightly colored geometric patterns. Over this the Huicholes wear a woven sash and an assortment of embroidered bags. Their broad-brimmed hats are woven from palm fibers and decorated with brightly colored felt and woollen tassels. – The Huichol women make embroidered blouses, bags, sashes, skirts and ribbons; for their religious ceremonies they make paper flowers, symbolic arrows, fans, gourds decorated with beads, miniature reproductions of everyday objects and animals and ritual objects in a variety of shapes and colors.

The **Cora** Indians, numbering about 7000, live in the coastal strip (see under Tepic, p. 254) and in villages in the Sierra Nayar, such as Dolores, Santa Teresa, Mesa del Nayar, Jesús María, San Francisco and Corapán. Their origins are unknown, but it is supposed that they came from the southwestern United States to the centrla Mexican plateau and were later driven down to the W coast. Although Christianized, they still practice some pagan rites, worshipping their old idols representing the sun, stars and water, as well as the Catholic saints. One of their important ceremonies is the expulsion of evil spirits from the bodies of the dead. Their cult rituals include a number of dances which are of pre-Christian origin but have taken on Catholic features. They have a form of self-government which is still largely independent of the state. Their festive dress is similar to that of the Huicholes, with some distinctive patterns of their own. – Cora craft products include handbags woven from maguey fibers and decorated with geometric flower and animal patterns, decorated woollen bags, colorful belts and embroidered shirts. – Their principal festivals in the Christian calendar are February 2 (Candlemas), Holy Week, October 15 (Santa Teresa) and All Souls (November 2).

Nogales
See under Sonora

Nuevo Laredo
See under Tamaulipas

Nuevo León

State of Nuevo León (N.L.). – Capital: Monterrey.
Area: 65,104 sq. km (25,136 sq. miles).
Population: 2,773,200.

ⓘ **Coordinación Federal de Turismo,**
Emilio Carranza 730 Sur, P.B.,
Monterrey, N.L.;
tel. (91 83) 44 01 72, 44 50 11, 44 11 69.

The state of Nuevo León has a short common frontier with the United States and is bounded on the W by Coahuila, on the S by San Luis Potosí and on the E and NE by Tamaulipas. The N of the state is arid and barren, the E is a region of subtropical vegetation, and in the S and W are forest-clad mountains. Nuevo León's industry and commerce give it a leading place in the economy of the country. The population consists mainly of Mestizos and Creoles (descendants of Spaniards). There are no pre-Columbian archeological sites of any consequence in the state.

HISTORY. – No Indian cultures developed in this region in pre-Columbian times, its barren territories being inhabited only by nomads. – The *Spaniards* began to settle the area in 1582–3, under the leadership of Luis Carvajal y de la Cueva, and by the end of the 16th c. the *reino de Nuevo León* included the present states of Tamaulipas, Coahuila, Zacatecas and Durango and parts of San Luis Potosí,

Mexico
United Mexican States
Estados Unidos Mexicanos

Nuevo León

**States
Estados**

1a	Baja California Sur	12 Aguascalientes
1b	Baja California Norte	13 Jalisco
2	Sonora	14 Guanajuato
3	Chihuahua	15 Querétaro
4	Sinaloa	16 Hidalgo
5	Durango	17 Colima
6	Coahuila	18 Michoacán
7	Nuevo León	19 México
8	Zacatecas	20 Morelos
9	San Luis Potosí	21 Tlaxcala
10	Tamaulipas	22 Puebla
11	Nayarit	23 Veracruz
		24 Guerrero
		25 Oaxaca
		26 Chiapas
		27 Tabasco
		28 Campeche
		29 Yucatán
		30 Quintana Roo

D.F. Distrito Federal (Federal District)

Texas and New Mexico. The present state was created in 1824, after Mexico achieved independence. During the war of independence (1810–21), the war with the United States (1846–8) and the French intervention (1862–6), there were frequent military encounters in this region, and in the later stages of the revolutionary wars (1917–19) there was bitter fighting between supporters of Venustiano Carranza and Pancho Villa. The economic development of the state in the 20th c. has been linked with the development of its capital, Monterrey.

ECONOMY. – A well-developed system of communications and the availability of energy resources in the form of hydroelectric power and natural gas have provided the basis for considerable industrial development, primarily around Monterrey. The main branches are steel production and the metalworking industries, together with plastics, glass, textiles, ceramics, cement, foodstuffs and beer. The state's *agriculture* produces cotton, sugar-cane, oranges and agaves. Contributions are also made to the economy by *livestock-farming, tourism* and *silver* and *lead mining*.

In addition to **Monterrey** (p. 189) the principal towns are **Linares** (pop. 65,000; hotels: Plaza Mira, Escondido Court), *Montemorelos* (pop. 29,000; Hotel Kasino), *Sabinas Hidalgo* (pop. 26,000; Hotel Álemo) and *Cerralvo* (pop. 12,000).

Oaxaca
(State)

State of Oaxaca (Oax.). – Capital: Oaxaca.
Area: 94,211 sq. km (36,375 sq. miles).

Population: 2,775,400.

ⓘ **Coordinación Federal de Turismo,** Matamoros 105 Esq. García Vigil, 6 01 44, 6 00 45, 6 01 23, 6 04 63.

Oaxaca, Mexico's fifth largest state, is bounded on the N by Puebla and Veracruz, on the W by Guerrero, on the S by the Pacific and on the E by Chiapas. Topographically it is one of the most varied of the states, with long stretches of beach, the rugged mountains of the Sierra Madre with their forests and deep valleys and great expanses of savanna covered with scrub and cactuses.

The highest point in the state is Cempoaltépetl (3400 m – 11,155 ft). Oaxaca ranks with Chiapas as the most "Indian" state in Mexico, with the descendants of the Zapotecs and Mixtecs who created two of the great pre-Columbian cultures. Together with no fewer than fifteen other Indian peoples living in the many little townships, they have remained relatively untouched by modern development.

Among the many pre-Columbian remains in Oaxaca, the most important are those of ****Monte Albán** (p. 189), *Etla, Huitzo, Dainzú* (p. 209), *Lambityeco* (p. 209), ***Yagul** (p. 294), ***Mitla** (p. 187), *Zaachila* (p. 210) and *Guiengola* (p. 256).

Mexico
United Mexican States
Estados Unidos Mexicanos

Oaxaca

States
Estados

1a	Baja California Sur	12	Aguascalientes
1b	Baja California Norte	13	Jalisco
		14	Guanajuato
2	Sonora	15	Querétaro
3	Chihuahua	16	Hidalgo
4	Sinaloa	17	Colima
5	Durango	18	Michoacán
6	Coahuila	19	México
7	Nuevo León	20	Morelos
8	Zacatecas	21	Tlaxcala
9	San Luis Potosí	22	Puebla
10	Tamaulipas	23	Veracruz
11	Nayarit	24	Guerrero
		25	Oaxaca

26	Chiapas
27	Tabasco
28	Campeche
29	Yucatán
30	Quintana Roo

D.F. Distrito Federal (Federal District)

HISTORY. – Around 1000 B.C. an Indian culture began to develop in the area near the present-day town of Oaxaca, and there came into being, originally under the influence of the *Olmecs*, the centers of Monte Albán, Huitzo and Dainzú. These were at first controlled by the *Zapotecs* and later by the *Mixtecs*. The origin of the Zapotecs is uncertain, but they may have come into the area from the Gulf coast, the home of the Olmecs. At some time before the beginning of the Christian era, influences from the Mayas in Guatemala began to make themselves felt, later followed by other influences from the Teotihuacán culture in the valley of Mexico. Evidently Oaxaca lay from the earliest times in the path of many migrant peoples and was exposed to a variety of cultural influences. In the 7th c. the Mixtecs came into the area and founded their first dynasty at Tilantongo on the Monte Negro; in the 9th and 10th c. they continued to expand, driving the Zapotecs out of Monte Albán and other cult sites. Although the Zapotecs were now in decline, they managed to preserve their separate identity and, like the Mixtecs have continued to do so down to the present. While the Zapotecs left a legacy of huge and elaborate buildings and large ceramic products the Mixtecs excelled in the production of fine pottery, jewelry and codices. In the second half of the 15th c. both of these peoples were attacked by the Aztecs and many of their cities became tributary to Tenochtitlán. – The *Spaniards* conquered part of this territory in 1521, adroitly taking advantage of the hostility between the Zapotecs and Mixtecs and the Aztecs. Cortés was granted large estates in the area, together with the title of Marqués del Valle de Oaxaca. – After Mexico achieved independence, Oaxaca became a state of the new Republic (1824). Two of the most famous Presidents of Mexico came from Oaxaca – Benito Juárez (1861–72), a pure-blooded Zapotec, and the mestizo Porfirio Díaz (1877–80 and 1884–1911).

ECONOMY. – Although Oaxaca is rich in *minerals* (silver, gold, coal, uranium, onyx) and has much fertile land, its weak economic and social structure makes it one of the poorest states in Mexico. It is hoped, however, that the working of its minerals, oil and timber, together with the growth of *tourism* and the marketing of its varied range of craft products, will mean a more prosperous future.

The Convents of the Mixteca Alta

In addition to the numerous relics of pre-Columbian times and the colonial period to be seen in and around the town of Oaxaca, every visitor's program should include a visit to the famous 16th c. Dominican convents in the Mixteca Alta. They are easily accessible, lying on or near Road 190 (Oaxaca to Puebla and Cuautla). The Mixteca is an upland region of high, cold valleys, in pre-Columbian times the heartland of the Mixtecs (the "men from the land of clouds"), who, between 1000 and 1521, established in this area large towns such as Tilantongo, Achiotla, Yanhuitlán, Coixtlahuaca, Tlaxiaco and Zopollán. – After the Conquest, in order to promote the colonization and Christianization of the region, the Spaniards built a series of magnificent Dominican convents. These are probably all designed by the same architect but have architectural variations attributable to local craftsmen. For the foundations of these convents the Spaniards used material from the Indian temples which they had destroyed. This region is still partly inhabited by relatively untouched Indian tribes, including the Amuzgos, Triques, Chatinos and Mixtecs.

At **Yanhuitlán**, 120 km (75 miles) NW of Oaxaca, there is one of these convents, built between 1541 and 1575.

The *church, a relatively plain but imposing building, has a façade which was originally Plateresque but was altered in the 17th c. in the Baroque spirit; it has six niches containing statues. The N doorway has a Gothic rose-window but in other respects is a typical example of the Plateresque style. The large nave has complex ribbed vaulting, and the windows are divided, Gothic-fashion, by vertical columns or ribs. The Mudéjar-style timber roof (*alfarje*) of the choir is

Landscape in Oaxaca state

particularly fine. The splendid *high altar (17th c.), with sculpture and paintings, is attributed to Andrés de la Concha. Above the altar, in the Chapel of the Rosary, is a unique polychrome marble relief of the Descent from the Cross. – On the way to the cloister visitors pass through a room in the **convent** containing a number of painted wooden statues. On the staircase are 16th c. frescoes. In the monks' cells are examples of colonial sculpture and photographs of convents in the surrounding area.

15 km (9 miles) farther NW, in Road 190, a side road goes off to **San Pedro y San Pablo Teposcolula**, 13 km (8 miles) SE. This little town, which still depends for its subsistence on the silkworm culture introduced by the Dominicans, has the remains of a convent destroyed by an earthquake and the passage of time. Although now in ruins, the *open chapel is one of the finest examples of 16th c. religious architecture in Mexico. With the exception of the central bays of vaulting, the whole building is in the purest Renaissance style. In the middle of the double row of arches is a hexagonal chamber with Doric columns, originally supporting a vaulted roof of which practically nothing survives.

Another 45 km (28 miles) SW on Road 125 is **Santa María Asunción Tlaxiaco**, which has a Convent of the Assumption dating from 1550, with a relatively sober Plateresque façade and Gothic vaulting; the altars are neo-classical.

Returning to Road 190 and continuing NW for 12 km (7 miles), we take a road on the right which comes in 24 km (15 miles) to **San Juan Bautista Coixtlahuaca**, once capital of the kingdom of Mixteca Alta and an important trading center. It was captured by the Aztecs under Moctezuma I in 1458 and became tributary to Tenochtitlán.

The **Dominican convent** has a *church* of 1546 with a fine façade predominantly in Plateresque style. It has the medallions characteristic of Plateresque together with niches containing figures and a Gothic rose-window over the doorway. The influence of the severe Herrerian style then coming into vogue can be detected. The façade of the side doorway is similar, but without the niches. The church has a large Churrigueresque altar, an interesting arch in the presbytery, a beautiful door leading into the choir and a finely carved pulpit. – Near the church are the ruins of a once magnificent Gothic *open chapel*. The once great convent lies in ruins.

Near the town were found a pre-Columbian site of the Late Classic period and a considerable number of tombs.

31 km (19 miles) NW of Oaxaca Road 131 branches off Road 190 towards Tehuacán and in about 90 km (56 miles) comes to the little town of **Teotitlán del Camino**. From here the turning on the R leads to **Huautla de Jiménez**, 68 km (42 miles) distant. This attractive district has not only become known for the hallucinatory fungi found here and for the cult associated with them, but also for an extensive system of *caves, including the deepest cave (1250 m/ 4102 ft.) in America – the fifth deepest in the world.

Other fine examples of colonial art and architecture in Oaxaca state are to be seen at **Oaxaca** (below), **Tlacolula**, *Tlacochahuaya* and *Cuilapan* (all described under Oaxaca, below).

Oaxaca (Town)

State: Oaxaca (Oax.).
Altitude: 1545 m (5069 ft). – Population: 245,000.
Telephone dialing code: 9 19 51.
ⓘ Coordinación Federal de Turismo,
Matamoros 105, Esq García Vigil,
tel. 6 01 44, 6 00 45, 6 01 23, 6 04 63.

HOTELS. – *Misión de los Angeles*, Calz. Porfirio Díaz 102, I, SP; *Señorial*, Portal de Flores 6, II SP; *Monte Albán*, Almeda de León 1, II; *Marquez del Valle*, Portal Claveria, II; *Plaza*, Trujano 112, II; *Francia*, 20 de Noviembre 212, II; *Central*, 20 de Noviembre 104, III; *San Fernando*, Díaz Ordaz 307, III.

RESTAURANTS in most hotels; also *Merendero El Tule*, Portal de Flores 3; *El Asador Vasco*, Portal de Flores II; *Guelatao*, Portal de Mercanderas 2; *Doña Elpidia*, Miguel Cabrera 413; *Catedral*, García Vigil 111.

RECREATION and SPORTS. – Swimming, riding, tennis, golf.

EVENTS. – Fiestas: last two Mondays after July 16, Guelaguetza; December 18, Virgen de la Soledad; December 23, Fiesta de los Rábanos.

The delightful town of **Oaxaca lies almost exactly in the center of Oaxaca state, in a valley luxuriant with subtropical vegetation and surrounded by the high mountains of the Sierra Madre del Sur. Unlike other colonial towns in Mexico, it has not suffered from industrialization or the population explosion and has largely preserved the character of a tranquil provincial capital in New Spain. It has an atmosphere all its own, a result of the mingling of Indian and Spanish elements.

Church of Santo Domingo, Oaxaca

HISTORY. – The Oaxaca valley was inhabited by primitive Indian tribes as early as 4000 B.C. The beginnings of an independent culture can be set around 1000 B.C., when the "Pre-Zapotecs" – who were perhaps themselves Olmecs (or at any rate were influenced by the Olmecs) – were in the process of evolving the culture known as Monte Albán I. In the subsequent periods, when the Zapotec and Mixtec cultures were expanding in the area round Oaxaca, there is no record of any settlement on the site of the present town. It was only in 1486 that the advancing Aztecs under their king Ahuítzotl established the military base of *Huaxyaca* (Náhuatl, "by the acacia grove"). – In 1521 the *Spaniards* arrived in this area under the leadership of Francisco de Orozco, defeated the Indians and founded a small settlement which in 1529 was given the name of *Antequera*. A mere three years later the Emperor Charles V raised it to the status of a royal town under the name of *Oaxaca*, derived from that of the Inca fortress. – The town played no part in the war of independence (1810–21). In 1830 Porfirio Díaz, a mestizo of Mixtec origin who was to become President of the Republic (1877–80 and 1884–1911), was born in Oaxaca. The national hero, Benito Juárez, a Zapotec Indian who also became President, resided in the town from 1847 to 1852 when he was governor of Oaxaca state.

SIGHTS. – The busy life of the town revolves around the ***Zócalo (Plaza de Armas** or *Plaza Central*), with its fine old trees, bandstand and cafés in the arcades around the square.

On the S side of the square is the colonial-style *Government Palace* (Palacio de Gobierno), and at the NW corner is the **Cathedral**, begun in the mid 16th c. and completed about 200 years later. It is a sturdy building designed to withstand earthquakes, with two low towers. The clock, which is original, was presented to the church by the Spanish king; its mechanism is entirely carved from wood. The Baroque façade has finely carved figures and bas-relief carving on the columns. The most notable features of the interior, which is in neo-classical style, are eight engraved glass windows and the chapels.

Not far from the Zócalo is the ***Market** (*Mercado*), which, like most of Oaxaca's markets, presents a lively and colorful scene. Its busiest day is Saturday, when the Indians flock into town from all over the surrounding area. Among the wares offered for sale here are woven articles, pottery, leatherware, knives and machetes.

Five blocks N of the Zócalo is the magnificent ***church of Santo Domingo**, a Dominican foundation of 1575. The church and the adjoining convent, almost earthquake-proof with walls 2 m (6½ ft) thick, occupy an area 150 m (500 ft) square. The imposing Baroque façade of the church has several niches containing statues.

The *INTERIOR, partly dating from the 18th c., has a profusion of gilded ornament and polychrome sculpture in high relief, in sumptuous contrast to the white ground of the walls and ceiling. The total effect is that of a palace rather than a church, while the countrified

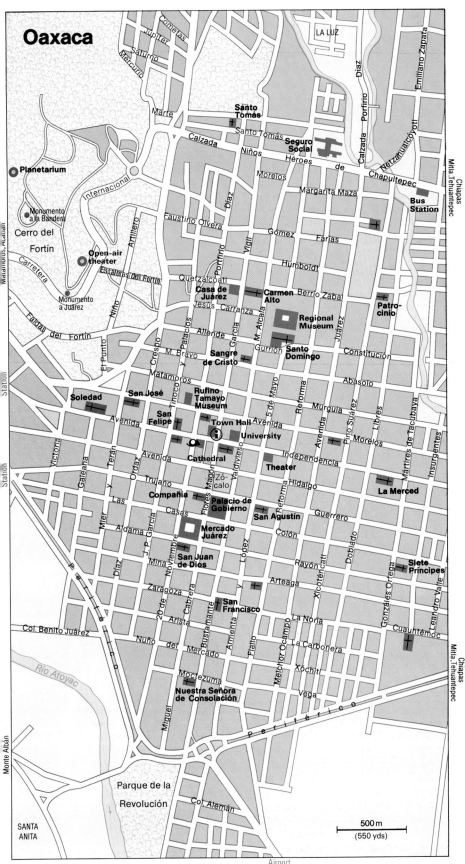

Oaxaca

LA LUZ

Planetarium

Monumento
a la Bandera

Cerro del
Fortín

Open-air
theater

Escaleras Del Fortín

Monumento
a Juárez

Faldas del Fortín

Santo
Tomás

Santo Tomás

Niños

Héroes

de

Chapultepec

Seguro
Social

Morelos

Margarita Maza

Gómez

Farias

Humboldt

Quetzalcóatl

Casa de
Juárez

Jesús

Carranza

Allende

Carmen
Alto

Berrio Zabal

Regional
Museum

Santo
Domingo

Gurrión

Constitución

Abasolo

Matamoros

Rufino
Tamayo
Museum

Sangre
de Cristo

Soledad

San José

San
Felipe

Avenida

Town Hall

University

Avenida

Morelos

Cathedral

Avenida

Independencia

Theater

Trujano

Zó-
calo

Hidalgo

Compañía

Palacio de
Gobierno

San Agustín

Guerrero

La Merced

Casas

Aldama

Mercado
Juárez

Colón

San Juan
de Dios

Rayón

Siete
Príncipes

Zaragoza

Arteaga

Cuauhtémoc

Arista

San
Francisco

La Noria

Nuño

del

Mercado

La Carbonera

Río Atoyac

Moctezuma

Xóchitl

Nuestra Señora
de Consolación

Vega

Bus
Station

Patro-
cinio

Parque de la
Revolución

Col. Alemán

SANTA
ANITA

Monte Albán

500 m
(550 yds)

Airport
Puerto Escondido , Puerto Ángel

Chiapas
Mitla,Tehuantepec

Chiapas
Mitla,Tehuantepec

Relief decoration on the ceiling of Santo Domingo

style of the colored sculptural decoration gives the nave, the choir arch and the chapels a distinctively Mexican note. On the ceiling above the entrance is a vine with golden stems and leaves out of which grow thirty-four portraits – the genealogical tree of San Domingo de Guzmán (d. 1221), who was related to the royal families of Spain and Portugal. – Of the church's eleven chapels the largest and finest is the *Chapel of the Rosary (Capilla de la Virgen del Rosario), which has its own choir, sacristy and towers. The ornate *altar, with a figure of the Virgin, ranks as one of the jewels of Mexican Rococo.

Most of the original altars and decoration of the church were destroyed in the 1860s, when it was used as a stable. The subsequent restoration was based on the originals.

In the adjoining convent, used for a long time as a barracks, is the *Regional Museum (Museo Regional de Oaxaca), which displays on two floors archeological and ethnological collections on the Indian cultures, as well as ecclesiastical and secular material of the colonial period.

The ETHNOLOGICAL COLLECTION contains costumes, masks, jewelry and ceremonial and domestic implements and utensils used by the various Indian tribes of the region, together with archeological material from Zapotec and Mixtec sites (stelae, urns, pottery, etc.) – all this supplemented by photographs, diagrams and maps. – The pride of the ARCHEOLOGICAL COLLECTION is the **Mixtec Treasure of gold, jade, turquoise and other semi-precious stones which was found in Tomb 7 at Monte Albán in 1932. The objects made from these materials included elaborately contrived bracelets, necklaces, ear ornaments, pectorals and masks. – The museum also contains historical documents on the history of the convent and the Dominican order and a variety of ecclesiastical and secular objects, including an old Spanish-style kitchen complete with utensils.

Five blocks W of the Zócalo is the *church of La Soledad (Basílica de Nuestra Señora de la Soledad), dedicated to the town's patroness. Built between 1682 and 1690, it has an atrium paved

with limestone slabs and surrounded by a covered walk on a higher level. The figure of the Virgen de la Soledad wears a black velvet robe embroidered with gold and precious stones and has a large pearl on her forehead. A variety of miracles are attributed to this royally clad Virgin, who is also regarded as the patroness of seafarers. – Adjoining the church is a small museum.

Other notable churches in Oaxaca are San Felipe Neri (elaborately decorated altars), San Juan de Dios (with an Indian depiction of the Conquest) and San Agustín (reliefs of St Augustine on the façade).

In a palace at Calle Morelos 503, four blocks from the Zócalo, is the *Rufino Tamayo Museum (Museo de Arte Prehispánico Rufino Tamayo), which was

A gold ornament from the Mixtec Treasure

The Tree of Tule

presented to the state by the famous artist of that name. Its five rooms contain an illuminating display of archeological material belonging to the principal Indian cultures (Olmecs, Zapotecs, Mixtecs, Mayas, Huaxtecs, Totonacs, Aztecs; Teotihuacán).

At Calle Garcia Vigil 609 is the house in which Benito Juárez worked as a servant between 1818 and 1828, now a *Juárez Museum* (Museo Casa Juárez) containing a variety of mementoes of this national hero, later President, who was born at Guelatao, near Oaxaca, in 1806.

On the *Cerro del Fortín de Zaragoza*, a hill rising some 100 m (330 ft) above the town, are two monuments, one to Benito Juárez and the other in honor of the national flag, and an *outdoor theatre*. Here the largest and most colorful fiesta in the country is held every year – the *Guelaguetza (Zapotec, "offering"), on the two Mondays following July 16. It includes both pre-Hispanic and Christian dances, performed by various Indian tribes of Oaxaca state in traditional costume.

SURROUNDINGS. – Some 10 km (6 miles) E of Oaxaca on Road 190 is the small village of *Santa María del Tule*. In front of a charming little church is the celebrated *Tree of Tule (*Árbol del Tule*), a huge specimen of a species of cypress (*Taxodium mucronatum*), estimated to be 2000 years old, which is 40 m (130 ft) high and has a girth of 42 m (140 ft).

10 km (6 miles) beyond this, a road goes off on the left to the nearby village of *Tlacochahuaya*, with the 16th c. church of San Jerónimo. The church is remarkable for its colorful paintings, in which Indian artists have given primitive and very individual expression to their own artistic and religious conceptions, covering the walls with stars, flowers, birds, suns and angels. – In another 3 km (2 miles) a road goes off to *Teotitlán del Valle*, 5 km (3 miles) away. This village with a history going back to pre-Hispanic times, built around a 17th c. church, is widely famed for its *sarapes* (woollen cloaks, rectangular in shape, with a hole for the head in the middle).

Soon afterward, a road goes off on the right to the archeological site of **Dainzú**. The excavations have shown that this was a very ancient settlement which was occupied from about 800 B.C. to A.D. 1400 (i.e., over the period covered by phases I to V at Monte Albán). The heyday of the site, which lies in a very beautiful setting, was probably in the late Formative period (800–300 B.C.). So far only a few buildings have been excavated at this great Zapotec cult center.

One of the largest of these buildings has a pyramidal base, and its construction is reminiscent of the North Platform at Monte Albán. On the S side of the lower story was found a gallery of very interesting stones carved with *reliefs which show Olmec influence and resemble the "Danzantes" of Monte Albán. Among the figures represented are ball-players and priests or divinities with jaguars as patrons of the ball game. The main staircase of this structure was of later date (about A.D. 700). Figures and scenes similar to those in the S gallery are carved in the rock on top of the hill. In the same complex was found the tomb of a ruler or priest. – In the lower part of the site can be seen a building (in course of excavation) with walls and staircases dating from the 3rd c. B.C. and, a little way apart, a *ball court* of the 10th or 11th c. A.D.

A few miles father on, close to the road, is the archeological site of **Lambityeco**. Its historical interest lies in the fact that it was evidently occupied only between the 7th and 9th c. A.D., the period at which Monte Albán was abandoned. There is a small pyramid, under which a house was excavated. Altogether seven tombs were found here. On the front of Tomb 5 are carved two heads, with names – perhaps the owner of the house and his wife. In Tomb 2, which was several times built over, were found two fine pieces of sculpture, figures of the Zapotec rain god Cocijo. – It is supposed that the inhabitants of Lambityeco, vulnerable to attack, abandoned it and moved to the older cult site of **Yagul** (p. 284), 5 km (3 miles) away.

Convent of Santiago Apóstol, Cuilapan

Some 2 km (1½ miles) farther on, down a short side road, is the ancient little Zapotec town of **Tlacolula**, with a fine parish church of 1647.

The **parish church** has a tripartite Baroque façade with round-headed arches, columns, niches and window lighting the choir. The interior is also mainly Baroque, though with the usual local peculiarities. Magnificent examples of the primitive wrought-iron work of the colonial period are the gate of the *Chapel of Christ* (Capilla del Santo Cristo), the choir screen and the pulpit rails. The chapel resembles the church of Santo Domingo in Oaxaca and the Rosary Chapel in Puebla in the riotous fancy and consummate craftsmanship of its stucco ornament. The decoration includes figures of Christ, the Virgin of Guadalupe and various martyrs carrying their heads under their arms. Other notable features are the gold-framed mirrors, some of them bearing the Habsburg double eagle, the silver chandeliers, the benches and the silver high altar. Although Indian influence is sometimes clearly visible it is not so strong as in many of the Poblano-style churches. – Inside the church was found a secret passage leading to a room in which valuable silver liturgical articles were found – hidden there during the revolutionary war (1911–20). They are on display at certain times.

Tlacolula is also noted for its picturesque *Sunday market.

12 km (7 miles) S of Oaxaca is **Cuilapan** (Náhuatl, "coyote river"). Situated on a hill are the church and convent of *Santiago Apóstol, one of the largest convents in Mexico.

The building of this massive **convent** was begun in 1555, but it was never finished. Behind the Renaissance façade of the roofless church are two interior colonnades, partly collapsed as the result of an earthquake. On the left-hand side is a stone pulpit approached by a short staircase. – The adjoining convent was abandoned in 1663, when the monks moved to Oaxaca. The walls are almost 3 m (10 ft) thick. At the entrance are wall paintings depicting the history of the order. A stone tablet bears the date 1555 in addition to pre-Columbian glyphs. The last room on the main floor served as a prison cell for Vicente Guerrero, the deposed President of Mexico, who was confined here by his enemies and shot outside the window of his cell in 1831. From the terrace on the upper floor, on which were the monks' cells, there is a fine panoramic view. – The *church*, the only part of the complex which is still in use, contains the tomb of the last Zapotec princess, daughter of Cocijo-eza, who took the name of Juana Donaje after her baptism.

An old-established activity at Cuilapan, formerly of considerable importance, is the manufacture of cochineal, a brilliant red dye made from the crushed bodies of the cochineal insect, which lives on cactuses.

6 km (4 miles) farther S on the same road is the village of **Zaachila**, site of the last capital of the Zapotec kingdom, the remains of which were discovered only in 1962. So far only the foundations of a number of structures on a hill behind the church of the Virgin of Juquila have been excavated.

In a patio within a rectangular platform were found two burials. Tombs 1 and 2. On the façade of *Tomb 1* were two jaguar heads; in the antechamber two stucco figures of owls with outspread wings; and in the tomb chamber itself stucco figures of two rulers of the underworld with human hearts hanging from their shoulders, each accompanied by a priest carrying a copal bag, named respectively "5 Flower" and "9 Flower", and, on the rear wall, an old man wearing a headdress and turtle-shell breastplate and holding flints in his hands. – Tomb 2 was less elaborately decorated but contained valuable grave goods of gold, jade and precious stones, now in the National Museum of Anthropology in Mexico City. As so frequently happened in the Oaxaca region, the Zapotec tombs here were later re-used by the Mixtecs. – In the village square can be seen monoliths with relief decoration which have been found in the surrounding area.

Following the main highway Oaxaca – Mexico City, about 32 km (20 miles) from Oaxaca, between the small towns of Huitzo and Suchilquitongo, is the recently discovered archeological site of Huijazoo (Náhuatl, "in the fortress of war"). Here nine highly original tombs were detected, particularly tomb no. 5 under an unexplored pyramid. The portal is formed by a snake mask, the interior (8.80 (29 ft.) × 4 m (13 ft.) is filled with finely carved jambs and multicolored murals depicting rulers and priests. The site is of Zapotec origin (A.D. 700–900) and is considered to be quite unique as far as architecture and painting are concerned. Currently it is not possible to visit the site.

Orizaba

State, Veracruz (Ver.).
Altitude: 1250 m (4100 ft). – Population: 273,000
Telephone dialing code: 9 12 72.
(i) **Coordinación Federal de Turismo,**
Av. Ignacio Zaragoza 20 Altos, Centro,
Veracruz, Ver.;
tel. (91 29) 32 70 26, 32 16 13.

HOTELS. – *Aries,* Oriente 6 Nr. 265, I; *Trueba,* Oriente
6 y Sur 11, I, SP, tennis; *Gran Hotel de France,* Oriente
6 Nr. 186, II; *Rossi,* Norte 4 Nr. 243, III; *San Cristóbal,*
Norte 4 Nr. 347, III.

RESTAURANTS in most hotels; also *El Gaucho,* Ote.
2 Nr. 155; *Paseo Real,* Ote. 6 Nr. 2–C; *Los Romanchu,*
Pte. 7 Nr. 208.

RECREATION and SPORTS. – Swimming, tennis,
golf.

**Orizaba lies in a fertile valley in the
Sierra Madre Oriental surrounded
by mountains, in a region of heavy
rainfall and moderate temperatures.
It is an important center of communications, situated 275 km (170
miles) from Mexico City and 150 km
(95 miles) from Veracruz, and one of
Mexico's major industrial centers. It
still, however, manages to preserve
something of its colonial character.**

HISTORY. – Originally an Indian township of no
particular consequence, the place was captured by the
Aztecs in the middle of the 15th c. and made into a
military base under the name of *Ahuaializapán*
(Náhuatl, "pleasant waters"). In the 16th c. the
Spaniards occupied this strategic point. Orizaba was
a favorite residence of the Emperor Maximilian and his
wife Carlota, who had a hacienda, Jalapilla, on the
outskirts of the town. In 1973 an earthquake
destroyed part of the old town, including the bullring.

The fertile soil and temperate climate of
the region have promoted the steady
development of the town as an agri-

cultural and industrial center. In the
surrounding area are coffee and fruit
plantations, marble quarries and power
stations, and within the town itself are
a large brewery, cement factories and
cotton spinning and weaving mills.

SIGHTS. – On the N side of the *Parque del
Castillo* is the massive fortress-like **parish
church of San Miguel,** built between
1620 and 1729. The rectangular *bell-
tower* also serves as a weather station.
One of the church's several towers is clad
with azulejos in Mudéjar style. The fine
sacristy has intarsia work, wall paintings
and pictures by the native artist Gabriel
Barranco (19th c.).

A striking and unexpected feature of the
town is the **Town Hall** (*Palacio Municipal*), a green and yellow building made
entirely of steel. Originally the Belgian
pavilion at the Paris International Exhibition of 1889, it was dismantled, transported across the Atlantic and re-erected
on its present site. – Also worth seeing are
the *churches* of *El Calvario, El Carmen* and
San Juan de Dios. – The *Escuela Federal*
(State School) in the Avenida Colón has
murals by José Clemente Orozco.

SURROUNDINGS. – 6 km (4 miles) E on Road 150 a
short side road leads to the dam and reservoir of
Tuxpango (*Presa de Tuxpango*) on the Río Blanco.
There is a cableway down to the village of Tuxpango,
almost 800 m ($\frac{1}{2}$ mile) below.

Some 30 km (20 miles) N of Orizaba, on the borders
of Puebla state, is Mexico's highest mountain, the
*Pico de Orizaba (5700 m – 18,700 ft). It is best
climbed from the W side (see p. 227).

Pachuca de Soto

State: Hidalgo (Hgo.).
Altitude: 2426 m (7960 ft).
Population: 180,000.
Telephone dialing code: 9 17 71.
(i) **Coordinación Federal de Turismo,**
Plaza de la Independencia 110, 3rd floor,
tel. 2 59 60, 2 48 60, 2 32 89.

HOTELS. – *Sahara,* Blvd. Felipe Angeles, I; *De Los
Baños,* Matamoros 205, II; *Noriega,* Matamoros 305,
II; *Plaza el Dorado,* Guerrero 721, II; *Juárez Gabino*
Barrera 11, III.

RESTAURANTS in most hotels; also *La Fogata,*
Matamoros 203; *Palacio,* Av. Juárez 200; *Giros,* Plaza
Independencia 110; *Kiko's,* Plaza Independencia 109.

RECREATION and SPORTS. – Swimming, tennis,
golf.

EVENT. – Fiesta on January 15 (Hidalgo State Day).

Neo-classical church, Orizaba

Pachuca, capital of Hidalgo state and the center of one of Mexico's oldest and richest mining areas, is surrounded on three sides by mountains. A town of steep and winding lanes, small squares and brown and beige houses, it has few features of tourist interest but lies in a region of beautiful and varied scenery containing towns and villages with interesting examples of early colonial art and architecture.

HISTORY. – The settlement of *Patlachiuhcán* is said to have been founded by the Aztecs around 1490 in order to work the gold and silver which lay just below the surface here. The Spanish town of *Pachuca* (Náhuatl *pachoa*, "confined space") was established in 1527 by Francisco Téllez, but its real rise began in 1555, when Bartolomé de Medina devised the process of amalgamation, separating metal from ore by treatment with mercury. New developments in the mid 18th c., due particularly to the enterprise of Pedro Romero de Terreros (later Conde de Regla), gave the town a further boost. This period saw the construction of the town's principal colonial buildings, also for the most part on the initiative of the Conde de Regla. In 1869 Pachuca became capital of the state of Hidalgo.

SIGHTS. – One of the most historically interesting buildings in Pachuca is the fortress-like house known as **Las Cajas** (1670), in which the Quinto Real, the "King's Fifth" which was levied on all minerals produced in New Spain, was stored.

Franciscan church, Pachuca

Also of interest is the former Franciscan convent, part of a huge complex which was built at the end of the 16th c. and subsequently rebuilt and extended several times. The legendary Count of Regla, who died in 1781 is buried in the church. In the *Capilla de la. Luz* stands the stately Churrigueresque *altar (18th c.). Recent additions to the complex include the *Centro Cultural Hidalgo*, with a Museum of Photography, an auditorium, several exhibition rooms and a shop selling archeological reproductions. The new *Museum of Regional History* houses archeological and ethnological collections (Teotihuacán, Huastecs, Chichimecs, Toltecs, Aztecs, Otomí, etc.) as well as military and religious exhibits.

Other notable buildings are the *Casas Colorados* (late 18th c.: now a lawcourt), and two 19th and 20th c. buildings, the *Teatro Efrén Rebolledo* and the *Torre del Reloj*, a 40 m (130 ft.) high clock tower with four sculptures in the niches, representing Freedom, Independence, Reform and the Republic; the carillon was imported from Austria and installed by a German, Albert Gross.

SURROUNDINGS. – S of Pachuca, just off Road 85, is the village of *Venta Prieta*, which is unusual in its strictly orthodox Jewish community, the descendants of Spanish Jews and Mexican Indians who came here from Michoacán at the end of the 19th c. to escape persecution.

12 km (7 miles) E of Pachuca, in a wooded mountain region, is the important old mining town of **Mineral del Monte** (formerly *Real del Monte*), which had one of the richest silver-mines in the world. – Another old mining town is *Mineral del Chico (Albergue Las Ventanas), 25 km (15 miles) N, reached by way of the *El Chico National Park*.

Some 35 km (22 miles) NE of Pachuca, in beautiful country, are the little towns of *Huasca de Ocampo*, **San Miguel Regla** (hotel: *Hacienda de San Miguel Regla, SP, riding) and *San Juan Hueyapan* (Hotel San Juan Hueyapan), which are excellent bases for the exploration of the surrounding area or the "Convent Route" to the N.

The Convent Route from Pachuca to Huejutla

Along this route, which runs through a beautiful and varied *landscape of rugged rock formations, gorges and fertile valleys, are a series of interesting 16th c. Augustinian converts.

34 km (21 miles) from Pachuca on Road 105 is **Atotonilco el Grande** (Náhuatl, "place of the hot water"; alt. 2138 m (7015 ft.) pop. 7000; August 28–31, Agricultural Show; market on Thursday), with an Augustinian convent of the mid 16th c. The façade

Augustinian convent, Atotonilco el Grande

of the church, only part of which survives, is in Renaissance style with Plateresque elements; the decoration includes medallions of Sts Peter and Paul. The long nave, with a lofty groined vault, has remains of frescoes. On the staircase of the convent are wall paintings depicting the great philosophers of antiquity.

30 km (19 miles) farther on, a road on the left leads (25 km – 16 miles) to **Metztitlán** (Náhuatl, "place of the moon"; alt. 1600 m (5250 ft.); pop. 6000), once capital of the independent Otomí territory of that name, which was never conquered by the Aztecs. The 16th c. Augustinian *convent has a large atrium with a stone cross, two *open chapels* and a *posa*. The relatively plain façade of the church is in Renaissance style with Plateresque features. In the cloister can be seen frescoes of the 16th c. and later. From the convent there is a magnificent *view out over the valley.

Returning to the main road and continuing N, we come in 10 km (6 miles) to *Metzquititlán*. The 16th c. Augustinian church of the Señor de la Salud has a beautiful Indian-Plateresque doorway in the style of the Tequitqui school of sculptors. – From Metzquititlán a country road leads towards San Nicholás. In 2.5 km (1 mile) a road on the left branches off across a stream to *Santa María Xoxoteco*. In 1974 impressive colored 16th c. frescoes were discovered in the little church. Some of these, representing very starkly historical religious subjects, are in the same style as those at Actopan.

Going N on Road 105 there is in 17 km (11 miles) a turning on the right leading in 9 km (6 miles) to *Tlahualompa*. This place is a center of bell-casting, and under certain circumstances the work can be viewed. Here, too, copper work is offered for sale by Indians living in the region. The area between Tlahualompa and the main road is rich in obsidian (a dark vitreous volcanic stone) which can be seen lying around.

Returning to Road 105 it is another 6 km (4 miles) to **Zacualtipan** (alt. 2020 m (6630 ft.); pop. 12,000; Hotel María Isabel; 16th c. Augustinian convent; church with Indian-Plateresque façade.

The next place of interest, some 35 km (22 miles) farther on, is the charmingly situated little town of **Molango** (Hotel Plaza Molango), named after the old Indian god, Mola. The Augustinian convent, built in 1546 on a pre-Columbian cult site, has a church with an unusual Spanish-Plateresque façade incorporating a finely executed Gothic rose-window. Note the carved inner surfaces (*alféizar*) of the pilasters at the entrance – a rare feature. The cloister, partly ruined, has a charming, harmonious beauty. Instead of a bell-tower Molango has the *"Espadaña"*, an extension of the atrium wall. – 6 km (4 miles) away is the attractive *Laguna Atezca*.

The last place on this route within Hidalgo state is **Huejutla de Reyes**, 95 km (60 miles) from Molango (alt. 180 m (591 ft); pop. 53,000; hotels: Posada de Huejutla, II; Juárez, III; fiestas: November 2, Día de los Fieles Difuntos; December 12, Día de la Virgen de Guadalupe; *market on Sunday); a Huastec town which has an Augustinian convent of the mid 16th c. The church has a Plateresque façade (with later alterations) and a stone font with stylized plant decoration. The location of the atrium in the town square is an unusual feature. – Huejutla is also famed for its pottery.

From Huejutla Road 105 continues through Veracruz state to the port of **Tampico** (165 km (105 miles): see p. 251).

Palenque

State: Chiapas (Chis.).
Altitude: 61 m (200 ft).

HOTELS. – *Chan-Kah*, 5 km (3 miles) from site, I, SP; *Las Ruinas*, 1 km (¾ mile) away, II, SP; *Nututún*, 10 km (6 miles) away on the road to Ocosingo, II, natural SP. – In the village of Palenque: *Tulija*, II, SP; *Tulipanes*, III; *La Cañada*, II; *Mizol-há*, II; *Casa de Pacal*, I; *Palenque*, II, SP; *Regional*, III. *Misión Palenque*, I, SP, Tennis.

RESTAURANTS in most hotels; also *Maya, Tarde, Nicte-há, La Selva*.

ACCESS. – *By road:* from Villahermosa 114 km (71 miles) on Road 186 to Cataja, then road on right to the village of Palenque (27 km – 17 miles) and another 9 km (6 miles) to the site; or from San Cristóbal de las Casas on a road which is still poor in places via Ocosingo (90 km – 55 miles) to Palenque (200 km – 125 miles). – *By air-taxi* from Villahermosa, Tenosique, San Cristóbal or Tuxtla Gutiérrez.

The great Maya Classic site of **Palenque lies at the foot of a chain of low hills covered with tall rain forest above the green floods plain of the Río Usumacinta. The local style of architecture and sculpture which developed here between A.D. 600 and 800 is unique in its beauty and technical perfection. Unlike the Mayas of northern Yucatán, who liked to locate their imposing buildings round great open plazas, the builders of Palenque preferred a more enclosed layout adapted to the hilly site.

HISTORY. – It is certain that the site, known by the Spanish name of *Palenque* ("stockade"), was already occupied before the beginning of the Christian era, during the Pre-Classic period (300 B.C. to A.D. 300). At that time the first Maya culture was flourishing in the southern area (Pacific coast and Guatemalan highlands), influenced originally by the Olmec culture and later by Teotihuacán. There is some evidence, however, of an independent Maya cultural development at a much earlier period.

However this may be, Palenque makes its first appearance in the historical record in the *Early Classic* period (A.D. 300–600), and its heyday as a religious and political center was between A.D. 600 and 800. Recent studies of the glyphs have made it possible to establish the genealogy of the kings of Palenque from the accession of Chaacal I in 501 to the death of Kuk in 783. During this period Palenque ranked along with Yaxchilán (Chiapas), Tikal, Piedras Negras, Quiriguá and Uaxactún (all in Guatemala) and Copán (Honduras) as one of the great cities in the central Maya territory; and it was during this period that some of the basic features of Maya culture were perfected, such as the corbelled vault, the hieroglyphic script, the art of carving stelae and the calendar. Formerly this classical period of Maya culture was known as the Old Empire, as distinct from the New Empire which followed it in northern Yucatán from the 10th c. onward. This division is, however, no longer tenable in the light of the advances in historical knowledge over the last twenty years or so.

Like all the other Maya cities in the central area, Palenque was abandoned in the 9th c. The latest date we have is A.D. 799, and only twenty years later Palenque had ceased to exist. The sudden abandonment of this and other Maya sites has long been a puzzle, and it is still not known what happened to bring this about. The most probable explanation is that there was a popular revolt against the increasingly harsh rule of the priestly caste. However this may be, the great cities in this region fell into ruin within a very short time and were swallowed up by the jungle.

The first to visit the site, in 1784, were Ordóñez y Aguiar, José Antonio Calderón and Antonio Bernanconi. They were followed two years later by the Spanish captain, José Antonio del Río, who sent the first account of Palenque to Charles III of Spain. In 1805 Guillermo Dupaix investigated the site and produced an illustrated report. From 1832 to 1834 the

controversial Jean-Frédéric de Waldeck lived at Palenque, and in 1841 J. L. Stephens and Frederick Catherwood also spent some time here. They were followed by a number of distinguished archeologists – Désiré Charnay, Teobert Maler, Alfred Maudslay and, in the 20th c., Eduard Seler, Sylvanus G. Morley and Frans Blom. In recent decades important excavations have been carried on by the Instituto Nacional de Arqueología e Historia (INAH) under the direction of Miguel Angel Hernández and Alberto Ruz l'Huillier.

THE SITE. – The area so far excavated measures some 300 m (330 yds) from E to W and 500 m (550 yds) from N to S, but this is only a fraction of the total area of the site, which is estimated to have an E–W extent of 8–9 km (5–6 miles). An underground aqueduct – the only one of its kind in Maya architecture – conveys water from the little River Otulum into the center of the town site.

Immediately right of the entrance to the site are the ruins of *Temples XII and XIII*, both probably built between A.D. 731 and 764. The next structure is the Temple of the Inscriptions (Templo de las Inscripciones) which was started by the ruler Pacal ("Shield", A.D. 603–683) in 675 and which was finished in 683. This is a sober and unadorned pyramid of classical type, standing 20 m (66 ft) high, including the temple on the summit, and is built up of nine superimposed tiers.

On the six pillars which frame the five entrances to the TEMPLE the remains of stucco figures can still be seen. On the walls to right and left of the main entrance to the rear chamber are carved a total of 620 *hieroglyphs. This inscription, from which the temple takes its name, appears to be mainly concerned with the family chronicles of the rulers of Palenque.

One of the greatest sensations in the history of pre-Columbian archeology was heralded by Alberto Ruz l'Huillier's discovery in 1949, in the central chamber of the temple, of a staircase buried under an accumulation of earth and rubble. It took three years' methodical work to excavate this secret entrance to the interior of the pyramid. The staircase led down to a masonry wall, at the foot of which were a variety of votive offerings (pottery, shells, jade objects and a pearl). After demolishing the wall, the excavators were confronted with a triangular slab of stone standing upright against another wall, in front of which were six skeletons of adolescents. Removing the stone, they found the entrance to a *crypt almost 7 m (23 ft) high, 9 m (30 ft) long and 4 m (13 ft) wide, lying 27 m (90 ft) under the temple platform, with numerous stalactites and stalagmites formed by water percolating down through the structure. On the walls were nine *stucco reliefs* of gods or priests, and on the floor were found two stucco *heads* which rank among the finest of their kind in the world. The chamber contained a *sarcophagus* with a cover slab measuring 3.80 by 2.20 m (12 ft 6 in. by 7 ft), carved in bas-relief with the figure of Pacal seated on a mask representing the earth god with his knees drawn up and his body leaning backwards. Above this figure is a cruciform device

Temple of the Inscriptions, Palenque

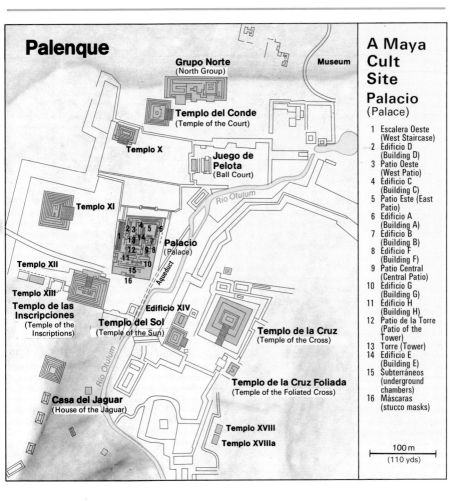

Palenque

Grupo Norte
(North Group)

Museum

Templo del Conde
(Temple of the Court)

Templo X

Juego de Pelota
(Ball Court)

Rio Otulum

Templo XI

Palacio
(Palace)

Templo XII

Templo XIII

Templo de las Inscripciones
(Temple of the Inscriptions)

Edificio XIV

Templo del Sol
(Temple of the Sun)

Templo de la Cruz
(Temple of the Cross)

Templo de la Cruz Foliada
(Temple of the Foliated Cross)

Casa del Jaguar
(House of the Jaguar)

Rio Otulum

Templo XVIII

Templo XVIIIa

A Maya Cult Site

Palacio
(Palace)

1 Escalera Oeste (West Staircase)
2 Edificio D (Building D)
3 Patio Oeste (West Patio)
4 Edificio C (Building C)
5 Patio Este (East Patio)
6 Edificio A (Building A)
7 Edificio B (Building B)
8 Edificio F (Building F)
9 Patio Central (Central Patio)
10 Edificio G (Building G)
11 Edificio H (Building H)
12 Patio de la Torre (Patio of the Tower)
13 Torre (Tower)
14 Edificio E (Building E)
15 Subterráneos (underground chambers)
16 Máscaras (stucco masks)

100 m
(110 yds)

which may represent the *ceiba*, the sacred tree of the Mayas, and above this again is a celestial bird; on either side of the figure are a number of symbolic death signs. On the sides of the slab are 52 glyphs. It is now believed that this is a symbolic representation of the death and rebirth of a ruler of Palenque, Pacal (reigned A.D. 615–683). In the sarcophagus was found a male skeleton, together with a jade mosaic mask which had slipped off the dead man's face and jade ornaments on his fingers, neck and arms. In each hand he had a piece of jade, and there was another in his mouth. This was the first time that a Maya pyramid had been found to serve as a funerary monument in the same way as the pyramids of Egypt.

The valuable **grave goods, together with a reconstruction of the crypt, can now be seen in the National Museum of Archeology in Mexico City.

Adjoining the Temple of the Inscriptions is the *Palace (*Palacio*), an unusual type of building in Maya architecture, on a huge artificial platform, trapezoid in shape, which stands some 10 m (33 ft) high and measures 100 by 80 m (330 by 260 ft). The part of the Palace now visible is thought to have been built in several stages between A.D. 650 and 770. The irregularly laid out complex consists of twelve buildings set around four courtyards, a series of underground passages (*subterráneos*) and a tower which dominates the whole group.

On the W staircase, to the left, is **Building D**, which has two parallel corridors. In its outer wall are five dóors, flanked by pillars bearing magnificent reliefs, some of them badly damaged. The subjects of the reliefs include a rite of consecration and the figure of Pacal, ruler of Palenque, dancing with his mother or wife. The inner side of Building D faces on to the *West Patio*.

The 15 m (50 ft) high *Tower, standing on an almost square base, was probably an observatory. It is unique in the ancient Indian architecture of Mexico, though there is room for doubt about the accuracy of the restoration.

From the Patio of the Tower we enter **Building E**, the rooms and corridors of which show the characteristic Maya corbelled vaulting. In this building was found an oval tablet with a relief of two seated figures, one of them presenting a headdress to the other, who sits on a higher level on a double-headed jaguar throne. The glyphs above this scene indicated that it represents Zac-kuk, queen of Palenque, and her son, Pacal, on the occasion of her accession to the throne (A.D. 615).

The largest and most interesting of the patios is the *East Patio*; enclosed by Building C on the W side, Building A on the E side and Building B on the S side.

Stucco head from Palenque

N of the Palace are the remains of the *Ball Court* (Juego de Pelota), and to the left of this Temple X. – Beyond this is the **Temple of the Count** (*Tempo del Conde*), so named because Frédéric de Waldeck lived here. Built between A.D. 640 and 650, it is the oldest structure so far excavated.

Characteristic of the **Palenque style** are the two parallel corridors, the rear one divided into three chambers. Here, too, can be seen the "mansard effect" produced by the steeply inclined outer walls, which are supported on internal arches. This distinguishes the Palenque style from the Puuc style of Yucatán, which had vertical outer walls between the middle and lower tiers. The Palenque style also uses stucco reliefs of figures and masks as decoration on the sloping walls above the middle tier, whereas stone mosaic decoration predominates in the Puuc area. The buildings at Palenque were frequently used as places of burial: thus under the floor of the Temple of the Count were found three tombs with grave goods which included jade beads, obsidian knives and shell ornaments.

Immediately NE is the **North Group** (*Grupo Norte*), consisting of Temples II, III, IV and V, built between A.D. 695 and 730. – Near this group is the small but very interesting **museum** of local finds (fragments of stucco work, stelae, grave goods, pottery).

The staircase leading up to **Building C** is flanked by stone slabs with reliefs of kneeling figures in attitudes of submission, apparently pointing to the glyphs which are also carved on the slabs. As far as they have been deciphered, these give the name of Pacal and the dates of his birth (A.D. 603) and accession (A.D 615).

In their extraordinarily complex calendrical system the Mayas set the starting point of their chronology at a hypothetical date corresponding to August 10, 3113 B.C. and indicated the total numbers of days since that date by combinations of date glyphs in their numbering system (a "vigesimal" system with a base of 20).

Standing in front of Building C, we see to the right of the staircase with the glyphs a slab with four larger glyphs, not yet deciphered. – The staircase of **Building A**, which stands opposite Building C, is flanked by large blocks of stone carved with large figures (four on the left, five on the right). Some of these figures, depicted in a submissive kneeling attitude, are thought to represent slaves or captives. The pillars between the entrances on the E front of the building have fine but much-damaged stucco reliefs. The two outer panels bear glyphs; the others have figures of rulers.

In this building is a *throne*, originally the main feature of a cult chamber divided into several parts, which is inscribed with glyphs yielding the date of A.D. 662. – The Palace also contains three latrines and a sweat bath which was used for ritual purification.

The Palace is believed to have been mainly an administrative building, though it also included apartments occupied by the rulers of Palenque.

Returning from here in the direction of the Palace, we pass the remains of the *aqueduct* and cross the River Otulum to reach the ***Temple of the Sun** (*Templo del Sol*). Completed in the year 692, this building, one of the most handsome at Palenque, stands on a four-tier platform.

The TEMPLE has three doorways providing access to two corridors and a shrine to the rear. A striking feature is the well-preserved *roof-comb*, a structural element once possessed by most of the buildings at Palenque which formed a continuation of the interior bearing wall and served a decorative function as well as increasing the apparent height of the building. – The pillars of the *doorways* are decorated with stucco human figures and glyphs, of which only fragments remain. – On the rear wall, opposite the central doorway, is a magnificently carved *relief*. In the center of this is a shield with two crossed lances, symbolizing the sun god; below is an altar borne by two seated figures, perhaps gods of the underworld; and on either side is a standing figure. The figure on the left is thought to be Pacal, ruler of Palenque (perhaps already deified?), the one on the right his son and successor, Chan-bahlum (snake-jaguar, A.D. 635–702). Both figures are surrounded by glyphs, and above the sun god's shield is an inscription giving the date of Chan-bahlum's accession.

Adjoining the N side of the temple is the building XIV, built by Kan-xul ("Precious Animal", A.D. 645–719?) after the death of Chan-bahlum in order to contain the menacing power of his deceased brother. It has a relief which shows the new ruler and his wife on the occasion of his accession to the throne (A.D. 702).

In the same group is the **Temple of the Cross** (*Templo de la Cruz*), which strongly resembles the Temple of the Sun and is likewise thought to have been built by Chan-bahlum in his own honor. It is believed, indeed, that he may have been buried in this temple. The large central relief from the rear shrine, now in the National Museum of Anthropology in Mexico City, depicts Chan-bahlum and his father, Pacal, on either side of a cruciform feature which may represent the *ceiba*, the sacred tree of the Mayas, and which gives the temple its name. The two lateral panels show (left) Chan-bahlum after his accession to the throne and (right) a god associated with the royal house, depicted smoking a cigar.

The **Temple of the Foliated Cross** (*Templo de la Cruz Foliada*), opposite the Temple of the Sun, is similar in plan to that temple and the Temple of the Cross and dates from the same decade. Here again the relief refers to the transfer of royal authority from Pacal to Chan-bahlum. The central feature is a cross which grows out of the sun god's head and has a sunbird perched on the top. The arms of the cross are formed by leaves of the maize plant decorated with human heads. To the right is a figure of Pacal, to the left his son and successor, Chan-bahlum.

Other buildings of interest are *Temples XVIII* and *XVIIIA*, to the S of the Temple of the Foliated Cross, and the *House of the Jaguar* (Casa del Jaguar), on the other side of the River Otulum.

SURROUNDINGS. – 20 km (12 miles) SW of Palenque on the Ocosingo road a side goes off on the right to the beautiful and romantically set waterfalls of **Mizol-há** ("waterfall" in Maya), which plunge from a height of almost 30 m (100 ft) into a large pool (bathing). – Some 50 km (30 miles) farther on, another road on the right leads in 4 km (2½ miles) to the *Agua Azul falls ("blue water"), where the water pours down in a number of wide cascades, amid luxuriant tropical vegetation, into the *Río Bascán* and later the *Río Tulijá*. The unusually clear water appears blue against the limestone river bed. There is excellent bathing in natural pools gouged from the rock by the river (modest restaurants, camp site, air-strip).

A recently built but poorly surfaced road leads in 100 km (62 miles) from Palenque to *Na-há* ("great water"), one of the last three settlements of the Lacandon Indians. Na-há can also be reached by air-taxi from Palenque, Tenosique and San Cristóbal de Las Casas. An equally rough road goes from Palenque to **Bonampak** (about 130 km (81 miles); see p. 82), which is not always passable and generally only by cross-country vehicles.

Papantla
See under El Tajín

Paricutín
See under Uruapan

Temple of the Sun, Building XIV and Palace, Palenque

The island of Janitzio in the Lago de Pátzcuaro

Parral (Hidalgo del Parral)

See under Chihuahua (town)

Lago de Pátzcuaro

State: Michoacán (Mich.).

ⓘ **Coordinación Federal de Turismo,**
Santos Degollado 340 Altos 1,
Morelia, Mich.
tel. (9 14 51) 2 05 22, 2 01 23, 2 84 98.

ACCOMMODATIONS. – ON THE LAKE: Motel San Carlos, Av. Caltzontzin, II; IN PÁTZCUARO: Posada de Don Vasco, Av. de las Américas 450, I, SP, tennis; Mesón del Gallo, Dr. Coss 20, I, SP; Mesón del Cortijo, extension of Av. A. Obregón, II; Posada de San Rafael, Plaza Principal 18, II; Motel Pátzcuaro, Av. de las Américas, II; Logs Escudos, Portal Hidalgo 73, II; Gran Hotel, Bocanegra 6, III. – Only restricted accommodations at present available in other towns and villages.

RESTAURANTS. – BY THE LAKE: Don Pepe. – IN PÁTZCUARO: Hostería de San Felipe, Av. de las Américas; El Gordo, Av. Lázaro Cárdenas; Las Redes, Lázaro Cárdenas 6.

RECREATION and SPORTS. – Swimming, rowing, sailing, water skiing, tennis.

EVENTS. – Fiestas IN PÁTZCUARO: Good Friday (Viernes Santo); December 8, Día de Nuestra Señora de la Salud. – IN JANITZIO: December 1–2, Noche de los Muertos. – IN QUIROGA: first Sunday in July, Día de la Preciosa Sangre de Cristo. – IN SANTA CLARA DEL COBRE (Villa Escalante): eighth day after Corpus Christi, Octavo Día de Jueves de Corpus; August 15, Copperware Fair.

The *Lago de Pátzcuaro is a large lake (length 19 km (12 miles), average breadth 5 km – 3 miles) lying at an altitude of 2050 m (6725 ft) amid forest-clad hills and extinct volcanoes. The lake is dotted with islands, the most important of which are Janitzio, Jarácuaro, Tecuén, Yunuén and Pacanda, and around its shores and in the surrounding area are Indian villages which have preserved much of their old way of life. The beauty of the lake and its setting give it a high place among Mexico's tourist attractions.

The principal town of this region is *Pátzcuaro, 4 km (2½ miles) from the lake ("place of the stones for temple-building" in Tarascan; alt. 2175 m (7135 ft); pop. 64,000; market on Friday), a charming little town which retains much of the atmosphere of the past. In this former Tarascan capital the Indian element is still predominant in the population, although the finest of its old buildings date from around 1550, when Pátzcuaro was a Spanish episcopal see. Here the memory of the great patron and teacher of the Indians, Bishop Vasco de Quiroga ("Tata Vasco", 1470–1565), is still very much alive. The history of the town, which received its charter from the Emperor Charles V in 1553, is closely bound up with that of Tzintzuntzan (p. 279) and Morelia (p. 196).

SIGHTS of Pátzcuaro. – In the colonial-style Plaza de San Agustín (Plaza Chica, Plaza Bocanegra) is the former church of

San Agustín, now housing the *Biblioteca Gertrudis Bocanegra*, which has murals by Juan O'Gorman depicting the history of Michoacán. Adjoining the square is the interesting *Market (Mercado)*.

From here either Calle Iturbide or Calle Zaragoza leads to the **Plaza Principal (Plaza Vasco de Quiroga, *Plaza Grande*), one of the largest and finest squares in Mexico. On the right is the Town Hall (*Palacio Municipal*), in an 18th c. palace. On the E side of the square is the *Casa del Gigante* ("House of the Giant"), with a beautiful doorway and decorated windows on the balcony.

At the SW corner of the square, in Calle Ponce de León, stands the old *Royal Custom House*. In the next block is the Baroque *church of San Francisco*, which contains a figure of Christ credited with miraculous powers. – 3 km (2 miles) W by way of Calle Ponce de León is an extinct volcano, the *Cerro del Estribo* ("Stirrup Hill"), from which there is a beautiful *view of the town and the lake.

SE of the Plaza Principal is the *Casa de los Once Patios* ("House of the Eleven Patios"), a former 18th c. convent building in which craft articles are displayed and on sale. Going N from here along Calle Enseñanza and passing the Hospital Santa María, we come to the *church of La Compañía* founded by Bishop Quiroga in 1546 and altered in the 18th c. – At the next corner is the *Colegio de San Nicolás*, a school founded by Bishop Quiroga in 1540 and now housing the *Museo de Artes Populares*, with an interesting collection of ethnological material and craft articles of both the past and the present. – Nearby is the Colegiata or *church of Nuestra Señora de la Salud*, founded by Bishop Quiroga in 1543 as a cathedral but never completed. It contains a statue of the Virgen de la Salud made from maize paste (*pasta de caña*) in a technique characteristic of Tarascan religious art. – Calle del General Serrato leads to the *Calvary chapel of El Humilladero*, just outside the town, with an unusual 17th c. doorway in a Renaissance style showing Indian influence, a crucifix bearing the date 1553 and an interesting altar.

4 km (2½ miles) from the center of Pátzcuaro is the quay (*muelle*) where boats can be hired for trips to the various islands on the lake. On the islands and around the shores of the lake are some thirty picturesque Indian villages, the inhabitants of which live mainly by fishing, using boats hollowed out of tree trunks and a variety of nets to catch the delicate whitefish (*pescado blanco*) and various species of perch and trout. The famous "butterfly nets" (*uiripu*) are now used almost solely for the benefit of tourists.

The most beautiful island in the lake is **Tecuén**; the most important, often crowded with tourists, is *Janitzio, reached in a half-hour boat trip. Above the picturesque fishing village of **Janitzio**, with its narrow twisting lanes and tile-roofed houses, rises a pompous *monument to José María Morelos*, one of the heroes of the struggle for Mexican independence. An internal staircase leads up to the head of the statue, from which there is a beautiful panoramic *view of the lake. On the walls of the staircase are frescoes by Ramón Alva de Canal depicting scenes from Morelos's life.

Janitzio is renowned for its impressive celebrations of the fiesta of *All Souls (Spanish *Día de los Muertos*; Tarascan *Animecha-Kejtzitakua*, "gifts for the dead") on the night of November 1–2, which combine Catholic and pagan elements. Before the fiesta there are special rites for the benefit of dead children and a ceremonial wild-duck hunt (*kuirisi-ataku*) on the lake, using throwing spears (*atlatl*).

On the W side of the lake, 18 km (11 miles) from the town of Pátzcuaro, is the attractive Tarascan village of *Erongarícuaro (Purepecha, "observation tower of the lake"; alt. 1980 m (6498 ft.); pop. 4000), in which a group of French Surrealists established themselves during the Second World War. The village has a fine Franciscan convent (1570) with an atrium, an open chapel and a Plateresque doorway showing Mudéjar features.

Fishing with the *uiripu* ("butterfly net")

Fiesta of All Souls on the Lago de Pátzcuaro

There is a colorful Sunday market at which village crafts such as fine hand-woven cambric and embroidery are offered for sale.

On the N side of the lake, some 25 km (16 miles) N of Pátzcuaro and 8 km (5 miles) from Tzintzuntzan, is the little town of **Quiroga** (alt. 1996 m (6551 ft.); pop. 11,000; accommodations in San Diego), with a 16th c. Franciscan convent, a noted center for the sale of *crafts and folk art from the surrounding area. – A short distance from Quiroga on the Zacapu road is the small lakeside resort of *Chupícuaro* (motel).

Some 40 km (25 miles) from Quiroga, on Road 15 (the Guadalajara road), is **Zacapu** (alt. 1980 m (6498 ft.); pop. 55,000; Hotel San Carlos; market on Sunday), which is believed to have been the first capital of the Tarascans (Purépecha) in the 12th or 13th c. Near the town are a number of archeological sites (Malpaís, La Iglesia) on which numerous tombs were found.

The 16th c. convent church has a Plateresque façade with Mudéjar features.

17 km (11 miles) from Pátzcuaro in the direction of Tiripetío is *Tupátero* and its simple brick church Santiago Apóstol (open on Sundays, otherwise only by special arrangement). The interior is resplendent, with a roof in Mudéjar style and an altar dedicated to St. James with strange paintings on wood. The colored paintings portray the life of Christ and the Virgin Mary in an impressive manner, just as they were presented to the Indians by 16th c. missionaries. A similar form of religious painting was discovered in two churches near Cuzco in Peru.

About 20 km (12 miles) S of Pátzcuaro lies **Villa Escalante** or **Santa Clara del Cobre** (alt. 2150 m (4906 ft); pop. 11,000; fiesta on August 15, Assumption; Copperware Fair; craft museum).

This old Tarascan town is widely famed for its fine beaten copperware: a craft which was practiced before the coming of the Spaniards but was promoted and encouraged by Bishop Vasco de Quiroga in the 16th c.

11 km (7 miles) W of Villa Escalante is the beautiful *Lago de Zirahuén (in Purépecha – Tzirahuen="where it steams") and to the village of *Zirahuén* (accommodation Cabañas de Ala). The same road runs on to join Road 14, which links *Morelia (p. 196) with **Uruapan** (p. 281).

Paz, La
See La Paz

Pico de Orizaba (Citlaltépetl)
See under Puebla (town)

Piedras Negras
See under Coahuila de Zaragoza

Popocatépetl and Iztaccíhuatl

Popocatépetl

States: México (Mex.) and Puebla (Pue.).

ⓘ Secretaría de Turismo,
Av. Presidente Masaryk 172,
Cuidad de México, D.F.;
tel. (9 15) 2 50 85 55.
Coordinación Federal de Turismo,
Blvd. Hermanos Serdán y Blvd. Norte,
Puebla, Pue.;
tel. (91 22) 48 29 77, 48 31 77, 48 30 44.

ACCESS. – From Mexico City via Chalco and Amecameca to the *albergue* (mountain hut) at Tlamacas (about 85 km – 53 miles). From Puebla via San Nicolás de Los Ranchos to the Paso de Cortes from where a branch road leads S in 5 km (3 miles) to Tlamacas (starting point for the ascent of Popocatépetl and another road goes N and in 7 km (4 miles) reaches La Joya (starting point for the ascent of Iztaccíhuatl).

The central Mexican highlands are bounded on the S by a volcanic chain extending across the country from the Pacific to the Atlantic. During the early and middle Tertiary era huge quantities of lava were deposited, and during the second phase of volcanic activity, which began in the Pliocene and is still continuing, Mexico's two great

Crater of Popocatépetl

mountain giants; **Popocatépetl (5452 m – 17,999 ft) and **Iztaccíhuatl (5286 m – 17,343 ft) came into being. These majestic snowcapped peaks in the Sierra Nevada form a ridge of mountains separating the Valley of Mexico from the Puebla plateau

The road from Amecameca to Tlamacas runs through the POPOCATEPETL-IZTACCIHUATL NATIONAL PARK, which lies between the two mountains, and over the *Paso de Cortés* (Cortés Pass), crossed by Cortés and his troops on November 3, 1519 on their march to Tenochtitlán. A road on the right leads to a mountain hut (*albergue*) at 3998 m (13,117 ft), the highest point accessible by car as a base for the *climb of **Popocatépetl (Náhuatl, "Smoking Mountain": 5452 m – 17,888 m). From here there are two possible routes to the summit (ascent and descent possible in a day long expedition, otherwise in two days with overnight camping: information and guides at Amecameca, Hotel San Carlos, or at mountain hut). The huge crater on the summit, with almost vertical walls, measures 826 by 400 m (2710 by 1310 ft). – The last major eruption was in 1802; there have been only small eruptions since, although there is frequently a cloud of smoke over the crater. Since the Spanish conquest large quantities of sulfur (originally used in the manufacture of gunpowder) have been extracted from the crater.

**Iztaccíhuatl or Ixtaccíhuatl (Náhuatl, "White Lady": 5286 m – 17,343 ft) is reached by taking the road to *La Joya*

Iztaccíhuatl

from the Paso de Cortés. Legend has it that this craterless mountain, 15 km (9 miles) from Popocatépetl, is a princess who died for love of the warrior Popocatépetl and was united with him in death. Seen from Mexico City, in good visibility, the summit of Iztaccíhuatl shows some resemblance to the head, breast and knees of a recumbent female figure. The strenuous climb requires a two days round trip (equipment for camping available).

From the Paso de Cortés it is 23 km (14 miles) to **Amecameca** (p. 75).

Puebla (State)

State of Puebla (Pue.). – Capital: Puebla.
Area: 33,995 sq. km (13,125 sq. miles).
Population: 3,672,800.

ⓘ **Coordinación Federal de Turismo,**
Blvd. Hermanos Serdán y Blvd. Norte,
Puebla, Pue.
tel. (91 22) 48 29 77, 48 31 77, 48 30 44.

The state of Puebla is bounded on the N and E by Veracruz, on the S by Oaxaca and Guerrero and on the W and NW by Morelos, México state, Tlaxcala and Hidalgo. It is a densely populated region of plateaus, fertile valleys and glaciated mountains which plays a major part in the economic and cultural life of the country. The population consists of
Creoles (descendants of Spaniards), mestizos and various Indian peoples (Nahua, Otomí, Totonacs, Mazatecs, etc.).

Although there are numerous archeological sites in Puebla, the only ones likely to interest the ordinary visitor are *Cholula (p. 106) and *Yohualichán (p. 266). Other sites of some importance are Las Bocas and Coxcatlán.

HISTORY. – The Puebla region, adjoining the great cultural centers in the Anáhuac valley, played a part of some importance in pre-Columbian times. In the Tehuacán valley archeologists discovered the earliest evidence of cultivation (gourds, avocados, chilies, cotton), dating to 6000 B.C. Later, from about 1200 B.C. to the Spanish conquest, the territory was occupied either successively or concurrently by the Olmecs, Zapotecs, Mixtecs, Toltecs, Totonacs and Aztecs (Mexica). The most important religious and political center during the Classic and Post-Classic periods was Cholula, whose influence extended widely for many centuries until the Conquest. – The Spaniards under Cortés arrived in this area in 1519 on their way from the Gulf coast to Tenochtitlán, and had settled it within a very short time. The later history of Puebla is bound up with that of its capital, Puebla de Zaragoza.

ECONOMY. – Soon after the Conquest Puebla became, and has remained, a region of major importance for its communications and its agricultural produce (wheat, maize, coffee, sugar-cane, maguey agaves). The principal minerals worked are gold, copper, coal, onyx and marble. The state is well supplied with hydroelectric power, which has contributed to the rapid development of industry. Industrial products include ceramics (particularly tiles), textiles, glass, soap, leather goods and automobiles (Volkswagen works at Puebla, with a total work force of about 12,000). Contributions are also made to the state's economy by craft products, tourism and the bottling of mineral water (Tehuacán).

In addition to the well-known tourist centers such as *Puebla, *Acatepec, *Cholula, *Huejotzingo and Teziutlán (see the entries for these places), the following towns in Puebla are worth mentioning:

Tehuacán (alt. 1670 m (5479 ft); pop. 84,000; hotels: Hacienda Spa Peñafiel, SP, golf, mineral water cures; Hotel México, Campestre y Balneario El Riego, SP, golf; Madrid; Reforma; Iberia; Harvest Festival in June; market on Saturday) is a quiet little spa noted for its thermal baths and mineral water. Also in Tehuacán are the churches of San Francisco (17th and 18th c.) and El Carmen (18th c.) and the Tehuacán Valley Archeological Museum.

Maize store at Calmeca (Puebla state)

Izúcar de Matamoros (alt. 1300 m (4265 ft); pop. 30,000; Hotel Posada de Cristóbal Colón, SP; fiesta July 25, Día de Santiago; Monday market), with a beautiful 16th c. fountain, a 16th c. Dominican convent with *posas* (processional chapels), a church (17th and 18th c.) and an open chapel.

San Martín Texmelucan (alt. 2270 m (7450 ft); pop. 36,000; Hotel La Granja; fiesta November 11, Día de San Martín; market Tuesday), with a convent and church (late 16th c.), a Churrigueresque parish church and a number of archeological sites in the surrounding area.

Huauchinango (alt. 1500 m (4920 ft); pop. 26,000; Hotel Rex, SP; March 10–20, Flower Fair; market on Saturday), an attractive little Indian town in a beautiful setting.

Acatlán de Osorio (alt. 1213 m (3980 ft); pop. 14,000; Hotel Romano; fiesta October 24, Día de San Rafael Arcángel; market on Sunday), a picturesque little Mixtec town famed for its *ceramics, particularly its painted pottery.

Visitors to north-western Puebla can make an interesting excursion to the curious rock formations in a valley near Zacatlán known as the *Piedras Encimadas* ("stepped rocks").

Mexico
United Mexican States
Estados Unidos Mexicanos

Puebla

States
Estados

1a Baja California Sur	12 Aguascalientes
1b Baja California Norte	13 Jalisco
	14 Guanajuato
2 Sonora	15 Querétaro
3 Chihuahua	16 Hidalgo
4 Sinaloa	17 Colima
5 Durango	18 Michoacán
6 Coahuila	19 México
7 Nuevo León	20 Morelos
8 Zacatecas	21 Tlaxcala
9 San Luis Potosí	22 Puebla
10 Tamaulipas	23 Veracruz
11 Nayarit	24 Guerrero
	25 Oaxaca

26 Chiapas
27 Tabasco
28 Campeche
29 Yucatán
30 Quintana Roo

D.F. Distrito Federal (Federal District)

Puebla de Zaragoza

State: Puebla (Pue.).
Altitude: 2162 m (7094 ft). – Population: 1,320,000.
Telephone dialing code: 91 22.
(i) **Coordinación Federal de Turismo,**
Blvd. Hermanos Serdán y Blvd. Norte;
tel. 48 29 77, 48 31 77, 48 30 44.

HOTELS. – *Mesón del Angel*, Hermanos Serdán 807, I, SP, tennis; *Hostal de Velasco*, 8 Oriente 213, I; *Posada San Pedro*, 2 Oriente 202, I, SP; *Lastra*, Calz. de los Fuertes 2633, I, SP; *Palacio San Leonardo*, 2 Oriente 211, I, SP; *Gilfer*, 2 Oriente 11, II; *Colonia*, 4 Sur 105, II; *Señorial*, 4 Norte 602, II; *Royalty Centre*, Hidalgo 8, II; *Augusta*, 4 Poniente 504, II; *Avenida*, 5 Poniente 306, III; *San Augustín*, 3 Poniente 313, III; *Gran Hotel del Alba*, Ave. Hermanos Serdán, 141, L. SP, golf, tennis.

RESTAURANTS in most hotels; also *La Fonda de Santa Clara*, Calle 3 Poniente 307; *El Cortijo*, 16 de Septiembre 506; *D'Armandos*, 7 Poniente 2105; *La Princesa*, Portal Juárez 101; *La Mansión del Marisco*, Priv. 37-A Oriente 406; *Los Delfines*, 17 Oriente 421; *Café Aguirre*, Calle 5 de Mayo 4.

RECREATION and SPORTS. – Swimming, tennis, golf, riding.

EVENT. – Fiesta on May 5 commemorating the battle of Puebla.

*Puebla, capital of the state of that name, lies in a fertile high valley surrounded by mountains, mostly volcanoes, including Popocatépetl (5452 m – 17,888 ft), Iztaccíhuatl (5286 m – 17,343 ft) and La Malinche (4461 m – 14,637 ft).** It is an old town with many historical associations and an abundance of colonial architecture, including no fewer than sixty churches. Long renowned as a center for the production of the brightly colored tiles which are used in many of its buildings, it has developed during the last decade or so into a considerable industrial center. It has, nevertheless, preserved much of its character as an old town of the colonial period.

HISTORY. – So far as is known, Puebla did not exist during the pre-Hispanic period. The town was founded in 1531 by Franciscan monks acting on the instructions of Bishop Julián Garcés of Tlaxcala and given the name of *Ciudad de los Angeles*. By 1537 it had a university, and in 1539 it became the see of a bishop under the name of *Puebla de los Angeles*. The town soon developed into the market center of the surrounding agricultural area and a traffic junction on the road between the Gulf of Mexico and the Pacific. GRThe manufacture of tiles (azulejos) in the Spanish mode, particularly in the style of Talavera de la Reina, began in the middle of the 16th c. As a Spanish foundation of predominantly European character,

Puebla was a natural competitor and rival of the old Indian city of Cholula, which it began to overshadow in the 17th c.

During the war between Mexico and the United States (1846–8) there was bitter fighting here between the troops of Generals Winfield Scott and Antonio López de Santa Ana, and the town was occupied for a time by US troops. – During the French intervention Puebla was the scene of a battle on May 5, 1862 in which Mexican forces under General Ignacio Zaragoza drove back the French, and the anniversary of that date is now a national holiday. A year later, however, the French took the town, and it remained in their hands until its recapture by General Porfirio Díaz in April 1867. – There was also bitter fighting here during the revolutionary wars (1910–20).

SIGHTS. – Streets running from E to W are called *avenidas*, those running from N to S *calles*. The Avenida de la Reforma (to the W) and Avenida Avila Camacho (to the E) divide the town into northern and southern halves (Norte and Sur), while Calle 16 de Septiembre (to the S) and Calle 5 de Mayo (to the N) similarly divide it into E and W (Oriente and Poniente).

The life of the town centers on the magnficient *Zócalo* (*Plaza de la Constitución*), surrounded by arcades (*portales*), with its tall trees, flower beds and fountains. On the S side of the square is the *Cathedral*, the second largest in Mexico after the Cathedral of Mexico City. It is an imposing building, mainly in Renaissance style, which was begun about 1575 but not completed until 1649. The N doorway, facing onto the square, has figures in high relief of the four Spanish Habsburg kings (Charles V, Philip II, Philip III and Philip IV), and under the arch the coats of arms of the Spanish kings. The main front and doorway, in sober and uniform style, already show the influence of the emergent Baroque style. The two towers are unusually high and slender; one dates from 1678, the other from ninety years later. A striking feature of the church is the huge dome, faced with azulejos.

The impressive INTERIOR (length 90 m (295 ft), width 47 m (155 ft), height 25 m – 80 ft) has three aisles and a large transept. Notable features are the neo-classical *high altar* (by Manuel Tolsá and José Manzo, c. 1800); the wrought-iron *choir screen* (by Mateo de la Cruz, 1679); the carved *choir stalls* (by Pedro Muñoz, 1719–22); two fine organs of the same period; the Baroque altar in the *Royal Chapel* and the Baroque retablo by the Flemish artist Diego de Borgraf in the *Capilla San José*; and a number of 17th and 18th c. pictures attributed to Pedro García Ferrer and Miguel Carbrera.

To the S of the Cathedral, in the beautiful old Archbishop's Palace, is the *Biblio-

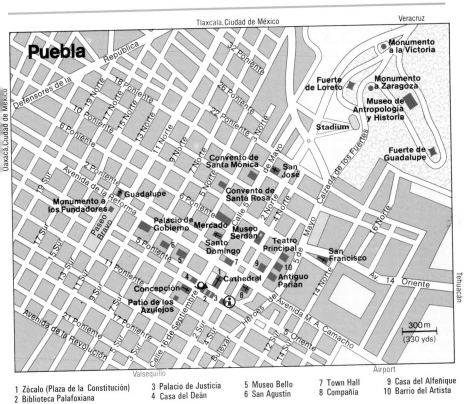

Puebla

1 Zócalo (Plaza de la Constitución) 3 Palacio de Justicia 5 Museo Bello 7 Town Hall 9 Casa del Alfeñique
2 Biblioteca Palafoxiana 4 Casa del Deán 6 San Agustín 8 Compañía 10 Barrio del Artista

teca Palafoxiana, a library, founded by Juan Palafox in 1646, which has a large collection of rare old books. – In the next block W is the **Dean's House** (*Casa del Deán*), a handsome old burgher's house in Renaissance style (1580). – Two blocks E of the Zócalo is the Jesuit **church of La Compañía** (1767), with a Churrigueresque façade and a blue and white tiled dome. In the very year in which the church was consecrated, the Jesuits were expelled from Mexico. In the sacristy, visitors are shown a tomb which is said to be that of an Asiatic princess who was captured by pirates, sold in Mexico as a slave and finally granted her freedom at the end of the 17th c. The picturesque *china poblana* costume which later spread throughout Mexico is said to have originated with her. – Adjoining the church is the former Jesuit college, now occupied by the **University**.

A little way N of the Compañía church on Calle 4 Ote, No. 416 is the *****Casa del Alfeñique** ("Almond-Cake House"), a late 18th c. building attributed to Antonio de Santa María Incháurregui which, with

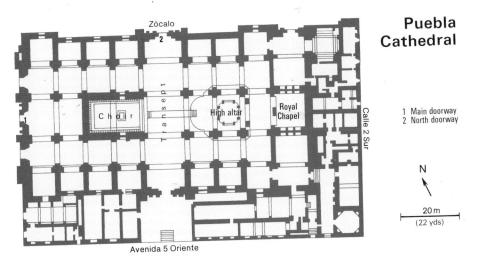

Puebla Cathedral

1 Main doorway
2 North doorway

its colored tiles, red brick and white stucco decoration, is a very typical example of the Poblano style, the local version of Baroque. It now houses the *Regional Museum* (pottery, arms and armor, pictures, costume, furniture). – Nearby is another building in similar style, the *Casa de Los Muñecos* ("House of the Puppets"). Proceeding, one finds the Museo de la Revolución (Museum of the Revolution) "Casa Arquiles Serdán" on 206 Ave. 18 de Noviembre, which contains interesting memorabilia of this fierce period (1910–20).

Two blocks N of the Zócalo is the **church of Santo Domingo** (1611), with a very individual Baroque façade. The *Chapel of the Rosary (Capilla del Rosario, 1690) is one of the most splendid achievements of Mexican Baroque. Every inch of the walls, ceiling, columns and doorways is covered with tiles, gold leaf, sculpture and carved woodwork. A particularly notable feature is an orchestra of cherubs caught up in a riot of arabesques from the center of which emerges the figure of God the Father. On the high altar is a richly attired figure of the Virgin of the Rosary surrounded by saints and apostles.

Church of Santo Domingo, Puebla

Some blocks farther N on Av. 18 Pte. 103 is the *Convent of Santa Mónica, founded in 1609 and altered in 1680. Although the convent was dissolved under the reform laws of 1857, the nuns continued to run it until 1934, when it was discovered. It now contains an interesting *museum* with a varied collection of religious art. – In Calle 3 Norte, two blocks away, is the **Convent of Santa Rosa**, which now houses the *Museum of Folk*

Art (Museo de Arte Popular), a library, shops and an authentic convent kitchen faced with tiles and equipped with original utensils. – Between Fort Loreto and Fort Guadalupe is the *Museo de Antropología e Historia*, with an interesting collection of archeological finds (Olmec, Toltec, Aztec) and enthnological material from the region.

Among Puebla's churches the following are particularly worth visiting: *San Francisco* (1551: Plateresque side doorway; 18th c. Churrigueresque main doorway; carved choir-stalls, mid-18th c.; altered in neo-classical style, c. 1800); *San José* (18th c.: Baroque, with a beautiful tiled dome); *La Concepción* (19th c. pictures); *San Agustín* (1629: Baroque); *San Miguelito* (17th c.: pictures by Diego de Borgraf); and the *Capilla de San Antonio* (magnificent Poblano-style stucco work in interior).

Other features of interest in the town include the *House of the Animal-Killer* ("Casa del que mató el Animal": Renaissance doorway of almost tapestry-like effect); the **Teatro Principal**, one of the oldest theaters in America (1759); *Fort Loreto* (Fuerte de Loreto, early 19th c.: 17th c. Loreto church, military museum, fine *view of the town) and *Fort Guadalupe* (Fuerte de Guadalupe); the *Museo de Arte José Luis Bello y González* (pictures, wrought-iron work, pottery, porcelain, copperware, furniture).

SURROUNDINGS. – 25 km (16 miles) S is the *Valsequillo reservoir* (also called Manuel Ávila Camacho) which has facilities for water sports. – Near here is *Africam*, a safari park with numerous exotic species of animals.

6 km (4 miles) from Puebla on Road 190 (the Oaxaca road) is **Tlaxcalancingo** (p. 70); 11 km (7 miles) farther on is *Acatepec (p. 68); and 1 km (¾ miles) beyond this, off the road to the right, is *Tonantzintla (p. 69).

31 km (19 miles) from Puebla, still on Road 190, we come to the attractive town of *Atlixco (Náhuatl, "place above the water"; alt. 1885 m (6185 ft.); pop. 82,000; hotels: Balmori, San Bernardo, Esparanza; Atlixcayotl fiesta September 29; market on Tuesday and Saturday), with a number of buildings in the Poblano style. Features of interest are the Chapel of the Rosary, part of the parish church (in the main square); the stucco façade of the former church of La Merced; and the fortress-like 16th c. church of the Franciscan convent on the Cerrito de San Miguel, with a restrained Plateresque façade. – Nearby is the *Hacienda de Cristo Grande*, with a doorway in neo-Mudéjar style.

32 km (20 miles from Puebla, on Road 150 (the Tehuacán road) is *Tepeaca (or Tepeyacac ("nose of

Pico de Orizaba (Citlaltépetl), Mexico's highest mountain (5700 m – 18,700 ft)

the hill"); alt. 2257 m (7407 ft.); pop. 12,000; Hotel Maria Elena; market on Friday). In the main square of this old posting station is a watch-tower ("Rollo") with Moorish and Renaissance features. It is said that the Spaniards chained Indian prisoners to this tower and whipped them. Opposite is the façade of a house which is reputed to have been built by Hernan Cortes and where he is thought to have lived after his defeat at Tenochtitlán (June 30, 1520). The fortress-like 16th c. Franciscan convent is one of the earliest of the kind in Mexico. – 20 km (12 miles) NE on Road 140 is **Acatzingo** (alt. 2160 m (7089 ft.); pop. 15,000; market on Tuesday), which has a similar 16th c. Franciscan convent with a beautifully carved font.

From Acatzingo there are two routes to the foot of Mexico's highest mountain, the *Pico de Orizaba (5700 m – 18,700 ft) or **Citlaltépetl** ("Mountain of the Star"). One route runs SE from El Seco on Road 140 to *Ciudad Serdán*; the other branches off 7 km (4 miles) N of El Seco and runs SE to *Tlachichuca*, where it is possible to hire an overland vehicle and drive to a mountain hut (4260 m (13,977 ft); overnight accommodations) on the Piedra Grande. The *ascent of this magnificent snow-capped volcano can be made by an experienced climber in a day. Before attempting the climb, inquire about means of access and routes.

From Puebla it is some 120 km (75 miles) to Tehuacán (p. 223) and 190 km (120 miles) to **Teziutlán** (p. 265).

Puerto Escondido

State: Oaxaca (Oax.).
Altitude: sea level.
Population: 23,000.
Telephone dialing code: 9 19 58.
ⓘ **Coordinación Federal de Turismo,**
Matamoros 105 Esq. García Vigil,
Oaxaca, Oax;
tel. (9 19 51) 6 01 44, 6 00 45.

HOTELS. – OUTSIDE THE VILLAGE: *Castel Bugambilias*, Playa de Bacocho, I, SP; *Rancho El Pescador*, on Acapulco road, I, SP, tennis, riding. – IN THE VILLAGE: with beach – *Las Palmas*, II; *El Rincón del Pacifico*, II; *Bungalows Villa Marinera*, II; *Santa Fé*, I, SP; without beach – *Paraíso Escondido*, II; *Naya*, II; *Lorén*, II; *Rocamar*, II.

RESTAURANTS in most hotels; also *Papagayo, La Palapa, La Posada, Casa de los Mariscos, La Estancia.*

RECREATION and SPORTS. – Swimming, snorkeling, diving, surfing, fishing, boat trips, tennis, riding.

ACCESS. – From Oaxaca 264 km (164 miles) on a winding road; or via Ejutla and Pochutla on the better Road 175 and Road 200 (305 km – 190 miles); from Acapulco 420 km (260 miles) on Road 200. – Regular flights by light aircraft from Oaxaca; further air services in larger aircraft are planned.

The little fishing village of Puerto Escondido lies in a sheltered bay on the Pacific, surrounded by hills with a luxuriant growth of vegetation and flanked by magnificent long *beaches (with heavy surf in places). Until recently it was a quiet little place frequented only by a few vacationers anxious to get away from the crowds; the construction of a new airport seems likely to attract larger numbers of visitors.

The village itself, straggling along the road, offers no features of particular interest. The *beaches, alternating with small bays, and the *lagoons have a rich bird life. Some stretches of coast afford excellent swimming, in spite of the surf, but in some places it is necessary to beware of the undertow. Puerto Escondido is popular with surfers on acount of its high waves.

SURROUNDINGS. – 83 km (51 miles) SE on Road 200 lies the charming fishing port of **Puerto Angel** (pop. 6000; hotels: Angel del Mar, I, SP; Soraya, II; La Posada Cañon del Vata, III). This resort, which only became popular a few years ago, has attractive beaches including Panteón, Santiago and Zipolite in a variety of settings. Some 40 km (25 miles) E of Puerto Angel in the Bay of Huatulco, the Mexican government and private investors are building a new vast sea resort. It is planned to open in 1988 for the public with over 1200 hotel rooms and is projected to surpass by the year 2000 the Caribbean resort of Cancún in every respect.

Puerto Vallarta

State: Jalisco (Jal.).
Altitude: sea level. – Population: 182,000.
Telephone dialing code: 9 13 22.

ⓘ **Coordinación Federal de Turismo,**
Presidencia Municipal, P.B.;
tel. 2 25 54, 2 25 55, 2 25 56.

ACCESS. – New roads from Tepic (165 km – 105 miles), Guadalajara (355 km – 220 miles) and Manzanillo (260 km – 160 miles). Ferry service from Cabo San Lucas (Baja California). – Direct air services from the largest towns in Mexico and from some foreign airports.

HOTELS. – *Fiesta American*, 2.5 km (1½ miles) away on road to airport, L, SP, tennis; *Camino Real*, Playa de las Estacas, L, SP, tennis, riding; *Buganvilias Sheraton*, on road to airport Nr. 999, L, SP, tennis; *Garza Blanca*, 5 km (3 miles) away on road to Barra de Navidad, L, SP, tennis, golf; *Posada Vallarta*, Av.

The holiday paradise of Puerto Vallarta

de las Garzas, L, SP, tennis; *Holiday Inn*, 3.4 km (2 miles) away on airport road, L, SP, tennis, riding; *Castel Pelícanos*, 2.5 km (1½ miles) away on airport road, I, SP; *Playa Conchas Chinas*, 2.5 km (1½ miles) away on road to Barra de Navidad, I, SP; *Hacienda del Lobo*, 5 km (3 miles) away on road to airport, I, SP, tennis; *Playa de Oro*, 2 km (1 mile) away on road to airport, I, SP, tennis, riding; *Calinda Plazas Las Glorias*, 2.5 km (1½ miles) away on road to airport, I, SP; *Posada Río Cuale*, A. Serdán 100, II, SP; *Océano*, Paseo Díaz Ordaz y Galeana, II; *Playa Los Arcos*, Manuel M. Dieguez 171, II, SP; *Encino*, Juárez 115, II; *La Lagunita*, Yelapa, II; *Yazmín*. Basilico Badillo 168, III; *Chulavista*, Juárez 263, III; *Elia*, 1.5 km (1 mile) away on road to airport, III; *Paraíso*, Morelos y Iturbide, III.

RESTAURANTS in most hotels; also *La Fonda del Sol*, Morelos 54; *Ostión Felíz*, Libertad 177; *Benito's*, Zaragoza 1601; *Pietro*, Zaragoza 245; *El Dorado*, Amapas y Púlpito; *Casa Blanca*, Paseo Díaz Ordaz 570; *Moby Dick's*, 31 Octubre 12: *Daiquiri Dick's*, Olas Altas 246; *Mismaloya Beach*, 31 Octubre 15; *Chico's Paradise*, 20 km (12 miles) away on road to Barra de Navidad; IN BUCERÍAS, 25 km (15½ miles) N: *El Chivero, El Corral, Rama Inn. Carlos O'Brien*, Av. Diaz Ordaj.

RECREATION and SPORTS. – Swimming, snorkeling, diving, boat trips, fishing, deep-sea fishing, water skiing, para-sailing, tennis, hunting, riding, donkey polo.

EVENTS. – Fishing competition; sailing regatta. – Fiesta December 12, Día de la Virgen de Guadalupe. – Market on Sunday.

*Puerto Vallarta, one of Mexico's most popular beach resorts, lies in a wide curving bay with a backdrop of luxuriantly wooded hills. Twenty years ago a remote and forgotten

Mexico
United Mexican States
Estados Unidos Mexicanos

Querétaro

States
Estados

1a	Baja California	12	Aguascalientes
	Sur	13	Jalisco
1b	Baja California	14	Guanajuato
	Norte	15	Querétaro
2	Sonora	16	Hidalgo
3	Chihuahua	17	Colima
4	Sinaloa	18	Michoacán
5	Durango	19	México
6	Coahuila	20	Morelos
7	Nuevo León	21	Tlaxcala
8	Zacatecas	22	Puebla
9	San Luis Potosí	23	Veracruz
10	Tamaulipas	24	Guerrero
11	Nayarit	25	Oaxaca

26	Chiapas
27	Tabasco
28	Campeche
29	Yucatán
30	Quintana Roo

D.F. Distrito Federal (Federal District)

fishing village, it is now one of the busiest vacation centers in the country.

HISTORY. – The town was founded only in 1851, and in 1918 was named after the then-governor of the state, Ignacio Luis Vallarta. This sleepy little place first came to public notice when the Hollywood film "The Night of the Iguana" was shot in the neighboring village of Mismaloya. Since the opening of a new road from Tepic in 1968, the town has developed rapidly.

SIGHTS. – Although Puerto Vallarta is an attractive town of cobbled lanes and whitewashed houses with tiled roofs, most visitors come here for the sake of the long beaches with their facilities for a variety of water sports, and the tropical setting.

The main attractions of Puerto Vallarta are to be found along the *Malecón* (seafront promenade), with its many hotels, restaurants, night spots and shops. There are also a small *archeological museum* and the *church of Guadalupe*, with a curious crown-shaped tower.

The *Bahía de Banderas ("Bay of Flags"), on which Puerto Vallarta lies, has a couple of dozen *beaches*, extending N and S of the Río Cuale, which divides the town into two. Among the best-known beaches N of the river are the *Playa de las Glorias, Las Palmas* (or *Las Cruces*: palm-grove), *Vallarta de Oro* (palm-fringed, near marina) and *Chino* (in Nayarit state: popular with picnickers). S of the river are

Playa del Sol (or *de los Muertos*: popular), *Las Amapas* and *Conchas Chinas* (below the cliffs), *Las Estacas, Punta Negra, Palo María* and *Gemelas* (all with pretty little creeks), *Mismaloya* (12 km (7 miles) S: Los Arcos rock formations, canoe trips to nearby lagoon, good diving area) and *Yelapa ("place of meeting"), in a beautiful setting, with a fresh-water lagoon, a waterfall and a good diving area.

SURROUNDINGS. – 15 km (9 miles) N of Puerto Vallarta on Road 200 lies the vacation center of *Nuevo Vallarta* (Nayarit) which is in course of development and farther on the fishing village of *Bucerías*. Continuing along the Carretera one reaches, on the far side of Punta Raza, the resorts of La Peñita de Jaltemba and Rincón de Guayabitos (see surroundings of Tepic, p. 262).

Querétaro (State)

State of Querétaro (Qro.). – Capital: Querétaro.
Area: 11,769 sq. km (4544 sq. miles).
Population: 844,000.
ⓘ **Coordinación Federal de Turismo,**
Puente de Alvarado 102–4,
Col. Carretas,
Querétaro, Qro.;
tel. (9 14 63) 4 32 73.

The state of Querétaro, lying almost exactly in the center of Mexico, shares with Guanajuato state the fertile plateau known as the Bajío, the country's granary, which lies at an altitude of between 1500 and

2000 m (5000 and 6500 ft) between the Eastern and Western Siera Madre. Querétaro is bounded on the S by México state and Michoacán, on the W by Guanajuato, on the N by San Luis Potosí and on the E by Hidalgo. It is made up of a hilly region rich in minerals, and the plains and valleys in which agriculture flourishes. The highest point in the state is the Cerro El Gallo (3350 m – 10,990 ft). The population consists of Mestizos, Otomí Indians and Creoles (descendants of Spaniards).

HISTORY. – The area now occupied by the state of Querétaro (Tarascan, "place of the ball game") was held by Otomí Indians until the middle of the 15th c., when it came under the control of the Aztecs. Evidence of the pre-Columbian cultures of this region has been yielded by the sites of Las Ranas, Toluquilla, Neblinas, El Lobo and Villa Corregidora. – The *Spaniards* first appeared in the area in 1532, and had settled within the next twenty-five years. During the colonial period and after Mexico became independent the history of the state was primarily tied to the development of its capital.

ECONOMY. – *Agriculture* (maize, clover, vegetables, fruit) and *livestock-farming* play a major part in the economy of Querétaro. The principal *minerals* are mercury and opals, together with silver, lead and copper. In recent years a variety of *industries* (agricultural machinery, motor vehicles, etc.) have been established around the capital.

Querétaro, like Hidalgo, Guanajuato, San Luis Potosí, northern Veracruz, northwestern Puebla, Tlaxcala and México state, is occupied by **Otomí** Indians, a widely distributed people numbering about 300,000 who speak a language of their own. Little is known about their origins, but it is thought that they were originally more closely concentrated in the central highlands and were driven back into the surrounding regions between the 8th and 9th c. Then, in the 14th and 15th c., they were conquered by the Aztecs (Mexica) and thrust back into even more inaccessible territories. During the Conquest they generally sided with the Spaniards against their Aztec oppressors.

The religion of the Otomí is a mingling of Catholic and ancient Indian practices. They perform sacrifices primarily to the earth goddess and are afraid that the souls of the dead may return to torment them. – Although the Otomí now for the most part dress in the same way as other country folk, the women sometimes wear traditional costume embroidered in bright colors. They produce a variety of artistic craft articles, including basketwork, pottery, woollens and furniture.

Querétaro (Town)

State: Querétaro (Qro.).
Altitude: 1836 m (6024 ft). – Population: 428,000.
Telephone dialing code: 9 14 63.
ⓘ **Coordinación Federal de Turismo,**
Puente de Alvarado 102–4,
Col. Carretas;
tel. 4 32 73.

HOTELS. – IN THE TOWN: *Real de Minas*, Av. Constituyentes 124, I, SP; *De Querétaro*, extension of Corregidora Sur 42, II; *Casablanca*, Contituyentes 69, II; *Del Marques*, Juárez Nte. 104, II; *Hidalgo*, Madero 11 Pte. III; *Mesón de Santa Rosa*, Pasteur Sur 17. – OUTSIDE THE TOWN: *Holiday Inn*, Carr. Constitución 13 Sur, I, SP; *Hacienda Jurica*, 229 km mark on road to San Luis Potosí, I, SP, tennis, riding, golf; *Motel Azteca*, 236 km mark on road to San Luis Potosi, II.

RESTAURANTS in most hotels; also *Fonda del Refugio*, Jardín Corregidora 26; *Polainas*, Plaza Corregidora y Andador 16 de Septiembre 13; *El Museu*, extension of Corregidora Sur 25; *Los Gauchos*, Av. Constituyentes 155 Pte.; *Disquemar*, 20 de Noviembre y Constituyentes Ote.

RECREATION and SPORTS. – Swimming, tennis, golf, fishing, riding.

EVENTS. – Fiesta on September 14; daily market.

Querétaro, capital of the state of the same name, lies amid rounded hills in a valley in the Mexican highlands, at the foot of the Cerro de las Campanas. It is notable for its *colonial architecture, and although there has been a considerable development of industry around the city in recent years, the old town has preserved much of the more tranquil atmosphere of the past.

HISTORY. – The town was founded by Otomí Indians long before the coming of the Spaniards, and was incorporated in the Aztec empire in the mid 15th c. The *Spaniards* gained control of the area between 1532 and 1550 and made the town a supply base for the rich mines in Guanajuato and Zacatecas. In 1699 Querétaro was raised to the status of a city and later was at the center of great historical events, to an extent equalled by few other towns in Mexico. It played a part in the early stages of the movement for Mexican independence led by Miguel Hidalgo (1810); the treaty of Guadalupe Hidalgo which ended the war with the United States was signed here in 1848; the last battle between the troops of President Benito Juárez and the Emperor Maximilian was fought at Querétaro in 1867, and Maximilian and two of his generals, Miramón and Mejía, were shot on the Cerro de las Campanas on June 19 in that year; and the Mexican constitution which is still in force was drafted at Querétaro in 1917.

SIGHTS. – Querétaro is renowned for its handsome colonial houses, churches and squares and for its beautiful parks,

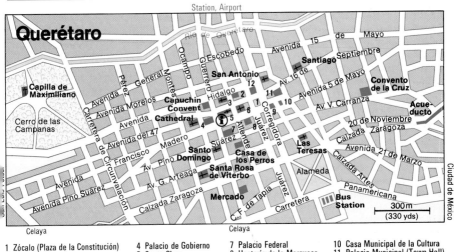

Querétaro

1 Zócalo (Plaza de la Constitución)
2 Casa del Marqués
3 El Carmen
4 Palacio de Gobierno
5 Santa Clara
6 San José de Gracia
7 Palacio Federal
8 Hostería de la Marquesa
9 Museo Regional
10 Casa Municipal de la Cultura
11 Palacio Municipal (Town Hall)
12 Teatro de la República

gardens and fountains. – A notable landmark is the impressive **aqueduct**, still functioning, which was constructed between 1726 and 1738 by the Marqués de la Villa del Villar del Aguilar. It has a total length of almost 9 km (6 miles), with 74 arches up to 29 m (95 ft) high.

To the S of the main square, the Plaza de la Constitución, is the **Convent of San Antonio**, founded in the mid 16th c. The church was rebuilt a hundred years later and the convent itself soon afterward. It now houses the interesting *Regional Museum* (Museo Regional), with works by the leading painters of the colonial period (17th–19th c.) and a collection of historical weapons, documents and other items.

Near the Museum, in Avenida 5 de Mayo, stands the **Town Hall** (*Palacio Municipal* or *Casa de la Corregidora*), a handsome 18th c. building with wrought-rion balconies. Here Josefa Ortiz de Domínguez warned those involved in the independence movement of the discovery of their plans (1810), which led to the premature outbreak of the war of independence. – To the S is the **Casa Municipal de la Cultura** (*Casa de Ecala*), another handsome building with wrought-iron balconies and sculptured decoration.

To the E, along Avenida Venustiano Carranza, is the *Convento de la Cruz* (Convent of the Cross), originally founded in the 16th c. but replaced a hundred years later by a Baroque building. The Emperor Maximilian had his headquarters here in 1867, and was confined in the convent for a time after being taken prisoner. In the convent garden is a curious species of tree, the needles of which grow in the form of a cross. – Opposite the convent is the *Capilla del Calvario*, built in the middle of the 17th c., on the spot where the Spaniards are said to have celebrated their first mass after taking the town in 1532.

From the Plaza de la Constitución the Avenida Francisco Madero runs SW, passing on the left the *Hostería de la Marquesa* (mid 18th c.) and on the right the *church of San José de Gracia* (late 17th c.). In a small garden at the corner of Avenida Madero and Calle Allende is the neo-classical **Neptune Fountain** (*Fuente de Neptuno*), by Francisco Eduardo Tresguerras (1797). – The adjoining **church of Santa Clara**, once belonging to a large convent, has a plain 17th c. façade.

In contrast to this unadorned exterior, the *INTERIOR of the church is an exceptionally fine example of the Churrigueresque style of the 18th c., with richly carved and gilded *retablos* bearing figures of apostles, saints and cherubim, flowers and a variety of other decoration. Particularly notable is the intricately carved wooden *choir screen*, with the figure of Christ in the middle and painted draperies on either side. Note also the fine wrought-iron *grille* above the sacristy doorway.

A short distance W, in Calle Guerrero, is the neo-classical *Palacio de Gobierno*. To the S along Calle Guerrero is the **Palacio Federal**, one of the finest buildings in Querétaro, originally an Augustinian convent dating from the first half of the 18th c. and attributed to Ignacio Mariano de las Casas. Its most notable features are the tripartite Baroque façade with niches containing statues and the magnificently carved arches and pillars of the *cloister. – Obliquely opposite, on the S side of Avenida Pino Suárez, are the plain façade of the late 17th c. *church of Santo Domingo* and the handsome Baroque front of the **Chapel of the Rosary** (by Mariano de las Casas, 1760).

Around the corner, in Calle Allende Sur, is the **House of the Dogs** (*Casa de los Perros*), once the residence of Mariano de las Casas. This little 18th c. palace takes its name from the gargoyles in the form of dogs on the outer wall and in the beautiful patio, which has an unusual fountain.

Turning right at the next corner into the Avenida General de Arteaga and continuing SW to Calle Ezequiel Montes, we come to the *church of Santa Rosa de Viterbo, one of the most interesting churches in the town. Also designed by Ignacio Mariano de las Casas, it was completed in 1752 but was later altered by Tresguerras. The most striking feature of the exterior is the pair of flying buttresses in the form of heavy volutes borne on square pillars.

The INTERIOR is notable for its richly carved Churrigueresque *retablos* and for a number of fine paintings of the colonial period. As in so many churches belonging to nunneries, there is a fine wrought-iron *choir screen*, behind which the nuns could participate in the mass. Other noteworthy features are the superbly carved *confessional*, the High Baroque *organ* and the life-size figures of the apostles at the Last Supper in the *sacristy*. Behind the Last Supper, covering the whole wall, is a painting by Tresguerras depicting St Rose of Viterbo surrounded by her nuns.

Other fine buildings in Querétaro include the *Cathedral* of San Felipe Neri (18th c.); the *churches* of *El Carmen* (17th and

Church of Santa Rosa, Querétaro

18th c.), *San Antonio* (17th and 18th c.) and *Santiago* (18th c.: cloister with arcading and neo-Mudéjar doorways); the *Capuchin Convent* (early 18th c.), in which the Emperor Maximilian was confined before his execution; the *Teatro de la República* (mid 19th c.), in which Maximilian and his two generals were tried and condemned to death; and the *Casa del Marqués* (first half of the 18th c.; patio with neo-Mudéjar features).

On the **Cerro de las Campanas** ("Hill of the Bells"), on the W side of the town, is the *Capilla de Maximiliano* (1901), built by the Emperor Franz Josef of Austria in memory of his brother, Maximilian, who was executed on this spot. Above the chapel towers a colossal *statue of Benito Juárez*, Maximilian's victorious opponent.

Around Querétaro is a productive opal-mining area, and these and other semi-precious stones including topaz, aqua marine and amethyst are cut and set in the town and can be purchased in speciality shops.

SURROUNDINGS. – 55 km (34 miles) SE (expressway) is the town of **San Juan del Río**, a center of basketwork and furniture making (alt. 1980 m (6498 ft.); pop. 40,000; hotels: *La Mansión, 172 km mark on road to México-Queretaro, I, SP, tennis, golf, riding; *La Mansión Galindo, 5 km (3 miles) in the direction of Amealco, L, SP, tennis, golf; Juárez, Av. Juárez Oriente 20, II; Villa de los Reyes, Av. Juárez Poniente 9, II; restaurants: La Balbaína, O'Punte, Ehlers), 26 km (16 miles) NE of San Juan del Río, on Road 120, is the charming spa of **Tequisquiapan** (alt. 1740 m (5740 ft.); pop. 15,000; hotels: El Relox, SP; Casablanca de Tequisquiapan, SP; La Plaza, Maridelfi, SP; Las Cavas, SP; restaurants: Las Brasas, Macondo, Lonchería Don Carlos), which attracts many visitors, particularly from Mexico City, with its thermal baths (radioactive water) and the facilities it offers for riding and fishing. 17 km (11 miles) N of Tequisquiapan on Road 120 a turning to the left in *Ezequiel Montes* leads to Bernal (about 17 km – 11 miles). The people living in this village, situated on a striking hill shaped like a hat, are noted for the production of heavy woolen *sarapes* and for their unusual dances. Returning to Road 120 and continuing N one reaches in 12 km (7 miles) **Cadereyta**, once a mining town but now noted for a large *cactus farm, Quinta Federico Schmoll, which ships cacti all over the world.

Some 30 km (19 miles) N of Cadereyta a good but winding road comes in 32 km (20 miles) to *San Joaquín* (alt. 2550 m – 8369 ft.), from where one can walk to the archeological sites of *Toluquilla* and *Las Ranas*. On return the main road can be followed through a magnificent scenic landscape over the watershed for 106 km (66 miles) to *Jalpan* (alt. 770 m (2527 ft,) pop. 500). Situated on the edge of the Sierra Gorda in an area devoted to coffee and sugar beet cultivation, Jalpan has a beautiful and interesting church, dedicated to St. James, which was built between 1751 and 1758. The man responsible for the building of this church with its magnificent *Baroque

Mexico
United Mexican States
Estados Unidos Mexicanos

Quintana Roo

States
Estados

1a Baja California Sur	12 Aguascalientes	
1b Baja California Norte	13 Jalisco	
	14 Guanajuato	
2 Sonora	15 Querétaro	
3 Chihuahua	16 Hidalgo	
4 Sinaloa	17 Colima	
5 Durango	18 Michoacán	
6 Coahuila	19 México	
7 Nuevo León	20 Morelos	
8 Zacatecas	21 Tlaxcala	26 Chiapas
9 San Luis Potosí	22 Puebla	27 Tabasco
10 Tamaulipas	23 Veracruz	28 Campeche
11 Nayarit	24 Guerrero	29 Yucatán
	25 Oaxaca	30 Quintana Roo

D.F. Distrito Federal (Federal District)

façade, and for missionary work among the Indians of the region was the celebrated Franciscan Junípero Serra. Brother Junípero later went to California where he founded missions, out of which grew towns such as Los Angeles and San Francisco. Father Serra and his padres also founded four other missions in the neighborhood of Jalpan: Concá (38 km – 24 miles), Landa (22 km – 13 miles), Tilaco (49 km – 31 miles) and Tancoyol (60 km – 37 miles). All these *four mission churches are definitely worthwhile seeing as their Indian style baroque façades have been recently restored.

84 km (52 miles) N of Jalpan is the town of Xilitla in the state of San Luis Potosí. 4 km (2½ miles) after leaving Xilitla on the road to Ciudad Valles, a dirt road on the left leads to the rancho La Conchita. Here you can explore the never finished jungle castle of Edward James. The recently deceased English millionaire constructed his bizarre surrealistic home into an area of fabulous tropic vegetation.

Quintana Roo

State of Quintana Roo (Q.R.). – Capital: Chetumal.
Area: 50,350 sq. km (19,440 sq. miles).
Population: 298,900.
(i) **Coordinación Federal de Turismo,**
  Av. Tulúm 81, Edif. FIRA,
  Cancún Q.R.;
  tel. (9 19 88) 4 32 38.

The state of Quintana Roo occupies the eastern and southern part of the Yucatán peninsula, bounded on the W by the states of Campeche and Yucatán and on the S by Belize (formerly British Honduras) and Guatemala. It is predominantly flat, covered with tropical forest and savanna and fringed by a long coastline on the Caribbean with magnificent *beaches, lagoons, coral reefs and islands. The climate is hot and humid. Along the coast and in the interior are numerous pre-Columbian sites, only a fraction of which have been excavated or even investigated. The population of the state consists mainly of Maya Indians.**

Among the principal Maya sites in Quintana Roo are ***Tulum, *Cobá, *Xel-há** and ***Kohunlich** (see the entries for these places), *El Rey,* ***Xcaret** (p. 75), *Tancah* (p. 292) and *Chunyaxché.*

COMMUNICATIONS. – In addition to regular *air services* to the Isla Mujeres, Cancún, Cozumel and Chetumal an excellent network of *roads* has been developed in recent years. From Mérida, Road 180 runs via Chichén Itzá and Valladolid to Puerto Juárez and Punta Sam (ferries to Isla Mujeres) and on to Cancún, from which the new coast road (No. 307) runs S via Puerto Morelos (ferry to Cozumel), Playa del Carmen (ferry to Cozumel) and Akumal to Tulum. It then turns inland and continues via the road junction to Felipe Carillo Puerto and Bacalar to Chetumal. From Tulum there is now a good road to the Maya site of Cobá, from which there is a connecting road to Nuevo X-can, 70 km (44 miles) E of Valladolid on Road 180. Road 295 provides a direct link between Valladolid and Felipe Carillo Puerto. There is also the southern route (Road 184) from Mérida via Muna and Oxkutzcab to Felipe Carillo Puerto, continuing S to Chetumal or turning N to Tulum. From Chetumal there is a road to Belize City, the largest town in Belize (formerly British Honduras). Chetumal is also the

Maya ruins on the coast of Quintana Roo

starting point of Road 186, which runs W across the southern part of the Yucatán peninsula to the road junction at Francisco Escárcega (Campeche state), from which there are roads S to Pelanque and Villahermosa and N to Champotón and Campeche.

HISTORY. – Archeological evidence indicates that the area of the present state of Quintana Roo was densely populated during the Maya *Classic period* (A.D. 300–900) and also to some extent in the *Post Classic period* (900–1450). – The *Spaniards* at first established themselves only at certain points on the coast, where they built forts to provide defense against constant raids by Indians and pirates, the greater part of the territory remaining in the hands of the **Mayas**. The first real Spanish settlement was established at Salamanca Becalar in 1544, but this was destroyed by pirates in 1652. A later settlement at Bacalar emained important as a stronghold and trading station until the middle of the 19th c., but this, too, was destroyed in 1858, during the "Caste War" by rebellious Mayas, who found support in the colony of British Honduras. The Maya rebellion was not quelled until 1901. A penal settlement for criminals and political prisoners was then established in Quintana Roo. In 1902 the territory of that name (after the 19th c. Mexican poet and leader of the independence movement, Andrés Quintana Roo) was formed from parts of Campeche and Yucatán states, and in 1974 Quintana Roo became the thirtieth state of the United Mexican States.

ECONOMY. – Until recently the economy of Quintana Roo, isolated as it was from the center of the country, depended mainly on the exploitation of its natural resources – *hardwoods, chichle, sisal* and *coconuts* – and on *fishing*. Today, with the development of the road system, the creation of a modern infrastructure (hotels, etc.) and the establishment of free trade zones, *tourism* is becoming increasingly important.

Salamanca

State: Guanajuato (Gto.).
Altitude: 1760 m (5775 ft).
Population: 123,000.
Telephone dialing code: 9 14 64.
ⓘ **Coordinación Federal de Turismo,**
Galarza 90,
Guanajuato, Gto.;
tel. (9 14 73) 2 01 23, 2 02 14, 2 02 44.

HOTELS. – *El Monte*, Juárez y E. Estévez, II; *Trevi*, Av. Hidalgo 221, II; *María Teresa*, Juárez y V. de Quiroga, II; *Posada Hidalgo*, extension of Hidalgo 1004.

RESTAURANTS in most hotels; also *El Cascabel*, 5 km mark on Irapuato road; *Camino Real*, Morelos 203; *La Fonda*, Guerrero 402.

RECREATION and SPORTS. – Swimming, tennis, riding.

The town of Salamanca lies on the N bank of the Río Lerma in the middle of the Bajío, a fertile plateau which extends over a large area in the states of Guanajuato and Querétaro. Although mainly known for its large oil refinery, it also possesses one of the most richly decorated churches in Mexico.

HISTORY. – In pre-Hispanic times, the site of the present town was occupied by the Otomí settlement of *Xidoo*, which after the coming of the Spaniards was renamed *Salamanca* by the brothers Juan and Sancho Barahoma, owners of a hacienda in the area. The official date of foundation of the town was 1603. During the 17th and 18th c. there was much building activity by the Church here. Like other places in central Mexico, the town was involved in the war of Mexican independence (1810–21). The revolutionary wars of the 20th c. and the epidemics which followed them set back the development of the region, but the last 40 years or so have seen great strides in agriculture and industry.

SIGHTS. – The most splendid monument of the colonial period in Salamanca is the **church of San Agustín** (begun 1615). It is a high and relatively narrow building, inconspicuously situated, with a plain façade. The entrance is flanked by severely unadorned columns with spiral fluting. An unusual feature is the placing of the crucifix on the highest point of the façade, under a conch.

The *INTERIOR of the church is almost completely covered with painted and gilded panelling. The decoration of the dome, in carved and gilded wood, and the wooden choir rails show strong Moorish

(Mudéjar) influence. One of the side altars, the *altar of San Nicholás de Tolentino*, is elaborately decorated with scenes from the life of this 14th c. friar against a net-like ground and shows consummate artistic skill. The high altar was replaced in 1832 by an uninteresting work in neo-classical style. Fortunately, however, two fine *side altars* dedicated to St Joseph and St Anne were preserved – magnificent examples of the Churrigueresque style, which in contrast to the rather flat modelling of the altars in the nave achieve a highly realistic rendering of the almost life-size figures of saints.

Also of interest is the old **parish church of San Bártolo**, with a "rustic" style Baroque façade. The *estípites* (pyramidal pilasters with the pointed ends downward), characteristic of the Churrigueresque style, are accompanied by sculpture by local artists using old Indian motifs such as the snake.

SURROUNDINGS. – Some 20 km (12 miles) NW is **Irapuato** (alt. 1795 m (5890 ft); pop. 215,000.; hotels: Flamingo, Blvd. Díaz Ordaz 72, I, SP; Real de Minas, Portal Carillo Puerto 1, II; Motel Florida, Av. Guerrero y Cedreo, II; Versalles, Pípila 16, II; Colonial, Cortázar 99, III; restaurants in most hotels; also El Cascabel, Blvd. Díaz Ordaz; El Rancho, Guerrero 1812; Rincón Gaucho, Blvd. Díaz Ordaz y Lagos; fiesta February 15, anniversary of town's foundation; April 2, Strawberry Fair market on Tuesday and Sunday). This rapidly growing town is, above all, the center of probably the largest strawberry growing area in the world. It has a number of interesting buildings, including the attractive neo-classical Town Hall (Palacio Municipal), the early 18th c. church of El Hospital (Churrigueresque façade) and the mid-18th c. parish church (richly decorated doorway). In the church of San Francisco are two notable pictures, Miguel Cabrera's "Virgin of Guadalupe" and the "Virgin of the Apocalypse" by Francisco Eduardo Tresguerras.

Saltillo
See under Coahuila de Zaragoza

San Blas
See under Tepic

San Cristóbel de Las Casas

State: Chiapas (Chis.).
Altitude: 2200 m (7220 ft). – Population: 93,000.
Telephone dialling code: 9 19 67.

(i) **Coordinación Federal de Turismo,**
Av. Central Pte. 1454.
Colonia Moctezuma,
Tuxtla Gutiérrez, Chis.;
tel. (9 19 61) 2 45 45, 2 55 09.

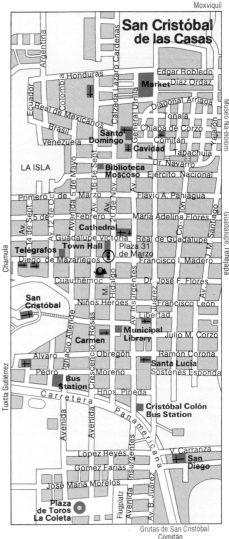

HOTELS. – *Posada Diego de Mazariegos*, Maria Adelina Flores 2, I; *Español*, 10 de Marzo 15, I; *Ciudad Real*, Plaza 31 de Marzo 10, II; *Na-Bolom*, Av. Vicente Guerrero 33, II, museum, library; *Santa Clara*, Av. Insurgentes 1, II; *Rincón del Arco*, Calle Ejército Nacional, II; *San Martín*, Calle Real de Guadalupe 16, III; *Posada de Abuelita*, Tapachula 18, III. – OUTSIDE THE TOWN: *Molino de la Arbolada*, Periférico Sur, I, horses available.

RESTAURANTS in most hotels; also *Olla Podrida*, Mazariegos 24; *Los Arcos*, Madero 6; *Casa Blanca*, Calle Real de Guadalupe; *La Galeria*, Dr Navarro 1.

RECREATION and SPORTS. – Swimming, riding, tennis, hunting.

EVENTS. – Fiestas: March 31, anniversary of town's foundation; July 17–25, San Cristóbal; December 10–12, Virgen de Guadalupe.

*San Cristóbal de Las Casas, the oldest Spanish settlement in Chiapas, lies in the Jovel valley surrounded by forest-clad hills, the

General view of San Cristóbal de las Casas

highest of which are Tzontehuitz (2858 m – 9380 ft) and Huetepec (2717 m – 8917 ft). Although it is a typical colonial town, with numerous churches and low houses with tiled roofs and wrought-iron window grilles, San Cristóbal is strongly marked by Indian influence. This gives the town a melancholy atmosphere of its own which lends it a particular fascination. The charm and interest to be found in San Cristóbal and the surrounding area make this one of the most attractive tourist centers in Mexico.

Until about ten years ago a remote and little-visited town, San Cristóbal has now developed a large tourist trade and has changed accordingly. The local shops and markets will tempt visitors with their displays of traditional costumes, leather goods, pottery and other craft products.

When visiting the Indian villages it should be remembered that many of the villagers dislike being photographed: visitors should therefore either refrain from taking photographs or seek permission to do so. – Many of the villages can be reached only in jeeps and similar vehicles suitable for cross-country travel. Apart from special festivals, markets are usually held on Sundays.

In spite of its southern latitude, San Cristóbal, lying as it does at a high altitude, has a very cool climate; this is particularly noticeable at sunset. It also has a fairly high rainfall, and there may be showers even during the dry season (November to May).

HISTORY. – The Maya settlement of *Huezecatlán* came under Aztec control at the end of the 15th c. The Spaniards had great difficulty in subduing the Maya tribes, and were able to make advances only after bitter fighting. In 1528 the conquistador, Diego de Mazagieros, founded the town of *Villa Real*, which was later renamed Cristóbal de Las Casas in honor of its patron saint, St Christopher, and the great patron of the Indians Bartolomé de las Casas, who was bishop of the town. Along with the rest of Chiapas, it was governed by the Spanish authorities in Guatemala until Mexico became independent. San Cristóbal was capital of Chiapas state until 1892, when it lost that status to Tuxtla Gutiérrez.

SIGHTS. – San Cristóbal has a large number of churches, although only a few of these are of real importance. In the

Church of Santo Domingo, San Cristóbal

Zócalo (Plaza 31 de Marzo) stands the **Cathedral**, begun in 1528 but much altered and redecorated in later periods. It contains a number of Baroque altars, pictures and sculpture of the 17th–19th c. and some fine woodcarving (e.g., the pulpit). – Adjoining the Cathedral is the *parish church of San Nicolás* (built 1613–20, restored 1815).

From the Zócalo, the Avenida General Utrilla runs N to the finest of San Cristóbal's religious buildings, the *****church of Santo Domingo**, built between 1547 and 1560 by Bishop Francisco de Marroquín of Guatemala. The present façade (17th c.), a typical example of Mexican Baroque, is, in terms of surface area, one of the largest in Mexico. Above the central doorway, with its grille and on either side, is the Habsburg double-headed eagle, the heraldic emblem of the Emperor Charles V.

The interior, overcharged with decoration, contains a number of pieces of sculpture and gilded wooden altars. The 19th c. pulpit, the base of which is made from a single piece of wood, is particularly ornate, ranking as one of the most remarkable examples of Baroque in the western hemisphere. – Adjoining the church is the *convent* to which it belonged, built at the same time. After being used during the 19th c. as a prison, it is now a cultural center.

Other churches worth seeing are the *Caridad, Merced, San Francisco, Carmen* (with the Arco del Carmen), *Guadalupe* and *San Cristóbal* (on the hill of the same name to the W of the town, with a magnificent *****view). – Near the church of Santo Domingo is the *****Market** (*Mercado*), where Indians from the mountain villages gather every day except Sunday.

With the building of a modern market hall some years ago, this lively and colorful market lost much of its character. Here can be seen primarily members of the two Maya peoples, the Tzotzil (about 110,000 representatives – Chamula, Zinacantán, Larrainzar. Huixtán and Chenel-hó) and the Tzeltal (about 100,000 – Tenajapa, Carranza, Amatenango del Valle, Oxchuc and Cancuc, wearing costumes which differ from village to village. The most easily recognizable are the Chamula and the villagers of Tenejapa and Zinacantán (see below under *Surroundings*).

Visitors to San Cristóbal should also visit the archeological and ethnological *****museum** and *library* in the *Na-Bolom* ("House of the Jaguar") guest-house. Both were founded by the Danish archeologist Frans Blom (d. 1963) and are devoted to the Indians of Chiapas and their culture. This very interesting establishment has been run since her husband's death by Mrs Gertrude Duby-Blom, a photographer as well as a student of the Indians. Also worth seeing is the home of Sergio Castro, 16 de Septiembre 32, which contains a notable private collection of Indian costumes.

SURROUNDINGS. – 10 km (6 miles) from San Cristóbal on the Comitán road, a short distance off the road to the right, are the **San Cristóbal Caves** (*Grutas de San Cristóbal*). The part open to visitors is only a very small section of this extensive complex of stalactic caves. – A few miles farther on, a road branches off on the left to *Ocosingo* (90 km – 55 miles) and **Palenque** (200 km (125 miles): see p. 213). Some 20 km (12 miles) along this road is *****Huixtán**, a village of the Tzotzil Indians. Here as in other mountain villages, following an ancient Maya tradition (compare the ceremonial centers), most of the population live, not in the village, but in the surrounding hills: in the village itself there are only the church, the village administrative office and a few shops.

Most of the men still wear their traditional wide white cotton trousers, held up by a broad red sash, and a white shirt, usually embroidered on the neck and arms. Over this is worn a black or brown woollen cloak. Their flat hats, locally made, are decorated with a red ribbon. – The women wear long dark-colored skirts with red belts, yellow-striped, cotton blouses with blue at the neck and white kerchiefs embroidered in colorful animal and flower patterns.

Of the 12,000 or so Huixtecos belonging to the Tzotzil tribe only about 10% live in the village of Huixtán. – Fiestas: May 14–16, San Isidro; June 27–30, San Pedro; September 28–29, San Miguel Arcángel.

50 km (30 miles) farther on is **Ocosingo**, a little town in the territory of the Tzeltal Indians which until recently was completely isolated. It is still of some importance as a center for the Indians of the surrounding area who live by tree-felling, gathering chicle and hunting. In the beautiful country around Ocosingo, some of it difficult to reach, there are various unspoiled Indian villages and haciendas (El Real, Australia, etc.) and the picturesquely situated village of *Alamirano*. 14 km (9 miles) NE of Ocosingo can be found the interesting archeological site of *****Toniná**. This Classic Maya site had its heyday in the 8th and 9th centuries. A considerable number of stelae, dated to between A.D. 495 and 909 were found here. The latter date is the latest ever found on a stela in Mesoamerica. In addition to two ball-game courts there can be seen circular calendar stones and more especially sculptures of headless humans. The site, extending altogether over seven terraces, includes an underground chamber with typical corbelled arches and a wooden lintel, as well as stone masks and stucco figures of – presumably – prisoners. The adjoining museum should on no account be missed.

Main square, Comitán

28 km (17 miles) NE of San Cristóbal is the Indian village of *Tenejapa, inhabited by only a few hundred of the 15,000 or so Tzeltal-speaking Indians who live in this area.

The men's costume consists of a black woolen tunic, short white trousers with embroidery on the legs and a pointed straw hat with broad colored ribbons. The women, who are noted for their skill in weaving and embroidery, wear richly embroidered blouses and dark blue skirts with narrow vertical stripes, a broad belt striped red and black and, over this, a narrow white belt. – Fiestas: January 23, San Ildefonso; July 24, Santiago Apóstol.

12 km (7 miles) W of San Cristóbal is *Zinacantán, a village of a few hundred inhabitants which serves as the religious and political center of the 14,000 Tzotzil-speaking Zinacantecos who live in the area.

The men wear a gray checked sash over short white trousers and a flat straw hat decorated with many-colored ribbons. The way in which the ribbons are worn (tied or untied) indicates whether a man is married or not. Fiestas: January 18, San Sebastián; August 8–11, San Lorenzo.

11 km (7 miles) NW of San Cristóbal is *San Juan Chamula, ceremonial center of the Chamula Indians, by far the largest Tzotzil-speaking group. Most of the Chamulas, who number over 40,000, live in small settlements scattered about the surrounding area. As in many Maya mountain villages, visitors will see three

large crosses, symbolizing the tree of life, in the village and on the hills.

The Chamula men wear white cotton shirts and trousers and white woollen cloaks, often with an orange-colored leather belt. On special feast days they wear straw hats with colored ribbons hanging behind. Men holding official posts in the community wear black cloaks. The women wear black wrap-around skirts reaching to mid-calf with sashes striped orange, red and green. Their blouses were formerly white, but they now prefer blue cotton or dark wool. – Fiestas: Carnival; Holy Week (Semana Santa); May 3, Santa Cruz; June 22–25, San Juan Bautista; August 30, Santa Rosa.

Other villages, less well known but equally interesting, particularly during their fiestas, are San Andrés Larrainzar, San Pedro Chenal-hó and Amatengo del Valle.

87 km (54 miles) SE of San Cristóbal, on Road 190 (the Panamerican Highway), is Comitán (alt. 1630 m (5350 ft); pop. 49,000; hotels: Robert's, Delfín, Lagos de Montebello, Internacional), a pleasant little colonial town in a garden-like setting (orchid growing), with a small museum in the Casa de la Cultura. – 16 km (10 miles) beyond this, on Road 190, a road goes off on the left to the *Lagunas de Montebello (p. 193), 40 km (25 miles) E. – 80 km (50 miles) from Comitán, on Road 190, is Ciudad Cuauhtémoc, on the Guatemalan border. The stretch of country before the border, which has beautiful scenery, a pleasant climate, many lakes and a variety of Maya remains, is to be developed as a new tourist area.

San Cristóbal de Las Casas is also a good base for trips by air-taxi to the Maya sites of **Palenque (p. 213), *Bonampak (p. 82) and *Yaxchilán (p. 296) in the rain forest of the Selva Lacandona, the Lacandón settlements of Lacan-há and Na-há and the waterfalls of *El Jabalí on the Río Santo Domingo and Río Dolores.

San Juan Chamula

Mexico
United Mexican States
Estados Unidos Mexicanos

San Luis Potosí

States
Estados

1a Baja California Sur	12 Aguascalientes	
1b Baja California Norte	13 Jalisco	
	14 Guanajuato	
2 Sonora	15 Querétaro	
3 Chihuahua	16 Hidalgo	
4 Sinaloa	17 Colima	
5 Durango	18 Michoacán	
6 Coahuila	19 México	
7 Nuevo León	20 Morelos	
8 Zacatecas	21 Tlaxcala	26 Chiapas
9 San Luis Potosí	22 Puebla	27 Tabasco
10 Tamaulipas	23 Veracruz	28 Campeche
11 Nayarit	24 Guerrero	29 Yucatán
	25 Oaxaca	30 Quintana Roo

D.F. Distrito Federal (Federal District)

San Luis Potosí (State)

State of San Luis Potosí (S.L.P.).
Capital: San Luis Potosí.
Area: 63,231 sq. km (24,414 sq. miles).
Population: 1,869,300.
(i) **Coordinación Federal de Turismo,**
Jardín Guerrero 14,
San Luis Potosí, S.L.P.;
tel. (9 14 81) 4 09 06.

The centrally located state of San Luis Potosí is bounded by the states of Zacatecas, Nuevo León, Tamaulipas, Veracruz, Hidalgo, Querétaro and Guanajuato. The mountainous eastern part of the state is crossed by the Sierra Madre Oriental, while the central and western areas are an arid plateau. The population consists mainly of Creoles (descendants of Spaniards), Mestizos and Otomí, Nahua, Huastec and Pame Indians.

Among the most important archeological sites in the state are *El Tamuín* and *El Ebano* (see under Tampico).

HISTORY. – In pre-Columbian times the dominant culture in the eastern part of the area was that of the Huastecs, who became tributary to the Aztecs in the second half of the 15th c. The rest of the state was inhabited by semi-nomadic tribes such as the Cuachichiles, Pames, Guamares, Copuces, Nahuas and Otomí, only a few of which have survived. – The *Spaniards* under Cortés reached the eastern part of the

state in 1522, but the region's considerable resources of precious metals were not discovered and exploited until seventy years later with the help of Tlaxcalans brought in for the purpose. During the war of independence (1810–21), a number of local men played leading parts. The state of San Luis Potosí was established in 1824, when the old Spanish government structure was abolished.

ECONOMY. – The state is rich in *salt* and *minerals*, particularly gold, silver, copper, lead, mercury and zinc. *Livestock-farming* plays an important part in the economy, as does *agriculture* in the tropical lowlands and irrigated areas (sugar-cane, coffee, tobacco, wheat, maize, beans and cotton). The states' *industries*, mainly centered in the capital, include tanning, metal founding, milling, brewing, textiles and furniture manufacture.

In addition to the capital, *San Luis Potosí* (see below), and its surroundings, the archeological sites and *Tamazunchale* (p. 252), the following places in the state are worth a mention:

Matehuala ("place of the green water": alt. 1614 m (5296 ft); pop. 59,000; hotels: Las Palmas Holiday Inn, El Pedregal, Motel El Dorado; fiestas: January 6, Fiesta del Cristo de Matehuala; June 13, Día de San Antonio). Although there is little to see in the town itself, it makes a convenient overnight stop.

Some 30 km (20 miles) NW of Matehuala, reached by way of a hilly road and a tunnel 2·5 km (1½ miles) long, is the remarkable ghost town of *Real de Catorce* (Hotel El Real). The name is said to commemorate

The ghost town of Real de Catorce

fourteen (*catorce*) Spanish soldiers who were killed by Indians here around 1700. This was an important mining town in its day, particularly at the end of the 19th c., when it had a population of 45,000 (only 700 today) and boasted a theater, a mint and an electric mine railway. A visit to the *Church of San Francisco*, which on October 4 every year is visited by thousands of pilgrims, is recommended. The pilgrims leave a considerable number of *votive tablets with expressions of gratitude for miracles which have occurred.

Around Real de Catorce grows the **peyotl cactus**, regarded by Indian peoples like the Huicholes and Tarahumara as a sacred plant, since they believe that in the hallucinated state induced by *mescalin* they receive messages from their gods. Since the peyotl does not grow in the regions where the Huicholes now live, they make a pilgrimage of up to 500 km (300 miles) to this area, which to them is the sacred land of Wirikuta. The pilgrimage involves elaborate ceremonies which end in the gathering of the cactus after it has been pierced by an arrow.

Ciudad Valles (see surroundings of Tampico, p. 252).

San Luis Potosí (Town)

State: San Luis Potosí (S.L.P.).
Altitude: 1877 m (6158 ft). Population: 665,000.
Telephone dialing code: 9 14 81.
ⓘ **Coordinación Federal de Turismo,**
    Jardin Guerrero 14;
    tel. 4 09 06.

HOTELS. – *Hostal del Quijote*, 3·5 km mark on road to Mexico City, L, SP; *Motel Cactus*, on road to Mexico City/Glorieta Juárez, I, SP; *Panorama*, Av. V. Carranza 315, I, SP; *Santa Fé*, on road to Mexico City/Glorieta Juárez, I, SP; *María Cristina*, J. Sarabia 110, II; *Filher*,

Av. Universidad 375, II; *Nacional*, M. J. Othón 425, III.

RESTAURANTS in most hotels; also *La Virreina*, Av. V. Carranza 830; *La Longa*, Aldama u Madero; *Villa Fontana*, 5 de Mayo 455; *Cazadores Potosinos*, Av. V. Carranza 700; *El Gaucho*, Vista Hermosa 116; *El Muelle 3*, Arista 1210.

RECREATION and SPORTS. – Swimming, fishing, tennis, golf, hunting.

EVENTS. – Fiestas: January 20, Día de San Sebastián; Easter Saturday, Procesión del Silencio; July 25, Día de Santiago Apóstol; August 25, Día de San Luis Rey; September 29, Día de San Miguel Arcángel; October 12, Día de la Virgen de los Remedios.

*San Luis Potosí, capital of the state of the same name, set on a steppe-like plateau, is an important traffic junction point and commercial center. In spite of increasing modernization, the town, with its handsome old buildings and beautiful parks, has preserved much of the character of the colonial period.

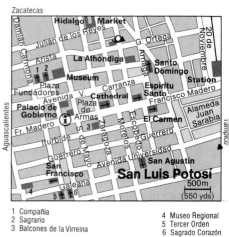

1 Compañía
2 Sagrario
3 Balcones de la Virreina
4 Museo Regional
5 Tercer Orden
6 Sagrado Corazón

HISTORY. – Little is known of the history of the place in the pre-Hispanic period. The site is believed to have been occupied by a settlement of the Cuachichil Indians named *Tanjamanja*. – The first Spaniards under the leadership of Miguel Caldera, soon followed by Franciscan friars, arrived in the area between 1585 and 1590. At this period, too, considerable quantities of silver and gold were discovered here and the town of *Real de Minas de San Luis Potosí* as founded, taking the latter part of its name from the Bolivian silver town of Potosí ("place of great riches" in Quechua). In 1658 the town received its municipal charter from Philip IV. Until 1824, San Luis Potosí was the chief town of a large *intendencia* which also included Texas. During the French intervention (1862–6) and for a short period thereafter, it was the seat of Benito Juárez's government after its expulsion from Mexico City.

SIGHTS. – In the center of the town is the *Plaza de Armas*, with the *Jardín Hidalgo*. On the W side of the square is the

Cathedral, San Luis Potosí

Government Palace (*Palacio de Gobierno*), a massive neo-classical building dating from the end of the 18th c.

On the E side of the square is the Baroque *Cathedral (1670–1740), preceded by an unusual hexagonal porch with niches containing statues of the twelve apostles.

The interior, overloaded with decoration, shows a mingling of various styles. – One block E is the 18th c. *church of El Carmen, with a façade which is a magnificent example of Mexican Baroque and a fine dome faced with colored azulejos. It has a Churrigueresque high altar and a side doorway with a very beautiful façade in Indian-Churrigueresque style.

In a former convent in Calle Galeana is the **Regional Museum** (*Museo Regional Potosino*), with archeological finds from the region (Huastecs, Totanacs, Aztecs) and ethnological material.

On the upper floor is the *Capilla de Aránzazu (early 18th c.), an outstanding example of the Churrigueresque architecture of New Spain. Note the carved *doors* of mesquite wood, the oversized *estípites* (pilasters with their pointed ends downward) carrying the vaulting, the *figure of Christ* in the porch (made from reeds coated with a resin mixture) and the *pictures* in the chapel and its annexes.

The 17th c. *Church of San Francisco* has a fine late Baroque façade with a particular Potosinic flavor. Opposite the Neo-Classic Teatro La Paz, dating from the end of the 19th c., stands the *National Museum of Masks* (*Museo Nacional de la Máscara*) which contains a formerly private collection of old and new masks from all regions of Mexico.

Other features of interest in the town are the *churches* of *San Agustín* (17th c., with a Baroque façade and neo-classical interior) and *Guadalupe* (18th c.); the *Alarcón Theater* (early 19th c.: neo-classical, by Eduardo F. Tresguerras) and The *House of Popular Art* (Casa de las Artesanías; articles for sale); the *House of Culture* (Casa de la Cultura); the *Hidalgo Market* (*rebozos, sarapes*, basketwork, pottery, etc.) and the *Museum of Bull-fighting* (Museo Taurino).

SURROUNDINGS. – 20 km (12 miles) E is the ghost town of **Cerro de San Pedro**. The gold and silver found here in the late 17th c. were the basis of the prosperity of San Luis Potosí.

Some 50 km (30 miles) S is **Santa María del Río**, an attractive little town renowned for its beautiful *rebozos*. – Near here are the spas (radioactive thermal springs) of *El Gogorrón, Ojo Caliente* and *Lourdes*.

San Miguel de Allende

State: Guanajuato (Gto.).
Altitude: 1910 m (6267 ft). – Population: 65,000.
Telephone dialing code: 9 14 65.
ⓘ **Coordinación Federal de Turismo,**
Galarza 90,
Guanajuato, Gto.;
tel. (9 14 73) 2 01 23, 2 02 14, 2 02 44.

Casa de Sierra Nevada, Hospicio 35, I; *Villa Santa Mónica*, Baeza 22, I, SP; *Hacienda de las Flores*, Hospicio 16, I, SP; *Villas El Molino*, Salida Real a Querétaro 1, I, SP; *Posada La Ermita*, Calle Pedro Vargas 64, I, SP; *Ranco El Atascadero*, extension of Santo Domingo, I, SP, tennis, riding; *Aristos Parador*, Calle Ancha de San Antonio 30, I, SP, tennis; *Misión de los Angeles*, 2 km mark on road to Celaya, I, SP; *Posada de la Aldea*, Ancha de San Antonio, I, SP; *Posada San Francisco*, Plaza Principal 2, II; *Villa Jacaranda*, Aldama 53, II, SP; *Posada de las Monjas*, Canal 37, II, *Mansión del Bosque*, Aldama 65, II; *Posada Carmina*, Cuna de Allende 7, II; *Sautto*, Hernández Macías 59, III; *Mesón de San Antonio*, Mesones 80, III; *Huéspedes Felíz*, Codo 30, III. – OUTSIDE THE TOWN: *Motel La Siesta*, 1 km mark on road to Celaya, II, SP; *Hacienda Taboada*, 8 km mark on road to Dolores Hidalgo, I, SP (thermal bath), riding.

RESTAURANTS in most hotels; also *El Circo*, Insurgentes 62; *Señor Plato*, Jesús 7; *La Princesa*, Recreo 5; *El Patio*, Correo 12; *Mama Mía*, Umarán 5; *El Carrusel*, Canal 15; *Pepe Pizza*, Hidalgo 15; *La Bugambilia*, Hidalgo 42.

RECREATION and SPORTS. – Swimming, riding (riding school), tennis, golf, fronton.

EVENTS. – Market on Sunday and Tuesday. – Fiestas: first Friday in March, Día del Señor de la Conquista; Palm Sunday (Domingo de Ramos); Good Friday (Viernes Santo); Corpus Christi (Jueves de Corpus); first Sunday after June 13, Día de San Antonio; September 16, Día de la Independencia; September

29 and following Saturday, Día de San Miguel Arcángel; December 16–25, Posadas de Navidad.

The town of **San Miguel de Allende, usually known simply as San Miguel Allende, lies on the slopes of a hill and in a beautiful valley. One of the few towns in Mexico to be designated as a national monument, it has been able to preserve almost intact its character as a colonial town.

General view of San Miguel de Allende

Although the façades presented to the street are often plain and unadorned, they conceal some very attractive houses with beautiful patios and gardens. The charm of the town and surrounding area and the agreeable climate have attracted many foreigners to San Miguel de Allende as either temporary or permanent residents. It has thus become a center of intellectual and artistic life, with a number of schools and colleges teaching painting, sculpture, music, literature and drama.

HISTORY. – In pre-Columbian times there were a number of Tarascan and Chichimec settlements in the area. Archeological remains of these settlements can be seen at the Hacienda Orduña and near Cañada de la Virgen. In 1542, Juan de San Miguel, a Franciscan friar renowned for his missionary activity in Michoacán, established an Indian mission here, naming it *San Miguel de los Chichimecas*. Soon afterward the population was increased by Indian settlers from Tlaxcala, who were exposed to frequent raids by warlike Chichimecs. In 1555 the village was raised to the status of a provincial town, soon to be renamed *San Miguel el Grande*. During the colonial period wealthy mineowners and landowners from Guanajuato and Zacatecas took up residence in the town, and some of the mansions they built are still among the town's principal architectural treasures. – Ignacio de Allende, born in San Miguel in 1779, was one of the leaders of the fight for Mexican independence which began in 1810. He was executed by the Spaniards in 1811, and in 1862 the town was named San Miguel de Allende in his honour. – In recent years, San Miguel has developed into an important cultural center without losing its traditional charm.

SIGHTS. – In the attractive main square, **El Jardín** or *Plaza de Allende*, is the town's principal landmark, the **Parroquia** (parish church), an unusual neo-Gothic structure built around 1880 in place of an earlier and more modest church. It was designed by an Indian architect, Ceferino Gutiérrez, on the model of certain European cathedrals. On the left in the Chapel of the Señor de la Conquista is the *Cristo de la Conquista*; this much revered 16th c. statue was made by Indians in Pátzcuaro out of a mixture composed of corn-stalk paste and a preparation of crushed orchid tubers. In this chapel, too, can be seen partly obliterated wall-paintings by Federico Cantú. The tombs in the spacious crypt include that of the former Mexican President, General Anastasio Bustamente (1770–1853). The *Camarín* behind the high altar in neo-classical style is the work of the all-purpose artist, Francisco Eduardo Tresguerras. – To the N of the parish church stands the 18th c. *church of San Rafael.* – At the SW corner of the square is a house with Baroque decoration, the birthplace of *Ignacio de Allende.*

At the NW corner of the square, in Calle Canal, is the imposing *Casa del Mayorazgo de Canal*, which mingles Baroque and neo-classical features and has an attractive inner courtyard. – On the N side of the square are the *Posada de San Francisco* and the **Town Hall** (*Palacio Municipal*), both handsome 18th c. colonial buildings.

One block W along Calle Canal we find the church and convent of **La Concepción**, begun in the middle of the 18th c. but not completed until the end of the 19th. The magnificent dodecagonal dome of the church, designed by Ceferino Gutiérrez, was completed in 1891. The church contains pictures attributed to Miguel Cabrera and Juan Rodríguez Juárez. The convent has a beautiful courtyard with fine old trees and two-story arcading. It now houses the *Centro Cultural Ignacio Ramírez* ("El Nigromante"), a state-run school belonging to the Instituto Nacional de Bellas Artes.

From the Convent of the Conception, Calle Hernández Macías runs S past a former prison and the headquarters of the Inquisition, standing opposite one another. Farther S, in the Calzada Ancha de San Antonio (on left), is a large and handsome 18th c. mansion which now houses the *Instituto Allende*, one of the town's two important art schools. To the E, beyond the Institute, is the *Parque Juárez*.

One block NE of the main square stands the late 18th c. **church of San Francisco**, with a fine Churrigueresque façade and a tall neo-classical tower. The interior, also neo-classical, is said to have been designed by Francisco Eduardo Tresguerras. In front of the church is a small park containing a monument to Columbus. On the W side is the *church of the Third Order*.

To the N, beyond Calle Mesones, is the early 18th c. **church**, the **Oratory of San Felipe Neri**, founded in 1712, which replaced the former Mestic ("Mulato") church, Ecce Homo. The façade of pink stone clearly reveals features of Indian style, especially in the five statues of saints in the niches. The church has a neo-classical altar with a number of pictures; in the S aisle is a painting of the Virgin of Guadalupe by Miguel Cabrera; the 33 scenes from the life of St Philip Neri are also attributed to Cabrera. – On the left in front of the high altar is the chapel of **Santa Casa de Loreto**, a copy of the original Santa Casa in Italy; it was built in 1735 at the expense of Manuel Tomas de la Canal. It contains a statue of the Virgin, as well as those of the donor and his wife

above their graves. On either side is a passage leading to the *Camarín, an octagonal room containing six altars, one neo-classical and five Baroque. The Baroque retablos, with their carved and gilded ornament in wood and stucco, are superb examples of Mexican Churrigueresque.

Adjoining San Felipe Neri on the E is the mid-18th c. **church of Nuestra Señora de la Salud**, the façade of which reveals the influence of early Churrigueresque style, with a large conch containing the Eye of God in the upper part. It contains neo-classical altars and a number of old pictures, including works by Miguel Cabrera, Antonio Torres and Tomás Xavier de Peralta.

Among the other churches in the town are *Santo Domingo, Santa Cruz del Pueblo, San Juan de Dios, San Antonio* and *Santa Ana*.

In San Miguel, as in neighboring villages and ranchos, there are a number of interesting Indian chapels in which can be seen, in primitive form, saints, crosses and other religious subjects, strangely represented in a very individual manner. In these chapels the Indians were able to conduct their worship in their mixed Indian and Catholic style, free of Spanish supervision.

A visit is recommended for those interested to the home of Stirling Dickinson (Santo Domingo 34), where *orchid growing is an important activity.

San Miguel de Allende

1 Town Hall	3 Birthplace of Ignacio de Allende
2 Casa del Mayorazgo de Canal	4 San Rafael
	5 Nuestra Señora de la Salud
	6 San Felipe Neri

Just outside the town on the road to Querétaro is a viewpoint, *El Mirador*, from which there is a fine *panorama of San Miguel and the surrounding area.

SURROUNDINGS. – In the immediate vicinity of the town, particularly to the NW, are a number of *thermal springs* (spas).

15 km (9 miles) N of San Miguel and 3 km (2 miles) off the road is the much frequented pilgrimage center of **Atotonilco** (Náhuatl, "place of the hot water"), a convent, with a much venerated statue of the Redeemer, which was founded by Father Felipe Neri de Alfaro in 1740. Passing this way at the head of his hastily gathered forces after proclaiming Mexican independence, Miguel Hidalgo took the image of the Virgin of Guadalupe from the church and fastened it to his banner, making the Virgin patroness of the Mexican liberation movement.

The **church** and various chapels have fine *frescoes, mostly by Miguel Antonio Martínez de Pocasangre, of folk themes. In the Camarín, behind the high altar, are statues of the Virgin and the apostles. To the right is the Chapel of the Rosary (frescoes of the battle of Lepanto), which leads into another *camarín* with a ceiling in the form of a shell. The whips sold in the vicinity of the church are said to be still used by many pilgrims.

28 km (17 miles) NW of Atotonilco is **Dolores Hidalgo** (alt. 1990 m (6529 ft); pop. 30,000; hotels: María Dolores; Posada Cocomacán; restaurant: La Fuente; market on Sunday). From the parish church of this little town Miguel Hidalgo y Costilla, the parish priest, launched the Mexican War of Independence on September 15, 1810 with the "Gritto de Dolores" ("Call of Dolores").

The *parish church (1712–78) has a fine Churrigueresque façade. In the same style, and no less impressive, are the two retablos, one on the left and the other on the right. The one on the left, richly gilded, has the famous image of the Virgin of Guadalupe. –

The *Casa de Don Miguel Hidalgo* contains a historical museum, mainly devoted to Hidalgo himself. – Dolores Hidalgo is also renowned for the attractive colored tiles (azulejos) which are made in the town.

Going NE on Road 110 from Dolores Hidalgo and crossing Carretera 57 one reaches in 8 km (5 miles) the attractive little town of **San Luis de la Paz** (alt. 2020m (6630 ft); pop. 19,000). From here it is about 10 km (6 miles) S to *Mineral de Pozos*. Once a prosperous mining town of 60,000 inhabitants it is now almost deserted, a *ghost town at the end of an interesting excursion.

San Miguel de Cozumel

See under Cozumel

San Miguel Regla

See under Pachuca

Sayil

State: Yucatáan (Yuc.).
Altitude: 28 m (92 ft).

ACCESS. – About 5 km (3 miles) S of Kabah on Road 261 a new road on the left leads in 4 km (2.5 miles) to *Sayil.

The archeological site of *Sayil is one of a group of Maya centers, built in pure Puuc style and also including

West front of the Palacio, Sayil

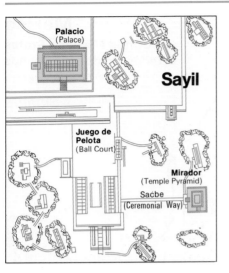

Palacio (Palace)

Sayil

Juego de Pelota (Ball Court)

Mirador (Temple Pyramid)

Sacbe (Ceremonial Way)

Xlabak and Labná, which have in the past attracted little attention from archeologists and visitors but have now been brought within easy reach by the construction of a new road.

HISTORY. – Since no precisely dated monuments have yet been found at Sayil ("place of the ants" in Maya), its age can be determined only by stylistic evidence. This suggests that the two principal structures on the site were built in the 9th c. A.D. – i.e., in the Maya *Late Classic period*. There was evidently no building activity after A.D. 1000.

THE SITE. – The dominating feature of the site is the *Palace (Palacio)*, a terraced structure (partly restored) which is one of the finest achievements of the Puuc style in Maya architecture. Each story of the building, which measures 80 by 40 m (260 by 130 ft) at the base, is set back from the one below, so that the roof of each story serves as a terrace for the one above. A large staircase runs up the S side to the summit of the structure, on the third story.

The most interesting part of the structure is the *WEST SIDE OF THE MIDDLE TIER, which has two doorways and four openings, each flanked by two columns with square capitals. Between these openings are groups of **clustered columns** imitating the timber posts of Maya huts, which create a remarkably harmonious effect. Above this is a **frieze**, in the middle of which is a huge *mask of the rain god Chac*, flanked by ornamental glyphs. The frieze also contains groups of small round columns and above the doorways, the stylized motif of the "diving god" between outward-facing snakes with open jaws.

At the NW corner of the Palace is a large cistern (*chultún*).

Other remains include the runs of a *ball court*, a small temple and the badly weathered temple known as the **Mira-**

dor, once connected with the Palace by a *sacbe* (ceremonial way). This stands on a platform and has a roof-comb of some size, once decorated with stucco ornament – relatively rare in the Puuc style, which usually preferred limestone mosaic work.

SURROUNDINGS. – 6 km (4 miles) E, on the road to Labná, is the archeological site of **Xlapak**. The most important of the restored structures is the Palace (Palacio), a typical example of the Puuc style.

On the main façade, above the unadorned ground floor and below a sill decorated with columns, is an interesting **frieze**. Above the central doorway is a kind of *tower* with an elaborate decoration of masks, and on either side are panels of geometric ornament, above which is a broad cornice. At the corners are other tower-like features built up in a complex pattern of superimposed *Chac masks*.

The road continues from Xlabak for another 3 km (2 miles) to the important Maya site of *Labná (p. 150).

Sinaloa

State of Sinaloa (Sin.). – Capital: Culiacán.
Area: 58,488 sq. km (22,582 sq. miles).
Population: 2,192,200.
ⓘ **Coordinación Federal de Turismo,**
Av. del Mar 1000,
Mazatlán, Sin.;
tel. (9 16 78) 1 42 12, 1 42 11, 1 42 10.

This long narrow state on the coast of the Mar de Cortés (Gulf of California) is bounded on the N by Sonora, on the E by Durango and Chihuahua and on the S by Nayarit. The coastal strip of bare tropical terrain rises in the E into the foothills of the Sierra Madre Occidental. The five rivers which flow down from the mountains into the Gulf have been harnessed by the construction of dams to supply extensive irrigation systems. The population consists mainly of mestizos and Creoles (descendants of Spaniards); in some areas there are still some Indians, mostly of the Mayo tribe.

Among the few archeological sites in the state – mostly consisting of cemeties and cave paintings – are *Camanito, Majada de Abajo, La Nanchita, Majada de Arriba, Imalá, Chametla* and *Guasave.*

HISTORY. – In the pre-Hispanic period, Sinaloa ("round hemp-bush" in Cahita) was strongly influenced by the cultures of central Mexico, as is shown by the archeological material (mainly vessels of alabaster and onyx and decorated pottery) found at

Mexico
United Mexican States
Estados Unidos Mexicanos

Sinaloa

States
Estados

1a Baja California Sur	12 Aguascalientes	
1b Baja California Norte	13 Jalisco	
	14 Guanajuato	
2 Sonora	15 Querétaro	
3 Chihuahua	16 Hidalgo	
4 Sinaloa	17 Colima	
5 Durango	18 Michoacán	
6 Coahuila	19 México	
7 Nuevo León	20 Morelos	
8 Zacatecas	21 Tlaxcala	26 Chiapas
9 San Luis Potosí	22 Puebla	27 Tabasco
10 Tamaulipas	23 Veracruz	28 Campeche
11 Nayarit	24 Guerrero	29 Yucatán
	25 Oaxaca	30 Quintana Roo

D.F. Distrito Federal (Federal District)

Chametla, Aztatlán, Culiacán and *Guasave.* This material is now dated to between A.D. 400 and 1400 and ascribed to influences from Teotihuacán, Tula (the Toltecs) and the Mixteca-Puebla culture. In the last 200 years before the Spanish conquest, the peoples living in this area were largely driven out or suppressed by nomadic tribes coming from the N. During this period some influence was also exerted by the Chimalhuacán league of states to the S.

The first *Spaniards* in the Sinaloa area probably came here under the leadership of Nuño Beltrán de Guzmán in 1531. Most of the settlements founded in the 16th c. were destroyed by the Indians, and the pacification of the region was achieved only in the second half of the 17th c., with the help of Jesuit missionaries like Juan Padilla, Juan de la Cruz and Eusebio Francisco Kino. Together with Sonora, Sinaloa belonged to the relatively independent western provinces of New Spain. Then in 1830, after Mexico had achieved independence, Sinaloa was separated from Sonora and became an independent state within the Republic.

ECONOMY. – In recent years, with the help of irrigation, Sinaloa has developed into an important agricultural region. The main products of its *agriculture* are wheat, cotton, tobacco, sugar-cane, winter vegetables and fruit. *Fishing* and the processing of fish products naturally make a considerable contribution to the economy. *Industry* produces mainly beer, tobacco goods, vegetable oils, soap, textiles and hardware. *Mining* yields salt, graphite, manganese and some precious metals. *Tourism*, a recent development, is making great strides. – Sinaloa has an excellent system of communications, in which the railways play an important part.

In addition to the important port and beach resort of **Mazatlán** (p. 156) the following places in Sinaloa are worth a mention:

The state capital is **Culiacán** (Náhuatl, "place where the god Coltzín is venerated" or "where two waters meet": alt. 65 m (213 ft); pop. 390,000; hotels: Executivo, I, SP; Los Tres Ríos, I, SP; Motel Los Caminos, I, SP; Valle Grande, II; Siesta III; restaurants: Los Arcos, El Rancho, La Pradera).

The town was founded by Nuño Beltrán de Guzmán in 1533 on the site of an earlier Nahua village and given the name of *San Miguel de Navito.* Later a mining town, Culiacán has developed in recent years into the center of an extensive agricultural area created by irrigation (cotton, sugar-cane, winter vegetables, etc.). The area is noted both for the legal cultivation of the opium poppy for the production of opiates and for the illegal cultivation of cannabis for the manufacture of marijuana.

Culiacán has little in the way of notable buildings, apart perhaps from the 19th c. *Cathedral*, the huge modern *community center* (Centro Cívico Constitución) and the interesting *museum* (archeological exhibits and displays of the plant and animal life of the region). – Popular elements in the life of Culiacán and of the state as a whole are the *bandas sinaloenses* like La Tambora – local bands which mingle military music with Dixieland jazz and Cuban rhythms.

In the immediate surroundings of Culiacán are the spas of *Carrizalejo, Macurimi* and *Imalá* (on the Río Tamazula: old Indian cave paintings in the vicinity). There is good fishing to be had in the *Sanalona* and *Adolfo López Mateos* reservoirs (bass, catfish, trout, etc.). – On the coast of the Gulf of California are the beautiful beaches of *Altata, Campo Aníbal* and *El Dorado.*

20 km (12 miles) N of Culiacán is *San Miguel Zapotitlán*, where old Mayo dances are performed on

the feast days of local saints, during Holy Week and at Christmas.

Guasave (alt. 36 m (118 ft); pop. 88,000; hotels: Del Rosario, Moctezuma; fiesta on first Sunday in October, Día de la Virgen del Rosario), where Mayo dances can also be seen.

Near the town is an archeological site (cemetery).

Los Mochis (alt. 73 m (240 ft); pop. 127,000; hotels: Las Colinas, I, SP; Santa Anita, I; El Dorado, II; Motel Posada Real, II; Monte Carlo, III; restaurants: El Farallón; Terome; Kowlon; Madrid), an important railway junction and center of a large agricultural area producing sugarcane, rice, vegetables and flowers (including a species of marsh marigold which is fed to hens to improve the color of the egg yolk). – Los Mochis is the starting-point of the spectacular *railway journey to the **Barranca del Cobre** (p. 79).

Topolobampo (alt. sea-level; pop. 10,000; fiesta June 1, Día de la Marina), terminus of the Chihuahua-Pacific railway line, with a ferry service to La Paz in Baja California. This fishing village, mainly occupied in the shrimp fisheries, lies in the large *Ohuira Bay*, which has some bizarre rock formations.

Some of the islands in the bay are mating areas for sealions.

Sonora

State of Sonara (Son.). – Capital: Hermosillo.
Area: 182,553 sq. km (70,484 sq. miles).
Population: 1,694,500.

ⓘ **Coordinación Federal de Turismo,**
Blvd. Eusebio Kino/esq. Román,
Yocupicio Edif. Pitic-6,
Hermosillo, Son.;
tel. (9 16 21) 4 73 99, 4 83 97, 4 84 07.

Sonora, Mexico's second largest state, is bounded on the N by the United States (Arizona), on the W by Beja California and the Gulf of California (Mar de Cortés), on the S by Sinaloa and on the E by Chihuahua. It is a region of deserts and semi-deserts studded with cacti, of mountains (the Sierra Madre Occidental) with great tracts of forest, of irregated valleys, or rocky and sandy coasts. Off the coast of Sonora lies Mexico's largest island, the Isla del Tiburón. The population, with a majority of whites and mestizos, also includes some Indian peoples still living an independent existence, such as the Pápagos, Opatas, Pima Seri, Yaqui and Mayo.

Of the few archeological sites in Sonora, near *Caborca, Sahuaripa, Yecora* and *La Pintada*, only those with cave paintings are really worth seeing.

HISTORY. – In pre-Columbian times Sonora (Spanish "resounding", from the sound made in working the local marble) was occupied by various nomadic and

Giant saguaro cacti in the Sonora desert

Mexico
United Mexican States
Estados Unidos Mexicanos

Sonora

**States
Estados**

1a Baja California	12 Aguascalientes	
Sur	13 Jalisco	
1b Baja California	14 Guanajuato	
Norte	15 Querétaro	
2 Sonora	16 Hidalgo	
3 Chihuahua	17 Colima	
4 Sinaloa	18 Michoacán	
5 Durango	19 México	
6 Coahuila	20 Morelos	
7 Nuevo León	21 Tlaxcala	26 Chiapas
8 Zacatecas	22 Puebla	27 Tabasco
9 San Luis Potosí	23 Veracruz	28 Campeche
10 Tamaulipas	24 Guerrero	29 Yucatán
11 Nayarit	25 Oaxaca	30 Quintana Roo

D.F. Distrito Federal (Federal District)

settled Indian tribes, whose descendants still live in certain restricted areas within the state. – The first *Spaniards* to reach this area, between 1531 and 1533, were conquistadors such as Francisco Vázquez de Coronado, Alvaro Núñez Cabeza de Vaca and Pedro Almindes Chirinos, who met with fierce resistance from the Indians. In 1567 an expedition under Francisco de Ibarra discovered the rich mineral resources of the region. In the course of the next hundred years, many Spanish settlements were destroyed in Indian raids, particularly by the Yaqui, and the area was pacified only after the arrival, in 1687, of the great traveller and missionary, Father Eusabio Francisco Kino, who established a network of *Jesuit missions.* After the expulsion of the Jesuits from New Spain in 1767, however, the Indian revolt flared again. At the beginning of the 19th c. Sonora and Sinaloa became part of the Western Provinces of the viceroyalty.

After the war of independence (1810–21), in which José María Hermosillo, a native of Sonora, played a leading part, Sonora was separated from Sinaloa and became an indepedent state. In 1825, 1875 and 1886 there were great *Indian risings* by the Yaqui and Mayo which set back the development of the state. – During the closing years of the 19th c., under the Presidency of Porfirio Díaz, the state's communications and the mining industry developed rapidly and rebellious Yaqui Indians were deported to Yucatán, from which they later returned to stage their last rising in Sonora in 1927. – During the revolutionary wars (1911–20), a prominent part was played by natives of Sonora, some of whom later became Presidents of Mexico, including Alvaro Obregón, Adolfo de la Huerta, Plutarco Elías Calles and Abelardo Rodríguez.

ECONOMY. – Until the Second World War, Sonora's principal resources were its *minerals* (gold, silver, copper, lead and tin). A considerable contribution to the economy is now made by *agriculture* in irrigated areas (cotton, fruit, vegetables, wheat maize, sugarcane, tobacco), as well as by *livestock-farming* and *fishing.* In recent years there has also been a steady

development of *tourism.* The state has good communications by rail and road.

In addition to the capital, **Hermosillo** (p. 138), the port of **Guaymas** (p. 136) and *Alamos* (p. 137) the following places in Sonora are worthy of mention:

Nogales (alt. 1179 m (3868 ft); pop. 122,000; hotels: Fray Marcos de Niza; Motel San Luis; restaurants: La Caverna; La Roca; El Trocadero; fiesta May 5, battle of Puebla) is of importance as a border town, lying opposite the town of the same name in Arizona (USA), and is also a commercial center.

Magdalena (alt. 693 m (2274 ft); pop. 24,000; hotels: Motel Kino, Cuervo; fiesta October 4, Día de San Francisco Xavier), 90 km (55 miles) S of Nogales, is a little colonial town with the church of San Francisco Xavier, in which the tomb of Father Kino was discovered in 1966. – Other old mission stations associated with Father Kino are *Cocospera, Caborca, Pitiquito, Oquitoa* and *Tubutama*.

A few **Pápago Indians** can still be found around *Sonoito, Quitovac, Caborca, Saric* and *Pozo Verde*. In southern Arizona there are about 12,000 members of this tribe, which is closely related to the Pima Indians; in Sonora only about 300. One theory is that the Pima-Pápagos are the descendants of the *Hohokum culture* which flourished in the southwestern United States between about A.D. 700 and 1400 (Pima: "the people which went"). This semi-nomadic tribe, which was perpetually at war with the Apaches, was partly

The Río Usumacinta at Tenosique (Tabasco)

Christianized by the Jesuits in the latter part of the 18th c. In the mid 19th c. there were major risings which were quelled by the Mexican government. The Pápagos now live by farming, hunting and food-gathering. Their religion shows only a limited number of Christian features: they believe in the immortality of the soul but include the sun and stars among their divinities. Their festivals, which involve old traditional dances, are mostly connected with the harvest and with hunting; their principal Catholic festival is October 4 (Día de San Francisco).

El Sumidero
See under Tuxtla Gutiérrez

Tabasco

State of Tabasco (Tab.). – Capital: Villahermosa.
Area: 25,337 sq. km (9783 sq. miles).
Population: 1,354,200.

ⓘ **Coordinación Federal de Turismo,**
Lerdo 101, 1st floor,
Malecón y Lic. Carlos A. Madrazo,
Villahermosa, Tab.;
tel. (9 19 31) 2 73 36, 2 74 56.

The state of Tabasco, lying along the southern shores of the Gulf of Mexico, is bounded on the E by Campeche state and Guatemala, on the S by Chiapas and on the W by Veracruz. It is a flat region with numerous lakes, rivers and areas of swamp and dense rain forest. Two navigable rivers, the Usumacinta and the Grijalva, cross the state on their way to the Gulf. The population consists mainly of Mestizos and Chontal Indians. Many species of tropical animals inhabit the forests,

Mexico
United Mexican States
Estados Unidos Mexicanos

Tabasco

States
Estados

1a	Baja California Sur	12	Aguascalientes
1b	Baja California Norte	13	Jalisco
		14	Guanajuato
2	Sonora	15	Querétaro
3	Chihuahua	16	Hidalgo
4	Sinaloa	17	Colima
5	Durango	18	Michoacán
6	Coahuila	19	México
7	Nuevo León	20	Morelos
8	Zacatecas	21	Tlaxcala
9	San Luis Potosí	22	Puebla
10	Tamaulipas	23	Veracruz
11	Nayarit	24	Guerrero
		25	Oaxaca
		26	Chiapas
		27	Tabasco
		28	Campeche
		29	Yucatán
		30	Quintana Roo

D.F. Distrito Federal (Federal District)

savannas and lakes and riveres of Tabasco.

Tabasco contains a number of pre-Columbian archeological sites, including **La Venta** (p. 91), one of the most important Olmec sites, *San Miguel* (also Olmec) and the Maya sites of *Comalcalco* (p. 290), *El Bellote, Jonuta, Balancán* etc. The principal modern towns, in addition to the capital, **Villahermosa** (p. 289), are *Frontera*, Emiliano Zapata, *Tenosique, Huimanguillo* and *Teapa*.

HISTORY. – In early times Tabasco ("damp earth") was, along with Veracruz, the original home of the mysterious **Olmecs**. Later it was inhabited by the *Chontal Indians*, who in pre-Hispanic times played an important part in the movement of peoples between central and southern Mexico and Yucatán. – The first Europeans to land here were Juan de Grijalva (1518) and Hernán Cortés (1519), but they were soon driven off by the Indians, and it was another twenty years before Francisco de Montejo was able to gain control of part of the region (1540 on). In 1824 Tabasco became a state in the Mexican republic. – In the 1860s Tabasco was the scene of battles with the French troops who occupied part of Mexico during this period. In the 20s and 30s of this century the radical governor in Tabasco, Tomás Garrido Canabal, waged a bitter war against the Church. Most churches were destroyed, the priests driven away and religious services forbidden. The persecution of these Christians inspired Graham Greene to write "The Power and the Glory".

ECONOMY. – The main *commercial crops* which flourish in Tabasco's hot and humid climate are bananas, coconut palms, cocoa, coffee and sugar-cane, together with *hardwoods, high-class woods* and the harvesting of *chicle*. *Livestock farming* and *fishing* also make important contributions to the economy. In recent years, however, the dominant feature in the development of Tabasco's economy has been its abundant reserves of *oil*.

El Tajín

See El Tajín

Tamaulipas

State of Tamaulipas (Tamps.).
Capital: Ciudad Victoria.
Area: 79,602 sq. km (30,734 sq. miles).
Population: 2,144,300.

(i) **Coordinación Federal de Turismo,**
2 y 3 Av. Carrera Torres 1510,
Ciudad Victoria, Tamps.;
tel. (9 11 31) 2 37 87, 2 38 41.

The state of Tamaulipas is bounded on the N by the United States (Texas), on the W by Nuevo León and on the S by San Luis Potosí and Veracruz. It has a long eastern coast-line on the Gulf of Mexico with great stretches of beach and numerous lagoons; in the western part of the state are the mountains and tropical valleys of the Sierra Madre Oriental; to the N is a region of vast arid plains. The population of the southern part of the state still consists mainly of Huastec Indians.

Mexico
United Mexican States
Estados Unidos Mexicanos

Tamaulipas

States
Estados

1a Baja California Sur	12 Aguascalientes
1b Baja California Norte	13 Jalisco
	14 Guanajuato
2 Sonora	15 Querétaro
3 Chihuahua	16 Hidalgo
4 Sinaloa	17 Colima
5 Durango	18 Michoacán
6 Coahuila	19 México
7 Nuevo León	20 Morelos
8 Zacatecas	21 Tlaxcala
9 San Luis Potosí	22 Puebla
10 Tamaulipas	23 Veracruz
11 Nayarit	24 Guerrero
	25 Oaxaca

26 Chiapas
27 Tabasco
28 Campeche
29 Yucatán
30 Quintana Roo

D.F. Distrito Federal (Federal District)

There are hardly any pre-Columbian archeological sites of any significance in Tamaulipas; the sites in this part of Mexico are mostly in the neighboring states of San Luis Potosí and Veracruz.

HISTORY. – In early times Tamaulipas ("high mountain") was inhabited only by nomadic tribes. Later some tribes adopted a settled way of life, and by 1100 B.C. there evolved a pottery-using culture which is generally ascribed to the Huastecs. These first phases of the Formative period are known as the *Pavón, Ponce* and *Aguilar* phases (to 350 B.C.), while the subsequent Pre-Classic and Post-Classic periods are labelled *Pánuco I–V*. It is not known with certainty when the Huastecs came into this area or where they came from, but it is supposed that they came in during the early Formative period from the Gulf coast, the probable cradle of the Meso-American cultures. The fact that their language belongs to the Maya group, together with other similarities, suggests that they are a Maya tribe which has traveled far from its original homeland. The area occupied by the Huastecs extended from Tamaulipas into parts of San Luis Potosí, Hidalgo and Querétaro and the northern part of Veracruz.

In the course of their long history, the **Huaxtecs** or *Huastecs* exerted a considerable influence on the cultures of the central highlands and northern Mexico. In early times there was a long period of cross-fertilization between the Huastecs and Teotihuacán. An ancient chronicle tells us that in a later period the Huaxtecs were involved in the dynastic conflicts in Tula (Tollan) which finally brought on the fall of the Toltec metropolis. It is also believed that Huaxtec influence extended N into the Mississippi and Ohio valleys. Finally, at the end of the 15th c., the Huaxtecs became tributary to the Aztecs, though they were not completely subjugated. – Other peoples, including the Aztecs, took over some of the Huaxtec divinities, including Quetzalcóatl (as the wind god Ehécatl), Tlazoltéotl, goddess of sexual love, Xipe Tótec, the "flayed god", a symbol of renewal, and Xochiquétzal, goddess of love and flowers. – Although Huaxtec cultural achievements cannot be compared with those of the southern Mayas, they were nevertheless important. Their delicate terracotta figurines and large stone figures of priests and nobles, and the ornaments and other articles made from metal, shells and semi-precious stones are of high quality. Their buildings are frequently circular and conical.

When the *Spaniards* arrived in this area, they found not a unified Huastec state, but a series of petty principalities which put up a fierce resistance to the invaders. The first Spaniards to come here were Hernández de Córdoba and Juan Grijalva (1518), but it was left to Francisco de Garay, Hernán Cortés and Gonzalo de Sandoval to bring the territory under Spanish control some years later (1521–6). Thereafter, the province was governed by Nuño de Guzmán, under whose harsh rule a lucrative slave trade with the Antilles grew up. The later history of the region was tied up with that of its largest town, Tampico (see below).

ECONOMY. – Its ports on the Gulf coast and its common frontier with the United States give Tamau-lipas one of the busiest economies among the Mexican states. Its main source of revenue is *oil*, followed by *agriculture* (cotton, maize, sorghum), *livestock farming* and *fishing*. The largest towns, important either as ports, commercial entrepôts on the frontier or agricultural centers, are **Tampico** (pop. 350,000: see below). *Nuevo Laredo* (pop. 282,000), *Matamoros* (pop. 404,000), *Reynosa* (pop. 325,000) and the state capital *Ciudad Victoria* (pop. 212,000).

Tampico

State: Tamaulipas (Tamps.).
Altitude: 12 m (39 ft). – Population: 560,000.
Telephone dialing code: 9 11 21.

ⓘ **Coordinación Federal de Turismo,**
2 y 3 Av. Carrera Torres 1510,
Ciudad Victoria, Tamps.
tel. (9 11 31) 2 37 87, 2 38 41.

HOTELS. – OUTSIDE THE TOWN: *Camino Real*, Av. Hidalgo 2000, L, SP; *Posada Tampico*, 2 km mark on Ciudad Mante road, I, SP. – IN THE TOWN: *Inglaterra*, Salvador Días Mirón 116 Ote., I, SP; *Impala*, Salvadodr Díaz Mirón 220 Pte., I, SP; *Colonial*, F. Madero 210 Ote., II; *Riviera*, Héroes del Cañonero y Colón, II.

RESTAURANTS in most hotels; also *Jardín Corona*, Av. Hidalgo 1915; *La Mansión Loredo*, Fresno 101; *Flamingo*, Av. Hidalgo y Nayarit; *Chinatown*, Av. Hidalgo y Av. Real; *Elite*, Díaz Mirón 211 Ote.; *Del Mar*, Aduana Sur 309.

RECREATION and SPORTS. – Swimming, tennis, golf, fishing, hunting.

EVENTS. – Carnival; February–March, fishing competition; November 3, San Martín de Porres.

Tampico, situated on the N bank of the Río Pánuco, is the most important port on the Gulf of Mexico (after Veracruz). Originally developed for the shipment of oil and cotton, it is now a busy and well-equipped port handling a considerable export trade, primarily to the United States, Europe and South America. It is a city of oil tanks, refineries and lively shipping activity, but around the city is a different landscape of river estuaries, lagoons and beautiful beaches.

The port of Tampico on the Gulf of Mexico

HISTORY. – The Tampico area was probably settled at a very early stage by the *Huastecs* (see under Tamaulipas), whose pottery can be traced back to before 1000 B.C. In the second half of the 15th c. the Huastecs became tributary to the Aztecs.

The first *Spaniards* to arrive here sailed down the river under Alonso Avarez de Pineda in 1519, and within ten years the Huastecs had been brought under Spanish control. In 1532 the Franciscan friar, Andrés de Olmos, built a convent on the ruins of an Aztec strong point, and around this the town developed. The settlement, then known as *San Luis de Tampico*, was granted the status of *villa* (a small town) in 1560. During the following hundred years, the town was exposed to frequent raids by Indian tribes (e.g., the Apaches) coming down from the N and by pirates coming in from the sea. In 1683 it was destroyed, and it was not rebuilt until 1823, after the war of independence. In 1829 it was occupied by Spanish forces, who were finally driven out by General (later President) Antonio López de Santa Ana. During the war with the United States (1846–8), it was again occupied for a short time by US troops under General Zachary Taylor, and then it was held by French troops for a time during the French intervention in Mexico.

The discovery of oil near Tampico at the beginning of the 20th c., during the presidency of Porfirio Díaz, brought US and British capital into the town, and the subsequent economic upsurge made Tampico for a time the largest oil port in the world.

SIGHTS. – The *Plaza de Armas* (Zócalo) is a vantage point where the busy life of the city, particularly in the evening, can be observed. In this square are the *Cathedral* and the *Town Hall* (Palacio Municipal).

Some 7 km (4 miles) N of the Plaza de Armas, in the satellite town of CIUDAD MADERO (pop. 200,000) the *Instituto Tecnológico* (closed on Saturday and Sunday) houses the interesting **Huastex Museum** (*Museo de la Cultura Huasteca*), which displays stone sculpture, terracotta figurines, pottery, ornaments and jewelry made of gold, silver, copper, shells and semi-precious stones, stone ritual objects, weapons and costumes produced by this interesting people (see above under Tamaulipas). – Popular beaches near the town are *Miramar* and *Altamira*.

SURROUNDINGS. – 60 km (38 miles) W on Road 70 is **Ébano** (S.L.P.); in the neighborhood a Huastec site was found which has interesting early building dating from the Pánuco I and II phases (350 B.C. to A.D. 200): i.e., from the Pre-Classic period. This is a dome-shaped structure almost 30 m (100 ft) in diameter and 3 m (10 ft) high, showing the circular cross-section characteristic of Huastec architecture. It was probably a temple of the wind god, Ehécatl. (The site is somewhat difficult to reach.)

44 km (27 miles) beyond this and 6 km (4 miles) before *Tamuín* a left turn toward San Vicente Tancualayab leads to the Huastec site of **El Tamuín**, 6 km (4 miles) distant. Although this was one of the most important towns in Huastec territory, the remains are neither spectacular nor well preserved.

Along the bank of the *Río Tamuín* extends an area of some 17 hectares (42 acres) studded with *platforms, altars, patios* and *earth mounds*. One structure brought to light by the excavators was a platform almost 3 m (10 ft) high with a large staircase, originally faced with painted stucco. Another low *temple platform* with conical altars, apparently dating from the 8th or 9th c. (i.e., the Classical period), still has visible wall paintings. Here, too, was found one of the finest and best known pieces of Huastec sculpture, the *statue of a youth* with the symbols of the wind god Ehécatl, standing 1.45 m (4 ft 9 ins.) high; it is now in the National Museum of Anthropology in Mexico City (copy in the Huastec Museum, Ciudad Madero).

30 km (19 miles) beyond Tamuín, on Road 70, one reaches **Ciudad Valles** (S.L.P.), the center of an agricultural area (alt. 90 m (295 ft); pop. 95,000; hotels – in the town: Valles, Piña; outside the town: Covadonga, Posada Don Antonio, Casa Grande; restaurant: Las Sillas; small archeological museum). In the surroundings of Ciudad Valles there are a number of thermal baths, caves and waterfalls.

Road 85 to the S leads in 106 km (66 miles) to **Tamanzunchale** (alt. 206 m. (676 ft); pop. 22,000; hotels: Quinta Cilla, SP; San Antonio, SP; Mirador; fiesta June 24, San Juan Bautista. – The *surroundings of this Huastec town, set amid luxuriant tropical vegetation, are a paradise for ornithologists and butterfly collectors. From here a road winds its way S amid orange groves into the state of Hidalgo, through the magnificent wild mountain scenery of the Sierra Madre Oriental.

Tapachula
See under Chiapas

Taxco de Alarcón

State: Guerrero (Gro.).
Altitude: 1670 m (5480 ft). – Population: 79,000.
Telephone dialing code: 9 17 32.
(i) **Coordinación Federal de Turismo**,
　　Costera M. Aleman 187,
　　Acapulco, Gro.;
　　tel. (9 17 48) 5 11 78, 5 13 03, 5 41 28,
　　5 22 84, 5 10 93, 5 15 95.

HOTELS. – *Monte Taxco, Lomas de Taxco, L, SP; tennis, golf, riding; *Hadienda de Solar, Paraje del Solar, L, SP, tennis, golf, riding; *Rancho Taxco Victoria, Carlos J. Nibbi 14, I, SP; De la Borda, Cerro del Pedregal 12, I, SP; Posada Don Carlos, Calle del Consuelo 8, I, SP; Loma Linda, Av. Pres. John F. Kennedy 52, I, SP; Los Arcos, J. Ruiz de Alarcón 12, II, SP; Santa Prisca, Cena Oscura 1, II; Posada de los Castillos, J. Ruiz de Alarcón 3, II; Agua Escondida, Guillermo B. Spratling 4, III; Meléndez, Cuauhtémoc 6; San Francisco Cuadra, I, SP.

RESTAURANTS in most hotels; also *Pagaduría del Rey*, Cerro de Bermejo; *Cielito Lindo*, Plaza Borda 14; *Señor Costilla's*, Plaza Borda 1; *Los Balcones*, Plazuela de los Gallos; *Alarcón*, Palma 2.

General view of Taxco

**Taxco, magnificently situated on the slopes of a group of hills, is one of the best known and most popular tourist centers in Mexico, presenting as it does the complete picture of an old colonial town with its low tiled houses, narrow lanes, little squares and picturesque nooks and corners.

RECREATION and SPORTS. – Swimming, tennis, golf, riding.

EVENTS. – Fiestas: February 22, Fiesta de Chavarrieta; Holy Week; September 29, Día de San Miguel; December 1, Silver Fair. Market on Thursday and Sunday.

HISTORY. – In pre-Columbian times the Taxco area was inhabited by a Nahua people, the Tlahuicas, whose settlement of *Tlachco* (Náhuatl, "where the ball game is played") lay some 10 km (6 miles) from the present town. The Tlahuica territory was attacked by the Aztecs under Itzcóatl and Moctezuma I, and was finally annexed to the Aztec empire in the middle of the 15th c. – The *Spaniards* came here in 1522 in quest of tin and silver, and in 1529 founded the township of *El Real de Tetzelcingo*, which in 1581 was renamed *Taxco*. The area's large resources of silver were not discovered until the middle of the 18th c., when José de la Borda found the large San Ignacio mine. In thanksgiving for the wealth which this brought him, Borda built the church of Santa Prisca.

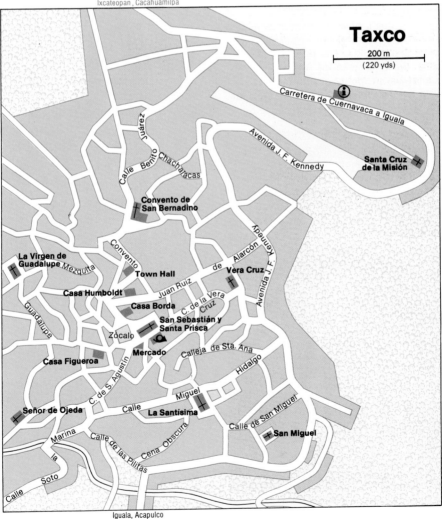

After the revolutionary wars (1910–20), the region became increasingly impoverished, until an American named William Spratling came to live in Taxco in 1930 and gave a fresh lease of life to the old craft of silversmithing, teaching the local people the techniques of the craft, design and marketing. Taxco now lives almost entirely from the tourist trade and the manufacture of silverware, which employs over 1500 craftsmen in several hundred small workshops. The metal used here is an alloy of 950–980 grams of silver and 20–50 grams of copper.

SIGHTS. – In the very picturesque little *Zócalo* (Plaza de la Borda) is the **church of San Sebastián y Santa Prisca**, a masterpiece of Churrigueresque architecture (by Diego Durán and Juan Caballero, 1751–8), built at the expense of the silver magnate, José de la Borda. The doorway is flanked on either side by a pair of Corinthian columns enclosing a series of sculptures. In the upper part of the façade, above the papal tiara, is a large medallion enclosing a representation of the baptism of Christ, replacing the central window commonly found here; above this is the choir window, topped by a round gable. The exuberant decoration of statues, coats of arms, foliage, scallops, ribbons, cherubim, etc., is carved with consummate skill. The uniformity of the side walls is relieved by a series of windows in richly sculptured frames. The towers which rise above the façade, each with four windows, are also richly

A picturesque street in Taxco

Sections

Grutas de Cacahuamilpa
(Cacahuamilpa Caves)

→ N
········· Paths

150 m
(165 yds)

Entrance

INTERESTING FORMATIONS

1	Chivo	
2	Fuentes	
3	Canastas	
4	Confites	
5	Aurora	
6	Tronos	
7	Portada de los Querubines	
8	Panteón	
9	Relicario	
10	Plaza de Armas	
11	Hornos	
12	Volcán	
13	Pedregal del Muerto	
14	Virginias	
15	Nacimiento	
16	Campanario	
17	Ánimas	
18	Água Bendita	
19	Puerto del Aire	
20	Bautisterio	
21	Lagunillas	
22	Torres de los Palmares	
23	Gloria	
24	Canastillas	
25	Emperatriz	
26	Infiernillo	
27	Órganos	

decorated, mainly with ornamented columns and grotesque faces. The dome, faced with blue and yellow azulejos, completes the total effect.

Notable features of the *INTERIOR are the superbly carved, painted and gilded Churrigueresque *retablos*, with numerous figures of apostles, angels and saints amid intricate patterns of flower and fruit decoration; pictures by Miguel Caberra above the entrance to the *Chapel of the Indians* (Capilla de los Indios), in the chapel itself and in the sacristy; the splendid *organ*; and the fine figure of Christ.

Other features of interest in the town are the *Market* (*Mercado*); the *churches* of *La Santísima* (1713, with later alteration; Baroque), *San Bernardino* (originally a 16th c. Franciscan foundation, rebuilt in neo-classical style after a fire in the 19th c.), *Guadalupe* (1877: *view of the Zócalo and Santa Prisca) and *Ojeda* (1822: magnificent *view of the town); the *Casa Borda* (1750: once the residence of José de la Borda, now municipal offices); the *Casa Humboldt* (18th c.; fine Mudéjar gateway; Humboldt slept here in 1803; exhibition of silver and sale of handmade articles); the *Casa Figueroa* (once the residence of the Conde de Cadena, later the Casa de Moneda, today a museum containing art exhibits, furniture and paintings); the *Calle Real de San Agustin* (shops, old houses); the *Plaza de los Gallos* (old Spanish atmosphere); and the *William Spratling Museum* (pre-Columbian antiquities, silver).

From the northern end of town a cable-car system ("teleférico") glides through the air giving breathtaking views of Taxco, arriving eventually at the mesa more than 240 m (800 ft.) above the city called Lomas de Taxco. Here one finds a large hotel, art galleries, tennis courts, a golf course, restaurants and a small airport for light planes.

Every year in the week before Easter, beginning on Palm Sunday and culminating on Maundy Thursday and Good Friday, curious **processions take place in Taxco, in which "penitentes" (penitents with their feet in chains), as well as "encruzados" and "flagelantes" (bearing heavy thornbushes on their naked shoulders or whipping themselves with leather straps) play a realistically dramatic part.

SURROUNDINGS – About 15 km (9 miles) S lies the romantic Taxco Viejo on the site of a former Tlahuica settlement. Around the town are a number of old *haciendas*, with the remains of earlier buildings.

30 km (20 miles) NW of Taxco (Roads 95 and 55), in the Cacahuamilpa National Park, are the stalactitic **Cacahuamilpa Caves** (*Grutas de Cacahuamilpa*, Náhuatl "in the cocoa grainfields"; Hotel El Parador, SP), located at an altitude of 1100 m (3600 ft). Since the caves were discovered in 1835, they have been explored for a distance of more than 16 km (10 miles) without the end of the system having been reached. Presenting an immense variety of stalactitic formations in sixteen chambers, up to 80 m (263 ft) wide and up to 67 m (220 ft) high, these are the largest and most interesting caves in Mexico. 26 km (16 miles) N of Cacahuamilpa lie the **Caves of Estrella** (*Grutas de la Estrella*), opened in 1976, which are reached in a comfortable ascent or descent of 15 minutes. The largest cave, which is about 1 km (⅔ mile) in length and which contains almost exclusively stalactites, is probably connected to Cacahuamilpa, but the connection has not yet been discovered.

40 km (25 miles) W of Taxco is **Ixcateopan**. Remains found under the altar of the 16th c. church were claimed to be those of Cuauhtémoc, the last Aztec ruler, who was killed in Honduras on Cortés's orders in 1525. The claim gave rise to a fierce controversy among historians.

Tehuacán

See under Puebla (state)

Tehuantepec

State: Oaxaca (Oax.).
Altitude: 110 m (360 ft). – Population: 39,000.
Telephone dialing code: 9 19 71.
ⓘ **Coordinación Federal de Turismo**,
Matamoros 105/Esq. García Vigil
Oaxaca, Oax.;
tel. (9 19 51) 6 01 44, 6 00 45, 6 01 23.

HOTELS. – *Calli*, I, SP; *Tehuantepec*, II, SP; *Oasis*, II.

RESTAURANTS in most hotels; also *Kike, Colonial*.

RECREATION and SPORTS. – Hunting, fishing, swimming (Salina Cruz beach).

EVENTS. – Fiestas: January 22, San Sebastián; June 24, San Juan Bautista; June 30, San Pedro; August 15, Assumption; December 10–12, Virgen de Guadalupe. Market on Sunday.

The town of Tehuantepec, which gives its name to the Bay and Isthmus of Tehuantepec (the narrowest part of Mexico, only 200 km (125 miles) across), is an important road and railway junction, located in a depression surrounded by low hills and the wide arc of the Río Tehuantepec. This hot and humid tropical town is set amid luxuriant vegetation. The population consists mainly of Zapotec Indians and mestizos.

HISTORY. – Tehuantepec (Náhuatl, "hill of the jaguar") must have had a long history in pre-Hispanic times as a *Zapotec* center. Around A.D. 1470, the town was occupied by an army led by the Aztec ruler Axayácatl. – When the *Spaniards* arrived in 1521–2 it was ruled by Cocijo-pii, son of the Zapotec king Cocijo-eza and an Aztec princess, who allied himself with the Spaniards against the Aztecs. In the early years of the colonial period, Tehuantepec was one of the possessions granted to Hernán Cortés.

This strategically important town, located on the shortest land route in Mexico between the Atlantic and the Pacific, suggested to Cortés, as it did to the Spanish viceroys and later to the Mexican government, the need to develop the town's communications in order to take full advantage of this situation. Roads were built, and in due time a railway, but plans to construct a canal were never put into effect. After the opening of the Panama Canal in 1914, Tehuantepec declined rapidly in significance. Only in recent years has the development of the oil industry increased the importance of the port of Salina Cruz and thus of Tehuantepec as well.

SIGHTS. – The town has few old buildings of any note. The **Cathedral**, originally a Dominican church founded in 1544, has been much altered and rebuilt but still preserves its old arches and domes. The **Town Hall** (*Palacio Municipal*) is a striking light-colored building borne on columns.

The **Market** (*Mercado*) presents a lively and colorful scene, dominated – like much else in the town – by the sturdy local women with their interesting costumes and ornaments.

SURROUNDINGS. – 18 km (11 miles) S is the port of **Salina Cruz** (alt. 70 m (230 ft); pop. 50,000; hotels: Jacarandas, Altamar, Miramar; restaurants: Aloha, El Barquito, Los Pericos), which has developed rapidly in the last few years as a center for the shipment and processing of oil. For visitors, however, its only attraction is its proximity to the extensive beach of *La Ventosa* (Posada Rustrian), 7 km (4 miles) away,

26 km (16 miles) E of Tehuantepec, on Road 190, is **Juchitán de Zaragoza** (alt. 38 m (125 ft); pop. 45,000; hotels: La Mansion; Motel del Rio, SP; fiestas: May 15, San Isidro Labrador; August 13, Vela de Agosto; September 3, Vela Pineda), of importance as the commercial center of the surrounding area. Its interest to visitors lies in its market and attractive traditional costumes, worn mainly at fiestas.

15 km (9 miles) W of Tehuantepec on Road 190, a track goes off on the right to the archeological site of **Guiengola**. Some 6 km (4 miles) along this track, a path runs along the hillside through a picturesque landscape of rocks, scrub and cacti to a hill rising some 400 m (1300 ft) above the valley (1 hour's climb) on which are the ruins of the last great stronghold of the Zapotecs.

Here can be seen the remains of a *wall* 3 m (10 ft) high and 2 m (7 ft) thick which once ran around the whole hill. In the main plaza are the remains of a large four-story *temple pyramid*, three smaller cult buildings and

a ball court. On the slopes of the hill there once stood the palace of the Zapotec king Cocijo-eza, who in 1496 successfully withstood an Aztec attack on his stronghold. – From the crags on this hill there is a magnificent *view of the Tehuantepec valley.

Tenayuca

State: México (Mex.).

ACCESS. – The archeological site of Tenayuca lies just outside the village of San Bártolo, near Tlalnepantla, 12 km (7 miles) N of the center of Mexico City.

On the outskirts of Mexico City stands the imposing *Serpent Pyramid of Tenayuca, which shows seven successive rebuildings between the 13th and 16th c. A product of the interaction between Toltec culture and the rising Chichimec kingdom, it is a classical example of the Aztec temple pyramid.

HISTORY. – According to the traditional story, a party of *Chichimecs* under their leader Xólotl ("monster") established themselves at Tenayuca (Náhuatl, "walled site") in A.D. 1224, after taking part in the destruction of Tula. Xólotl and his successors, Nepaltzin ("revered cactus fruit") and Tlotzin ("falcon"), finally defeated the Toltecs in their new home in Culhuacán (1246), and at the beginning of the 14th c. the Chichimecs, already strongly "Toltecized", moved their capital to Texcoco. Tenayuca was in turn exposed to the influence of various other peoples, including the Tepanecs, the Tlahuicas and the Mexica. From the middle of the 15th c., the inhabitants of this region were for the most part under the control of the neighboring city of Tenochtitlán. – After the Conquest the *Spaniards* destroyed the temple which stood on the pyramid and appointed Rodrigo de Paz Moctezuma, son of the Aztec ruler Moctezuma II, as governor of Tenayuca.

The excavation of the site was begun by Leopoldo Batres around 1900 and continued by Ignacio Marquina in 1931 and 1957.

THE SITE. – The *Serpent Pyramid, which was dedicated to the sun god, appears to have been rebuilt (i.e., covered with a new structure) every 52 years at the end of the Aztec calendrical cycle. The most recent overbuildings, mainly under Aztec influence, were in 1351, 1403, 1455 and 1507. Two earlier overbuildings, in 1247 and 1299, may have taken place under Chichimec and Toltec influence.

The first pyramid measured 31 by 12 m (102 by 39 ft) and stood 8 m (26 ft) high; the last 66 by 62 m (217 by 203 ft) and 19 m (62 ft) high. Although nothing in the nature of an observatory was found by the excavators, it seems probable, from specially sited posts in the walls and certain other features, that the

Stone serpent, Tenayuca

structure served for astronomical observations or that its orientation was determined by the positions of celestial bodies. The posts were found to point to the precise spots where the sun sets on March 21 and September 23, so that here, as at Chichén Itzá and Teotihuacán, the N–S axis of the structure is displaced 17 degrees to the E.

The remains now visible date mainly from the last three overbuildings. In general, the final structure resembles the principal temple of Tenochtitlán, which was almost totally destroyed or buried under later buildings. The pyramid is surrounded on three sides by a base decorated with serpents, 138 of which can be seen in this "Serpent Wall" (Coatepantli). There are believed to have been 800 serpents originally. Set beside small platforms (two on the N side and one on the S) are coiled "fire serpents" or "turquoise serpents" (*xiuhcóatl*), probably porters of the sun, which date from the fifth overbuilding. – To the right of the pyramid is a *crypt* decorated with skulls and human bones, perhaps symbolizing the earth into which the sun sinks and disappears every evening. – Originally there were two staircases leading up the four tiers of the pyramid to the double temple on the summit.

Facing the pyramid is a small **museum** containing finds from the surrounding area, but which has been closed for some time.

SURROUNDINGS. – 3 km (2 miles) N in a well-maintained garden setting, is the completely restored **temple pyramid of Santa Cecilia Acatitlán**, probably dedicated to the sun and the rain god Tláloc. The temple itself has also been restored, so that the whole structure gives an excellent impression of Aztec religious architecture in the late Post-Classic period. Adjoining the pyramid is a very interesting museum in a house with a patio (various Aztec sculptures).

Tenochtitlán
See p. 30 and under Distrito Federal and Mexico City
See p. 30 and under Distrito Federal and Mexico City

Teotihuacán

State: México (Mex.).
Altitude: 2281 m (7484 ft).
(i) **Secretaría de Turismo,**
Av. Presidente Masaryk 172,
Ciudad de México, D.F.;
tel. (9 15) 2 50 85 55.

HOTELS. – *Villas Arqueológicas*, L, SP, tennis; *Posada Pirámides*, I.

RESTAURANTS in hotel; also *La Gruta* and restaurants in *Museum*.

ACCESS. – The site, at San Juan de Teotihuacán, is some 50 km (30 miles) from Mexico City and 88 km (55 miles) from Pachuca.

**Teotihuacán, situated on the treeless fringes of the Anáhuac valley, is the largest pre-Columbian site so far excavated in Meso-America, and one of the most impressive complexes of ruins in the world, notable for the symmetry of its layout and the unity of its architecture. During the first 600 years of the Christian era, Teotihuacán was the most influential political, religious and cultural power in Meso-America.

HISTORY. – Nothing is known of the builders of Teotihuacán (Náhuatl, "place where man becomes a god"), their language or history. It used to be thought that it was a Toltec city, but excavations at Tula have shown that Teotihuacán was abandoned or destroyed some 200 years before the Toltecs established their authority. The names of the site and of the individual structures are either Náhuatl or of modern origin, and bear no relationship to the original names.

During the period which can be designated as *Proto-Teotihuacán* (600–200 B.C.) village groups were formed, and toward the end of the period a large village with an area of 6 sq. km (2½ sq. miles) developed in the NW part of the site of the later town. It was at this time that the first obsidian workshops were established. This glass-like generally green and grey stone was indespensible as the raw material for finely made implements and as an object of trade. The actual development of the community into a town occurred during the *Teotihuacán I* phase (200 B.C. until the end of the pre-Christian era), in which the N–S axis of the "Street of the Dead" and the first parts of the Sun and Moon Pyramids were built. During this phase Teotihuacán was influenced by Oaxaca, as is shown by finds belonging to phase II of Monte Albán. During the following phase, *Teotihuacán II* (A.D. 0–350), the city reached its greatest extent, estimated at over 20 sq. km (7½ sq. miles), an area which exceeded that of Rome at that time. This period saw the completion of the Pyramid of the Sun and the Pyramid of the Moon, the erection of the Temple of Quetzalcóatl and the Citadel, as well as the creation of important pottery ("thin orange") and monumental sculptures. During *Teotihuacán III* (A.D. 350–650), the heyday of the city when the population reached 200,000, most of the upper stories – including those of the Temple of Quetzalcóatl and the Pyramid of the Moon – were undertaken. The Palace of Quetzalpapálotl and a considerable number of wall paintings are also of this period. The process of cultural cross-fertilization and trading exchanges between Teotihuacán on the one hand and Monte Albán, El Tajín, Pánuco, Cholula, Guerrero and the southern Maya territories on the other, were on an astonishing scale. During the 5th and 6th c. the metropolis exercised the widest sphere of influence in Meso-America. Whether this was achieved by invasion or by peaceful expansion as a result of political moves, by trade or through religion is not clear. At any rate strong indications of Teotihuacán cultural influence have been found in widely separated places, including Xochicalco (Morelia), Cacaxtla (Tlaxcala), Kaminaljuyú (Guatemala) and in Petén (Guatemala, especially in Tikal). During the final phase, Teotihuacán IV (A.D. 650–750), at the beginning of which the "Street of the Dead" was extended and fine wall paintings and pottery were still being produced, the cult site was suddenly and forcefully brought to an end.

This collapse was paralleled by that of other classic cultures of Meso-America, but occurred here 200 years earlier. Although the causes are still not known, the methodical destruction of the ceremonial center leads to the conclusion that the priests themselves destroyed their temples in the face of pressure from an external enemy (barbaric tribes from the NW?). Perhaps other reasons – for example, internal revolts or an economic crisis also contributed to the debacle. The once great metropolis was reduced to a regional center, and its population of about 30,000 lived amid the ruins communally with the primitive foreign intruders. Without doubt the collapse of Teotihuacán sent a shock wave throughout Meso-America, since the power centers decayed and the trade links were broken, all of which must have contributed to a general economic decline.

To later peoples like the Toltecs and Aztecs, the abandoned site of Teotihuacán was the abode of spirits, a city of mythological origin. – When the Spaniards passed this way in 1519 after their defeat in Tenochtitlán (the "Noche Triste" or "Sad Night"), the site was covered with earth. The first excavations were carried out by Almaraz in 1864, followed in the 1880s by Leopoldo Batres and Désiré Charnay. In the early years of the 20th c. some of the principal buildings were reconstructed, sometimes destroying or distorting the original forms. Excellent excavation and restoration work was later done by Manuel Gamio and Ignacio Marquina in the 1920s, the Instituto Nacional de Arqueología e Historia from 1962 on, under the direction of Ignacio Bernal and since 1980 under Rubén Cabrera, as well as René Millon of the University of Rochester, N.Y.

THE SITE. – In the center of the extensive archeological zone of some 20 sq. km (8 sq. miles), only part of which has been excavated, is the ceremonial center proper, covering an area of 4.2 sq. km (1½ sq. miles). If the architecture within this precinct now appears rather featureless, it should be remembered that originally all the façades were faced with multi-colored stucco and decorated with sculpture.

Adjoining Parking Lot 1 is the Unidad Cultural, with a small museum which gives an excellent survey of the development of Teotihuacán in a wide range of exhibits, chronological tables, maps and plans, etc. This part of the site was once occupied by an extensive complex of buildings, including the city's principal market.

Just beyond this is the Miccaotli or main street of the city, erroneously named the *Street of the Dead (Calle de los Muertos), 45 m (150 ft) wide, which runs S from the Pyramid of the Moon for a distance of 4 km (2½ miles). Crossing this, we come to an imposing square courtyard, bounded by four platforms, known as the Citadel (Ciudadela); it is thought to have contained cult buildings and the dwellings of priests and official dignitaries. This shows the talud-tablero style (an alternation of vertical and sloping wall surfaces) so common at Teotihuacán, with a predominance in this case of the vertical surfaces with panels framed in moldings. The panels and frames were originally faced with a thick coat of mortar covered with many-colored frescoes. – The talud-tablero style was adopted, usually in slightly altered form, at other pre-Columbian sites, including Monte Albán, Xochicalco, Kaminaljuyú and Tula.

In the center of the Citadel is the *Temple of Quetzalcóatl, a pyramid, twice built over, which is notable for its sculptured figures, originally 366 in number – an unusual feature on a site which has yielded little sculpture.

It is not known to which god this temple was dedicated, but it was evidently associated with rain and with maize. The sculptured figures are of two types, which alternate around the façade of the temple. One represents a serpent, its head framed in flower petals or feathers and its body surrounded by shell and spiral motifs symbolizing water. The other is a stylized mask, perhaps of the rain god Tláloc or a maize god, with large round eyes and two fangs. There are some remains of coloring on the figures, which were originally coated with stucco.

Going N along the Street of the Dead toward the Pyramid of the Moon, we come in 400 m (¼ mile), on the left, to the Two-Story Buildings (Edificios Superpuestos), originally comprising a porch with six columns, a large courtyard with a staircase, small temples, arcades and various other structures. On some of the walls are remains of frescoes which show resemblances to those of El Tajín. – Opposite this is a group of remains known only as the 1917 excavations (Excavaciones de 1917). – Beyond this group is the Viking Group (Grupo Viking),

Sculptured serpents and masks on the Temple of Quetzalcóatl, Teotihuacán

named after the American foundation which worked here. In one of the two courtyards around which this complex is built were found two layers of mica 6 cm (2½ in.) thick, the purpose of which can only be guessed at.

Beyond the *Priests' House* (Casa de los Sacerdotes), on the right of the road, a broad staircase leads up to the *Plaza of the Pyramid of the Sun* (Plaza de la Pirámide del Sol), some 70 m (230 ft) wide. In the middle is an *altar*, at the corners remains of temples and other buildings.

On the E side of the plaza towers the largest structure at Teotihuacán, the **Pyramid of the Sun** (*Pirámide del Sol*). This gigantic monument, exceeded in size in Meso-America only by the pyramid of Cholula, is located so that on the day of the summer solstice the sun sets exactly opposite the main façade.

The area covered by the Pyramid of the Sun (220 by 225 m (720 by 740 ft) is almost as great as that of the Pyramid of Cheops in Egypt; its height (63 m (207 ft), or 74 m (243 ft) with the original temple), is about 70 m (230 ft) less. Its volume, mostly consisting of adobe bricks, has been calculated as 1 million cubic metres (35,000,000 cubic feet). These figures under-state its original bulk, since in the course of an ill-conceived restoration in the early years of this century a layer of stone and stucco some 7 m (23 ft) thick was removed from the facing of the pyramid.

A double flight of steps leads up to the first level of the pyramid, from which a broad *staircase* runs up the higher levels to the summit, once occupied by the temple. From here there is a magnificent *view* of the whole archeological zone.

In 1971 a shaft 7 m (23 ft) deep was discovered by chance at the foot of the main staircase. From the foot of this shaft a passage 103 m (340 ft) long leads to a group of chambers arranged in clover-leaf formation. In these chambers (not yet open to the public) were found remains of pottery and mica discs (mirrors?) which had evidently escaped the attentions of robbers. The purpose of this underground complex, probably constructed about A.D. 250, can only be conjectured (place of sacrifice, burial vault, cult chamber in honour of the rain or maize god?).

On a terrace on the opposite side of the Street of the Dead are the remains of four temples, forming a complex known as the *Patio of the Four Little Temples* (Patio de los Cuatro Templitos). – Beyond this, on the right of the road, is a long stretch of crudely built walling which is ascribed to the Chichimecs, and behind this, under a protective roof, are interesting *wall paintings* depicting a jaguar some 2 m (6½ ft) long. – Just before the plaza in front of the Pyramid of the Moon is reached, we see on the left the *Temple of the Mythological Animals* (Templo de los Animales Mito-lógicos) and the *Temple of Agriculture* (Templo de la Agricultura). The Temple of the Mythological Animals containing remains of frescoes depicting animals, some of which are now in the National

Pyramid of the Sun, Teotihuacán

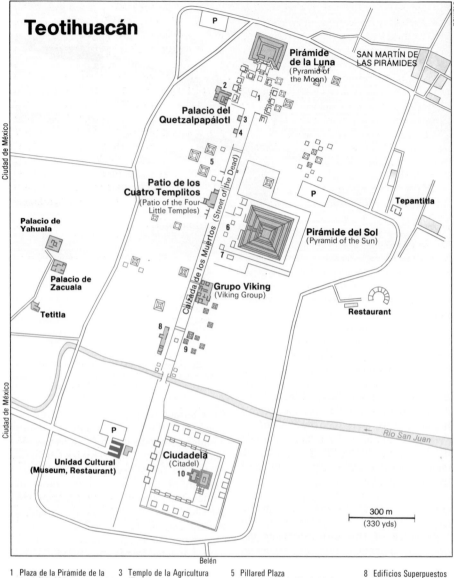

Teotihuacán

Ciudad de México

Ciudad de México

Pirámide de la Luna (Pyramid of the Moon)

SAN MARTÍN DE LAS PIRÁMIDES

Palacio del Quetzalpapálotl

Patio de los Cuatro Templitos (Patio of the Four Little Temples)

Calle de los Muertos (Street of the Dead)

Palacio de Yahuala

Palacio de Zacuala

Tetitla

Pirámide del Sol (Pyramid of the Sun)

Tepantitla

Grupo Viking (Viking Group)

Restaurant

Río San Juan

Belén

Unidad Cultural (Museum, Restaurant)

Ciudadela (Citadel)

300 m (330 yds)

1 Plaza de la Pirámide de la Luna (Plaza of the Pyramid of the Moon)
2 Palacio de los Jaguares (Palace of the Jaguars)
3 Templo de la Agricultura (Temple of Agriculture)
4 Templo de los Animales Mitológicos (Temple of the Mythological Animals)
5 Pillared Plaza
6 Plaza de la Pirámide del Sol (Plaza of the Pyramid of the Sun)
7 Casa de los Sacerdotes (Priests' House)
8 Edificios Superpuestos (Two-Story Buildings)
9 1917 excavations
10 Templo de Quetzalcóatl (Temple of Quetzalcóatl)

Museum of Anthropology in Mexico City; the Temple of Agriculture had frescoes of plants, now replaced by copies.

The *Plaza of the Pyramid of the Moon* at the end of the Street of the Dead is the most impressive example of architectural planning at Teotihuacán, notable alike for the symmetry of its layout and the harmony of its proportions. It is surrounded by a series of staircases and pyramidal platforms, mostly of four stories, which were originally topped by temples in the same way as the principal pyramid. In the middle of the plaza is a large square *altar*.

On the left of the plaza is the **Palace of the Quetzal Butterfly** (*Palacio del Quetzalpapálotl*), discovered in 1962, the most magnificent mansion in the city, probably the residence of the chief priests. It is richly decorated and has well-preserved frescoes. A staircase with a large serpent's head leads up to a porch or antechamber decorated with wall paintings, and beyond this is a small arcaded courtyard with square columns covered with interesting bas-reliefs depicting the mythological figures of the Quetzal butterfly together with bird and water symbols. The reliefs were originally painted and had inset discs of obsidian, some of which have been preserved. Note also the highly stylized figures painted on a red ground and the jagged points on the roof bearing year glyphs.

The adjoining **Palace of the Jaguars** (*Palacio de los Jaguares*) has notable early wall paintings depicting felines with human heads and jaguars blowing conch shells. In one frieze are the symbols of the rain god and the year. – From here a tunnel leads into part of what is probably the oldest structure in Teotihuacán, known as the **Substructure of the Feathered Snail-Shells** (*Subestructura de los Caracoles Emplumados*), lying under the Palace of the Quetzal Butterfly. The largest of the surviving façades, originally belonging to a temple, is decorated with magnificent *reliefs of snail-shells decorated with feathers (musical instruments?), green birds (parrots?) and four-petalled flowers.

On the N side of the plaza is the imposing *Pyramid of the Moon** (*Pirámide de la Luna*), the front of which is formed by a five-story pyramidal structure in *talud-tablero* style. A broad staircase leads up to the pyramid proper, which consists of four stories, each set back from the one below. The pyramid covers a total area of 140 by 150 m (460 by 490 ft) and stands 46 m (151 ft) high. Although it is 17 m (56 ft) lower than the Pyramid of the Sun, the rise in the ground means that its summit is on the same level. The staircase extends only to the third level. From the top of the pyramid there is another fine *view of the site.

Some distance away from the ceremonial center, and best reached by car, are some interesting remains of dwelling houses. The **Tepantitla** complex (Náhuatl, "place of thick walls"), 500 m (550 yds) E of the Pyramid of the Sun, has fine *wall paintings of richly attired priests, the god Tláloc rising from the ocean and dispensing rain, the paradisiac world of the rain god, etc.

1.5 km (1 mile) from the Pyramid of the Sun, on the W side of the Street of the Dead, is the site of **Tetitla** (Náhuatl, "place of stones"), which also has fine frescoes dating from two different building periods. They depict jaguars with feather headdresses, richly clad priests, the rain god Tláloc, the quetzal bird, symbolic hands, etc.

100 m (100 yds) away are the *Zacuala Palace* (Palacio de Zacuala) and the *Yahuala Palace* (Palacio de Yahuala), both evidently fortified residences.

400 m ($\frac{1}{4}$ mile) W of Tetitla is the interesting site of **Atetelco** (Náhuatl, "on the stone wall by the water"), with two patios dating from different building periods. One of these, on a lower level, has magnificent *frescoes of priests, coyotes, birds' heads, etc. The White Patio, the older of the two, has three fine colonnades and frescoes of jaguars and coyotes with feather headdresses and Tláloc symbols.

The *son et lumière* show, put on six evenings a week during the dry season, is highly impressive.

10 km (6 miles) from Teotihuacán is the imposing fortified convent of **Acolman** (p. 70).

Tepic

State: Nayarit (Nay.).
Altitude: 915 m (3000 ft). – Population 200,000.
Telephone dialling code: 9 13 21.
ⓘ **Coordinación Federal de Turismo,**
Av. Mexico Sur 253A, 1st floor,
Local;
tel. 3 09 93, 2 09 45.

HOTELS. – *Fray Junipero Serra*, Lerdo 23 Pte., I, SP; *Motel La Loma*, Paseo de la Loma 301, I, SP; *Sierra de Alicia*, Av. México 180, I; *Motel del Sol*, Insurgentes 284 Ote, II; *Tepic*, Dr. Martínez 438 Ote, III.

RESTAURANTS in most hotels; also *Roberto´s*, Paseo de la Loma e Insurgentes; *Chante Clair*, Laureles y Góngora; *La Terraza*, Insurgentes 98 Pte.; *El Farallón*, Av. Insurgentes 276 Pte.

EVENT. – July 25, Día de Santiago Apóstol.

Tepic, capital of Nayarit state, lies at the foot of the extinct volcano of Sangangüey (2360 m – 7743 ft), in a setting of green wooded hills 50 km (30 miles) E of the Pacific coast. To the E of the town extends a wide plain with tobacco and sugar-cane plantations. Until the beginning of the 20th c. Tepic led the tranquil life of a remote provincial town but it now has many modern features.

HISTORY. – The settlement of Tepic (Náhuatl, "hard stone") was founded by Nuño Beltrán de Guzmán (1531) near the old Indian town of Nayarit, and was granted a charter by Philip V in 1711. During the colonial period and the first century of Mexican independence, it was largely isolated from the center of the country, partially as a result of repeated attacks by rebellious Cora and Huichol Indians. The modern development of the town and surrounding area began only when a railway line to Tepic was opened in 1912.

Street scene, Tepic

fishing. – About 70 km (43 miles) from Tepic, in the direction of Guadalajara, Road 15 traverses a bizarre area, strewn with lava bolders (Ceboruco Volcano). To the township of **Ixtlan del Rio** (Nahuatl, "place of the obsidians"; alt. 1024 m (3360 ft); pop. 17,000; Hotel Calle Real; fiestas on last Sunday in October, Día de Cristo Rey and December 8–12, Virgin of Guada-lupe). – 3 km (2 miles) farther, on the L, lies one of the few archeological sights in western Mexico (*Centro "Ceremonial Rincón de Ixtlan" y "Los Toriles"*) not consisting solely of cemeteries. The site, part of which has been excavated, appears to have been inhabited as early as the 6th and 7th c. A.D., though the remains now visible probably date from the early Post-Classic period (A.D. 900–1250), when Toltex influence was certainly being felt here. Among the interesting structures are an L-shaped building on a low platform with remains of many square columns and a round building with cruciform windows and two altar platforms, which was presumably dedicated to Quetzalcóatl in his capacity as god of the winds. Nearby are more dwellings, platforms and altars, as well as several buildings which have not yet been excavated.

40 km (25 miles) S of Tepic is **Compostela** (alt. 1020 m (3350 ft); pop. 20,000; Hotel Flores; fiestas: first Friday in December, Día del Señor de la Misericordia; July 25, Día de Santiago Apóstol), an old mining town situated in a tobacco-growing area; it has an interesting 16th c. parish church.

SW of Compostela on bays of the Pacific are several small fishing villages which have recently become popular seaside resorts; among them are *Rincón de Guayabitos* (hotels: Suites Costa Alegre, Playa de Oro, Estancia San Carlos, Fiesta Mar; bungalows: El Delfín, El Rinconcito, La Hacienda, María Teresa, Villa del Sol Dorado) and *La Peñita de Jaltemba* (hotels: La Siesta, Miramar, Posada Hilda, San Juanito, Rosita; bunga-lows: Las Palmas).

50 km (30 miles) W of Tepic is the bathing beach of *Playa Miramar*, with the fishing village of Santa Cruz, and 23 km (14 miles) N of this is **San Blas**, which has developed in recent years into a popular seaside resort (pop. 6000; Suites San Blas, Aticamas y Las Palmas, SP; Motel Las Brisas, Cuauhtémoc 106 Sur, SP; Posada Casa Morales, Cuauhtémoc; Bucanero, Juárez Pte. 75; Los Flamingos, Juárez 105 Nte.; rstaurants: La Isla, Torino; fiesta: February 3, Día de San Blas). During the colonial period San Blas was an important commercial port handling trade with East Asia, as is indicated by the remains of an old Spanish fort. From this picturesque little fishing town, attrac-tive *boat trips can be made on the local rivers and lagoons, notable for their abundance of bird life. Among the beautiful long *beaches near the town are the *Playa de Matanchén*, to the S, and the *Playa de los Cocos*.

Another popular bathing beach is the *Playa Los Corchos*, 100 km (60 miles) NW of Tepic via *Santiago Ixcuintla*. – 25 km (16 miles) from the coast an attractive excursion can be made to the *Laguna Mexcaltitán*, 25 km (16 miles) N. The village of **Mexcaltitán** (fiesta: June 29) lies like a miniature Venice on an island in the lake, which is well stocked with fish and the sanctuary of numerous waterfowl. Some historians believe that this island is the legendary Aztlán, the original homeland of the Nahua peoples and thus of the Aztecs.

SIGHTS. – Tepic has little to offer in the way of historic buildings, but it is a good base for excursions to the beaches on the coast or to the villages of the local Indians (who can also be encountered on their visits to the town).

In the Plaza Principal is the mid-18th c. *Cathedral*, with two neo-Gothic towers. The church of *La Cruz de Zacate* (mid 18th c.) contains a cross from Zacategras which is venerated by the Indians. The *Amado Nervo Museum* is devoted to the well-known Mexican poet of that name, a native of Tepic. There is also an interesting ***Regional Museum** (*Museo Regional de Antropología e Historia*), with archeo-logical finds from the region, pictures of the colonial period and ethnological material on the Cora and Huichol Indians.

SURROUNDINGS. – Huichol and Cora villages in Nayarit and Jalisco can be visited by light aircraft. Roads are under construction to some of these remote settlements. – The mountain villages of these tribes can also be visited from **Acaponeta**, either in light aircraft, in a cross-country vehicle like a jeep or on a mule. The Cora Indians live not only in the mountains but also in the coastal region, particularly in the villages of *Rosamorada* and *Huajicori*, N of Acaponeta.

40 km (25 miles) SE of Tepic is the *Laguna Santa María*, a crater lake which offers good swimming and

Tepotzotlán

State: Mexico (Mex.).
Altitude: 2270 m (7450 ft). – Population: 27,000.
ⓘ **Secretaría de Turismo,**
    Av. Presidente Masaryk 172,
    Ciudad de México, D.F.;
    tel. (9 15) 2 50 85 55.

ACCESS. – From Mexico City 42 km (26 miles) N on
Road 57, then minor road (2 km – 1¼ miles) to
Tepotzotlán.

Tepotzotlán, an attractive little colonial town within easy reach of Mexico City, was once one of the major centers of religious education in New Spain. Its *convent now houses a museum of religious art of the greatest interest, and the excellently restored church is a gem of Mexican Baroque architecture.

Church of San Francisco Xavier, Tepotzotlán

HISTORY. – Tepotzotlán (Náhuatl, "place of the hunchback") was an old Otomí settlement in which the Jesuit *Colegio de San Martin* was founded in 1582. The buildings were erected by local craftsmen with the support of the Indian caciques (or chiefs). Here the Spaniards were taught the Náhuatl and Otomí languages and the sons of the Indian élite were given a religious education. During the 17th and 18th c. the convent was considerably enlarged. One of the principal contributors to this rebuilding was Pedro Ruiz de Ahumada, who financed the reconstruction of the church of St Francis Xavier, which was reconsecrated in 1682 but not completed until 1762. After the expulsion of the Jesuits from New Spain in 1767, the college and the church passed into other hands, but after Mexico became independent, the Jesuits returned to Tepotzotlán – although their influence was now much reduced – and remained there until the dissolution of the convent in 1859. – Some years ago responsibility for the convent and the church was transferred to the Instituto Nacional de Antropología e Historia. In 1964 a museum of religious art was installed in the college, and the church now also serves a similar purpose.

SIGHTS. – The **façade of the *convent church**, mainly built between 1628 and 1762, ranks with the façades of the Valenciana church at Guanajuato and Santa Prisca at Taxco as one of the supreme examples of the Chirrigueresque style in Mexico. The work of a number of different artists between 1760 and 1762, it is a magnificently harmonious composition of *estípites* (pilasters with their narrower ends downward), niches containing statues and medallions of relief carving. Above the window is a statue of St Francis Xavier, and in the lateral niches are figures of SS. Ignacio de Loyola, Francisco de Borja, Luis Gonzaga and Estanislao de Kotska, the leading personalities of the Jesuit order. The two-story tower also has *estípites*. The small

tower to the rear of the church belongs to the Santa Casa de Loreto.

The **INTERIOR of the church, which is entered through the convent, is notable particularly for the seven sumptuously gilded altars, mostly of carved wood, in typical Churrigueresque style. The tripartite **high altar**, similar in design to the façade of the church, has a statue of St Francis Xavier in the middle, together with very expressive sculptures of the Immaculate Conception (upper central part) and St John the Baptist (left-hand niche). The reredos to the right is dedicated to St Luis Gonzaga, the one on the left to St Estanislao de Kotska. – Other notable features are the altars and chapels, dating from between 1733 and 1758, of *San Ignacio de Loyola* (figures of the founders of the Jesuit order), *Nuestra Señora de Guadalúpe* (pictures of the Virgin of Guadalupe, patroness of Mexico, and frescoes on the same theme by Miguel Cabrera), *Neustra Señora de la Luz* (superb statue), the *Relicario de San José* (picture by José Ibarra, very beautiful small retablo) and *Nuestra Señora de Loreto* (copy of the Santa Casa of Loreto in Italy, reredos with an early Italian statue).

Adjoining the Loreto chapel is an octagonal chamber, the **Camarín**, which is one of the peak achievements of Mexican High Baroque. The hand of Indian

Camarín, San Francisco Xavier

artists can be detected in the form and decoration of the retablos and the ceiling. Particularly notable are the figures of the Archangels and the silver ornamentation, now blackened by oxidation. The early groined vaulting still shows Mudéjar influence. The magnificence of the total effect is enhanced by the light filtering through the alabaster windows.

The old Jesuit college now houses the ***National Museum of the Vice-royalty** (*Museo Nacional del Virreinato*). In the *Fountain Cloister* (Claustro de los Aljibes) are oil paintings by Cristóbal de Villalpando. From here we enter the *House Chapel* (Capilla Doméstica), in the porch (*portería*) of which are pictures by Miguel Cabrera.

The vaulting of the **Capilla Doméstica**, which dates from the mid 17th c. but was subsequently altered, bears the emblems of the six principal religious orders which carried out missionary work in New Spain. It has a very fine *altar*, with sculpture, mirrors and pictures of Jesuit saints. To the left can be seen the kneeling figures of the donor, Pedro Ruiz de Ahumada.

The numerous rooms and corridors of the museum contain a rich display, varied from time to time, of **religious art** of the 16th–19th c. from all parts of the Viceroyalty of New Spain, including sculpture, altarpieces and pictures by the leading artists of the colonial period together with furniture, porcelain, arms and armor and liturgical utensils and articles of all kinds. Some rooms in the college are regularly used for concerts and dramatic performances.

SURROUNDINGS. – 27 km (17 miles) SW by way of *San Miguel Cañadas* is an aqueduct of several tiers built by the Jesuits in the 18th c. to supply water to Tepotzoltán, **Los Arcos del Sitio**. It is the highest in Mexico (60 m – 200 ft).

26 km (16 miles) NW of the turning for Tepotzotlàn, on Road 57, a side road branches off on the right for Tepeji del Rio and the great Toltec site of **Tula* (20 km (12 miles): see p. 272).

Tepoztlán
See under Morelos

Tequila
See under Jalisco

Texcoco de Mora

State: Mexico (Mex.).
Altitude: 2278 m (7474 ft). – Population 68,000.
Telephone dialing code: 9 15 95.
ⓘ **Secretaría de Turismo,**
Av. Presidente Masaryk 172,
Ciudad de México, D.F.;
tel. (9 15) 2 50 85 55.

ACCESS. – From Mexico City via Los Reyes on Road 190 and then on 136 44 km (27 miles); on Roads 85 or 85D and 99 about 46 km (29 miles). A direct road via the Texcoco lake is planned. From the archeological site of Teotihuacán it is 35 km (22 miles) to Texcoco.

HOTELS. – *Posada Santa Bertha*, Netzahualcóyotl 213; *Iberia*, Bravo 100.

RESTAURANTS in hotels; also *Haus María Elisabeth*, Netzahualcóyotl 6; *Cortijo La Morena*, Callejón de San Pablo 107; *La Parroquia*, Plaza Constitución 152.

Between the 14th and 16th c. Texcoco, then situated on the shores of Lake Texcoco (now dried up), was a place of some importance which rivalled the Aztec capital of Tenochtitlán, built on an island in the lake. The modern town, well situated within easy reach of Mexico City, is a market town for woolen clothing, pottery and glass, with many archeological sites and treasures of colonial art and architecture in the surrounding area.

HISTORY. – At the beginning of the 14th c. the Chichimecs, who had founded Tenayuca in the previous century during the reign of their ruler Xólotl, transferred their capital to Texcoco (Náhuatl, "place of the great rocks"), which had been founded during the Toltec period. In the second half of the 14th c. the town came under the control of the Tepanecs of Atzcapotzalco (Náhuatl, "anthill of men"); but in 1428 the Tepanecs were defeated by an alliance of the Mexica and Texcoco, and in 1431 the kingdom of Texcoco was restored. Its general ruler *Netzahualcóyotl* ("Hungry Coyote", 1418–72), who won legendary fame as poet and warrior, entered into an alliance with Tenochtitlán and Tlacopán (Tacuba). Thereafter Texcoco, although politically subject to the warlike Mexica, enjoyed its heyday as a center of art and culture. After the death of Netzahualcóyotl's son and successor, *Netzahualpilli* (1472–1515), there were disputes over the succession which the Mexica exploited to the disadvantage of Texcoco.

Monument to Netzahualcóyotl, Texcoco

Arches at the entrance to the atrium of the church at Papalotla

After the *Spaniards* captured Texcoco in 1521, encountering little resistance, they launched from here the ships which they had built at Tlaxcala and which played a decisive part in the conquest of Tenochtitlán. It is estimated that Texcoco had a population of over 150,000 when it was taken by the Spaniards. Soon after their arrival, the Franciscans built a convent school here for the instruction of the Indians. In 1575–6 the population was decimated by plague, and a century later Texcoco was still a small town of no consequence.

SIGHTS. – Little is left to recall the former splendor of Texcoco. Of the *convent*, which was built beside Netzahualpilli's palace, there remain only the porch and a Renaissance cloister. The *church* has a finely decorated N doorway.

SURROUNDINGS. – 7 km (4 miles) N is the village of *Chiconcuac* (market: Tuesday) which is renowned for its woolen goods (*sarapes, rebozos*). Nearby is *Papalotla*, which has the attractive little church of Santo Toribio (Baroque retablos of carved wood; intricately carved *arches at entrance to atrium, 18th c.).

22 km (14 miles) NE of Texcoco is *Tepetlaoxtoc*, with a Dominican convent (1529; cloister with remains of frescoes), a beautiful fountain and an 18th c. church.

7 km (4 miles) E of Texcoco is the hacienda of *Molino de las Flores* ("Mill of Flowers"), established in 1616 but now much dilapidated. Notable features are the small Baroque chapels and the beautiful gardens. In the vicinity, on the *Cerro de Texotzingo*, are remains of Netzahualcóytl's sumptuous summer residence, with baths and "hanging gardens".

3 km (2 miles) S of Texcoco is *Chapingo*. In the main building (Edificio Principal) of the College of Agriculture (Escuela Nacional de la Agricultura) has some of Diego Rivera's finest *frescoes, depicting the Mexican agrarian revolution, the fertility of the earth and the prospect of a better future for mankind.

A short distance from Chapingo is **Huexotla** (Náhuatl, "place of meadows"), once a town of some importance, though under the political control of Texcoco. It still retains the walls which surrounded the sacred precinct (Teocalli) – an extensive archeological zone of which only a fraction has been investigated. – Other features of interest are a small and modest Franciscan convent of 1541, with two 16th c. stone crosses in the atrium, and – in striking contrast – the ornate Churrigueresque façade of the church of San Luis Obispo (17th and 18th c.), with marked Indian features. The church has a fine stone pulpit of the 16th c., also showing Indian features.

Farther S is the village of *San Miguel Coatlinchán* (Náhuatl, "house of the snake"), with an attractive church dedicated to St Michael, a fortified structure with a Baroque façade and a tile-faced tower. Near here was found the huge stone figure, weighing no less that 167 tons, of the water goddess Chalchiuhtlicue, sister and wife of the rain god Tláloc, which now stands at the entrance to the National Museum of Anthropology in Mexico City.

25 km (16 miles) from Texcoco is the famous convent of *Acolman (p. 70), and 35 km (22 miles) away is the site of *Teotihuacán (p. 257).

Teziutlán

State: Puebla (Pue.).
Altitude: 1990 m (6529 ft). – Population: 59,000.
Telephone dialing code: 9 12 31.
ⓘ **Coordinación Federal de Turismo,**
Blvd. Hermanos Serdán y Blvd. Norte,
Puebla, Pue.;
tel. (91 22) 48 29 77, 48 31 77, 48 30 44.

HOTELS. – *Virreinal*, Hidalgo 78, I; *Central*, Hidalgo 801, II; *Valdés*, Hidalgo 903, II.

RESTAURANTS in most hotels; also *A.D.O.*, Allende 25; *Plaza*, Hidalgo 901.

EVENTS. – Beginning of August, fair, with performances by Voladores; market on Friday and Sunday.

The attractive colonial town of Teziutlán lies among forest-clad hills on a winding road cut from the rock. Although the town itself has no features of major tourist interest, it is conveniently situated on one of the routes from Mexico City to the Gulf of Mexico and is a good base from which to explore the interesting hill country in the surrounding area.

SIGHTS. – The town, founded in 1520, has many fine old colonial buildings and a pretty main square with the *church of El Carmen.*

SURROUNDINGS. – 15 km (9 miles) W are the *Chignautla* springs. – 46 km (29 miles) W of Teziutlán, just after Zaragoza, a side road runs N (17 km – 11 miles) to **Zacapoaxtla** (alt. 1800 m (5900 feet); pop. 18,000; fiesta at beginning of May; market on Wednesday; accommodations: Jardin, and at Apulco, 6 km (4 miles) N), in a magnificent mountain setting but frequently shrouded in mist, where visitors will find great tracts of unspoiled country and the settlements of various Indian tribes which have preserved their old way of life and customs. The traditional festivals of the Nahua, Otomí and Totonacs are among the most interesting and colorful in the whole of Mexico. In the town itself there are the churches of Guadalupe and San Pedro.

35 km (22 miles) N on a magnificent mountain road is *Cuetzalán ("place of the quetzal": alt. 1022 m. (3354 ft); accommodations: Posada Jackelin, Posada Cuetzalán, Las Garzas, Rivello; between Cuetzalán and Zacapoaxtla: Tres Arroyos; fiestas: July 15–18, local festival; October 2–6, San Francisco and Coffee Fair; December 12, Guadalupe; market on Sunday).

The picturesque little town of Cuetzalán (Puebla state), in the Sierra Norte, is the center for various groups of Indians, who flock into the town on market days and festivals in their colorful costumes. – The town is renowned for its annual **festivals, at which the best folk groups in the region (Quetzales, Negritos, Santiagos, Voladores) perform their characteristic dances. – The main features of interest in Cuetzalán are the weekend *market*, the *Town Hall* (Palacio Municipal), in a rather European style of architecture and a small ethnographical museum; nearby is the Parroquia with an unusual tower; in the main square stands a clock tower and just outside the town the *Church of Guadalupe* before which are graves artistically decorated with flowers. – The economy of Cuetzalán and the surrounding area is centered on the growing and processing of coffee.

For archeological enthusiasts there is an interesting excursion (50 minutes in a vehicle suitable for cross-country driving) to the archeological site of *Yohualichán (Náhuatl, "house of the night").

This cult center, built on four different terraces, is the only one in a style similar to El Tajín (p. 125). Visitors can see four structures, three of which have been partly restored. The most interesting of these, on the second terrace, is a seven-story **pyramid** which, like the other buildings on the site, has the niches characteristic of El Tajín. The site's ball-court (juego de pelota) with a length of approx. 90 m (295 ft.) is

one of the largest in Mesoamerica. Since Yohualichán, like El Tajín, was inhabited by Totonacs when the Spaniards arrived, the large structures on both of these sites were long attributed to that people. It is still not known with certainty who were the builders of these cities of the Classic period (A.D. 300–900). The results of the excavations so far carried out show that Yohualichán did not achieve the artistic level of El Tajín, and there is much evidence to suggest that it was an earlier foundation.

Tijuana

State: Baja California Norte (B.C.N.).
Altitude: 29 m (95 ft). – Population: 1,200,000.
Telephone dialing code: 91 66.

(i) **Coordinación Federal de Turismo,**
Linea Internacional,
Puerta Mexico, Planta Alta,
Col. Federal;
tel. 82 33 47–9, 86 54 01–5.

HOTELS. – *El Presidente Tijuana*, Blvd. Agua Caliente 1, L, SP; *Lucerna*, Paseo de los Heroes y A. L. Rodríquez, I, SP, tennis; *El Conquistador*, Blvd. Agua Caliente Sur 700, I, SP; *Country Club*, Tapachula 1, I, SP; *Palacio Azteca*, Av. 16 de Septiembre 213, I, SP; *Padre Kino*, Blvd. Agua Caliente, II; *Tecate*, Calle 6a y Constitución:, II; *Álvarez*, Callejón 1, Naciones Unidas 167, III; *Nan King*, Calle 2a 390, III; *Las Palmas*, 3 km (2 miles) on Ensenada road, III.

RESTAURANTS in most hotels; also *Matteotti*, Blvd. Agua Caliente 222; *Reno*, Calle Hidalgo 1939; *La Costa*, Galeana 150; *Pedrín*, Av. Revolución 1115; *El Abajeño de Guadalajara*, Blvd. Agua Caliente 101; *Cesar's*, Calle 5a y Av. Revolución; *Arizona*, Blvd. Agua Caliente 106.

RECREATION and SPORTS. – Swimming, water skiing, surfing, fishing, tennis, golf, riding.

EVENT. – Fiesta on September 16, Dia de la Independencia.

Tijuana is the largest Mexican town on the border with the United States (California), and of all Mexican towns the one most exposed to American influence. Living mainly

Street scene in Tijuana

from tourism, it draws many millions of visitors every year, principally from the Californian cities of San Diego, 25 km (16 miles) away, and Los Angeles (260 km – 160 miles). It is the starting-point of the Carretera Transpeninsular, which runs S through the entire length of Baja California.

HISTORY. – Tijuana (from Cochimí *Ticuán*, "nearby water") has had a short history, having grown out of a cattle-rearing hacienda named *Tía Juana* ("Aunt Jane") established by José María Echandi in 1829. The town's rise began during the Prohibition period, when it provided ready access to liquor for deprived US citizens.

SIGHTS. – One of the few notable buildings in the city is the *Cathedral* (20th c.), dedicated to the Virgin of Guadalupe. The great attractions of Tijuana lie in its shops, offering duty-free goods from all over the world as well as Mexican folk art and souvenirs, its wide range of entertainments (bullfights, horse and dog races, jai alai, baseball) and its night life. The life of the city, particularly on weekends, centers on the main square, the *Parque Municipal Guerrero*, the shopping area around the *Avenida Revolución* and the *Bulevar Agua Caliente* with its numerous hotels, restaurants, shops and sports arenas.

SURROUNDINGS. – 10 km (6 miles) S are the beautiful beaches of *Playas de Acapulco*.

50 km (30 miles) E on Road 2 is *Tecate* (alt. 107 m (351 ft); pop. 78,000; hotels: El Dorado, San Carlos; El Refugio, Indotel; fiestas: first Sunday in July; December 12, Día de Nuestra Señora de Guadalupe), an agricultural and industrial center with a large brewery; border crossing into the United States. – 66 km (41 miles) E on the Mexicali road is *La Rumorosa*, with bizarre rock formations from which there are magnificent *views of desert country. – Some 30 km (20 miles) beyond this is the *Laguna Salada*, which lies below sea level.

From Tecate it is 140 km (87 miles) to **Mexicali** (alt. 3 m (10 ft); pop. 730,000; hotels: Holiday Inn, La Cachanilla, Del Norte, Lucerna, La Siesta, Bahía; restaurants: La Misión Dragón, Chu-Lin, Palacio Mandarín, Mandolino, Del Mar, Bum Bum.) Until 1898 this was a village of the Cucapá Indians named Laguna del Alamo: it is now the dynamic capital of Baja California Norte, an important agricultural center (cotton, fruit, vegetables, etc.) and a border town opposite its sister city of *Calexico* in the United States. SE of Mexicali, near the little town of Nuevo León, is the geo-thermal zone of *Cerro Prieto*. ***Laguna Volcán** is that rare phenomenon, a mud volcano.

200 km (125 miles) S of Mexicali is the fishing village of *San Felipe* (pop. 18,000; hotels: Castel San Felipe, Riviera; fishing competitions), now a popular vacation resort. Deep-sea fishermen come here to catch the totoaba, a 1.50 m (5 ft) long sea bass which is found here and nowhere else.

Tlacolula
See under Oaxaca

Tlaquepaque
See under Guadalajara

Tlaxcala (State)

State of Tlaxcala (Tlax.). – Capital: Tlaxcala.
Area: 4027 sq. km (1555 sq. miles).
Population: 613,100.
ⓘ **Coordinación Federal de Turismo,**
Blvd. Mariano Sánchez 11B, 1st floor,
Tlaxcala, Tlax.;
tel. (9 12 46) 2 23 69.

Tlaxcala, the smallest but also one of the most densely populated states in Mexico, is bounded on three sides by Puebla, on the W by México state and on the N by Hidalgo. It is a region of forests and cultivated land lying at a relatively high altitude, with a pleasantly cool climate. Within the state is Mexico's fifth highest mountain, La Malinche or Malantzín (4461 m – 14,637 ft). The population consists mainly of Otomí Indians.

Among the relatively few pre-Hispanic sites in the state are *Tizantlán,* *Cacaxtla* (both p. 270) and *San Miguel del Milagro*.

HISTORY. – Little is know of the early history of this area. The first inhabitants may have been incomers from the Gulf coast (Olmecs?) between 1000 and 500 B.C. About the middle of the 14th c. A.D., Nahua Indians of the *Tlatepotzca* tribe came here from Texcoco and mingled with the *Otomí* then living in the area. There then came into being the state of Tlaxcala, a kind of republic made up of four autonomous territories which played an important part in the resistance to the Aztecs (Mexica) of Tenochtitlán. After a period of expansion which extended their authority as far as the Gulf coast, the Tlaxcalans were driven back to their original heartland by the Aztecs in the second half of the 15th c. There they were beleaguered for many years, until at the beginning of the 16th c. the Aztecs concluded a treaty with the still unconquered Tlaxcalans under which military operations were thereafter confined to periodic skirmishes designed to secure prisoners for sacrifice to the gods. This was the practice known as the Xochiyáoyotl or Flower War.

When the *Spaniards* arrived in 1519, the Tlaxcalans at first put up fierce resistance, but soon concluded an alliance with Cortés against the hated Aztecs. Only Xicoténcatl, one of the four rulers, refused to join this

Mexico
United Mexican States
Estados Unidos Mexicanos

Tlaxcala

States
Estados

1a	Baja California Sur	
1b	Baja California Norte	
2	Sonora	
3	Chihuahua	
4	Sinaloa	
5	Durango	
6	Coahuila	
7	Nuevo León	
8	Zacatecas	
9	San Luis Potosí	
10	Tamaulipas	
11	Nayarit	
12	Aguascalientes	
13	Jalisco	
14	Guanajuato	
15	Querétaro	
16	Hidalgo	
17	Colima	
18	Michoacán	
19	México	
20	Morelos	
21	Tlaxcala	
22	Puebla	
23	Veracruz	
24	Guerrero	
25	Oaxaca	
26	Chiapas	
27	Tabasco	
28	Campeche	
29	Yucatán	
30	Quintana Roo	

D.F. Distrito Federal (Federal District)

alliance and two years later was executed by the Spaniards. Even after the first unsuccessful Spanish attempt to take Tenochtitlán (the "Noche Triste" or "Sad Night"), the Tlaxcalans remained faithful to the alliance, and Cortés and his men were based in Tlaxcala while making preparations for the final siege of the Aztec capital. From here were launched the brigantines which carried out the decisive attack on Tenochtitlán by water, and with this Tlaxcalan help Cortés and his troops were able to capture the city and destroy it in 1521. In gratitude for their help, the Tlaxcalans were granted certain privileges by the Spanish crown. There continued to be a strong bond between Tlaxcala and the Spaniards, and when the struggle for independence broke out in 1810, the Tlaxcalans supported the continuance of Spanish rule. During the French intervention and the conflicts between Conservatives and Liberals (the Guerra de Reforma), there were a number of battles on Tlaxcalan soil (1862–4). A peasant revolt against President Porfirio Diaz which broke out in 1910 initiated the revolutionary wars of the following decade.

ECONOMY. – The state's *agriculture* centers on the cultivation of wheat and the maguey agave and on livestock-farming. Also of importance to the economy are the craft and industrial production of *woolens* and *clothing* and the manufacture of *pottery*.

Tlaxcala (Town)

State: Tlaxcala (Tlax.).
Altitude: 2255 m (7399 ft).
Population: 51,000.
Telephone dialing code: 9 12 46.
ⓘ **Coordinación Federal de Turismo,**
Blvd. Mariano Sánchez 11 B, 1st floor;
tel. 2 23 69.

HOTELS. – *Jeroc's*, Blvd. Revolución 4, II; *Mansión Xicohtencati*, Juárez 15, II; *Albergue de la Loma*, Guerrero 58, II; *Chalets Tlaxcala*, Blvd. Revolución, III.

RESTAURANTS in most hotels; also *La Fuente*, Blvd. Revolución; *Hostal del Cid*, Blvd. Revolución 6.

EVENTS. – End of October and beginning of November, Trade Fair; market on Saturday.

*Tlaxcala, capital of the state of the same name, lies in the Mexican highlands on the slopes of the Sierra Madre Oriental. Once the center of the process of fusion between Spaniards and Indians and of the Christianization of Mexico, it is now a rather sleepy little provincial town with only a few old buildings as reminders of its great past.

HISTORY. – Tlaxcala (Náhuatl, "place of maize") later became known as Tlaxcala de Xicoténcatl after the native ruler of that name who opposed the Tlaxcalan alliance with the Spaniards. The town was founded about the middle of the 14th c. by *Tlatepotzca* Indians, a Nanhua people from Texcoco, and for almost 200 years was a place of considerable importance, capital of a republic which held out against the Aztec empire surrounding it. The pre-Hispanic history of the town was closely tied to that of the Tlaxcalan state (see above under Tlaxcala state).

The *Spaniards* reached the town in 1519 on their way to Tenochtitlán, and after some initial resistance the Tlaxcalans made an alliance with them against the Aztecs. After their first defeat and retreat from Tenochtitlán (the "Noche Trist"), the Spaniards were able to regroup and re-equip themselves in Tlaxcala; without this help, and the supplies and reinforcements which the Tlaxcalans provided, they might not have succeeded in capturing the Aztec capital. The first Franciscans came to Tlaxcala in 1523 to assist in the rebuilding of the town and begin the process of converting the Indians. Soon afterward, the Emperor Charles V granted Tlaxcala a municipal charter and special privileges in recognition of the support it had given the Spaniards. Then a populous city – one of the largest in Mexico – it suffered a catastrophic loss of population by plague in 1544–6 from which it never recovered, and thereafter it played only a very modest part in history.

The Camarín, Ocotlán

SIGHTS. – In the *Plaza de la Constitución* is the **Town Hall** (*Palacio Municipal*), built about 1550, with fine window arches in Indian-Moorish style on the second floor. – Adjoining the Town Hall is the **Government Palace** (*Palacio de Gobierno*), begun in 1545, in the corridors of which are modern frescoes depicting the history of the town by the Tlaxcalan painter Desiderio Hernández Xochitiotzin. – Here, too, is the *Palacio de Justicia* (Law-courts), on the site of the old Chapel Royal (Capilla Real). This building, begun in 1528, was partially destroyed in the 18th c. by fire and again in 1800 by an earthquake. Interesting bas-reliefs, depicting the arms of Castile and León as well as those of the House of Austria, are to be seen on the frieze at the entrance to the chapel. This church which was dedicated to Charles V served as an Oratory for the baptised nobles of Tlaxcala. – Behind the main square, adjoining the market, stands the Parroquia San José with a red brick façade, covered with tiles.

Government Palace, Tlaxcala

Near the square, to the NE, are the convent and church of *San Francisco (1525), one of the earliest convents to be founded in Mexico. The main buildings were erected between 1537 and 1540. The church has a magnificent *cedar wood ceiling in Moorish style (Alfarje), spangled with stars. In the Chapel of the Third Order is the font at which the four rulers of

Tlaxcala are said to have been baptized. – On a lower level, down two flights of steps, is the Gothic *open chapel (Capilla de los Indios), one of the earliest of its kind in Mexico. In the atrium are remains of two of the four original *posas* (processional chapels).

Above the town, 1.5 km (1 mile) away, is one of Mexico's finest churches, the ****Basilica of the Virgin of Ocotlán** (Náhuatl, "place of the pine-tree"), built in the middle of the 18th c. by an Indian architect, Francisco Miguel (photograph, p. 65). The white stucco decoration of the inner part of the Churrigueresque façade and the towers stand out magnificently against the vaulted outer sections with their facing of hexagonal red tiles. This combination and the very realistic effect of the "shell arch" give this Baroque building its notable elegance. Above the doorway is a figure of St Francis bearing the three worlds which symbolize his three orders, and above this is a crowned figure of the Virgin. The stucco decoration and the glazed tiles for the church were made in Puebla.

The INTERIOR was completed in the mid 19th c. and partly restored in the 1930s. Features of the original building which survive unchanged, however, are the **high altar**, the two *side altars* and the octagonal ****Camarín** (a niche or chamber containing an image of the Virgin) – in this case a small chapel behind the high altar with multi-colored stucco decoration showing Indian influence. The *dome* of this sumptuously decorated chapel has figures of the Virgin and the apostles within a golden ring, with the Holy Ghost hovering above their heads. Especially fine is the *Camarin Table* (1761) consisting of a single piece with a diameter of 2.05 m (6 ft 9 ins), with eight legs representing monkeys (ozomatli), the old Indian symbol of joy. – Ocotlán is still a very popular place of pilgrimage.

SURROUNDINGS. – 5 km (3 miles) NW of Tlaxcala on the road to Apizaco is **San Esteban Tizatlán**, once one of the four cities which made up the republic of Tlaxcala. Here are the remains of Xicoténcatl's palace and two altars with interesting pre-Columbian *frescoes in the style of the Mixtec pictographs. These depict mythological figures such as Xochiquetzal, the patron goddess of Tlaxcala, Tezcatlipoca ("Smoking Mirror"), war god of the North, Mictlantecuhtli, lord of the underworld, and Tlahuizcalpantecuhtli, god of the morning star. In the ruins is a church with an open chapel (16th c.).

About 10 km (6 miles) S of Tlaxcala extends the pretty Acuitlapilco Lake (Laguna) which contains great numbers of fish. 20 km (12 miles) N on Road 119 is *Apizaco*, from which Road 136 runs 27 km (17 miles) SE to **Huamantla de Juárez** (alt. 2560 m (8399 ft); pop. 34,000; accommodations: Rosita, Vallejo), which has a Franciscan convent founded in the 16th c. with a Baroque church (rebuilt in the 18th c.). The *fiesta held here in the first half of August, with its intricately patterned carpets of flowers (*xochipetate*), attracts large numbers of visitors.

35 km (22 miles) SW of Tlaxcala, 1 km (¾ mile) NW of the village of *San Miguel del Milagro*, is the archeological site of *Cacaxtla. This site, consisting of several pyramids and temples on which little excavation work has been done, became famous overnight in 1975 when tomb-robbers tunnelling into the remains came upon pre-Hispanic wall paintings, which they then very properly reported to the authorities.

On the evidence of old chronicles it is presumed that the original builders of this site on its commanding hill were Olmec-Xicalanca who had penetrated inland from the Gulf Coast. This ethnic group who are not identical with the Pre-Classic Olmecs and which are not easy to classify, probably controlled the Puebla Valley between A.D. 650 and 1200. It is accepted that Cacaxtla had its heyday between A.D. 700 and 900. It was during this period that the impressive *frescoes were created. These reveal clear features of the Maya style, like those of the final phase of Teotihuacán. Unmistakable characteristics of this culture appear − although in a slightly different form − with the Talud-Tablero style (inclined walls/steep walls) in the architecture of Cacaxtla. Until recently it was thought that Cacaxtla, on the evidence of its frescoes, might have been a Maya settlement, but now the general opinion is that merely small groups, and especially artists, from the central Maya region lived in Cacaxtla and like those in Xochicalco exercised their creative influence.

On the right, on Hill B (Montículo B), the visitor comes to the part of the archeological area called Los Cerritos ("the little hills"). Here there is the base of a three-storied pyramid which has not yet been completely excavated. After crossing a depression the visitor stands before the great pedestal (Gran Basamento), an enormous terraced complex on which are situated a great number of structures of various types, including palaces, colonnades, platforms, patios, altars etc. The most interesting feature for the visitor is Building A, or Building of the Painters (Edificio A o de las Pinturas) in the NE of the complex. Inside can be seen five multicolored wall paintings which mostly represent symbolically Quetzalcóatl (winged snakes) and Tláltoc (rain god). Maya features can be seen in a long-nosed mask, the cross-band motif on the belts etc. There is a striking bas relief in clay of the profile of a seated person. − Equally worth visiting is Building B (Edificio B) on the N side of the Gran Basamento. Here can be seen a large painting known as "the battle" (La Batalla). It depicts in a cruel manner a bloody conflict between the victorious jaguar warriors and the defeated bird men. Maya influence is shown in the deformity of the heads and in the breastplates. The conflict within the duality between jaguar and bird may symbolize the conflict between day and night.

Cacaxtla is only one part of an area not yet archeologically explored. Excavations of this site and its surroundings in the near future will certainly provide fresh facts about the mingling of distant cultures in Meso-America. The site is sometimes closed to the public; if open it should be visited before 1 pm.

Tollan
See Tula

Toluca de Lerdo

State: México (Mex.).
Altitude: 2680 m (8793 ft). − Population: 510,000.
Telephone dialing code: 9 17 21.
ⓘ **Coordinación Federal de Turismo,**
Av. Vicente Villada 123,
Col. Centro;
tel. 4 42 49, 4 89 61, 4 03 04.

HOTELS. − *Del Rey Inn*, at km 63 on Mexico City road, L, SP; *Castel Plaza Las Fuentes*, at km 57 on Mexico City road, I, SP; *Neuvo Hotel San Carlos*, Portal Madero Pte. 210, I; *La Mansión de Miled*, Hidalgo Pte. 310, I; *Maya*, Hidalgo Pte. 315, II; *Rayón*, Rayón 210 Sur., III.

RESTAURANTS in most hotels; also *La Fonda Rosita*, Morelos 402; *La Cabaña Suiza*, at km 63 on Mexico City road; *Le Marquis*, Sor Juana Inés de la Cruz 1105; *Concorde*, A. Serdán 111; *El Mesón de las Ramblas*, Matamoros 107.

RECREATION and SPORTS. − Swimming, tennis, golf, riding.

EVENTS. − July 16, fiesta of Virgen del Carmen; market on Friday.

Toluca, capital of México state, lies in the Valley of Mexico, 64 km

Pre-Columbian frescoes, Cacaxtla

Pottery market, Toluca

Fruit and vegetable market, Toluca

(40 miles) from Mexico City. It is the highest city in Mexico, an important commercial town and center of communications. In recent years it has also developed into a considerable industrial center. The town itself has less to offer the tourist than the surrounding area.

HISTORY. – During the Classic period the area around Toluca (from the Náhuatl *Tollucán*, "place of reeds") seems to have been under the influence of Teotihuacán. It is not clear when the *Matlatzinca* (Náhuatl, "they who have small nets"), a Nahua people showing linguistic affinities with the Otomí, as well as marked Toltec features, established themselves here. During the 14th c. the Matlatzinca came under the control of various princes ruling in the Anáhuac valley. At the beginning of the 15th c. they were allied with the Aztecs, but were later conquered by them, many of the tribe being driven out and seeking refuge in the Michoacán area. Several Matlatzinca risings against the Aztecs were quelled with heavy loss of life. – The people of Toluca gave some assistance to the *Spaniards* in the taking of Tenochtitlán. In 1521 a Spanish party led by Gonzalo de Umbría explored the Toluca valley, and the Franciscans founded their first convent in the town in 1529. In 1667 *Toluca de San José* was granted a municipal charter. – In 1830 Toluca became capital of the state of México, and, at the end of the 19th c., "de Lerdo" was added to its name in honor of the statesman Sebastián Lerdo de Tejada.

SIGHTS. – In the attractive *Zócalo* (Plaza de los Mártires) stands the *Cathedral*, a 19th c. building in neo-classical style. On the N side of the square is the *Government Palace* (Palacio de Gobierno), built in

1872. One block to the right of the Zócalo is a long shopping street with 120 arcades (*portales*). Near here is the 18th c. Baroque *church of El Carmen*. – Not far away lies the ***Market** (*Mercado*), one of the largest and most interesting in Mexico. – Other features of interest are the *Museum of Art* (Museo de Bellas Artes), the *Museo de Charrería* and the *Casa de las Artesanías* (showrooms for the sale of local handicrafts).

SURROUNDINGS. – 8 km (5 miles) N of Toluca on the Querétaro road a turning on the left leads in 2.5 km (1½ miles) to the pre-Columbian site of **Calixtlahuaca** (Náhuatl, "place with houses on the plain"), a cult center whose origins and early history are wrapped in obscurity. The remains of buildings found here belong to the Teotihuacán culture, and in the early Post-Classic period show affinities with Xochicalco and the Toltecs. Later the site came under the control of the Matlatzinca, who ruled here until they were driven out by newcomers from the Anáhuac valley. The Aztecs occupied Calixtlahuaca for the first time in 1474 and thereafter exerted a major influence on building activity here. A number of abortive risings by the Matlatzinca against the Aztecs ended with the destruction of the Matlatzinca temples.

Calixtlahuaca

On a great terrace surrounded by a wall is the most important building of this site, the *Temple of Quetzalcóatl (Estructura 3) which has several times been built over. The four-tiered circular pyramid has a broad open staircase and bears an altar. The temple was dedicated to the wind god Ehecatl, who was adopted by the Huastecs and identified with Quetzalcóatl. A statue of the god found here can now be seen in the museum in Teotenango. On a higher level (not open to inspection) is a complex of buildings consisting of the Temple of Tláloc (Estructura 4) and a pyramid platform (Estructura 7) with a broad staircase. In the same location stands an interesting T-shaped Altar of Skulls (Tzompantli) with projecting skulls. A third even higher level reveals the partly overgrown remains of two platforms (Estructura 5 and 6) and two stone slabs. When leaving the site in the direction of the cross-roads, the fourth group of Calixtlahuaca, called Calmecac (Estructura 17) after the elite Aztec school, lies to the W. The group consists of several rooms and platforms around a large rectangular courtyard.

8 km (5 miles) SE of Toluca is the little town of Metepec, with a beautiful convent church (16th and 17th c.). The town is noted for the green stoneware and polychrome terracotta figures produced here.

25 km (16 miles) S of Toluca on Road 55 is Tenango del Valle (or de Arista), near which is the large archeological site of Teotenango (Náhuatl, "place of the divine wall"), the origins of which go back to at least the 7th c. A.D. The heyday of the site was between the 10th and 12th centuries. Here, too, there is a mingling of various cultures – late Teotihuacán, the Toltecs, the Matlatzinca and the Aztecs – but the predominant influence is that of the Matlatzinca. A large part of this, formerly the most important ancient Indian *cult center in the Toluca valley, a site which bears primarily the stamp of the Matlatzinca, has been excavated in the last fifteen years. The central section has been called the North Group (Sistema Norte) and divided into six associated complexes (conjuntos). These include groups of buildings which, with their courtyards, form an architectural unit. Typical of these are the pyramidal platforms with three of four recessed tiers (diagonal wall with ledge) on which the temple buildings once stood. They were reached from the extensive ceremonial open spaces by staircases, often of considerable size.

The visitor comes first to Complex A (Conjunto A) on the Concourse of the Jaguar (Plaza del Jaguar). On the second tier of the supporting wall can be seen a relief of a jaguar and carved on the left the glyph "2 rabbit" ("2 tochtli") and on the right the glyph "9 house" (9 calli). – Complex E (Conjunto E) behind complexes B and C reveals a ball court (juego de pelota), 23 m (75 ft) long and 10 m (33 ft) broad, as well as the remains of a sweat bath (temazcal) and living rooms which were sacrificed when the ball court was built.

The most extensive area in the North Group is represented by Complex D (Conjunto D). As well as platforms, dwellings and patios the complex includes a construction, 120 m (394 ft) long and 40 m (130 ft) wide, known as the "Snake Base" (Basamento de la Serpiente). In front of it extends the Plaza de la Serpiente, bounded on the W by the Street of the Frog (Calle de la Rana) and on the N by the Square of the Peach (Plaza del Durazno) which might possibly have been the town's market place. The first two names are the result of the discovery of a snake relief and a frog sculpture.

In the interesting site museum are important archeological finds of the State of Mexico, principally from Teotenango, Malinalco and Calixtlahuaca. Especially notable are the statue of Ehécatl from Calixtlahuaca and the carved wooden drum (panhuehuetl) from Malinalco. – From Teotenango it is 24 km (15 miles) to Tenancingo (p. 154) and 40 km (25 miles) to *Malinalco (p. 153).

A recommended excursion from Toluca is to drive SW via Roads 103, 134 and 3 for some 50 km (31 miles) to the extinct and often snowcapped volcano, the *Nevado de Toluca or Xinantécatl (Náhuatl, "naked man"; alt. 4475 m (14,687 ft); hut at 3750 m –12,304 ft). The road goes as far as the Laguna del Sol (Lake of the Sun) and the Laguna de la Luna (Lake of the Moon) at 4200 m (13,784 ft). From the peaks around the rim of the crater there are superb *views of the Toluca valley, the mountains of Guerrero, the forest regions of Michoacán and the peaks of the Sierra Nevada (Popocatépetl and Iztaccíhuatl: p. 221).

75 km (47 miles) W of Toluca is the attractive vacation resort of *Valle de Bravo (alt. 1880 m (6170 ft); pop. 16,000; hotels: Motel Avándaro, SP, tennis, riding; Motel Montiel, SP; De Los Arcos, SP, golf, riding; Avándaro Courts, SP; Posada Rincón del Bosque; restaurants: Los Veleros, Taverna de León, El Capitán, La Michoacana, lying on the shores of a man-made lake (Presa de Valle de Bravo or Presa Miguel Alemán; facilities for water sports), surrounded by hilly country and luxuriant vegetation. – Near the town are the interesting rock formations of La Peña and the waterfall of Salto de Ferrería.

Tonantzintla
See under Acatepec

Torreón
See under Coahuila de Zaragoza

Tula (Tollan)

State: Hidalgo (Hgo.).
Altitude: 2030 m (6660 ft). – Population: 19,000.
ⓘ Coordinación Federal de Turismo,
Plaza de la Independencia 110, 3rd floor;
Pachuca, Hgo.;
tel. (9 17 71) 2 59 60, 2 48 60, 2 32 89.

HOTELS. – Motel Cuellar, 5 de Mayo; Motel Lizbeth, Melchor Ocampo 200.

ACCESS. – From Mexico City, Road 57 (direction Querétaro); then in 68 km (42 miles) turning to Tepeji del Río and Tula (20 km – 12 miles) and a further 3 km (2 miles) to the ruins. From Pachuca it is 90 km (55 miles) to Tula.

On a hill near the little town of Tula de Allende, separated from it by a river, are the remains of *Tollan,

once capital of the Toltecs, who not only dominated the early Post-Classic period in central Mexico but also had considerable influence on the Maya culture of Yucatán, 1200 km (750 miles) away.

HISTORY. – The Tula area was originally inhabited by Otomí Indians, who later mingled with the Chichimecs, the Náhuatl-speaking nomads who pushed into the region from the NW in the 9th c. It was probable that at this time another group arrived in Tollan from Tabasco on the Gulf Coast; these were the Nonoalca (Náhuatl, "where the speech changes"). The traditional accounts of subsequent events are such a mixture of reality and myth that they must be viewed with scepticism. We are told that Mixcóatl ("Cloud Serpent"), the legendary founder of the Toltec dynasty, made his way into the Anáhuac valley and married Chimalma ("Recumbent Shield"), a princess of Tepoztlán, who in A.D. 947 gave birth to Ce Acatl Topiltzín ("One Reed Our Prince"). After studying in the cult center of Xochicalco, which was dedicated to the god Quetzalcóatl, he took over the leadership of the Toltecs and in A.D. 968 founded the new capital of **Tollan** ("place of reeds"). As a teacher of the arts and sciences, he promoted the peaceful cult of Quetzalcóatl and as a priest-king adopted the name of Quetzalcóatl. Some twenty years later, he came into conflict with his mythical rival Tezcatlipoca ("Smoking Mirror"), the warlike god of night and patron of evil spirits. Having been defeated in this contest, Topiltzín left Tollan in 987 and went to Cholula. After spending some time there, he moved on by way of Veracruz into Yucatán, bringing Toltec culture to the Mayas and, as the god-king Kukulcán, initiated a renaissance of Maya culture. According to another version Quetzalcóatl sailed away from his country by sea, promising to return. As a result of recent research it is now believed that the Nonoalca-Toltecs returned to their original home at Tabasco in the second half of the 10th c., and then went to Chichén Itzá and finally conquered it. The result of the mingling of Toltec militarism with Maya genius was the Post-Classic renaissance of Maya art. It is obvious from the striking similarity in architecture and sculpture between the Post-Classic Chichén Itzá and Tula that the artistic quality of the latter is incomparably lower. It seems logical that of two similar works of art the better executed must be the original. From this it is now presumed that the main elements of the Toltec-Maya style were once again brought to Tula.

After the victory of the warlike party in Tollan, the city developed into a militarist state, the backbone of which was formed by the warrior orders of Eagle Knights and Jaguar Knights. It seems likely that the Toltecs also introduced the practice of mass human sacrifice to appease the gods. The decline of Tollan began in A.D. 1125 with a quarrel between the two founder groups, the Chichimecs and the Nonoalcas, which led to the first emigration to Cholula and its conquest. There followed the great fire of Tollan and the arrival of other groups of Chichimecs who took part in the battle around Cholula. The end of the Toltec dynasty finally came in A.D. 1175 under the two rival rulers Topiltzín Quetzalcóatl and Huémac. One after the other they fled to the south, where according to another legend Topiltzín burned himself to death, only to return as the god of the morning star; history here confuses the first with the last ruler Topiltzín. Huémac is said to have commited suicide in Chapultepec and to have been reborn as king of the underworld. The Toltecs found new homes in the Anáhuac valley or traveled farther afield to the Gulf coast and into Chiapas, Guatemala and Nicarágua. The Náhuatl-speaking Pipil Indians who live in these regions are probably remnants of this mass emigration. – The *Aztecs* who later gained control of the Tula area felt themselves to be the heirs of the Toltecs and took over many features of their culture, particularly of their religion.

The 16th c. accounts, particularly those of Bernardino de Sahagún and Fernando de Alba Ixtlilxóchitl, referred to the mysterious city of Tollan, but for four centuries the site of this city could not be found. It was therefore erroneously assumed until about forty years ago that Teotihuacán had been the Toltec capital. Although Antonio García Cubas in 1873 and Désiré Charnay in 1880 discovered archeological remains near **Tula**, it was not until 1938 that Wigberto Jiménez Moreno found the site of the ancient city. Systematic excavation was begun by Jorge R. Acosta in the 1940s, and this made it possible to identify the site with certainty as the old Toltec metropolis. In the 70's it was established through work directed by Eduardo Matos Moctezuma that in its heyday Tollan occupied an area of 13 sq. km (5 sq. miles) and probably had a population of 60,000.

THE SITE. – The first structure encountered on entering the site is *Building 1* (Edificio 1), a palace, several times overbuilt, which was probably a dwelling house for priests. On the N side of the central plaza is the *Temple of the Morning Star* (*Templo de Tlahuizcalpantecuhtli*), also known as the *Pyramid of Quetzalcóatl* or *Building B*. From the plaza a staircase leads up to the summit platform of the five-story pyramid (10 m (33 ft) high, 40 m (130 ft) square) on which the temple once stood.

The columns and colossal *Atlantean figures* which were found on the site have been re-erected on the

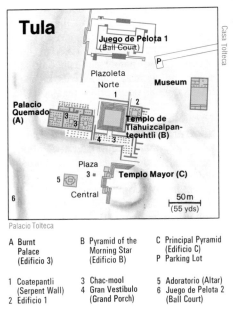

Tula

Juego de Pelota 1
(Ball Court)

Casa Tolteca

P

Plazoleta
Norte

Museum

Palacio
Quemado
(A)

Templo de
Tlahuizcalpan-
tecuhtli (B)

Plaza
Central

Templo Mayor (C)

50 m
(55 yds)

Palacio Tolteca

A Burnt Palace (Edificio 3)	B Pyramid of the Morning Star (Edificio B)	C Principal Pyramid (Edificio C)
		P Parking Lot
1 Coatepantli (Serpent Wall)	3 Chac-mool	5 Adoratorio (Altar)
2 Edificio 1	4 Gran Vestibulo (Grand Porch)	6 Juego de Pelota 2 (Ball Court)

Pyramid of the Morning Star, Tula (Tollan)

platform; the left-hand Atlantean figure is a reproduction. These magnificent statues, 4.60 m (15 ft)
high, which once stood on the roof of the temple,
represent warriors who symbolize the god Quetzalcóatl as the morning star. In their right hand they hold
a spear-thrower (atlatl), in the left a sheaf of arrows, a
pouch containing incense and a small sword. They
wear a breastplate in the form of a butterfly. The
rear belt buckle is interpreted as the setting sun. – The
rectangular columns bear reliefs with the symbol of
the earth (a crocodile's head) and representations of
warriors and weapons; the unfinished column has the
head of Quetzalcóatl. The round columns are decorated with delicate reliefs of feather patterns,
representing the body of the feathered serpent whose
head originally formed the base of the column. – Along
the sides of the pyramid, which are in a variation of the
talud-tablero style, can be seen remains of friezes
depicting jaguars and eagles devouring the human
hearts which they hold in their claws. – In the large
porch (the Gran Vestíbulo) in front of the pyramid
some of the columns have been re-erected. At the NW
corner of the colonnade are remains of painted reliefs
depicting a procession of warriors and priests. To
the right of the staircase is the headless figure of a
Chac-mool.

In many respects this structure resembles the Temple
of the Warriors at Chichén Itzá. Typical "exported"
features of Toltec architecture – serpent columns,
friezes with reliefs of striding jaguars and eagles, small
Atlantean figures supporting altars, Chac-mools, etc.
– are to be found in many areas in Meso-America, but
nowhere more than at Chichén Itzá.

Along the N side of the Temple of the
Morning Star runs the "Serpent Wall"
(Coatepantli), 2.20 m (7 ft) high and 40 m
(130 ft) long. On this are carved, below
spiral patterns and geometric ornaments,
reliefs of snakes devouring human
skeletons. – On the other side of the small
plaza (Plazoleta Norte), to the N of the
temple, is Ball Court 1 (Juego de Pelota
1), 67 m (220 ft) long and 12.50 m (40 ft)
across, unfortunately almost completely
destroyed. It resembled in its measurements the ball court of Xochicalco.

To the SW of the ball court is Building 3,
the **Burnt Palace** (Palacio Quemado),
which originally comprised a number of
large halls, colonnades and courtyards. In
the central courtyard are two Chac-mools,
and at its NW corner, set in the wall, is a
panel with painted reliefs depicting a
procession of richly attired nobles.

To the S of the palace, in the middle of the
Central Plaza (Plaza Central), is a small
altar (adoratorio) on a rectangular platform. – On the E side of the plaza is
Building C (Edificio C), the **Principal**

Atlantean figure, Tula (Tollan)

Temple (*Templo Mayor*), on the staircase of which is still another Chac-mool. On a stone slab to the right of the staircase can be seen the glyph for the planet Venus, one of the symbols of Quetzalcóatl.

There is an interesting **museum** displaying finds from the site.

In the little town of **Tula de Allende**, founded by Franciscans in 1529, stands a *fortified church* built in 1550–3 with a façade in pure Renaissance style. The interior vaulting is very fine.

SURROUNDINGS. – 1.5 km (1 mile) N of the ruins, near the archeological site of Little Tula (Tula Chico) is a curious monument known as *El Corral*. The main structure is circular, with two rectangular annexes on the E and W sides. An interesting altar which stood here is now in the Tula museum.

On a hill known as *El Cielito*, 6 km (4 miles) SE of Tula, are the ruins of an Aztec palace built on an earlier Toltec site. The palace was still occupied in the early years of Spanish rule, when it was the residence of Pedro Moctezuma, son of the luckless Aztec ruler Moctezuma II. This Aztec prince, educated in the first Franciscan school for the Indian élite, was appointed cacique of Tula by the Spaniards.

On the *Cerro de la Malinche*, a hill on the other bank of the Río Tula, interesting glyphs dating from the reign of Ce Acatl Topiltzín were found carved on a smoothed rock face.

18 km (11 miles) from Tula, near Road 57, is **Tepeji del Río** (alt. 2175 m (7136 ft); pop. 21,000; hotel: Paradero 20 de Noviembre; fiesta on Good Friday), which has an interesting 16th c. church with a fine colonial-Plateresque façade.

Tulum

State: Quintana Roo (Q.R.).
Altitude: 14 m (46 ft).

HOTELS. – *Crucero*, 1 km (¾ mile) before the site at the turning of Road 307, II. On the coast road to the S, from the ruins at the sea: *Cabañas El Paraiso*, 1.3 km (¾ mile), III; *Cabañas Chac-Mool*, 5.5 km (3½ miles), III; *Los Arrecifes*, 7 km (4½ miles). II; *Cabañas de Tulum*, 7.5 km (4¾ miles), II; *Boca Paila Fishing Lodge*, 22 km (15 miles), I; *Pez Maya Fishing Beach Resort*, 25.5 km (16 miles), L; *Punta Allen*, 55 km (35 miles), simple lodging.

*Tulum is the only known Maya fortified town of any size located on the coast. It occupies a prominent site on 12 m (40 ft) high cliffs above the Caribbean, here fringed by a beach of white sand, and is protected on the landward side by a wall. Although architecturally it falls short of other Maya sites in interest, its unique *situation and the wall paintings which have been found here make it one of the Maya sites in the Yucatán peninsula most worth visiting.

Tulum, on the Caribbean

HISTORY. – Little is known of the history of Tulum ("fortress" in Maya), the original name of which is said to have been *Zamá* ("daybreak"). It is now assigned to the late *Post-Classic period* (after A.D. 1200) – i.e., to the time of the "Mayanized" Toltecs. The principal buildings were probably erected as late as about A.D. 1450. A stela dated to A.D. 564 has been found at Tulum, but it is now believed that this came from somewhere else, perhaps the neighboring Classic site of Tancah.

The first Europeans to discover the site were a party of Spaniards under Juan de Grijalva, who sailed along the Yucatán coast in 1518. The town seems to have been still occupied in 1544, when the Spaniards conquered northeastern Yucatán. Toward the end of the 19th c., during the "Caste War", Maya Indians again entrenched themselves within the walls of the ancient fortress. The first accurate and illustrated description of the site was given by Stephens and Catherwood, who visited Tulum in 1842. During the 20th c., excavations have been carried out by Morley and Howe for the Carnegie Institution and later by Angel Fernández and various Mexican organizations.

THE SITE. – The relatively small site of Tulum, 132 km (82 miles) S of Puerto Juárez and 248 km (154 miles) N of Chetumal, is, like the late Post-Classic Maya sites of Mayapán and Ichpaatún (both of which show Toltec influence), surrounded on the landward side by a **defensive wall**. The area enclosed by the wall measures 380 m (415 yds) from N to S and 165 m (180 yds) from E to W. The wall, built of stone, originally stood between 3 and 5 m (10 and 16 ft) high and had an average thickness of 7 m (23 ft), with five gates faced with stone slabs. This suggests that Tulum was not only a cult center but a populated town as well. Along the top of the wall ran a walk protected by a parapet. At the two inner corners are small temples which are thought to have served as watchtowers.

Archeologically, the most interesting building in Tulum is the **Temple of the Frescoes** (*Temple de los Frescos* or *Building 16*), which stands roughly in the

center of the walled area, half-way along the E–W axis. The main parts of the structure were probably built about 1450, in the late Post-Classic period. As commonly happened with Maya religious buildings, the temple was several times built over in the course of time.

The GROUND FLOOR consists of a single chamber, with an entrance (divided up by four columns) on the W side. Above this is a double cornice broken up into three *niches*. In the central niche is a stucco figure of the "Diving God"; the other two contain seated stucco figures with elaborate headdresses. At the ends of the cornice are large masks in low relief, formerly painted, which probably represent Itzamná, the old sky god of the Mayas of Yucatán.

The UPPER FLOOR has a *niche* above the doorway with remains of a stucco relief, probably of the Diving God. The wall of the inner chamber has interesting **paintings** in the style of the codices, the subjects being Maya but the style more Mixtec. In the upper part of the wall, facing each other, are two figures of the sky god, Itzamná, flanked on the right by the rain god, Chac. In the central register is Itzamná's wife, the moon and fertility goddess Ixchel, together with two unidentified figures. In the lower part, to the right, is another representation of Ixchel, this time in a marine setting with stylized fishes.

On an altar in front of the temple is *Stela 2*, 1.30 m (4 ft) high, bearing a date in the Post-Classic Maya calendar which has been deciphered as A.D. 1261.

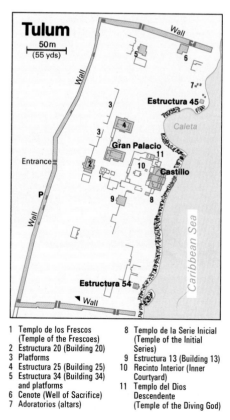

1 Templo de los Frescos
   (Temple of the Frescoes)
2 Estructura 20 (Building 20)
3 Platforms
4 Estructura 25 (Building 25)
5 Estructura 34 (Building 34)
   and platforms
6 Cenote (Well of Sacrifice)
7 Adoratorios (altars)

8 Templo de la Serie Inicial
   (Temple of the Initial
   Series)
9 Estructura 13 (Building 13)
10 Recinto Interior (Inner
   Courtyard)
11 Templo del Dios
   Descendente
   (Temple of the Diving God)

Tulum – a general view of the remains

The largest and most striking structure on the site is the **Castillo** (*Building 1*), which stands on the edge of the cliffs half-way along the E side. It has been established that this was built in three different phases. A broad staircase leads up to a terrace on which stands a two-chambered temple. In front of the temple is a stone, presumably an altar for human sacrifices. The entrance to the temple is divided up by two serpent columns. In the niche above the central doorway is a stone figure of the Diving God.

At the NE corner of the plaza is the **Temple of the Diving God** (*Templo del Dios Descendente*) or *Building 5*, built on the site of an earlier structure. An unusual feature is that the walls slope in toward the ground, so that the floor area is less than the area of the roof – a device apparently intended to give the building increased stability.

The **Temple of the Diving God** consists of a single chamber. In the niche above the entrance is a *stucco* figure of the Diving God, who is depicted with wings on his arms and shoulders and a bird's tail. There are various interpretations of this divinity, who appears so frequently at Tulum – as a bee flying down, as the evening star or the sun at its setting, as lightning. – Practically nothing is left of the painting on the main façade of the temple and the E wall of the interior.

At the SE corner of the plaza is the *Temple of the Initial Series* (Templo de la Serie Inicial, Building 9), named after Stela 1, which was found here by Stephens and has been dated to A.D. 564 (see above under *History*).

Other features of the site are *Building 25*, with a polychrome figure of the Diving God; *Building 35*, erected over a small *cenote*; and *Building 45*, with a circular platform and a magnificent *view of the sea and the Castillo.

SURROUNDINGS. – 24 km (15 miles) S of Tulum on Road 307 is **Chunyaxché** (Muyil), a large site (2.5 sq. km – 1 sq. mile) lying close to the road, with

various pyramids, temples and palaces of the Late Classic and Post-Classic periods. The highest structure is a pyramid 19 m (62 ft) high. Most of the remains on this site, on which little archeological exploration has been done, are covered with vegetation. From here there is a road to the *Laguna Chunyaxché*, a beautiful lake which offers good swimming and fishing.

Along the cost N of Tulum, and in the southern part of Quintana Roo, there are many pre-Hispanic Maya remains. Among the most notable sites are *Las Milpas, San Miguel de Ruz, Chamax, Chacmool* (Santa Rosa) and *Tupak.*

Tuxpan
See under El Tajín

Tuxtla Gutiérrez

State: Chiapas (Chis.).
Altitude: 530 m (1739 ft). – Population: 235,000.
Telephone dialing code: 9 19 61.

ⓘ **Coordinación Federal de Turismo,**
Av. Central Poniente 1454,
Col. Moctezuma;
tel. 2 45 35, 2 55 09.

HOTELS. – *Castel Flamboyant*, Blvd. Dr. B. Domínguez 1081, I, SP; *Safari*, 2a Av. Norte Ote 635, I, SP; *Bonampak*, Blvd. Dr. B. Domínguez 180, I, SP; *Gran Hotel Umberto*, Av. Central Pte. 180, I; *Lacanjá*, Blvd. Dr. B. Domínguez 1380, I, SP; *La Mansión*, la Pte. Norte 121, II; *Serrano*, Av. Central Pte. 224, II; *María Teresa*, 2 Nte. Pte. 259B, III; *Riverpal*, 5a Nte. Pte. 331, III.

RESTAURANTS in most hotels; also *Flamingo*, Pasaje Zardain; *London*, 2a Nte. y 4a Pte.; *Las Pichanchas*, Av. Central Ote 837; *Chung Shan*, 1a Nte. Pte.; *Bávaro*, Blvd. Dr. B. Domínguez 302.

RECREATION and SPORTS. – Swimming, tennis, hunting, boat trips, fishing.

EVENTS. – Fiestas: April, 25–29, San Marcos; August 16, San Roque.

Tuxtla Gutiérrez, capital of the state of Chiapas, lies on the Panamerican Highway in a fertile subtropical valley. Due to its central location and the discovery of oil in Chiapas, it has developed in recent years into a large modern town.

HISTORY. – In the region around present-day Tuxtla there lived people of Maya stock, the Zoque, who called the place Coyactocmo (in Zoque, "place of rabbits") which later became, in Náhuatl, Tuxtlán with the same meaning. The first Spanish monks arrived in the 16th c. and were followed by groups of Spaniards who settled here. The latter had often to defend themselves against the Zoque Indians who formed the majority of the population. At the beginning of the

19th c., when Comitán had already been granted the status of a town and when San Cristóbal de Las Casas had already held that status for almost 300 years, Tuxtla was still a small place. In 1848 Tuxtla received the additional name of Gutiérrez and in 1892 it replaced San Cristóbal as the capital of Chiapas. Today it has acquired considerable importance as an administrative, cultural and commercial center.

SIGHTS. – There are relatively few old buildings in Tuxtla Gutiérrez. Among them may be mentioned the *Cathedral* (much altered and rebuilt) and the white and red *Government Palace* (Palacio de Gobierno).

Fountain, Chiapa de Corzo

In the NE of the town, in Parque Francisco Madero, a new building for the **Regional Museum of Anthropology and History** (*Museo Regional de Antropología e Historia*) was recently completed; (archeological finds of the Olmec and Maya periods; ethnological exhibits from the area, etc.).

In the same district is the modern **Theater Emilio Rabasa** and the **Botanical Garden.** SE of Taxtla, on a site embracing some 100 hectares (250 acres) lies the ***Miguel Álvarez del Torro Zoological Garden**, exclusively devoted to animals of Chiapas and which is worth visiting.

SURROUNDINGS. – 22 km (14 miles) N there is a good view into the very impressive ****Sumidero Canyon** (*Cañón del Sumidero*). From the rim of the canyon it is fully 1000 m (3300 ft) to the *Río Grijalva* (Río Grande de Chiapa), pursuing its winding course far below.

Here, it is said, in 1528 there occurred a mass suicide of the Chiapanecs who were being oppressed by the Spaniards. From Chiapa de Corzo dramatic boat trips could be organized along the river.

18 km (11 miles) W on the Panamerican Highway is the little town of **Chiapa de Corzo** (alt. 415 m (1362 ft); pop. 18,000). Just at the turning off the main road can be seen a single-story pyramid (restored) which was found to contain a tomb.

Excavations by the New World Archeological Foundation showed that the Chiapa de Corzo area, like Izapa (p. 96), was one of the oldest pre-Columbian sites in Meso-America. The pottery found here indicated that the site was inhabited from 1400 B.C. to A.D. 950, i.e., from the beginning of the Early Formative period to the Classic period. Here, too, was found the earliest dated inscription in America (Stela 2, dated to December 9, 36 B.C. currently exhibited in the Regional Museum in Tuxtla Gutiérrez). It is not known who the builders of this cult center were, though it has been labeled as transitional from Olmec to Maya or as Proto-Maya. The Conquistador Diego de Mazariegos founded the present-day place in 1528 around a gigantic ceiba tree (ceiba pendantra) which was revered by the Indians and which today is still called "La Pochota" (Náhuatl, póchotl="the hunchback").

The *Church of Santo Domingo* (mid 16th c. with later alterations) is also worthy of a visit. – In the Zócalo is a curious 16th c. octagonal **fountain*, begun by Father Rodrigo de León in 1552 and completed ten years later, in Moorish style, shaped like the Spanish crown. – Also in the Zócalo is the little *Lacquer Museum* (Museo de Laca), with an excellently displayed collection comparing local and Chinese lacquerware.

There are a number of large reservoirs in the area around Tuxtla Gutiérrez, some of which offer excellent facilities for water sports. 35 km (22 miles) N is the *Chicoasén* reservoir (Presa Chicoasén), with one of the largest hydro-electric plants in Latin America. 88 km (55 miles) away via *Octotzocuatla* lies the *Netzahualcóyotl* or *Mal Paso* reservoir, and 68 km (42 miles) SE the *Angostura* reservoir.

Tzintzuntzan

State: Michoacán (Mich.).
Altitude: 2100 m (6890 ft).

ACCESS. – 18 km (11 miles) N of Pátzcuaro. From Morelia 40 km (25 miles) W on Road 15 (direction Guadalajara), then road on left to the village of Tzintzuntzan (8 km – 5 miles).

The Tarascan site of Tzintzuntzan lies on a hill above the village of the same name, with a magnificent view of the nearby Lago de Pátzcuaro. Built in an unusual architectural style, this was once the principal cult center of the Tarascans.

HISTORY. – Tzintzuntzan ("place of the humming-birds" in Tarascan) appears to have been founded in the 11th c. A.D. Together with Pátzcuaro and Ihuatzio it later became one of the three dominant cities of the Tarascan league. It is not known where the *Tarascans* (*tarascue*, "son-in-law"). who called themselves *Purépechas*, originally came from, but it is probable that, like other groups they were incomers from the NW in the 10th and 11th c., that is in the Toltec period, but that they did not continue to penetrate into the Valley of Mexico. Their original center seems to have been Zacapu, but under their ruler, Hireticátame ("Stout King"), in the 14th c. and later, in the 15th c. (i.e., in the late Post-Classic period), they spread over the whole of Michoacán and large areas of Jalisco and

Sumidero Canyon near Tuxtla Gutierrez

Colima (some 65,000 sq. km – 25,000 sq. miles). But the true founder of the Tarascan state, a league of three cities, was the legendary hero Tariácuri, who united the various tribes living in the area. Tzintzuntzan, with an area of 6.7 sq. km (2.6 sq. miles) and a population of about 35,000, became the dominant city of the Tarascans, who proved themselves an increasingly warlike people. In 1478, under their ruler, Tzitzipandácuri, and with the help of their excellent copper weapons, they defeated the Aztecs, then pressing forward under their leader, Axayácatl, after capturing Toluca. Later attempts by the Aztec king, Ahuítzotl, to conquer the Tarascans were equally unsuccessful.

Ruins of temple, Tzintzuntzan

The *Spaniards* arrived here under the leadership of Cristóbal de Olid in 1522, and persuaded the Tarascans, without striking a blow, to accept Spanish rule. In 1529, however, the notorious conquistador, Nuño Beltrán de Guzmán, killed the Tarascan ruler, Tangaxoan II, an act which led to risings against the Spaniards. Peace was restored by the priest and legal scholar Vasco de Quiroga (1470–1565), who became bishop of Michoacán in 1537. The see, originally in Tzintzuntzan, was later transferred to Pátzcuaro. Vasco de Quiroga fostered the craft skills of the Indians and promoted the various handicrafts which are still practised in the region.

The **Tarascans** lived mainly by fishing, hunting and cultivating maize. The population was divided into two main classes, the military élite and the priests on one hand, and the fishermen, peasants and slaves on the other. Their principal god was the fire god, Curicaveri; other important divinities were Cuerauáperi ("Earth Mother"), Tata Uriata ("Father Sun") and Nata Cutzi ("Mother Moon"). – Although predominantly a warrior people, they excelled over most other peoples of Meso-America in the working of metal (gold, silver and copper). The limited distribution of copper-working in Meso-America suggests that this technique was introduced from Peru or Colombia. The Tarascans were also famed throughout Meso-America for the high quality of their feather-work, pottery, textiles and obsidian objects. They also produced crude stone sculpture of archaic appearance, including figures resembling the Chac-mool of the Toltecs. Their architecture was relatively simple but markedly individual, its characteristic features being the *yácatas* (temple platforms with circular superstructures).

Tzintzuntzan was described in detail in the old Spanish chronicles, but the first excavations were those of Charles Hartfort in 1878, followed by Carl Lumholtz at the turn of the century and by Alfonso Caso, Daniel Rubín de la Borbolla and Jorge Acosta in the 1930s and 1940s and Román Piña Chan in the 1960s.

THE SITE. – The remains are of interest for their architectural style and general effect rather than their details of workmanship. On the huge **platform**, 425 by 250 m (1395 ft by 820 ft), there were originally five low T-shaped *temples* (yácatas; Náhuatl, yácatl="nose"), with rectangular substructures ending in oval platforms. These platforms, originally crowned by circular superstructures, were evidently tombs, while the yácatas were cult centers dedicated to the fire god Curicaveri.

Excavation of the circular structure of Temple V brought to light the tombs of Tarascan rulers and their families, with numerous grave goods. On the E side of the fortress-like structure was a monumental **staircase** 30 m (100 ft) wide leading up to the terrace. The yácatas numbered I to V (starting from the right, facing away from the lake) had twelve tiers or steps 0.90 m (3 ft) high, with staircases leading up to the top. They were built of flagstones laid without mortar, held in place by walls of stone blocks, and were faced with a volcanic stone called *xanamu*, bound with a mixture of clay and pebbles.

On the opposite side of the road to Quiroga is the present-day town of **Tzintzuntzan** (alt. 2050 m (6725 ft); pop. 10,000; fiestas: February 1–7, Día de Nuestro Señor del Rescate; Holy Week; Corpus Christi), which has a Franciscan convent (rebuilt 1570) with a large atrium and old olive trees, rarely found in Mexico (the planting of the olive was forbidden in the Spanish province of New Spain). The church, which was damaged by fire in 1944, has a colonial-Plateresque façade. There are some interesting paintings inside the church, including a "descent from the cross" attributed to Vecellio Titian. – The town is noted for its painted pottery, woodcarving, stone carving and basketwork.

SURROUNDINGS. – From the road to *Pátzcuaro (p. 218), a side road on the right leads to *Ihuatzio* (Purépecha, "place of the coyotes"; 4 km – 2½ miles). This former Tarascan capital, which once extended over 1.3 sq. km (½ sq. mile) and had a population of about 5000 has a few ruins, among them three yácatas, but they are poorly preserved and are likely to be of interest only to specialists.

Uruapan de Progreso

State: Michoacán (Mich.).
Altitude: 1610 m (5280 ft). – Population: 262,000.
Telephone dialing code: 2 06 33.
ⓘ **Coordinación Federal de Turismo,**
Santos Degollado 340, Altos 1,
Morelia, Mich.;
tel. (9 14 51) 2 05 22, 2 01 23.

HOTELS. – *Real de Uruapan,* Nicolás Bravo y 5 Febrero, I; *Mansión de Cupatitzio,* Parque Nacional, I, SP; *Plaza Uruapan,* Ocampo 64, I; *Victoria,* Cupatitzio 13, I; *El Tarasco,* Independencia 2, I, SP; *Motel Pie de la Sierre,* 3 km (2 miles) on Carapán road, I; *Uruapan Continental,* N. Bravo 33, II; *Hernández,* Portal Matamoros 19; *Villa de Flores,* E. Carranza 15, II; *Mirador,* Ocampo 9, III.

RESTAURANTS in most hotels; also *Los Manjares de Caltzonzin,* B. Juárez 153; *Mercado de Antojitos,* Portal; *Las Palmas,* D. Guerra 2; *Emperador,* Portal Matamoros 18.

RECREATION and SPORTS. – Swimming, tennis, riding.

EVENTS. – Fiestas: Palm Sunday; Holy Week (Handicraft Fair); July 22, Día de Maria Magdalena; July 25, Día de Santiago Apóstol; October 4, Día de San Francisco; October 24, Festival de Coros y Danzas.

Uruapan, still relatively little frequented by tourists, lies in wooded country. Its mild climate, luxuriant vegetation and beautiful parks are its principal attractions.

In the Eduardo Ruiz National Park

HISTORY. – The town of Uruapan (Tarascan, "where the flowers bloom") was founded by the Franciscan friar, Juan de San Miguel, in 1532 under the name of *San Francisco de Uruapan.* It was laid out on a regular plan and divided into nine districts (*barrios*), which still preserve much of their individual characters.

SIGHTS. – The main square (*Plaza Principal*) was laid out in early colonial times as a large market. In the square is the *Guatápera* or *Huatápera Chapel,* also called Santo Sepulcro, the chapel of the hospital founded by Juan de San Miguel, with a fine Plateresque *doorway and a

Paricutín and the half-buried church of San Juan Parangaricutirorícuaro

statue of the founder ("Santo de Uruapan" or "Tata Juanito"). The Hospital, which has a beautiful patio, now houses the **Museum of Folk Art** (*Museo de Artes Populares*), noteworthy for the lacquerware which has been made in the town since the 16th c.

The finest of the town's beautiful parks are the *Jardín de los Mártires* (Garden of the Martyrs) and especially the *Eduardo Ruiz National Park* in the gorge of the Cupatitzio (Purépecha, "where the waters meet"). Amid luxuriant vegetation are waterfalls, rocks, springs, etc. – In the daily *market* visitors will be tempted by the local lacquerware, handwoven fabrics and traditional costumes.

SURROUNDINGS. – 10 km (6 miles) S of Uruapan is one of Mexico's most beautiful waterfalls, *La Tzaráracua* (Tarascan, "sieve"), in a beautiful wooded setting on the *Laguna Cupatitzio*, with a drop of almost 40 m (130 ft).

Some 70 km (45 miles) beyond this, on Road 37, is the reservoir of *El Infiernillo* ("Little Hell"), a man-made lake more than 100 km (60 miles) long formed by a dam 175 m (575 ft) high and fed by the rivers *Tepalcatepec* and *Balsas*. It is planned to develop the tourist potentialities of the area. 30 km (19 miles) W of Uruapan toward Patzcuaro lies the township of Tingambato (Purépecha, "place of warm weather") where a site has recently been partly excavated.

36 km (22 miles) N of Uruapan, on Road 37, is *Paracho de Verduzco* (pop. 18,000; local fiesta August 8, handicraft fair November 16–26, which is renowned for its furniture, guitars, violins, toys and other articles made from wood.

A side road on the left off Road 37, 14 km (9 miles) N of Uruapan, leads via *Cocinas* to *Angahuán* (20 km – 12 miles; pop. 16,000), with the 16th c. church of Santiago (Plateresque façades showing Mudéjar influence, open chapel). Near this village is the extinct volcano of **Paricutín** (Tarascan, "that which lies in front": 2575 m – 8449 ft), which came into the news when it erupted on February 20, 1943 and buried several villages in its lava. The eruptions continued for almost three years and left over 5000 people homeless. Horses can be hired in Angahuán for the 40 minutes' ride to the huge *lava field*, from which protrudes the half-buried village church of San Juan Parangaricutirorícuaro.

Uxmal

State: Yucatán (Yuc.).
Altitude: 12 m (39 ft).

HOTELS. – *Hacienda Uxmal*, I, SP; *Villa Arqueológica*, I, SP, tennis; *Misión Inn Uxmal*, I, SP.

The famous Maya site of **Uxmal** lies on a scrub-covered plain in northwestern Yucatán 80 km (50 miles) S of Mérida. Although not one

Mérida

Uxmal

1 Juego de Pelota (Ball Court)
2 Casa de las Tortugas (House of the Turtles)
3 Palomar (Dovecot)
4 Cuadrángulo (Quadrangle)
5 Pirámide de la Vieja (Pyramid of the Old Woman)
6 Templo del Cementerio (Temple of the Cemetery)
7 Grupo de las Columnas (Group of the Columns)
8 Grupo Noroeste (Northwest Group)
9 Grupo Oeste (West Group)

of Mexico's largest archeological sites, Uxmal, predominantly built in the Puuc style of the Maya Classic period, is one of the finest and most complete complexes of pre-Columbian architecture in the whole country.

HISTORY. – Uxmal (Maya, "the thrice built") is believed to have been founded by a tribe from Petén (Guatemala) in the 6th c. A.D., during the Maya *Classic period*. It is possible, however, that there was an earlier settlement here, perhaps in the Pre-Classic period. The most splendid phase of Uxmal's architecture was in the 9th and 10th c. Although the Indian chronicles assert that Uxmal was founded about the year 1000 by the *Xiú*, a people from the Mexican highlands, the city had already passed its peak at that time. It is more probable that the Xiú settled in and around the abandoned town not until the 13th or 14th c., and after the destruction of Mayapán in the mid 15th c. moved on to Maní, their final establishment before the coming of the Spaniards.

The first Spaniard to give an account of the site was Father Alonso Ponce, who visited it in 1586. Uxmal was explored by Jean-Frédéric de Waldeck in 1836, and John L. Stephens and Frederick Catherwood spent some time here in 1841. The first systematic excavations were carried out by Frans Blom in 1929, and ten years later José Erosa Peniche worked on the site in the first of a series of Mexican expeditions which were continued in subsequent years.

THE SITE. – The excavated area – which, as at so many other pre-Columbian sites, represents only a small part of the archeological zone – measures 700 by 800 m (750 by 850 yds). In contrast to Chichén Itzá, Toltec features are almost wholly absent, so that Maya architecture is seen here in its pure form. Unlike other Maya cities in Yucatán, too, Uxmal was not built around one or more *cenotes*, since this type of natural water-hole does not exist in this area. The place of the cenotes was taken by *aguades* (holes in the ground faced with watertight material) and *chultunes* (man-made cisterns) in which rainwater was collected. The lack of ground water gave the rain god Chac a position of predominant importance, as can be seen from his frequent appearance in the sculptured decoration of the site.

Opposite the entrance is the tallest structure on the site, the *Pyramid of the Magician or Soothsayer (Pirámide del Adivino)*, which stands 38 m (125 ft) high. Legend has it that it was built in a single night by a dwarf with the help of his mother, who was a witch. In fact it was built and rebuilt over a period of more than three centuries, in five superimposed structures which can be clearly distinguished from one another.

The pyramid has an oval base instead of the usual rectangular one. On the W side, the foundations of **Temple I**, the oldest structure on the site, can be seen at the foot of the pyramid. This dates from the 6th c A.D., as is shown by the date 569 on a door lintel. On the façade, richly decorated with masks of the Maya rain god Chac, was found the famous figure of the "Queen of Uxmal" which is now in the National Museum of Anthropology in Mexico City, depicting a tattooed priest's head held in the jaws of a snake.

Temple II (*Templo Interior Oriente*), with a pillared inner chamber, is entered through an opening in the upper part of the E staircase. – **Temple III** (*Templo Interior Poniente*), built on to the rear of Temple II and not visible from outside, consists of a small central

shrine and an antechamber. – The steep *staircase* (60°) on the W side has no balustrade in the traditional sense but is flanked by stylized Chac masks. It leads up to **Temple IV** (*Templo Chenes*), which is entered through the open jaws of a stylized mask. Unlike other buildings at Uxmal, where the Puuc style predominates, this temple is in pure Chenes style. The entrance is a typical example of the style, and the façade of this cube-shaped structure is entirely covered with the Chac masks and lattice ornament which are characteristic of the Chenes style.

Temple V, also known as the *House of the Magician* or *Soothsayer*, which belongs to the final building phase, is reached either by the staircase on the E side or by two narrow staircases alongside the Chenes Temple on the W side. This rectangular structure, a smaller copy of the Governor's Palace (below), appears to date from the late 9th c. Part of the façade of the temple, which has three chambers, has lattice ornament. – From the top of the Pyramid of the Magician there are magnificent *views of the other buildings on the site and of the surrounding area.

Immediately NW of the Pyramid of the Magician is the magnificent *Nunnery Quadrangle (Cuadrángulo de las Monjas)*, so named by the Spaniards because of the numerous "cells". The four long buildings set around a trapezoid courtyard measuring 64 by 46 m (210 by 150 ft) stand on terraces of varying height and were built at different times.

The *patio* is entered through the corbel-arched entrance of the **South Building**, the second oldest building in the complex. The arch lies on the same axis as the badly ruined *ball court* in front of the Nunnery Quadrangle. On the E side of the central corridor are eight rooms, half of them looking S, the others looking N into the patio. The frieze above the doors has reliefs of Maya huts against a background of lattice ornament.

On the opposite side of the patio, standing on a platform almost 7 m (24 ft) high, is the oldest and largest building in the complex, the 81 m (265 ft) long **North Building**. The broad *staircase* is flanked by two small temples. The one to the left (W) is known as the *Temple of Venus*, because a motif on the frieze is believed to represent the planet Venus. It is borne on

Pyramid of the Magician, Uxmal

four columns, and is the only building with columns at Uxmal. The North Building contains a total of twenty-six rooms and has eleven entrances opening off the patio. As is usual in Puuc architecture, the lower story is undecorated. Above the cornice are four *towers*, each with four superimposed Chac masks. Other decorative elements include reliefs of thatched huts, monkeys and snakes.

The third oldest structure is the **East Building**, which has five entrances. The cornice is decorated with *snakes*, with their heads looking out on the N side; the frieze is relatively plain, consisting mainly of lattice-work; and there are also panels containing owls' heads.

The most recent range of buildings, the **West Building**, has seven entrances. Its *frieze is the most elaborate in Puuc architecture. Above the main entrance is a canopied *throne*, originally occupied by a seated figure which was half man and half turtle. The main part of the frieze shows an alternation of Maya huts, rows of masks, geometric ornament and coiled snakes forming meander-like patterns. The snakes, which were a later addition, are one of the few Toltec features found at Uxmal. – At each of the corners of the building are three superimposed masks of the rain god Chac.

From the Nunnery Quadrangle a path leads S to the **House of the Turtles** (*Casa de las Tortugas*), one of the most harmoniously proportioned of the build-ings at Uxmal, almost 7 m (23 ft) high and 29 m (95 ft) long. From the E side three entrances lead through the undecorated lower story into the interior. Above the middle cornice is a frieze of closely set columns. The building takes its name from the stylized turtles on the upper cornice.

Immediately S of this is the **Governor's Palace** (*Palacio del Gobernador*), per-haps the finest example of pre-Hispanic architecture in America. Set on a huge platform on a terrace, the palace is 98 m (322 ft) long, 12 m (39 ft) across and 8 m (26 ft) high. It consists of a central structure and two wings flanking two vaulted corridors, which were later closed off by cross walls.

The lower story has an undecorated façade with eleven entrances and another entrance at each end.

These give access to twenty-four chambers, all with the characteristic corbelled vaulting. – Above the middle cornice is a *frieze 3 m (10 ft) high, the upper part of which consists of an almost continuous row of Chac masks, together with a profusion of geometric patterns, Maya huts and stylized serpents. The lower part has a series of S-shaped ornaments forming a serpent which originally ran around the whole building. The figure with a headdress of quetzal feathers above the central entrance (restored) may represent a ruler of Uxmal. It is estimated that some 20,000 pieces of dressed stone weighing between 20 and 30 kg (45 and 67 lb) each were used in this huge stone mosaic.

In front of the palace is an *altar*, in the middle of which is a double-headed jaguar. This figure, cut from a single block of stone, may have served as a throne and a symbol of authority; it was discovered by Stephens in 1841.

SW of the Governor's Palace is the **Great Pyramid** (*Gran Pirámide*), which has recently been partly restored. Originally nine stories and standing 30 m (100 ft) high, this had a summit platform which was not occupied by a temple but by four small palace-like buildings on the four sides. The top story has Puuc-style ornament of masks, lattice-work, flowers and meanders.

One of the masks is so arranged that the nose forms a step or a throne, as on the Codz-pop at Kabah.

To the W is the **Dovecot** (*Palomar*), which, like the Nunnery Quadrangle, is built around a courtyard, measuring in this case 60 by 40 m (200 by 130 ft). This structure, which has been only partly restored, gets its name from the unusual form of its roof-comb, consisting of nine triangular structures with numerous small openings like pigeonholes rising above a long series of columns. This interesting building is thought to be about 200 years older than the Nunnery Quadrangle and the Governor's Palace: i.e., it was probably built between A.D. 700 and 800.

Dovecot, Uxmal

To N and S of the Dovecot are two other structures (not yet restored) on a similar plan, the *South Group* (Grupo Sur) and the *Quadrangle* (Cuadrángulo). – To the SE is the *Pyramid of the Old Woman* (Pirámide de la Vieja), not yet excavated, which may be one of the oldest structures at Uxmal. The top of this pyramid is a good point from which to photograph the Governor's Palace.

From the Pyramid of the Old Woman, a path runs 400 m ($\frac{1}{4}$ mile) S to the remains of a building to which the name of *Phallus Temple* (Templo de los Falos) has been given, after the row of sculptured phalluses, some of which serve as gargoyles (rainwater spouts). – The path to the exit runs past a group of buildings, some 200 m (220 yds) from the ball court, which includes the *Temple of the Cemetery*. Here a number of buildings, some of them badly ruined, stand around a square courtyard. On the N side is a pyramid with an almost completely ruined temple on the summit platform. Only on the W side is there a relatively well-preserved building with three entrances.

The roof-comb of the temple is similar to that of the Dovecot, suggesting that this is also a building of earlier date. The complex is named after four small platforms, probably altars, which are covered with carved skulls and cross bones and hieroglyphs. This seems to reflect Toltec influence, so rarely found at Uxmal.

Near the Temple of the Cemetery is the *Platform of the Stelae* (Plataforma de las Estelas), with five stelae up to 3 m (10 ft) high. There is a new museum which is part of the service building.

SURROUNDINGS. – The road from Uxmal via Muna to Maxcanú comes in 35 km (22 miles) to the village of *Calcehtok*. 3 km (2 miles) S are the interesting Caves of Calcehtok. About 1 km ($\frac{3}{4}$ mile) north of the caves a turning on the left leads to the great ruined Maya site of **Oxkintok**, which is now considered one of the oldest known Maya centers in Yucatán. In this very overgrown site a door-lintel was found which has been dated to A.D. 475, that is to the early classic period. The latest date discovered here was A.D. 849 found on a stele. The early classic architecture of Oxkintok corresponds to the Petén style, the late classic to the Puuc. Calcehtok can also be reached from Mérida on Road 180 in 74 km (38 miles) via Maxcanú.

Between *Becal* and *Pomuch*, on Road 180 to the S of Maxcanú, there are a number of villages with Maya remains and attractive colonial buildings (see under Campeche town).

Valle de Bravo
See under Toluca

Venta, La
See under Laguna de Catemaco

Veracruz (State)

State of Veracruz (Ver.).
Capital: Jalapa.
Area: 71,896 sq. km (27,759 sq. miles).
Population: 6,022,200.
(i) **Coordinación Federal de Turismo,**
Av. Ignacio Zaragoza 20 Altos, Centro,
Veracruz, Ver.;
tel. (91 29) 32 70 26, 32 16 13.

Veracruz, one of the most populous states in Mexico, is bounded on the N by Tamaulipas, on the W by San Luis Potosí, Hidalgo, Puebla and Oaxaca and on the SE by Chiapas and Tabasco. The landscape of the state is full of variety: between the rugged peaks of the Sierra Madre Oriental and the long beaches on the Gulf of Mexico coffee plantations alternate with fields of maize, industrial towns with great expanses of vanilla, oilfields with primeval tropical forest. Once the homeland of the legendary Olmecs, the state is mainly populated by mestizos, together with the descendants of Negro slaves and Totonac, Huastec and Nahua Indians.

There are important Olmec sites at *Cerro de las Mesas, Tres Zapotes* and *San Lorenzo Tenochtitlán* (see under Laguna de Catemaco). Remains of the Huastecs and Totonacs are to be found at *Zempoala or Cempoala* (p. 288), *Castillo de Teayo* (p. 127) and *El Tajín* (p. 125).

HISTORY. – After the Olmecs (c. 1200 to 400 B.C.), whose influence extended over much of Mexico, came the *Huastecs* and *Totonacs* and later the *Aztecs*, who gained control of the area by military conquest. The *Spanish conquest* began with Cortés's landing in 1519 near present-day Veracruz. The first Spanish settlement, with the name of Villa Rica de la Veracruz was founded near Quiahuitlán, which was renamed La Antigua in 1924. Not until the end of the 16th c. was the local Spanish headquarters transferred to the site of the present-day town of Veracruz.

Mexico
United Mexican States
Estados Unidos Mexicanos

Veracruz

States
Estados

1a Baja California Sur	12 Aguascalientes
1b Baja California Norte	13 Jalisco
	14 Guanajuato
2 Sonora	15 Querétaro
3 Chihuahua	16 Hidalgo
4 Sinaloa	17 Colima
5 Durango	18 Michoacán
6 Coahuila	19 México
7 Nuevo León	20 Morelos
8 Zacatecas	21 Tlaxcala
9 San Luis Potosí	22 Puebla
10 Tamaulipas	23 Veracruz
11 Nayarit	24 Guerrero
	25 Oaxaca
26 Chiapas	
27 Tabasco	
28 Campeche	
29 Yucatán	
30 Quintana Roo	

D.F. Distrito Federal (Federal District)

ECONOMY. – In addition to its *plantation agriculture*, producing a varied range of tropical and subtropical crops, Veracruz has a well-developed *industry*; among the principal products are beer, spirits, tobacco, soap, cement, chemicals, glass and leather goods. Contributions are also made to the economy by the *transport industry*, *livestock farming*, *fishing*, the *oil industry* and, increasingly, *tourism*. Its well-balanced economic structure has made Veracruz a wealthy state, in which such regional centers as Jalapa, Veracruz, Córdoba, Orizaba (see the entries for these places), Poza Rica, Minatitlán and Coatzacoalcos have developed and prospered.

Veracruz (Town)

State: Veracruz (Ver.).
Altitude: 3 m (10 ft). – Population: 680,000.
Telephone dialing code: 9 12 93.
ⓘ **Coordinación Federal de Turismo**,
   Av. Ignacio Zaragoza 20 Altos, Centro;
   tel. 32 70 26, 32 16 13, 32 99 42.

HOTELS. – *Exelaris Hyatt*, Mocambo 4300, L, SP; *Calinda*, Av. Veracruz y Carr. 150, L, SP; *Hostal de Cortés*, Blvd. Camacho y B. de Las Casas, L, SP; *Mocambo*, Calzada Mocambo, I, SP; *Acuario*, Av. J. de Diós Pesa 1015, I, SP; *Playa Paraíso*, 3·5 km (2 miles) on road to Ocambo, I, SP, tennis; *Villa del Mar*, Blvd. M. A. Camacho, I, SP; *Colonial*, Miguel Lerdo 117, I, SP; *Baluarte*, Francisco Canal 265, II; *Ruíz Milan*, Paseo del Malecón, II; *Acapulco*, Uribe 1327, II; *Guadalajara*, Mina 1053, II; *America*, H. Cortes 892; *Bravo*, Av. Bravo 1115, III; *Cielo*, S. Pérez Abascal 580, III.

RESTAURANTS in most hotels; also *Prendes*, Zócalo; *Los Cedros*, Calz. Mocambo; *El Caballo Bayo del Puerto*, Gen. Figueroa 407; *El Pescador*, Zaragoza 335; *El Chato Moyo*, Landeros y Coss 142; *La Ley del Monte*, 20 de Noviembre Esq. Azueta; *Cayetano*, Molina 88. – IN BOCO DEL RÍO: *Pardino*, Revolución 10; *Las Brisas del Mar*, Zamora Esq. Juárez.

RECREATION and SPORTS. – Swimming, fishing, sailing, diving, tennis, golf.

EVENT. – Carnival.

The old town of Veracruz, Mexico's principal port, lies just above sea level on a sandy beach in the hot climatic zone and is connected with Mexico City, 425 km (265 miles) away, by two railway lines and several roads. The town's importance as a port and customs station and as the main center for the

Zócalo, Veracruz

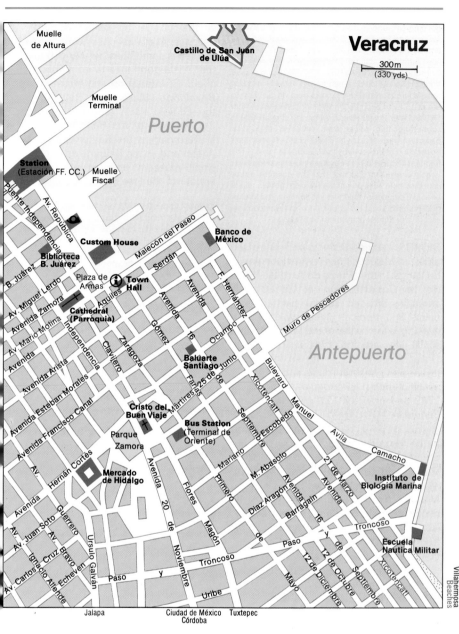

Veracruz

Muelle de Altura

Castillo de San Juan de Ulúa

300m (330 yds)

Puerto

Muelle Terminal

Station (Estación FF. CC.) Muelle Fiscal

Custom House

Banco de México

Biblioteca B. Juárez

Plaza de Armas · Town Hall

Cathedral (Parroquia)

Baluarte Santiago

Antepuerto

Muro de Pescadores

Cristo del Buen Viaje

Parque Zamora

Bus Station (Terminal de Oriente)

Mercado de Hidalgo

Instituto de Biología Marina

Escuela Náutica Militar

Jalapa   Ciudad de México   Tuxtepec
          Córdoba

Villahermosa Beaches

coastal region on the Gulf of Mexico and the tropical hinterland has given it an eventful history. In spite of its warm and humid climate, Veracruz is a lively and attractive town which is popular with Mexican vacationers and offers an agreeable mingling of colonial and modern architecture.

HISTORY. – In the centuries before the Christian era, the area around Veracruz (Spanish, "True Cross") was probably inhabited by the mysterious *Olmecs* and later by the *Totanacs*. The capital of the kingdom of this people was Zempoala, some 40 km (25 miles) distant from present-day Veracruz. – On Good Friday in 1519 (April 22) Hernán Cortés landed here with his Spanish troops, and later received an embassy from the Aztec ruler Moctezuma II. Moctezuma took Cortés to be the returning Quetzalcóatl, the legendary ruler who had

been driven out of the Toltec capital of Tula (Tollan) about 530 years before and had disappeared over the sea, promising that he would come back. Cortés resolved to remain, and founded the town of *Villa Rica de la Vera Cruz*. The site of the town was changed several times, until in 1598 *Nueva Veracruz* was established on the position of the present town. Although the town itself was slow to develop, the port was of prime importance in the movement of shipping between Mexico and Spain (Cádiz and Seville). During the 16th c., and increasingly in the 17th, the town suffered from raids by British, French and Dutch pirates. Toward the end of the war of independence, in 1821, the Mexican general, Agustín de Iturbide, defeated the last Viceroy of New Spain, Juan O'Donojú, at Veracruz, after which the Viceroy signed the treaty of Córdoba recognizing Mexico's independence.

In 1838 Veracruz was occupied by French troops sent to enforce the payment of compensation to their government, and in 1847, during the war between Mexico and the United States, it was occupied for a time by US troops. – The intervention by Spain, France and Britain in the conflict between Liberals and Conservatives in Mexico led to a further occupation of Veracruz by a French expeditionary force. – In 1864 Maximilian of Habsburg landed here on his way to Mexico City to become Emperor; and three years later his fate was finally sealed when the French troops supporting him sailed from here on their final departure from Mexico. – There was a further brief occupation of the town by the US army in 1914. – The frequent occupation of Veracruz by foreign troops was largely a result of the fact that the customs duties collected here were one of the Mexican government's principal sources of revenue; accordingly, the foreign governments sought to gain control of this income as security for debts due to them by Mexico.

SIGHTS. – Although the town is one of the oldest in Mexico, it has few major colonial buildings. In the *Plaza de Armas (Plaza de la Constitución or Zócalo), an attractive arcaded square planted with palms and tropical plants which in the evening is the center of the town's relaxed social life, are the 17th c. Town Hall (Palacio Municipal), with an interesting façade and a beautiful patio, and the former parish church (La Parroquia), dedicated in 1743 and now the Cathedral of Nuestra Señora de la Asuncion.

In the Plaza Gutiérrez Zamora stands the church of Santo Cristo del Buen Viaje, said to be the oldest church in Mexico. – At Calle Zaragoza 397 is the Museo de Arte e Historia Veracruzana, with excellently displayed collections of archeological material and art from the Olmec, Totonac and Huastec cultures.

It is well worthwhile to walk along the Malecón (Quay) and observe the busy activity of the Harbor. From the harbor a boat can be taken to the Castillo de San Juan de Ulúa, a large island fortress which is one of the town's landmarks. The Spaniards began to build this fort in 1528 to protect the coast from attack by sea – an objective not always achieved. In later times it was used primarily as a prison. The Island is also connected with the town by road. – Another boat trip from the harbor is to the Isla de los Sacrificios, so called because the Spaniards witnessed a human sacrifice here. The island now attracts many visitors to its beaches.

The bathing beach nearest to the town is the Playa Villa del Mar. 8 km (5 miles) farther S is the beach of Mocambo. Beyond the fishing village of Boca del Río

is the village of Mandinga with its beaches. At the beaches nearer the town, the sea is sometimes heavily polluted, so that it is a good idea to go a little farther afield. Of interest are the Museum of the Revolution (Museo de la Revolución) in the Edificio Faro Venustiano Carranza, the Museum of the Reform (Museo de la Reforma) in the Edificio Faro Benito Juárez and, in the Baluarte de Santiago, a small museum housing weapons and armour of the time of the Conquista.

SURROUNDINGS. – 25 km (16 miles) N of Veracruz on the coast road (No. 180) a side road leads to the fishing village of La Antigua, where Cortés landed in 1519 and established his temporary headquarters. He then burned his boats in the bay in order to emphasize that there was to be no turning back from his campaign of conquest. In 1524 a Spanish settlement – removed to the present site of Veracruz in the late 16th c. – was established here. Remains of the fort, now riven by tree roots, and of the first church built on Mexican soil can still be seen.

10 km (6 miles) farther along Road 180, beyond José Cardel, a side road goes off on the left to *Zempoala or Cempoala (in Náhuatl, "twenty waters"; 3 km – 2 miles), which from the 13th c. to the Spanish conquest was the last capital of the Totonacs. In the second half of the 15th c. the Aztecs defeated the Totonacs and exacted payment of tribute from them. 23 days after his landing in Mexico Cortés met the Totonac king Chicomacatl (known as Cacque Gordo = "fat chief") on May 15, 1519 in Zempoala. The Conquistador succeeded in securing the alliance of the Totonacs, who were the natural enemies of the Aztecs.

The *ARCHEOLOGICAL SITE of Zempoala (Cempoala) covers an area of some 5 sq. km (2 sq. miles) and comprises ten groups of buildings – though visitors can now see only the few buildings that have been restored. They date from the last 300 years before the arrival of the Spaniards, and some of them show definite Aztec features. It is probable, however, that the site was already occupied during the first millennium A.D.

On the N side of the plaza is the Principal Temple (Templo Mayor) or Temple of the Thirteen Steps. The pyramid stands 11 m (36 ft) high; each of the tiers, 85 cm (33 in.) high. The platform on which it stands measures 67 by 40 m (220 by 130 ft). On the summit

Zempoala

1 Altars
2 Templo de las Chimeneas (Temple of the Chimneys)
3 Templo de las Caritas (Temple of the Little Heads)

Templo Mayor, Zempoala

platform the remains of a rectangular temple can still be seen. – On the E side of the plaza is the **Temple of the Chimneys** (*Templo de las Chimeneas*), a six-story structure with a broad staircase leading up to the platform and the remains of columns from which the temple takes its name. – On the W side of the plaza is the **Great Pyramid** (*Gran Pirámide*), a later structure which consists of a series of superimposed platforms, each smaller than the one below. – A little way E of the plaza is the interesting **Temple of the Little Heads** (*Templo de las Caritas*), similar in structure to the Great Pyramid, with niches in the walls which once contained a total of 360 small terracotta heads. – At the entrance to the archeological zone is a small museum with a few exhibits.

Villahermosa

State: Tabasco (Tab.).
Altitude: 11 m (36 ft). – Population: 380,000.
Telephone dialing code: 9 19 31.

ⓘ **Coordinación Federal de Turismo**,
Lerdo 101, 1st floor,
Esq. Malecón y Lic. Carlos A. Madrazo,
tel. 2 73 36, 2 74 56.

HOTELS. – *Exelaris Hyatt*, Av. Juárez 106, L, SP; *Cencali*, Juárez y Paseo Tabasco, I, SP; *Maya Tabasco*, Av. Grijalva y Blvd. Mina, I; *Villahermosa Viva*, Blvd. Grijalva y Paseo Tabasco, I, SP; *Manzur*, Av. F. I. Madero 422, I; *María Dolores*, Aldama 404, II; *Casa Blanca*, Río Samaria 200, II; *Balboa*, Bastar Zozaya 505, III.

RESTAURANTS in most hotels; also *Club de Pesca*, 27 de Febrero 812; *Pelícanos*, Paseo Tabasco 401; *Chez Vaglia*, Av. 27 de Febrero 703; *Country Steakhouse*, Cedro 209; *Los Pericos*, CICOM; *Chon Cupón*, Parque La Choca Tabasco 2000; *Capitán Beuló* (ship restaurant starting from Paseo Malecón).

RECREATION and SPORTS. – Swimming, tennis, hunting, fishing, boat trips.

EVENT. – Carnival Tuesday (Shrove Tuesday).

Until a few years ago Villahermosa, capital of Tabasco state, was a rather sleepy town in a tropical setting on the banks of the Río Grijalva; but the building of new roads and the discovery of large reserves of oil in Tabasco and Chiapas have transformed it into a rapidly growing modern city, an important center of communications and commerce. It lies in a depression crossed by various rivers and waterways and has a hot and humid climate with heavy rainfall.

HISTORY. – Nothing is known of the pre-Hispanic history of the area. As early as 1518 the Spanish Conquistador Juan de Grijalva explored the region and met strong resistance from the Indians. In 1596 *Villa Felipe II* was founded and two years later was renamed *San Juan Bautista de la Villa Hermosa* (Spanish, "beautiful village"). In time it developed into Tabasco, the largest town in the state (see history of Tabasco p. 250).

SIGHTS. – Villahermosa has few historic buildings, apart from the *Cathedral* (1614), but it possesses two of the most interesting archeological *museums* in Mexico.

In the great new cultural complex **CICOM** (*Centro de Investigaciones de las Culturas Olmeca y Maya*), opened in 1980 on the west bank of the Río Grijalva, is the *Carlos Pellicer Camara Regional* **Museum of Anthropology** (*Museo Regional de Antropología Carlos Pellicer Camera*), named after the celebrated poet, collector and founder of museums Carlos Pellicer (1897–1977).

In the considerable collection of relics of various cultures of Mexico are stone sculpture, pottery and jade figurines of the *Olmecs* (Náhuatll, "people from the land of rubber"); pottery, masks and everyday objects from *Teotihuacán*; copies and originals of *Aztec* sculpture; pottery and sculpture from the *W coast* of Mexico; terracotta heads of the *Totonacs*; *Zapotec* and *Mixtec* pottery and urns; and terracotta figures, pottery, urns, stelae, copies of manuscripts (codices) and reproductions of wall paintings of the *Mayas*.

Also in the CICOM complex are an auditorium, a library, the *Esperanza Iris State Theater*, exhibition and sale rooms for handicrafts, restaurants, shops, etc., and in process of construction an art gallery and a garden of art.

On the south-west shore of the *Lake of Illusions* (Laguna de los Ilusiones) is an outdoor archeological museum, the ****Museo de la Venta**.

Olmec stone altar in Museo de la Venta

In this tropical park are artefacts of the **Olmec culture** (*La Venta culture*), including altars, stelae, sculptured figures of animals and the colossal heads from **La Venta**. In this museum, the Mexican anthropologist, who came from Tabasco, Carlos Pellicer set out to display the remains of a great culture in an appropriate setting, and the result is immensely impressive. The original find-spots lie in inaccessible areas of swamp in the states of Tabasco and Veracruz.

Some archeologists regard the **Olmecs** as the originators of all the Meso-American cultures; it is certain that this mysterious people evolved the oldest known culture in Mexico, which strongly influenced large areas of the country. As far as we know, the Olmecs were the first people to develop a glyphic script and a system of numbers, and they are accordingly regarded as the forerunners of the Mayas. The earliest known dating of the Olmecs is 31 B.C., on Stela C at Tres Zapotes. As well as producing their magnificent large-scale sculpture, they showed consummate craftsmanship in the delicate modelling of terracotta figures and the intricate working of jade. Their heyday was between 1200 and 400 B.C., but their influence continued to be felt until the 4th c. A.D. Major Olmec sites in addition to La Venta are *San Lorenzo*, *Tres Zapotes* and *Cerro de las Mesas*.

It is still a puzzle how the people of this Stone Age culture were able to move the huge blocks of basalt from which they cut their **colossal heads**, standing up to 3 m (10 ft) high and weighing up to 20 tons. Some of the faces show Negroid features; in others there is a mingling of human and animal (jaguar) characteristics. The un-Indian aspect of these faces has given rise to the most far-fetched theories. It has been suggested on the one hand that they represent Nubian princes sent by Ramesses III of Egypt to look for the underworld in the west, and on the other, that they depict potentates of the prehistoric megalithic cultures of southern England and northern France. It need not be mentioned that there is not the slightest evidence to support such hypotheses. Farther W lies the new complex of '*Tabasco 2000*', which includes the planetarium, a conference center, department stores, the City Hall, etc. – Still farther W on the east bank of the Rió Carrizal extends *La Choca Park* (Parque La Choca).

SURROUNDINGS. – 52 km (32 miles) NW via Nacajuca or 82 km (51 miles) along Road 180 via Cárdenas and then on Road 187 is the town of **Comalcalco** (Náhuatl, "in the house of the Comales"; comalli=tortilla pan; pop. 20,000; accommodations: Imperial, Lerdo, Morelos). 3 km (2 miles) NE of the town lies the archeological site of *Comalcalco, the most westerly of all the more important Maya sites. It dates from the late Maya classic period (A.D. 600–900) and probably reached its zenith in the 8th century. The layout of the temple, the style and use of stucco embellishment and the ornament of the tomb which was discovered there, have a certain similarity with the art of Palenque. It is striking to note that, since stone was in short supply, and on account of the proximity of the sea, kiln-fired bricks and mortar made from crushed mussel shells were used, a practice which is unique in the classic Maya period. The first explorer in Comalcalco was Désiré Charnay in 1880. Frans Blom and Oliver La Farge worked here in 1925 for the University of Tulane. In recent years the I.N.A.H. (Instituto Nacional de Antropología e Historia) has embarked on new excavations and restoration.

The visit should begin in the northern part of the site with the extensive *Plaza Norte* (North area). On the W side stands a great pyramid of several tiers with the remains of *Temple I* on the top; on the left at the foot of the open staircase can be seen damaged stucco figures. On a mound on the N side stands *Temple II*; the only other buildings worth mentioning, such as *Temple group III*, are only just being revealed. To the S stands the *Acropolis*, forming a great man-made platform and enclosing the concourse of the same name (Plaza de la Acropolis). On it stand the little *Temples IV and V* and a building known as the '*Palace*' (Palacio). Not far from Temple IV Frans Blom discovered the most interesting tomb of the 'Nine Men of the Night' (Tumba de los Nueve Señores de la Noche). Nine stucco reliefs, three on the wall on each side of the tomb, may represent the nine rulers of the underworld. Originally the figures were painted red and they only partly reveal classic Maya features. The sarcophagus in the tomb-chamber has fallen victim to tomb robbers. Somewhat lower down on a stepped platform is another group of buildings. *Temple VI* has on its steps an impressively modelled stucco mask. *Temple VII* is also decorated with stucco on the southern side, including a sitting figure in profile. Recently opened at the site is a museum in which are interesting sculptures, pottery and figurines found in Tabasco.

From Comalcalco it is 20 km (12 miles) to *El Paraíso* (pop. 10,000; Hotel Centro Turístico). Near this town and also some 75 km (47 miles) E in the vicinity of

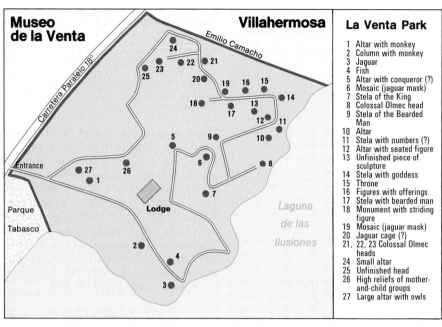

Museo de la Venta

Villahermosa

La Venta Park

1 Altar with monkey
2 Column with monkey
3 Jaguar
4 Fish
5 Altar with conqueror (?)
6 Mosaic (jaguar mask)
7 Stela of the King
8 Colossal Olmec head
9 Stela of the Bearded Man
10 Altar
11 Stela with numbers (?)
12 Altar with seated figure
13 Unfinished piece of sculpture
14 Stela with goddess
15 Throne
16 Figures with offerings
17 Stela with bearded man
18 Monument with striding figure
19 Mosaic (jaguar mask)
20 Jaguar cage (?)
21, 22, 23 Colossal Olmec heads
24 Small altar
25 Unfinished head
26 High reliefs of mother-and-child groups
27 Large altar with owls

Frontera (pop. 26,000; hotels: Maya del Grijalva, San Agustín) are several attractive beaches. Frontera is a significent port for Tabasco.

58 km (36 miles) S of Villahermosa is *Teapa* (alt. 72 m (236 ft); pop. 18,000; hotels: Quintero, Jardín). Nearby lie the interesting caves, *Grutas de Coconá* (Maya, "water which falls from the sky") which were once used as a pirate lair. Close at hand, too, are the sulfur springs of *El Azufre.* There is another cave, *Cuesta Chica,* near *Tapijulapa* about 30 km (19 miles) distant.

In the eastern part of Tabasco lies the little town of *Emiliano Zapata* (alt. 30 m (98 ft); pop. 10,000; hotels: Bernat Colonial, Maya Usumacinta, Ramos, San Agustín) a center of cattle rearing and the junction for the road to Palenque (Chiapas). About 50 km (31 miles) NE of Emiliano Zapata is *Balancán* (alt. 18 m (59 ft); pop. 9000; Hotel Delicias). This is a region for shooting, fishing and archeological sites; Balancán itself has a new archeological museum (Museo Dr. José Gómez Panaco), housed in the Casa Cultura. From Emiliano Zapata it is about 70 km (43 miles) SE to the little town of **Tenosique de Pino Suárez** on the Río Usumacinta (alt. 60 m (197 ft); pop. 25,000; hotels: Don José, San Juán, Azulejos; carnival; starting point of the annual boat race marathon to Villa Hermosa). Thanks to its excellent situation the town is a good base for expeditions into the jungle. – The air-taxi trip from Tenosique to the sites of *Bonampak (p. 82) from *Yaxchilán (p. 296) is cheaper and faster than the trip from Palenque or San Cristóbal de las Casas.

Xel-há

State: Quintana Roo (Q.R.).

ACCESS. – The Caleta (bay) de Xel-há lies 1 km (⅔ mile) off Road 307, 117 km (73 miles) S of Puerto Juárez (12 km (7 miles) S of Akumal) and 228 km (142 miles) N of Chetumal (16 km (10 miles) N of Tulum).

The interesting *nature reserve of Xel-há contains within a relatively small area a fresh-water lake, a bay on the Caribbean and a variety of Maya remains. Its rich flora and fauna, both under water and on land, will fascinate swimmers, snorkelers and strollers.

Now a popular weekend resort, this site was discovered only in 1959 during underwater exploration by the Club de Exploraciones y Deportes Acuáticos de México (CEDAM). Xel-há ("where the waters were born" in Maya) seems, more than other coastal sites in this region, to have been an important Maya cult center during the Classic period: this is shown by the size of the lagoon and the archeological finds that have been made in and around it.

The remains found here included a *defensive wall* of the Post-Classic period and several *altars* lying under water, including one in a cave which was evidently a shrine of some kind.

Here were found the remains of two hearths, giving rise to theories that the Mayas carried out cremations in this sanctuary. Unfortunately, parts of the altar have been removed in recent years as well as at some earlier period. The cave, which lies on the S side of the lagoon near the channel connecting it with the sea, can easily be reached by a good swimmer, though at times only by diving.

Ruins

Xel-há

P

Laguna

Caribbean Sea

■ Altar Cave

● Caves, reefs,
interesting spots under
water

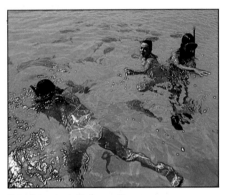

Xel-há – a snorkeller's paradise

The mixture of fresh and salt water which is regularly found in the bays of Quintana Roo produces a rich and varied underwater life in this natural aquarium, with its crystal-clear water and its reefs and rocky islets. The shores of the lagoon, with their alternation of caves, inlets and backwaters and their exotic plants, form a pictureque frame for the colorful *underwater world. Xal-há offers every facility for swimmers and snorkelers (restaurant, changing rooms, snorkel rentals, etc.).

SURROUNDINGS. – On a hacienda 10 km (6 miles) S is the Maya site of **Tancah**, with a cenote. The temples here are similar to those at Tulum, though some of them appear to be considerably older. It is thought that Tancah was a dependency of the nearby city of ***Tulum** (p. 275) in the late Post-Classic period A.D. 1200 on).

Xochicalco

State: Morelos (Mor.).
Altitude: 1525 m (5005 ft).

ACCESS. – From Cuernavaca 28 km (17 miles) S to Alpuyeca, then 8 km (5 miles) to the turning for Xochicalco (4 km – 2½ miles).

The fortress-like site of *Xochicalco lies 130 m (430 ft) above an extensive plain, on a conical hill on which platforms have been formed partly by the removal of soil and partly by building it up. The history of this site is one of the great riddles of Meso-American archeology, since practically nothing is known of the people who built it and the remains so far excavated show influences from a number of different cultures.

HISTORY. – Xochicalco (Náhuatl, "in the house of flowers") was probably established around A.D. 500, and seems to have developed into an important cultural and trading center in the 7th and 8th c. It is believed that the earliest settlers in this area were Mixtec-speaking Indians. The site, lying at the meeting-place of the advanced cultures of northern and southern Mexico, shows the influence of Teotihuacán as well as of the Maya, Zapotec, Mixtec and Toltec cultures. Later Xochicalco became an important teaching center, at which Ce Acatl Topiltzín is said to have received, about the middle of the 10th c., the education which later enabled him to become the legendary god-king of Tula and the bringer of culture under the name of Quetzalcóatl.

Xochicalco seems to have been fortified only in the 9th c. After A.D. 900 the town declined and its end came shortly afterwards, when it was either conquered by other peoples or abandoned for economic reasons. In time the population was absorbed by the Toltecs, Tlahuicas and Aztecs. – The first Spanish account of Xochicalco was written by Bernardino de Sahagún in the 16th c., and the first excavations were carried out by Father José Antonio Alzate in 1777. A little later Guillaume Dupaix arrived and

General view of Xochicalco

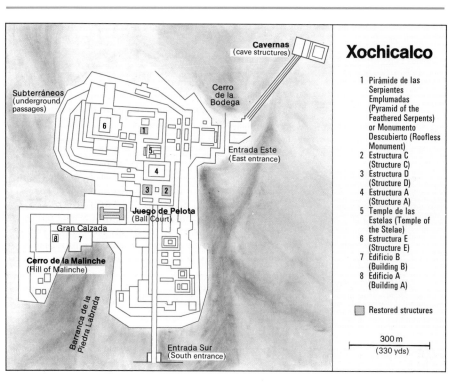

Xochicalco

1 Pirámide de las
  Serpientes
  Emplumadas
  (Pyramid of the
  Feathered Serpents)
  or Monumento
  Descubierto (Roofless
  Monument)
2 Estructura C
  (Structure C)
3 Estructura D
  (Structure D)
4 Estructura A
  (Structure A)
5 Temple de las
  Estelas (Temple of
  the Stelae)
6 Estructura E
  (Structure E)
7 Edificio B
  (Building B)
8 Edificio A
  (Building A)

▨ Restored structures

300 m
(330 yds)

Alexander von Humboldt came here at the beginning of the 19th c. Excavation and restoration work was done by A. Peñafiel in 1877 and Leopoldo Batres in 1910. Since the 1960s, further excavations have been carried out by the Instituto Nacional de Arqueología e Historia under the direction of Eduardo Noguera and César A. Sáenz.

THE SITE. – The total area of this religious and military metropolis is more than 12 sq. km (4½ sq. miles); the cult center itself measures some 1200 m (1300 yds) from N to S and 700m (750 yds) from E to W. From the top of the hill there are magnificent *views of the surrounding hills, plains and lakes.

The tour of the site begins at the *Lower Plaza* (Plaza Inferior), on which are two restored pyramids built up in steps, known as *Structures C and D*. On the Altar of the Stele of the Two Glyphs (Adoratorio de la Estela de los Dos Glifos) between the two pyramids a large *stela* inscribed with glyphs, almost 3 m (10 ft) high and weighing 6 tons was found. – Passing the poorly preserved Structure A, we come to the *Pyramid of the Stelae* (Pyrámide de las Estelas) on the highest level of the site, where a 15 m (50 ft)-wide staircase leads up to the temple. Here were found three highly interesting 1.8 m (6 ft)-high stelae with reliefs of the deities Tláloc and Quetzalcóatl as well as number glyphs of the Maya and Zapotec an Mixtec year glyphs. These stelae, the only ones

bearing glyphs so far found in central Mexico, are now in the National Museum of Anthropology in Mexico City. On the right of the base of the staircase can be seen the former sanctuary, the sacrificial chamber (cámera de las ofrendas) in which were found various sacrificial gifts (stone figurines, a jade head, arrow heads made of obsidian, human bones etc.).

A short distance N can be found the most important building of Xochicalco, the *Pyramid of the Feathered Serpents* (*Pirámide de las Serpientes Emplumadas*), also known as the *Roofless Monument* (Monumento Descubierto), measuring 21 by 18.60 m (69 by 61 ft); it is thought to have been built in honor of an important assembly of priest-astronomers.

The pyramid consists of two stories, of which only the LOWER PART is preserved in its entirety. It is built in the *tulud-tablero* style (with an alternation of sloping and vertical wall surfaces), but here, in constrast to the usual pattern at Teotihuacán, the sloping wall predominates. This is decorated with magnificent *reliefs of eight feathered serpents entwining various glyphs and seated figures. Originally they were painted white, red, black, blue and yellow, but in a final phase they were overpainted in red, the color of death, probably in token of the city's imminent fall. The glyphs on either side of the staircase (three day symbols) may refer to a correction of the sacred calendar. – Along the sides of the vertical wall are poorly preserved reliefs of seated figures, stylized serpents and calendrical glyphs. Above the projecting cornice over the vertical wall of the upper story is a frieze of stylized shells, probably associated with the god Quetzalcóatl.

Of the UPPER PART of the pyramid only the slopping wall remains, part of it covered with poorly preserved reliefs. The wall bounds an almost square *temple* (11 by 10.50 m (36 by 34 ft), which some archeologists believe was open to the sky: hence the name, "Monumento Descubierto". This view, however, is not generally accepted. – On the walls set at right angles to the entrance can be seen the figure of a coyote and the symbols for fire.

Monumento Descubierto, Xochicalco

Going W from the Pyramid of the Feathered Serpents to *Structure E* and continuing down the N side of the hill, we pass on the left the entrance to a series of **underground passages and chambers** (*subterráneos*). From a large entrance hall, a broad staircase leads by way of three landings into a corridor. Another passage from the entrance hall runs up to a room (19 m (62 ft) long, 12 m (39 ft) wide, 3.50 m (11 ft) high) with three rectangular columns (4 by 2 m – 13 by 6 ft 6 in.). In the corner is a light shaft which may have been used for astronomical observations. There are a number of other underground passages in the complex, some of them excavated, others

Features of different Mexican cultures found at Xochicalco:	
Mayas:	Ball courts, reliefs of seated figures, bars and dots as numbers, sweat baths
Teotihuacán:	Variant of *tablud-tablero* style, glyphs, figurines, pottery
Zapotecs:	Pottery, bars and dots as numbers
Toltecs:	Names of warriors and priests, pottery
Mixtecs:	Year glyphs, pottery

awaiting excavation. (These subterranean rooms and passages are sometimes closed to visitors.)

In the middle of the cult center is the **Ball Court** (*Juego de Pelota*), the only one of the ball courts on the site which has been restored. It measures 69 m (225 ft) from E to W, with sloping walls along the sides and ends. In the side walls were set the stone rings which served as "goals" in the ritual ball game (*tlachtli*). – In its layout and in its furnishings the Ball Court here reveals striking similarities with many of those in the Maya territory. The later ball court in Tula is almost identical in its layout and measurements. – From the Ball Court a path, the Gran Calzada, leads W to a series of buildings. Parallel to the 20 m (66 ft) wide roadway stands a row of low circular platforms which may have been altars. We then reach *Building B*, also called a palace (Edificio B, El Palacio; priests' residences, sweat bath and patios), then *Building A* (Edificio A, a cult building) and finally the *Hill of Malinche* (Cerro de la Malinche), a man-made mound in the form of a flat-topped pyramid, with a terrace. From the top there is a fine view.

SURROUNDINGS. – 20 km (12 miles) from Xochicalco (4 km (2½ miles) from Mazatepec) is *Coatetelco* (Náhuatl, "hill of snakes"). On the edge of an archeological zone on the shores of Lake Coatetelco is the small partially excavated site of *Cuahtetelco* with a museum exhibiting stone sculpture, pottery and other material belonging to various cultures (Teotihuacán, Tlahuicas, Aztecs, etc.).

Xochimilco
See under Mexico City

Yagul

State: Oaxaca (Oax.).
Altitude: 1650 m (5414 ft).

ACCESS. – 34 km (21 miles) from Oaxaca on Road 190 (direction Tehuantepec), a side road goes off on the left to the site, 2 km (1¼ miles) away.

*Yagul, once an important Zapotec and Mixtec political and religious center, lies on the slopes of a hill NE of Tlacolula in a landscape studded with tall cacti. The temples and palaces, built on three levels, are

Yagul

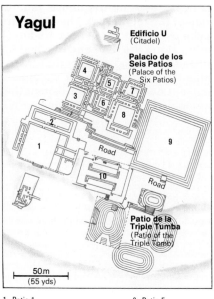

Edificio U
(Citadel)

Palacio de los
Seis Patios
(Palace of the
Six Patios)

Road

Road

Patio de la
Triple Tumba
(Patio of the
Triple Tomb)

50 m
(55 yds)

1 Patio 1
2 Sala del Consejo (Council Chamber)
3 Patio D
4 Patio A (formerly Patio 2)
5 Patio B
6 Patio E
7 Patio C
8 Patio F
9 Patio 3
10 Juego de Pelota (Ball Court)

dominated by a fortress on the hilltop commanding panoramic views of the Oaxaca valley.

HISTORY. – Yagul (Zapotec, "old village") was occupied in the late Formative period (800–300 B.C.), i.e., in the Monte Albán I phase. Excavation has brought to light more than thirty tombs, ranging in date from 300 B.C. to A.D. 1400. Building activity on the site reached a peak between A.D. 900 and 1200 (Monte Albán IV), when Monte Albán was abandoned and the decline of the Zapotecs began. During this period Mixtec influence increased, and there seems to have been a similar development at Mitla,

15 km (10 miles) away. It is still not known with any certainty, however, which people established the pre-Columbian sites around Yagul. – The site was rediscovered in the late 1950s, and thereafter was excavated and restored by the University of the Americas and the Instituto Nacional de Arqueología e Historia under the direction of Ignacio Bernal. Part of the site remains unexcavated.

THE SITE. – On the lowest level, most of which has been excavated, is the *Patio of the Triple Tomb* (Patio de la Triple Tumba), with four temples and, in the middle of the patio, a place of sacrifice. On the left-hand side of the patio is a sculptured figure of a squatting toad which symbolizes the rain god. – From a platform in the middle of the patio, the left-hand opening leads down into a *tomb* with three chambers, which have elaborately carved façades and were found to contain the remains of high dignitaries and rich grave goods.

Palace of the Six Patios, Yagul

General view of excavations, Yagul

On the second level is the *Ball Court (*Juego de Pelota*), one of the largest and finest yet found in Meso-America. Like other ball courts in Oaxaca, it lacks the heavy stone rings normally set into the side walls. – Adjoining on the W is *Patio I*, framed with terraces and building. This courtyard, measuring 30×36 m (98×118 ft) has several tombs with decoration on the front and is bounded on the N by the *Council Hall* (Salla del Consejo), 34 m (112 ft) long and 6.3 m (21 ft) wide which is divided into three by two 2 m (6½ ft) broad columns.

On the third level is the complex known as the *Palace of the Six Patios* (Palacio de los Seis Patios). Here, too, Mixtec structures have been built over earlier Zapotec ones. In this labyrinth, which may have been a residence for the élite of the city, the rooms have from one to three doorways opening off the various patios. In one of the long narrow passages there are remains of stone mosaic decoration in the style of Mitla.

The stiff climb up to the *Citadel* is worthwhile for its interesting architecture and for the magnificent *view it affords.

SURROUNDING. – Soon after the turn for Yagul, another side road branches off on the right to the interesting site of *Caballito Blanco*, with the remains of white drawing of stylized human figures on a flat rock face. A stepped path leads up to the sparse remains of a structure resembling Building J at Monte Albán; it has been dated to 240 B.C. (Monte Albán II).

Yanhuitlán
See under Oaxaca (state)

Yaxchilán

State: Chiapas (Chis.).
Altitude: 320 m (1050 ft).

ACCESS. – By air-taxi direct from Tuxtla Gutiérrez, San Cristóbal de la Casas, Palenque of Tenosique; or by light aircraft to Agua Azul on the Río Usumacinta and from there down the river by boat to Yaxchilán.

The large Maya site of *Yaxchilán in eastern Chiapas is almost complete-ly surrounded by a loop of the Río Usumacinta, here 200 m (220 yds) wide, which forms the border with Guatemala. The site can barely be seen from the river, since much of it is overgrown by the dense vegeta-tion of the rain forest. The Maya city once extended for almost 1.5 km (1 mile) along the river and reached far inland on to a series of high terraced hills. The remains so far excavated make it one of the most fascinating archeological sites in Mexico.

HISTORY. – During the *Classic period* (A.D. 300–900) Yaxchilán ranked with Palenque (Chiapas), Piedras Negras, 50 km (31 miles) down stream, Tikal and Quiriguá (all in Guatemala) and Copán (Honduras) as one of the great religious and political centres of the central Maya territory in the lowland region. In its heyday, during the 8th c., Yaxchilán appears to have controlled a number of other towns in the area, including Bonampak. Glyphs which have recently been deciphered record the chronicles of a dynasty whose principal representatives were two rulers named "Shield Jaguar" and "Bird Jaguar" and whose authority extended throughout the region. Like other Maya sites in the central Maya territory, Yaxchilán was abandoned in the 9th c. for reasons that are unknown. Until recent years, nomadic Lacandón Indians still celebrated their ancient rites in the ruins of Yaxchilán.

Edwin Rockstroh came here in 1881 from Guatemala, but the first scientific discovery of the site was by an Englishman, Alfred P. Maudslay, who came here in 1882 and named it *Menché* (Maya, "green tree"). Soon afterwards he was followed by a Frenchman, Désiré Charnay. Maudslay was also responsible for removing the seven door lintels which are now on view in the British Museum and which he exported by permission of the government of Guatemala which, at that time, was believed to be the responsible authority for this territory. The Austrian archeologist Teobert Maler worked on the site between 1897 and 1900 and gave it the name of *Yaxchilán* (Maya, "place of green stones") after the nearby stream of that name. In the early years of the 20th c., the US archeologists A. M. Tozzer, Sylvanus G. Morley and H. Spinden also worked here. In recent years restoration work has been carried out by the I.N.A.H. and Roberto García Mol.

THE SITE. – Only a small proportion of the structures which extend along the banks of the Río Usumacinta and over the neighboring hills have been excavated and restored. The greater part of the site is still covered by primeval forest or has been overgrown again after excavation, and therefore access is difficult. The remains

The Río Usumacinta at Yaxchilán

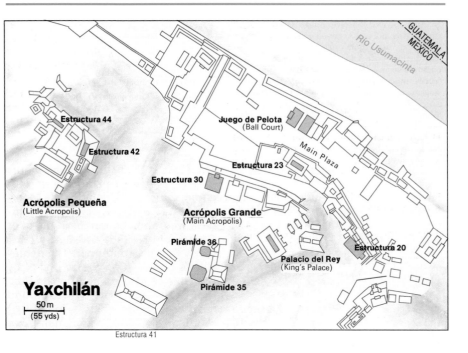

Estructura 44
Estructura 42
Acrópolis Pequeña
(Little Acropolis)
Juego de Pelota
(Ball Court)
Main Plaza
Estructura 23
Estructura 30
Acrópolis Grande
(Main Acropolis)
Pirámide 36
Palacio del Rey
(King's Palace)
Estructura 20
Yaxchilán
50 m
(55 yds)
Pirámide 35
Río Usumacinta
GUATEMALA
MEXICO
Estructura 41

extend in four groups from the banks of the river up the slopes of the hills toward the W. The buildings show no unusual architectural features; they are not so much temple pyramids as palaces, usually with three entrances and two parallel corridors. The upper parts of the façades and the roof-combs (*cresterías*) were originally decorated with stucco and stone figures. As at Pelenque, the roofs show the so-called "mansard effect", with the roof-combs rising in the middle.

Notable features at Yaxchilán are the *reliefs, of consummate delicacy but powerful effect, carved on stelae, altars, lintels and steps.

Up to now *inscriptions have been found on 114 of these stone slabs, ranging in date from A.D. 514 to 810. The reliefs frequently show two figures, evidently symbolizing a transfer of power from one ruler to another; the face of the larger and more important figure is shown in profile, but the body and legs are depicted frontally and the feet turned outward, while the smaller figure is shown entirely in profile. Other reliefs depict rituals of dedication and human sacrifice, battle scenes and prisoners. – Some of the stelae and altars are broken or damaged; others have been removed. Many of the reliefs discovered here are now in the National Museum of Anthropology in Mexico City (e.g., Lintels 9, 12, 18, 26, 32, 33, 39, 43, 47, 53, 54, 55 and 58 and Stelae 10, 15 and 18), in the British Museum (e.g., Lintels 15, 16, 17, 24, 25, 35 and 41) and in large museums in other countries.

Among the buildings in the first row, along the banks of the river, the most notable are the *ball court* (*Structure 14*; 5 sculptures) and *Structures 18* (8 stelae),

16 (Lintels 38 and 40), 6 and 5 (staircase with glyphs 1). – Those in the next row, on the far side of the Main Plaza, include *Structures 19* (Labyrinth – El Laberinto; Altars 1 and 2), 23 (Altars 7 and 18), 22 (Temple of the Inscriptions – Templo de las Inscripciones; Lintel 22, Altars 17 and 20), 20 and 21 (Temple of the Sacrifice of Birds – Templo de las Ofrendas des Ave; Lintel 14; Stelae 5, 6 and 7).

On an isolated hill, reached by a flight of steps, is the complex known as the Main Acropolis (Acrópolis Grande). The largest building in this group is *Structure 33*, or the **Palace of the King** or of Quetzalcóatl (Edificio 33, Palacio del Rey), which probably dates from A.D. 757.

This imposing structure measures 22 by 5 m (72 by 16 ft) and stands 7 m (23 ft) high, with the roof-comb adding another 6 m (20 ft). The last step of the staircase leading up to the palace is covered with

Palacio del Rey, Yaxchilán

handsome *glyphs*. The three entrances have *threshold stones* (Nos. 1, 2 and 3) carved with scenes from the life of the "bird-jaguar" ruler and above them are niches which once held stone figures. The frieze still preserves some remains of decoration. – The double *roof-comb is particularly fine, with eight rows of rectangular recesses. In the middle there originally stood the statue of a ruler with a magnificent headdress, 2.50 m (8 ft) high. – In front of the building is the torso of a figure, known as the "King" (Rey), which was found inside the palace; the head lies nearby (until recently the Lacandón-Maya worshipped their deity Hachakyum who lived in this headless figure). Just outside this building is Stela 31.

Farther uphill is another group comprising *Structures 39* (Altars 4, 5 and 6), *40* (Stelae 12 and 13, Altars 13, 14 and 15) and *41* (Stelae 16, 19 and 20). This complex was originally connected to a platform 100 m (110 yds) down the hill by a large staircase.

NW of the King's Palace is the group known as the *Little Acropolis* (Acrópolis Pequeña), consisting of *Structures 42–52*. In the ruins of Structure 42 were found the remarkable Lintel 42 and, in Structure 44, Lintels 44, 45 and 46 as well as the Stelae 14, 17, 21, 22 and 23 and the hieroglyph staircase 3.

It should be pointed out that in Yaxchilán many of the fallen lintels and overturned stelae have been set up in other places on the site. Before visiting the site, it is a good idea to inquire about the condition and the accessibility of the remains.

Yucatán

State of Yucatán (Yuc.). – Capital: Mérida.
Area: 38,508 sq. km (14,868 sq. miles).
Population: 1,161,700.

ⓘ **Coordinación Federal de Turismo,**
Av. Itzaes 501,
Mérida, Yuc.;
tel. (9 19 22) 3 60 75, 3 69 75, 4 65 96,
4 53 67.

The state of Yucatán occupies only part of the large peninsula of that name, which also includes the Mexican states of Campeche and Quintana Roo and the northern parts of Guatemala (Petén) and Belize (formerly British Honduras). The peninsula is bounded on the W and N by the Gulf of Mexico and on the E by the Caribbean. The western and northern coasts consist mostly of sandbanks, lagoons and mangrove swamps, while the E coast is fringed by coral reefs and islands (Cozumel, Isla Mujeres). Yucatán is a huge lowlying limestone plateau rising gently toward the S, a karstic region largely covered by savannas and scrub forest.

The rainfall, increasing toward the S, seeps rapidly through the thin layer of earth and underlying limestone to form underground rivers and lakes. The collapse of the roofs of underground caverns

Mexico
United Mexican States
Estados Unidos Mexicanos

Yucatán

States
Estados

1a	Baja California Sur	12	Aguascalientes
1b	Baja California Norte	13	Jalisco
		14	Guanajuato
2	Sonora	15	Querétaro
3	Chihuahua	16	Hidalgo
4	Sinaloa	17	Colima
5	Durango	18	Michoacán
6	Coahuila	19	México
7	Nuevo León	20	Morelos
8	Zacatecas	21	Tlaxcala
9	San Luis Potosí	22	Puebla
10	Tamaulipas	23	Veracruz
11	Nayarit	24	Guerrero
		25	Oaxaca
		26	Chiapas
		27	Tabasco
		28	Campeche
		29	Yucatán
		30	Quintana Roo

D.F. Distrito Federal (Federal District)

has led to the formation of several circular water-holes, large and small, which are known as *cenotes* (from the Maya word *dzonot*). In pre-Hispanic times the Maya Indians built their great cult centers around these cenotes; they are still of importance as contributors to the water supply of the region.

ANIMAL LIFE. – The dense scrub of Yucatán is still the home of jaguars and ocelots, although they have increasingly retreated to the remoter parts of the region. The alligator, ruthlessly hunted in the past, is also disappearing. Other animals include deer, wild pigs, pheasants, wild duck, wild turkeys and monkeys. Reptiles include the iguana, the boa constrictor and other snakes. There are also many tropical birds, including parrots, toucans, flamingoes and humming-birds.

ECONOMY. – A major contribution to the economy of the state is made by the cultivation and processing of *sisal* (henequen) from agaves, although this is now less important than in the past as a result of the development of man-made fibers. *Timber-harvesting* and *fishing* also play a considerable part. Until the 20th c., Yucatán's economic relationships tended to be with Europe rather than with central Mexico, and it was only in the 1950s that it acquired rail and road connections with the rest of the country. The most important *port* is Progreso, on the Gulf of Mexico, which handles much of the region's trade. In recent years *tourism* has developed on a substantial scale, bringing large numbers of visitors to the Maya sites and the beach resorts on the coast.

HISTORY. – Archeologically, Yucatán is a region of great importance, with numerous remains of the *Maya culture* of the Classic (A.D. 300–900) and Post-Classic (900–1450) periods. – The first contacts between the *Spaniards* and the natives of Yucatán took place between 1512 and 1519, when the great Maya sites, with only a few exceptions, had already been abandoned. It took twenty years of hard fighting before the Spaniards, under the leadership of the two Montejos, father and son, were able to gain control of somewhat less than half the peninsula. During the colonial period, Yucatán, owing to its remoteness, was a province of little importance. Rebellious Maya tribes repeatedly tried to recover their lost territories, and there was particularly bitter fighting in the second half of the 19th c., when, during the "Caste War", an independent state was established in this region for a time. It was only in the early years of the 20th c. that the Mexican government was able to establish full sovereignty over Yucatán. Many of the defeated Indians then withdrew into the deserts of Quintana Roo. – Apart from numbers of pure-blooded Spaniards in and around Merida, the population of Yucatán state consists mainly of Maya Indians and mestizos. In some areas only the Maya language is spoken.

Among the principal *Maya sites* in the state of Yucatán are **Chichén Itzá, Izamal, Dzibilchaltún, **Uxmal, *Kabah, *Sayil** and *Labná (see the entries for these places), *Xlapak* (p. 245) and *Mayapán*. Other major sites in the peninsula are in the states of Campeche and Quintana Roo.

Few parts of Mexico have so many archeological sites as Yucatán. The **Maya** Post-Classic culture (A.D. 900–1450), evolved by a combination of local and incoming Maya tribes and Toltec incomers from the Mexican highlands, created a magnificent architecture in which early Maya elements mingled with Toltec features. The pottery and stone sculpture, however, fell short of the high quality achieved in the Early and Late Classic periods (A.D. 300–900), particularly in southern Campeche, Chiapas, Guatemala, Belize and Honduras.

In the Post-Classic period, too, the "Long Court", the Maya calendar which counted every day from the beginning of the Maya epoch being the day zero (August 13, 3114 B.C. in our calendar), was used only in an abbreviated form. This *Maya calendar* is claimed to be the most complete and most accurate ever devised. The Mayas were the first people to use the number zero, which enabled them to calculate dates over very long periods of time. The earliest date definitely established goes back to A.D. 292 (Stela 29 at Tikal, Guatemala). – The Mayas were also distinguished from other pre-Columbian cultures in possessing a fully developed *hiero-glyphic script*, which until recently could be only very partially deciphered. A scientific break-through came in 1958, when Heinrich Berlin, a German domiciled in Mexico, found the so-called '*Armorial Glyph*'. He discovered that certain characters always appeared in particular places; from this the glyphs of the eight classic Maya centers – Palenque, Yaxchilán (Mexico), Tikal, Piedras Negras, Quiriguá, Seibal, Naranjo (Guatemala) and Copán (Honduras) could be identified. Berlin presumed therefore that their history was inscribed on the stelae and other monuments of these sites. Subsequently Tatiana Proskouriakoff of the Carnegie Institute ascertained that the dating in particular groups of stelae indicated each time an average life-span, from which the dates of the reign of a ruler and later also the dates of birth and marriage could be worked out. At the same time the names of certain rulers and members of their family were successfully established. In the 70s it was possible for Linda Schele, Peter Matthews and Floyd Lounsbury of the University of Texas to demonstrate the genealogy of the ruling dynasties of Palenque from A.D. 465 until the demise of the city.

In *Mérida (p. 157), Izamal (p. 144), *Valladolid* (p. 101), *Motul, Tikul* and indeed almost every town in the state there are fine examples of *colonial art and architecture*, particularly the Franciscan churches and convents of the 16th and 17th c. Some of these are still to be found in an original setting and atmosphere and are well worth a visit. Among these places SE and SW of Mérida are *Kanasín* (Church of St Joseph – Iglesia de San José; well-known for Yucatán regional dishes); *Acaceh* (Church of Our Lady of the Nativity – Iglesia de Nuestra Señora de la Natividad, in the square near a Maya pyramid); *Tecoh* (Church and Convent of the Assumption – Iglesia y Convento de la Asunción; henequén (sisal) growing; many cenotes); *Maypán* (ruined Maya sites – see surroundings of Mérida p. 159); *Tekit* (Church of St Anthony of Padua – Iglesia de San Antonio de Padua); *Mama* (Church and Convent of the Assumption – Iglesia y Convento de la Asunción, with an attractive espadaña and an old bucket-wheel in the convent); *Chumayel* (Church of the Immaculate Conception – Iglesia de la Purísima Concepción, with a black Christ above the altar; the place is also known through the discovery of one of the "Books of the Chilam Balam", the great Maya chronicle); *Teabo* (Church of St Peter and St Paul – Iglesia San Pedro y San Pablo; Posada de los Presidentes); *Tipical* (Church of Mary Magdalene – Iglesia de la Magdalena, on a hill); *Maní* (Church and Convent of St Michael – Iglesia y Convento de San Miguel – see surroundings of Labná p. 151); *Oxcutzcab* (Church and Convent of St Francis of Assisi – Iglesia y Convento San Francisco de Asís; cultivation of citrus fruits; nearby a system of caves similar to those at Kukikán and especially the *Cave of Lultún (Gratas de Lultún), 7 km (4 miles) S – see surroundings of Labná p. 151); *Tikul* (Church of St Anthony – Iglesia de San Antonio; reproductions of Maya sculptures and pottery; Hotel Otilia Zapata; restaurant Los Alemndros); *Muná* (Church and Convent of the Assumption – Iglesia y Convento de la Asunción; cenotes; tobacco growing) and *Umán* (Church and Convent of St Francis of Assisi – Iglesia y Conventu de San Francisco de Asís; cenotes, henequén growing and processing; 17 km (11 miles) from Mérida).

Yuriria
See under Celaya

Zacatecas (State)

State of Zacatecas (Zac.).
Capital: Zacatecas.
Area: 73,454 sq. km (28,361 sq. miles).
Population: 1,244,500
ⓘ **Coordinación Federal de Turismo,**
Blvd. López Mateos 923A,
Zacatetas, Zac.;
tel. (9 14 92), 2 67 50, 2 67 51.

The state of Zacatecas, a high region of low rainfall with only a few permanent rivers, is bounded on the N by Coahuila, on the W by Durango, on the S by Jalisco and Aguascalientes and on the E by San Luis Potosí. It is a country of rugged mountains and sandy plateaus, rich in minerals. The population consists mainly of Creoles (descendants of Spaniards) and mestizos, together with the Huichol Indians of the area around Colotlan. In Zacatecas there are two large colonies (La Batea and La Honda) of Mennonite settlers who left Canada in 1923.

In addition to such well-known archeological sites as *La Quemada* (Chicomóztoc) and *Chalchihuites*, there are numbers of lesser sites such as *Teul de González Ortega, Las Ventanas* and *Canutillo*.

HISTORY. – In pre-Hispanic times Zacatecas (Náhuatl, "land where zacate grass grows") was inhabited by various Indian tribes, including the Caxcanes, Tecuexes, Hachichiles, Huicholes, Cora and Tepehuanos, all but the last three of which have now disappeared. During the Post-Classic period it lay within the area of the Chalchiuites culture, which was probably under Toltec influence. The Aztecs probably bypassed this region in their migration from the NW into central Mexico. – The *Spaniards* under Pedro Almíndrez Chirinos, who came here after the Conquest in search of precious metals, soon became involved in fighting with the local Indians. Later the first rich silver mines were discovered with the help of the local tribes, then partly reconciled to Spanish rule. The mines brought prosperity to the state, and this prosperity was reflected in a great flowering of richly decorated buildings both sacred and secular. During the Guerra de la Reforma (1858–61) and the revolutionary wars (1910–20), there was bitter fighting in the state, and particularly in some of the towns.

ECONOMY. – Among Mexican states, Zacatecas is one of the richest in *minerals*, mainly gold, silver, copper, zinc, mercury and lead. Its *industry* is confined to the processing of these minerals and of sugar-cane, agaves, wool and cotton. Crop *agriculture* (wheat, sugar-cane, maguey agaves) is less important than *livestock-farming. Tourism* is now beginning to develop.

In addition to the capital, *Zacatecas (see below) and various places of interest in the surrounding area like *La Quemada* (Chicomóztoc), *Jérez Garcia de Salinas* and *Fresnillo* (see under Zacatecas town) the following places are worthy of mention:

Sombrerete (alt. 2351m (7714 ft); pop. 16,000; fiesta February 2–10, La Candelaria – Candlemas), a picturesque little town with the churches of San Francisco

Mexico
United Mexican States
Estados Unidos Mexicanos

Zacatecas

**States
Estados**

1a Baja California Sur	12 Aguascalientes
1b Baja California Norte	13 Jalisco
	14 Guanajuato
2 Sonora	15 Querétaro
3 Chihuahua	16 Hidalgo
4 Sinaloa	17 Colima
5 Durango	18 Michoacán
6 Coahuila	19 México
7 Nuevo León	20 Morelos
8 Zacatecas	21 Tlaxcala
9 San Luis Potosí	22 Puebla
10 Tamaulipas	23 Veracruz
11 Nayarit	24 Guerrero
	25 Oaxaca

26 Chiapas
27 Tabasco
28 Campeche
29 Yucatán
30 Quintana Roo

D.F. Distrito Federal (Federal District)

(16th c.), Santo Domingo (18th c., with a Churrigueresque façade) and San Juan Bautista (18th c.)

51 km (32 miles) SW of Sombrerete lies the township of *Chalchihuites* (Náhuatl, Chalchíhuitl = "green stone"), from where it is another 7 km (4 miles) to the beginning of the extensive archeological zone of Chalchihuites, also known as Alta Vista. Little is known of the builders of this site, which extends over the haciendas of Alta Vista, El Vergel and El Chapin. Some of the structures were built in the 4th c., but its most prosperous period was between the 5th and 6th centuries. It is accepted that the site was abandoned about A.D. 1050.

The site appears to have been founded here predominantly on astronomical grounds, practically on the Tropic of Cancer. It attained a far-ranging reputation in this mining region (flint, jade, turquoise, etc.), both as a religious and as a trading center. It is interesting to note that the early phase of the site was under the influence of Teotihuacán. Features of the Meso-American culture of Chalchihuites later spread N into the SW of the USA (Hohokam-culture).

Among the features of this low-lying site is a corridor, surrounded by a wall, which is known as the "Labyrinth" and which, from its position and furnishings obviously served as an observatory (looking towards the El Piacho Mountains). Nearby are the Snake (Quetzalcóatl) Wall with corresponding designs, the Hall of Columns (Salón de las Columnas) with 28 pillars, and priests' courts with altars for sacrifice and fire. Also of interest are the symbols of a cross, cut into the rock of the Cerro El Chapín; these, like almost all the buildings, were fashioned according to precise astronomical rules.

Zacatecas (Town)

State: Zacatecas (Zac.).
Altitude: 2496 m (8189 ft). – Population 188,000.
Telephone dialing code: 9 14 92.
ⓘ **Coordinación Federal de Turismo,** Blvd. Lopez Mateos 923A; tel. 2 67 50, 2 67 51.

HOTELS. – *Calinda*, López Mateos y Callejón del Barro, SP, tennis, I; *Aristos*, Lomas de la Soledad, SP, tennis, I; *Motel del Bosque*, Cerro de las Peñitas, I; *Posada de los Condes*, Av, Juárez 18, II; *Reina Cristina*, Av. Hidalgo 703, II; *Posada de la Moneda*, Av. Hidalgo 413, II; *Rio Grande*, Calzada de la Paz 513, III.

RESTAURANTS in most other hotels; also *Mesón de la Mina*, Av. Juárez 15; *Caballo Loco*, at km 101 on Guadalupe road; *Vila del Mar*, Ventura Salazar 340.

RECREATION and SPORTS. – Swimming, tennis.

EVENTS. – Fiestas: Augustus 27, Día de la Morisma; September 14, Día de Nuestra Señora del Patrocinio.

The charming colonial town of *Zacatecas, capital of the state of the same name, lies in a narrow gorge dominated by the hills of La Bufa, Mala Noche and El Padre. Surrounded by a plateau broken up by mountains, the town was for centuries an important silver-mining center. With its attractive old buildings and cobbled lanes, it is now one of the most beautiful of Mexico's colonial towns.

HISTORY. – The area around Zacatecas (Náhuatl, "land where zacate grass grows") was inhabited in pre-Hispanic times by various Indian peoples of whom very little is known. They appear to have been at one time under the influence of the cultures of Chalchihuites and La Quemada (Chicomóztoc). – The town was founded in 1546 by a group of conquistadors searching for silver under Juan de Tolosa and, rapidly becoming wealthy by mining the local silver, was granted a municipal charter by Philip II in 1585. During the revolutionary wars there was a hard-fought battle here between the forces of the dictator Victoriano Huerta and Pancho Villa, in which the latter was victorious

Zacatecas Cathedral

SIGHTS. – In *Plaza Hidalgo* stands the magnificent ***Cathedral**, regarded by many as the supreme example of Mexican Churrigueresque. Begun in 1612 on the site of an earlier church, it was given its present form mainly between 1730 and 1760. The richly decorated **façade, very typical of the exuberance of Spanish-Mexican Baroque, has figures of Christ with the twelve apostles, four Fathers of the Church around the choir window and, in the upper part, God the Father surrounded by eight angel musicians, showing a mingling of Romanesque elements with Indian conceptions. The dome was rebuilt in 1836. The interior, primarily neo-classical in style, is disappointing; most of the sumptuous furnishings (gold and silver articles, European pictures, etc.) were removed during the Guerra de la Reforma and the revolutionary wars. – Also in Plaza Hidalgo is the *Government Palace* (Palacio de Gobierno), an 18th c. mansion with fine wrought-iron balconies and frescoes treating historical themes of Zacatecas.

The Callejón de Veyna leads to the **church of Santo Domingo**, a plain mid-18th c. Baroque building with a façade which is notable for being in the form of a "spanish wall" (biombo). Features of the interior are eight beautifully carved retablos in Churrigueresque style, a neo-classical high altar and the paintings by Francisco Antonio Vallejo (18th c.) in the sacristy. – Adjoining the church is the former *Jesuit College*, with a beautiful cloister.

Once the most magnificent sacred building in Zacatecas but now mostly in ruins, the *Church of San Agustín* has a side doorway with a *Plateresque façade; this represents the conversion of St Augustine and is one of the finest in the country.

A landmark in the town is the Cerro de la Bufa (2700 m – 8861 ft), on which stands the *Capilla de los Remedios*, or *Virgen del Patrocinio Señora de los Zacatecos*, built at the end of the 19th c. This notable height, 4 km (2½ miles) from Zacatecas, provides excellent views over the town and is the starting point of the cableway which crosses the town to the Cerro El Grillo, 650 m (711 yards) away. Another recommended visit is to the disused mine, *El Edén*, within the town boundaries. A visit should also be made to the new *Museum Francisco Goitia* in the former Casa del Pueblo; this neo-classical building houses the works of the expressionist and chronicler of the Revolutionary War, Francisco Goita (1884–1960) who was born in Fresnillo (Zacatecas). Other sights include the unique metal construction of the *Market of Jesús González Ortega* (late 19th c.), the *Church and Convent of San Francisco* (16th/17th c.; Gothic cloister), the *Calderón Theater* (late 19th c.), the *Folk Museum of the Huichol Indians*

(Museo de Arte Huichol) and the *Aqua-duct* (late 18th and early 19th c.).

SURROUNDINGS. – 7 km (4 miles E is **Guadalupe**, which is famous for its convent.

The *Convent of Nuestra Señora de Guadalupe, founded by Franciscans in 1707, is now a well stocked museum (Museo de Arte Virreinal). It contains a private *library* and a *collection of valuable *paintings* of the colonial period, including works by such artists as Cristóbal de Villalpando, Rodríguez Juárez, Migual Cabrera, Antonio Torres and Antonio Oliva. – The church (consecrated 1721) has an interesting Baroque façade. On either side of the doorway is a niche containing a statue, flanked by two columns. The columns, like those on the upper part of the façade, are divided into three sections with different decorative patterns (figures, spirals and interlace). Above the door is a group in high relief of the Apostle Luke painting the Virgin of Guadalupe. The upper part of the façade, in the style of the local native craftsmen, is reminiscent of the façade of Zacatecas Cathedral. The effect is spoiled by the left-hand tower, added in the late 19th c. The interior is notable for the neo-classical *Capilla de la Purísima* (also known as the Capilla de Napoles), dating from the middle of the 19th c., which is lavishly decorated with gold-leaf and enriched with old paintings. The *parquet floor of mesquite wood is exceptional; it is laid out in an artistically contrived imaginative pattern of compass-cards, signs of the zodiac and holy scripture.

53 km (33 miles) S of Zacatecas is the pre-Columbian site of **La Quemada** or *Chicomóztoc* (Náhuatl, "seven caves"), a cult center built on a large hill which probably originated in the early Classic period. It is doubtful, however, whether this site can be identified with the legendary Chicomóztoc from which the seven Nahua peoples are said to have set out on their journey to the S. (What is certain is that La Quemada, like Calchihuites (above, p. 301) and other places in Zacatecas and Durango, lies in an area which marks the northern limit of the cultures of Meso-America.

This fortified town, probably the most important in the northern region, had its heyday in the 10th and 11th c. A.D., that is in the Post-Classic period and must have been destroyed at the beginning of the 13th c., probably by fire. As early as 1650 Pater Antonio Tello described this site, which he called Tuitlán. The first scientific description was by G. F. Lyon in 1826. In 1903 excavation was begun under Leopoldo Batres and was continued in the 50s and 60s by José Corona Nuñez and Pedro Armillas. In spite of Meso-American influence (e.g. step pyramids, ball courts, round pillars, elevated roads), the ruins can in no way be compared in their architecture with the old Indian centers farther to the south. The structures, extending over a mountain ridge (1500 m – 4923 ft from N. to S.), and overlooking the plain 150 m (492 ft) below, are built primarily of small flat stone slabs and adobe bricks.

On the left we first come to a complex called the *King's Palace* or *Cathedral* (Palacio del Rey or La Catedral); this consists of a broad terrace (67×64 m – 220× 210 ft) which is bounded by low walls and forms a courtyard. On the E side an entrance leads into the *Great Pillared Hall* (Salón de las Columnas; 40×31 m – 131×102 ft). The eleven stone pillars are up to 5 m (16 ft) high and have a diameter of up to 2 m (6½ ft); it is not known whether this, presumably the most important building, La Quemadas, had a roof. Not far N of the palace is a small platform from which a

roadway, 10 m (33 ft) wide, leads to the *Ball Court* (Juego de Pelota), which is very rare in this region. Adjoining is the impressive structure, the *Votive* or *Sun Pyramid* (Pirámide Votiva or Pirámide del Sol). This restored structure, consisting of two stories, has sides 17 m (56 ft) long, 11 m (36 ft) high and has a flat top. Higher up to the W of the Votive Pyramid are groups of buildings designated as the *Citadel* or *Acropolis* (Ciudadela or Acrópolis). On the level called the Second Landing (Segundo Cuerpo) lies a large courtyard surrounded by platforms on all four sides. A flight of steps, flanked by 7 m (23 ft) high walls, leads N to a courtyard which is dominated by a severely damaged pyramid. In the western part of the courtyard can be seen the ruins of a number of interconnected rooms of various sizes. The Third Landing (Tercer Piso) is reached by a staircase resting on a supporting wall up to 10 m (33 ft) high. On an open sunken courtyard stands an attractive five-story pyramid with sides 11.7 m (39 ft) long; this is called the *Temple of Sacrifices* (Templo de los Sacrificios). Steps on the S lead to a small rectangular altar which is believed to have been used as a place of sacrifice (Altar de Sacrificios). In the well-preserved east wing of the courtyard is a rectangular hall; it measures 22×30 m (72×98 ft) and has a bay window. The highest level of the site is reached by a stairway and a narrow passage; here are a series of ruined buildings with terraces and galleries. From the building known as *La Terraza*, access to which entails a climb up the steep steps on the S side, there is a magnificent view over the whole archeological area and further afield.

55 km (34 miles) SW of Zacatecas is **Jérez de García Salinas**, a town of rather Andalusian atmosphere (alt. 2190 m (7185 ft); pop. 34,000; Hotel Jardín; fiestas: January 23, Día de San Ildefonso; Easter Saturday; September 8, Día de la Virgen de la Soledad).

65 km (40 miles) NW of Zacatecas is the old silver-mining town of **Fresnillo** (alt. 2250 m (7380 ft); pop. 117,000; hotels: Casa Blanca; El Fresno, Plaza, Las Vegas; fiestas: August 23 Foundation Day; at Plateros, 7 km (4 miles) away, on June 15 Day of Santo Niño del Huarachito). Near the town are thermal baths.

Zihuatanejo and Ixtapa

State: Guerrero (Gro.).
Altitude: sea level. – Population: 32,000.
Telephone dialing code: 9 17 43.

(i) **Coordinación Federal de Turismo,**
Paseo de Zihuatanejo,
Zihuatanejo, Gro.;
tel. 4 28 35.

HOTELS. – IN ZIHUATANEJO: *Villa del Sol, I, SP; Irma, II, SP: Posada Caracol, II, SP; Sotavento, II; Catalina, II; Calpulli, II, SP; Las Urracas, II; Casa Bahía, III; Casa Aurora, III; Las Gatas Beach Club II. – IN IXTAPA: *Camino Real, L, SP, tennis; Holiday Inn, L, SP, tennis; *Sheraton, L, SP, tennis; *Dorado Pacífico, L, SP, tennis; Krystal, L, SP, tennis; El Presidente, L, SP, tennis; Club Méditerranée, I, SP, tennis; Aristos, I, SP, tennis; Castel Palmar, I, SP; Riviera del Sol, I, SP, tennis.

RESTAURANTS in most hotels; also in ZIHUATANEJO: *La Mesa del Capitán, Kontiki, El Sombrero, La Tortuga, El Taboga, Tucán, Punta Arenas. – IN IXTAPA:

Playa de las Gatas, Zihuatanejo

Da Bafone, Villa de la Selva, Villa Sakura, Betos y Quiques.

RECREATION and SPORTS. – Swimming, snorkeling, diving, water skiing, fishing, deep-sea fishing, hunting, golf, tennis (Ixtapa only).

ACCESS. – From Acapulco 240 km (150 miles) on Road 200; from Playa Azul, to the NW, 130 km (80 miles); direct road from Mexico City via Toluca and Ciudad Altamirano recently provisionally completed. Air services from Mexico City and from other Mexican and US airports.

The former fishing village of Zihuatanejo, situated in a sheltered *bay, is surrounded by beautiful beaches, wooded hills and rocky crags. Along with the fashionable resort of Ixtapa, founded only in 1975, it is one of the most relaxing resorts on the Pacific coast of Mexico.

HISTORY. – Zihuatanejo (Náhuatl, "dark wife") is said to have been a favorite winter resort of Tangáxoan II, last king of the Purépecha (Tarascans). – During the colonial period, the town became for a time a commercial port of some consequence. The sleepy little fishing port was discovered in the 1960s by vacationers seeking isolated beaches, and the establishment of the new resort of Ixtapa (Náhuatl, "above, where it is white"), 10 km (6 miles) away, led to further development at Zihuatanejo as well. The little town has been modernized, but has lost much of its original charm in the process.

SIGHTS. – The fishing village of Zihuatanejo, a huddle of low houses, offers little of particular interest. Its five beaches (in order from the airport towards Ixtapa) are the **Playa de las Gatas* (best reached by boat; according to a legend there is a stone wall in the water, not far from the beach, which goes back to the time when the Indian king Tangáxoan II wished to bathe here in privacy; the bay is well suited

to snorkeling and diving), *Playa Calpulli* and *Playa de la Ropa* (suitable for swimming); *Playa de la Madera, Playa del Malecón* and *Playa de Majahua* (between Zihuatanejo and Ixtapa).

Before reaching the modern seaside resort of **Ixtapa**, a bare 10 km (6 miles) from Zihuatanejo, we come to the *Playa de la Vista Hermosa*. Then follow the attractive beaches of *Don Juan, San Juan de Díos, Casa Blanca, Cuata* and *Quieta*. Among the offshore islands with pleasant beaches, generally good facilities for snorkeling and abundant vegetation and animal life (especially birds), are the *Isla Ixtapa* (Isla Grande), *Isla de la Pie* and *Moro de los Pericos*.

The SURROUNDINGS of Zihuatanejo and Ixtapa, with their fishing villages, coconut, banana and coffee plantations, offer scope for a variety of attractive excursions.

Practical Information

Market scene, Oaxaca

When to go

A vacation in Mexico can be enjoyed at any time of year, since even in winter the temperatures are agreeable. During the winter dry season, however, the vegetation dries up and it can sometimes be very hot on the coast for lack of any cooling rain. The heavy rain which usually falls between June and September lasts only a few hours as a general rule, and enhances the beauty of the countryside with a riot of luxuriant vegetation.

Weather

Although Mexico's large area and topographical diversity are reflected in its range of different climatic zones, there are a number of constant factors which apply over wide areas.

Almost everywhere in Mexico there is much less rain in winter than in summer, with rainfall reaching its maximum in July,

August and September. An exception to this rule is the area around Tijuana in the extreme N of Baja California, where the heaviest rainfall is in winter.

In the coastal regions subject to the moderating influence of the sea, the temperature variations between day and night and between summer and winter are relatively small. Inland and at higher altitudes the range of variation increases, reaching an extreme in the northern highlands, where, for example, the day temperature in January can rise above 20°C (68°F) while the night temperature can fall well below freezing point.

For a more detailed account of climatic conditions in Mexico see pp. 17–21.

How to get there

For those not traveling by car, and with limited time at their disposal, the best way to get to Mexico is by air. There are services to Mexico City International Airport from many cities in North America. Among the major airlines serving Mexico are American Aeromexico, Mexicana, Eastern and Pan Am.

Time

Mexico is divided into four time zones with an hour's difference between each. The eastern part of the country (Campeche, Yucatán, Quintana Roo) observes the *Hora Oficial del Este* (US Eastern Time), the central zone the *Hora Oficial del Centro* (US Central Time), in the adjoining western areas (Nayarit, Sinaloa, Sonora, Baja California Sur), the *Hora Oficial de las Montañas* (US Mountain Time), and in Baja California Norte the *Hora Oficial del Pacifico* (US Pacific Time). – There is no Daylight Savings Time in Mexico, since there is relatively little difference in the length of the day over the year.

Health hints

The climate of Mexico can give rise to health problems for visitors who neglect certain simple precautions. Protection against strong light and sunburn is essential. Many people require a period of acclimatization to get used to the high altitude, and the tropical mugginess of the lowland regions can also be trying. The climate, particularly in southern Mexico, increases the risk of certain diseases such as malaria. In the hot humidity food does not keep well and microorganisms flourish, so that stomach and intestinal disorders are common.

Light conditions in Mexico (Hints for photographers)

Visitors from more northerly latitudes should remember that as Mexico lies closer to the Equator, the length of the day varies less over the year than it does at home. In northern Mexico the longest summer day lasts only 13 hours and the shortest day in winter lasts 11 hours; in southern Mexico the difference between the length of the day in summer and in winter is even less. The period of twilight is also shorter. It very rapidly becomes light enough to take photographs in the morning, and darkness falls with corresponding speed in the evening. The middle of the day is less suitable for taking color photographs than in more northerly countries, since the sun stands high in the sky; both light and shade are hard, and the gentler side lighting required for some subjects is lacking.

Electricity

Usually 120 volts 60 cycles, but occasionally 125 or 220 volts AC. Power sockets normally take US type plugs.

Travel documents

For entry into Mexico beyond the border towns a passport **tourist card** is required. This can be obtained free of charge from a Mexican consulate, a travel agent, an airline affiliated to the International Air Transport Association (IATA) or from border officials. A tourist card is normally issued for a period of 30 days, but can also cover a period of 90 or even 180 days if required. Within Mexico an extension up to a maximum of 180 days can be obtained on application on the Ministry of Home Affairs (Secretaría de Gobernación). Border towns can be freely visited for a period up to 72 hours without a tourist card, but for longer stays and for further travel into the interior the card is required. Canadian citizens require a passport in addition to the tourist card. A US or Canadian **driver's license** is valid in Mexico for a period of up to 6 months. – Visitors arriving in Mexico by car must obtain a Mexican car permit, issued at the frontier without formality. Proof of ownership, registration and license are required. A car taken into Mexico must be exported again: it cannot legally be sold within Mexico. – *Car insurance* is not compulsory in Mexico, but it is essential for a visitor to take out comprehensive insurance at the frontier. – Visitors planning to enter Mexico from the USA in a rented car should bear in mind that most car rental firms, if informed of such a proposal, are liable to withdraw from the contract. Cars can, of course, be rented in the normal way within Mexico.

Customs regulations

Personal effects and vacation equipment may be taken into Mexico for a temporary period without payment of duty. There are also duty-free allowances for each adult of 200 cigarettes or 9 oz of tobacco and 1 quart of liquor or one bottle of wine. – Mexican brands of tobacco goods and spirits are cheaper than those sold in duty-free shops at airports, etc.

The export from Mexico of gold and antiquities is prohibited.

Postal rates

(are raised several times a year)
Postcards and airmail letters (up to 20 grams (0·706 oz) cost presently 100 pesos to the USA and Canada, 140 pesos to Europe and 50 pesos within Mexico. As a rule, mail service in, from and to Mexico is slow.Telegrams can be sent from *oficinas de telégrafos.*

Currency

The unit of currency is the Mexican *peso* ($, with one vertical bar: not to be confused with the sign for the US dollar, which has two vertical bars). There are 100 *centavos* to the peso.

As of January 1, 1987 there are banknotes for 500, 1000, 2000, 5000, 10,000, 20,000 and 50,000 pesos and *coins* in denominations of 1, 5, 10, 20, 50, 100 and 200 pesos.

Exchange rates
Are based on the US dollar and therefore fluctuate against European currencies; since July 11, 1985 there is a controlled dollar rate for certain payments for trade – and financial transactions; the free rate is valid for tourists and is being changed upwards almost daily, more or less keeping up with the inflation rate of the economy, currently over 100% p.a.

The rate of exchange on December 23, 1986 was the following:

1 US$	900 pesos
1000 pesos	1·11 US$
£1 sterling	1290 pesos
1000 pesos	£0·76 sterling

Exchange regulations
There are few restrictions on the import and export of Mexican currency; unused Mexican money can normally be changed back in limited amounts before leaving the country. – It is preferable to take *travelers' checks* (in US dollars) or US dollar bills. Hotels, car rental firms and large shops accept the standard credit cards.

Traveling in Mexico

Driving

The *road system* of Mexico (233,000 km – 145,600 miles) varies according to the density of population in the various states. Thus in the N – Baja California Norte and Sur, Sonora, Chihuahua and Coahuila – the network is relatively thin, the best developed part of the system being the

Car rental (*coches de alquiler*). – In all the larger towns and vacation centers there are car rental firms. The cars provided by the international rental companies are usually in good condition; those supplied by small local firms, though mechanically in good order, tend to be less well maintained in other respects. – The use of credit cards for car rental is accepted; customers paying in cash are required to put down a security deposit.

Driving in Mexico. – At junctions and intersections between roads of equal status, vehicles coming from the right

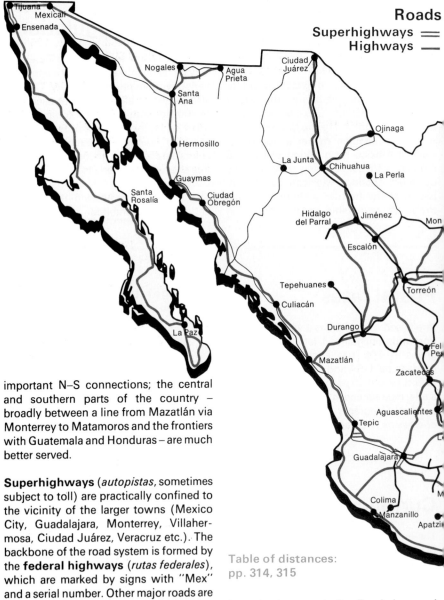

Roads
Superhighways ═══
Highways ────

important N–S connections; the central and southern parts of the country – broadly between a line from Mazatlán via Monterrey to Matamoros and the frontiers with Guatemala and Honduras – are much better served.

Superhighways (*autopistas*, sometimes subject to toll) are practically confined to the vicinity of the larger towns (Mexico City, Guadalajara, Monterrey, Villahermosa, Ciudad Juárez, Veracruz etc.). The backbone of the road system is formed by the **federal highways** (*rutas federales*), which are marked by signs with "Mex" and a serial number. Other major roads are **state highways** (*rutas estatales*), also numbered, which are maintained by the individual states. *Secondary roads*, often unsurfaced, serve the smaller towns and villages and the remoter areas of the country.

Table of distances: pp. 314, 315

have, in theory, priority. Road signs and markings are in accordance with international standards. A sign with an "E" in a circle means "parking" – "estacinamiento". If accompanied by the word "no" or if crossed out by a diagonal bar, the

meaning should be obvious. *Speed limits* are indicated by signs. Speed limit and mileage signs are in kilometers (0.62 mile). Typical speed limits are 100 k.p.h. (62 m.p.h.) and 80 k.p.h. (50 m.p.h.).

It cannot be assumed that local drivers, particularly in the larger towns, will strictly observe the traffic regulations. Visiting drivers, therefore, should be constantly on their guard; driving in the busy traffic of Mexico City, or in the rural areas where animals, pedestrians and cyclists share the roads, is an experience which calls for steady nerves and quick reactions.

Warning! – During the rainy season, unsurfaced roads usually become impassable for normal cars, and even four-wheel-drive vehicles may find it difficult to negotiate them.
Before setting out on a journey, therefore, inquire about the condition of the roads. For long journeys the most reliable source of information is a bus driver.

Railways
— **Main lines**
— **Branch lines**

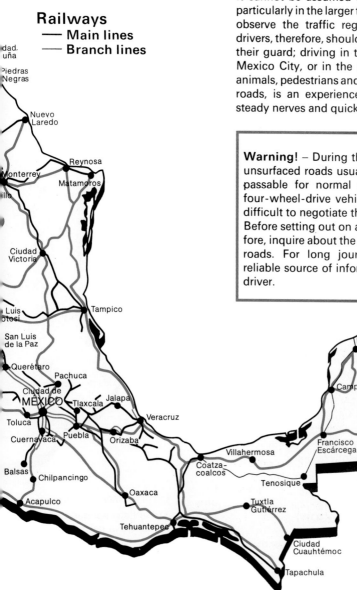

Buses
(camiones, autobuses)

Mexico is served by a dense network of bus routes reaching into the remotest parts of the country. On the main highways there are fast and comfortable coaches with first and second class ("super de luxe" and "de luxe"); fares are low, and the difference between first and second class fares is not great. On other

roads there are third class buses, which are less comfortable but provide an excellent opportunity for making contact with the local people. – On the first class bus services it is advisable to book in plenty of time (at least a day in advance); and in general it is desirable to check up on departure times and tickets well before the bus is due to leave. Seat reservation tickets *(fichas)* are frequently issued.

Gasoline prices
(subject to alteration)

Prices are usually somewhat lower than in the USA and much cheaper than in Europe. At present regular gasoline (Nova Plus) cost 155 pesos, Premium (Extra)

180 pesos and Diesel 140 pesos a liter (1,057 quarts). Unleaded gasoline is designated "sin plomo" and is available in a silver pump.

Railways

The network of the Mexican railways *(ferrocarriles, FFCC)* with a total track of 25,800 km (16,215 miles), is thinly spread except in the area between Manzanillo on the Pacific and Veracruz on the Gulf of Mexico. Most of the main lines are run by the state-owned **Ferrocarriles Nacion-**

ales de México (*National Railways of Mexico*). Other lines handling passenger traffic (some of them narrow gauge) are *Ferrocarril del Pacífico, Ferrocarril de Chihuahua al Pacífico, Ferrocarril Sonora-Baja California, Ferrocarril Coahuila-Zacatecas, Ferrocarriles Unidos*

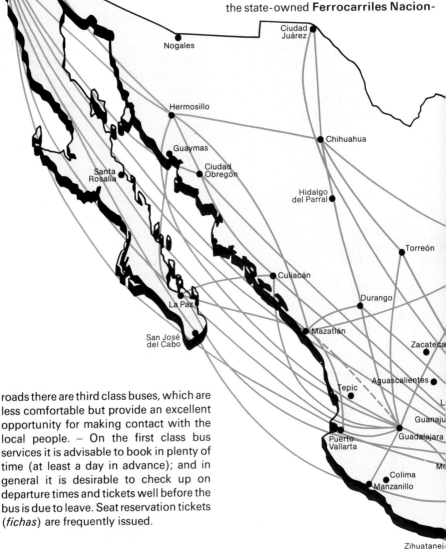

de Yucatán and *Ferrocarril del Sureste*. There are also a few lines handling only freight.

Railway fares are lower than on the long-distance buses, but standards of comfort and punctuality are not high, and the journeys are long and slow. Visitors should always travel first class, particularly for overnight journeys (reclining seats and simply equipped sleeping compartments available at extra charge).

A magnificent sightseeing experience is the trip on the Ferrocarril de Chihuahua al Pacífico, through the grand and rugged scenery of the **Barranca del Cobre** (*Copper Canyon*) in the northern Sierra Madre Occidental. On this mountain stretch the line goes through some 90 tunnels, over 30 bridges and climbs to a height of 2480 m (8140 ft).

Car ferries

There are car ferries (*transbordadores de coches*) linking the ports of Guaymas, Los Mochis, Mazatlán and Puerto Vallarta with La Paz and San Lucas in Baja California. There are also ferries between the islands of Cozumel, Cancún and Isla Mujeres and the nearest ports on the NE coast of the Yucatán peninsula (Quintana Roo).

There are also small ferries across some of the lagoons on the coast of the Gulf of Mexico.

Air services

Mexico's principal international airport is the Aeropuerto Internacional of Mexico City, to which there are flights (in some cases with intermediate stops) from the principal airports in North America.

The state-owned airlines **Aeroméxico** and **Mexicana** (*Compañía Mexicana de Aviación*) fly services to the United States, transatlantic routes to Madrid and Paris and a large network of domestic services, as well as services to Panama City (Panama), Bogotá (Columbia), Caracas (Venezuela), Havana (Cuba), San Juan (Puerto Rico), Guatemala City (Guatemala) and San José (Costa Rica).

The great distances between different parts of the country and the low air fares make air travel an important means of travel in Mexico, bringing the larger towns and vacation centers within easy reach.

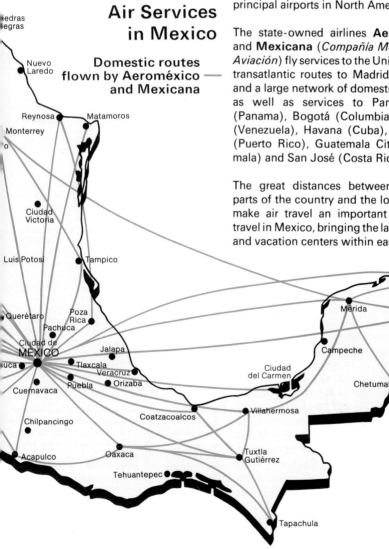

Air Services in Mexico

Domestic routes flown by Aeroméxico and Mexicana

Distances by road (in kilometers) between selected Mexican towns	Acapulco	Chetumal	Chihuahua	Ciudad Juárez	Durango	Guadalajara	Guanajuato	Hermosillo	La Paz	Manzanillo	Metamoros	Mérida	Mexico City	Nogales	Nuevo Laredo	Oaxaca	Piedras Negras	Puebla	Querétaro	San Luis Potosi	Tampico	Tapachula	Tijuana	Veracruz	Villahermosa
Acapulco		1849	1852	2227	1300	949	762	2372	4700	1195	1334	1946	397	2677	1588	656	1714	497	619	821	869	1326	3283	821	1278
Chetumal	1849		2832	3308	2352	1984	1804	3407	5781	2292	2078	446	1449	3684	2346	1275	2558	1323	1671	1873	1556	1256	4290	1054	571
Chihuahua	1852	2832		375	709	1144	1161	1921	4221	1469	1141	2960	1455	2198	1048	1971	1036	1581	1233	1031	1276	2630	2804	1869	2308
Ciudad Juárez	2227	3308	375		1084	1519	1536	2297	4596	1844	1516	3350	1830	2573	1423	2346	1411	1956	1608	1406	1723	3076	3179	2255	2737
Durango	1300	2352	709	1084		600	609	1212	3512	925	938	2408	903	1489	825	1419	833	1029	681	479	871	2088	2095	1327	1766
Guadalajara	949	1984	1144	1519	600		301	1423	3723	325	1010	2040	535	1700	998	1051	1124	706	348	354	746	1720	2306	1004	1398
Guanajuato	762	1804	1161	1536	609	301		1724	4031	626	866	1860	355	2001	977	881	1103	491	133	210	602	1540	2607	789	1218
Hermosillo	2372	3407	1921	2297	1212	1423	1724		2300	1634	2150	3463	1958	277	2057	2519	2045	2129	1781	1691	2083	3143	883	2427	2821
La Paz	4700	5781	4221	4596	3512	3723	4031	2300		3934	3450	5852	4303	2239	3357	4819	4345	4429	4081	3991	4383	5549	1457	4727	5210
Manzanillo	1195	2292	1469	1844	925	325	626	1634	3934		1335	2348	843	1911	1323	1274	1449	969	667	679	1071	2004	2517	1267	1706
Metamoros	1334	2078	1141	1516	938	1010	866	2150	3450	1335		2149	960	2427	348	1445	765	1024	858	656	492	1892	3033	1024	1507
Mérida	1946	446	2960	3350	2408	2040	1860	3463	5852	2348	2149		1505	3740	2409	1346	2599	1379	1727	1929	1627	1327	4346	1125	642
Mexico City	397	1449	1455	1830	903	535	355	1958	4303	843	960	1505		2280	1191	516	1317	126	222	424	468	1185	2841	424	863
Nogales	2677	3684	2198	2573	1489	1700	2001	277	2239	1911	2427	3740	2280		2334	2796	2322	2406	2058	1968	2360	3465	822	2704	3143
Nuevo Laredo	1588	2346	1048	1423	825	998	977	2057	3357	1323	348	2409	1191	2334		1652	756	1284	969	767	752	2152	2940	1284	1767
Oaxaca	656	1275	1971	2346	1419	1051	881	2519	4819	1274	1445	1346	516	2796	1652		1833	408	738	940	953	669	3402	421	704
Piedras Negras	1714	2558	1036	1411	833	1124	1103	2045	4345	1449	765	2599	1317	2322	756	1833		1443	1095	893	972	2372	2928	1504	1987
Puebla	497	1323	1581	1956	1029	706	491	2129	4429	969	1024	1379	126	2406	1284	408	1443		348	550	532	1077	3012	298	737
Querétaro	619	1671	1233	1608	681	348	133	1781	4081	667	858	1727	222	2058	969	738	1095	348		202	539	1407	2664	646	1085
San Luis Potosi	821	1873	1031	1406	479	354	210	1691	3991	679	656	1929	424	1968	767	940	893	550	202		392	1609	2574	848	1287
Tampico	869	1556	1276	1723	871	746	602	2083	4383	1071	492	1627	468	2360	752	953	972	532	539	392		1370	2966	502	982
Tapachula	1326	1256	2630	3076	2088	1720	1540	3143	5549	2004	1892	1327	1185	3465	2152	669	2372	1077	1407	1609	1370		4026	868	685
Tijuana	3283	4290	2804	3179	2095	2306	2607	883	1457	2517	3033	4346	2841	822	2940	3402	2928	3012	2664	2574	2966	4026		3310	3704
Veracruz	821	1054	1869	2255	1327	1004	789	2427	4727	1267	1024	1125	424	2704	1284	421	1504	298	646	848	502	868	3310		480
Villahermosa	1278	571	2308	2737	1766	1398	1218	2821	5210	1706	1507	642	863	3143	1767	704	1987	737	1085	1287	982	685	3704	480	

Language

The official language of Mexico is **Spanish**, with a sprinkling, in its spoken version, of words taken over from the Indian language. *Náhuatl*. In pronunciation and speech melody, Mexican-Spanish resembles the Spanish of Andalusia.

As the mother tongue of more than 320 million people, Spanish is the most widely spoken of the Romance languages and second only to English as a world commercial language. Many of its words are of Arabic origin. – Although English is widely spoken in the larger towns and tourist centers, which are used to large numbers of visitors from the United States and Canada, it is desirable to have at least a smattering of Spanish when traveling in Mexico – if only to avoid the unflattering designation, "gringo". For those departing from the beaten tourist track, some knowledge of Spanish is indispensable.

Pronunciation. – Vowels are pronounced in the "continental" fashion, without the diphthongization usual in English. The consonants *f, k, l, m, n, p, t* and *y* (consonantal) are normally pronounced much as in English; *b* has a softer pronunciation than in English, almost approximating to *v* when it occurs between vowels; *c* before *e* or *i* is pronounced like *s* (in Castilian Spanish like *th* in "thin"), otherwise like *k; ch* as in English; *d* at the end of a word or between vowels is softened into the sound of *th* in "that"; *g* before *e* or *i* is like the Scottish *ch* in "loch", otherwise hard as in "go"; *h* is silent; *j* is the Scottish *ch; ii* is pronounced like *l* followed by consonantal *y*, i.e., like *lli* in "million" (sometimes like *y* without the *l*); *ñ* like *n* followed by consonantal *y*, i.e., like *ni* in "onion"; *qu* like *k; r* is strongly rolled; *x* usually as in English, but in some proper names between vowels (México, Oaxaca) like Scottish *ch*, and before consonants like *s; z* like *s* (in Castilian like *th* in "thin"). In many words of Indian origin *x* is pronounced like *sh*.

Stress. – The rule is that words ending in a vowel or in *n* or *s* have the stress on the second-to-last syllable; words ending in any other consonant have the stress on the last syllable. Any departure from this rule is indicated by an acute accent on the stressed vowel. Thus Tampico and Esteban, with the stress on the second-to-last syllable, and Cozumel and Veracruz, with the stress on the last syllable, are spelled without the acute accent, unlike México, Tonalá, Yucatán, Juárez, etc. For this purpose the vowel combinations *ae, ao, ea, oe, oa* and *oe* are regarded as constituting two syllables, all other combinations as monosyllabic:

Distances by road (in miles) between selected Mexican towns

	Acapulco	Chetumal	Chihuahua	Ciudad Juárez	Durango	Guadalajara	Guanajuato	Hermosillo	La Paz	Manzanillo	Matamoros	Mérida	Mexico City	Nogales	Nuevo Laredo	Oaxaca	Piedras Negras	Puebla	Querétaro	San Luis Potosí	Tampico	Tapachula	Tijuana	Veracruz	Villahermosa
Acapulco		1149	1151	1384	809	590	474	1474	2921	743	829	1209	247	1663	968	408	1065	309	385	510	540	824	2040	510	794
Chetumal	1149		1760	2056	1462	1233	1121	2117	3592	1424	1291	277	900	2289	1458	792	1590	822	1038	1164	967	780	2666	655	355
Chihuahua	1151	1760		233	441	711	721	1194	2623	913	709	1839	904	1366	651	1223	644	982	766	641	793	1634	1742	1161	1434
Ciudad Juárez	1384	2056	233		674	944	954	1427	2856	1146	942	2082	1137	1599	884	1458	877	1215	999	874	1071	1911	1975	1401	1701
Durango	809	1462	441	674		373	378	753	2182	574	583	1273	561	925	513	882	518	639	423	298	541	1297	1302	825	1097
Guadalajara	590	1233	711	944	373		187	884	2313	202	628	1268	332	1056	620	653	698	439	216	220	464	1069	1433	624	869
Guanajuato	474	1121	721	954	378	187		1071	2504	389	538	1156	221	1243	607	547	685	305	83	130	374	957	1620	490	757
Hermosillo	1474	2117	1194	1427	753	884	1071		1429	1015	1336	2152	1217	141	1278	1565	1271	1323	1107	1051	1294	1953	549	1508	1753
La Paz	2921	3592	2623	2856	2182	2313	2504	1429		2445	2144	3636	2985	1391	2086	2995	2700	2752	2536	2480	2724	3448	905	2937	3237
Manzanillo	743	1424	913	1146	574	202	389	1015	2445		829	1459	524	1187	822	792	900	602	414	422	666	1245	1564	787	1060
Matamoros	829	1291	709	942	583	628	538	1336	2144	829		1335	597	1508	216	898	475	636	533	408	306	1176	1885	636	936
Mérida	1209	277	1839	2082	1273	1268	1156	2152	3636	1459	1335		935	2324	1497	836	1615	857	1073	1199	1011	825	2700	699	399
Mexico City	247	900	904	1137	561	332	221	1217	2985	524	597	935		1417	740	321	818	78	138	263	291	736	1765	263	536
Nogales	1663	2289	1366	1599	925	1056	1243	141	1391	1187	1508	2324	1417		1450	1737	1443	1495	1279	1223	1467	2153	511	1680	1953
Nuevo Laredo	968	1458	651	884	513	620	607	1278	2086	822	216	1497	740	1450		1027	470	798	602	477	467	1337	1827	798	1098
Oaxaca	408	792	1223	1458	882	653	547	1565	2995	792	898	836	321	1737	1027		1139	254	458	584	592	416	2114	262	437
Piedras Negras	1065	1590	644	877	518	698	685	1271	2700	900	475	1615	818	1443	470	1139		897	680	555	604	1474	1819	935	1235
Puebla	309	822	982	1215	639	439	305	1323	2752	602	636	857	78	1495	798	254	897		216	342	331	669	1871	185	458
Querétaro	385	1038	766	999	423	216	83	1107	2536	414	533	1073	138	1279	602	458	680	216		126	867	874	1407	401	674
San Luis Potosí	510	1164	641	874	298	220	130	1051	2480	422	408	1199	263	1223	477	584	555	342	126		244	999	1599	527	800
Tampico	540	967	793	1071	541	464	374	1294	2724	666	306	1011	291	1467	467	592	604	331	867	244		851	1843	311	610
Tapachula	824	780	1634	1911	1297	1069	957	1953	3448	1245	1176	825	736	2153	1337	416	1474	669	874	999	851		2501	539	426
Tijuana	2040	2666	1742	1975	1302	1433	1620	549	905	1564	1885	2700	1765	511	1827	2114	1819	1871	1407	1599	1843	2501		2057	2302
Veracruz	510	655	1161	1401	825	624	490	1508	2937	787	636	699	263	1680	798	262	935	185	401	527	311	539	2057		298
Villahermosa	794	355	1434	1701	1097	869	757	1753	1060	1060	936	399	536	1953	1098	437	1235	458	674	800	610	426	2302	298	

thus *paseo* has the stress on *e*, *patio* on *a*, without the need of an acute accent to indicate this. The acute accent is, however, required when the first vowel in the combinations *ia, ie, io, iu, ua, ue, ui, uo* and *uy* is to be stressed (e.g., *sillería, río*), and when the second vowel in the combinations *ai* or *ay, au, ei* or *ey, eu, oi* or *oy* and *ou* is to be stressed (e.g., *paraíso, baúl*).

The **article** is *el, la, lo* (masculine, feminine and neuter), plural *los, las, los*. The possessive is indicated by *de*, "of", the dative by *a*, "to", which combine with the masculine singular to form *del* and *al*. The accusative is the same as the nominative, except that in the case of persons and personified objects it is expressed, like the dative, by the preposition *a*.

Everyday expressions

Good morning!	¡Buenos días!
Good afternoon!	¡Buenas tardes!
Good evening, good night!	¡Buenas noches!
Goodbye!	¡Adiós! / ¡Hasta la vista!
Yes, no	Sí, no (señor, etc.)
Please!	¡Por favor!
Thank you (very much)!	¡(Muchas) gracias!
Not at all! (You're welcome!)	¡De nada!
Excuse me! (for a mistake, etc.)	¡Perdón!
Excuse me! (e.g., when passing in front of someone)	¡Con permiso!

Do you speak English?	¿Habla Usted inglés?
A little, not much	Un poco, no mucho
I do not understand	No entiendo
What is the Spanish for ...?	¿Cómo se dice en español ...?
What is the name of this church?	¿Cómo se llama esta iglesia?
The Cathedral (of St John)	La catedral (de San Juan)
Where is Calle ...?	¿Dónde está la calle ...?
Where is the road to ...?	¿Dónde está el camino para ...?
To the right, left	A la derecha, izquierda
Straight ahead	Siempre derecho
Above, up	Arriba
Below, down	Abajo
When is it open?	¿A qué horas está abierto?
How far?	¿Qué distancia?
Today	Hoy
Yesterday	Ayer
The day before yesterday	Anteayer
Tomorrow	Mañana
Have you any rooms?	¿Hay cuartos libres?
I would like ...	Quisiera ...
A room with private bath	Una cuartos con bano
With full board what does it cost	¿Con pensión completa cuánto vale?
Everything included	Todo incluído
That is too expensive	Es demasiado caro
Check, please! (to a waiter)	¡Mesaro, la cuenta (nota)!
Where is the bathroom?	¿Dónde está el baño?
Wake me at six!	¡Llámeme Vd a las seis!

Where is there a doctor?	¿Dónde hay un médico?
Where is there a dentist?	¿Dónde hay un dentista?
Where is there a chemist?	¿Dónde hay una farmacia?

Road signs

Aduana	Customs
¡Alto!	Stop
Aparcamiento	Parking lot
¡Atencion!	Caution
Autopista	Superhighway
Avenida	Avenue, wide road
Bifurcacion	Road fork, junction
Calzada	Road (formerly road on dam)
Canada	Track for livestock
Carretera	Highway
Carretera de Cuota	Turnpike
¡Cedo el paso!	Give way
Cerro	Hill
Collectivo	Minibus
¡Cuidado!	Caution
Curva Peligrosa	Dangerous bend
Desviacion	Diversion
Direccion unica	One way only
Doble traccion	Four-wheel drive
Grua	Crane, tow-away service
Gruta	Grotto, cave
Llevar la derecha (la izquierda)!	Keep to the right (left)
Malecon	Road on river bank
Muelle	Mole, pier, quay
Niebla	Fog
¡Obras!	Road Works
¡Al Paso!	Dead slow
Paso a nivel	Level crossing
Paso prohibido	No entry
Pavimento	Surfaced road
Peaje (cuota)	Toll
Peatones	Pedestrians
¡Peligro!	Danger
Pesero	Minibus
Playa	Beach
Prohibido el adelantamiento	No overtaking
Prohibido estacionarse	No parking
Puente angosto	Narrow bridge (the first driver to flash his lights has priority)
Sentido contrario	No entry (one way street)
Sentido unico	One way street
Topes	Rumble strips (metal strips or uneven surface to compel drivers to slow down)
Transbordador	Ferry

Traveling by train and bus

All aboard!	¡Viajeros al tren!
Arrival	Llegada
Baggage	Equipaje
Bus	Camión, autobus
Change here!	¡Cambiar de tren!
Conductor (ticket collector)	Revisor
Departure	Salida
Fare	Precio, importe
First class	Primera clase
Junction	Empalme
Luggage	Equipaje
No smoking (compartment)	No fumadores
Platform	Andén, plataforma
Railway	Ferrocarril
Second class	Segunda clase
Smoking (compartment)	Fumadores
Stop	Parada
Ticket	Billete, boleto
Ticket collector (conductor)	Cobrador
Ticket window	Taquilla de boletos
Timetable	Horario de trenes
Train	Tren
Waiting room	Sale de espera

Numbers

0	cero
1	uno (una)
2	dos
3	tres
4	cuatro
5	cinco
6	seis
7	siete
8	ocho
9	nueve
10	diez
11	once
12	doce
13	trece
14	catorce
15	quince
16	dieciseis
17	diecisiete
18	dieciocho
19	diecinueve
20	veinte
21	veintiuno
22	veintidós
30	treinta
31	treinta y uno
40	cuarenta
50	cincuenta
60	sesenta
70	setenta
80	ochenta
90	noventa
100	ciento (cien)
101	ciento uno
153	ciento cincuenta y tres
200	doscientos
300	trescientos
400	cuatrocientos
500	quinientos
600	seiscientos
700	setecientos
800	ochocientos
900	novecientos
1000	mil
1 m.	un millón

Ordinals

1st	primero (primera)
2nd	segundo
3rd	tercero
4th	cuarto
5th	quinto
6th	sexto
7th	sétimo/séptimo
8th	octavo
9th	nono/noveno
10th	décimo
20th	vigésimo
100th	centésimo

Fractions

$\frac{1}{2}$	medio (media)
$\frac{1}{4}$	un cuarto
$\frac{1}{10}$	un décimo

Compass points

Norte (Nte)	North
Sur (S.)	South
Este, Oriente (Ote.)	East
Oeste, Poniente (Pte.)	West

At the post office

Address	Dirección
Air mail	Por avión
Letter	Carta
Mailbox	Buzón
Postage	Porte, franqueo
Postcard	Tarjeta postal
Poste restante	Lista de correos
Postman	Cartero
Post office	Correo
Printed papers	Impreso
Registered letter	Carta certificada
Stamp	Timbre
Telegram	Telegrama
Telephone	Teléfono

Geographical, architectural, etc., terms

Adobe	Clay bricks, air-dried
Alfiz	Molding around Moorish arch
Artesanía	Arts and Crafts
Artesonado	Coffered ceiling
Audiencia	Administrative court; court of appeal
Avenida	Avenue
Azulejos	Glazed tiles (originally blue – azul)
Bahía	Bay
Barranca	Gorge, ravine, canyon
Barrio	District, quarter (of a town)
Biblioteca	Library
Bolsa de Valores	Money market, stock exchange
Brecha	Field path
Cabo	Cape
Cantina	Bar, tavern
Capilla	Chapel
Capilla abierta	Open chapel
Capilla Mayor	Principal chapel, containing the high altar
Carretera	Main road
Casa de huespedes	Inn
Cementerio	Cemetery
Cenote	(Maya) water-hole, sacred well
Cerro	Hill
Ciudad	City, town
Claustro	Cloister
Colegio	College, seminary
Convento	Monastery, convent
Coro	Choir
Cuesta	Slope, hill
Cueva	Cave
Cumbre	Summit
Custodia	Monstrance
Embalse	Reservoir, man-made lake
Ermita	Small country church, pilgrimage chapel
Estrella	Rose-window
Faro	Lighthouse
Fonda	Inn, small restaurant
Fuente	Fountain, spring
Gruta	Cave
Hamaca	Hammock
Huerta	Fertile irrigated area
Ídolo	Idol (pre-Columbian clay or stone figure)
Iglesia	Church
Indígena	Native Indian
Lago	Lake
Laguna	Lagoon, lake
Llano	Plain
Loma	Hillock
Mar	Sea
Mercado	Market
Mirador	Viewpoint, roof terrace
Monasterio	Monastery
Palacio	Palace
Palacio Arzobispal	Archbishop's Palace
Palacio Episcopal (Obispal)	Bishop's Palace
Palacio Municipal	Town hall
Pantano	Swamp
Parroquia	Parish church
Paseo	Avenue, promenade
Paso (geog.)	Pass
Patio	Courtyard
Plata	Silver
Playa	Beach
Posa	Processional chapel
Portería	Hall
Presa	Reservoir, man-made lake
Puerta	Door(way)
Puerta del Perdón	Door of Absolution (name of principal entrance to many cathedrals, so called because those entering were sure of absolution)
Puerto	Port, harbor, pass
Punta	Point, headland
Quinta	Country house
Reja	Grill, grating
Retablo	Reredos, altarpiece
Rio	River
Sacristía	Sacristy
Sagrario	Sacristy, chapel
Sala capitular	Chapterhouse
Secretaría	Ministry
Selva	Wood, forest
Sierra	Mountain range
Sillería	Choir-stalls
Tianguis	Market
Torrente	Mountain stream
Tumba	Tomb, grave
Zócalo	(Principal) square

Abbreviations

C and F = caliente and frío	= hot and cold on faucets (sometimes H & C is used)
Edo = Estado	= state
E.U.A. = Estados Unidos de America	= USA
E.U.M. = Estados Unidos Mexicanos	= United States of Mexico
INI = Instituto Nacional Indigenista	= National Institute of Indian Affairs
IMSS = Instituto Mexicano de Seguro Social	= Mexican Institute of Social Affairs (runs a considerable number of hospitals)
JLP = José Lopez Portillo (former President of Mexico, 1976–1982)	
Lic. = Licenciado	= Lawyer

MMH = Miguel de la
Madrid Hurtado
(President of
Mexico from
1.12.1982)
PB = Planta Baja   = Ground floor
PEMEX = Petroleos   = National Mexican
Mexicanos   Oil Company
M/N = Moneda Nacional   = National currency
(Mexican peso)
S.A. = Sociedad Anónima   = Limited Company
UNAM = Universidad   = Autonomous
Nacional   University of
Autónoma de   Mexico in Mexico
Mexico   City

The grammatical structure of **Náhuatl** is totally different from that of the Indo-European languages; it is a "polysynthetic" language, which can express a whole sentence in a single word. The characteristic double consonant of Náhuatl, the *tl*, has been reduced in the course of time to a simple *t*, so that the language is now generally called *Náhuat* or *Náhua*. The spelling and pronunciation of Náhuatl – which before the Spanish conquest was written only in a glyphic alphabet – was stabilized only with the adoption of the Latin alphabet. Since the language has only about twenty different sounds, this gave rise to no difficulty. – Words taken from Náhuatl into Spanish are mainly the names of plants and animals.

Indian languages. – Most of the peoples which evolved the advanced cultures of pre-Columbian times belonged to the *Náhuatl* language family, one of the components of the Uto-Aztec linguistic group, which comprises several different dialects and is still spoken by almost a million people. It is estimated that some 3% of the Mexican population speak only Indian languages.

Other Indian languages still spoken in Mexico are *Otomi, Maya, Tarascan* (Purepecha), *Mixtecan, Zapotecan, Totonacan, Mazatecan* etc., which are quite different from each other and from Náhuatl. It is characteristic of most of the Indian languages of Meso-America that they were originally spoken by a cultured and educated upper class but that after the disappearance of that class they sank to the level of purely peasant languages.

Manners and customs

Even more importance is attached in Mexico than in Spain to the forms of politeness – a trend which has sometimes led to the development of overly formal rules of etiquette. Arrogant or inconsiderate behavior is poorly received in Mexico, and tact is of the very essence of social intercourse. Impatience is an emotion the Mexicans do not seem to feel themselves or appreciate in others, and in general punctuality – as that term is understood in North America or northern Europe – is not a Mexican habit. Visitors should be ready, therefore, to allow at least half an hour's grace in relation to appointments, opening times, etc. An exception to this rule is the bullfight, which always begins punctually at the time stated. – The midday **siesta** between 2 and 5 p.m. is a sacred institution, and most Mexicans will be upset by any disturbance to it.

Mexicans are very ready with invitations and offers of hospitality. If it is not repeated and no precise time is suggested, the invitation is a merely polite one, and even the person giving it does not expect it to be taken seriously. If a rendezvous is arranged, it is likely to be in a restaurant or café: an invitation to the host's home is a great proof of confidence and a genuine distinction. If a guest expresses appreciation of something belonging to the host, the host will often offer it to him; this, too, is a polite form of speech which the guest must not take literally.

Although many friendly offers by Mexicans are mere empty flowers of speech, the helpfulness of local drivers to other motorists in difficulty is very genuine. In certain circumstances, too, an offer of an appropriate sum of money can work wonders. Thus public officials, who tend to be poorly paid, will expect some pecuniary recognition even for services (e.g., customs clearance) which are part of their official duties. To Mexicans this seems perfectly in order, and they do not see it as implying bribery and corruption.

Tipping plays an important part in Mexican life. In hotels and restaurants the bill does not include a service charge, and at least 15% of the amount should be given in tips.

Porters expect about 500 pesos for each piece of luggage, hotel chambermaids, etc. 500 pesos per night. Taxi drivers may be given a few pesos on top of the fare.

Shops in Mexico have fixed prices, but in the markets, bargaining is normal – if only as a means of engaging the other party in conversation. As a broad rule of thumb, it can be said that the prospective buyer should counter the price asked by the seller with an offer about a third less, and can expect to settle at somewhere around 75% of the original figure. In places with a large tourist trade, the original prices are likely to be set higher and the buyer's offer should therefore be correspondingly lower.

Finally, one or two points on relations with the Indian population. These shy but very hospitable people – particularly so in the remoter parts of the country – have lived for centuries in the shadow of the European incomers to their country. They appreciate it when visitors approach them on equal terms and are careful to avoid the appearance of patronizing them. – In recent years there has been an increasing reluctance on the part of the Indians to be photographed by tourists, most noticeable in Chiapas state with its very colorful religious ceremonies. It is advisable, therefore, to get permission from the village headman before trying to take any photographs; it is a matter of ordinary tact, at least, to refrain from using flash in churches and at solemn religious celebrations, and to respect the wishes of any Indians who object to being photographed.

Accommodations

Hotels and guest-houses

The **hotels** (*hoteles*) of the higher categories in large towns and resorts offer excellent standards of comfort and amenity. Like too many American hotels, however, they tend to have efficient service but little atmosphere. Hotels under Mexican management have, on the whole, more individuality. There are also hotels under German and Swiss management which are pleasant and comfortable. Outside the main tourist centers, visitors may find somewhat lower standards of comfort.

At present there is in Mexico an official classification system for accommodations which ranges in five categories from the highest, GT (Gran Turismo), down to establishments with one star. The room prices are, on average, fixed twice a year by the Ministry of Tourism and maintained with varying success. The prices also depend on geographical zones and can often be negotiated on the spot on an individual basis.

Hotel category		Double room
official	in this Guide	per night (pesos)
★★★★★	L	45,000–85,000
★★★★	L	25,000–45,000
★★★	I	14,000–28,000
★★	II	9,000–16,000
★	III	5,000– 9,000
no star		3,000– 5,000

Youth hostels

The youth hostel movement has so far made relatively little headway in Mexico, and there are only a few youth hostels (*albergues de la juventud*) in the entire country.

Camping and trailering

These are not yet popular in Mexico. There are a number of properly equipped sites, particularly on the Pacific coast, which are mainly patronized by visitors from the United States, but elsewhere in the country camping and trailer sites are few and far between, and usually have fairly spartan facilities. Send $4.00 and $1.00 to cover air mail return postage (money order only) to Margarita, Apartido Postal 5–599, Mexico 5, D.F. for an English language guide to over 500 camp and trailer parks in Mexico and Central America.

Food and drink

The culinary traditions of the Indian population, combined with influences brought in by Spaniards and other incomers, produce a distinctively Mexican cuisine, with local variations in different parts of the country. The large hotels also, of course, serve the usual international dishes.

Mexican meals are usually substantial, consisting of a series of different courses. Many restaurants also offer a tourist menu (menu turistico) or set menu (*comida corrida:* about 6000 pesos) or one-course meals (from about 3000 pesos). – Lunch is eaten between 2.00 p.m. and 4.00 p.m., dinner not before 8.00 p.m.

An almost ubiquitous item in a Mexican meal is the tortilla, a maize pancake which is served either as an accompaniment to the main dish or on its own with a filling of meat, vegetables, spices, cheese, etc. Also very popular are the various species of peppers (chilis) and a range of sauces. Poultry appears frequently on the menu, and in the coastal regions there is excellent seafood, though surprisingly few kinds of fish. Popular side dishes are *frijoles refritos* (beans fried in oil with various spices) and rice. Potatoes and pasta are rarely served. – A popular dish for festive occasions is *mole poblano*, an elaborate sauce made according to an Indian recipe, with numerous ingredients (several kinds of pepper, bitter chocolate, etc.).

Reading a Mexican menu
(*lista de comidas*)

Tablesetting *cubierto*; spoon *cuchara*; teaspoon *cucharita*; knife *cuchillo*; fork *tenedor*; plate *plato*; glass *vaso*; cup *taza*; napkin *servilleta*: corkscrew *sacacorchos*. – Breakfast *desayuno*; continental breakfast *café con panes*; second breakfast *almuerzo*; lunch *comida, almuerza*; dinner *cena*. – Those who want their food not too highly seasoned should order it *sin picante*.

Hors d'œuvres (antojitos). – Guacamole avocado salad; *tacos* stuffed rolled tortillas; *frijoles refritos* fried beans; *ostiones* oysters; *coctel de camarones* prawn cocktail.

Soups (sopas). – Pozole veracruzano maize soup with chopped vegetables, spices, etc., served separately; *cocido* thick soup; *gazpacho* cold vegetable soup; *menudo* soup made with offal of veal, pork or poultry. *Sopa de arroz* rice pilaf (not really a soup).

Egg dishes (platos de huevos). – Huevo egg (*crudo* raw, *fresco* fresh, *duro* hardboiled, *tibio* softboiled); *huevos revueltos* scrambled eggs; *huevos rancheros* fried eggs with highly seasoned sauce.

Fish and seafood (pescado y mariscos). – Frito fried, *asado* roasted, *cocido* boiled, *ahumado* smoked. – *Trucha* trout; *carpa* carp; *anguila* eel; *bagre* catfish. – *Atún* tuna; *bonito* bonito, white tuna; *corvina* sea raven; *jurel* yellowtail; *lisa* mullet: *mero* sea bass; *lenguado* sole; *sardina* sardine; *sierra* mackerel pike; *pez espada* swordfish; *marlin* fanfish; *bacalao* dried cod; *tiburón, cazón* shark. – *Camarón* shrimp; *langosta* crayfish; *langostino* lobster; *jaiba, cangrejo* crab; *pulpo, calamar* octopus; *ostión* oyster, *abalone* abalone, ear shell; *tortuga* turtle.

Meat (carnes). Asado roast, *pierna* leg, *chuleta* chop, cutlet; *gordo, graso* fat. – *Carnero* mutton; *cerdo* pork; *cochinillo, lechón* sucking pig; *cordero* lamb; *ternera* veal; *vaca* beef; *carnitas* roast pork; *bisteck* steak; *rosbif* roast beef; *carne estofada* stew; *carne salada* salt meat; *carne ahumada* smoked meat; *tocino* bacon; *fiambre* cold meat; *jamón* ham; *salchichón* salami-type sausage; *chorizo* highly seasoned sausage; *longaniza* spiced pork sausage; *tamales* minced meat steamed in corn husks and seasoning. – *Poultry (aves):* guajolote turkey; *faisán* pheasant; *ganso* goose; *pato* duck; *perdiz* partridge; *cordorniz* quail;

pichón pigeon; *pollo* chicken. – *Game (caza):* venado venison; *jabalí* wild pig; *liebre* hare;: *conejo* rabbit.

Sauces (salsas). – Mole poblano a sharp sauce made with bitter chocolate; *salso verde* sauce made with herbs, peppers and green tomatoes; *pipián colorado* made with tomatoes, chilis and herbs; *salsa borrocha* made with pulque and herbs.

Vegetables (verduras). – Aguacate avocado; *alcachofas* artichokes; *calabacitas* courgettes; *flor de calabaza* pumpkin flowers; *col* cabbage; *col lombardo* red cabbage; *col de Bruselas* Brussels sprouts; *coliflor* cauliflower; *repollo* white cabbage; *acelgas* chards; *cebollas* onions; *espárragos* asparagus; *espinacas* spinach; *guisantes* peas; *garbanzos* chick peas; *judías* beans; *frijoles* kidney beans; *jitomatoes* tomatoes; *zanahorias* carrots. – *Salads (ensalada, lechuga):* pepino cucumber; *apio* celery; *escarola* endive; *vinagre* vinegar; *aceite* oil; *pimienta* pepper (*molida* ground); *sal* salt (*salado* salted, salty); *mostaza* mustard.

Tortillas. – Chilaquiles tortillas with meat and cheese; *tacos* stuffed rolled tortillas fried in oil; *enchiladas* tortillas with sharp chili sauce and meat; *chalupas* tortillas with upturned edges fried in oil with meat, sausage and salad; *tamales* filled with minced meat and wrapped in maize husks.

Desserts (postres). – Helado ice; *postic, flan* pudding. – *Fruit (frutas):* cerezas cherries; *higos* figs; *tunas* prickly pears; *fresas* strawberries; *manzanas* apples; *melocotones* peaches; *melones* melons; *naranjas* oranges; *peras* pears; *pinas* pineapples; *plátanos* bananas; *uvas* grapes. There are also various tropical fruits like papaws, mangoes, guavas and zapotes.

Drinks

Beer (*cerveza*) is increasingly displacing the old national drink, pulque. Excellent light-colored (*clara*), semi-dark (*semioscura*) and dark (*oscura*) beers are brewed in Mexico.

Pulque, which has an alcohol content of about 3%, is made from the juice of the maguey agave. This juice (*agua miel* or "honey water") is also distilled to produce a strong spirit, **tequila**, and a similar spirit of higher quality, **mezcal**. – **Aguardiente**, a colorless brandy, and **rum** (*ron*) are distilled from sugar-cane.

Wine (*vino*): production is increasing and today some good quality wines are available.

Coffee (*café*) is a popular drink. The beans are roasted to a very dark color. Black coffee (*café solo*) is preferred in the Mexican highlands, coffee with milk (*café con leche*) on the coast.

Mexico is the homeland of **chocolate** (*chocolate*), which – whipped into a froth and flavored with vanilla – is a regular feature of the Mexican breakfast.

Soft drinks (*refrescos*), **fruit juices** (*jugos*) and **mineral water** (*agua mineral*, Tehuacán: *con gas* carbonated, *sin gas* non-carbonated) are widely available.

> Visitors who eat unpeeled fruit or salads, drink water from the tap or buy food or drinks from a street vendor may catch a disagreeable but usually harmless intestinal infection which can be a nuisance during a short vacation. If they are staying in Mexico for some time they would be well advised not to run the risk of infection.

Sports and recreation

Water sports

The numerous man-made lakes (reservoirs) in inland Mexico offer facilities for a wide range of water sports (*deportes acuáticos*) – boating, sailing, windsurfing, water skiing, etc. – On the open Pacific coast (W coast of Baja California and the coast on the mainland S of Mazatlán) the heavy swell coming in from the ocean affords excellent surfing. – Bathing beaches: see p. 323.

Diving (*buceo*) enthusiasts are also well catered to. Snorkelers and scuba divers will find plenty of scope, particularly off the E coast of Yucatán (Cancún, Cozumel, Isla Mujeres). The plant and animal life of the coral reefs in this area provide magnificent subjects for underwater photography.

Tennis

Formerly confined to a few fashionable private clubs, tennis (*tenis*) has now developed on a considerable scale to meet the needs of vacationers. Many of the larger hotels have their own courts, and the clubs welcome visitors.

Riding

The Mexicans are great horselovers, and Mexico is noted for its cross-bred horses. Some hotels have facilities for riding (*equitación*), and on a visit to a hacienda a ride can usually be arranged.

Golf

There are golf-courses, usually belonging to local clubs or to hotels, near the larger towns and tourist centers.

Shooting (hunting)

Although many of the rare species are now to be found only in the remoter parts of the country, Mexico still has plenty of game. There is good wildfowling (mainly duck) on the lagoons of the Pacific coast. – Hunting permits are issued by the local authorities.

Fishing

The coastal waters and continental shelf of Mexico are abundantly stocked with fish and attract large numbers of coastal and deep-sea fishers. Boat trips in search of the larger game fish are popular. – There is relatively little fresh-water fishing in Mexico, since there are few rivers with a flow of water throughout the year. Many lakes and reservoirs do, however, offer good fishing.

For rod fishing (*pesca con caña*) a fishing permit (*permiso de pesca*) is required. In the inland regions this is usually issued by the local authority, on the coast by the local harbormaster or branch office of the Ministry of Industry and Commerce.

Climbing

Mexico offers only limited scope for real mountaineering (*alpinismo*), but there is excellent mountain walking to be had in the main ranges, the Eastern, Western and Southern Sierra Madre. Since the tree-line lies at about 4000 m (13,000 ft), the mountain regions don't have the Alpine character of European peaks. There is little in the way of overnight accommodations, so that climbers must confine themselves to day trips unless they are prepared to spend the night in an Indian village.

The landscape pattern is often masked by the dense vegetation, and it is therefore necessary to be prepared to deviate from the direct route and negotiate gorges which cannot be seen from a distance.

Three peaks of genuine Alpine character are the snow-capped volcanoes *Popocatépetl* (5452 m – 17,888 ft), *Ixtaccíhuatl* (5286 m – 17,343 ft) and *Citlaltépetl* (Pico de Orizaba, 5700 m – 18,700 ft); but even for these, stamina, rather than high mountaineering skill, is required. Rock-climbing is possible at heights of up to about 4000 m (13,000 ft), but the rock is often much weathered and crumbling. At higher altitudes there are great expanses of volcanic ash and isolated pinnacles of rock.

Mountaineering Club;
Club Citlaltepetl de Mexico,
Calle Dr. Mora 9 – 25C,
Mexico. 1. D.F.
Tel. 5 12 35 34.

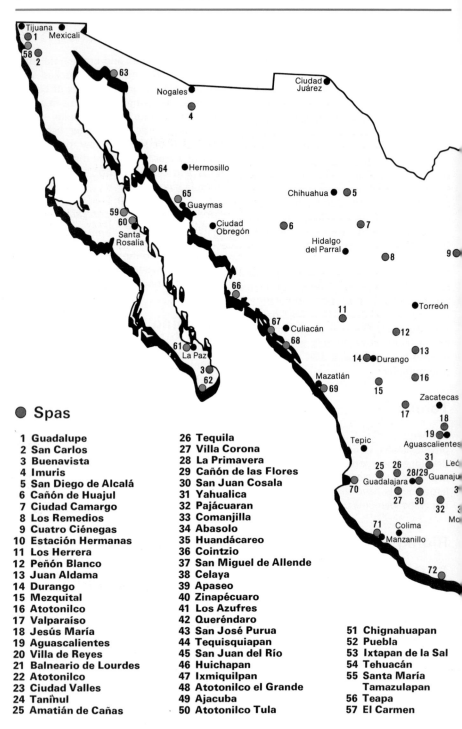

● Spas

1 **Guadalupe**	26 **Tequila**
2 **San Carlos**	27 **Villa Corona**
3 **Buenavista**	28 **La Primavera**
4 **Imuris**	29 **Cañón de las Flores**
5 **San Diego de Alcalá**	30 **San Juan Cosala**
6 **Cañón de Huajul**	31 **Yahualica**
7 **Ciudad Camargo**	32 **Pajácuaran**
8 **Los Remedios**	33 **Comanjilla**
9 **Cuatro Ciénegas**	34 **Abasolo**
10 **Estación Hermanas**	35 **Huandácareo**
11 **Los Herrera**	36 **Cointzio**
12 **Peñón Blanco**	37 **San Miguel de Allende**
13 **Juan Aldama**	38 **Celaya**
14 **Durango**	39 **Apaseo**
15 **Mezquital**	40 **Zinapécuaro**
16 **Atotonilco**	41 **Los Azufres**
17 **Valparaíso**	42 **Queréndaro**
18 **Jesús María**	43 **San José Purua**
19 **Aguascalientes**	44 **Tequisquiapan**
20 **Villa de Reyes**	45 **San Juan del Río**
21 **Balneario de Lourdes**	46 **Huichapan**
22 **Atotonilco**	47 **Ixmiquilpan**
23 **Ciudad Valles**	48 **Atotonilco el Grande**
24 **Taninhul**	49 **Ajacuba**
25 **Amatián de Cañas**	50 **Atotonilco Tula**

51 **Chignahuapan**
52 **Puebla**
53 **Ixtapan de la Sal**
54 **Tehuacán**
55 **Santa María**
Tamazulapan
56 **Teapa**
57 **El Carmen**

Spas

The great majority of Mexican spas are in the southern part of the Sierra Madre Occidental and the southern central highlands.

Properly organized spas with all necessary facilities are available only in the large resorts of *Aguascalientes* and *Tehuacán*.

Elsewhere there are only very simple facilities; in many places there are mineral springs which are still in their natural state and are used only by the population of the immediately surrounding area.

From Tehuacán comes the best-known Mexican mineral water (Agua Tehuacán).

Spas and Bathing Beaches in Mexico

● Bathing Beaches

58 **Ensenada**	75 **Puerto Escondido**
59 **San Carlos**	76 **Puerto Ángel**
60 **Santa Rosalia**	77 **Puerto Madero**
61 **La Paz**	78 **Tulum**
62 **Cabo San Lucas**	79 **Isla Cozumel**
63 **Puerto Peñasco**	80 **Isla Cancún**
64 **Bahía Kino**	81 **Isla Mujeres**
65 **Guaymas**	82 **Progreso**
66 **Topolobampo**	83 **Ciudad del Carmen**
67 **Altata**	84 **Coatzacoalcos**
68 **El Dorado**	85 **Alvarado**
69 **Mazatlán**	86 **Veracruz**
70 **Puerto Vallarta**	87 **Nautla**
71 **Manzanillo**	88 **Tecolutla**
72 **Playa Azul**	89 **Tuxpan**
73 **Zihuatanejo/Ixtapa**	90 **Tampico**
74 **Acapulco**	

This is only a selection of the most easily accessible and best equipped of Mexico's many beaches.

Bathing beaches

Mexico has a coastline of about 10,000 km (6000 miles) on the Gulf of Mexico and the Pacific, with a great range of bathing beaches (*playas*) of varying character. On the Gulf coast the sea is calmer, since the offshore islands provide shelter from the Atlantic swell. This is true also of the Gulf of California, which is protected by the long peninsula of Baja California. The open Pacific coast is exposed to heavier surf and to marine currents.

Apart from the immediate surroundings of the large Atlantic ports of Tampico, Veracruz and Coatzacoalcos the quality of the water ranges from good to excellent. – Water sports; see p. 321.

National Parks

State	National Park	Nearest place
Baja California Norte	Constitución de 1857	Ensenada, B.C.N.
Baja California Norte	Sierra de San Pedro Martir	Ensenada, B.C.N.
Coahuila	Balneario Los Novillos	Cd. Acuna, Coah.
Colima	Nevado de Colima	Tuxpán, Jal.
Chiapas	Cañon del Sumidero	Tuxtla Gutiérrez, Chis.
Chiapas	Lagunas de Montebello	Comitán, Chis.
Chiapas	Palenque	Palenque, Chis
Chihuahua	Cascada de Bassaseachic	Cuauhtémoc, Chi.
Chihuahua	Cumbres de Majalpa	Chihuahua, Chi.
Distrito Federal	Cerro de la Estrella	Itztapalapa, D.F.
Distrito Federal	Cumbres del Ajusco	San Miguel Ajusco, D.F.
Distrito Federal	El Tepeyac	Gustavo A. Madero, D.F.
Distrito Federal	Fuentes Brotantes de Tlalpan	Tlalpan, D.F.
Distrito Federal	Historico Coyoacán	Coyoacán, D.F.
Distrito Federal	Lomas de Podierna	Distrito Federal
Distrito Federal	Molino de Belén	Distrito Federal
Guerrero	Gral Juan Álvarez	Chilpancingo, Gro.
Guerrero	Grutas de Cacahuamilpa	Taxco, Gro.
Guerrero	El Veladero	Acapulco, Gro.
Hidalgo	El Chico	Pachuca, Hgo.
Hidalgo	Los Mármoles	Zimapan, Hgo.
Hidalgo	Tula	Tula, Hgo.
Mexico	Bosencheve	Zituácuaro, Mich.
Mexico	Desierto del Carmen	Tenancingo, Mex.
Mexico	Insurgente Miguel Hidalgo	Cuajimalpa, D.F.
Mexico	Iztaccíhuatl-Popocatépetl	Amecameca, Mex.
Mexico	Lagunas de Zempoala	Huitzilac, Mor.
Mexico	Molino de Flores	Texcoco, Mex.
Mexico	Nevado de Toluca	Toluca, Mex.
Mexico	Los Remedios	Naucalpan, Mex.
Mexico	Zoquiapan y Anexas	Río Frío, Mex.
Mexico	Sacromonte	Amecameca, Mex.
Michoacán	Barranca de Cupatitzio	Uruapan, Mich.
Michoacán	Lago de Camécuaro	Zamora, Mich.
Michoacán	Cerro de Garnia	Cd. Hidalgo, Mich.
Michoacán	Insurgente José M. Morelos	Morelia, Mich.
Michoacán	Pico de Tancitaro	Uruapan, Mich.
Michoacán	Rayón	Tlapujahua, Mich.
Morelos	El Tepotzteco	Tepoztlán, Mor.
Nayarit	Isla Isabel	San Blas, Nay.
Nuevo León	Cumbres de Monterrey	Monterrey, N.L.
Nuevo León	El Sabinal	Cerralvo, N.L.
Oaxaca	Benito Juárez	Oaxaca, Oax.
Oaxaca	Lagunas de Chacahua	Pinotepa Nacional, Oax
Querétaro	Cerro de las Campanas	Querétaro, Qro.
Querétaro	El Cimatario	Querétaro, Qro.
Quintana Roo	Tulum	Tulum, Q.R.
San Luis Potosí	El Potosí	Santa Caterina, S.L.P.
San Luis Potosí	Gogorrón	Villa de Reyes, S.L.P.
Tlaxcala	Malinche o Matlalcuéyatl	Huamantla, Tlax.
Tlaxcala	Xicoténcatl	Tlaxcala, Tlax.
Veracruz	Cañon de Río Blanco	Orizaba, Ver.
Veracruz	Cofre de Perote	Perote, Ver.
Veracruz	Pico de Orizaba	Cd. Serdán, Pue.

Owing to the economic situation some of the National Parks have not been maintained to a very high standard.

Folk traditions

Bullfighting

The bullfight (*corrida de toros*) has become a national institution in Mexico, to which it was imported from Spain. All the larger towns have bullrings (*plazas de toros*), the one in Mexico City being the largest in the world (60,000 seats). During the main bullfighting season (November to March; in northern Mexico, the summer) the leading bullfighters (*toreros, matadores* or *espadas*), many of them from Spain, perform; outside this season the bulls are fought by novice bullfighters. The corridas are usually held on Sundays and public holidays, beginning at 4.00 p.m.; and, contrary to the usual custom of the country, they start punctually at the time stated. The best seats are on the shady side of the arena (*sombra*), the cheaper ones on the sunny side (*sol*).

A *charro*

The fighting bulls (*toros bravos*) are bred on specialized haciendas and, after a careful process of selection, are sent to the arena at the age of four or five.

The **bullfight** (*lidia*) has three main parts (*suertes*). After a brief prologue during which the *capeadores* tease the bull by playing it with their brightly colored capes (*capas*), there follows the *suerte de picar* or *suerte de varas*, in which the mounted *picadores* provoke the bull to attack them, plunge their lances (*garrochas*) into its neck and withstand the charges of the infuriated beast as best they can. When the bull has been sufficiently weakened (*castigado*) by his wounds (*varas*), the second stage, the *suerte de banderillas*, begins. The *banderilleros* run toward the bull carrying several *banderillas* and, skilfully eluding its charge at the last moment, stick them into its neck. The normal banderillas are sticks 75 cm (2 ft 6 in.) long, with barbed points and paper streamers; the *banderillas a cuarta* are only 15 cm (6 in.) long. If a bull is too quiet or of uncertain mood, the banderilleros provoke it by plays with a cloak (*floreos*). When three pairs of banderillas have been planted in the bull's neck, the *suerte suprema* or *suerte de matar* begins. The *espada* or *matador*, armed with a red cloth (*muleta*) and a sword (*estoque*), begins by teasing the bull with the cloth and seeks to maneuver it into a position in which he can give it the death stroke (*estocada*), after which the *coup de grâce* is administered by a *punterillo* with a dagger. If the bull has shown itself courageous and aggressive, it will be loudly applauded. Unskilled bullfighters will be vociferously criticized and booed. – The show is repeated six or eight times until the onset of darkness.

Cockfighting

Cockfighting (*pelea de gallos*) is widely popular in Mexico. The cocks, carefully selected for their fighting spirit, have sharp steel blades fixed to their feet with which they can inflict bloody wounds. There is heavy betting on the outcome of the contest.

The charreada

The charreada is the Mexican equivalent of the US rodeo, a tradition derived from the days of the large haciendas with their mounted cattle herders. They are usually put on by associations of *charros* ("horsemen") in their own stadiums. After an opening parade in picturesque costumes, the charros show their riding skill, using the lasso and catching wild steers and unbroken horses. During the intervals there are folk dances and mariachi music.

Jai alai (frontón)

This game, known in Spain as pelota, originated in the Basque country and was brought to Mexico by the Spaniards, like so many other Mexican sports. Surely the fastest and most dangerous ball game in the world, it is played on a rectangular court surrounded on three sides by high walls and usually roofed over. The players, usually in teams of two, have on their right hand a long scoop-like basketwork "glove" with which they drive a hard ball some 6 cm ($2\frac{1}{2}$ in.) in diameter against the wall at great speed. There is heavy betting on the result of the match. – A variant is *frontenis*, played with tennis rackets.

Folk dances

Many of the folk dances (*bailes folklóricos*) still danced in Mexico originated

Dancers, Oaxaca

in pre-Columbian times; others were brought in from Europe. While the conquistadors tried to put a stop to the pagan dances of the Indians, the Franciscan and Dominican missionaries sought to integrate the old traditional songs and dances into Catholic ritual. Thus an Aztec dance symbolizing the conflict between day and night, between good and evil, became an expression of the Church's fight against the powers of the devil; similarly the ceremonial dances in honor of the Aztec Earth Mother, Tonantzín, are still danced with little modification to honor the Virgin of Guadalupe. – Dancing is an essential feature of the numerous Mexican fiestas.

In the **Quetzal dance** in the states of Veracruz and Puebla the dancers wear colorful costumes and a huge circular headdress.

The **Viejito dance** ("dance of the little old men") recalls the defeat of the Tarascans by Cortés, when the Tarascan ruler appeared before his conquerors in the symbolic role of an old man in order to express his submission. The dancers, wearing masks, imitate the weary movements of old men and then gradually change back into young men.

The **Venado dance** (Stag dance) of the Yaqui, Mayo and Tarahumara Indians of northwestern Mexico is danced to bring good fortune in the hunt. Similar to this, but simpler, is the ritual **Matachín dance**.

In Oaxaca there is the **Penachos dance** (Feather dance), named after the feather headdresses, decorated with mirrors, worn by the dancers.

The **Sonajero dance**, in which the dancers wear elaborate headdresses and carry rattles and bows and arrows, does honor to the symbol of the Cross and the forces of nature.

The **Conchero dance**, danced mainly in central Mexico, is accompanied by plucked string instruments made from armadillo shells.

The most popular ballroom dances are mostly based on Spanish tunes and Spanish steps. Among them are the *jarabe tapatío* of Guadalajara, the *zandunga* of Tehuantepec, the *huapango* of Veracruz and the *jarana* of Yucatán. The *danzón* is popular with the working classes, particularly in Mexico City.

Costumes

Only a generation ago the *charro costume*, originally the festive dress of cattle herders and rancheros, was still worn by men in many parts of the country. This consists of a jacket and breeches of fine leather, decorated with rows of silver buttons, a gathered shirt and a broad-brimmed felt hat trimmed with gold and silver brocade. It is now worn only by members of charro clubs and mariachi groups. –The *china poblana* costume worn by women, consisting of a skirt embroidered in red and green, worn over several petticoats, with a white blouse and a woollen shawl (*rebozo*), is said to have been brought into Mexico by a Chinese woman from the Philippines. It is now seen, for all practical purposes, only at fancy dress balls and on folk occasions.

The traditional *Indian costumes* can still be seen in many parts of the country, particularly in areas remote from the larger towns. The ancient methods of spinning and weaving are still practiced, although the old vegetable dyes have now given place to modern synthetic dyes. A varied range of traditional costumes can be seen in the states of Oaxaca, Veracruz, Yucatán and Chiapas. It is mainly the women who cling to the traditional dress; most of the

Indian headdresses

men wear modern dress, perhaps a plain white manta shirt and trousers with a woven belt. Protection against cold and rain is provided by heavy woolen cloaks (*sarapes*) in geometric patterns. In the warm regions on the Gulf of Yucatán, the men wear open-necked pleated shirts (*guayaberas*) with several pockets, while the women wear the *huipil*, a square of embroidered cotton with openings for the head and arms. A similar garment worn in northern and central Mexico is the *quechquémetl*, made of two lengths of material. The straw hat (*sombrero*) was imported from Spain. Pre-Hispanic costumes are to be found primarily among the Tarahumara, Huichol, Tzotzil, Tzeltal and Amuzgo Indians.

Arts and crafts

The quality and variety of Mexican folk art can withstand comparison with any country in the world. While it is true that in recent years there has been a tendency toward the industrial mass production of articles of poorer quality, there is still a wide choice of craft products of excellent workmanship and imaginative design. Like so much else in Mexico, folk art shows an attractive mingling of Spanish and Mexican elements. Many parts of the country have developed their own artistic styles, so that a visitor travelling around Mexico will encounter a constantly changing range of tempting products.

Pottery (*cerámica*) of excellent quality is found particularly in the states of Michoacán, Jalisco (notably at Tonalá and Tlaquepaque), México and Guanajuato and in the Federal District.

Basketwork (*cestería*), using straw, sisal, palm leaves, osiers, etc., is produced in the states of México, Querétaro, Michoacán, Jalisco, Oaxaca, Guerrero, Campeche and Yucatán.

Sarapes (woolen or cotton cloaks worn by men) and **jorongos** (poncho-like cloaks) are found in the states of México, Guanajuato, Michoacán, Coahuila, Jalisco, Oaxaca and Tlaxcala, embroidered **blouses** (*blusas bordadas*) in the Federal District and in the states of México, Michoacán, Guanajuato, Jalisco, Puebla, Oaxaca, Chiapas and Yucatán.

Silverware (*objetos de plata*) and other precious metals should be bought only in reliable shops. Silverware is produced in Mexico City and in the states of Guerrero (Taxco), Michoacán, Jalisco and Guanajuato. – **Gold filigree work** (*filigrana de oro*) is produced in Oaxaca and Yucatán.

Semi-precious stones (*piedras semipreciosas*) – opal, amethyst, rock crystal, agate, garnet, jadeite, nephrite, obsidian – are used in the manufacture of jewelry and ornaments, particularly in Querétaro, Guanajuato and Durango.

An Indian girl spinning

Hand-blown glass (*vidrio soplado*) is found in Mexico City and the states of Jalisco, Guerrero and Oaxaca.

Lacquerwork (*lacas*), particularly painted bottle-gourds, can be bought in Michoacán, Guerrero, Oaxaca and Chiapas.

Carved wooden articles (*labrados de madera*) – sculptured figures and everyday objects – come from Michoacán, Guerrero and Oaxaca.

Leather articles (*objetos de cuero*) are produced in Jalisco, Zacatecas, Oaxaca and Chiapas.

Hammocks (*hamacas*) are made in Veracruz, Tabasco, Campeche, Yucatán and Chiapas.

Sombreros can be bought all over the country, but those produced in Michoacán, Campeche and Yucatán are of particularly high quality.

Markets

The market (*mercado*) plays a central role in Mexican life. When the Spaniards first arrived in the country, they were astonished by the size of the market-places, the range of goods on sale and the excellent organization; the markets of Mexico are still conducted with much less noise and bustle than in other southern countries. Bargaining over prices is normal, and indeed is expected. The abundance and variety of the wares on sale – local craft products, folk art, flowers, fruit, vegetables and much else – make colorful and fascinating scene. – The travelling Indian markets are known as *tianguis*.

Well-known markets

Acámbaro, Gto.	daily except Thursday
Acatlán de Osorio, Pue.	Tuesday and Sunday
Acatzingo, Pue.	Tuesday
Acaxochitlán, Hgo.	Wednesday and Sunday
Acolman, Hgo.	Wednesday

Pottery market

Actopán, Hgo.	Wednesday
Aguascalientes, Ags.	daily
Álamos, Son.	Sunday
Alvarado, Ver.	Sunday
Amecameca, Mex.	Sunday
Anguangueo, Mich.	Saturday and Sunday
Apan, Hgo.	Sunday
Apatzingán, Mich.	Saturday and Sunday
Apizaco, Tlax.	Sunday
Arriaga, Chis.	daily
Atlacomulco, Mex.	Sunday
Atlixco, Pue.	Tuesday and Saturday
Camargo, Chih.	Monday and Saturday
Celaya, Gto.	Tuesday and Saturday
Chalco, Mex.	Friday
Chetumal, Q.R.	daily
Chiconcuac, Mex.	Tuesday and Sunday
Cholula, Pue.	Wednesday and Sunday
Ciudad Hidalgo, Mich.	Sunday
Cosamaloapan, Ver.	Saturday and Sunday
Cuauhtémoc, Chih.	daily
Cuernavaca, Mor.	Sunday
Cuetzalán, Pue.	Sunday
Dolores Hidalgo, Gto.	Sunday
Ejutla, Oax.	Wednesday
Etla, Oax.	Wednesday
Fortín de las Flores, Ver.	Sunday
Fresnillo, Zac.	Sunday
Guadalajara, Jal.	Sunday
Guanajuato, Gto.	Sunday
Huamantla, Tlax.	Wednesday and Sunday
Huauchinango, Pue.	Saturday
Huejotzingo, Pue.	Thursday and Saturday
Huichapan, Hgo.	Sunday
Iguala, Gro.	Saturday and Sunday
Irapuato, Gto.	Tuesday and Sunday
Ixmiquilpan, Hgo.	Monday
Ixtapan de la Sal, Mex.	Sunday
Izúcar de Matamoros, Pue.	Sunday and Monday
Jilotepec, Mex.	Friday
Jiquilpan, Mich.	Saturday
Jocotepec, Jal.	Sunday
Juchitán, Oax.	Sunday
León, Gto.	Monday and Tuesday
Lerma, Mex.	Saturday
Manzanillo, Col.	Saturday and Sunday
Matehuala, S.L.P.	daily
Mérida, Yuc.	daily
Metepec, Mex.	Monday
Metztitlán, Hgo.	Sunday
Miahuatlán, Oax.	Monday
Mitla, Oax.	Sunday
Morelia, Mich.	Thursday and Sunday
Moreleón, Gto.	Sunday and Monday
Motul, Yuc.	Monday
Nochixtlán, Oax.	Sunday
Nuevo Casas Grandes, Chih.	daily

Oaxaca, Oax.	daily (esp. Saturday)
Ocotlán, Jal.	Saturday and Sunday
Ocotlán, Oax.	Friday
Ozumba de Alzate, Mex.	Tuesday and Friday
Papantla, Ver.	Sunday
Parras, Coah.	Saturday and Sunday
Pátzcuaro, Mich.	Tuesday, Friday and Sunday
Perote, Ver.	Sunday
Poza Rica, Ver.	daily
Puebla, Pue.	Thursday and Sunday
Puerto Vallarta, Jal.	Sunday
Querétaro, Qro.	daily
Quiroga, Mich.	Sunday
Sabinas, Coah.	Saturday and Sunday
Salamanca, Gto.	Tuesday and Sunday
Saltillo, Coah.	daily
Santiago Tlaquistengo, Mex.	Tuesday
San Cristóbal de las Casas, Chis.	daily except Sunday
San José Purúa, Mich.	Sunday
San Juan de los Lagos, Jal.	daily
San Juan del Río, Qro.	Sunday
San Martín Texmelucan, Pue.	Tuesday and Friday
San Miguel de Allende, Gto.	Tuesday and Sunday
Silao, Gto.	Tuesday and Sunday
Tamazunchale, S.L.P.	Sunday
Taxco, Gro.	Thursday and Sunday
Tecali, Pue.	Tuesday and Friday
Tecamachalco, Pue.	Saturday
Tehuacán, Pue.	Saturday
Tehuantepec, Oax.	Sunday
Tenancingo, Mex.	Thursday and Friday
Tenango, Mex.	Thursday and Sunday
Tepeaca, Pue.	Friday
Tepeji del Río, Hgo.	Monday
Tepoztlán, Mor.	Wednesday and Sunday
Tequisquiapan, Qro.	Sunday
Texcoco, Mex.	Friday and Sunday
Teziutlán, Pue.	Friday and Sunday
Tierra Blanca, Ver.	daily
Tlacolula, Oax.	Sunday
Tlaxcala, Tlax.	Saturday
Toluca, Mex.	Friday
Tonalá, Chis.	daily
Tula, Hgo.	Sunday
Tulacingo, Hgo.	Monday and Thursday
Tuxtla Gutiérrez, Chis.	daily
Uruapan, Mich.	daily
Valle de Bravo, Mex.	Thursday and Sunday
Veracruz, Ver.	daily
Villahermosa, Tab.	daily
Xochimilco, D.F.	Thursday and Saturday
Zaachila, Oax.	Monday
Zacapu, Mich.	Sunday
Zacatlán, Pue.	Friday and Sunday
Zacualtipán, Hgo.	Sunday
Zimapán, Hgo.	Saturday and Sunday
Zitácuaro, Mich.	Sunday

Fiestas

Every town and village in Mexico has a fiesta in honor of the local saint or patron of the place, and there are numerous other seasons for celebration, including the main church festivals and national holidays. In the fiestas old Indian rituals, Christian

Folk performer in traditional dress

practices and the Mexicans' natural *joie de vivre* combine to produce a lively and colorful pageant which may last several days. Mexicans of all social classes are prepared to go to considerable expense to play their part in these celebrations.

Public and religious holidays

January 1	*Año Nuevo* (New Year's Day)
January 6	*Día de los Reyes* (Twelfth Night)
February 5	*Día de la Constitución* (Constitution Day)
March 21	*Birthday of Benito Juárez* (b. 1806)
May 1	*Día del Trabajo* (Labour Day)
May 5	*Anniversary of Battle of Puebla* (1862)
September 1	*Día de la Nación* (National Day)
September 16	*Día de la Independencia* (Independence Day: 1810)
October 12	*Día de la Raza* (Day of the Race, Columbus Day)
November 1 and 2	*Todos los Santos, Día de los Muertos* (All Saints, All Souls)
November 20	*Día de la Revolución* (Revolution Day: 1910)
December 12	*Día de la Virgen de Guadalupe* (Feast of the Virgin of Guadalupe: 1531)
December 25	*Navidad* (Christmas)
Moveable festivals	*Semana Santa* (Holy Week) *Jueves de Corpus* (Corpus Christi)

Folk dancers

Particularly important fiestas are the *Día de los Reyes* (Day of the Kings, i.e., Twelfth Night) on January 6, when children are given presents; *Candlemas* (Día de la Candelaria, February 2); *Carnival*, which incorporates both European and Indian features; *Holy Week* (Semana Santa), strongly influenced by Spanish practice; *Corpus Christi* (Jueves de Corpus), with a strong Indian element; *Independence Day* (Día de la Independencia, September 15/16), when the celebrations last several days; *Revolution Day* (Día de la Revolución, November 20); *All Saints* and *All Souls* (Todos los Santos, Día de los Muertos: November 1–2), when the dead are remembered and a symbolic family meal is eaten at the grave; the fiesta of the *Virgin of Guadalupe* (December 12), with an Indian pilgrimage to Mexico City; the *Posadas* (nine days beginning December 16), symbolizing Mary and Joseph's journey to Bethlehem; and *Christmas* (Navidad), an occasion for gay and noisy celebrations.

Opening times

Mexican *shops* have no standard closing time, and usually remain open into the evening and on Sundays. In the hotter parts of the country there is a lunch break between 2.00 p.m. and 5.00 p.m.

Banks are open Monday–Friday from 9.00 a.m. to 1.30 p.m.

Museums are open from 9.00 a.m. to 5.00 p.m. daily except Monday, when they are closed. There are reduced admission charges on Sundays.

Shopping and souvenirs

The varied range of Mexican craft products make popular souvenirs. They are cheapest where they are made and in markets. On no account should gold and silver articles be bought from a street trader; the best place to get them is from the man who made them, or failing that, in a reliable shop. Taxco is the best place for silver. Genuine silver articles must bear a stamp ("sterling" or "925").

Visitors should not buy antiquities, since their export is prohibited; but excellent replicas can be bought in the National Museum of Anthropology in Mexico City. The "finds" which visitors are frequently offered on archeological sites are mostly fakes, which may have been buried some time previously for greater verisimilitude. Since the potters producing them are highly skilled in traditional techniques of manufacture they may be difficult to distinguish from the real thing, even for an expert.

Information

Secretaría de Turismo (SECTUR)
(*Ministry of Tourism*)

Avenida Presidente Masaryk 172,
Mexico City 5, D.F.;
tel. (9 15) 2 50 85 55.
250 42 98 (Regional Office)

24 hr hotline for tourists (915) 250 01 23

Offices of the Secretaría de Turismo (SECTUR) in the United States

Peachtree Center, Cain Tower, Suite 1201,
Atlanta, GA 30303;
tel. (404) 659 2409.

9701 Wilshire Boulevard, Suite 1201,
Beverly Hills, CA 90212;
tel. (213) 274 6315.

John Hancock Center,
875 North Michigan Avenue, Suite 3612,
Chicago, IL 60611;
tel. (312) 649 0090.

Two Turtle Creek Village, Suite 1230,
Dallas, TX 75219;
tel. (214) 526 6950.

First Denver Plaza Building,
633 17th Street, Suite 2010,
Denver, CO 80202;
tel. (303) 893 6823.

C. E. Lummus Tower, Suite 1370,
3000 South Post Oak Road,
Houston, TX 77056;
tel. (713) 840 8332.

100 Biscayne Boulevard, Suite 2804,
Miami, FL 33132;
tel. (305) 371 8037.

1 Shell Square Building, Suite 1515,
New Orleans, LA 70139;
tel. (504) 525 2783.

405 Park Avenue, Suite 1002,
New York, NY 10022;
tel. (212) 755 7212 and 755 7261.

GPM South Tower, Suite 240,
800 N.W. Loop 410,
San Antonio, TX 78216;
tel. (512) 341 6212.

San Diego Federal Building,
600 B Street, Suite 1220,
San Diego, CA 92101;
tel. (714) 236 9314

50 California Street, Suite 2465,
San Francisco, CA 94111;
tel. (415) 986 0992.

5151 E. Broadway, Suite 1535,
Tucson, AZ 85711;
tel. (602) 745 5055.

1156 15th Street N.W., Suite 329,
Washington, D.C. 20005;
tel. (202) 296 2594.

Offices of the Secretaría de Turismo (SECTUR)

1 Place Ville Marie, Suite 2409,
Montreal, P.Q. H3B 3M9;
tel. (514) 871 1052.

101 Richmond Street West, Suite 1212,
Toronto, Ontario M5K 2E1;
tel. (416) 364 2455.

700 West Georgia Street,
Vancouver, B.C. V7Y 1B6;
tel. (604) 682 0551.

Within Mexico, information can be obtained from the *Coordinaciones Federales de Turismo* in the state capitals and larger tourist resorts. Some states maintain their own information offices in places frequented by tourists.

Asociacion Mexicana Automovilistica (*AMA*)
Orizaba 7,
Mexico, 06700, D.F.;
Tel. (9 15) 5 88 70 55.

There are AMA offices in the larger towns.

Airlines

Aeroméxico
Paseo de la Reforma 445,
Mexico City 5, D.F.;
tel. (9 15) 553 57 33.

Mexicana
Head Office
Ave. Xola 335
Mexico City, 03100 D.F.;
tel. (915) 660 44 44
           660 44 33.

Mexican Embassies

2829 16th Street N.W.,
Washington, D.C.;
tel. (202) 234 6000.

130 Albert Street,
Ottawa, Ontario;
tel. (613) 233 8988.

Embassies in Mexico

USA:
Paseo de la Reforma 305,
Mexico City, D.F.;
tel. (9 15) 211 00 42.

Canada:
Schiller 529
Mexico City, D.F.;
tel. (9 15) 254 32 88.

Telephoning

In Mexico only local calls can be made from a coin-operated telephone. At the moment these calls are free due to coin adjustment problems. Long distance calls (llamadas telefónicas de larga distancia) can be made at special places which show the sign "Larga Distancia", usually in shops, except in Mexico City, where there are telephone offices. For calls within Mexico dial **02**, for international calls (English speaking operators) dial **09**.

Emergency calls

The main highways are patrolled by the green vehicles ("green angels") of the road emergency service (tel. 250 48 17) run by the Ministry of Tourism. The National Automobile Association (AMA) also runs a breakdown service; its service vehicles are painted yellow and bear the letters "AMA".

Ambulance Red and Green Cross (Cruz Roja and Cruz Verde)   **557 57 58**
     557 57 59
Police (Policía Distrito Federal y Transito)   **588 51 00**
Police (Policía de Caminos)   **684 21 42**
Fire Service (Bomberos)   **768 37 00**
Missing Persons Service (Locatel)   **658 11 11**

Baedeker's Travel Guides

What's there to do and see in foreign countries? Travelers who rely on Baedeker, one of the oldest names in travel literature, will miss nothing. Baedeker's bright red, internationally recognized covers open up to reveal fascinating A-Z directories of cities, towns, and regions, complete with their sights, museums, monuments, cathedrals, castles, gardens and ancestral homes—an approach that gives the traveler a quick and easy way to plan a vacation itinerary.

And Baedekers are filled with over 200 full-color photos and detailed maps, including a full-size, fold-out roadmap for easy vacation driving. Baedeker—the premier name in travel for over 140 years.

Please send me the books checked below and fill in order form on reverse side.

☐ **Austria** $14.95 0-13-056127-4	☐ **Mediterranean Islands** $14.95 0-13-056862-7
☐ **Caribbean** $14.95 0-13-056143-6	☐ **Mexico** $14.95 0-13-056069-3
☐ **Egypt** $15.95 0-13-056358-7	☐ **Netherlands, Belgium, and** **Luxembourg** $14.95 0-13-056028-6
☐ **France** $14.95 0-13-055814-1	☐ **Portugal** $14.95 0-13-056135-5
☐ **Germany** $14.95 0-13-055830-3	☐ **Provence/Cote d'Azur** $9.95 0-13-056938-0
☐ **Great Britain** $14.95 0-13-055855-9	☐ **Rhine** $9.95 0-13-056466-4
☐ **Greece** $14.95 0-13-056002-2	☐ **Scandinavia** $14.95 0-13-056085-5
☐ **Israel** $14.95 0-13-056176-2	☐ **Spain** $14.95 0-13-055913-X
☐ **Italy** $14.95 0-13-055897-4	☐ **Switzerland** $14.95 0-13-056044-8
☐ **Japan** $15.95 0-13-056382-X	☐ **Tuscany** $9.95 0-13-056482-6
☐ **Loire** $9.95 0-13-056375-7	☐ **Yugoslavia** $14.95 0-13-056184-3

Please turn the page for an order form and a list of additional Baedeker Guides.

A series of city guides filled with colour photographs and detailed maps and floor plans from one of the oldest names in travel publishing:

Please send me the books checked below:

☐ **Amsterdam** $10.95 0-13-057969-6	☐ **Madrid** $10.95 0-13-058033-3
☐ **Athens** $10.95 0-13-057977-7	☐ **Moscow** $10.95 0-13-058041-4
☐ **Bangkok** $10.95 0-13-057985-8	☐ **Munich** $10.95 0-13-370370-3
☐ **Berlin** $10.95 0-13-367996-9	☐ **New York** $10.95 0-13-058058-9
☐ **Brussels** $10.95 0-13-368788-0	☐ **Paris** $10.95 0-13-058066-X
☐ **Copenhagen** $10.95 0-13-057993-9	☐ **Rome** $10.95 0-13-058074-0
☐ **Florence** $10.95 0-13-369505-0	☐ **San Francisco** $10.95 0-13-058082-1
☐ **Frankfurt** $10.95 0-13-369570-0	☐ **Singapore** $10.95 0-13-058090-2
☐ **Hamburg** $10.95 0-13-369687-1	☐ **Tokyo** $10.95 0-13-058108-9
☐ **Hong Kong** $10.95 0-13-058009-0	☐ **Venice** $10.95 0-13-058116-X
☐ **Jerusalem** $10.95 0-13-058017-1	☐ **Vienna** $10.95 0-13-371303-2
☐ **London** $10.95 0-13-058025-2	

PRENTICE HALL PRESS

Order Department—Travel Books

200 Old Tappan Road

Old Tappan, New Jersey 07675

In U.S. include $1 postage and handling for 1st book, 25¢ each additional book. Outside U.S. $2 and 50¢ respectively.

Enclosed is my check or money order for $_____

NAME_____

ADDRESS_____

CITY_____STATE_____ZIP_____